Maintaining the Right Fellowship

Studies in Anabaptist and Mennonite History

No. 26

Maintaining the Right Fellowship

A narrative account of life in the oldest Mennonite Community in North America

John L. Ruth

Studies in Anabaptist and Mennonite History

Edited by Cornelius J. Dyck, Leonard Gross, Leland Harder, Guy F. Hershberger, John S. Oyer, Theron Schlabach, J. C. Wenger, and John H. Yoder

Published by Herald Press, Scottdale, Pennsylvania, and Kitchener, Ontario, in cooperation with Mennonite Historical Society, Goshen, Indiana. The Society is primarily responsible for the content of the studies, and Herald Press for their publication.

1. Two Centuries of American Mennonite Literature, 1727-1928°
   By Harold S. Bender, 1929
2. The Hutterian Brethren, 1528-1931
   By John Horsch, 1931
3. Centennial History of the Mennonites in Illinois°
   By Harry F. Weber, 1931
4. For Conscience' Sake°
   By Sanford Calvin Yoder, 1940
5. Ohio Mennonite Sunday Schools°
   By John Umble, 1941
6. Conrad Grebel, Founder of the Swiss Brethren
   By Harold S. Bender, 1950
7. Mennonite Piety Through the Centuries
   By Robert Friedmann, 1949
8. Bernese Anabaptists and Their American Descendants°
   By Delbert L. Gratz, 1953
9. Anabaptism in Flanders, 1530-1650
   By A. L. E. Verheyden, 1961
10. The Mennonites in Indiana and Michigan°
    By J. C. Wenger, 1961
11. Anabaptist Baptism: A Representative Study
    By Rollin Stely Armour, 1966
12. Lost Fatherland: The Story of Mennonite Emigration from Soviet Russia, 1921- 1927
    By John B. Toews, 1967
13. Mennonites of the Ohio and Eastern Conference°
    By Grant M. Stoltzfus, 1969
14. The Mennonite Church in India, 1897-1962
    By John A. Lapp, 1972
15. The Theology of Anabaptism: An Interpretation
    By Robert Friedmann, 1973
16. Anabaptism and Asceticism
    By Kenneth R. Davis, 1974

° *Out of print but available in microfilm or photocopies.*

Maintaining the Right Fellowship

A narrative account of life in the oldest Mennonite community in
North America

John L. Ruth

Commissioned by the Franconia Mennonite Conference
of the Mennonite Church, and the Eastern
District Conference of the General
Conference Mennonite Church

HERALD PRESS
Scottdale, Pennsylvania
Kitchener, Ontario
1984

Library of Congress Cataloging in Publication Data

Ruth, John L.
  Maintaining the right fellowship.

  (Studies in Anabaptist and Mennonite history;
no. 26)
  Bibliography: p.
  1. Mennonite Church. Franconia Conference—History.
2. General Conference Mennonite Church. Eastern
District Conference—History.   3. Mennonites—Penn-
sylvania—History.   4. Pennsylvania—Church history.
I. Title.   II. Series.
BX8117.P4R87   1984   289.7'748   83-18579
ISBN 0-8361-1259-8

In appreciation of all those persons
Unmentioned in this book—
Young and old,
Male and female,
"Ethnic" or bringing new backgrounds,
Ordained or "unordained"—
Who, in the past three centuries,
Have helped to maintain the fellowship of Christ,
As it has taken shape
In the Franconia
and
Eastern District
Mennonite Conferences

No record was kept of our Forefathers when they came to this country, which was then a wilderness, and hence many things will be forever dark—oh what a pity! How easy a matter would it be if every father would keep a record all his life time and then hand it over to some one else to continue where he left off. . . .

My poor heart often feels sorry that so little is known about them. All the old people are gone, and no one here anymore to give me the desired information. What might have been handed down to the coming generation with ease is now out of reach, and as the reader will see, I can only describe what is yet possible. May God give his blessing. . . .

—Isaac B. Tyson
1864

The history of the [Franconia] Mennonite congregation is hard to chronicle as no records are kept by the congregation from time to time, and, therefore, undoubtful much of interest is left unwritten. But like the husbandman in the harvest field there is always something left for the gleaner.

—John D. Souder
1886

Old Grandmother Hiestand had 10 children—said some must spread—couldn't all stay near home—one went to Canada—rode there on horseback—carried willow whip, then planted it. . . .

Grandfather Bowers . . . would take clean shirt and go to creek for bath & change clothes then go back to house—sit on porch and sing.

—Mary Latshaw Bower
1920

. . . I have walked many, many miles, and I have spent many, many hours in weary labor . . . so that the past happenings may not be lost to the present as well as the coming generations. I learned some things . . . that no living soul knows anything about anymore, which were given to me by the older people in their declining years, and which I feel it my call and duty to write down and put it in book form so that the coming generations can read and ponder over it. . . . And let me tell you, dear reader, that this history is not only written for today but for . . . a hundred years hence.

—Henry D. Hagey
1932

It is hoped that someday we will have more detailed color of those early days.

—Freeman H. Swartz
1947

Contents

General Editors' Preface

Studies in Anabaptist and Mennonite History has been fortunate to include several regional histories in its series. Certainly one of the most interesting is John L. Ruth's *Maintaining the Right Fellowship*. Ruth captures the unique flavor of eastern Pennsylvania Mennonites and capitalizes on the renewed interest in Mennonite unity. He has demonstrated the linkages as well as the contrasts between the Franconia Conference of the Mennonite Church and the Eastern District of the General Conference Mennonite Church.

The Mennonite Historical Society is delighted to recognize the 300th anniversary of Mennonites in North America with this distinctive piece of historical research and writing. We are pleased to join the sponsoring committee to add this fresh contribution to Mennonite self-understanding.

John A. Lapp
Theron F. Schlabach

Editorial Committee's Preface

The vision for a new interpretative history of the first Mennonites in the New World became a matter of record in the minutes of the Mennonite Heritage Council meeting on July 19, 1978. By September 19 of the following year the editorial committee held its first meeting in the recently opened Family Heritage Restaurant, Franconia, Pennsylvania. This committee consisted of three representatives of the Franconia Mennonite Conference and five representatives of the Eastern District of the General Conference Mennonites. It was convened by the chairman of the planning committee for the 1983 celebration, Walton Hackman, and it was this planning committee to which the editorial committee was responsible throughout the duration of the preparation of the book manuscript.

The parent 1983 planning committee throughout took full responsibility for the financing of this venture with its fund-raising efforts headed ably by one of its members, Mary Jane Hershey, while the editorial committee focused upon such items as the book's length, the nature and extent of its documentation, its style, the authorizing of research assistants and expenditures. The editorial committee also continually monitored the progress of the project, and it explored the requirements for the book to be included in the esteemed Studies in Anabaptist and Mennonite History series (hereafter designated SAMH). Finally, its members read and responded to the manuscript itself.

The original editorial committee suffered the loss, through a prolonged illness, of one of its beloved members and cochairmen, Esko Loewen. His vacancy was filled in both capacities by Esko's successor in the pastorate of the Zion Mennonite Church, Souderton, Pennsylvania, Richard Early.

Two research assistants made substantial contributions: Robert Ulle of Blooming Glen, Pennsylvania, whose special competence is in the Germantown part of the story; and James O. Lehman, Harrisonburg, Virginia, bringing extensive acquaintance with the responses of the Mennonites during the Civil War.

We are deeply indebted to the author, John L. Ruth, for his skill in writing and his years of research far exceeding the amount of time for which he was remunerated; to Theron Schlabach, Goshen, Indiana, one of the coeditors of the SAMH; and to John A. Lapp, also of Goshen, Indiana, who by special appointment served as editor of this particular SAMH volume. The editorial committee is further indebted to Professor Burton G. Yost, chairman of the Religion Department, Bluffton College, Bluffton, Ohio, and to minister J. Herbert Fretz, coordinator of Church and Seminary Relations at the Associated Mennonite Biblical Seminaries at Elkhart, Indiana, for giving the manuscript their critical reading with the benefit of their long association with the General Conference Mennonite Church. We, lastly, express our gratitude to the research assistants already mentioned, for their dedicated labor in the particular areas of their expertise. It is with such a series of links that the publication of this new history has been made possible.

Representing the Eastern District of the General
Conference Mennonite Church:

Richard Early°
John E. Fretz
James Gerhart
Ray K. Hacker, secretary
Esko Loewen°
Wayne Mumbauer

Representing the Franconia Mennonite Conference:

John E. Lapp
S. Duane Kauffman
Gerald C. Studer°

°Cochairmen of the Editorial Committee

Author's Preface

Having at first promised my sponsoring committee an "interpretive history" of three centuries of Mennonite life in eastern Pennsylvania, I soon felt overwhelmed by the task, and chose a working-title that promised less: "Pages from a Story." But as I wrote at these pages, I found I was indeed interpreting in almost every sentence. In the very casting of my material in narrative form, I was reminding the reader that a spiritual community had been maintained across time, distance, and change. This continuing, I realized, was the theme I felt carried by. I then chose a title from the pen of an elderly Mennonite minister near the Rhine River in "Germany," who would have many descendants in the community I was describing.

Two months after William Penn had received his vast American land grant, Hinrich Kassel wrote that those who have joined the Christian church "maintain the right fellowship with each other with bread and wine in memory of the great love and benevolence Christ has shown ("*halten dann die rechte Gemeinschaft wider einander mit Brot und Wein zum Gedächtnis der grosse Liebe und Wohlthat die Christus bewiesen hat*"). In this brief remark on the Lord's supper I hear hints of the flavor of the historical Mennonite family: (1) Christians' experience of salvation is intrinsically bound up with their relation to each other; (2) it is possible to discern what kind of fellowship is consistent with Christ's teaching; (3) this fellowship must be kept and renewed. As Mennonites used to say, we must "keep house" in the church, according to "the rule of Christ" as found in the eighteenth chapter of Matthew.

This book is an attempt to give access to the attic of memory in the spiritual household of the oldest Mennonite community in North America. It is meant to be less a ledger in which a researcher can "look up facts" than a story on which a musing reader may meditate. It has been written with an ordinary, rather than an intellectual, reader as its intended main audience. Of course the writer, who has been trained in literature rather than history, has tried to present only what is true and demonstrable from evidence. But he has written less for fellow-historians seeking data for the proof of a thesis than for the reader feeling a hunger for a story where only outline has been available. The book has been written as though to persons who wished, as I have wished all my life, that they could listen to the conversation, feel the texture, savor the idiom of the life before theirs in the family of faith.

I feel keenly how barely I have sketched the story. Though some readers have already questioned the inclusion of so many family names, I have anticipated rather the disappointment of those who will find their own missing. I know of much material I have still not gone through, and feel that only now, having gained an overview of three centuries from 1648 to 1947, would I have been ready to begin interpreting. I think daily of episodes or vignettes collected in my research that should have been in these pages, and I find it painful to read almost weekly material just appearing, especially on the original migration to Pennsylvania, that would have enriched my story considerably had I been able to read it a year or even six months ago.

Then there is the period since 1947, when my account breaks off. There is a revealing story in these recent years of ferment and change, not all easy to hear, but to do justice to it would have taken many months longer. This omission will certainly disappoint the goodly number of small congregations which have been born since 1947. Two of them—Garden Chapel and Levittown (both of the Franconia Conference)—contributed useful summaries of their own history, in expectation of such inclusion. These may serve future historians.

I have built on the work of at least five dozen prior historians, whose writings are listed in the bibliographical note. Of course, no other source was of as much help as John C. Wenger's substantial *History of the Mennonites of the Franconia Conference*, written when he was in his mid-twenties and published by the Franconia Mennonite Historical Society in 1937. It is significant that even then the Eastern District Conference made its historical records available for research on the project. Having bought my copy for $3.00 at the Herald Bookstore in Souderton where I was working at the age of twenty-one, and annotated it profusely, I finally wore out the binding thirty years later as I studied it daily while writing my own book. Now long out of print, and eagerly bought at local auctions, it remains indispensable for anyone researching the topic, a storehouse of necessary information on both the Franconia and Eastern District conferences.

Here should also be recorded my appreciation for the work of Wilmer Reinford, who, in the period after the death of historian John D. Souder, took strong initiative in building up the small collection of what has become the extremely valuable Mennonite Library and Archives of Eastern Pennsylvania. Wilmer's was a key role, and his commitment to this ministry the most persistent and fruitful, at a crucial time for the preservation of our historical materials. In the Eastern District too, under Ray Hacker's leadership, John E. Fretz, and Marvin Rosenberger have been careful stewards of their growing collection, which was merged in 1967 with that of the Franconia Mennonite Historical Society.

Another stimulus to Mennonite historical consciousness in the two local conferences was the making available, by owner Charles Hoeflich of the Blooming Glen congregation, of a fine old building for a "Heritage Center" in Souderton. This prompted the formation of a new organization, the Mennonite Historians of Eastern Pennsylvania, headed in its first years by Ray Hacker. The wealth of both its museum and the library was made maximally useful to me by archivist Joseph Miller, who brought to my crowded study many items needed for research.

I am indebted for favors extended to me by the staffs of the Musselman Library at Bluffton College, the Menno Simons Historical Library at Eastern Mennonite College, the Mennonite Historical Library at Goshen College, the Schwenkfelder Library, and the libraries of Ursinus College, the Lancaster Mennonite Historical Society, the Historical Societies of Bucks and Montgomery Counties, the Historical Society of Pennsylvania, the *Heimatstelle Pfalz* in Kaiserslautern, and the *Mennonitische Forschungstelle* at the Weierhof—both of the latter in the Federal Republic of Germany. The Archives of the Mennonite Church at Goshen, Indiana, overseen by Franconia Conference native Leonard Gross, were of special importance and of great help in making manuscript copies of old correspondence available. Barbara Coffman of Vineland, Ontario, supplied a collection of significant letters, as did Amos Hoover of the Muddy Creek Farm Library.

The unique pile of materials assembled by Robert F. Ulle on colonial Mennonite history became the point of departure for my research, and will enrich his own forthcoming writing on the Germantown Mennonite experience. Similarly, a documented first-draft account based on the research of James O. and Dorothy Lehman served as the backbone of my Chapter 11, on the Civil War period. The unselfish sharing of Robert Ulle and James Lehman was a demonstration to me of the unconventional nature of "the right fellowship" which is the theme of this book.

In countless conversations and telephone calls over the past three years I have drawn especially on the generously given historical knowledge of Joel Alderfer, John E. Fretz, James Gerhart, Alan G. Keyser, Isaac Clarence Kulp, Jr., Harrison Landis, John E. Lapp, Oliver Nyce, Marvin Rosenberger, and Howard Shelly. Most of all, J. C. Wenger of Goshen, Indiana, helped me eliminate numerous errors of detail. I am all too well aware that the errors remaining are my own. The quality of many of the illustrations was enhanced by the careful photographic reproductions of my son, John A. Ruth. Thomas Nolan helped me greatly with the index.

Both the Eastern District Conference and the Franconia Conference contributed heavily to the expenses of this project. The most remarkable demonstration of this separated family's joint support came in response to a fund-gathering led by Mary Jane Lederach Hershey. The widespread participation of interested individuals showed that the call for a new history touched a spiritual nerve in both conferences.

Under the Mennonite Heritage Council formed several years earlier by the Franconia Conference for my guidance and support in creative projects on Mennonite themes, I had already written over half of a history I was calling "The Split." This was an account of the 1847 division which had produced "The East Pennsylvania Mennonite Conference." Under the guidance of the editorial committee for this book, it was decided to integrate the material in my manuscript on "The Split" into the tercentenary history of both conferences. The patience of the editorial committee was repeatedly tried as my writing took over a year more than they had arranged for. In spite of the fact that there was no financial obligation to me for this extra time, I was given further remuneration. To Walton Hackman, who took strong and friendly initiative in this matter, and to others involved, I owe a debt of thanks.

The Salford Mennonite congregation, in which I have been serving as an associate pastor for over a decade, has allowed me liberty to range widely in my work and research, while at the same time providing a supportive home base. One might travel far before finding, as I have found in the very place of my youth, just such a favorable combination of attitudes.

One special word, to members of the Eastern District Conference. Your trusting such a work to the hand of someone from the Franconia Conference is a gracious gesture. Undoubtedly my Franconia Conference orientation shows even more definitely than I am aware. If it proves unfair at any point, I ask your forbearance, and that you regard the expression of my bias as a part of the process of reaching toward a better mutual understanding. May this cooperation, which has enhanced our friendship as we have explored our common rootage, point us more faithfully in the direction of a right fellowship in Christ.

John L. Ruth
Vernfield
January 31, 1983   Harleysville, Pennsylvania

Maintaining the Right Fellowship

Chapter 1

"For the Sake of Their Faith"

1648-1681

In a little vine-growing village on the Pfrimm River a two-hour westward walk from the free imperial city of Worms, a man stared into the eastern sky before daylight in April 1665. A bright, long-tailed comet, seeming to point toward the earth, filled him with misgivings. It was the third of such stars to appear in the past quarter-year. "What they mean," mused Yillisz Kassel, father of one of a dozen local Mennonite families, "I am afraid many people will learn with sorrow and misery." The glowing tail of the star looked to him like a rod—the sign of God's wrath for disobedient human beings.

Yillisz (Julius or Yillis) Kassel, whose family would carry his rough sketches of the three comets to the forests of a transatlantic colony, was hardly jumping to conclusions. "For in the year 1618," he recalled somberly, "I saw also the great comet star."[1] 1618! History pupils for centuries to come would recognize the year as the beginning of the sustained catastrophe they were taught to call the "Thirty Years' War." And the common people of the Palatinate who endured it, as had Yillisz and his family, could only recall this interminable "great misery in Germany" with the bleakest of feelings.

The fertile Rhineland, by virtue of its central location and wealth of food, had become the cockpit of brawling Christian nationalities—Catholic, Lutheran, and Reformed—trying to maintain or redefine Europe politically and religiously. It was a war to be remembered for its unspeakable bitterness, by the people whose farmland it tormented. No atrocity too gross had been left uninvented, no known store of food unrifled, no castle or farmstead or village within reach unwrecked. Historians have repeatedly confessed the inadequacy of words to evoke the degradation and brutality and cynicism of the spectacle—Swedish, Spanish, Dutch, Swiss, French, and German soldiers tramping back and forth over the suffering Palatine landscape, foraging, looting, smashing, raping, killing, and burning. Something in the richness of "that Fruitful and Delicious Countrey" seemed to evoke the worst in the demoralized and hungry mercenaries fighting for the meaningless honor of their distant kings. And when, in 1648, it had ended in exhaustion in the Peace of Westphalia, with hardly a stone on top of another, wolves roaming empty lanes, once-lush fields scrub-forested, and, in places, a tenth of the population left, the old Catholic German Empire had become a shell. Sixty-one cities and some 300 petty princes paid lip service to it, the map of their holdings a splotchy puzzle.

The largest piece in the Rhineland was the "electoral" Palatinate *(Kurpfalz)*, straddling the north-flowing Rhine, pocked by free cities like Worms and Speyer, and crazy-patched with dozens of other little duchies and earldoms. The elector was headquartered in Heidelberg, just east of the Rhine, where the huge castle looked down over the Neckar. Yillisz Kassel's hamlet of Kriegsheim was in Palatine holdings, and thus under the administration of the elector *(Kurfürst)* himself, but at one edge it touched the little Leiningen-Dagsburg-Falkenberg earldom. However small, each such hereditary realm had its ruined castle and wasted fields. Villages, or even single farmsteads, called "hofs," might be divided among two or three baronies or church properties, each with its peculiar set of taxes, tithes, and excises. Small farmers might own modest plots, but their feudal landlords still lived by inherited, multiple, and endless revenues.

Some twenty communities in the general area of Kriegsheim, just west of the sprawling and multi-channeled Rhine, had in a recent census been designated as containing Mennonite inhabitants. Yillisz Kassel's name had been ninth on a list of such people as Jan Clemens of neighboring Niederflörsheim, Peter Bechtel of Gundersheim, Peter Schumacher of Osthofen, Heinrich Fritt of Aspisheim, Heinrich Kolb and Thomas Rohr of Wolfsheim, Jan Bliem of Spiesheim, Johannes Herrstein of Obersülzen, Heinrich Jansen of Rodenbach, and Heinrich Kassel of Gerolsheim.[2] These families, unlike the Mennonites of Holland, were not really citizens of their "country," the Palatinate (in German called the *Pfalz*). As "*Manisten*" (Mennonites) they were rather "tolerated" people who paid, as did the local Jews, special taxes for the privilege of living and working among the citizens. They did not fit any of the three religious categories—Catholic, Lutheran, and Reformed—that were recognized under the treaties made at the end of the Thirty Years' War. Nor were they appreciated by the clergy of the three official churches. These pastors felt that they had enough of a struggle to administer their decimated parishes without the irritating presence of people who looked after their own spiritual concerns, did not "go to church" or the official sacrament, "let their children run about

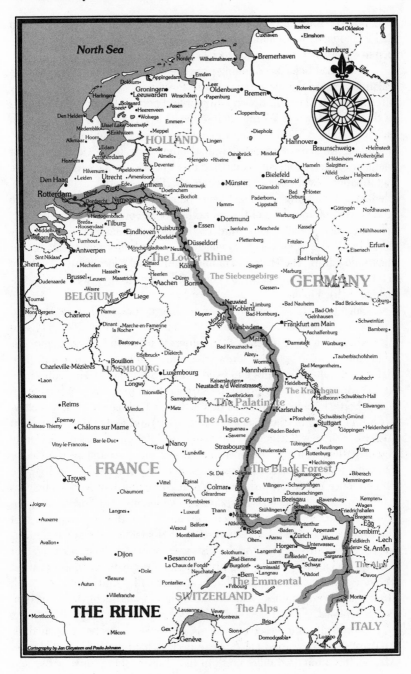

THE RHINE

Cartography by Jan Gleysteen and Paula Johnson

unbaptized," sometimes held "their services boldly in the forest," and even had the audacity to "solemnize marriages" on their own.[3] What would happen to society in general if such social variety were tolerated?

There had been a continuing presence of these stubborn people in the Palatinate since the early days of the Protestant "Reformation," shortly after Martin Luther had defied emperor and pope at the imperial congress in the nearby town of Worms. Before the Thirty Years' War they had been called "Baptizers" *(Täufer)*, or even, more ominously, "Re-baptizers" *(Wiedertäufer*, Anabaptists), and they had often been linked in the popular memory to the violent Anabaptist radicals who had, in the early days of the Reformation, established by force an abortive "kingdom" in the Westphalian city of Münster. A few years before the war had broken out, no fewer than 106 members of this group had been counted in Kriegsheim itself—between a half and a third of the local population.[4] Though they could be harried from village to village, it seemed impossible to stamp out their fellowships. The Herrstein family, complained a local pastor, "will not let themselves be instructed or converted, even if they were to be immediately fried in oil."[5]

Once the war was ended, however, their notorious diligence attracted the favor of the new elector, the Protestant Karl Ludwig (1648-80), who needed nothing more urgently than settlers to restore his ravaged land. His mild immigration policies drew not only Catholics, Lutherans, and Reformed, but Mennonites and even a small *Bruderhof* of Hutterites from far-off Moravia as well. And so the surviving Palatine Anabaptist communities shortly became the base for new settlements of harassed fellow-believers from both north (the "Siebengebirge" area) and south (Switzerland and Alsace). Whereas Catholic, Lutheran, and Reformed pastors jealously resented their coming, the government—or more accurately the elector himself—from economic motives—was more tolerant. Already in 1652 the church office in Niederflörsheim, the next village north of Kriegsheim, was complaining that foreign "Anabaptists," adherents of a "dangerous, obstinate sect," had slipped into their community.[6] In the same years, east of the Rhine in the Kraichgau district south of Heidelberg, secret forest meetings of newly arrived Swiss Anabaptists were occurring. Thus occurred that mixing of Dutch-speaking Rhenish Mennonites with German-speaking Palatine and Swiss Anabaptists that in another half century would establish strong new communities between the Delaware and Schuylkill Rivers in North America.

Shortly after the Peace of 1648, as a little room was being opened for Anabaptists in the wasted Palatinate, especially hard times descended upon Mennonites a hundred miles north in the "Lower Rhine" area, above and

THE LOWER RHINE

Cartography by Jan Gleysteen and Paula Johnson

below Krefeld "in the land of Meurs," in the duchies of Jülich and Cleves, and in the Siebengebirge region of present-day Bonn. Here some five or six hundred Mennonites, toughened by a century of persecution, had first won a toehold in the cottage weaving industry of the region, and then threatened to dominate it. Since they tended to take such good care of each other, and had what seemed to others to be an uncanny network for letting each other know of available land or economic opportunities, they were sometimes resented. Like Jews, they were highly motivated, and knew their living lay not in their social status but in their work. They were by heritage religiously separate and self-sufficient.

The town of Krefeld itself had a long-standing reputation for extraordinary tolerance, and so Mennonite weavers, bleachers, and dyers tended to resettle there, bringing the town eventual wealth, by their productivity, that far surpassed that of the neighboring towns that had banished them. In this region lived the parents of the people who would be founders of "Germantown." In 1652 we may observe the Mennonite Wilhelm Lukens being expelled from the village of Dahlem. Four of his children—one the wife of a Mennonite deacon—would be Germantown pioneers. Fleeing from Gladbach to Krefeld in 1654 were the parents of Jan Lensen, who with his wife, Mercken, would be the first Mennonites of Germantown. In the same community of Jülich we find a ruckus going on in the home of Matheis Doors, who would have no fewer than six children among the Germantown pioneers. The bailiff had hit Matheis' pregnant wife in the face, and the baby, born a few days later, was forcibly baptized Catholic. The father, a Mennonite by conviction, was fined 100 guilders, and joined the Reformed Church—for which, at least, there was legal provision in this Catholic-ruled province.[7]

Likewise in the Löwenberg or Siebengebirge district, a little farther south along the Rhine near Bonn, an inventory of Anabaptists was called for in 1652. Sixty-one households were listed, including such names as Clemens, Hendricks, Krey, Rohr, and Schomecker. Most were weavers and vine-dressers. The newly Catholic government gave these people, many of whom owned only a few acres of land, two years to vacate the territory. Not everyone could move to the town of Krefeld; some of those who tried to do so had to stay on neighboring farms. And so it was the Palatinate, where "High German" rather than "Low Dutch" was spoken and where officials admitted there was "more than too much open space," that became for some of these harassed people the best option. We may observe Arnold Schomecker's widow and her children selling the family "house and hof" at Niederdollendorf, "for the sake of their faith." Three of the six children are still minors. Loading their "movables" on a boat, they sail upstream, south toward Mainz, from which they will eventually reach and settle in Kriegs-heim, the Palatine home of Yillisz Kassel.[8] Perhaps, for all we know, the Kassels themselves are part of this migration. In any case, Peter Schomecker (Schumacher), one of the oldest sons, will one day be a citizen of Germantown, and his Kolb grandsons will be among the founders of the daughter settlement, Skippack.

Except for Holland, European countries had not yet learned the tolerance which would one day give Mennonites freedom of conscience. Even in Krefeld, the Catholics were allowed to worship only in a convent church, and had to pay fees for baptism, marriage, and death rites to the dominant Reformed Church. All groups, including Mennonites, had to have their marriages announced in the Reformed Church. Down in Amsterdam, the Mennonites were already much freer. Their merchants had advanced so swiftly to wealth, culture, and power that they could heavily influence government policy. But even under Holland's laws, when it came to the colony of New Amsterdam across the Atlantic, the Dutch Reformed Church was still trying in the 1640s to practice a monopoly. Its officials were afraid to let even a Lutheran pastor hold meetings there, for fear the Mennonites who met privately on Long Island and read, rather than preached to each other, would be emboldened "to introduce like public assemblies." And "even the Jews," they noted, would like "to erect a synagogue" in New Amsterdam "for the exercise of their blasphemous religion." If Jews, Mennonites, and "English Independents" all had the freedom of public worship in the new colony (which would one day be New York), "a very Babel" might result. The church must "employ all diligence to frustrate all such plans, that the wolves may be warded off from the tender lambs of Christ." Means had to be found "by which the true Reformed Religion will be maintained, and all other sects excluded. . . ."[9]

Thus for the Mennonites of Europe, who had to live in the crevices of the social establishment, it sometimes made little difference whether the government was Catholic or Protestant. Either one might be intolerant. The very fiercest of their tormentors were in fact the Swiss Reformed clergy and officials. As recently as fifty years earlier, the main leader of the Zurich Anabaptists, Hans Landis, had been publicly beheaded, and his son Felix had expired in prison as late as 1642. Local Reformed clergymen had found it unforgivable that the Bachmans, Eglis, Fricks, Heges, and Landises should have their own unofficial church, and then refuse, while quoting the words of Christ, to swear legal oaths or take up the sword in military service. Several farms were confiscated from young Henry Frick, a former ensign who had refused to go back into military duty; the church treasury had been confiscated, and the chief members roughly jailed in the Oetenbach convent.[10] Even letters of protest from wealthy Dutch Mennonites and officials did no good. Under sustained harassment, the small Zurich Anabaptist fellowship then disappeared, its weary members turning up a few years later in Bern, Alsace, and the Palatinate.

The old Täufer or Anabaptist community in the Bernese valleys proved a bigger challenge to the authorities. There were too many Anabaptists, and they had too many sympathizers and even recent converts, for them to be dealt with easily. Complaints were made by Bernese Reformed officials that the Anabaptists were spreading. Their criticism of the established church made other people lose respect for it. "Not only do these people not attend official church services," report the officials, "they preach and baptize without legal authorization, and they exercise church discipline according to their own conceptions." In alarm, the Canton of Bern organized a special "Anabaptist Committee" to hunt down and break up the congregations of these "stiff-necked" people.

Anyone who wants to understand the traditional "Franconia" or "Lancaster" Mennonite temperament must ponder this era, when these Swiss mountain-farmers stood in sustained tension with church and city officials, and their attitudes were sealed into their fellowship by innumerable incidents. From the earliest years of the Reformation their Swiss ancestors— led by such persons as Conrad Grebel, Felix Mantz, and Georg Blaurock— had learned to read the New Testament as though it applied directly to everyday life. It had broken in upon their minds that the kingdom of God was to be recognized not just as a biblical figure of speech, to be heard in sermons, but as an impinging, overwhelming, and definitive reality. It created, in the midst of the world, its own new social order. For acting on this basis the leaders of the Anabaptist movement had been executed by both Catholic and Protestant governments, tightly allied with their official churches.

Whether or not the church officials felt that the populace was willing to live by the ethos of the Sermon on the Mount, the Swiss "Brothers" (and Sisters) were ready to try. Postponing the practice of this teaching to a future millennium, or "excusing" Christians from its requirements because of human "weakness," were considered by these simple Christians to be forms of disobedience. The gospel had been given to be obeyed, not just known. When Jesus had said, "Swear not at all," and "Love your enemies," he had not merely been offering a set of higher ideals; he had been describing the actual behavior of those who believed that the kingdom of heaven was at hand. Not only had he announced the new order; the manner of his life had been narrated at such length in the gospels because it was to be seen as our example. It was meaningless to talk about knowing Christ unless one was

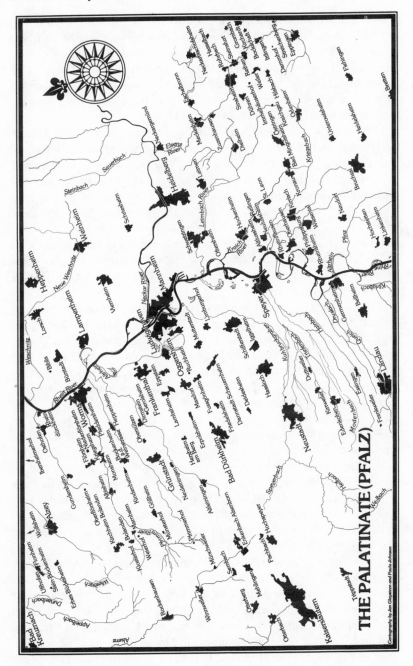

THE PALATINATE (PFALZ)

Cartography by Jan Gleysteen and Paula Johnson

following Christ in one's individual and social behavior. Theologizing by
church leaders of an "invisible church" had the result of avoiding the possibility of spiritual accountability—"binding and loosing"—among church
members. Allowing people who fought and swore and intrigued and
adulterized to come to the Lord's supper because one didn't want to
"judge," and then confiscating the property of those who stayed away for
conscience' sake, were not signs of the church of Christ.

So thought the tough Anabaptist Stauffers and Gerbers and Meyers
and Funks and Haldemans. The Bernese government, made jittery by
recent peasant unrest, tried jailing, exile, flogging, brandings, fines, and
even sentences to row as galley slaves. But many of the Swiss Brothers and
Sisters, sometimes hiding in mountainside huts, could not be moved. As a
Dutch Mennonite wrote a few years later, they knew that "no body can be
put to, or endure greater suffering, than to be forced to believe and do
contrary to what he can in Conscience understand and take out of God's
holy Word." And surely the Reformed ministers, themselves bitterly critical
of the Catholic persecutions, knew that "no body can be made a good
Christian by Force...."[12]

Reluctantly, in quiet leave-takings that did not always get into legal
records, some of the Bernese Anabaptists vanished from the meadows in the
foothills of the Alps, to reappear by 1650 on the records as renters of war-
wasted Palatine hofs several hundred miles to the north, on the east side of
the Rhine. Here the Bachmans, Freys, Fricks, Heges, and Landises of
Zurich joined Dirsteins, Funks, and Senns of Bern on ruined estates which
they immediately began to help restore. They settled just where, thirty
years earlier, the two fiercest battles of the Palatinate had been fought, and
the destruction was most complete. These Anabaptists were, it should be
understood, only a small percentage of an extensive northward Swiss influx
into these depopulated lands. But they soon numbered over 400, and included such additional names as Groff, Meyer, Musselman, Oberholtzer,
Rosenberger, Ruth, and Sauter.[13] Their grandchildren would one day help
to carve new communities out of North American forests, migrating there
side-by-side with such Swiss-born neighbors as the Lutheran Altdörfers and
the Reformed Hirtzells.

The district east of the Rhine, in modern times called Baden (though
then part of the Palatinate), is of special interest to our story. The
"Kraichgau," or region drained by the Kraich River, is a major source of
early emigrants to the American Mennonite community later to be called
the "Franconia Conference." Here the Anabaptists, taking on the name of
"Menists" (which had better standing in Holland), clustered on wrecked
hofs and in villages like Steinsfurt, Reihen, or Kirchardt, halfway between

Heidelberg and Heilbronn. Almost immediately, they sent two of their ministers, Hans Mayer and Hans Körber (John Moyer and John Gerber) to petition the elector for permission to meet for worship as their brothers and sisters on the left side of the Rhine were doing. A prominent merchant of Worms, claimed as a member of their faith, also was to see the elector regarding the possibility of their holding meetings.[14] No permission was given, but neither was a prohibition declared, and so these Swiss immigrant "Menists" had quietly gathered, in the summer in the feudal forest near Steinsfurt, occasionally in a monastery building, and for two successive winters in the dwelling of a widow. Their vigorous work won the respect of an official in nearby Hilsbach, who filed a report that the hofs of Streichenberg, Immelhaus, Steinsfurt, and Reihen were being restored by Anabaptists. "They keep clearing forests," he wrote, "make swamps tillable," and "diligently discharge their obligations." Of special note was their manner of helping their poorer members to pay the various taxes. One would hardly find, among the other inhabitants, people "who could farm such properties." "The manorial hofs would have to lie empty and spoiled if these families were to move away."[15]

A German Mennonite *Hof* in the general *Kraichgau* area, as it appeared in the 1950s, just before several buildings were razed. The *"Ursenbacherhof."* (Walter Schmutz, Daisbach)

But not everyone was content to have these people around, and in the evening of March 2, 1661, officials broke in upon a meeting in the widow's house. The fifty-three "Anabaptist persons" present were just beginning to sing a hymn—doubtless from their collection of martyr ballads called the *Ausbundt*. The whole gathering was arrested—"man, wife and child"— and a hearing was held by which the officials determined that the people were "pure Swiss." We may note that whereas one of the Anabaptists arrested two decades earlier in Zurich had been named Rudolph Hege, now there was a Rudi Hege among those caught here at Sinsheim in the Palatinate.° These distressed Menists protested that they had been holding their meetings "in all quietness and without the knowledge" of anyone else. No one had been tempted to come with them to the meetings. It was so important to them to be allowed to worship together, they said, that "before they would give up these meetings they would rather leave the land."[16]

On the following October 23, to their great dismay, the electoral regime decreed a major fine of 100 Reichstaler, each person having been caught at the meeting to be assessed proportionately to his means.[17] Again they protested in vain. They were told that they might now again meet in peace, but that on every such occasion there was to be a fine strictly reckoned for each person present, young or old. A religious head tax, in other words. The same arrangement was imposed on the other side of the Rhine at Wolfsheim, home of the Heinrich Kolb family northwest of Yillisz Kassel's Kriegsheim. There too an angry church inspector reported meetings of over 200 persons among the Anabaptists, whose fellowship had lately been augmented by new Swiss immigrants. Further, he claimed, the Anabaptists were trying to mislead members of the Reformed Church.[18]

The consternation which now spread among the Palatine Mennonites was complicated at Kriegsheim by a recent division in the congregation. Some six years earlier, very soon after the Dutch-speaking immigrants from the Lower Rhine had arrived, an itinerating English Quaker minister named William Ames had been in the community, preaching a Christianity as stringent as that of the Mennonites, but much more outspoken, and with another kind of orientation to governmental authority. The Quakers preached against the payment of such taxes as served for military exemptions, or which purchased the right to hold public worship. No monetary price, they insisted, could be set on such things. Honor should be given to God, not human beings; thus, hats should not be taken off in deference to officials or anyone else.

°There were also participants by the name of Groff, Landes, Mayer, Oberholzer, Rohr, and Rosenberger.

Ames won not only a hearing but also a number of converts from the Kriegsheim community, including members of the Hendricks, Schomecker (now Schumacher), and eventually the Kassel families. Other Quaker missionaries traveled about the Continent preaching fearlessly, often with jail-stays as their reward, and winning small groups of converts, though only in Mennonite communities. One of the Kriegsheim converts, Jan Hendricks, traveled with William Ames on a preaching mission as far as Danzig. The reports of such trips were joyfully read by Friends in England as possible foretastes of a European harvest among people now covered with great spiritual "darkness."

These English missionaries displayed a truly astonishing strength of purpose and willingness to endure derision and beatings "for the sake of the truth." Indefatigable visitors, they made all kinds of hopeful acquaintances, even checking into the little Hutterite Bruderhof in the city of Mannheim. Ames and others who followed in the work actually made friends with the elector himself, as well as with his sister Elizabeth. On occasion they were invited to dine with this unusual prince in his castle, where he displayed a cordiality and willingness to hear the case of their "Friends" which they interpreted as love. He gave no evidence of displeasure when they ate at the table in his and other noble persons' presence without removing their hats, or when they addressed him with the familiar *"du und dich"*—"thee and thou." More than once, claimed these Quakers in their letters home, the elector told them not to obey the mean-spirited Reformed churchmen who denied them their normal rights. He excused the behavior of the state clergy by saying that their support was a political necessity in his state. At times the Quakers thought they were on the verge of receiving full toleration by electoral fiat, but eventually they learned that the prince's personal friendliness was one thing, and the practical functioning of the Reformed and Lutheran clergy, whose friendship he also cultivated, another.

At any rate, there were now two sectarian congregations for the Kriegsheim officials to worry about. The Quakers made more difficulty by their refusal of some of the traditional taxes the Mennonites had been willing to pay. When the local Reformed clergy understood that these people would now decline to pay the "tithes" which helped pay salaries in the state church, the Quakers were regarded as "the offensivest, the irregularest, and the perturbatiousest people that are of any sect."[19] But as their leader, ex-Mennonite Hans or Jan Philip Labach protested, "It seems strange to us that money is demanded from us for payment regarding the freedom of our conscience and meeting." In such matters of faith "no assessment can be made ... nor money charged."[20] The Mennonites, on the other hand, while they complained over the raising of their taxes for freedom from guard duty, mentioned only their poverty—they said they barely had bread—and the economically draining task of restoring unproductive fields.[21]

Holding out stoutly against the taxes, the Kriegsheim Quakers finally saw seven of their men jailed, with heavy confiscations made on their property. Eight cows were taken. George and Peter Schumacher, having arrived only five years earlier, each lost a bedstead, possibly the main furniture they had brought up the Rhine when expelled from their ancestral home. Hendrick Gerretsen, whose son would one day live in America, lost two cows. Cabbage and turnips and sheep and swine were likewise forcibly taken and sold to satisfy the guard-duty and meeting taxes in the spring of 1664.[22]

All this unhealthy commotion deeply disturbed the mayor of Kriegsheim. By refusing the taxes, some of which, he claimed, were ancient and never previously questioned even by Mennonites, and not even letting crops lie in the field where they could be quietly picked up, the Quakers have caused, he complained, "such confusion ... among the common people that nobody wants to obey anyone else any more, so that an uprising is to be feared in the whole community, and the best inhabitants will leave the village of Kriegsheim and settle elsewhere."[23] At the same time the Mennonites filed a complaint of another kind of trouble—the attempts of certain people in the community to reclaim from Mennonite ownership, paying only the original price, the properties these recent immigrants had rebuilt. The Mennonites appealed directly to the elector that this practice of the *Auslösungsrecht* should be disallowed. If this is not done, they inform their prince, "very many people who have already pretty much made up their minds to move from Holland to the Electoral Palatinate will be frightened off and will stay back."[24]

The Mennonite-toleration issue was now reaching a crisis. English Quaker missionaries returned periodically to strengthen their precious flock at Kriegsheim, once with the ostensible reason of helping their friends with the wine harvest. Missionary Ames was able to visit the elector, where he told of the difficulties of the Kriegsheim Friends. Around the same time a written appeal came from the Mennonites of the Alzey district, which included Kriegsheim. This congregation too hoped for a better hearing from their prince than from local religious officials. The poll tax or fine for holding meetings, they claimed, was higher than they had the resources to pay. "We had greatly rejoiced, certainly, when we heard that we might live in the dear fatherland ... to enjoy freedom and the exercise [of our religion] and your Electoral most serene Highness's most gracious protection, and in response to this not only brought our possessions and livelihood, but applied and spent our bodily strength, in order to bring into a handsome up-building and improvement the wastage of houses and property, and we also caused many of our relatives in the faith to come into the land, so that it might be re-inhabited." But now, if no relief from the recently imposed fines is to be had, "dire need will force us to leave the dear fatherland and bring us into misery." There is no danger, these Mennonites imply, of any civil disobedience on their part, outside of these impossible taxes. They are "willing," in fact, "to render the most devoted obedience with body and property, so far as we can."[25] This reverent, biblically based but almost medieval-sounding principle of dutiful subjection to rulership, visible in many American Mennonites and Amish in America three centuries later, had another flavor than that of the Quakerism born in the atmosphere of the English Revolution. It was also a great deal milder than some of its earlier Anabaptist precedents.

The elector, who was loath to lose the economic benefit of his Mennonite farmers, finally reacted with a special "Concession," issued on August 4, 1664. Acknowledging the Mennonite peculiarity of abstaining from defense and war activities, he reminds his officials that the Palatinate nevertheless has the highest need for subjects who can "rebuild and bring into proper condition" the emptied countryside. Therefore, after an exact

Karl Ludwig, Elector (*Kurfürst*) of the Palatinate from the end of the Thirty Years' War in 1648 until his death in 1680. This "pious and learned Prince," who granted the important "Concession" of 1664 to the Anabaptists of his regime, was a grandson of the English King James I. (Museum of Palatinate History, Speyer)

registry of Mennonites has been drawn up, they may be allowed to meet in their villages for worship, but in groups representing no more than twenty families, and without allowing any members of the official churches to attend. Any Mennonite who fails to be registered will be severely fined, and other inhabitants are to give such a person no lodging. In return for this declared "freedom," each Mennonite household will be charged six guilders a year, under the title, "Mennonite Recognition Money."[26]

This official act was a watershed; it gave the Mennonites more security than they had previously known. In some verses written during the year following the Concession, we find Yillisz Kassel acknowledging the divine gift of "peace and freedom." But hardly had the Mennonite registry been recorded, listing some ninety families west and north of Worms, when another misery descended on the struggling local villages. Troops of marauding soldiers, involved in one of the recurrent border battles the elector was too weak to control, once again threatened the safety and property of the area. To make things worse for Yillisz Kassel, he became seriously and painfully ill, to the point that death seemed a likelihood. Gravely concerned now for his family, he prayed for God to "show me a place" in which to hide from the dangers of war.

When he had watched the "three stars" earlier in the year Kassel had hardly guessed trouble would come so soon, but now he confessed that "we have well earned this punishment" by being more concerned with "temporal goods" than salvation, and have lived "in many things like the world." Now danger of civil breakdown had the community on the brink of flight from their homes, and Yillisz broke off his verses in a state of anxious prayer.

When he next took up his pen, it was to thank God heartily for the refuge they had found in the nearby city of Worms, "among people who show me love and loyalty." He was as sick as ever, and lay awake at night in pain, writing his verses while others slept, but at least his family was safe. Frightful reports of pillage and murder in the countryside were afloat. Yillisz mused sadly on the account the plunderers must finally render to God, and contrasted with their attitude his own profoundest hope to be saved "through the blood of Christ." His own righteousness was "much too small" to trust for salvation. "*Ach nein, ach nein, das thu ich nicht,*" he recoiled ("Oh no, oh no, that I'll not do!"), even though some Lutheran critics of the Mennonites accused them of trusting, like Catholics, in their own "good works."

.After many months of suspense, the chaos subsided, and the Kassel family, with Yillisz still painfully ill, was able to return to Kriegsheim. The countryside was in an appalling condition:

> Many a person brought into need,
> Mistreated to the point of death;
> Many fair houses knocked apart,
> People even stripped of clothes,
> Cattle and crops have disappeared,
> Barrels split open, the wine all spilled,
> Thus folk are cheated of their keep.[27]

Yillisz saw it all in biblical terms, as when God punished Israel for unfaithfulness.

Another subject also saddened his thoughts, one that was harder for him to discuss openly in Kriegsheim. In his verses, where he could speak "as before God," he grieved over the division in his congregation between Mennonites and Quakers. His homespun couplets on the topic declare a parable about a wealthy king. This gracious ruler had placed high up on a mountain a desirable jewel which no one but those who climbed the mountain could receive. In response to a challenge and invitation from the king, some people began to climb, but before long a difference of opinion broke out regarding the proper path. The climbers began to accuse and scorn each other with great clamor, and divided, "as two flocks in a meadow."

> Who now will speak a verdict true
> About this family split in two?
> Nothing to say, have I decided,
> But that they both are to be chided . . . .
> The Lord, Who every heart can see—
> He knows how sad it is to me . . . .[28]

Despite his strong feelings, Yillisz wished his poem to remain anonymous. The person who wrote these lines, he concludes, "lives in Germany, and would gladly see the congregation's welfare." The poem, perhaps meant to be a tract (the local Quakers did publish one), was doubtless never printed, but found its way in Yillisz's original manuscript to a settlement in the New World which was opened up, in part, by the very Kriegsheim Quakers here alluded to. It appears that Yillisz had descendants in both Mennonite and Quaker "flocks."

As these verses were being penned (1667), the greatest single influx of Mennonite refugees into the Palatinate was still three or four years in the future. This was to result from the climactic efforts of the Reformed pastors of the Swiss canton of Bern, several hundred miles south of the Palatinate, to convert or rid themselves, once and for all, of the Anabaptists in their parishes. Those who would not take an oath of allegiance to the Canton of Bern were given two weeks to leave. Property was confiscated, forty men and women were jailed in the town of Bern (one eighty-year-old man died there), some were whipped, branded, and sent across the border into Burgundy, and six men were even shipped in chains to Venice, where they were to be handed over to officials to be made galley slaves.[29]

These ominous moves finally broke the grip many local Anabaptists had on their immemorial homeland, especially those whose homes were taken and sold. By November 2, 1671, 200 of them were reported as arriving, destitute, in the Mennonite communities of the Palatinate, with bundles on their backs and children in their arms. The group included crippled persons. Only a few horses were available to carry the weak or elderly. Ninety-two-year-old Bishop Christian Stauffer, patriarch of seventy-eight living descendants, arrived with his seventy-year-old second wife. Christian was a veteran *"Taüfer"* who had spent time in a Bernese prison over a quarter of a century earlier. Not all of his married descendants who came along on the trek had their spouses with them. One grandson, twenty-seven-year-old Hans Stauffer, was still a bachelor. As he settled here with his relatives in the desolate countryside along the Rhine, it would have been shocking for him to realize that he would make his next move, thirty-seven years later, to a plantation along a river called "Schuylkill" on another continent.

Along with the Stauffers came thirty-six-year-old Anna Neuschwanger, with only one of her six children, and without her husband. Daniel Stauffer, cousin of Hans, and his pregnant wife also had only their oldest child along, with five more remaining back in Bern. They did have two sets of bedclothes. Babe Schlappe, an eighteen-year-old girl, had left a family of parents and eight sisters. With her was Fronia Engel, a fifteen-year-old orphan. Neither had any money. Fifty-year-old Margaret Bieri had left her husband and four children behind. Some of the spouses who did not come along were of the Reformed Church, and thus were not in legal difficulty. Incredibly, among the group was found ninety-five-year-old Michael Shenk.[30]

By the beginning of 1672 no less than 787 of such Bernese refugees were reported as having streamed north into the Palatine Mennonite communities, 359 west of the Rhine, and 428 on the east.[31] It took Deacons Valentin Hütwohl and Georg Liechten four days of traveling from village to village in their region to get a complete roster. Valentin and Jan Clemens, in whose villages some fifty were housed, then sent the list to an influential Mennonite merchant and deacon at Amsterdam, asking for aid.[32] The Dutch Mennonite churches, touched to the heart, sent substantial gifts of 15,466 guilders back to the Palatinate during that "Anxious Year" of 1672.[33] Such remarkable brotherly compassion, felt by the prosperous, cultured

Dutch Mennonites for the poverty-stricken Swiss-Palatines related to them only by faith and through letters, would continue for six decades, with appeal after appeal being followed by substantial monetary response. This story of brotherhood has been insufficiently preserved by American historians. As concerned as any of the Dutch was Thielman van Braght, recent compiler of the monumental *Martyrs Mirror*. Recognizing in this new Swiss migration an extension of his Mennonite saga of persecution, he now hurried down to the Palatinate to see the exodus firsthand. Thirteen years later he included the story of it in his expanded second edition.[34]

The question was where to absorb these care-worn pilgrims. We may select the example of one Mennonite community—Ibersheim, a ruined estate with several hofs some six miles down the Rhine from Worms. Here, for reasons unexplained by historians, there had been latitude for the Mennonites to own land even before the great Electoral Concession. It was already nicknamed "the Mennonistenhof." Its meadows and fields lay on either side of the great river, and some crops had to be ferried across. A Reformed chapel still stood in the main hof, but since the recent owners were mostly Mennonites, it was little used. This situation had greatly disturbed the Reformed pastor of the district, who felt he was watching a deterioration of his own charge. He complained bitterly that babies on the hof were no longer being baptized, and that some of his parishioners had attended the Mennonite meetings. When questioned, one Mennonite replied, "We don't put any watchman at the door, but we let it stand open, prevent no one, tell no one to go in—they go at their own privilege." As the Reformed pastor continued to submit official objections, the Mennonites reaffirmed their willingness to live by the terms of the Electoral Concession, as far as their "conscience and teachings" would permit. But on the point of actually preventing people from coming to the meeting, or turning away those who wanted to seek their soul's salvation along with the Mennonite congregations, here "one must obey God rather than man."[35]

Now that the "strange Anabaptists from Switzerland" had begun to arrive, local Mennonites such as Deacon Valentin Hütwohl were reported to be helping them move to the region of Ibersheim.[36] Noting large meetings, nervous officials clamped down on the Ibersheimers with a heavy fine for baptizing in front of the assembled congregation a man who had been Reformed, though his grandparents had been Mennonite. The fine money was to be used to repair the Reformed chapel, which had only fifty members on the roll.[37]

Then the Stauffers and their companions in misery arrived at the "Mickenhäuserhof," a farmstead at the west end of the Ibersheimerhof. This new Bernese breed, according to one report, was even more "obstinate" than the Mennonites of previous immigrations. Their toughness was certainly necessary to cope with the situation they found at their new home. When they first arrived a gang of bandits was housed in some castle ruins, from whom the would-be settlers hid during the night in bushes

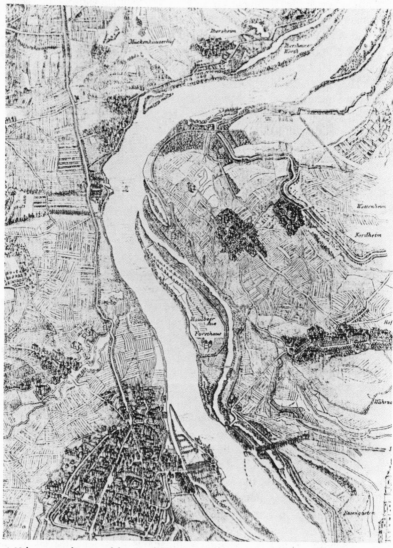

A 19th-century drawing of the city of Worms, on the Rhine. The Mennonite *Mückenhäuserhof* and *Ibersheim* are shown where the northward-flowing Rhine bends east and north. (Fritz Kehr, Ibersheim)

along the sprawling, marshy Rhine. But after the elector's troops had routed the bandits, the Swiss refugees went to work among the weed-covered fields and collapsed buildings.[38] Grazing and fishing rights came with the property. Here, except in years such as 1674 and 1688, when the Palatinate again turned into a battleground, the industrious Swiss farmers found peace and economic stability. Such family names as Hiestand, Reiff, and Hackman became identified with the community, intermarrying with the hardy Stauffers or the Dutch-speaking Clemens family.

Why all these strands of local history? Because they are the preparation of that spiritual family which, having mixed itself together in the Palatinate, would, first in 1683 and then again from 1707 to 1774, transplant a part of itself to American soil, as the eventual "Franconia" and "Eastern" Mennonite districts. But before we see that process of transplantation beginning, we must meet another man and another community—both Quaker.

The man, of course, is William Penn, brilliant son of a British admiral in good standing with the royal family of the Stuarts. Young William had been enrolled at Oxford, but while listening to a Quaker preach, had felt a mystical "opening of joy" that was not a part of the classical curriculum, and had left the university because of his growing nonconformist beliefs. He weakened somewhat, and served in the military in Ireland (the time of his famous but ironically—for a pacific Quaker—armored portrait). There too, however, he heard a Quaker preach—George Fox had commissioned Friends to go everywhere with the truth of the light. Thus it was in Ireland that Penn experienced his maturer Christian "convincement," after which he shortly began to preach himself, and to be jailed like other Quaker preachers, a total of at least six times. Prison gave him time to write, and he began to publish the first of his 150 pamphlets and books, such as *No Cross, No Crown,* while becoming ever more deeply involved in both Quaker and business affairs. From his father he had learned never to compromise his conscience.

After some Quakers in London had been locked out of their place of meeting he spoke to them in the street, and was thrown into a "stinking" jail. But the trial which followed proved to be a turning point in British legal history. "Shall I plead to an indictment," he challenged his accusers, "that hath no foundation in law?"

"You are a saucy fellow."

"The question is not whether I am guilty of the indictment, but whether this indictment be legal. . . ."

"You are an impertinent fellow. . . ."

"I design no affront to the Court, but to be heard in my just plea."

"Take him away...."

"Is this justice or true judgment? The Lord of heaven and earth will judge between us...."

"Be silent there."[39]

The mayor of London himself became so exasperated that he shouted, "Stop his mouth! Jailer, bring fetters and stake him to the ground!"[40]

Yet it was this youthful author of *The Great Case of Liberty of Conscience*, not the British government, who saw more deeply into justice and human nature, and events continued to confirm the young philosopher's promise. When Quakers, looking for a place to live their beliefs, settled in west New Jersey and got into disagreements, Penn helped to construct for them a constitution. He was equally absorbed in politics and religion, and soon after his return from America we find him on a missionary tour on the Continent of Europe with several Quaker companions. After a meeting with the Quakers of tiny Kriegsheim that was attended by "a coachful" of curious dignitaries from nearby Worms, Penn's party went on to Mannheim in hopes of another Quaker interview with Elector Karl Ludwig. The ruler having unfortunately just left for his headquarters in Heidelberg, Penn sent his thoughts in a letter. He commended the "Great Prince" for his "indulgence" to religious dissenters, and asked "what encouragement a colony of virtuous and industrious families might hope to receive" to "transplant themselves into" the Palatinate. It was, of course, far from Penn's imagination that he himself should, in another five years, be owner of a territory larger than the Palatinate. He called the elector's attention to the little flock of "Friends at Kriegsheim," who just the day before had been forbidden by local officials to hold meetings. This, Penn wrote, contradicted the indulgence the elector had himself allowed. Finally, the thirty-three-year-old preacher gave the aging prince some spiritual advice, and signed off as "Thy unknown, but sincere friend."[41]

Making a quick trip by Rhine boat and on foot, Penn's little party arrived the next morning, a Sunday, back in Kriegsheim, where a good many of the villagers were present for a Quaker meeting. It lasted from ten until three o'clock, and during this interval the local Mennonites as well as their Quaker relatives must have heard a discourse from a visitor destined to be famous beyond peer among their children and grandchildren on another continent. But as to Penn here issuing them an invitation to follow him to the New World, as historians have liked to suggest, there could have been small likelihood. As we have seen, Penn was still considering the Palatinate empty enough to be itself a goal for migrants.

The Kriegsheim meeting, Penn felt, was a "good" one, with "the Lord's power sweetly opened to those present." Behind the barn in which they met stood the local constable, suspiciously listening at a door. He heard nothing, he reported later to the local clergyman, "but what was good." In the evening the seven-family Quaker congregation met again by themselves, when their visitors were greatly impressed by the "lovely, sweet, and true sense among" them. "They were greatly comforted in us," wrote Penn of those Hendrickses, Kassels, and Schumachers. "Poor hearts! a little handful surrounded with great and mighty countries of darkness. . . ."[42] The next day, after still another meeting, Penn's party walked back to Worms with several Kriegsheimers. He had begun an acquaintance which, in less than a decade, would blossom in an as yet undreamed of American village of "Germans," where he and George Keith, a Scottish Quaker who had come along on the tour, would meet again some of the people to whom he had preached here in Kriegsheim near the Rhine.

Penn also knew and appreciated the Mennonites of Holland, and on his way back to England, after a meeting with friends in Amsterdam, he and George Fox had a friendly debate with a leading Mennonite minister, the liberal Galenus Abrahamsz. After five hours of discussion which ended in "general satisfaction" if not agreement, Penn and Fox departed, along with another Quaker missionary named Benjamin Furly.[43] This latter person, though an Englishman, was becoming a successful merchant in Rotterdam, and would be, in a few years, Penn's indispensable agent through which Quakers and Mennonites would purchase land in America.

This missionary trip may have been the occasion, at Kriegsheim, when Johannes Kassel, apparently a son of Yillisz, became a Quaker. Among his Kassel relatives this move caused unhappiness. Hinrich Kassel, minister or perhaps bishop at nearby Gerolsheim, issued a "writing" about this time, entitled *An Exposé of the Quakers or Tremblers*, in which he expressed his deep grief that some of his Mennonite blood-relatives had become Quakers, and now stood in opposition to him and his family. A quick retort by a Quaker, *The Exposer Exposed*, appeared in Amsterdam in 1678.[44]

Just at this time, another small Quaker congregation was taking shape some 200 miles down the Rhine from the Palatinate, in the old linen-weaving town of Krefeld. Our last glimpse at this scene along the "Lower Rhine," where "Germany" and Holland meet, had found persecuted Mennonite weavers fleeing to Krefeld's tolerant walls in the 1650s, and now as we return in 1679, we find the former refugees and their children working peacefully at their looms. Nevertheless, they are still not allowed to have their own building for meetings. Here are op den Graeffs, grandchildren of a Mennonite bishop who signed the "Dortrecht Confession" of 1632. There are Tysons and Jansens and Lukens and Lensens and Neuses—all of Mennonite families from Krefeld or towns in the surrounding duchies of Meurs,

Jülich, and Cleves. A short hour's walk from the west bank of the Rhine, Krefeld is humming with a weaving, bleaching, and dyeing industry that will soon make it a notable industrial center.

Just as among the Dutch-speaking Mennonites who had migrated down to the Palatinate there had earlier been a favorable reception to Quaker preaching, here at Krefeld there was now (1679) being gathered a Friends' Meeting. Two English Quaker women had recently been among them, and had moved down to Kriegsheim, where the community was agog over their distribution of tracts and—amazing thought—even preaching. Back in Krefeld two other Quaker missionaries drew from among the Mennonite congregation between twenty and thirty followers, and set up regular meetings for First Day (Sunday) and Fourth Day (Wednesday).[45] There is no record of opposition to this development from the other Mennonites, many of whom now had siblings and in-laws in the smaller fellowship. But the Reformed officials of the city were not at all happy about this new complication in their society. The Reformed Synod received complaints that these former Mennonites no longer practiced baptism or the Lord's supper (claiming these were entirely spiritual matters), held separate meetings, and for some irritating reason would not doff their hats even when greeted in the street.

Hermen and Grietgen (Margaret) op den Graff's family motto, from a window of their house in Krefeld, 1630. Translation: "To be God-fearing, devout, and of good morals; zealous, hospitable, and truthful in speech—is Christian, and pleases the Lord; brings favor, and sets many a one to great honor." (Klaus Reymann, Krefeld)

Just how angry this made some Krefelders was evidenced by the ex-pulsion of the new Quaker, weaver Herman op den Graeff, and five other persons by armed men who led them out of the city. After the Quakers had cautiously returned, they were re-expelled, with a local deputy swearing by his soul's salvation that if they came back again he would personally see them whipped and branded. After they had nevertheless slipped unobtru-sively back into their homes, still another Krefeld Quaker, Johannes Bleijckers, who failed to tip his hat to two of his neighbors, was thrown down, kicked, and dragged by his hair until he was too seriously injured to walk.[46] So we will not be surprised to find both Herman op den Graeff and Johannes Bleijckers, three years later, sailing toward America in search of another society.

When the news of this rough treatment reached England, William Penn wrote directly to the Prince of Orange, asking him to check the persecution of "these poor, inoffensive people" in Krefeld. How could Protestants criticize Catholics for persecution, he asked, if they themselves persecute other Protestants? "Indulge" these "dissenting inhabitants," Penn pleaded; "it is Christian, it is Protestant, it is human. . . ."[47] And before long Benjamin Furly, the affluent Quaker merchant in Rotterdam, had also protested to the authorities. By August of 1680 things had settled down to where there could actually be Quaker public meetings in Krefeld, attended by "many" local "inhabitants" who listened without "scoffing." By the next summer, when Herman op den Graeff's brother Dirk was mar-ried, the public wedding was "in the manner of Friends."[48] Yet before long most of this new congregation would abandon their European town for a new start on the American frontier.

We must now conclude our review—all too hasty—of these regions of Europe special to us because they bred the pioneers of the first permanent Mennonite community in the New World. We have arrived at the year 1681, in which Charles the Second, "By the grace of God King of England Scotland France and Ireland" set his signature to an ornate parchment granting William Penn an unmeasured tract of land north of Maryland, west of the Delaware, and "as far" northward "as plantable." For this colony, Penn preferred the name "New Wales," being "much opposed" to "Pennsylvania," which he feared "should be lookt on as a vanity in me. . . ." But when the name was fixed, he accepted it, and confessed he believed his God would "bless and make it the seed of a nation."[49] His busi-ness instinct awoke sharply, and almost immediately he began to advertise for settlers, with a pamphlet entitled *Some Account of the Province of Pennsylvania in America.* His campaign would bear fruit within a few years among both Quakers and Mennonites in both Krefeld and Kriegsheim. By

July 1681 Penn, ever ready to mix business, politics, and religion, had
begun to sell land to English Quaker "First Purchasers," who had to
promise to settle their tracts within a stipulated time. The "Proprietor"
could hardly guess at the fame—and the grief—this plantation would bring
him.

Our story will focus on one small community in this new enterprise.
But we have hardly paused long enough anywhere in the three decades we
have surveyed, except with Yillisz Kassel of Kriegsheim, to hear the voice of
this community—the Mennonites. We know its people were a quietly stubborn lot, willing to sacrifice everything rather than let the surrounding
state-supported churches dictate, in the name of a homogenous society, the
practice of their faith. We know that Quakers found, on the Continent, no
more willing listeners to their revolutionary witness of the light within than
among these Mennonites. We know they had been, in recent decades, a
noiseless, well-behaved fellowship, so industrious as to invite jealousy. We
know such things, but we have only briefly reflected on what it was they
believed. Were they Christians, in terms of orthodox theology?

For an answer, we may turn to Hinrich Kassel, veteran leader at
Gerolsheim in the Palatinate, and possibly a brother of Yillisz. In the very
months of William Penn's new grant, preacher or bishop Kassel is putting
together a little document for a young preacher, "J.H.," of his community.
There is, after all, no seminary for Mennonites, who tend to make ironic remarks about "the educated ones." But Hinrich is engaged in education all
the same, with this "ABC," as he calls it, or elementary direction book for
"a beginning preacher."[50] It will articulate the traditional Mennonite views
on the Christian faith, baptism, and communion, and then, promises the
title, will explain the "rules and order of the Mennonite or *Taufgesinnte*
[misspelled Tauffsgesinds] fellowship." It is written out of an intense desire
that the Mennonite order, as Hinrich has learned it, should be maintained
"according to this pattern and form."

Unfortunately for us, the author, who had just come through a "very
hard fever," and wrote this "all on my bed" out of "the pressure of my feelings," was not to complete his document. Perhaps death interrupted the
work, which is broken off after sixteen pages, just after Hinrich had completed his articles of faith, and prepared to describe the marks of faith in
human behavior. But he had gotten far enough in his counsel to his
"beloved friend in Christ" to make it clear to us that his theology would be
basically unobjectionable to many evangelical Protestants. One must come
to God in faith, he writes, as the one, eternal, and almighty Creator. This
God has given us his Son, in whom we must believe, and at whose command we must be baptized as a response of faith. God also gives us his

Spirit, to comfort and teach us. We acknowledge these three—Father, Son, and Holy Spirit—as "one eternal almighty God, and not three gods or persons . . . though they have three names." All this, except for the emphasis on the need for personal faith in baptism, is most customary. No one would be persecuted for such beliefs in a Christian country.

But perhaps in Hinrich Kassel's description of the Christian church we can catch more clearly the special note of the Mennonite Fellowship. Lacking any reference to hierarchy or sacrament or tradition other than that found in the New Testament itself, this simple confession places on record the essential Mennonite themes: membership in the body of Christ by individual faith, the Lord's supper as a symbolic memorial, accountability to Christ through the discernment of the brothers and sisters, mutuality, and compassion. Written in the Palatinate, and taken by his descendants to "Skippack" in Pennsylvania, it may stand here as a summation, and an introduction to the spiritual family whose American story we are about to unfold:

> We believe . . . in one holy, general Christian church, out of many people who together believe the Gospel, and are baptized at the command of Christ into one community, of which Christ is the head, [and] whom he has bought with his blood and made to be kings and priests before God, his heavenly Father. These then maintain the right fellowship with each other, with bread and wine in memory of the great love and benefit that Christ showed. They also bear concern for each other as one heart and one soul, so that their fellow-members will be cared for in daily need, each one doing his duty regarding his poor brother and sister, so that the saints will thus be bound together in the bond of love. They also have a sympathy for all poor people, of whom there are many.[51]

Chapter 2

"Only Ancient Forest"

1682-1700

When we Americans who have European ancestors tell how and why they "came across," we like to speak colorfully, simply, and above all, spiritually. But the vagueness of our knowledge inflates our rhetoric, and fails to confront us with history's complexity.

It was, in August 1609, an *Englishman* on a *Dutch* boat looking for a way to the wealth of *China* who gave a white man's name to an *Indian* river we know by a *French* one—"Delaware." Henry Hudson called it the "South River," and after deciding that this was not a passage through the continent to the riches of the East, found another one which he called the "North River," though we remember it by his own name. It was then a *German* born along the Rhine, Peter Minuit, who founded the *Dutch* New Amsterdam which became the *English* New York, and the same doughty captain established a colony for the *Swedes* on the Delaware. At both of these American locations—the "North River" and the "South River"— small groups of Mennonites settled before "Pennsylvania" had even been dreamed of.

Both groups were Dutch, eddies in the outward stream of Hollanders in that colonizing, mercantilist era. And so we run across an occasional "Mennist" name in the ledgers of New Amsterdam, such as that of the carpenter Pieter Pieterson who, in 1654, is assessed with twenty other lot owners along the banks of a new canal through Manhattan.[1] Another Mennist family was causing a problem for the local Reformed Church. Though attending services faithfully, they did not wish to have another baptism on top of their Mennonite one. Some of the Reformed people, considering the Dutch Mennonites unsound on the doctrine of the Trinity, felt a new baptism was necessary before these Mennonites could "partake with us of the Lord's Supper." By the time they had finally decided to admit the thirty-

year-old Mennonite to communion, he and his family were moving on to a
new home in "the West Indies," where the Dutch flag was also flying.[2] In
addition, we have already heard of the "Mennonists" of Gravesend on
Long Island who, in the words of a Dutch Reformed official in 1657, "meet
together," when "the one or the other reads something for them."[3] This is
all we hear about this earliest American Mennonite community, unless it be
they to whom some Germantown Mennonites refer in a letter six decades
later that mentions New York: "There are people here who call themselves
Mennisten, who would like to have the articles of faith translated into
English...."[4]

The Mennonite settlement below the "South River," on the Delaware
shore just across the bay from Cape May, was more definite, but of shorter
duration. Here, eight years after Peter Stuyvesant had conquered several
lonely Swedish outposts in the name of Holland, some two dozen Dutch
Mennonite families established a colony. They had sailed from Amsterdam
in May 1663, animated by their founder's dream of a new, classless, Christian society. What possessed them to settle at the mouth of the Horekill, on
the very site of Swan Valley (Zwaanandael), where three decades earlier the
bones of thirty-three European settlers had been scattered by angry Indians?

Their visionary leader, a native of the Dutch coastal town of Zierikzee
where the Mennonites had a distinctly liberal flavor, had signed a contract
with the burgomasters of Amsterdam. In return for monetary support, this
document committed the twenty-four enlisted Mennonite families "to
reside" in the new transatlantic settlement, "and to work at the cultivation
of the land, fishing, handicraft, etc....." This would be a preparation "for
other coming persons and families": the Amsterdam merchants were clearly
hoping for a spreading Dutch establishment on the American coast.[5] The
dreamer they were subsidizing, Pieter Cornelisz Plockhoy, had addressed
the Dutch public in a recent *Short and Clear Plan*, describing a *Volck-plant-
ing ... aen de Zuyt-revier en Nieu-nederland*. In this pamphlet appears no
information of his Mennonite association, nor any appeal directed especially
at Mennonites (though they were the only ones who joined). A set of "Spur-
ring Verses" quoted at the end sounds like a typical commercial planters'
exaggeration. In the New Netherlands, it promises,

> The birds obscure the sky, so numerous in their flight,
> The animals roam wild, and flatten down the ground.
> The fish swarm in the waters, and exclude the light,
> The oysters there, than which no better can be found,
> Are piled up heap on heap, till islands they attain;
> And vegetation clothes the forest, mead and plain.[6]

But Plockhoy's basic plan was not just another economic venture: it was an experimental mutual society based on equality of standing. Six hours of labor a day were to be "for the common Profit." Although this socialism was not pure—profits were to be paid out in equal shares to the individuals making up the joint company—no one would be a mere hired hand. "The name of servant or servant-maid has no place among us. . . ." The stipulation that no kind of "lordship or servile slavery shall burden our company" is claimed to be the first written reaction against slavery in North American history. In fact, a fundamental grudge against any kind of "lording," spiritual or economic or social, seems to be Plockhoy's driving motive. Weary of religious wrangling, he had joined the "Collegiants" in Holland—an association which did not require giving up one's original church membership. Now he would prove to the contentious, sect-wracked society of Europe that humans could live without anyone being boss over the rest! A large central meetinghouse, arranged in the plan of an ampitheater, would allow everyone equal opportunity to speak at meetings for worship.

The Swan Valley venture was actually not the first place of Plockhoy's attempts. Five years earlier he had sailed to England, spoken personally with Oliver Cromwell, and published several prospectuses for a new social commonwealth which would model humanity to the rest of society. It was only after Cromwell died that he had returned to Holland, attracted a following among the Amsterdam Mennonite congregation (nicknamed "Plockhoyisten"), and organized his new colonizing company. He was, though he would have denied it, a utopian, to whom history would give only a footnote.

Soon after his colony of fellow Mennonites had arrived "with their baggage and utensils" at Zwaanandael, one of them filed an ominous report with the Amsterdam officials. The local Indians, went the letter, "declared they had never sold the Dutch any land to inhabit." And more serious than this was an unforeseen European development. Charles II, King of England, made a grant to his brother of "all New England from the St. Croix to the Delaware." Dutch control was to be eliminated. In July 1664 an expedition headed by Robert Carre left England, to arrive the last day of August in view of the town and fort of Manhattan. A week later the Dutch surrendered, and a month after that the Dutch holdings on the Delaware were similarly taken over. The little Mennonite colony at Swan Valley was quashed in its infancy, with the only historical record being Carre's boast that his men had destroyed the property of "the quaking society of Plockhoy" to the last nail.[7]

What became of the Mennonites themselves remains unknown. Plockhoy and his wife were granted lots in the new English town of Lewis (Lewes) eight years later, and we shall catch only one more glimpse of them, old and helpless, at the end of the chapter. Defeated, certainly, but leaving a testimony of idealism, as well as the first record of a body of people with Mennonite background in North America, Plockhoy had anticipated the more famous Germantown settlement by two decades.

The Welcome, bringing William Penn to his new colony, docked along the Delaware at the former New Amstel, now New Castle, on October 27, 1682. Penn had written ahead in friendly fashion to the Indians whose countryside he now "owned," and to thousands of acres of which he had already issued deeds to some 470 English purchasers. Eventually he granted 43,000 of such acres to Dutch and German-speaking purchasers, through Penn's fellow missionary, translator, and agent at Rotterdam, the Quaker businessman Benjamin Furly. The deals were already very much in the making as Penn arrived to take charge of the frontier itself. Here, several hundred Swedes, Finns, and Dutch had been dividing the white man's trade among the Indians. The colony-planter now became a law-giver, and began by assigning his largest town, Upland, a new name— Chester. By December he called the first meeting of a new "General Assembly," and in the following March met its second session in a newly surveyed town near the juncture of the Delaware with the Schuylkill. What had been the village of Shackamaxon to the Indians now became a row of riverside houses and a projected gridwork of rule-straight streets called Philadelphia. New laws and a spate of letters inviting European settlers poured forth.

Most of the "First Purchasers" of William Penn's land, to whom he sold 860,000 acres, were English and Welsh Quakers. Many of them never saw the land to which they held title; in fact it often took years before the acreage for which they held a parchment was actually surveyed at a specific location. First Purchasers, while being allowed privileges such as lots in the city of Philadelphia, had to promise to find settlers for their land within a stipulated time. The feudal tradition of "quit-rent"—an annual payment per acre in addition to the original purchase price—was required. Penn hoped by this to have a continuing income, but history was running in another direction, and quitrents proved difficult or impossible to collect. Real life proved far less orderly than Penn's dream of regularly laid out townships, each with a meetinghouse at its center, extending back from the Delaware River, and radiating in on the capital "greene countrie towne" of Philadelphia.

Having made many acquaintances in his missionary travels on the

Continent, Penn was hopeful of attracting from there some German and
Dutch settlers. He had an especially favorable impression of their character.
Two or three sorts of his religious contacts had seemed particularly promis-
ing—Quakers, Mennonites, and "Pietists." When he had been in the Rhineland, he had also visited the town of Frankfurt on the River Main, which
was a kind of center of Pietist life. It was here that in 1670 a Bible-discussing
cell-group or house-gathering had been organized by the Lutheran pastor
Philipp Jacob Spener, a native of Strasbourg. His emphasis was on practical
Christianity, a personal sense of salvation, love, and spiritual edification.
From this and related currents would flow, in a few more decades, such
movements as the Dunkers, Moravians, and Methodists. The group which
met at Frankfurt in a house called the "Saalhof" was among the first to
catch William Penn's enthusiasm for a colony where Christianity could start
over in a New World setting. They read the printed materials describing
Pennsylvania, and even got letters personally written by Benjamin Furly. As
these merchants and other well-to-do Bible-students went on discussing,
some of them began to believe that they had decided to migrate. By
November 1682 they were ready to lay out money for a tract of Pennsylvania land, and considered asking a devout young lawyer, presently away
on his educational "grand tour" of Europe, to manage their new venture.[8]

Before they had received their deeds, a trio of Dutch-speaking
"merchants" had also responded to Furly's advertising campaign. A Mennonite investor at Krefeld, Dirk Sypman; a Reformed linen-merchant from
nearby Kaldenkirchen, Jan Streypers; and a traveling ex-Mennonite Quaker
preacher and merchant from Amsterdam, Jacob Telner—each had paid 100
pounds and gotten a deed for 5,000 acres of Pennsylvania land on March 9
and 10, 1682/3 (old style).[9] The fact that their purchases came at the same
time suggests that Furly may have come up from his warehouse at Rotterdam and closed this sale of 15,000 acres at Krefeld. In any case, it was the
first actual purchase in response to Penn's advertising on the Continent.

Who were these three affluent men who were the first non-British participants in the Pennsylvania investment?

Of Sypman the Mennonite and resident of Krefeld, we know the least.
He was the only one of the three who would never visit the planned-for
colony in whose finances he was becoming involved. Most of his 5,000 acres
would not even be laid out by the time he would sell his rights to them a
decade and a half later. When they would be located for the next purchaser,
they would turn out to be an area called "Skippack."[10]

Jan Streypers, the Reformed linen-merchant from Kaldenkirchen (his
stepson-in-law was one of the expellees from Krefeld in 1680), had a sizable
set of relatives who were willing to start life again in a frontier colony. Jan

himself was not yet ready, but he was willing to let his teenage son Leonart go, since Jan's older brother Willem would be in the group, and a young Mennonite weaver, Jan Lensen of Krefeld, was ready to teach Leonart the trade in exchange for two year's loan of a loom. Further, Jan's wife, Entgen Tyson (Theissen), daughter of a Mennonite family who had turned Reformed to escape persecution, had a whole set of siblings who were willing to consider migrating. These Tysons (literally "children of Matheis"), now almost entirely Quaker in persuasion, were to be the largest grouping among the local families who would help to settle Germantown. There was Elizabeth, who had married Peter Keurlis; Helen, wife of former Mennonite Thones Kunders; Gertrude, wife of Paul Kuster; Agnes, wife of Lenart Arets; and two single brothers, Reinert and Herman. This adds up to at least six in-laws, as well as a wife, a brother, and a son, of investor Jan Streypers. With so many relatives involved, it seems strange that he would sell so little of his land, and would make the journey only years later, and then, for reasons unknown, without his wife.

Historians have given the third investor, Jacob Telner of Amsterdam, credit for being the most vigorous pusher of the Krefeld emigration. Perhaps this is due to his leaving more traces in the records. Although he had been baptized a Mennonite at Amsterdam in 1665, he had been one of those responding to the Quaker preaching. Some of the Quakers felt that Jacob tended to get "pretty hie," and wrote to him warning against "much talking" and always striving for "some great attainments." Apparently he was not afraid to disagree with the founder George Fox himself. His approach may be guessed from William Penn's comment that he had been "much pressed by Jacob Telner concerning . . . business." On the other hand, when he had appeared on the other side of the Atlantic and visited Friends in west and east New Jersey "on Truth's account," his "service" had been "well accepted." This had occurred before Penn had received his grant from the king. And within a year or two after the founding of Germantown, in which he would be the largest single landowner, Telner and his wife and daughter would emigrate themselves.[12] There would even be, eventually, a large tract of land next to Skippack that for years would be called "Telner's Township." But we have no evidence that he had any contingent of friends or relatives in the venture, such as Jan Streypers'.

We now have in view two groups of people: the eight well-to-do Pietists of Frankfurt, and the three investors of Kaldenkirchen, Krefeld, and Amsterdam. Hundreds of miles apart, they are linked in their contact with Penn's agent Benjamin Furly, their German-Dutch nationality, their dissatisfaction with religious conditions in Europe, and their approaching interconnection in Pennsylvania. There was also a person—a young schoolteacher and lawyer with a doctor's degree and the ability to speak Latin, French, and Italian—whom the two groups would shortly have in common. His name was Francis Daniel Pastorius.

Coming back to Frankfurt from a grand tour of nineteen months, he looked up his spiritual friends at their meetings in the "Saalhof." There, mysteriously full of enthusiasm, were assembled Pastor Spener himself, a local ceramics manufacturer, a notary, a judge, a woman who was to write several devotional books, and others. Their talk was all of William Penn and his colony. "Finally," Pastorius was later to recall, they could no longer "withhold" their "secret": they were actually buying 25,000 acres, and several had made up their minds "to transport themselves families and all" to help found a new German society in the "howling wilderness" of Pennsylvania.[13] The idealistic plan swept the thirty-one-year-old lawyer off his feet. The corruption he had observed in his just-completed tour had convinced him that Europe was about to collapse under its own sin anyway. William Penn, according to the printed letters the Frankfurters showed Pastorius, was giving to the German "nation a . . . promise" of opportunity unprecedented in their history. Twenty five thousand acres? It would be a little principality. Who would refuse such an opportunity?

Having the least to lose of any in this proposed "Frankfurt Land Company," Pastorius soon got his father's permission and gave his books to a stepbrother. Six of the Frankfurters gave him a "power of attorney" to go ahead and get a colony going in the "Province in America which heretofore was called New Netherland." The paper gave Pastorius the right to do anything but sell their land. He was to "order the tillage of the ground . . . according to his best diligence, hire Labourers, grant parts of the land to others, take the yearly Revenues or Rents"[14]—it must have been a very heady prospect for the bachelor lawyer. Word went to Mr. Furly that the Frankfurters wanted land "set out on a Navigable River." Furly, in turn, knew a Quaker businessman in London who also wanted to emigrate, and negotiations began with him for ship passage. Furly must have expected to have both sets of his customers—Frankfurters and Krefelders—in one boat. The London Quaker, James Claypoole, reported that he had found just the item—the 500-ton, fifty-man crew *Concord,* "ye best that sails to ye West Indies."[15]

As this correspondence grew serious, Pastorius was looking for a corps of workers to accompany him on the voyage, and help open the new settlement in preparation for the arrival of the Frankfurt Pietist owners themselves. One place he went as he got ready was a village we know—Kriegsheim, west of Worms down along the Rhine. We can guess that the reason he knew about Kriegsheim had something to do with Penn's earlier visit to both Kriegsheim and Frankfurt on his tour of five years before. At any rate, in Kriegsheim Pastorius conferred with Quakers (and ex-Mennonites) Peter Schumacher, Gerhard Hendricks, and Arnold Kassel, all of whom would, in a few years, follow him to America. At this moment, only one Schumacher, a Jacob said to be from Mainz, was ready to go along.[16]

With his new "power of attorney" and a purse of "Reichsthaler" from his father, Pastorius set out for England on April 2, 1683. In a brief stop at Cologne he had almost convinced a Danish diplomat to join his Frankfurt venture, when the man's wife balked. A few days later Pastorius arrived, on foot, at the weavers' town of Krefeld, where emigration was in the air. Several weeks earlier Jan Streypers had sold 100 of his 5,000 acres to his brother Willem (Pastorius still had no deeds for the Frankfurt land). Now the Pietist pilgrim talked especially with Streypers' brother-in-law Thones Kunders and a set of three weavers, the brothers Dirck, Herman, and Abraham op den Graeff who were probably cousins of Streypers. These four men were all former Mennonites, the grandfather of the op den Graeffs having been a well-known Mennonite bishop of Krefeld. Since two local investors—Streypers and Dirck Sypman—had already bought 10,000 acres in Pennsylvania, the talk must have been about how the two colonizing ventures of "Krefeld" and "Frankfurt" might cooperate. Surely, as "Dutch" and "Germans," they would be placed side by side in Penn's mostly English woods. Then Pastorius hurried on down the Rhine to the busy port of Rotterdam,[17] where he could deal directly with agent Furly, and meet the third Krefeld sponsor, merchant Jacob Telner, who had come over from nearby Amsterdam.

By mid-May 1683, Pastorius had moved on to London, where we find him putting together for the Frankfurters' dream-venture a group of German, Dutch, Swiss, and English "servants." Much to Claypoole's chagrin, "Pastorius and his friend"—Jacob Schumacher?—were talking of "going in another vessel," the *America*, only half the size of the *Concord*, but scheduled to sail six weeks earlier.[18] Probably hoping for a commission, Claypoole wrote frequent letters to Furly in Rotterdam, asking when the main body of Pastorius' "Frankfurts" could be expected, and extolling the advantages of the *Concord*, on which he himself intended to emigrate. The captain, who had taken the ship across the Atlantic "7 or 8 times," was "a very civil man." The ship itself, "130 feet" in length and "32 feet" broad, was "convenient for passengers," having space "for a very considerable family" where they could eat and sleep' privately. No more than 180 passengers would be taken (later reduced to 120), and the captain had promised to stow a third of the twenty-six cannon "in ye hole." Those who booked the voyage could choose the "Butcher Baker and a Brewer."[19] With such salesman-like information Claypoole also sent along to Furly greetings from the Quaker leader George Fox, who was just then a guest at Claypoole's house.

Three days later, on May 18, Claypoole wrote another urgent letter, wondering what was happening with "the Frankfurts." If they did "intend to go" in the *Concord,* they would need to hurry and make definite arrangements.[20] Then came a letter from Furly with a list of thirty-three names of people from Krefeld, not Frankfurt, who were now organizing and had agreed to take passage on the *Concord* to Philadelphia. Claypoole immediately reserved place for them, and wrote back to Rotterdam that they would have to be on hand by "the 6th of July, which is the day lymited for sailing from Gravesend." Severe financial penalties would be charged if the boat had to wait longer. "So before the last day [of June] they ought to be here."[21] As for Pastorius, he had already left London with his little band of servants to sail from the port of Deal on the *America* in a few days. No "Frankfurts" had arrived to go with him.

Could Pastorius have known, as the *America* headed into the stormy Atlantic "with a good wind," that none of his formerly so optimistic Frankfurt backers would ever follow through on their emigration plans, he might have had a most gloomy voyage. The weather certainly was threatening enough. Not being able to speak English, he nevertheless found pleasure in conversing in Latin with fellow-passenger Thomas Lloyd. But as the little vessel pitched and lurched among the waves almost all of the passengers became seasick. No one died, but Dutch Isaac Dillbeck, the healthiest-looking of Pastorius's motley group, remained sick the longest. A Swiss servant took "a heavy fall," another one was "badly hurt," and "the English maid had the erysipelas." Pastorius himself, though only briefly seasick, was on one occasion hurled against the ship's clock, and another time, during a storm at night, he "fell so violently upon the left side" that he had to stay in bed for several days. Yet the same boisterous wind chased this polyglot "Noah's Ark," the *America,* over to Philadelphia in ten weeks.[22]

More important to our story are "thirty-three" Krefelders, still busy getting their affairs in order while Pastorius was already under sail. Well over a dozen land-purchases took place among them between the 7th and 22nd of June. The smallest purchase, or rather agreement to pay quitrent, was made by the one couple in the group who had remained Mennonite, young Jan and Mercken Lensen. They made a deal with investor Jan Streypers of Kaldenkirchen: in return for fifty acres of land in the new settlement, and the use for two years of "a linnen weaving stool with 3 combs," Jan promised to teach the boy Leonart Streypers the weaving trade in the new colony, and presumably keep him in room, board, and clothing.[23] And although Mercken's father had earlier been driven out of his hometown of Gladbach, he had been able to leave her his "small estate" there, so that now she and her husband, Jan, needed to make a legal disposal. Their "power of attorney" to two friends says that they want to sell the property because they "intend, God willing, to go on a journey by way of Holland and England further into foreign territory and provide ourselves with a dwelling there. . . ."[24] Similarly with the Lukens, an old Mennonite family now become Quaker, a brother and two sisters—Jan, Beatrix, and Mercken—each with a spouse, also filed a document stating, "We intend to journey away from our parents . . . to Pennsylvania, and probably will not come back here in our lifetimes. . . ."[25] Not only was this prophecy true, but one of the men, Mercken's husband, Jan Siemens, would not live through the first two winters in the new colony.

Another man signing up for land was Johannes Bleijkers, the Quaker who, as we have previously learned, had been badly beaten by his Krefeld neighbors. His purchase was, for some reason, from the Frankfurt Company.[26] He was planning to make the trip although his wife was in the later stages of pregnancy. A sixth man, weaver Lenart Arets van Aaken, was apparently of more means, and bought 1,000 acres on the same day that two other new investors from Krefeld, Mennonites Jacob Isaacs van Bebber and Govert Remke, each bought an equal amount.[27] Van Bebber would migrate shortly after the main body of Krefelders, but Remke would not.

The other seven Quaker families preparing to migrate fall into two groupings we have already met, and they were probably linked as cousins and through marriage: relatives of main investor Jan Streypers and the op den Graeffs. The first family included Jan's brother Willem (who was permanently leaving behind his wife and children) and four brothers-in-law: Peter Keurlis, Thones Kunders (who had just buried a child), Lenart Arets, and the yet unmarried Reynier Tiessen.[28] It may strike us as strange that at least two of Streypers' brothers-in-law bought their land from someone else. Streypers' large American holdings, in fact, would not be sold or settled before his death, over twenty years later. The other migrating family, the op den Graeff clan, included not only weavers Dirck, Herman, and Abraham, but their fragile widowed mother and an unmarried sister. This family too had means, and jointly bought 2,000 acres of land from Jacob Telner.[29] They were also expected to serve as agent for Dirk Sypman, who, though he came to Rotterdam with Streypers and Telner to complete the land-dealings, sold very few of his acres.

Meanwhile, agent James Claypoole fretted in London as "the 33 Dutchmen" for whom he had booked passage failed to appear. He was "well assured," he wrote to Furly, that the latter would "not make me engage and then leave me," but he felt there should be reserved adequate "time to take up and ship their goods and buy some necessaries" before the *Concord* hoisted anchor.[30] He had already written that "butter and cheese may do well," and that tools ought to be bought in England; any iron equipment in ships from the Continent which "touched" at English ports would incur fearfully high customs duties. By June 19 Claypoole was "glad to hear the Crevill friends are coming,"[31] but by July 3 he was anxious again. The same stormy weather that was buffeting Pastorius' ship on the high seas was now slowing the Krefelders' trip between Rotterdam and Gravesend. A "grown daughter" of one of the eleven families died in this passage. We will try, wrote Claypoole, to hold the *Concord* in port "upon one pretence or another," but the danger of losing the money was growing.[32] Finally on July 7 he became mildly despondent, writing that the situation "troubles me much," and once again recommending the ship. Already fourteen oxen have been slaughtered, thirty barrels of beer have been installed, and there is enough bread for 120 passengers. The master "intends ... to be gone with the first fair wind" ten days hence, which would mean the unfortunate "loss of [the Krefelders'] money which I have pd to the Mr long since."[33]

But on that very day the ship of the Krefeld party finally arrived at Gravesend, and there were several weeks left, as it turned out, to stock up and stow away their goods on the reassuringly substantial *Concord*. In among their chests, apparently, was the family Bible of the Lukens, already 86 years old: it was a "Biestkens" edition—long a favorite of the Dutch Mennonites, as in Switzerland and the Palatinate the Swiss "Froschauer" Bible had an analogous status. Thones Kunders, a Quaker, had his ancestral Mennonite martyr book. We may also envision Jan Lensen's loom and weaving gear being lowered into the hold. At least two of the families looking over their new sea-home must have been wondering how it would go with their mothers' late-term pregnancies. A small flock of children, counting as half fares on the register, and making the number of souls in the party exceed the official count of "thirty-three," followed at the heels of parents or older siblings. Finally, on July 24, the wind was fair, and Master William Jeffries gave the command to sail.

It was much calmer now than when Pastorius' ship had left some six weeks earlier. In contrast to his voyage, the Krefelders were blessed with "a very comfortable passage," in which they remembered they "had our health all the way." Weaver Herman op den Graeff would even call it "a wonderfully prosperous voyage." Johannes Bleijckers' wife gave birth to a baby boy promptly named Pieter, and both she and the other woman who had a baby girl were "easy in labor and soon well again."[34] Though it took all of three weeks to lose sight of England, another seven would bring them to Philadelphia.

In that far-off frontier town of sixty new houses and 300 equally recent farmsteads, William Penn was parleying with Indian chiefs, and eagerly anticipating both the Krefelders' and Pastorius' arrival. While they were all on the high seas Penn was writing to Benjamin Furly that he must now try to persuade the main Mennonite preacher in Amsterdam to bring over a large colony. For 800 pounds sterling, Penn would offer Galenus Abrahamsz and his people a little realm *(Herrlichkeit)* of 20,000 acres. Why should they stay in decadent European cities when an opportunity beckoned to live out their principles "far from fleets and armies"?[35] Putting these 20,000 acres next to the 43,000 being sold to the other Dutch and German societies would make a most impressive "Dutch" tract. But the liberal Galenus had other inclinations, including the forming of a seminary for Dutch Mennonite preachers.

His storm-wracked crossing accomplished, Francis Daniel Pastorius gazed down curiously from the deck of the *America* as it anchored briefly in the Delaware River near Chester. Two nearly naked Indians, "strong of limb, dark in body" and with "coal black hair," were paddling up in a canoe. Intrigued, the learned young lawyer offered them "a dram of brandy," and in return they wanted to pay him half a shilling. When he refused, they shook his hand and said, apparently in English, "Thanks, Brother!" And up in Philadelphia an equally friendly reception awaited him from Penn himself, who would point him out to other Indians as a "Teutschmann." It was something of a jolt, though, to find the town of Philadelphia so framed by "forest and brush" that Pastorius could hardly find his way from the river bank to a nearby house. His friends at home in Europe could well imagine, he wrote, "what kind of impression such a town made on me, who had just visited London, Paris, Amsterdam, and Gent." But dining with William Penn, whom Pastorius found very impressive, discussing with him the future of a German nation in Pennsylvania, and setting his menservants to work building a new temporary house must have kept him from melancholy. As the house was finished he placed a little Latin sign over the door that made Penn laugh to read: "Little House but Good Friends: Keep away ye Profane!"[36]

The first houses tended to be made of the logs chopped down to make room for them, and to be set half in the ground, so that the bottom half might be called a "cave." A servant who had been sent ahead for James Claypoole had already completed one such, though it would strike the soon-to-arrive owner as more "like a barn." Pastorius' men lacked proper experience for this new scene; the Dutchman Isaac Dillbeck could not have been used to forestry, and even Jacob Schumacher soon cut himself so badly with an axe that he could not work for a week. Yet by the time the *Concord* docked at Philadelphia on October 6 Pastorius had his little house "one-half under the earth and half above," and it turned out to be large enough to accommodate, in this emergency of guests, twenty of the homeless Krefelders.[37]

These twenty were doubtless the most fortunate of the Krefeld party, and there must have been immediate anxiety to get something built for them all in the face of rapidly approaching winter. William Penn was most sympathetic to them, and once "said openly" among his "counselors and those standing about," "The Frankfurters I am very fond of, and wish that you would love them also."[38] In view of the fact that there were only one or two Frankfurters who had come, he must have had in mind the "Krefelders" as well, who were considered joint settlers with the other society. Penn was willing to advance the new arrivals, many of whom had spent their means on the voyage, "some stores" for the winter, and six days after their coming issued a warrant for the surveying of 6,000 acres to be equally divided by the Frankfurt and Krefeld groups.

Since these are the people in whose midst the first permanent Mennonite community in America is about to take root, let us look briefly through their curious eyes at their new landscape. In the town of Philadelphia they are startled to see "Blacks or Moors . . . as slaves to labor"—a thing they consider a contradiction in Christianity and especially for Quakers. The populace has a kind of frontier-town honesty; posters declare where lost items may be reclaimed. The Indians' black hair contrasts spectacularly with the snow-white hair of the children of the old Swedish settlers. The Indians are not to be feared, especially those who have not been corrupted by the Europeans. The Swedes and Dutch are careless farmers, letting their cattle roam the woods. Everywhere it is "only ancient forest," with "beautiful sweet violets" in the underbrush as late as October 16, and vines of small wild grapes. What was needed, Pastorius kept thinking, was a dozen foresters from the Tyrol to deal with the woods.[39]

William Penn was just as eager for the Germans to live in separate settlements as they themselves were to do so. At one point Penn even suggested to Pastorius a name for the Frankfurt holdings: "New Franconia."[40] Now Pastorius, with his few servants representing the Frankfurters, and the Krefeld group which was three or four times as large, requested that their land be designated along a river. All the Delaware-side lots had, unfortunately, been sold long ago. But when Penn's land office showed the new arrivals a spot along the other river, the Schuylkill (the site of present-day

Roxborough), they were far from pleased. It was much too hilly for Krefelders, who were nearly all weavers anyway, to farm or garden. They asked for another option, and so we find some seven men, including surveyor Thomas Fairman, walking with Pastorius six miles northeast out of Philadelphia on October 24. Here, on gently rolling land beside hills that reminded Herman op den Graeff of München-Gladbach, and which the old Swedish and Dutch settlers remarked was the best land available, the new purchasers discovered "fertile black soil ... girt round and round with charming springs" of "delicious" water. The eight men conferred beside an old Indian trail. They were two miles from the Schuylkill, but there were two nearby streams—the Wissahickon and Wingohocking—capable of driving mills, and the land was much better than that along the Schuylkill. They agreed to accept 6,000 acres here, to be equally divided between the two societies, and Fairman immediately surveyed fourteen house lots of three acres each, on either side of the trail which he laid out as a sixty-foot-wide central road. Each lot had about 180 feet of frontage, and was about 800 feet deep. After every sixth lot there was to be a "cross-street." This historic act finished, the eight men apparently spent the night in the woods. On their way back to Philadelphia the next day they celebrated by chopping down a tree embraced by a massive grapevine bearing some "four

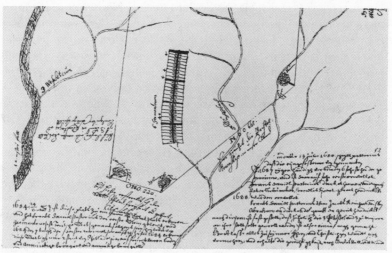

Map of Germantown, drawn up for the Frankfurt Company in 1688, five years after the original settlement. Fifty-four lots are shown on both sides of the main road, with four cross streets. The Mennonite meetinghouse was built twenty years later, on the east side of the road, three or four lots south of the fourth cross street. Jan and Mercken Lensen, the first Mennonite arrivals, had the third lot from the bottom (south end) on the east side. (Samuel W. Penny-packer, *The Settlement of Germantown*)

hundred clusters." After everybody had "had enough," each one carried a hatful, as Israel's ancient spies in Canaan, back to Pastorius' half-underground cabin.[41]

There, several German families and the Krefelders cast lots for locations in their new jointly owned village. On the east side the first lot went to Peter Keurlis, who would later have in his house a simple inn. Next was Thones Kunders, in whose house meetings for worship would first be held. Next was the one Mennonite—weaver Jan Lensen. Then came another weaver, Lenart Arets, who held title to a thousand acres, not yet surveyed. Then came the young, unmarried Reinert Tiessen, and finally the brothers-in-law Jan Lukens and Abraham Tunes. Across the road, on the Schuylkill side, the first lot was in the name of Jan Streypers, though he had not come along. His brother Willem's lot was on the other side of three adjacent op den Graeffs, Dirk and Herman and Abraham having their weavers' establishments next to each other. Next came a German, and the last was Johannes Bleyckers.[42] Jan Siemens, for whom no lot is listed on a 1688 plan, was not to live a great deal longer; his widow would marry Willem Streypers in 1685.

But the very first to die would be the elderly mother of the op den Graeffs, who passed on a mere six weeks after arriving in the New World. Her funeral at Philadelphia, in the third week of November, came in the midst of house-building. Already calling their village Germantown (though the majority spoke "Low Dutch"), the settlers made a German pun referring to their poverty by calling it also "Armentown" (Poortown). The depth of their neediness but also their "Christian contentment and persistent industry" in these first bleak months would be impossible to describe to "coming generations," remarked Pastorius, "nor would it be believed...."[43] The dozen hastily thrown up huts along a "street" 1300 feet in length, two hours walk from Philadelphia, would have been unimpressive, to say the least, to European eyes. Yet before long flax was being spun beneath these roofs, and a little granddaughter of the deceased Greitgen op den Graeff was the first American-born baby of the settlement. A community was taking shape, and William Penn wanted more people for it. "Come, come here," he wrote to Germany, "and serve God with me in a virgin wilderness, which already begins to blossom like the rose."[44]

But all was not roses. There was more discord in the growing town of Philadelphia than Penn had expected, and on New Year's Day he poured out public prayers for an increase of love so fervent that the listening Pastorius found them "impressive and thrilling." Another subject of prayer, doubtless, was Beatrix Tunes, wife of Abraham and sister of Jan Lukens, who became so ill that she had to be taken to Pastorius' little house in

Philadelphia, where she remained for a long time "out of her mind."[45]

A more cheerful note is struck in a letter from one of the settlers, probably Herman op den Graeff, who reported that though it was very cold, the cattle had enough to eat in the woods. As he sat writing in his makeshift house, several Indians came in, including a squaw with her child wrapped in fur. As they gazed fascinated at the movements of his pen, he took the hand of one, closed it around the pen, and went on with his letter for a line or two: ". . . in the town have one lot seven rods wide, 3 acres in size, also forty acres. . . ."[46] Such Indians seemed to be scarcer as the winter months progressed. They had a superstition, reported Pastorius, "that just as many Indians must die annually as there are Europeans who come here."[47] Certainly the "good road" that had grown out of the earlier Indian trail by the "repeated wanderings" of the forty-two Germantowners "back and forth" to Philadelphia, was a sign to the Indians of the white man's way of taking possession. And as more lots were laid out, pushing the town northward until it became a mile long, the Indians faded farther away.

During the following year another Mennonite family arrived—that of Krefeldian Isaac Jacobs van Bebber, a brother of Herman op den Graeff's wife. Having purchased a thousand acres, he was given a house lot between Jacob Schumacher and one assigned to Jacob Telner, who had also come over with his wife and daughter, but was temporarily preaching and disturbing clergymen in New York.[48] Since there were only two Mennonite families in Germantown in 1684, they probably met for worship, at least for the time, with their Quaker relatives in dyer Thones Kunders' house. Here they would fellowship with the majority of the old Krefeld Friends' Meeting, transferred to the New World.

And what of the Palatine village of Kriegsheim of which we heard so much in the last chapter, where Penn and Pastorius had also visited Quakers? Here, where church officials continued to complain, the Quakers were definitely having a harder time than their Mennonite relatives. The latter were typically reported to be "quiet, industrious and neighborly." One officer observed, "It must be acknowledged by everyone that they behave quietly, secluded, and peacefully . . . and are diligent in their work, are always more obedient than others to the government . . . and have contributed with a good will to the bearing of all burdens."[49] But a negative bias could also appear, as that expressed toward Tielmann Kolb of Wolfsheim, son-in-law of the Quaker Peter Schumacher. With his wife and seven children, observed one critical official in 1685, Tielmann "behaves very neighborly, but is still malicious, and so should not be considered unworthy of legal punishment."[50]

The "injuriousness" of the Mennonites in the critics' minds consisted in the fact that "they do not want to fill any office, and draw away the sustenance of the other subjects," presumably by their unusually hard work. "They are useful people as far as paying the rent goes," argued another report, "and they have the appearance of being pious, but in actuality they are not, as they are real masters in helping each other whenever a good piece of land becomes available, in order to bring it into their possession."[51] Another local report simply states that "their peculiarity consists in the fact they swear no oaths, carry no weapons, do not baptize their children before they understand what baptism is, [have] an exhorter who is otherwise however a farmer, as they are too, who encourages them to good works and if one of them sins, brings such a person before the meeting. . . ."[52]

But when it came to the tax-resisting, publicly testifying Quakers, the official reaction was much stronger. They are "a foolish sect," maintained one officer, "a kind of brothers who are generally irritating and regard no one but themselves."[53] And when, in May 1685 three such men—Gerrit Hendricks, Peter Schumacher, and Hans Peter Umstat—handed in a request for a certificate allowing them to "cross over into Holland" with their belongings, the official reported that the news gave "great joy" to "the whole community."[54] Still, the document was so long in coming that the Quakers had to ask for it again. Their experiences of years past, when their cattle and crops had been confiscated for nonpayment of taxes, had toughened them so that they were not easily intimidated. One of the prospective émigrés was, in fact, the elderly Hendrick Gerrits, who had lost two cows in 1663, and was now ready to go to Germantown with his young son, Gerrit Hendricks.

By August 16 we find the Hendrickses and old widower Peter Schumacher in the seaport of Rotterdam, signing an agreement with Dirck Sypman of Krefeld, who had not been able to get settlers for the land he had so hopefully bought over three years before. Now "Pieter Schoenmaker last residing in Krysheim in the palatinate" promised to settle with his children on 200 acres in "Jerman town," for which he would pay Sypman an annual quitrent of "two Rix dollars" which would be remitted "exactly in sound current money without any reduction, whatsoever the pretence may be. . . ."[55] Apparently Sypman had not been finding his land investment very dependable. But with no down money required, he now granted tracts to both Schumacher and Hendricks. Having signed the indentures on the very "point of departure" for London, they were met in the latter city by Quaker leader George Fox, who came up to visit these "Germaine frids yt were going to pensilvania."[56]

Less than two months later the party of nearly twenty Quaker souls, the majority of the Kriegsheim Friends' Meeting, arrived on the *Francis and Dorothy* at Philadelphia. "Gerhardt" Hendricks and his father took two lots on the undeveloped eastern side of the main street in Germantown, behind which was a stream where Gerhardt planned to build a mill. Schumacher and Umstadt took lots on the other side. Half a year later the rest of the Kriegsheim Quakers arrived, led by forty-seven-year-old Johannes Kassel.[57] This helped to make Germantown so full that three new villages were planned, the first to be called "Krisheim" in reference to the European home of the most recently arrived contingent.

This migration from Kriegsheim, which was not much smaller than the original one from Krefeld, bolstered the Quaker community to the point that collections could be taken for a meetinghouse (1686). Perhaps this is the place to note that Germantown was, in the beginning, a predominantly Quaker affair, though to be sure these Quakers were all converted Mennonites. The Quaker way of life had made them more trouble than even the Mennonites had experienced, and so the Quakers had found the Pennsylvania dream attractive before the Mennonites. The presence of the latter built up much more slowly; it was fifteen years before a minister would be selected among them, and twenty-five before they would have baptisms and a meetinghouse. Germantown was never a "Mennonite" town, and we serve no factual accuracy in claiming that more than one of the "original thirteen families" was Mennonite.

On the other hand, a modest Mennonite presence was accruing, as Mennonites in the Krefeld area had been responding to reports of the new settlement from their Quaker relatives. In the very year when Thones Kunders, in whose house the Quakers had been meeting, made one of the largest contributions toward a new meetinghouse, his original Mennonite congregation back at Goch was baptizing his younger first cousin, Jacob Gaetschalck.[58] The latter would, after delaying fifteen more years, come to Germantown too, and become the first American Mennonite bishop. And already in 1687 another of the Mennonite van Bebbers came over, to be followed shortly by two Dutch businessmen and their families—papermaker Willem Ruttinghuysen[59] and silk-merchant Dirck Keyser.[60] Jan Lensen, the first Mennonite to have come, now had enough fellow-members for them to "begin to have a meeting" in the van Bebber house, at which they "endeavored to instruct one another." Sometimes Dirck Keyser would read "a sermon from a book by Jobst Harmonsen."[61]

Willem Ruttinghuysen, who had been successful in his papermaking business in Holland for over a decade, came to Germantown via New York with his sons Gerhard and Claus and daughter Elizabeth. Already in August 1687 he purchased one of the last fifty-acre lots at the northern end of the now filled-up village. Claus traveled back up to Manhattan over a year later (1689) to marry a Dutch Reformed girl who had migrated from Leeuwarden. Claus, recorded by the Reformed officials as "living on the South river"[62] (*i.e.*, the Delaware), then brought his bride back to tiny Germantown, where both his father and he would eventually be papermakers and Mennonite preachers. Dirck Keyser, a Mennonite silk merchant who had lost two wives, also arrived in Germantown via New York on October 10, 1688, bringing with him two sons. A daughter, Johanna, died on the trip down from New York, and was buried at a plantation en route.[63] Dirck's trade in "Amsterdam dyed silk" and his coat-of-arms type of copper plate advertisement bespoke a Dutch Mennonite worldliness that would not please Palatine or Swiss Anabaptists. Yet his grandfather had been a signer of the 1632 Dortrecht Confession, and in Germantown he took a visible role at the informal Mennonite meetings.

It was the interval between the Ruttinghuysen and Keyser arrivals that produced what may be Germantown's most famous expression: a protest against slavery. This was in the form of a two-page letter signed on May 18, 1688 by four Germantown men, and addressed to the local Quaker "Monthly Meeting." The first signature is that of "garrett Henderiks," followed by two of the op den Graeff brothers—"Derick" and Abraham— sandwiching the name of Francis Daniel Pastorius. Having met all of these men before, we realize that none of them was, as has been claimed here and there, Mennonite (the op den Graeffs had been Mennonite earlier). Further, they were not all Quaker; Pastorius gave his boys Lutheran baptism as infants. It is equally intriguing to note that the Frankfurt Company of which Pastorius was the agent had in its charter a provision reserving to its owners all revenues from not only "products of the ground . . . Cattle" and manufactures, but "Slaves" as well.[64]

This Germantown protest was actually directed not to the general public, but to the Quakers who owned slaves, and it was meant to be discussed at Quaker meetings. Well might the first signer, Gerrit Hendricks, with his family's memory of having their property confiscated at Kriegsheim, recall to Friends their own reasons for emigration: "In Europe there are many opprssd for conscience sake. . . ." How ironic, now, having moved to Penn's Holy Experiment, to find among Quakers themselves "those opprssd wh are of a black colour"! How frightened the emigrants had themselves been, on occasion during their sea voyage, if they had seen "a strange vessel—being afraid it should be a Turk and they should be . . . sold for slaves into Turkey. Now what is this [slavery] better [than] Turks do?" Pennsylvania might have a reputation for freedom of conscience, but in this it is worse than "Holland and Germany" (the writers' origins). If something like this "is well done, what shall we say is done evil?"[65]

Crude as its English may be, this is a memorable document, and cherished by the descendants of the very Quakers it challenged. While affirming both its derivation and prophetic tone as solidly Quaker, we may still detect in the background some flavor of Mennonite conscience, inherited from the signers' origins. Rarely, in recent centuries, have the strong but quiet Mennonite scruples been thus given the articulation of the Quaker gift for public prophecy. Interestingly, we hear very little after this from miller Gerrit Hendricks, while weaver Abraham op den Graeff leaves on Germantown records a trail of general contentiousness.

By the year 1690, when the Rittenhouse paper mill was built on the nearby Monoshone Creek, the population of Germantown had reached 175. About two thirds were natives of Krefeld and Jan Streypers' Kaldenkirchen, with most of the rest coming from the Palatinate around Kriegsheim.[66] William Penn now presented the town with a charter allowing them to be a self-governing corporation. The idea was that the Germans might have their own local laws. But this, alas, did not make for brotherly love. The religious gatherings on Sunday morning were, as we have seen, separate, with, on a given Sunday morning, Jacob Telner preaching among the Quakers and Dirck Keyser reading to the Mennonites. At least a dozen Mennonite men were in the group of sixty-two who were "naturalized" on May 7, 1691,[67] and new names were coming, such as Jan Krey and Paulus Kuster. The new civil organization of the town, requiring a sheriff and other aspects of law enforcement, raised questions of conscience for the Mennonites and some Quakers as well. In this ambiguous moment a local Quaker minister charged several "Public Friends," including Jacob Telner, with weak Christology and wielding the sword of the state. Arguments and a serious split now ran through Germantown. George Keith, the center of the controversy, issued pamphlets, and his opponents signed accusations against him. The op den Graeff brothers divided over the question. Keith publicly called Dirck, who opposed him, "an impudent rascall." Perhaps the most interesting observation regarding the Mennonite view of all this was made by a Quaker historian, who said it was no wonder that people like the Mennonites, "who count it unlawful for a Christian to bear the sword of magistracy," would favor Keith's criticism of Quakers who used the law and police.[68] The agitator soon sailed for England and was ordained an Anglican missionary, thus satisfactorily proving his insincerity to many fellow Quakers. When he returned to Philadelphia and tried to preach at a Quaker Yearly Meeting, exasperated Friends shoved him out into the street.[69]

Later in the year of Keith's departure to England (1694), we find the recently organized Germantown court with an interesting piece of business in hand. An old and helpless pauper couple had turned up in the village, and they needed a place to live. The man was blind. The court instructed Willem Ruttinghuysen and Jan Doeden, both Mennonites, to take up an offering in the town, so that a little cottage could be built, with a garden, for the resourceless couple. A tiny lot less than twenty feet wide was marked off at the "end street of the town," near the Ruttinghuysen and Keyser homes. The little house was built and a tree was planted in front of it. And who were these guests for whom the town felt a special compassion? None other than Cornelisz Plockhoy and wife, who had been driven out of their own utopian colony on the Delaware Bay thirty years earlier, and had now come to throw themselves upon Mennonite hospitality.[70] All record of their whereabouts in the interval has been lost to history.

From time to time reports drifted over from Europe of the old religious intolerance. The Palatinate had again been unbelievably ravaged by the French, with the elector's castle at Heidelberg itself being left in ruins. Hinrich Kassel and other ministers reported almost unbearable losses and burnings to their Mennonite friends in Amsterdam and Hamburg. The Kriegsheim Quakers had left for Pennsylvania just in time. Over half of the 400 Mennonite families in the Palatinate lost their homes. Fifty households from between Heidelberg and Heilbronn had wandered to their Mennonite "brothers" in Holland, then on to "Holstein," seeking for a place to earn bread and clothing. Some Mennonite refugees had escaped to little islands in the middle of the Rhine River, where they built rough huts of straw and sticks, and stayed alive by eating snakes and frogs.[71] And in 1694 there had been new persecution of Mennonites in Rheydt—a town not far from Krefeld. Under a new Catholic regime, people had been routed out of their homes at night and forced to pay astounding fines.[72] One of those expelled and interrogated was Altgen Lukens, mother of children in Germantown. Perhaps, in this crisis, she envied them. In any case, her spinster daughter Elizabeth, about to marry the Mennonite widower Jan Neuss,[73] would soon help to swell the Mennonite community at Germantown.

But moving in the opposite direction across the Atlantic was one of Germantown's major backers, merchant Jacob Telner, who had failed to make a great business success with his 5,000 acres.[74] Dirck Sypman, too, back in Krefeld, now gave up (1698), and sold what was left of his 5,000 acres on paper to Mathias van Bebber of Germantown.[75] The third original investor, Jan Streypers, was complaining that he had yet, after fourteen years, to collect any quitrent from the property he had placed in Jan Lensen's hands.[76] And perhaps more disgusted than anyone else was Pastorius, who had never gotten any support but money from the Frankfurters who had talked him into moving to Pennsylvania as manager of their

Jean Metz Kraybill, a descendant of the Kulps who settled at Skippack, reads the inscription, "Thielmann Kolb 1699," on the door of a formerly Mennonite hof in the vineyard-surrounded village of Wolfsheim, north of Alzey in the Palatinate. By 1699 Minister Thielmann Kolb's Quaker father-in-law, Peter Schumacher, had been living in Germantown, Pennsylvania, for fourteen years. Five sons of the Thielmann Kolb family became influential Mennonite leaders, one in the Palatinate and four at Skippack. See Note 19, Chapter 3. (Paul N. Kraybill)

colony. He now resigned from the company, which had become only a commercial thing in function.

This survey brings us to a significant moment in the life of the Germantown Mennonites. From the beginning of their settlement, they had found that they "could not agree" with their Quaker relatives. Though they had neither preachers nor "ordinances," they had nevertheless begun "to have a meeting," trying "to admonish one another." Their ancestors had had lengthy experience in doing without church buildings and educated leaders. For some time Dirck Keyser had read sermons to them. Now, in 1698, still more Mennonites were arriving, such as Jan Neuss and his brother Hans. Coming to the Mennonite meetings in Isaac van Bebber's house, the new arrivals asserted that it would "be better for the edification of the church to choose by election a preacher and a deacon."[77] There was certainly a large enough congregation now to warrant this. And so the first selection of Mennonite leaders in North America took place. For this

spiritual responsibility the loosely organized congregation chose two of their
best men. For minister, America's first papermaker, Willem Ruttinghuysen.
For deacon, Krefeld weaver, Jan Neuss.[78] At the end of a century had come
the beginning of an American church.

Yet neither baptism nor communion was possible. It was one thing to
read or exhort at the wish of one's friends in the faith, but quite another to
claim the authority of that covenanted body of the "defenseless" Church of
Christ whose hallmark was that it "maintained" a disciplined church. Why
was this infant church so slow to take up spiritual autonomy? Surely not because it did not care what form it might take. It was rather, at least in part,
because its members did not want to erode the authority of their fellowship,
as they had known it in Europe, to "bind and loose." The social situation
was confusing enough. The ragged edges of this frontier Mennonite family
threatened, here and there, to fray off into Baptist, Quaker, or Reformed
circles. There was no aggressive articulation of the Anabaptist ecclesiastical
vision.

True, a quorum had now been gathered who were solidly committed
to nonresistance and mutual accountability as essential marks of the church
of Christ. But without specifically transmitted authority to "maintain the
right fellowship . . . with bread and wine" or baptism, their church life
remained weakly ordered. Its future in Pennsylvania was not assured. A
firm texture of leadership and identity would not emerge until there had
been woven across the warp of Germantown's Dutch-speaking Mennonites
some sober homespun from the Palatinate.

Chapter 3

"They Are a Sober People ... And Will
Neither Swear Nor Fight"
1700-1716

As the new century began, nearly sixty families were strung out along the mile-long road that was Germantown. At least a dozen were Mennonite. Conversation was in "Low Dutch," or the "broken Hollandish" of Krefeld, as one visitor called it. Though only a twenty-fifth of the size of Philadelphia, the village had a reputation for quality linen and paper manufacturing. There was a Quaker meetinghouse and a makeshift jail, but still no school. With its neighboring settlements of "Krisheim," "Crefeld," and "Somerhausen" (present-day Mount Airy and Chestnut Hill), it was really still on the verge of the wilderness. The only area to the north that had a specific white man's name was "Plimouth." A map sent over to Europe to drum up immigration in 1704 shows a colonizing scene centering in the Delaware-Chesapeake region and New Jersey, with Germantown hardly noticeable at the northern edge.[1]

Yet this frontier village was the goal of five Mennonite families and friends who set out from Hamburg, Germany, in March 1700. This group of nearly thirty souls was the first of a half dozen "waves" of immigration that would build up the Mennonite community in southeastern Pennsylvania. Their own congregation at Hamburg had prospered on the whaling trade, and had won a place in the life of the city that allowed them to substitute fire-watch for military duty. Yet its internal peace had been troubled by doctrinal differences drifting up from the Mennonite scene in Amsterdam.

The little migrating group included members who were seriously concerned with the life of the church. Prominent among them were the three related families of Isaac van Sinteren, Claes Berends, and Harman Karsdorp, the latter a "shipwright." The first two had married sisters from

75

Amsterdam, daughters of Cornelius Classen. Now, as Isaac sold his house in Hamburg and met his father-in-law in Amsterdam to talk about financial arrangements, the older man surprised him by saying that "he also had it in mind to come after them to Pennsylvania." Then there was Hendrick van Sinteren, probably Isaac's nephew; a widow, Trientje Harmons of the strict "Huiskoper" wing of the Mennonites; and Isaac Karsdorp, obviously linked with Herman of the same name. Paul Roosen, a relative (grandson?) of the affluent, devout, and now aged Hamburg preacher Gerrit Roosen, brought his family along, but not for long. Finally, there were the Arnold van Fossens, probably related to the van Sinterens. If the latter had as many as four children, the whole group arriving in Germantown from Hamburg in 1700 would have numbered at least thirty.[2]

This new source of immigration seemed to please William Penn's agent in Rotterdam, Benjamin Furly. His attorney was empowered to make an exception in requiring quitrent from Isaac Van Sinteren and Herman Karsdorp, who were, as Furly wrote, "at present bound from London to the . . . province [of Pennsylvania]."[3] The more immigrants from "Germany," the more sale there would be for the thousands of acres owned by Penn's "First Purchasers," some of whom had been waiting nearly two decades for a return on their investment.

Another effect of this group's coming was to interlink their parent congregation at Hamburg with a developing Germantown-Krefeld-Amsterdam correspondence. The widely respected author Gerrit Roosen at Hamburg, the ministers of the Dutch Mennonite "Jerusalem" at Amsterdam, and the many relatives of the Germantowners back at "Krefeld and Goch"—this set of transatlantic "friends" now provided the little Pennsylvania fellowship with a circle of awareness and spiritual concern. And as for the other significant community we have been observing—that of the Palatine villages near Worms—it too was in touch with this "circle." Two young men of the Kassel family, Hendrick and Johannes, had been baptized up at Hamburg,[4] and a Hendrick Kassel would turn up before long in Germantown. The Kolb family of at least nine sons and daughters had a Quaker grandfather, Peter Schumacher, and a number of cousins living in Germantown, and must have been receiving American mail. Or young Gerhardt Clemens, of nearby Nieder Flörsheim, might well have had Pennsylvania on his mind. At his wedding to Anneli Reiff in 1702, for which Anneli's stepfather Hans Stauffer contributed an ox, a sheep, and a pig, Gerhardt may well have been joshed about taking his bride to the New World.[5]

The thirty Hamburg immigrants were apparently not entirely pleased with the still weakly organized condition of the Mennonite fellowship they found in Germantown. Minister William Rittenhouse (the English spelling), whose paper mill washed down the Monoshone Creek in a flood the next spring was now, in the words of William Penn, a "decrepit old man."[6] Not only had this businessman-preacher not performed any baptisms among the rising generation (his own son Claus, partner in the paper business, was still not listed as a member eight years later); there was no observance of communion, that commemoration of such vital importance to Mennonites for discerning who was "in unity" with the congregation. Perhaps such considerations helped to discourage the Paul Roosens, who sailed back to Hamburg before long, and then wandered on to Russia.[7] Claus Berends wrote back to Hamburg expressing "some anxious concerns" about what would be proper procedure in ordination, baptism, and communion, when no bishop was available. He seems to have raised the question of having a bishop sent over from Hamburg to "lay hands" on and ordain a bishop at Germantown.[8]

Even without a bishop, of course, some of the Germantown Mennonites had maintained their traditional scruples. Linen-weaver Jan Lensen, though apparently not objecting to keeping an inn for a while, excused himself from serving as a committeeman in the town government "because his conscience would not allow of it."[9] He did submit his financial "controversies and debates" with Krefeld land-owner Jan Strepers to arbitration.[10] Two other Mennonites, Claus Jansen and Hendrick Sellen, were among those with the unwelcome assignment of collecting a special tax to build a more substantial jail.

Another new arrival who also asked to be excused from jury duty was Jacob Gaetschalck.[11] Coming with his family late in 1701, he brought with him a certificate of good standing in the old Mennonite congregation at Goch, north of Krefeld. His father had once been a servant for the Neus family, of whom Jan had become the first Mennonite deacon in Germantown. Jacob's older brother was now a minister in the Goch congregation, and their family stretched back in unbroken connection with the beginnings of the Anabaptist fellowship along the Lower Rhine.[12] Unlike his older cousin Thones Kunders, in whose house the Germantown Quakers had first met for worship, it had been important for Jacob to maintain his Mennonite affiliation. Now in his mid thirties, this "turner" or carpenter was to impress his Germantown friends so favorably that they would approve him as a preacher within a year of his arrival.

Germantown was now so full of people that the need for a school could no longer be denied. Francis Daniel Pastorius, weary of being secretary or attorney for the failing "Frankfurt" company, took up the work, and at least ten of the Mennonite families made financial contributions. Coming back from a European business trip was prospering merchant Mathias Van Bebber, who had bought Dirk Sipman's allotment of land, and now wanted to have it "laid out" somewhere in the area designated for the "Dutch," some fifteen miles north in the "Perkiomen" region. Jacob Telner, though now living and doing business in London, still held title to a section near the Perkiomen Creek that was big enough to be called "Telner's Township." Next to this, on both sides of the "Skepek" Creek, 6,166 acres of woods would soon be called "Van Bebber's Town," or "Bebberstaun," in which Germantown would have an outlet for its recent arrivals bent on homesteading.

But first the church had to be put on a firmer basis. The Hamburg ministers had replied to Claus Berends, after discussing the Germantown situation in their *Lehrdienst*. It was too far, and too difficult, they wrote, for them to think of sending over a bishop to ordain one for Germantown. They could see no other way out of the problem than for the "membership" at Germantown to "pray earnestly for a season" that the Lord would "look graciously on the preachers there," and "overlook the weaknesses in them," and enable one of them to take up the bishop's role. In the case of such a need in the spiritual community, an exception would have to be made to the usual procedure. Even in the early church, commented the Hamburg preachers, there was the example of a deacon, Philip, performing a baptism on the Ethiopian "treasurer," when there was no bishop or even minister present. This "opinion" was sent from Hamburg in March 1702, and a copy filed with the Mennonite leaders down at Amsterdam.[13]

With this encouragement, the Germantown Mennonites appointed two more ministers on the following eighth of October. One was Hans Neuss, brother of deacon Jan Neuss, and the other was the recently arrived Jacob Gaetschalck. Apparently neither of them had a gift for public speaking; they "ministered to the church by reading only." And in spite of the advice of the Hamburg ministers, neither of the newly ordained men took up a bishop's role. The congregation still seemed to lack assurance to take the weighty step of "establishing" one of their new "teachers." They still looked across the Atlantic for proper confirmatory authority. Perhaps they were still insufficiently unified. It was some time in the next few years that the Lower Rhenish Hans Neuss, one of the two new "teachers," became offended with Hamburger Arnold van Fossen. The latter, who had moved on to the Rittenhouse property on the main road while the Rittenhouses were rebuilding their mill along the Monoshone Creek, now sold a small lot along the road to deacon Jan Neuss. This was in obvious anticipation of building a meetinghouse. Why the deacon's brother felt wronged by Arnold we shall probably never know, but he was so grieved that he quit not only his preacher's office but the church itself—for good.[14] At the least, this suggests instability in the infant congregation, with its miscellaneous membership collected from three European sources—the lower Rhine, Holland, and Hamburg. Though a lot had been purchased, no building was erected, and no baptisms occurred, for another five years.

By this time some of the members were buying sections of land from Mathias van Bebber, a native of Krefeld. His 6,166 acres had finally been located along the Skippack by patent on February 22, 1703 (1702/03 Old Style).[15] This made Mathias, whose father and brother were also businessmen, into a veritable Dutch "patroon." Before long he would be referred to as "Gentleman," and move to Maryland, leaving his Skippack affairs in the hands of the Reformed Hendrick Pannebacker, a surveyor. In Maryland Mathias would become involved in government office as well as business, and trade his Mennonite affiliation for an Anglican one. His father and brother Isaac remained members of the Germantown Mennonite congregation, though Isaac too moved to Maryland. Mathias's land along the Skippack had hardly been laid out before Mennonites like Jan Krey and Claus Jansen of Germantown bought tracts, and settled next to Hendrick Pannebecker. Across the Skippack, around "Telner's Township" (near present-day Evansburg and Collegeville), the settlers were Welsh or English, or, if German or Dutch-speaking, of Lutheran and Reformed background.

Down in Germantown, life was not all pleasant. Though Pastorius had gotten rid of his Frankfurt Company responsibilities (their land was finally laid out by others at "Manatawny"), he had great difficulty getting men to hold office in the Germantown government. The Mennonites would serve as fence inspectors, but not as constables. Abraham op den Graeff, the skilled linen-weaver, seemed to be involved in continuous quarrels, until a neighbor was heard to say, "No honest man would be in his company." For that, Abraham sued.[16] Lutherans were also suing each other over who owned Manatawny (present-day Pottstown area). None of the Dutch or Germans felt completely secure in the ownership of their property, sensing that the surrounding majority of English people still considered them "foreigners." An appeal for "naturalization" was submitted for "about 150 . . . high and low Germans," including "some Mennists, who (with their Predecessory for some 150 years past) could not for Conscience sake take an Oath."[17] While all this was going on, the royal government suddenly canceled Germantown's charter, and the dream of complete self-government for the Germans in Pennsylvania disappeared for good. Over in England, William Penn was spending months in debtors' prison, and would gladly have sold his rights to Pennsylvania for a fair price.

But if the year 1707 marks the end of "German" independence in Pennsylvania, it was also a very positive turning point for the Germantown

Mennonites. So far, their story had not been much different from the record of Dutch Mennonites on Long Island a half century earlier. Would the Germantown group be absorbed by Philadelphia as the others had seemed to fade into New York? The signs were not very good. Though they had three ministers, and the aging Willem Ruttinghuysen was trying to get their "articles of faith" printed in English, the congregation felt too poor to pay for the project. But now, whereas a quarter-century's accumulation of Dutch-speaking Mennonites had been unable to get a full-fledged church life under way, a new thrust would come from "high German" Mennonites in the Palatinate.

While Pennsylvania had been knitting herself into a Quaker-led society, the Palatine farmers had been grievously tested by war and taxation. Most of the Mennonites were either immigrants themselves to the Palatinate, or the children of such immigrants. Religiously they were tolerated, but economically they were depressed. As pamphlets singing the praises of opportunity in Pennsylvania became more frequent, a mythical image of a golden land began to float in the Palatine imagination. Letters from Pennsylvania claimed that its farmers had no taxes to pay—only a modest quitrent. What must that have sounded like to farmer Hans Stauffer, who, in these years, had to "keep" a military "horseman" from time to time at his family's expense, pay taxes to burgomasters of local towns, tolls to ferry his lord's crops over the Rhine, and tithes to support the local Protestant church activities—all before he could contribute to his own Mennonite deacon's fund?[18] No wonder that, in 1709, a valve would seem to blow out in the Palatinate, and a horde of its citizens head like lemmings toward Rotterdam, the gateway to the Atlantic and Pennsylvania.

This mad rush was anticipated by two years by a little migration from the family of Thielman Kolb, living three or four hours northwest of Hans Stauffer, in Wolfsheim. In retrospect, the Kolb family stands out as leaders in the Mennonite communities in both the Palatinate and Pennsylvania. The oldest of the children, Peter, would be an influential bishop. At least four of the other six sons were destined to be minister or deacon. It is surprising indeed that they have never, in the years since they helped to found the Mennonite fellowship in America, been looked at more carefully by historians. The name "Thielman," so common in the Kolb family, echoes that of an earlier Thielman Rupp, member of a staunch Anabaptist family that had migrated north from Bern even before the Thirty Years' War. If we note the reiteration of the given names Arnold, Jacob, Heinrich, and Peter in the Bucholtz, Kolb, and Schumacher families, we become fairly sure that they are all cousins of some sort, as they are certainly Mennonites or ex-Mennonite Quakers.[19]

Early in the year 1707 three of the Kolb sons left their Palatine home for Pennsylvania: Martin, Johannes, and Jacob. All in their twenties (with Jacob still unmarried), they left behind two older and two younger brothers. Peter, the bishop, was in his mid-thirties, and the youngest, Thielman, Jr., was only sixteen. Henry, the second oldest, was strongly inclined to go along, as was Arnold, the second youngest. Eventually all but Peter would cross the Atlantic. As the first three brothers left in 1707, there was an awareness in the wider Dutch-speaking Mennonite circle that the little Palatine band was connecting another European Mennonite group with Pennsylvania. The earlier emigrants from Kriegsheim had been Quakers.

In a new exchange of letters we find the family of Wynand Bowman asking for financial help in Holland, and the ministers at Hamburg writing to Amsterdam about some "brethren" on their way to Pennsylvania. As the Kolbs and Bowmans prepared to take ship, the Hamburg ministers recommended to the leaders of the conservative "Sun" church at Amsterdam that they meet as quickly as possible to give the Palatines guidance on the church-order questions coming from Pennsylvania.[20] For some reason the advice of five years earlier had not been acted on at Germantown. This time, recommended the Hamburg leadership, the letter that went from Amsterdam to Pennsylvania should be signed by the congregations at both Amsterdam and Hamburg. Perhaps this would make a more reassuring impression on the Germantowners, who had so far been hesitant, in the words of the Hamburg ministers, "to accept our counsel." Accordingly, a letter was written on April 16 by Hermanus Schyn and his colleagues at Amsterdam, reassuring the Germantown church of their spiritual right to proceed with baptism.[21] Since the Kolbs and Bowmans were expected to sail in May, it does not seem unlikely that they carried with them this letter. Apparently the Kolbs had means to pay their own way, whereas the Bowman family needed a loan. More Palatines wanted to come, but the Amsterdam Mennonites refused further donations, saying that these were not true refugees—they merely wanted to better their living conditions.[22] This refusal might have kept people like Henry and Arnold Kolb at home, since when they did come two years later, they were among a group found to be "altogether very poor."

The effect of this Palatine migration on the Germantown Mennonites was, at first, mixed. So far, the tone had been set by Dutch-speaking immigrants. For a full year, the Kolb brothers and the Bowmans apparently "kept to themselves" and would not worship with the Mennonite congregation they found, still without a meetinghouse. We might speculate that they found fault with businessman Willem Rittenhouse, or perhaps someone like the influential Dirck Keyser (who later would perform the marriage of one

of the Kolb brothers). A Germantown legend would have Dirck wearing a
long silk coat that offended Mennonites from Skippack by its finery.[23] In
any case, the letter from Amsterdam brought "joy" to old minister Rittenhouse. There were persons requesting baptism, and he now at last "fully
resolved" to proceed with them. Yet for some reason he had still not gone
ahead when, over half a year later, both he and his wife were struck down
by a brief and fatal illness. The bewildered little congregation then had only
carpenter Jacob Gaetschalck as a minister, and he was still unable to give an
actual sermon of his own. But out of this low moment came a heartening
renewal. In the weeks after Rittenhouse died, for reasons we can only guess
at, the Kolbs and Bowmans changed their behavior and "united" with the
other Germantown Mennonites.[24]

With Rittenhouse gone, it fell to Jacob Gaetschalck to act as bishop,
and several "elections" were planned for at once. First three deacons were
chosen—Isaac Van Sinteren, Hendrick Kassel, and Conrad Jansen. Added
to silversmith Jan Neuss, this made the rather startling total of four "deacons and overseers" for a congregation of under forty members. Then, a
month later on March 22, 1708, two more ministers were selected: Herman
Karsdorp from Hamburg, now about fifty, and Martin Kolb, oldest of the
three brothers in Pennsylvania, not quite thirty.[25]

This set of ordinations expresses a surprising if uncertain unity, since it
linked in shared authority emigrants from three discrete European
regions—Hamburg, the Lower Rhine, and the Palatinate. A log meetinghouse was now built on the former Rittenhouse and Van Fossen
property, and the thirty-four members agreed there should be a baptismal
service. On May 9, 1708, eleven applicants were thus received, and two
weeks later they all "celebrated," in what must have been a deeply moving
moment, "the suffering and death of our Savior by observing the Lord's
Supper." Jan Lensen's family must have continued twenty-five years, since
the founding of Germantown, without a service such as this. After long
desire, hesitation, and some dissension, it was all there: leadership, baptism,
communion, and a meetinghouse such as they would not have been
allowed in the Palatinate or in some sections of the Lower Rhine. Jacob
Gaetschalck remembered this moment as a time of "good peace" in the
fellowship.[26] It was the American inauguration of what minister Hinrich
Kassel of the Palatinate had called maintaining "the right fellowship."
Through this meeting flowed the future of the Franconia and Eastern District Mennonite conferences.

But even though Jacob Gaetschalck could report back to Amsterdam
that "we went ahead with the administration of baptism," and that the congregation had rejoiced to find that one of their two new preachers was

capable of giving "two sermons" over the next four months, the situation felt incomplete. The Kolb brothers had told of a Mennonite "preacher" over in Europe, "embued with love and faithfulness," who was "inclined to come over." Presumably he lacked sufficient means as yet, and Germantown now asked the leaders at Amsterdam to "be helpful to him on his way."[27] There had also been a suggestion from the Hamburg leaders that the oldest of the Kolb brothers, Peter, become involved in the process of getting a bishop to Germantown. Peter was either to be named bishop himself, or to elect one (the letter alluding to this is difficult to interpret). Well over a century later a deacon at the Salford congregation whose father had been born in 1710 would claim that the first choosing of an American minister by the traditional casting of lots had indeed taken place in Europe, with the results being sent back to Germantown by letter. This story too is not fully clear, but it certainly points to a special procedure involving both communities.[28]

At this point we might remember the three other Kolb brothers left in Europe: Henry, Arnold, and Thielman, Jr. Since the oldest, Henry, is now twenty-nine, and since we know that we would eventually sign a statement of faith with his name next to Jacob Gaetschalck's, we may venture an educated guess. Might Henry be the "preacher" in Europe who the Kolbs of Germantown knew was "inclined to come over"? Might he indeed be ordained to baptize by his brother Peter, who was rapidly becoming a major spokesman for the Palatine Mennonites? We can only theorize, of course, but our theory becomes more interesting as we find Henry Kolb, six or seven months after the above topic had been mentioned by the Germantowners, preparing to emigrate to Pennsylvania, where he would serve as one of the main leaders.

When he left home with his wife, Barbara, and their three young daughters in March or April 1709, Henry Kolb was not alone. Nor was the group of nearly seventy Mennonite souls with whom he traveled alone. They were borne on the crest of a veritable wave of pilgrims that had suddenly welled up in the Palatinate, and cascaded down the Rhine toward the port of Rotterdam. The city was taken by surprise; it had all happened so fast that the reasons for it were unclear, and later historians have continued to sift for the answer to why this *Völkerwanderung* broke out just when it did.[29]

Perhaps the freezing of the Rhine, which flows at a brisk fourteen miles an hour, evokes for us as well as anything the shockingly fierce winter of 1708-9. Already the previous autumn Hans Stauffer had sensed something odd, and had made a rare nonfinancial observation in his family account book: "On the apple trees, apples and blossoms hung together on the same tree or twig. And this was found on many trees."[30] At the beginning of October a clinging cold set in that was more intense than any in living memory. Birds fell dead from the air, saliva crackled before it hit the ground, and grapevines were killed by overpowering frost at their roots. For a vinedresser like Henry Kolb, with apparently little or no money, the economic future looked bleak. And during it all, down in Bern, Switzerland, Mennonite bishop Benedict Brechbill was shivering in jail, enduring the inhuman frigidity either in "a special hole" or "working at the wool." The Reformed Church in Bern was on another of its drives to expel or convert its Anabaptist neighbors.

Numerous pamphlets had been advertising Pennsylvania, and there was a Quaker preacher from Philadelphia moving about in Germany, as spring came. Meeting many Mennonites, he called them "a great people ... who are very near to the truth," and felt that there might be a rich "harvest" among them, "spiritually speaking." Perhaps he occasionally invited them to Pennsylvania. He could not remember that he had "ever met with more tenderness and openness in people than in those parts of the world."[31]

Not far from the homes of the Kassels and Kolbs, we find twenty-eight-year-old Gerhart Clemens puzzling over his own family record book. As a vine-dresser who also works as a weaver, he is looking for a better place to earn his living. He and his wife, Anneli, have decided to take their two little boys to Pennsylvania. He has sold both a cow and a horse to his wife's stepfather, Hans Stauffer, and wants to make sure he has computed their worth correctly, making "everything balance": "My father-in-law reckoned to me for the horse 35 rix dollars and for the cow 12 rix dollars. Now is that right?" Perhaps Gerhart, whose grandparents had come up the Rhine from closer to Holland, was more familiar with Dutch money. His father Jacob gave him a parting sum of "126 guilders."[32]

In these very days (early March 1709), the Palatine Mennonite leaders on both sides of the Rhine were commissioning a delegation to visit "many places" among the Mennonites of Holland. Amsterdam had been the source of a lifeline of deeply appreciated aid for decades. Now the Palatines had heard that there might have been complaints related to the way they had disposed of these financial gifts. In order to quiet this disturbing talk, the leaders wanted to send official clarification through the personal representation of Bishop Peter Kolb of Kriegsheim and "established deacon" Hans Bechtel from east of the Rhine. On March 13, sixteen ministers and bishops from west of the Rhine, meeting at the Ibersheimerhof, added their signatures to the letter which Kolb and Bechtel would take on their trip. One of the signers was the father of the Kolb brothers, Tielman.[33] The name of Henry, who we have theorized above as another possible minister, is not on the list. But that in itself is inconclusive, for Henry had just about then taken his family toward Rotterdam. Thus Bishop Peter and his younger brother, Henry, would have gone to Holland at about the same time, though with differing purposes: Peter to visit and return, and Henry to emigrate.

A few weeks later, in any case, Rotterdam was stirred by the unannounced arrival of hundreds of Palatine refugees who threw themselves on the city's charity, and asked for transportation to England. Official "passes" or visas were being granted by an English diplomat at the Hague, and so the only problem was financial. Queen Anne, insisted the refugees, had a special affection for the German Protestants, and would help them travel to British colonies in America, where they would be able to support themselves. As the group swelled quickly to eight or nine hundred, something had to be done; the burgomasters of Rotterdam paid out first 450 and then 300 more guilders for relief, and some private charity began to flow. The city hired a Mennonite iron-merchant and minister, Hendrick Toren, to see that relief was distributed (amounting to about six cents per person per day), and to book passage for the refugees to England. For a while Toren was helped by another local Mennonite merchant and deacon, Jan Suderman.[34]

Amidst this anxious crowd of emigrants were found "9 or 10 families from around Worms and Frankenthal" who identified themselves as Mennonites. Among them were the Clemens and Kolb families. Presenting themselves to the Rotterdam Mennonite leaders, they showed letters of membership in Palatine congregations. They were probably aware not only of the long tradition of Dutch aid to Swiss and Palatine sufferers, but of the specific assistance, about two years earlier, that had allowed the Wynant Bowman family to emigrate to Germantown. Now, desperately hoping to better their own lot, they asked aid for themselves. They impressed the Rotterdam leaders as "altogether very poor," and an inquiry was immediately sent up to Amsterdam, some forty-five miles distant, as to whether any funds might be left in the treasury of the Mennonite "Committee for Foreign Needs." The Amsterdamers replied that there were, but that encouraging Palatines who had no money for fares themselves to go to Pennsylvania was "useless and entirely unadvisable."[35] The opinion at Amsterdam was that Hendrick Toren was too independent an operator.

We may wonder ourselves how really "poor" someone like Gerhart Clemens was, with his guilders and rix dollars. Perhaps he was one of the vinedressers who, "encourag'd by their friends abroad in Pennsylvania," had among his baggage "vine plants . . . for a new start in the plantations."[36] But the group of Mennonites as a whole was indeed so poor that they had brought "hardly anything that is necessary in clothing and shoes, much less money for fare . . . to England" or for passage over the Atlantic. And who, in addition to those of Gerhart Clemens and Henry Kolb, were these Mennonite families stopping at Rotterdam? Since they were registered several times during their journey, and since they do represent the largest group of Mennonite émigrés so far in our story, we may give them the honor of a special list.[37]

Husband's Name	Age	Occupation	Children and Their Ages
Christman, John	41	vinedresser	sons 7, 5; daus. 9, 2
Clemens, Gerhardt	28	vinedresser and weaver	sons 5, 1½
Halteman, Ulrich	40	carpenter ("turner")	sons 10, 4; daus. 9, 5, 2
Hoherluth, Geo. Adam	45	weaver	sons 19, 12; daus. 17, 14
Hubscher, Andrew	50	farmer ("husbandman")	son 22; daus. 13, 9, 8, 5
Kolb, Henry	30	farmer and vinedresser	daus. 6, 3, ½
Nusbaum, John	46	shoemaker	sons 13, 9, 6, 2; daus. 9, 2
Oberholtzer, Mark	45	farmer	sons 10, 8, 3; daus. 6, 1
Schrager, Andrew	53	farmer	daus. 23, 20
Volweider, Jacob	27	farmer and vinedresser	
Wingart, John	46	vinedresser	sons 18, 13, 11, 8, 6
Wismar, Jacob	50	farmer and tailor	son 20; dau. 22

In addition, five single persons were listed:

> Bauer, Christina, 23
> Bien, John, 24
> Eshelmans, Anna, 37 (a widow)
> Graeff, Jacob, 10 (parents living in Pennsylvania)
> Kolb, Arnold, 22

The total of these persons who identified themselves as Mennonites (the English enrollers usually called them "Baptists") is seventy-three. But with them came also the illiterate twenty-five-year-old Lutheran weaver Michael Ziegler,[38] who was soon to wed Andrew Schrager's daughter Katharina, and later become a Mennonite minister. And on the same boatload out of Rotterdam as Ulrich Halteman were the Mennonite-sounding families of Christian Ruth and Henry Frick, accompanied by another Ruth family of seven persons.[39] One other observation we might make on our list is that the fact that all but two of the fathers were forty or older leaves a strong impression of economic motivation.

By late April Hendrick Toren had four ships engaged. In what must have been a crowd-drawing, noisy scene at Rotterdam's embarkation

The *Hoofdport*, or main dock at Rotterdam, where oceangoing passengers boarded ship. (Frank Reid Diffenderfer, *The German Exodus to England in 1709*)

facility, the "Hoofdport," Toren and Suderman supervised the loading and registry of 852 Palatines, including seven of the above-listed Mennonite families. But so many new refugees were now swamping the city's environs that a few weeks later, on May 12, 1,283 more would be sent to England, with another 4,000 to follow inside a month. Rotterdam was becoming genuinely alarmed at the size—and the cost—of this human swarm.

Arriving in London, the milling refugees were housed in barns, inns— from twenty-eight to thirty to a room—and warehouses, and when these were full, in a sea of army tents pitched on half a dozen locations, such as at the Blackheath, along the Thames, and at the edge of the city. On Sundays crowds gathered to stare at the "poor Palatines," or taunt the Catholics among them. As the flood of arriving immigrants remained unabated, Queen Anne, recently widowed, rode out to assess the phenomenon, and to hear the reasons for the emigration from the Palatines themselves in her husband's native tongue. An official free will "collection" was legislated, and benevolent Quakers distributed free shoes and shirts. Hundreds of Bibles were passed out, wagonloads of bread hauled in—it was a vast relief operation testing the limits of London's capacity for charity. Women cooked in holes in the ground, incessant multiple burials were performed, and officials stewed over where to ship or how to employ the Palatines arriving at the rate of a thousand a week. Although 2,776 more had come by early July, another 2,000 were waiting back at Rotterdam. What they hoped was for the queen to pay their fare to "Carolina" or Pennsylvania, and give them an allowance to set up housekeeping there. They had read books that promised this, they pleaded.[40]

In London, of course, there were no Mennonites for Henry Kolb to report to, unless we call Jacob Telner, the ex-Germantown Quaker merchant, by the affiliation of his youth in Amsterdam. Visiting the camps, Telner was as amazed as anyone by this influx, and discovered amidst the crowds some fourteen families of Mennonites, whom he considered as his "own flesh."[41] "About sixty" of those who had come with the first group applied as "Minists" to the London Quakers, who interviewed them and found that they had left the Palatinate "on account of General Poverty and Missery." Since "some Charitable persons" had already given them "a dayly allowance," the Quakers at first left it up to "particular friends" to help them, but arranged for "a quantity of friends Books in high Dutch . . . to hand to the Minists and others."[42] By this time the sixty-nine Mennonites we have earlier observed were no longer in one group. Eight of the families were "about to transport themselves" to Pennsylvania on June 24, whereas six, who in Jacob Telner's opinion "ought" also to go there, simply lacked the means to pay the fare. One option they did have was to petition that they might be included in an expected Swiss emigration to "Carolina." When the Quakers learned that the eight families were on the verge of departure, they asked "what sum" would be appropriate to help with "the passage to Pennsylvania." They then made a donation of fifty pounds, which impressed Jacob Telner as a generous amount. Struck with pity for the six families left behind, which seem to include those of John Nusbaum and Jacob Wismar, Telner wrote to Amsterdam and Haarlem, admonishing wealthy Mennonites there to "let some crumbs fall" to those "poor sheep."[43] Did it occur to him that every Mennonite who could get to Pennsylvania was a potential homestead-purchaser, perhaps even in "Telner's Township"?

Some of the "eight families" were, in fact, on their way to neighboring Skippack. "Herewith come the Palatines," wrote William Penn to his agent James Logan at Philadelphia. Logan was to treat them "with tenderness and love," and help them to get established so that they would send back to Europe an "agreeable" description of Pennsylvania. Penn hoped for more settlers like them. "They are a sober people," he wrote, "and will neither swear nor fight." Logan was to make sure that the ship captain, by the name of Guy, "used them well" during the voyage.[44] We may name five of the "eight families" whom we suspect to be on Guy's ship: John Christman (a Hans Chrisman turns up in the area of Telner's Township), Gerhardt Clemens, Henry Kolb, Marcus Oberholtzer and Andrew Schrager, with Arnold Kolb, Michael Ziegler and John Bien almost certainly included. Their vessel was bound for Philadelphia, and in early October we already find Gerhardt Clemens buying a horse from deacon Henry Kassel of the Germantown congregation.[45]

The "six" remaining Mennonite families, in what must have been a severe disappointment, were left among the 10,000 refugees in London to try to arrange other transportation or support. By fall the arriving refugee count had swelled to some 13,000, forcing both London and Rotterdam to take new actions. Already in August Rotterdam had sent Hendrick Toren and Jan van Gent on yachts up two branches of the Rhine, to stop the oncoming flood of migrants. By warning of difficulties, and paying return fares to the Palatinate, the two Mennonite merchants believed they had turned back "probably a thousand people." But even after this, Toren shipped another 1,100 on to England. The government there was now fed up with the uncontrolled influx, and was shipping back not only Catholics but other late arrivals. A royal declaration, translated into colloquial German, was sent over to the Continent, announcing that all who might still "be intentioned to come here" should "cancel their journey," as they would certainly find it "fruitless unless they are prepared to support themselves."[46]

The campaign was effective; the masses reluctantly stopped coming. But one Mennonite family of eight whose plans remained unchanged was that of Hans Stauffer of Alsheim near Worms. On November 5 they "set sail" down the Rhine with son-in-law Paulus Friedt, and after at least ten stops got to Rotterdam on December 17. By late January they had arrived among the penniless Palatines in London.[47]

Some of these refugees had by now been disposed of by putting them into military service, some had been sent to Ireland, and others to the West Indies. For the destitute families of John Nusbaum and Jacob Wismar, the best remaining option must have seemed to be a voyage to North Carolina at the queen's expense. This was becoming possible through the plans of two Bernese entrepreneurs, Christopher von Graffenried and Franz Luis Michel. For a scheme to develop thousands of acres in North Carolina, they needed dependable settlers. One source of them seemed to be a group of Anabaptist families which the Canton of Bern was just then attempting to deport from Switzerland, and the crowds of "poor Palatines" in London had become another. From among the latter, von Graffenried and Michel picked out 650 of the most healthy and industrious, promising each family of settlers 300 acres in Carolina, free clothing and ocean fare, and a cow and two pigs on credit.[48] Among the takers were the Nusbaum and Wismar families, the fathers being a shoemaker and tailor, respectively, and Wismar having a twenty-year-old son.

Not before January 1710, when members of the "eight" families had already purchased land in Pennsylvania, did the Carolina ships sail from London. Among the 650 Palatines aboard were doubtless some of the other "six families" of Mennonites, but Nusbaum's and Wismar's were the only ones that would actually get land at "New Bern." We do know that the ships were packed so full, and the stormy voyage took so long, that only half of the Palatines survived. As they neared the Virginia coast, a French pirate-ship plundered one of the vessels so severely that there were hardly enough clothes left to wear, and the naive Palatines drank so much fresh water and ate so much fresh fruit that many sickened and died.[49] So perhaps the Wismar and Nusbaum families lost some of their Mennonite friends before they reached Carolina.

Graffenried himself stayed back to wait for the Swiss Mennonites who were about to be deported from Bern, but in this expectation he was disappointed. The whole boatload of Mennonite prisoners had been freed from their Swiss guard while coming down the Rhine—the sick women and children already at Mannheim, and the long-bearded men at the first stop in Dutch territory. Most of the men had then gone back to hunt for their families among Mennonite friends in the Palatinate. William Penn, over in England, had his eye on the group. He had an understanding, in fact, with Graffenried's partner Michel, and so wrote to Holland to make sure that this "company of 50 or 60 Switzers, under one Mitchell," would be allowed through the country.[50]

Another group of "twenty-nine" Palatine Mennonites bound for America came into Rotterdam on April 10, asking Hendrick Toren for financial aid. Toren and Jan van Gent applied to the Foreign Aid Committee of the Amsterdam Mennonites, who responded that though there were too "many such requests" for all to be fulfilled, "since the lack is only 200 florins and without which the voyage can not be made," the request would be granted.[51] And so the little Palatine group went on to London. A ten-week delay ensued, in which it turned out that they would go to Pennsylvania instead of Carolina, as the Rotterdam Mennonites had been led to believe. After at last boarding their ship on June 24, these future pioneers of the Lancaster Mennonite Community wrote a letter of report and thanks to their "dear friends" at Amsterdam who had made their departure possible by their financial gift.[52] Signing the letter were Martin Oberholtzer, Martin Kündig, Christian and Hans Herr, Jacob Müller, and Martin Meili—about to become the founders of the largest Mennonite community in the New World.

After waiting for a "Russian convoy," they sailed toward Philadelphia in the same general fleet that carried the frustrated Graffenried toward Carolina. A month after their arrival in Pennsylvania these diligent Palatines were having land surveyed for them some sixty miles west of Philadelphia, along the Pequea Creek. There seemed to be at least ten families by now, one being the Wynant Bowmans who had emigrated some three years earlier, and now came along from Germantown. By thus moving west to a colony of their own rather than north into nearby Skippack where the Kolb brothers, Andrew Shrager, and earlier Mennonite immigrants had begun to settle, these Palatine farmers of Zurich ancestry established a Mennonite community that would have a slightly different flavor than the Lower Rhenish and Palatine mix of the older Germantown-Skippack settlement. From their very American beginnings these two communities— "Lancaster" and "Skippack" (or "Franconia")—maintained their specific concerns, while also cultivating continuous fraternal contacts. Sometimes siblings from the Palatinate would be divided between "Pequea" or "Conestoga" (which had a large "Bernese" component) and "Skippack." And both communities, in a quirk of American linguistic transformation, soon found

Date-stone in the house of Hans Ulrich Berge, Mennonite pioneer in Lower Salford. (George and Delpha Dee Wolfe)

themselves part of a larger cultural community in which the Palatine dialect (to be called "Pennsylvania Dutch") replaced their earlier Dutch or Swiss accents. Already, Dutch and German were mixing at Skippack.

After the 1709-10 "wave," Mennonite immigration seemed to pause. The European "War of the Spanish Succession" may have put a damper on sea travel. But along the Skippack life was tranquil. There were no Indian troubles. By 1712 Jacob Gaetschalck could record that the congregational membership of "Germantown and as far as Skippack," two and a half hours northwards, had reached ninety-nine. Apparently the good farming land was already taken, for Hans Stauffer, arriving a half year after the Henry Kolb-Gerhart Clemens-Andrew Schrager group, settled ten miles southwest across the Schuylkill. Even Bishop Jacob Gaetschalck had moved out to "Towamencin," and his name was on the list of petitioners for a road to Farmar's Mill (Skippack Pike) in 1713.[53] Near him, two of the original Krefeld "thirteen," now elderly men, bought new acreage for their families: Jan Lukens (Christopher Dock School farm) and his brother-in-law Abraham Tunes. Expanding out of Skippack was Jan Krey, who in 1714 got land along the Schuylkill, as Marcus Oberholtzer, of whom we have heard nothing since his coming with the Kolbs and Clemenses in 1709, was also attempting to do.[53]

If Marcus's prosperity was slow in coming, it was far preferable to what his Mennonite neighbor in the Palatine camp in London—Jacob Wismar—had experienced in North Carolina. There Jacob's and John Nusbaum's names had been placed on the map of "New Bern," showing that each had a house along the broad street laid out by Lord Graffenried.[54] The Palatines had gone to work with their usual energy, and had quickly surpassed in prosperity the British settlers in the neighborhood. But there was a war on between the British government and the Tuscarora Indians whose traditional lands this new settlement was crowding. On September 22, 1711, the Tuscaroras fell upon New Bern in groups of six or seven, and managed to slaughter over a hundred of the terrified Palatines. To have survived their miserable ocean voyage for such a fate! Elderly Jacob Wismar and probably his wife survived the raids, but family tradition would hint that their twenty-four-year-old unmarried daughter was among the slain. Her brother, two years younger and apparently also named Jacob, eluded death, according to the story, by holding out toward the enraged Indians some tobacco, which made them relent. Having escaped, "he walked and ran ninety miles in one day."[55] Eventually, it was said, he reached a Quaker community on the northeastern outskirts of Philadelphia, and by 1726 we shall find him settling in a part of Bucks County later called Plumstead, along with a son of the Marcus Oberholtzers with whom he had shared the Palatine camp experience at London.

Now the American Mennonite mix was underway. Amsterdam Mennonites helped by having printed in their city a *Confession of Faith* (1712) in English, as the Germantowners had requested four years earlier. Palatine preacher Martin Kolb's first wife having died, he married one of Deacon van Sinteren's Dutch-speaking daughters, and a year later Martin's single brother Jacob took another. Both had already moved to Skippack, or "Bebberstown," with their brother John. The other brother, Henry, doubtless of unique spiritual status by virtue of a European ordination, was also a Skippacker.

How much better a life this was than the one they had left in the Palatinate, which, in 1716, was getting a new, Catholic elector—Charles Philip! Since this prince was doubling the Mennonites' protection fee and limiting their land-purchasing privileges, there was new distress in the thirty-odd Mennonite communities of the realm. Charles Philip did renew the Mennonite "Concession," but he did not respond to requests that he relax edicts which kept Mennonites from practicing trades. Taxes remained heavy. And so, in 1716, it was reported again, from the Steinsfurt area east of the Rhine where Meyers, Landeses, and Altdörfers were thickest, that "three families have just recently left to move to Pennsylvania."[56] A new Palatine wave, dwarfing the previous one, was about to arrive in the port of Philadelphia, and flood out past Skippack to "Salford," "Schuylkill," "Swamp," and "Goschenhoppen." Wedded to the Lower Rhenish influence of the original Germantown church, it would produce the unique family that would become the "Franconia" and "Eastern District Conferences."

Chapter 4

"In Their Own Way and Manner"
1717-1755

As the children of the dozen Mennonite families at "Bebberstaun" became aware of their forested surroundings, most of the "Original People," as the local Delaware Indians called themselves, had already moved west. Their land "on the Perkioming" had been released by their Chief Manghougsin to William Penn twenty-five years before the Kolbs and Clemenses had taken it up for money. The present Chief Sassoonan, as well, had already (1709) moved with his Unami subtribe to where the Allegheny Trail crossed the Susquehanna River (later Harrisburg).[1] A relative few straggled behind, and one eastern tributary of the Perkiomen would be called "Indian Creek," pronounced "Inching Krick" by the incoming Germans. Some of the stragglers did odd chores, eagerly accepting, in pay, the white woman's bread, which they would allow to roll down the hill on the way home as dogs snapped at it and everyone was in high glee.[2] When particularly pleased, they might walk away singing in happiness. In a group, they might make "sounds peculiar to themselves" to express satisfaction. A single Indian would carry a bag of grain down the new Skippack Road to Farmar's Mill, skirting "four very bad swamps," for a leaf of tobacco.[3]

One local legend preserves a memory of the sadness which the Indians also felt. A white man and an Indian—so goes the story—were sitting together on a log at Skippack (other locations are sometimes claimed). The Indian, without explanation, began to sit closer and closer to the white man. The latter moved over toward his end of the log. Still the Indian pushed closer. Finally there was no room left, and the white man had to sit on the ground. When he asked the Indian what he meant by crowding him off the log, the Indian replied that this was to symbolize what the white man had done to the Indian, in regard to the land.[4]

The Mennonites of Skippack had not come to the New World to preach to the Indians (as the Moravians did a bit later) or to anyone else. They seem rather to have been seeking relief from heavy taxation and religious restrictions. They probably even found little time, in the midst of their chopping and seeding and weaving, to write letters back to Europe. One settler who never learned to write at all was the formerly Lutheran Michael Ziegler, who by 1717 was not only a Mennonite but something of a leader, and then or soon thereafter a minister. But his wife, Catharina (Schrager), could write, and when she and Michael named their second child, born in 1714, Christopher, they may well have had in mind a European relative or friend who would not only soon join them on the Skippack frontier, but teach their children to write.[5] Certainly the thirty or more Mennonite children of the community at Bebber's Town would need a teacher before long. And the teacher in Germantown—Francis Daniel Pastorius—was becoming quite elderly.

There was also another Kolb brother left in the Palatinate—the youngest—and he had finally married (1714) the widow Elizabeth Schnebeli of Mannheim. The Mennonite congregation of this town was full of talk of migration to Pennsylvania. Refugees were still coming up from Bern; and many of those who had been expelled in 1710 had not found permanent homes in either Holland or the Palatinate. Leaders such as Benedict Brechbill and Hans Burghalter had been traveling and conferring on a variety of options. The king of Prussia wanted Mennonites to clear his swamps. The king of England was inviting them to build a colony west of the Allegheny Mountains in Pennsylvania, with the false information that this was only "about thirty miles from the sea." The cautious Palatine and Swiss Mennonites asked the advice of the Dutch Mennonite "Committee" at Amsterdam, and were told that there would be no contributions for ocean fare.[6]

But pressure to emigrate was again building up throughout the Palatinate, and once again there would be a Mennonite current in an outflowing wave. The "great freedom" William Penn had received from his king had been "made ... known ... everywhere" in the Germanies. And to the Mennonites had come a personal emissary from Pennsylvania—Martin Kendig (Kündig) of the Pequea settlement some sixty miles west of Bebber's Town. This little colony, having found wonderfully good land, was already purchasing many more acres, and in 1715 had sent Kendig back to relatives in the Palatinate to appeal to these friends to join them on the frontier. Several generations later a member of the Boehm family would relate that it was the persuasion of Martin Kendig that had brought his grandparents to cross the ocean.[7]

And so, in spite of blunt warnings of no support from Amsterdam Mennonites who had repeatedly given heavily to the needy Swiss refugees, their Committee suddenly got word on March 20, 1717, that over a hundred of their coreligionists had left the Palatinate for Rotterdam. The greatest of all Mennonite "waves" of immigration to Pennsylvania had broken loose. "In the year 1717, the 21st of March we left for Ibersheim in the Palatinate," wrote Tielman Kolb (Jr.), recording his own small family's journey toward Rotterdam.[8] Three weeks later the Mennonite businessmen of that city were greeted with the sight of not one but three hundred poor Palatine Mennonites who said thirty more were on the way. Most of them—a mixture of Swiss and Palatines—seemed to have enough money, but four families would be stranded without help. Leaders Benedict Brechbill, Hans Burghalter, and Hans Rup undoubtedly made a strong case, but the Dutch Mennonite Committee responded with a stern official refusal. Then they immediately agreed privately that as far as their own personal feelings were concerned, these Palatine "friends" were to be helped "as much as possible." Though several Mennonite leaders from Haarlem wrote advising against any help at all, the Rotterdam businessmen bypassed official church procedure to aid the Palatine "émigrés" whether or not the Committee could agree to do so.[9]

There is no list of the Mennonite families in this 1717 "wave." We do know that three shiploads of Palatines, including 363 persons, landed briefly in Britain, and then arrived in Philadelphia late that summer.[10] It is obvious that this was a full-scale, community-considered Mennonite migration, since influential leaders were involved. Another bishop, in addition to Brechbill and Burghalter, was Valentine Klemmer.

As though in anticipation of this major influx, there was a transaction back in Bebber's Town at about the time of the sailing from Rotterdam. The Mennonites on the Skippack bought from Mathias Van Bebber a 100-acre plot, at a somewhat reduced rate, to be used for the "benefit ... of the poor of the ... Menonists ... in Bebberstownship...." Here we notice the traditional Mennonite arranging for support of indigent or incapable or otherwise struggling members. The Mennonites of Zurich, Switzerland, had had such a farm "for the poor" a century earlier. This would also be the site "to Erect a meeting house," and "a place" for anyone who lived in Bebberstownship "to bury their dead." There would also be room for "a school house ... to have their Children ... taught & Instructed...." The ownership of the plot was to be entrusted only to such as "Continue in unity & religious fellowship ... & remain members" of the Bebberstownship "meeting of the people Called Menonists."[11] The 100 acres were chosen from the area near the oldest clump of Mennonite farms—the Dutch speaking Jansens and Kusters—not far from the Skippack Creek (and the later border with Worcester Township). This left the larger German Kolb-Zie- gler-Clemens family clump at a distance of about two miles. It was to be the first Mennonite-sponsored school of the New World, and its appearance would symbolize the interesting fact that here at the edge of the frontier the Mennonites were quicker to achieve community stability than either their Reformed or their Lutheran neighbors. The latter had to wait for regularly ordained leaders from Europe, whereas the Mennonites, choosing from the ranks of their farmers and weavers, had a supply of trusted men close at hand.

The memorable teacher of the new Mennonite school was, it seems probable, already on his way to America as this agreement was being drawn up. Christopher Dock, who seems to have settled in with the Michael Zieg- ler family (and perhaps married a sister of Michael's wife Catharina?) ar- rived at least no later than 1718 in Skippack, where he at once began teach- ing. Since his two daughters would carry the same name as two of Michael's, and since Michael's second son had already been named Christopher before the new schoolmaster arrived, we may suspect a prior relationship or at least acquaintance.[12] There must have been some special reason for so sensitive a man as Christopher Dock (pronounced and written in English by himself and others as "Duck") to align himself so closely, and for so many years, with the expanding Mennonite community at Skippack. Almost all the known "1717" Mennonite immigrants who stayed in eastern- most Pennsylvania moved beyond Skippack, while Christopher stayed there for at least seven years, and even then, though he moved into a Reformed and Lutheran community in Upper Salford, traveled back to teach at schools in three Mennonite meetinghouses. As Michael Ziegler (his brother- in-law?), who seems to have come from a Lutheran background, the pietist Christopher Dock found a niche in the Mennonite fellowship that gave him a home in a strange land.

Of 330 Mennonites mentioned at Rotterdam, or the 363 Palatines referred to at Philadelphia in 1717, we may guess that between a third and a half stayed in the settlements east of the Schuylkill. At this point the "high German" influence would overwhelm the earlier "Dutch" which reigned at Germantown. But whereas the "Pequea" and now "Conestoga" Men- nonites, of predominantly Swiss origin, would continue meeting for worship in their homes, "Skippack" was already preparing to erect a meetinghouse better than the one at Germantown, and which would show a "Dutch" in- fluence. The incoming Palatines, though now in the majority, would be in- fluenced at the outset by the counsel and tastes of the first established bishop, the Dutch-speaking Jacob Gaetschalck. This factor would be absent in the more distant "Pequea" and "Conestoga" settlements.

How good a list of these "1717" immigrants to the eastern community can we make? Unfortunately, there are no ship lists to consult. Pennsylvania Governor William Keith did become alarmed, as he heard of the "great number of fforeigners from Germany" who "had dispersed themselves over the country." These newcomers had not produced "any certificates from whence they came," and so Keith felt they should be asked to take some sort of oath of loyalty to the British king. Understanding that some of the 363 "fforeigners" were "said to be Menonists, who cannot for conscience sake take any oaths," Keith stipulated that such people "be admitted upon their giving any Equivalent assurances in their own way and manner."[13] But it was already too late. Life is always more than civil ordinances can keep up with, and in this case the taking of oaths or making of affirmations left no orderly record for us to peruse. It was the same with the books recording quitrent payments, which were a jumbled and inconsistent set of notations.

Gathering some data as we can from family records and land purchases, we could compile an incomplete and correctable list which

Name	Place of Settling	Known to Arrive by
Allebach, Christian	First Swamp, eventually Salford	1718
Bauer, Hans	"Goschenhoppen"	1717
Cassel, Hupert	Schuylkill	1717
Detweiler, Hans	Skippack	1725
Dock, Christopher	Skippack	1718
Fretz, John & Christian	Salford? (later Deep Run)	1717?
Funck, Henrich	"Indianfield"	1718
Grubb, Henry	(Frederick Township)	1718
Hunsberger, Hans, Jacob & Ulrich	(Franconia Township)	1723
Hunsicker, Valentine	Swamp, then Skippack	1717
Klemmer, Valentine	Swamp	1717
Kolb, Dielman	Salford	1717
Landes, Johannes	Swamp	1717
Lederach, Andreas & Johannes	Salford	1717
Meyer, Christian & Hans	Salford	1719
Reiff, Abraham	(Franconia Township)	1719
Reiff, Hans	Salford	1718
Rupp, Hans	Germantown area	1717
Ruth, Henrich	Salford	1718
Weirman, Willem	Skippack	1725
Wenger, Heinrich	Manatawny	1717

would include the following Mennonite immigrants arriving in 1717 or shortly thereafter:[14]

Perhaps every one of the above families came in the actual year 1717. From that point on, it was later remembered, Mennonite immigrants came to the "Skippack" and related communities "almost every year" until 1740. By 1726 we may be certain of the arrival of the following additional families:[15]

Bechtel, Hans Jacob	Manatawny (Schuylkill)	1720
Bergey, Hans Uli	Salford	1726
Borneman, Daniel	Hanover	1721?
Brenneman, Christian	Towamencin	1720
Buckwalter, Francis	Schuylkill	ca. 1720
Hiestand, Abraham	?	1726
Hoch, Melchior and Rudolph	Manatawny, Hanover	1726
Landes, John Heinrich	Schuylkill	1722
Longenecker, Daniel	Schuylkill	1719-21
Roth, Johannes	Schuylkill	1719
Souder, Jacob	Built mill at Salford	1726
Yoder, Hans	Saucon	1720

Again, perhaps some of these families were already in Pennsylvania in 1717.

Whereas twenty-one of the "1717" immigrants were granted land out at "Conestoga" on the same day (September 27, 1717), their eastern coreligionists fanned out over a variety of "German" settlements over the next year or two. We may wonder why some of the Swiss who were in the original group deported from Bern in 1710 did not go along out to Conestoga. Hans Rupp, it seems, stayed around Germantown, and Heinrich Wenger found land up in Manatawny (Pottstown area). Others believed to be Swiss went to outlying area: Hans Bauer to "Goschenhoppen" (later Hereford area); Henry Grubb to the territory later called Frederick; and the Buckwalter and Longenecker families to "Schuylkill." This area, on both sides of the river, reached from present-day Phoenixville to present-day Pottstown, and had been opened up for development at about the same time as Bebber's Township. Several Palatines like Hupert Cassell (son or grandson of Yillisz), Hans Jacob Bechtel (already or soon to be a preacher), Johannes Roth, and even Marcus Oberholtzer—a name we saw in the 1709 migration—all chose land in the general Schuylkill area. John Roth's farm would eventually be the site of the Vincent meetinghouse, and Marcus Oberholtzer's the location of the one at Coventry. The Buckwalters and Longeneckers settled among the loops of the river across from the site of present-day Phoenixville. And also near where the Coventry meetinghouse would be built—across the river from present-day Pottstown—were Bechtels, Hochs, Landeses, and Schweitzers.

Another "German" pocket was developing in the "Great Swamp" region of Bucks County, later to be called "Milford." Bishop Valentine Klemmer, who had brought along his seventeen-year-old grandson Valentine Hunsicker, chose this location, and both weaver Christian Allebach and Marcus Oberholtzer looked it over. Jacob Schelly did purchase land there, as well as Johannes Landes, two of whose brothers had gone west with the Conestoga group. Just north across a hilly range, in "Saucon," Hans Yoder found his home.

All around the Germans, of course, were English and Welsh Quakers, Baptists and Anglicans, both speculating and establishing farms reaching back from the first-settled banks of the Delaware. The energy of the German pioneers actually pushed back the tentative edges of the English and Welsh settlements. Thus, as the strong 1717 German influx took place, David Powell of Philadelphia barely got 3,000 acres of land bought between the Skippack and Perkiomen in time to retail it to the "Palatines" in tracts of 100 to 300 acres. This area, reaching northeast from Bebber's Town toward the Bucks County Line (present-day Salford and Franconia), proved one of the most popular locations of all for the Mennonite newcomers. Here names like Rees Williams disappeared as names like Hans Uli Bergey came in. Dielman Kolb got 300 acres about a mile from his four brothers' farms at Skippack, and was surrounded by fellow immigrants like Andrew and John Lederach, Hans Uli Bergey, Hans Reiff, and weaver Henrich Ruth (on the site of the future Salford meetinghouse).

Gerhart Clemens and Michael Ziegler had both been prospering, and Gerhart himself took 690 of Powell's 3,000 acres on both sides of the Branch Creek, while Michael bought another 100.[16] And pushing farther up between the Skippack and the Branch and along the Indian Creek were the newly arrived Meyer brothers Hans and Christian, the promising young Henrich Funck (Christian Meyer's son-in-law), and Henrich's brother-in-law Abraham Reiff. These names have a very Palatine ring, whereas three Hunsberger brothers, arriving in the area perhaps a bit later, may have come directly from Switzerland. The whole area later called Salford and Franconia was then referred to as Skippack or, in German, "Schüpbach." The origin of this name is uncertain, but we may note the presence of a village called Schüpbach on the Emme River, in the heart of the Mennonite community in Bern, Switzerland, to which the origins of many of the Palatine Mennonites can ultimately be traced.

Although Governor Keith had stated that the Palatines showed no certificates of origin, many must have carried some kind of "attestation." The family of Johannes Roth, who settled at "Schuylkill," preserved two such papers which allow us a glimpse into the act of migration from the Palatine to the Pennsylvanian setting. One, dated June 14, 1719, is from the city of Worms. Identifying Roth as an "assessor" by occupation and a "Menonist" by religion, it calls him "a good subject," and requests all officials to "let him pass with wife and children everywhere free and unmolested. . . ." The other paper, issued two weeks earlier on May 30, is witnessed by four Mennonite "servants . . . of the church in the Palatinate," including Bishop Peter Kolb, who himself had five younger brothers who had migrated. It is addressed to Mennonite leaders in Holland and Pennsylvania. Now that Johannes and Barbara Roth and their little children have expressed a "desire and pleasure . . . to journey to Pennsylvania," the home church wishes them well. "As to their conduct as brethren and sisters we can say nothing else than that we are satisfied with their honesty and sincerity, and therefore request of all to whom they may come to recognize and receive them and to give them all good advice. To hear of such kindness will give us much pleasure."[17]

Such a paper might be shown to the leaders at Skippack, where communion was more likely to be celebrated at first than in the smaller and more scattered Mennonite community at "Schuylkill." At Skippack the congregation was growing more rapidly than anywhere else. A large brown sandstone "Vorgader Hausz" (Dutch for meetinghouse) was being constructed. Under its gambrel roof were open, hand-hewn joists. The main meeting room contained backless benches and two stoves (later three). There was another "Kammer" (room), perhaps related to the school held in the building, leaded windows, and, outside, a "stall" for horses.[18]

The Hunsicker family would recall that their pioneer Valentine had helped as a young man with the masonry of the meetinghouse, and apparently the wider community assisted, for a Lutheran neighbor named Hallman also helped, and later had his family burial plot there. Since Valentine Hunsicker was said to have come to Skippack from Swamp in 1720, perhaps the meetinghouse was built that summer. Christopher Dock had already been teaching school for at least two years, and on February 17, 1721, several traveling Quaker preachers, "at the Request" of some of the local Mennonites, "had a Meeting in the Baptist Meetinghouse near Skippolk." After they had experienced "a comfortable time to General Satisfaction," the Friends "parted lovingly," and moved on to a meeting the next day among Quakers at nearby "North Wales."[19] It would not be the last time a member of another denomination would preach in this Mennonite meetinghouse.

In those busy years of clearing and building, not everything got done in proper sequential order. A "Declaration of Trust" governing the use of the 100-acre Mennonite farm, school, and meetinghouse at Skippack was not drawn up until March 30, 1725.[20] This was also the year when thirty-four men of the Bebber's Town community appealed for the laying out of a township to be named Skippack. Half of these men were Mennonite. Three Frieds had now moved in, and the names of Hans Detweiler and Willem Weirman made their appearance on the list. Next to the name of prosperous minister Michael Ziegler was that of schoolteacher Christopher Dock, though before long he would buy a farm in Salford.[21]

Still another document on which Michael Ziegler needed to set his "mark" involved the whole Pennsylvania Mennonite community. Gathering from "Canastoge" as well as "Shipack," Germantown, "Great-Swamp," and "Manatany" were sixteen ministers and bishops, to proclaim their loyalty to the Mennonite teaching as written in the 1632 Dortrecht *Christian Confession of the Faith of the harmless Christians, in the Netherlands known by the name of Mennonists*. This was now, in 1725, issued in English for the American reading public,[22] the important *Appendix* by Tielman Tielen van Sittert being translated. The Dutch Mennonites had sent over a translation of the *Confession* itself in 1712. Van Sittert's eloquent *Appendix*, which had first appeared in 1664, explained that the Mennonite understanding of "Revengeless" Christianity was, rather than "something new or strange," the understanding of Christ's teaching that the Anabaptists had cherished since the days of the Reformation. Apparently this was a point the "Skippack" and "Conestoga" Mennonites wanted to make to their American neighbors at the very outset.

"We lovingly desire thee," pleaded these busy Mennonite pioneers of their English-speaking reader, "not to look so much on the meanness of the Wording of this little Book." If this "Christian Reader" could overlook the fact that the Mennonites were "not exquisite in the English language," and pay attention instead to "the Grounds and Truths" of van Sittert's essay, he would see that "one of the weightiest Articles of our Doctrine and Religion" was "that without any Worldly might or Fleshly Defence or Weapons, the Lord Christ must be preached, and followed Revengeless." This teaching that Christ is to be "followed" as well as praised, that he is an "Example gone before us" providing norms for our own behavior, is candidly laid before the Pennsylvania public, with the sixteen Mennonite leaders acknowledging that they "do own" this *Confession* and *Appendix* "and also, have took the same to be wholly ours."[23] This action took place at what must have been a significant conference in 1725. From Skippack Bishop Jacob Gaetschalck seems to be the first to sign, followed by Henry Kolb and his brother Martin, Claes Jansen, and Michael Ziegler. There are only three names from Germantown (showing that Skippack is already a stronger community): John Gorgas, John Conerads, and Claes Rittinghausen. From Swamp came Bishop Velte (Valentine) Clemer, and upper and lower Manatawny are presented, respectively, by Jacob Beghtly (Hans Jacob Bechtel) and Daniel Longenecker. Five Conestoga leaders were also present to sign the statement. In this joint action we see the close linkage that originally existed between what would eventually be called the "Franconia" and "Lancaster" conferences. Their completely translated document (dated 1725) was issued in 1727 from the Philadelphia press of Andrew Bradford, an early customer of the Rittenhouse paper mill.

Although they now had something in English to show to government officials when questions of oath or war arose, other resources would be needed in the dialogue with German pietist fellowships who were also appearing in Pennsylvania. Closest in spirit to the Mennonites, and migrating initially, like them, from Krefeld, were the "New Baptists" or "Dunkers," so called because of their requirement of baptism by immersion. Their first baptisms in Europe had not taken place until a year after the first three Kolb brothers had come to Germantown, but by a decade later, when a contingent arrived in Philadelphia (1719), they had won sufficient following and preached boldly enough to alarm officials in half a dozen German regions. They too believed that true Christianity must be "revengeless" or without coercion, but, unlike the Mennonites, they had not become "quiet" in manner or witness. Their arrival in America was followed by a lull in their outreach, caused perhaps by some initial disunity, the sheer work of settlement, and the effects of wide dispersion. But on Christmas Day, 1723, the American Dunkers regrouped and held their first baptisms in the Wissahickon Creek near Germantown. An outburst of spiritual fervor then occurred, perhaps anticipating the atmosphere of the somewhat later "Great Awakening" across the Eastern Seaboard.

From this very beginning a few Mennonites became involved with the Dunkers, thus initiating a sometimes curious dialogue between the two nonresistant fellowships. It usually found the Dunkers in an evangelizing, and the Mennonites in a defensive, role. One of Henrich Funck's neighbors along the Indian Creek was Dunker preacher Johan Jacob Preisz (1720), and it may have been partly in response to immersions occuring there that Bishop Funck would later write a book on the proper understanding of baptism. Up at Schuylkill Johannes Heinrich Landes and his wife, having just recently arrived in Pennsylvania, became interested in Dunker teaching, and traveled to Germantown, where they were two of the six persons baptized at the Christmas revival in 1723.[24] Less than a year later the elder

Peter Becker established a Dunker congregation at Coventry, near the Landes farm. Eventually this congregation would take in a significant number of former Mennonites.

This may have been the first case of what would be experienced in almost every generation henceforth among the Mennonites: some of their members finding more satisfaction in a more "charismatic" fellowship. Many a fencerow debate over the Dunker insistence on immersion would occur. Interestingly, since the Dunkers were solidly "nonresistant" and of course practised "believer's baptism," a Mennonite could join them without losing these most basic of Anabaptist convictions. In the ongoing interchange, the Dunkers generally gained more than they lost, with the result that some Mennonites nursed something of a historic grudge. A Mennonite born as late as 1836 could say, in the 20th century, "Die Dunker sin net ehrlich riwwer kumma, un sie sin noch net ehrlich"[25] (The Dunkers didn't come over here honestly, and they still aren't honest.) On the other hand, intermarriage often occurred, an occasional Dunker joined the Mennonites, and neighbors of both fellowships were often the best of friends.

Back in the Palatinate the relatives of the recent Mennonite emigrants were eager for news. A letter from Heppenheim, just west of the Rhine, arrived in Philadelphia addressed to "Johannes Roth, on the Schuylkill, in Pennsylvania." It was from Peter Roth, a brother, telling of deaths in the family and sending greetings from relatives. "And . . . tell us," Peter wrote, "how you got along on your journey and what it cost you, and . . . how you like it in that country and also whether you could advise me to come, or would you rather be with us again? . . . Tell us the condition of the land and the place. . . . We hope you will tell us the truth."[26] By 1726, when the Skippack community had developed to the point that Gerhart Clemens or his son John was having a gristmill built, the letters sound increasingly unhappy. "We would have come to you," wrote Peter Roth, "if we only had the traveling money. We are burdened very heavy. We must pay militia tax, palace tax, building tax and monthly tax and an order has also been issued by the civil authorities to sequester the property of all Mennonites for their earnest money."[27] And even this was not as bad as the experience of a Mennonite family by the name of Landes, who had just bought (1725-26) an estate near Alzey (northwest of Worms). Some Catholics in the region objected, and a decision was handed down from the electoral regime that the sale should be nullified. Further, from then on any member of the Catholic, Lutheran, or Reformed churches could legally demand that land purchased by Mennonites must be returned (the purchase price being refunded). Only after a strong appeal from the Mennonites was this "*jus retractus*" law limited to future purchases.[28] This denial of normal rights to purchase land once again sent a shock of dismay through the Mennonite community, and must have made Pennsylvania seem even more inviting to Mennonite farmers.

Conditions were bad enough that the wealthy Amsterdam "Committee," after repeated warnings and refusals to aid Palatine emigrants, broke down and gave 300 florins for passage money to the family of one Hubert Brower of Neuwied. The Browers, whose passport is dated May 4, 1726, soon appeared as neighbors of the Roth family near the Schuylkill River.[29] To help their European relatives and to keep them from trying to migrate too, the Dutch Mennonites were sending substantial donations to the Palatinate. On the Sunday before Christmas the congregation at Rotterdam, having less than three hundred members, gave an amazing offering of 1487 guilders for this purpose.[30]

But if they thought this would cool the climbing Pennsylvania fever they were mistaken. All over the Palatinate, for the third time since 1709, among Lutheran and Reformed as well as Mennonites, another "wave" was gathering in the spring of 1727. We find twenty-six year-old Abraham Schwartz, a native of Gerolsheim who had already been married by Bishop Hans Burghalter to his second wife, Elizabeth Hystant, receiving from his father an old Bible which he now, in March, had rebound "immediately."[31] The Schwartzes and their two little boys were among "150" Mennonites, some without money, who were about to flock to Rotterdam. This rerun of the 1709 and 1717 outpourings would be, for Mennonites, the second largest wave. The Amsterdam "Committee," realizing that the move would not be stopped no matter what they said, asked to be informed as to how many were coming, and how many of these "would arrive without means."[32] There were at least seventy-four of such persons by late July, costing the Committee well over 3,000 florins. This provoked from them an urgent message to Pennsylvania that the preachers there should "announce emphatically . . . from the pulpit that they must no more advise their needy friends to come out of the Palatinate."[33] The preachers were to say, rather, that if the Palatines stayed at home they would receive help there. Of course, if the Pennsylvania Mennonites wanted to help pay the ocean fares themselves, that was their own business.

Already in June ships were again being loaded with hopeful Palatines in the Rotterdam harbor. The *Friendship* of Bristol, on which Abraham Schwartz and his brother Andreas embarked, had forty-six Palatine families making 200 persons, including Cassels, Croessmans, Hackmans, Hiestands, Meyers, Valentine Kratz, Preacher John Oberholtzer, and Mathes Schweitzer.[34] The voyage was lengthy, and among the fifth of the passengers who did not survive it were Preacher Oberholtzer and the baby

Johannes Schwartz. The latter's mother Elizabeth must also have found the crossing miserable, as she was to die, in her husband Abraham's words, "when I had been in the land four weeks."[35] Abraham then seems to have married Anna (b. 1708), a daughter of Preacher Henry Kolb of Skippack.

This new flood of Palatines triggered the Pennsylvania government into requiring a promise of loyalty from all newcomers, and a proper list of names to be taken already when the boat was loaded in Europe. On September 21, 1727, the first 109 Palatines signed a declaration of allegiance to the British king in the Philadelphia Courthouse. This was to become such a common occurrence, in the ensuing years, that it is reflected in what the *Pennsylvania Gazette* reported as an example of "thoughtless questions" heard in Philadelphia:

"What does the bell ring for?"   "From the Palatinate."
"They are about to swear some Palatines."   "Where is that?"
"Where do all these Palatines come from?"   " 'Tis in Germany."[36]

But at least these new procedures, which reflected the shock some English-speaking authorities felt at seeing the massive influx, helped to ensure better records. From them we can recover many names in this fourth "wave" by which the easternmost Mennonite community was largely augmented. Even so, of course, we are certain that our list is incomplete. But among those who entered the port of Philadelphia in the fall of 1727 were:[37]

If we bring together the names of known immigrants in the next three

Name	Place of Settlement
Bach, Jacob	Schuylkill (time of entry uncertain)
Bachman, Hans Georg	Saucon
Cassel, Yelles	Skippack
Halteman, Nicholas (& brothers)	Salford
Hiestand, Jacob	Swamp or Upper Milford
Hiestand, Johannes	?
Jung, Valentine	Saucon
Kendig, Martin	(Indianfield?)
Kratz, Valentine	Salford
Landes, Jacob	Indian Creek
Meyer, Johann Vincent	Skippack
Reser, Hans	Saucon
Schumacher, Georg	?
Schwartz, Abraham	Skippack (later Deep Run)
Schwartz, Andreas	Salford (later became Franconia)
Schweitzer, Mathes	Schuylkill (Coventry)
Zug, Peter & Ulrich	Swamp

years (1728-30) with names among persons naturalized in 1730, we are probably including some which should be in the list above:[38]

Name	Place of Settlement	Known to Arrive by
Acre, Casper & Jacob	Schuylkill (Coventry)	1730
Bechtel, Hans Georg (minister)	Goschenhoppen	1728
Beidler, Ulrich	Goschenhoppen (Hereford)	by 1729
Drissel, John	Swamp	by 1730
Greder, Jacob	Skippack	by 1730
Geissinger, Philip	Saucon	by 1730
Klemmer, Hans	Salford	1730
Klemmer, Heinrich	(Franconia)	1730
Kolb, Dielman (son of Bishop Peter)	(Eventually) Deep Run	1729
Latscha, Johannes Franz	Goschenhoppen (Hereford)	1728
Metz, Jacob	Towamencin	by 1730
Moll, Johann Peter	Goschenhoppen (Hereford)	1728
Musselman, Jacob	Swamp (Richland)	1730
Neukommet, John	Saucon	by 1730
Rosenberger, Heinrich	Indianfield	by 1729
Weis, Jacob	Swamp	1728

This German "wave" filled in vacant tracts at the edges of Skippack and on over toward Bucks County. Roads were laid out leading toward "Goschenhoppen," the wilderness-edge are of Maxatawny, and to Gerhard Clemens' new mill in Salford, on the northeast Branch of the Perkiomen. Another contingent of Dunkers came in 1729, and all around were many new Reformed settlers, often from the very same villages in Europe as their Mennonite neighbors along the Skippack and Indian Creeks. An attempt to get a Reformed church going in Skippack failed, although a building was erected—the first for this denomination in America. Mennonites at "New Goschenhoppen" in the "Hanover" area in northern Philadelphia County joined Lutheran and Reformed people in sponsoring what must have been a union meetinghouse and school. In this region occurred the only recorded local Indian scare, in May 1728. A few Shawnees on the warpath scuffled with several white men, wounding one in the belly and causing a few other injuries. Alarmed Episcopalians near Bebber's Town whipped up a petition to the government on behalf of those who feared for the safety of their wives and children, who meant "more to us than Life." One man signed forty-four of the attached seventy-seven names, which included many Mennonite ones.[39] For some reason, the name of Johannes Kolb is missing, while those of his four brothers at Skippack are all there. Interestingly, each of these four brothers was, or soon would be, a minister or deacon.

This was a moment of rapid expansion and organization. New townships were set up: Salford in 1728, Franconia in 1731, and Milford in 1734. And just as this new density of settlement was occurring, Christopher Dock decided to quit the schoolroom. He found 100 acres in (Upper) Salford and went to farming as almost everyone else was doing. With no sons of his own and only two daughters, he was probably kept as busy as everyone else establishing and improving his farm amidst the towering oaks near Old Goschenhoppen. Did one reason for his withdrawal lie in the fact that the community at Skippack hardly paid enough for a man to support his family by teaching? Something of Christopher's unusual kind of piety may be indicated in an oral tradition that he was so religiously conscientious that he refused to wear linen and wool mixed together.[40] Or was there an economic basis for this scruple? Another legend suggests that he was such a peaceful man that even crude insults from a workman by a roadside could draw from him no angry reply.[41]

For whatever reason, this best of the German schoolteachers of Pennsylvania did not return to his "calling" for a decade, just when the communities of Skippack and Salford were filling up with growing families. In Skippack alone there were at least seventeen Mennonite landowners by 1734, which would easily have provided for the presence of seventy school-age children. And Salford was not far behind. Later Dock would confess that his conscience disapproved of this forsaking the youth of the community, and he would ask God's forgiveness. Perhaps his temporary retreat is explained by the fact that, as he later remarked, his profession was not "established" by the government in Pennsylvania, as it was in his previous community in Germany. The basic means he had of dealing with unruly youth in his frontier classroom was "love."[42]

The flow of immigration from "Germany" rose and fell from year to year. Though 1731 brought few new Mennonite faces (Jacob Schumacher and Jacob Hackman on the *Britannia*), the Palatines in general were very much on the move. Some 800 passed through Rotterdam during the summer, just as the Synod of the Dutch Reformed Church was in session there. The whole Synod went out to visit the crowd of refugees, sang and prayed with them, and arranged for relief supplies.[43] Among the Reformed members was the family of William Gerges (Garges), who would find a niche on some undeveloped land in Lower Salford near Gerhard Clemens. Several members of his family would join the Mennonite community through marriage. On the same ship which brought the Gergeses arrived Dutch-speaking Gesbert and John Boors. First Methacton, and then the Towamencin Mennonite congregation, where Hendrickses and Gottschalcks also spoke

Dutch, would absorb members of this family.

Then, in 1732, after Skippack and Salford were already full, and new land was being bought at "Perkasie" and "Deep Run," there came another spurt of Mennonite immigration. We can see it coming down the Rhine in May, when "eleven large vessels" full of "Men, Women and Children" were observed passing the town of Wesel. They were reported to be fleeing "hard usage, intolerable servitude, and Religious grievances," and to be heading for "the English Colonies in America."[44] Watching the shore slip by were Mennonites like twenty-eight-year-old Jacob Benedict Gehman and his wife, with his older brother Christian, who was still single. Michael Derstein, also single, had received financial help from "some of his friends" to make the trip.[45]

Once again, Mennonite travelers arriving in Rotterdam appealed for aid to their wealthy Dutch brothers in the faith. But the Dutch Mennonites were at last coming to the end of their patience with these impulsive and, to their minds, unnecessary migrations. One of the deacons at Rotterdam, the affluent distiller Oliver van Vlierden, allowed some forty Palatine Mennonite families to lodge in his dark warehouse while waiting for shipping, but made a charge of two stivers per person per night. This, observed a later Dutch historian, did not please his guests.[46] Van Vlierden's son-in-law Isaac Hope actually owned a substantial shipping firm, which took quite a few Palatines to Philadelphia. It was mostly such businessmen, rather than the Rotterdam Mennonites in general, who had dealings with the Palatines. These refugees often arrived unannounced, and something had to be done about them immediately, before the congregation as a whole could be consulted. For this, executive-type action was useful. It also was helpful to have business connections to arrange for the gathering of food supplies, such as the twenty-four pounds of smoked meat, fifteen pounds of cheese, and seventy pounds of Zwieback which were part of the recommended ration for each adult voyager.[47] But although businessmen handled the matter, the whole congregation helped with the expenses.

When over three thousand of various religious persuasions had once again descended on Rotterdam, the Mennonite Committee finally decided they had had enough. On June 15, 1732, they passed a resolution that they would no more, for any reason whatsoever, help the Palatines travel, except back to where they had come from.[48] This stern action seems to have had considerable effect among the 600 or more Mennonite families remaining in the Palatinate. Their migrations fell off sharply, and except for a modest spurt nearly twenty years later, never regained its former volume, as far as the "Franconia Conference" area is concerned ("Lancaster" did have strong immigration again in the early 1750s). Almost a year after their action, the Dutch Committee announced that they were no longer troubled with requests for migration money.[49] They also circulated discouraging stories of trials aboard ships crossing the Atlantic. One shipload of 150 Palatines, they said, had wandered nearly half a year on the ocean, with the passengers forced to eat rats while most of them starved.

Of the "ten ship loads" totaling 3,000 Palatines coming to Philadelphia in 1732, one had a particularly bad time, taking four months to cross, and losing sixty passengers en route. The rest were "nearly all sick" and "weak," and quite a few died after the ship had docked. Nicholas Ish (Esht), coming on the *Plaisance*, was listed as sick on arrival, but later recovered.[50] Some weeks earlier, on August 11, had come the *Samuel*, said to be carrying "106 Palatines and their families," making a total of 279 persons. These included widower Jacob Oberholtzer, Michael Dierstein, two Gehman brothers, and over a dozen younger unmarried people with "Mennonite" names.[51]

A list of Mennonite-connected immigrants of 1732 to 1734 might thus include the following:[52]

Name	Place of Settlement	Known to Arrive by
Altdörfer, Friedrich (Lutheran)	Salford (Redemptioner)	1733
Bassler, Ulrich	Upper Milford	1732
Beidler, Christian		1732
Dierstein, Michael	Rockhill, Hilltown	1732
Gehman, Benedict	Saucon	1732
Gehman, Christian	Hereford	1732
Hottel, John	Oley	1732
Lapp, John	(New Britain)	1733
Longenecker, Ulrich, Sr., Ulrich, Jr., & Jacob	Schuylkill	1733
Mininger, Abraham, John & Joseph		1734
Oberholtzer, Jacob	Hereford?	1732

Many a younger person came along without the means to pay his or her own fare; such were forced to "sell themselves," as one report put it, for "3, 4, 6 to 8 years," to a master who in return would pay the fare and give them a place to live. "When their time is out," one Germantown resident wrote warningly back to Europe, "they receive nothing but a poor suit of clothing."[53] Much depended, of course, on the kind of master involved. "Some hundreds" of Reformed people, wrote two of their ministers, "are in the service of English people...."[54] Mennonites probably had a greater cohesiveness as a group, and thus needed the indentured servant system less than some other groups, but they too were involved as both servants and masters. Jacob Beidler[55] apparently began his American life as a servant in Chester County, and young farmer Hans Klemmer of Lower Salford took in eighteen-year-old Lutheran Friedrich Altdörfer,[56] formerly of Steinsfurt, east of the Rhine. Just as in the Palatinate there had been a mixture of Lutheran, Mennonite, and Reformed populations, here Friedrich not only bound himself to the Mennonite family of Hans Klemmer, but when the latter died three or four years later, married his widow Anna. From this union came many Mennonite Alderfers in the Salford congregation. In the same manner other names, such as Hechler and Schwerdle,[57] would also become a part of the Mennonite family. There were, of course, sad cases in the neighborhood, where servants and masters were unhappy with each other, with flight, suicide, and even, in Upper Hanover, a frightful murder of a Schwenkfelder woman by a Swiss servant who felt his term of service was too long.

The immigration that formed the later "Franconia Conference" was about three-quarters completed, we may estimate, by the middle of the 1730s. Most of the good land had been taken between the Perkiomen and the Bucks County Line. Well over half of the landholders in Bebber's Town were Mennonites; throughout the northern part of Philadelphia County, later called Montgomery, we may count about eighty Mennonite farms.[58] Although several Welsh families had settled at the springs of the Skippack Creek (later the site of Souderton), only the name "Welshtown" would linger where Benners, Souders, and Hunsbergers would take over. Up in the Swamp area, the "great tract" of investor Joseph Growden had been "sold mostly to Dutchmen,"[59] who had their own Mennonite, Lutheran, and Reformed culture in peaceful coexistence with English-speaking Quakers in nearby Richland. An advancing column of Germans would soon push over into Gwynedd, New Britain, Hilltown, and Rockhill, where the earlier settlers had been Welsh Baptists, and Quakers. Though Abraham Schwartz had 100 acres in Bebber's Town, he would soon be moving to a new homestead at Deep Run, where many of his neighbors would be the grown-up children of Mennonite immigrants who had settled at Skippack and Schuylkill. Deacon Jacob Kolb of Bebber's Town had bought land in "Freetown" (Rockhill) by 1731, and in 1737 it was taken up by his son, "Strong Isaac."[60] Living next to Isaac would be his brother-in-law Michael Derstine.

Some unused land, though not the best for farming, was found for a new group of "Germans" arriving in the 1730s—the Schwenkfelders from Silesia. The Methacton (pronounced "Modetchy" in German) region across the Skippack Creek from Bebberstown was one area where large acreage could still be had for contiguous settlement. Several pockets in Towamencin, a corner of Lower Salford, and larger sections of the New Hanover and Goschenhoppen areas also drew parts of this devout, spiritualistic, nonresistant fellowship. The main body arrived at Philadelphia in 1734 with favorable memories of European Mennonites. They had fled Catholic territory after years of threats and harassment, and arrived at Hamburg as resourceless refugees. There a wealthy Mennonite named Hinrich van der Smissen had fitted out three ships to take them to Amsterdam, and given them good food and drink to take along. At Amsterdam the Mennonites put them up while shipping to America was being arranged. A family from Haarlem paid their fare to Pennsylvania on the *Saint Andrew,* and sent along 224 rix thaler for the care of the poor. From that time on, the Schwenkfelders were to maintain a charity fund that was based on this initial Mennonite donation.[61] In Pennsylvania they lived as close neighbors with many Mennonites. Occasional intermarriages would bring into the Mennonite family such Schwenkfelder names as Anders, Hedrick, Heebner, and Kriebel. In later years, after the Schwenkfelders overcame their earlier scruples against building meetinghouses, the special relationship with the Mennonites would be evident in the sharing of "harvest home" services. But already in the first war troubles of the 1750s and 1770s it would be seen that this group was somewhat less committed than the Mennonites to a refusal of war-service for Christian reasons.

Some of the Schwenkfelders who settled at Goschenhoppen lived among both Catholic and Mennonite neighbors. A tradition of the good interdenominational relations of this region is held in the local story of the Catholics' first arrival in the "Butter Valley" at present-day Hereford. Winter was at hand, and the newcomers were without food supplies. At this point, runs the folk memory, the already established Mennonites shared the meat they were butchering with the Catholic group.[62] Throughout the following centuries this tradition of neighborliness would remain strong, with such expressions as the Catholics helping to build a new Mennonite meetinghouse. Since there was so little similarity between the two communions, there was no issue of young people being drawn across from one to the other. Thus the Mennonites might experience less friction with the Catholics than with a group much "closer" to them, the Dunkers. This latter fellowship in 1733 organized a congregation on the edges of the Mennonite community in the Swamp region; a few years later its communion was being attended by people with such "Mennonite" names as Frick, Longenecker, Rhodes, Schleiffer, and Zug. Down in Germantown, the Mennonites and Brethren apparently seemed so much alike to one Philadelphian observer that he saw them as part of the same communion: Germantown, he reported, had "a high German Mennonite Church, and a

similar one in which the Crefeld or broken Hollandish is used."[63] Many of
the Dunkers had immigrated, of course, directly from Krefeld, and both
Mennonite and Dunker congregations met in log houses for worship along
the same side of the Germantown Road, less than a mile apart.

These mid-1730s were a time of regularization of community and
spiritual life. Meetinghouses were built at Hereford, Swamp, and Saucon
(at the latter place, it would later be claimed, Indians sometimes attended
the services, leaving bows and arrows at the door).[64] Salford drew up a deed
for a lot from the farm of Henrich Ruth in 1738, the year Christopher Dock
returned to teach there and at Skippack.[65] On the deed, apparently signed
by most of the male heads of families at Salford and a number from Franconia township, was an indication that a building already stood on the land.
A road petition mentions a meetinghouse by 1728. Doubtless all but the
stone building at Bebber's Town were of logs, and most if not all would
have served for school as well as church purposes (though good teachers
were almost impossible to find). The geographic center of a *"Gemeinde"* or
congregation might have a meetinghouse, whereas worship meetings in its
outlying districts could be held in homes. This seems to have been the case
in Coventry, or in Franconia, where the memory persisted of gatherings in a
Detweiler home.[66] The leading Bebber's Town *Gemeinde* reached out on
all sides, into Towamencin, Providence, and Worcester (and later into
Frederick), as is made evident in the records of its "Alms Book" which was
now (1738) begun. Such an extended, multicentered "congregation," once
each area had its own meetinghouse, would eventually form a "bishop district."

Five such regions or districts contributed to a conference of "servants"
or ministers on February 12, 1735. Such a gathering in the winter season
when travel was likely to be difficult suggests that some urgency may have
been felt. Later conferences would be held in the more convenient months
of May and October. This early coming-together, a foreshadowing of the
strong intercongregational feeling that would bind the "Franconia Conference" into a self-conscious unit, included representatives from Skippack,
Schuylkill, Germantown, Great Swamp, and Goschenhoppen. This was the
order in which Hupert Cassel of Skippack, who considered the event important enough to register on the flyleaf of one of his books, placed the
communities.

The three topics of discernment which Hupert lists are "the
constable's office," "taking out warrants," and "footwashing."[67] The latter
topic, we may guess, might have had connections with the testimony of the
Dunkers. Would the reception of the formerly Amish Zug family of Swamp
into the Dunker fold be also related? Whether or not to practice footwash-

ing as an ordinance would be an issue in the Franconia Conference until the 20th century, and actually occasion the organization of a separate congregation at Skippack over a century after this 1735 conference. The necessity of a constable for each of the townships being newly formed in this decade was also no minor issue for these Mennonites. In Europe they were not even considered citizens, and here they were being invited, sometimes requested, to take on forms of civil authority. Thirty-five years later they would explain to Mennonites in Europe that they refrained from governmental offices because these required the use of "force." But in these first years, we find Christian Clymer (1737) appointed constable in Milford Township,[68] and here and there other communal responsibilities of a civil nature were occasionally taken by Mennonites. Although they believed strongly that social organization came under two separate kingdoms, Christ's and this world's, new freedom in Pennsylvania was challenging them to redefine the borders of those kingdoms.

The most innocent kind of civil function might be serving as guardian for the estate of a friend or relative, as Jacob and Dielman Kolb were called to do, with Deacon John Conrad of Germantown, when Hans Rupp died without leaving a will.[69] Claus Jansen at Bebber's Town had also served as tax collector for his area. Taxes were minimal, though on occasion there might be a special levy, as in 1738 when Philadelphia County was assessed to pay bounties for "wolves and crows destroyed."[70] (These were the days when bear, beaver, and wild turkeys were also a part of the scene. Fifty years later six wild turkeys would be shot at Rittenhouses' Mill.)

Another kind of collection—the annual quitrent payment written into the land patents from the Penns—was apparently neglected for decades, but after 1732 it too was demanded. "I do not find that a Quitrent had been paid for [Bebber's] Towneship," wrote land agent James Steele in 1735, "Since the date of the patent granted to Mathias Vanbebber wch I take to be about Thirty years since." Now that all three of Penn's sons were living in Pennsylvania, a new and largely vain effort was being made to realize this hereditary income by which William Penn had once hoped to make his family wealthy. Steele had earlier written to the surveyor and informal leader of Bebber's Township (Skippack), Hendrick Pannebecker, and asked him to collect the quitrent, but there had apparently been almost no response from the local landowners. In adjacent Salford, conscientious people like Gerhart Clemens, Dielman Kolb, and Johannes Lederach had paid up. But in all of Bebber's Town, where over half of the landowners were Mennonites, only Minister Michael Ziegler, it seems, had paid. Taking a new initiative, agent Steele then wrote to Ziegler, asking him "to speak with the inhabitants of Bebbers Township and let them know that the

Quitrents . . . must be forthwith paid . . . so that the [Penns] may be paid wt has been so long due to them." Ziegler, now prospering in his mid-forties and still signing papers with his "mark," seems to have held a reputation of trustworthiness. Steele wrote that the "best way" to proceed would be for Bebber's Town people "to meet and pay to thyself [or] any other that they might think fit."[71] This seems to indicate that Michael had by now achieved a position of both spiritual and economic leadership in his neighborhood. But his neighbor, deacon Jacob Kolb, apparently also functioned as a collector of the quit rent.[72]

Although many Palatines continued to reach Philadelphia, in the later 1730s the Mennonite immigration fell off sharply. Individual families did continue to filter in. Among the 388 persons reported on the ship *Harle* arriving in September of 1738 was Christian Souder.[73] A few other young men, such as Jacob Schantz[74] (1737), the Reformed Hans Georg Delp[75] (1738), and John Adam Gotwals[76] (1739) continued to arrive, eventually finding land in the already occupied Lower Salford, Schuylkill, Franconia, and Skippack communities. Schantz, coming directly from Switzerland, found a place beside the Schuylkill where the young Martin Bechtel, ordained minister in 1729, had a ferry.

Christian Souder first bought land from a Welsh family by the name of James in what would be "New Britain." From this Baptist clan of Jameses there went emigrants, around this time, to South Carolina, apparently in search of more open land. Surprisingly to us, in that distant frontier settlement the James family from Bucks County would mingle with Mennonites who had come down to this "Welsh Tract" from Skippack. These Skippackers represented one of the very first remigrations to occur by Mennonites who had come from Europe. They were the family of Johannes Kolb, the only one of at least five brothers in America who was not a deacon or minister at Skippack. Around the year 1739 Johannes seems to have taken his grown-up family to the new homestead along the Peedee River in South Carolina.[77] What his connections here might have been we do not know. Jacob Wismar, Jr., of Deep Run had gone back to visit his father's holdings in North Carolina after Jacob, Sr., had died in 1725,[78] but the Welsh Tract in South Carolina was a great distance from the earlier "New Bern" settlement. Perhaps there was a family connection between the Skippack Kolbs and the New Britain Jameses. There certainly would be intermarriage eventually (Skippack minister Claus Jansen's youngest son would also marry a Welsh woman from the James family of "Montgomery"). By January 1738 the Jameses who had moved to South Carolina had organized the Welsh Neck Baptist Church, and fourteen years later, when a new congregation, the Catfish Baptist Church was chartered, among its first members were men named Henry, Jacob, Martin, and Tilman Kolb.

Even more interesting may be the fact that by 1735 there had been among the Carolina Welsh settlers members of the Jacob Buckholt family. This is probably a still closer link with the Kolbs: there had been Bucholzers among the Mennonites of Kriegsheim near the old Kolb home in the Palatinate; a Bucholz family had come to Germantown in 1685; and a Jacob Buckholts was in the Schuylkill Mennonite settlement in 1726. In any case, the Carolina Kolbs seem to have kept their Mennonite identity for a generation or so, being considered by Carolina Moravians as "pure Baptists or Mennonites" with "three meetinghouses" as late as 1763. But by the outbreak of the Revolutionary War they would seem to have been fairly well assimilated by the surrounding Baptist ethos. Johannes Kolb's grandson Abel Kolb (whose given name had been common among the James family in Hilltown), would be an outstanding leader in the local militia, in the area called "Culp's Neck" on the Peedee River. Back at Skippack, the Johannes Kolb homestead was sold, after several years, to John Adam Gotwals, who had come to Pennsylvania in about the year the Kolbs moved south.

Another family leaving Skippack for more open territory did not have to go nearly so far. Abraham Schwartz joined Mennonites Jacob Wismar, Jr., and Martin Overholt near the Deep Run in Bucks County, as land there, including some that had once been the property of original investor Jan Streypers, became available in the 1720s from developer William Allen. Next to Abraham's new plantation were three others belonging to three of his in-laws, two sons and a daughter of the deceased Skippack minister Henry Kolb (d. 1730). Marrying into this emerging Mennonite fellowship at Deep Run would be a son of Huguenot immigrant Peter Loux. A strong community of Mennonites and Lutherans (later to be joined by Scotch-Irish Presbyterians) was well in place before Bedminster Township was founded in 1742. At least ten of the thirty-five petitioners for the township were Mennonites.[79] Already in 1738 they selected Abraham Schwartz as their first minister. A meetinghouse is mentioned in a deed as early as 1744. Thus Deep Run, though farther east, had a congregation before such communities as "Perkasie" (Blooming Glen), New Britain (Line Lexington), and Plains. So did Upper Saucon, where about the same number of Mennonites signed the appeal for a township in June 1742.

This filling-up of the land motivated the Penn brothers, the "Proprietors" of Pennsylvania, to prepare more of their frontier holdings for individual sales. Thomas Penn had reorganized the Proprietary Land Office in 1732, and now wanted to make definite some vague boundaries in the old Indian treaties of his father. One of these treaties had a base line beginning near the Delaware River (Wrightstown) and running north through Bucks

County. When this was now brought up to date, the result was the infamous "Walking Purchase" of September 19-20, 1737. The white agents employed trained runners to "walk" two days out from the river. At least one of them got twice as far—above the Pocono Mountain—as the Delaware Indians had expected the old purchase of 1686 to extend. This shady deal may represent to us the early stages of an increasing breakdown of trust between the Pennsylvania government and the Indians.[80] Although Mennonites were not particularly involved in this, they began to be troubled by the noticeable drift toward hostility along the frontier. As warlike European events sent ominous rumors floating through Pennsylvania, they began to look to their Mennonite friends in Holland for reassurance.

Of course the immigrants from the Palatinate remembered well what war could do to the farming countryside. Even now, the news must have reached Skippack, Swamp, and Deep Run of the miseries recently experienced back at the Ibersheimerhof along the Rhine. Another war had broken out; rough French soldiers had ridden onto the hof demanding 5,000 florins worth of grain and hay. They had torn up the barn roof, damaged house furnishings, ridden off with the poultry, and used twenty-five of the hof's draft animals to haul grain down to the French military headquarters in Worms.[81] Certainly such news would reach Franconia Township, where we begin to notice the presence of a Hackman family, of which at least three "Ulrichs" remained back at Ibersheim.

Transatlantic mail arrived from time to time, occasionally being advertised in a new German newspaper issued by Christopher Saur in Germantown. Almost none of this correspondence survives, but we do find minister Martin Kolb writing to his wife Magdalena's Classen cousins in 1738, telling them that his father-in-law, deacon Izaak van Sintern, has died, and disclaiming any debts to a European nephew.[82] Another death that was doubtless reported to Agnes, wife of miller Jacob Galle at Uffhofen in the Palatinate, was that of her brother, deacon Jacob Kolb of Skippack. While pressing cider on October 4, 1739, he was killed by a falling beam, "to the exceeding grief ... and concern" of his "numerous" family and relatives. He had been held "in great esteem," noted editor Saur, by "his friends and neighbors."[83] This left in Skippack only Martin, the oldest, and Dielman, the youngest, of the original Kolb immigrant brothers. "Strong Izaak," Jacob's oldest son, would become the main leader at Rockhill. Interestingly, it was only two weeks after Jacob's untimely death that the Conestoga Mennonites suffered a similar tragic loss of a respected minister. Ulrich Brechbill, only son of immigrant Bishop Benedict, was suddenly killed in a wagon accident on "the Philadelphia Road."[84]

The same month brought news of open war between England and

Spain, and Pennsylvania Governor George Thomas began to try to gather a militia. These were days when the Quaker-dominated assembly, with whom the Mennonites were in sympathy, was beginning a long, futile struggle to keep military doings out of the colony. "Why did they come among us," asked one Quaker, referring to nonpacifist immigrants, "if they could not trust themselves with our principles. . . ?"[85] When the Mennonite leaders of Skippack "made application" to the assembly, "in case of . . . an outbreak, to be exempt from the bearing of arms," they were disturbed to learn that the Quaker officials did not have "power to grant the request." The worried Mennonites were told they would have to appeal directly to "His Royal Highness, the King of Britain."[86]

Another topic of conversation in these months was the presence of the stirring revival preacher George Whitefield, who arrived in Philadelphia on April 14, 1740. Gathered at the separatist Schwenkfelder Christopher Wiegner's farm at Towamencin were some two thousand listeners, doubtless including many local Mennonites. One Peter Bohler preached in "Dutch," and Whitefield himself, who recorded that "few of these people could speak English," held forth in that language. "I never saw more simplicity," was his reaction to this meeting in "Wilderness country, Thirty miles distant from Philadelphia."[87] Apparently not much came of this meeting, but Wiegner, whose home was a rallying point for religious enthusiasm, in the following month hosted another famous leader who could speak German—Count Nicholas Ludwig von Zinzendorf of Saxony. This forty-year-old pietist, whose godfather had been none other than the Philip Spener who had so influenced young Francis Daniel Pastorius at Frankfurt, had left his king's court to become a Lutheran clergyman. On his hereditary estate, Herrnhut, he had gathered the remnants of the old "Bohemian Brethren," whose origins dated back before the Protestant Reformation. Zinzendorf had developed a reputation among Lutherans as an independent operator with a passion for evangelism and for unifying all evangelical believers into one "brotherhood." In his wide travels he had met the Mennonites of Holland, and had even won a well-known Amsterdam Mennonite pastor, Johannes Deknatel, to affiliate with the "Moravian Brethren," though still holding on also to his Mennonite membership. Zinzendorf had celebrated communion in Deknatel's home.

The Mennonites of Philadelphia County would prove less ready for such innovations. After the Count arrived in Philadelphia in 1741, he held a series of "Unity" conferences, beginning in Germantown and ranging as far as Oley. All German "sects" were invited to the talks. Mennonites too were present. On his way to Falckner Swamp (New Hanover) for the second meeting, Zinzendorf seems to have stopped at the home of "a venerable . . .

Mennonite leader" at Skippack to see if this man's people might participate further. We might expect this to be Martin Kolb, now over sixty, but perhaps it was Martin's elderly fellow minister Yellis Cassel. Whoever it was "received the Count graciously, listened patiently, but declared the time was too short to send qualified delegates" to the next meeting.[88] The Falckner Swamp discussions, reportedly, "grew violent," and an account of the following session, on February 21-23 at Oley, suggests that Zinzendorf was felt to be too domineering by some participants. One of the Count's severest critics later recalled that Yellis Cassel had attended this third meeting, and had been asked by the Count to "subscribe" to the unity movement in the name of the Mennonites. The following interchange then took place, as Zinzendorf challenged Cassel:

"I'll wager with you whatever you wish, that in less than a year half the Mennonites will be Moravian."

"I have no wager to make."

"Why won't you wager?"

"Wagering is for idle fellows and light-minded people. I'll wager nothing and I won't sign either."[89]

This attempt to interest Mennonites in an organizational change was, of course, almost entirely futile. One "single brother from Goschenhoppen, of Mennonite parents," was baptized by a Moravian bishop in 1745.[90] This Abraham Groff, who died a few years later, was atypical, but he can be seen as one of the first of those American Mennonites who, in every subsequent generation, would be wooed from their specific tradition of "peoplehood" to a more pietistic and conversion-emphasizing fellowship. Zinzendorf's fellowship did crystallize into "visible" congregations at Germantown and Bethlehem a few months after the Oley conference, but with no recorded Mennonite members.

Even before this had happened, Yellis Cassel had been at a smaller meeting with five other local Mennonite pastors to discuss a topic that gave them considerably more concern: the rising war atmosphere and its potential effect on the younger Mennonite generation. Many of the latter had grown up with parents who had been preoccupied with planting and building; now special educational measures might be called for.

Sometime during the course of this year (1742) the old hymnal of the "Swiss Brothers," the *Ausbund*, was reissued from Saur's press in Germantown.[91] To this first American edition was added an appendix written nearly a century earlier, telling how the Anabaptists of Switzerland—great-grandparents of the Pennsylvania Mennonites—had remained faithful under persecution. The contents of the appendix were actually two reports that had been sent to the Dutch Mennonites. Now the Skippack ministers were turning almost instinctively in the same direction, asking their friends in "Amsterdam and Haarlem" for advice and help. They themselves felt "weak, helpless, and powerless to seek" in their "humble way," the favor of the English Court for their old scruples against participating in war. But the Skippackers remembered that some of the older ministers who had settled in Lancaster had received a valuable promise when passing through Amsterdam and Haarlem on their way to Pennsylvania in 1717. The Dutch Mennonites had promised that, should the Pennsylvania pioneers "suffer on account of freedom of conscience," Dutch leaders "would report the matter to their brethren in Holland." Now, perhaps, such a moment had arrived, when the men of Skippack might be "compelled against [their] consciences to bear arms . . . to the great burdening of [their] consciences." Matters looked so serious that the Skippackers confessed, "We recognize . . . that we have made a mistake in coming to this far off country with insufficient assurances in the matter of freedom of conscience."[92]

Indeed the political atmosphere of Pennsylvania was changing; a nasty riot broke out at the next election on Market Street in Philadelphia. The Quakers, through the assembly they dominated, had been holding out for nonviolence, whereas nonpacifists were worried about containing Indians at the frontier, as well as the French on the high seas and the local rivers. Christopher Saur's editorializing strongly influenced the German vote in sympathy with the Quakers. A group of sailors, commissioned by an anti-Quaker, stormed the election, swinging clubs at "Broad-brims and Dutch dogs."[93] This scandalous outbreak only solidified the Quaker-German pacifist voting alliance. Their opponents complained from time to time that the "Dutch" (Germans) came down from the country in "shoals" to vote at the Philadelphia elections. Editor Saur, who brought out a remarkably fine quarto-sized German Bible in 1743, was much resented for his voting advice by people like the rising printer Benjamin Franklin. Saur kept his readers at Skippack, Tulpenhocken, Swamp, or Indianfield up to date, complaining of Indian unrest due to unfair squatting by white immigrants, and reporting European news. "This is a time," he mused, "when one hears from no single place or people where there is not war and shouts of war, as well in the natural and church realms as among the leaders in the Scriptures."[94] Pennsylvania's governor called on his people to arm themselves, whereas the Quaker assembly kept on refusing to appropriate funds for military needs. Then "King George's War" brought England into declared conflict with the colonizing Spanish and French.

Worried now about their status of citizenship, Pennsylvania Mennonites again petitioned the assembly for some means by which they could show loyalty without taking an oath or promising to take up arms. An act was passed containing language that satisfied them at least for the moment. Whereas an earlier law stipulated that applicants for citizenship present "Certificates of their having taken the Sacrament of the Lord's Supper in some Protestant or Reformed Congregation" in Pennsylvania, this requirement was dropped for "Quakers, or such who conscientiously scruple to take an oath." In the three days of April 11-13, 1743, about eighty Mennonite men from the "Skippack" (Franconia Conference) region "subscribed the qualifications," rather than swearing, and became naturalized citizens of Pennsylvania.[95] To this date, as much as any other, can the American citizenship of the thousands of their Mennonite descendants in eastern Pennsylvania be traced. Mixed among Schwenkfelders and a surprising number of conscientious members of the German Reformed Church, these Mennonite farmers of Bucks, Philadelphia, Chester, Berks, and Northampton counties could also socialize, as they waited for the proceedings to take place, with a dozen or so Mennonites from Lancaster County.

For these years, our list of new Mennonite immigrants is sparse. We do catch sight of Joseph Bieri (Berks County) in 1739, Jacob Ledterman (Deep Run) in 1741, and Hans Rothrock (Saucon), Jacob Groff, and Heinrich Schleiffer (Upper Milford) in 1743.[96] Then for half a decade our list of immigrants to the Mennonite community east of the Schuylkill is blank.

A new leader was emerging among the "Skippack" Mennonites at this time—Henrich Funck, miller along the Indian Creek in Franconia Township. He seems to have emigrated from near the village of Bonfeld,[97] east of the Rhine, in 1717, and to have had relatives of the same family name in the "Conestoga" settlements. The quality of his family is evident in that three of his four sons would be chosen bishop, minister, or deacon, and the fourth would be a prosperous miller. Apparently the first Mennonite minister (and bishop, or "full minister") in Franconia Township, Henrich would be involved in three or four publishing ventures drawn forth by the issues of his times. He first felt a need for a clear setting forth of Mennonite teaching on baptism. A mile down the Indian Creek that drove his mill lived a Dunker preacher who insisted that baptism by immersion was a necessary requirement for membership in the Christian church. Perhaps the Martin Funk from Conestoga, who in 1744 joined the Seventh-day Dunker Cloister on the Cocalico Creek, was a cousin of the Franconia Funks. In any case, during that year Henrich brought out a ninety-four page book entitled *A Mirror of Baptism*[98]—the first book by a Mennonite in the New World. Pietist publisher Saur, himself perhaps a Dunker, printed it, but kept his name off the title page.

The hallmarks of this miller-author's style are simplicity, clarity, sobriety, a lack of name-calling or even using the name Mennonite, and an easy familiarity with both Old and New Testaments. He asks his reader to accept the testimony of Scripture rather than other "histories" of the subject. There are many varieties of baptism, he observes, among those who claim the name Christian: some "dip" adult believers "three times forward," some "pour water on the head," and others do not baptize at all, "saying, the baptism of the Holy Ghost is all-sufficient." Funck prefers to see the subject of how to baptize with water enveloped by two related "baptisms": the pouring out of the Holy Spirit, found already in the Old Testament, and the "baptism of suffering," in which Christ's followers are identified with him in carrying the cross. Moving from Scripture to Scripture with sometimes hardly an extra comment, Funck articulates the traditional Anabaptist position: if "uninstructed" people or "infants, who cannot discern between their right hand and their left" are "baptized . . . we cannot see that it is an evangelical baptism . . . seeing they do not receive it by faith. . . ." Further, those who wish to unite themselves with Christ "should be willing to be baptized with the same baptism of suffering and shedding of blood wherewith [our] Lord and Master was baptized . . . and this is the allegiance of all the true disciples of Jesus Christ, in this world." Not only the apostles, but "many thousands . . . since . . . were baptized with the baptism of suffering. . . ." Finally, Funck warns against requiring immersion, arguing that although both John the Baptist and his "subjects" must have been standing in the Jordan River, "it is to be believed that the Baptist baptized his subjects with water, that is, *with* the water that he had out of the Jordan, whether in his hands or in a vessel, whether by pouring or sprinkling, which are almost the same. . . ."[99]

Although the Dunkers would strenuously reject such exegesis, they very much agreed on the normality of Christians' suffering with their Lord. And so the Seventh-day Dunkers at Ephrata, some sixty miles west of Henrich Funck's home, could make their first publication (1745) an edition of Anabaptist writings about the suffering church of Christ: *Golden Apples in Silver Bowls.* It has been claimed that this was actually done at Henrich Funck's direction. He was certainly involved in a campaign for the Cloister's next publication of the same year, a 120-page excerpt from the massive Dutch record of Anabaptist persecution, *The Bloody Spectacle, or Martyrs Mirror,* translated by a Dunker calling himself "Theophilus."[100]

By the fall of 1745 the Skippack leaders felt not only "anxiety and fear" but disappointment. Their letter to Amsterdam of three and a half years earlier had received no reply. "The flames of war," they saw, were now "rising higher," and something would have to be done to "prepare" their people "for firmness and perseverance in faith." They had been vainly wishing "for several years" to have the Dutch *Martyrs Mirror* "translated into the German language" so that their "many young people" could read it. Now there was a German publisher in Germantown, and some interested persons had offered to do the translating (the Ephrata Dunkers?), but the Mennonites were not ready to trust them fully for an accurate version of their treasured book. At length there seems to have been a conference, and "all the ministers and deacons . . . agreed" that their leaders should write another letter to "the brethren in Holland."[101] Just recently one of the Skippack ministers, Dutch-speaking Claus Jansen, had died, bequeathing his own old copy of "ye Book called the Book of Martyrs" to his wife.[102]

At about the time of Claus's death, we catch a tantalizingly quick glimpse of three other Skippack ministers—Martin Kolb, Yellis Cassel, and Michael Ziegler—at another funeral. The date is September 26. The elderly wife of a Lutheran neighbor had died. Her husband had helped the Mennonites build their meetinghouse, and his family preferred burial there rather than at the just-constructed Lutheran church on the other side of the Perkiomen. So Heinrich Melchior Muhlenberg, the influential new Lutheran pastor, had come over to Skippack to conduct the service there. Since it was an exceptionally hot day, after the body had been covered with earth Muhlenberg prepared to preach his sermon to the "large crowd" under a nearby tree. But the Mennonite ministers came to him saying that he was welcome to have his sermon in their "roomy" meetinghouse. He replied that he did not wish to disturb them in the religious "freedom" Pennsylvania gave them. But the ministers persisted, asking him not to "disdain" their "house." Muhlenberg then consented, but as they went in, the oldest minister (probably Yellis Cassel) said in the visitor's ear that he hoped "no strange ceremonies" would be performed. After the sermon the aged man begged Muhlenberg's pardon for this remark; he had not known what to expect, apparently, from a Lutheran pastor. All three ministers thanked their guest "with weeping eyes" for having "sounded the trumpet of repentance, as they called it, in their house."[103]

By the end of the following year Muhlenberg had come to feel quite at home at this large stone meetinghouse, having preached at least four more funeral sermons there, with the ministers always present and expressing "friendship and neighborliness."[104] After another sermon that dealt with repentance, one of the Mennonite ministers quoted to Muhlenberg, "with a deep sigh," a verse from Deuteronomy: "O that there were such an heart in them, that they would fear me, and keep all my commandments during all their life."[105]

On October 19, 1745, while the "air" was "filled with rumors of war," the three Skippack ministers met with Bishop Jacob Gottschalck of Towa-

Pewter communion cups of three Colonial Mennonite congregations. L. to r.: Deep Run, Line Lexington, Plains. The Deep Run cup is believed to have been given to the congregation by land merchant William Allen at the founding of the congregation. (Mennonite Heritage Center, Souderton, Pennsylvania)

mencin, Dielman Kolb of Salford, and Henrich Funck of Franconia to write another urgent "appeal" to their Dutch brethren. How much would it cost, they inquired, to have a thousand copies of the *Martyrs Mirror* translated into German, printed and bound in Holland, and shipped to Pennsylvania? How much extra would illustrations cost (as in the last edition sixty years earlier)? The inquiry, written this time in duplicate to insure its safe reception, was to be delivered "in haste" to the church council of the Mennonites of Amsterdam, in the hope that a favorable reply would come back "as soon as possible."[106]

This hope too was to prove vain. The Dutch Mennonites, in an era of commercial prosperity and spiritual decline, had doubtless lost enthusiasm for their own martyr-strewn heritage, let alone the fostering of it on the strange American frontier. No answer came back for two years, and then only in the form of a half-hearted suggestion: one of the Skippack leaders might translate some of the *Mirror's* stories into German, and the young students could then copy them out in long hand.[107]

As the Pennsylvania Mennonites waited, their community was growing by the rapid enlargement of families. Two new ministers were added at Skippack: Michael Ziegler's son Andrew, and son-in-law Jacob Shoemaker. The former had married Dielman Kolb's only child, Elizabeth, and was destined to be a bishop. Over at Deep Run the Mennonites received a gift of fifty acres from developer William Allen, along with a pewter communion cup to be used at the new meetinghouse they built. At Hereford a potentially hurtful situation was overcome by good will. Several years earlier a Catholic chapel—rare for Pennsylvania—had been built not far from the Mennonite meetinghouse erected just two years before. Both Mennonites and Schwenkfelders had contributed to the Catholic project. Now, in 1747, one of the Mennonite settlers, Ulrich Beidler, had fallen out of the good graces of his own congregation, and apparently been disowned. Reacting in anger, he warned that he would plant a "thornbush" among his Mennonite members that would not let them forget him. The meetinghouse, for which there was no deed, stood on his land. He sold the property to a Catholic, thinking that the Mennonites would thus lose possession, or at least inherit contention, and then moved to regions near the Susquehanna. But the Catholics and Mennonites proved such good neighbors that about eight years later the latter were allowed to buy back their land from their Catholic friends for two pounds, ten shillings, and put a better meetinghouse there.[108] Another Mennonite whose plantation had been the site of a meetinghouse, Henrich Ruth of Salford, also moved in 1747, but only to the Welsh New Britain area, near the new plantations of several Rosenberger families. A new Mennonite congregation (Line Lexington) was about to appear there.

Although mail from Europe was continuing to arrive, the best part of a year had gone by without word from Holland. Dielman Kolb and Henrich Funck then seem to have decided to accept an offer of the Ephrata Cloister to do the vast *Martyrs Mirror* project.[109] The Dunker commune was uniquely blessed with low cost labor, and a complex of at least three mills including a paper mill. Protecting themselves by promising to buy copies only if the translation proved acceptable, and agreeing not to sponsor a competing edition, the Mennonites now looked to the celibate and saintly

Peter Miller, earlier a young pastor in the Reformed church at Skippack, to oversee the effort and do the actual translating. It was gossiped that he understood fourteen languages. Just before the agreement was reached, one of the Cloister's mills burned down (September 5, 1747), and had to be rebuilt. Once this was accomplished, the great new task began, and lasted through three wearying years. Though the title page seems to have been printed in the first year, 1748, it was more likely 1751 before copies could be bought. (Izaak Kolb, nephew of sponsor Dielman Kolb, would not get one until 1752.)

As persistent news of Europe's wars kept appearing in Christopher Saur's journal, fifteen men at the Cloister were toiling over the largest book to appear in America before the Revolutionary War. Four worked at composing the type, four were "pressmen," and six were occupied with making the thick paper. The heavy boards in the covers were obviously being crafted to survive for generations. Translator and superintendent Peter Miller, in his white monk's garb and hood, claimed that while the project was underway he got no more than four hours of sleep nightly. Henrich Funck and Dielman Kolb, though living sixty miles to the east, had such "love" for the book that they read proof line by line for every one of the over fourteen hundred folio-sized pages, and claimed to find in Miller's translation not a single false note. Some twelve hundred of the huge volumes were printed, of which seven hundred had been sold within three years, at the modest price of "twenty-one shillings." Miller commented to a visitor that the Cloister had no intention of making a profit.[110]

Back at Skippack Dielman Kolb, though only in his mid-fifties, may not have had the best of health. Part way through the project he wrote his will, naming his fellow proofreader, Bishop Henrich Funck, as one of his trustees. Dielman's brother Martin, though nearly a decade older, was quite vigorous. An episode in his life that reveals a surprising role in the larger community occurred in 1749, when he was called down to Whitemarsh to preach a sermon at the unexpected funeral of a friend. It was the first German Reformed minister in America, schoolmaster John Philip Boehm, originally of Worms. "For thirty years," wrote editor Christopher Saur approvingly, these two uneducated but devoted ministers, one Reformed and one Mennonite, had "labored side by side in concord." Like Kolb, Boehm could be found by a visitor working on his farm to support himself between ministerial duties. When no Reformed preacher was available in the emergency of Boehm's sudden death, that most un-European thing had occurred: a Mennonite was called in to preach at a Reformed minister's burial. No other event could have more eloquently brought home to the Skippack Mennonites the unique blessing of Pennsylvania's freedoms.[111]

The restored home (1740s) of Minister Dielman Kolb, Lower Salford Township, presently owned by Philip Detweiler. (Photo by Jay Ruth)

For some reason Dielman Kolb "could not use [his] pen" for a while around 1750. Then, in early August, he received a letter from his "good friend" editor Saur of Germantown, hinting that Kolb had been ill, but asking now for his help in regard to another "good friend," Christopher Dock. Saur considered the Skippack and Salford schoolmaster to be "equipped by God with special gifts" for his calling, and yearned to get his methods of "school-management" into print for readers in both Pennsylvania and Germany. None of Dock's unique ways of "dealing with children" would lack interest. And now that the teacher was approaching old age, it would be too bad if his remarkable understanding of children should die with him.[112]

Dielman's home was on Dock's way to the Skippack school, and so it is not surprising to find that the schoolmaster stopped in with his friend within a few days of Saur's letter. By August 8 he had taken pen in hand, and was prefacing his thoughts with the name of his home region, "Salford" (present-day Upper Salford, near the "Old Goschenhoppen" Church). Protesting that he wished to gain no "reputation" or "ill-smelling honor" for his efforts, Dock writes conscientiously that he can nevertheless not "completely refuse" a request that is related to the glory of God and the welfare of human beings. The result is a very valuable essay in which we can envision a colonial Pennsylvania German schoolroom, and get insight into a truly gentle character—doubtless standing in contrast with many contemporary country teachers. While this is not the place for a lengthy study, a few excerpts from the essay, *A Simple and Thoroughly Prepared School Management*[113] will be appropriate:

> ...When the lesson is assigned, they learn it by repeating it aloud. To keep them all learning I walk about in the room until I think they have had enough time to learn their lesson. Then I strike the blackboard with my rod and everyone suddenly becomes quiet. The first one then begins to recite.... [Misbehavers] are given their choice, whether they prefer to wear [a] yoke or receive a rap on the hand. They seldom choose the yoke but usually hold out their hand to the rod.[114]

> The [child] who can point first to the letter with his finger, I grasp his finger and hold it until I have made a chalk mark beside his name.... To the child who has received most chalk marks during the day ... I owe something, perhaps a flower drawn on paper or a bird.[115]

> In ... Pennsylvania many things that concern the school are different.... The teacher in Germany ... cannot be easily deposed by the common man ... if he treats the children too sharply. Nevertheless I freely confess, even ... though I had the power from God and high authority to use severity, it is after all given only for correction, not for harm. Experience ... proves that a child that is slow in learning is harmed rather than helped when he is punished severely, whether with words or with the rod.[116]

> The poor beggar's child in filth, rags, and lice, if he is otherwise good and willing to be taught, must be as dear to [the schoolmaster] (even if he should not receive a penny for it in this life) as the child of a rich man....[117]

> I must thank God sincerely that after I was assigned to this vocation by him, he also imparted to me the grace of a special love for youth. If this love did not exist, it would be an intolerable burden to me to be among youth....[118]

> ...Love, discipline, and instruction in the Lord together form a threefold cord which is not easily broken.[119]

This unusually sensitive and modest man, feeling it a duty to see "love enhanced" in his community, tried to link in friendship the students of his "two schools" held in Mennonite meetinghouses some five miles apart. He taught three days a week at each school. In a section of his book entitled "How Letters are Exchanged," he explains that

> When I returned to the school in Salford the pupils in Skippack gave me letters to take along, and when I came back the Salford pupils did likewise. It was arranged that the pupils of the same grade exchanged letters.... The salutation was simply this: My friendly greeting to N.N. The content of the letter was a brief rhyme or a Bible verse; besides this something of their school practice was added.... [120]

It appears that there has survived, from the hand of pupil Christian Stauffer of Lower Salford in 1767, at least one modified example of such "letters." The format is much like the usual *Vorschrift* or "writing sample." Beginning with a laboriously copied German hymn, for which Schoolmaster Dock seems to have provided the ornamental first letter and Fraktur top line, the exercise moves on to some moral apothegms copied out in an ungainly English:

Beauty without virtue is like a painted Sepulchre.

Contentmend makes amany hapy without a fortune.

How much you write regart not but how well.

If you a [fault] have done for which you are chid take cer.

Labour for that wich goeth not to decay.

The bottom margin contains a rhyme naming both writer and recipient of this schoolboy's exercise:

> Yilles Kassel thu ich nennen
> und dhu ihn gar wohl kennen
> Christian Stauffer bin ich genan
> und bin dier auch nicht unbekand.

To make the letter's purpose and origin even clearer, a note on the back reiterates, "A friendly greeting to you Yilles Kassel, written by me Christian Stauffer in Lower Salford Township." [121]

Could a book like Dock's *Schul-Ordnung*, without known parallel in the colonies, have come from the pen of an ordinary Palatine Mennonite? It would not seem likely. Yet, if Dock was not Mennonite by background, he does seem, as we have observed, to have married a Mennonite wife, lived with a Mennonite family, and passed up a Lutheran and Reformed school much nearer to his farm than either Salford or the five-mile-distant Skippack. The Lutheran pastor at Old Goschenhoppen, where Dock lived, considered him a Mennonite,[122] and Catharine, the older of the Docks' two daughters, married Peter, the son of a Mennonite minister at Skippack, Claus Jansen. Perhaps even stranger is the fact that, more than two centuries after the death of this saintly poet, teacher, and folk artist, his European origins had yet to be discerned. His much-discussed "Fraktur" art (in which some of his pupils considerably surpassed his talent), had to await systematic examination that was only possible after cumulative efforts by collectors.[123] But his gentle admonitions were continually consulted and quoted by those following his vocation in a Mennonite high school named for him, nearly two centuries after his death, situated on the Towamencin homestead of the Lukens family from old Krefeld.

Now our story must return to the immigration. A sixth and final "wave" must be registered for the years 1749-51, in which at least fifteen more families came to the edges of our Mennonite community. Out west of the Conestoga there was more room, and so a greater contingent of the Mennonite newcomers went there among a flood of new Palatines, and increasing numbers of Scotch-Irish "Presbyterians." But Hans Durstine, brother of Michael at Rockhill, and arriving on September 9, 1749, probably meant to stay east. Unfortunately, sickness caught up with him— there were great complaints in these years of disease-ridden ships holding people quarantined in the Philadelphia harbor—and shortly after his funeral there was an auction for the contents of three well-filled chests he had brought across and sent by wagon out into the country. A glance at the auction inventory gives us a more intimate sense of how migrating Mennonite families packed their belongings and invested in items to sell when they arrived in the new world. It would appear that Hans was a weaver, as nearly 200 yards of a considerable variety of cloth was included. The chests also contained, among other items,

> a great Bible and several other books
> 3 new hats, a spice box and a looking glass
> small box with doctor's stuffs
> a tin butter box
> 3 whetstones and a powder horn
> 2 old bags with rags
> 6 pewter plates and 6 pewter spoons
> 12 small iron kettles
> 12 Dutch [as opposed to English] scythes
> an old gun
> 2 timber chains
> turner's [carpenter's] tools.[124]

Coming on the same ship, the *St. Andrew*, were Jacob and John Rohr,[125] the former of whom turned up shortly in New Britain, where he was trustee for the land of a new congregation.

Henry Rickert,[126] coming on the *Patience* ten days later, settled at the eastern edge of Hilltown, and the following week on the *Isaac* arrived Rudolph Landes,[127] to become a resident of Bedminster. "From time to time" Rudolph would write letters back to the village of Oberflörsheim, west of Worms, where a decade before his migration to America he had been "received in great poverty and ill health and taken up in the congregation of Jesus Christ."[128]

A family of five Schowalters from Switzerland,[129] as well as three Basslers, now found contiguous land at some distance from the main community—just west of the northward bend in the Lehigh River. This group of eight families would remain settled there less than a generation. In 1751 Jacob Galle (Geil)[130] came to the Springfield area. He too would move after a few decades to Virginia. Jacob and Peter Stauffer, sons of Christian Stauffer of Lower Salford, moved to the northern Shenandoah Valley, where in 1749 Peter bought 438 acres of land and laid out a town called "Staufferstadt" (later Strasburg).[131] In 1750 members of the Hottel family also left the Swamp region for the Shenandoah Valley.[132] Eventually Funks, Geils, Hottels, Trissels, and Schowalters who had formerly lived in these northeastern settlements would form a significant contingent of the Mennonite community in Virginia.

Another new area for homesteading was west of the Susquehanna, whither Abraham Bauer, son of pioneer Hans at Hereford now moved.[133] We have earlier noted that Ulrich Beidler moved west from the Hereford Community about this time.

The family of Isaac Krall, Mennonite "shoemaker in Skippack" (near present-day Kulpsville), accepted into their home an immigrant English couple. The husband, Richard Elwood, was a stonemason. After the Kralls had given or lent means for living to the resourceless arrivals (to the value of fourteen pounds), the latter suddenly vanished, leaving additional debts in the neighborhood. Krall then sent in a notice of their disappearance to Christopher Saur's paper, the *Pennsylvania Berichte* (News).[134]

We may observe that the more recent arrivals generally could not find room in the dense Skippack-Salford-Franconia Mennonite corridor. This pattern held in the few years that remained before the "French and Indian War" slammed the door on further immigration. It was to the less central Swamp area that latecomers like Christian Biehler and Abraham Zetty (1752), or Valentine Nold and Georg Schimmel (1753, 1754) would go. In eastern Plumstead appeared Hans Georg Schaddinger, and in western

Coventry, as a redemptioner with John Steiner, young Georg Hechler (1754) from Alsace.[135]

We see further evidence of Mennonite expansion in the appearance of new meetinghouses at Perkasie (Blooming Glen), where two sons of Bishop Henrich Funck, along with Cassels and Meyers from Skippack and Indianfield, had settled, and at New Britain (Line Lexington), where Ruths, Lapps, and Rohrs were beginning to replace some of the Welsh farmers. Soon there would be another meetinghouse on the "Plains" near Gwynedd, also mostly Welsh in recent years. Over at Coventry, too, land had finally been bought for this purpose in 1751. Not only was the countryside almost solidly occupied from the Schuylkill to the Delaware by 1755; a few of the children of the pioneers were beginning to move on to more open frontier, where the Indians, on their painful retreat west and north, could barely keep ahead of the creeping Scotch-Irish squatters' settlements.

By 1755 the major Mennonite immigration to this easternmost of the Pennsylvania communities was history. We are now looking at a community that had transplanted from the Rhineland a spiritual family with many of its traditions still very much intact. Since the coming of Jan Lensen to Germantown in 1683 there had been a mixing of Dutch and German-speaking families that by now must have numbered over 1,000 souls (we have named about 150 other immigrants, mostly heads of families). The fellowship had taken spiritual as well as economic root. It had shown its coherence by consulting European leaders, ordaining ministers, organizing congregations, building meetinghouses, aiding its poor, holding conferences to establish discipline, and employing an excellent teacher for some of its children. The center of influence had shifted from Germantown to Skippack, and many children of the Skippack congregation were in the newer community at Deep Run. Permanent communities were at Hereford and Hosensack (Upper Milford), and at Swamp and Saucon. Others were firming up along the Schuylkill and along the southeastern flanks of what the Mennonites from "Conestoga" referred to in general as "Skippack." Basic teaching had gotten into print: there was a *Confession of Faith* in the official language of the colony, a hymnbook, and a book on believer's baptism by one of the ministers. This man's cousin, in the Franconia Township of 1756, could leave to his wife "my new Bible, my Martyr Book, one of my new hymn books, one of my Golden Apples (a hymn book) and one of my Psalm Books."[136]

Certainly the seven-decades-long migration had been variously motivated, sporadic, and informal. It had left ragged edges in Europe. "My sons . . . have been lost sight of several years ago," stated the aged Anna Maria Fretz of Ketterich in 1729, "and it is not known whether they are still living."[137] But at far-off "Deep Run," where the Fretz brothers settled, as at Skippack, Schuylkill, Goschenhoppen, and Swamp, it was becoming evident that these people had not come to Pennsylvania to forget who they were. The Lutheran pastor Muhlenberg, who tended in his diary to use the term "so-called Mennonites," was almost envious of the functioning of their brotherly aid. They had received "good support," he wrote hintingly to his own European friends, "from their spiritual brethren in . . . Germany."[138] This helpful Mennonite correspondence was now beginning to drop off, and after several decades would cease. But the Skippack Mennonites were already giving evidence of a commitment to "maintain the right fellowship" which had come down to them through two centuries of a suffering, "revengeless" church of Christ. The strength of that commitment, and the fabric of their covenant community, were about to be tested by wars and rumors of wars.

Chapter 5

"Unlimited Freedom" and
"The Flames of War"

1756-1786

Ordinary preachers among the Mennonites were called "servants." Their function was to teach and admonish. But a *Gemeinde* or congregation also needed deacons to look out for its poor or weak members, and proven ministers entrusted with the important role of "keeping house" (*haushalten*) in the church—seeing that "the right fellowship" was "maintained" in accordance with "Matthew 18." For this role a lay minister (and apparently even a deacon) could be "established" or "confirmed." Later, Pennsylvania Mennonites would call such a leader a "bishop."

The first person to function thus among Pennsylvania Mennonites had of course been Jacob Gaetschalck, who was in later life a carpenter at Towamencin. His continuing presence in the fellowship for over half a century after the first Lord's supper he had overseen at Germantown in 1708 must have given younger bishops a sense of continuity with the American "beginning." Whereas his Lower Rhenish background would have helped him in writing letters to Holland, he may have had fewer contacts with the "Conestoga" Mennonites, sixty miles west, than his colleague at Swamp, Valentine Klemmer. The latter bishop, it would be remembered, died in a fraternal visit among Conestoga friends, and was buried at "Mellinger's." Since "breaking of bread" was celebrated once a year, it was not difficult for five bishops to meet the needs of all the congregations from the Schuylkill to the Delaware. Doubtless already by 1750 or 1760 all the "servants" conferred with the bishops at least annually at the "Indianfield" (Franconia) meetinghouse. Earlier, there may have been "conferences" or "councils" (the German word used was *Rath*) at other meetinghouses. But the ministers' habit of gathering in centrally located Franconia would eventually give to the larger Mennonite set of congregations the name "Franconia Conference" in place of the earlier "Skippack." Still, the most influential center remained the Skippack settlement.

Between the years 1756 and 1763, leadership largely passed into new hands. Abraham Schwartz, the immigrant of 1727 who had married a daughter of immigrant preacher Henry Kolb, was now (1738) selected as the first bishop at Deep Run. Martin Bechtel was selected at Schuylkill (1738), Izaak Kolb at Rockhill (1760), Andrew Ziegler at Skippack (1763), and Jacob Meyer in the Swamp district (1763).[1] Ziegler was "confirmed" in the year prior to Jacob Gaetschalck's death in the latter's nineties. This new bishop lived closer to Salford than even the Funks, but his connections were more toward Skippack. He was a saddler, and his brother Michael, Jr., a tanner; together they had commercial and personal contacts in Philadelphia, now the largest city in the British colonies. They were acquaintances of the important Quaker merchant Israel Pemberton, and functioned as general contact between Quakers and Mennonites well before Andrew became a bishop. Having doubtless learned to write in Christopher Dock's classroom (where English as well as German was given to the pupils on models of writing), Andrew sent an occasional crudely spelled letter to the Philadelphia Quakers.

When Indian attacks darkened Pennsylvania's outlook in 1756 (and deacons Valentine Hunsicker and Christian Meyer gathered contributions for relief of refugees), Andrew apparently led a meeting near Skippack on the question of collecting money for the Indians. This was a Quaker-sponsored project, also well-supported by the Schwenkfelders, to pacify the aggrieved Indians. After the meeting Andrew wrote to ask Pemberton: "Please to let us know whether our Governor is at Home." "Some of our friends," he added, "have a minde" to talk to him.[2] A few months later both Andrew and Michael were again conferring with the Philadelphia Quakers on the same subject.[3] In the interval Andrew's well-known father-in-law, Dielman Kolb, had died, leaving Andrew most of his large landholdings (near present-day Lederach).

Because these were busy and nontheoretical people, we have only scant written records from which to evoke the tenor of their daily life. Yet we are able to find Andrew Ziegler exemplifying honesty by advertising a watch his son had found along the road,[4] writing legal papers for neighbors, showing displeasure with his alcoholic son Michael, being called an "honest" man in Christopher Dock's will, or stating his convictions with blunt emotion in a conference of ministers. Or, next to the nearby Salford Meetinghouse, we might observe distiller and deacon Jacob Clemens, whose careful family account book gives us a view of the community going about its business: getting a redemptioner from the boat in Philadelphia; helping a young married couple get started; working all day in the fields for the pay of one chicken; engaging a hired man "for one year for 10 pounds in money, one pair of shoes, one linen shirt and one pair of linen breeches"; or Christopher Dock buying a barrel of cider.[5] We find a new stone meetinghouse being built at "Clemens' " (Salford) in 1760 (with half of the expenses being said to be paid by Peter Freed).[6]

By reading the newspaper these people read we can find them advertising that "strange" cattle have joined their herds, describing their bells, brandmarks, or color. Demonstrating that their life too had its shadows is a notice by one Jacob Clemens of Towamencin that his wife has left him. Philip Geissinger of Saucon lets the public know a man has come to his house, asked to sell a horse, and then disappeared, with the horse still at the Geissingers.[7] Or, by reading the wills these people wrote, we find other revealing glimpses: Andrew Lederach designating for his wife "our large chest which we brought from Germany and our cupboard in the old house,"[8] or Jacob Sellen, shopkeeper of Worcester, willing "one fourth of my estate to benefit of the Poor amongst Mennonist ... persons belonging to ye Meeting House now erected in ye township of Perkyome and Skepack ..." (apparently, in 1759, there was still no regular meetinghouse at Methacton itself).[9]

The most interesting will of all is that of author Henrich Funck of Franconia, written out by himself in German, after his wife had died and he felt a "presentiment" of his own "departure."[10] Carefully dividing his estate among his nine children, he pays special attention to his crippled daughter Esther. Referring to "poor Esther" again and again, he admonishes the other siblings to make sure she is to stay with whoever will care for her best; they are instructed to keep her "clean in washing and mending," and free from lice. She receives a trust fund larger than the worth of the mill, which goes to her brother Abraham, and more than twice the worth of the plantation at "Perkasie" which had gone to her brother Henry, Jr. The deacons at Franconia and Rockhill are asked to keep Esther's caretakers accountable to the church for the performance of their duty. Another special note in this will is the emphasis on a peaceful execution of its directives. Everything is to be arranged "in accordance with brotherly love, Christian forebearance and righteousness." All outstanding accounts are to be collected

> as I have always done—by using no force against any man; and what is lost, or is regarded as lost, may be lost, and my heirs shall leave all such debts ... uncollected, because I hope the blessing of God will bring it after to them in some other way, which point I desire may not be forgotten.

Perhaps Henrich was working, at this time (1759), on the manuscript of his second book, which would be published by his family after his death a year later. This was over three times the size of his earlier *Mirror of Baptism*, and took on the large theme of *Restitution, or an Explanation of Certain Chief Points of the Law*.[11] In this 308-page essay Henrich is at pains to show that Jesus Christ fulfills the "law of Moses," or the Old Dispensation, in all points, major and minor. Ranging incessantly from Genesis to Revelation, its effect is to provide an overview of the Scriptures with Christ as the touchstone to their meanings. Each cultic item in the Hebrew religion has its better spiritual counterpart in Christ the fuller and final revelation. Reading this book, we are in the world of the traditional Mennonite sermon. We hear a Scripture-oriented call to repentance, regeneration, humility, and discipleship. The view of post-biblical history is taken from the *Martyrs Mirror*. It makes the Mennonites the spiritual heirs of the Waldenses, and renders the Mennonite story in terms of its sufferings, "especially and longest in Switzerland," where persecution has "still not come to an end."[12] For Henrich Funck, the topic of sacrifice in the Old Testament is of vital interest, in its preparation for Christ's offering of himself, which is in turn reenacted in the suffering church. Thus all biblical and current history is focused on one drama. It is now our solemn opportunity to identify with this Lord and Lamb of history; to become one with Christ "in a true faith" which expresses itself in "genuine repentance and betterment in a new life." This will be marked by "humility and lowliness," "love and hope," and obedience to "the commandments of Christ." "In sum," what we must do is follow Christ "in cross and suffering . . . to the death."[13] The persecution may be gone, but the old Anabaptist call to die to the world has not been blunted.

When Henrich Funck died in 1760, he was replaced in the office of bishop by "Strong Izaak" Kolb of Rockhill. An unpleasant moment occurred soon thereafter at a "large meeting" of ordained men, when Kolb heatedly declared that he would not "serve" in his office along with the deacon at Franconia. His reason was that the latter—Christian Meyer, Jr.— had not treated Bishop Funk (his own brother-in-law) fairly. Whatever lay behind this, it made "much trouble" in the community for several years. Izaak moved from hilly Rockhill to a flat area of Gwynedd in 1764, in the years when a new congregation was gathering at "Plains." Five years later, when a younger bishop was needed (Izaak experienced illness in his old age), the candidates were Samuel Bechtel and Christian Funk. The former had moved down from Saucon to buy Izaak's farm at Rockhill, and the latter was a son of Bishop Henrich Funck. This ordination also caused some heavy discussion. Deacon Meyer thought a new bishop was not needed. As the other ministers tried vainly to get him to agree, he was "called out" of their meeting for a quick conference with his wife, Magdalena. When he returned to the discussion, he had changed his mind. Lots were then cast, and the new bishop turned out to be Christian Funk.[14]

The Funks were apparently an outspoken clan. The new bishop's older brother, Henry, who had moved from "Perkasie" to "Hosensack," was ordained at the latter place (for Upper Milford?), but after about three years of preaching was silenced for being "too absolute," and wanting "the whole [Mennonite] Society to be subject to him."[15] Another Funk, Jacob, who was a cousin to Christian and also a preacher at Franconia, would later get into serious controversies at Germantown. And Christian himself, the new bishop, would be the center of sustained, racking dissensions in his congregation during the approaching years of the Revolutionary War.

This was of course the direct opposite of the tone of Bishop Henrich's admonition to peacefulness in his will, or to the spirit of their teacher Christopher Dock, who had also written his own will—but in English. The labored phrasing of this document gives the modern reader a bit of a shock, especially in the context of our knowledge of him as a gentle spirit. Writing of his "two Daughters," he mentions that "de eldest named Margareth Duck She is married with Henry Stryckers, and Dwellth upon my Plantation in the Downship aforesaid de jungest her Name is Catharine Duck She is married with Pieter Jansen of Skippack in Bebber Township. . . ." Regarding his "Household goods," he is in agreement with one of Henrich Funck's stipulations: "It is not my Will to sell it upon a Public Vandue, my order is dit, to chose Man, two upright Man can do it, let them bring it in two like part and worth as good she can. . . ."[16] Of course it is not all this rough, and in his native tongue Dock could be quietly eloquent. Apparently still teaching "in his great age," he wrote a parting hymn for his pupils that is still being read and sung by "Plain People" across North America in 1983: "Mein Lebensfaden lauft zu Ende. . . ."[17]

> My thread of life runs to its ending,
>   My pilgrimage is nearly done.
> O God, a guide to me be sending,
>   To keep me on the pathway home,
> Who'll with me at the rudder stand
> As I the final storm withstand. . . .
>
> And now good-night, beloved children,
>   God bless you, and take care of you,
> Adorn your souls with humble virtue,
>   And bring you to his kingdom true.
> Good night again to one and all,
> Both young and old, both great and small.

This and other writings by Dock were published in Christopher Saur's occasional periodical, the *Geistliches Magazien*. By 1769 Dock had considerably outlived his own expected life-span, and finally, nineteen years after he had composed it, allowed the manuscript of his *School-Management* to be prepared for publication. Saur read it with "much pleasure," but immediately lost it among the papers in his shop. After vainly hunting and advertising for it, and being told by Dock not to worry about it, the editor suddenly found it, and published it in 1770.[18] In October of the following year Dock died. A story lingered in the community that he had been found lifeless on his knees after dismissing his pupils from the Skippack school, where he had been praying for them.

The Indian troubles along the Pennsylvania frontier in these years touched the eastern Mennonite community only at its northern edges. West of Bethlehem, where the Lehigh River bends northward, was one of the latest Mennonite communities to form. By 1760 they had a meetinghouse, where Baers, Basslers, Showalters, Siegfrieds, and others could worship (occasionally, it would be said, disturbed by Indians). One Saturday morning, October 8, 1763, Ulrich Showalter was working on the roof of a building on the west bank of the Lehigh, near the "Indian Falls," or "Siegfried's Bridge." From this vantage point his attention was caught by a group of Indians crossing the Lehigh. He counted twelve.[19] What he did not realize was that they were on a mission of revenge for ill-treatment, and shortly they had tomahawked several of the neighbor's children. In later years it would become evident that they had been severely provoked by certain white persons' dishonest dealings. This was the era of "Pontiac's War," which saw the grandson of William Penn, now governor of Pennsylvania, offering high bounties for the scalps of Indians, children as well as adults. It was the time of the "Paxton Boys' " raids, in which peaceful Indians living among Mennonite settlements in Lancaster County were ruthlessly slaughtered because they were Indians. The peaceful Quakers, and the German pacifists who had followed them to Pennsylvania, were of course profoundly shocked—this could not be happening in Penn's Woods! Perhaps such experiences were a factor in the moving of the Showalter and Bassler clans away from the Lehigh area to Chester and Lancaster counties, beginning in 1771. The congregation at Siegfrieds' would never thrive after this, and would in fact produce a colonel in the Pennsylvania Militia.

While this edge of the Mennonite fellowship was eroding, however, other pockets were expanding. The eastern wing of the Swamp congregation seems to have erected a new building about 1771, and Methacton seems also to have gotten one about this time. In Chester County, where Phoenixville would later appear, a better meetinghouse was built in 1772, and at the eastern edge of the fellowship a new building appeared in New Britain (later called Doylestown). A meetinghouse was built about the same time for the western wing of the Hereford congregation in Colebrookdale (later Boyertown). Salford and Deep Run had gotten stone meetinghouses in 1760 and 1766, and even Germantown had one built under the supervision of Jacob Knorr in 1770. Knorr, later to serve as one of the ministers in the congregation, was a well-known carpenter-contractor, having overseen the woodwork for of an imposing stone house for the family of Pennsylvania's Chief Justice William Chew a few years earlier, just up the road (present-day "Cliveden"). The strength of these walls would be proved a few years later when cannonballs could not breach them.

After a peace was concluded between England and France in July 1763, so few new Mennonite immigrants came as not to constitute any "movement." Nor were these latecomers land-seekers as their predecessors had been. Young Jacob Gross, arriving in 1763 or 1764, was a shoemaker, and apparently lived for a while with Jacob Rohr in New Britain.[20] Thirty-year-old Hendrick Roosen, a member of the Hamburg Mennonite congregation, was in Philadelphia by 1765, then returned home briefly before reemigrating. A confectioner in Philadelphia, he joined the Germantown congregation and married a Stauffer.[21] Three children of the deceased Andrew Hage arrived on October 19, 1767. Eighteen-year-old Hans Jacob was to become a well-known clockmaker in Franconia Township.[22] On the same ship five years later arrived another eighteen-year-old, Johannes Schwerdle of Eppingen, east of the Rhine. As a "redemptioner" or "indentured servant," he worked in New Britain and then for Deacon Henry Rosenberger in Franconia, eventually marrying Henry's daughter.[23] Johannes had a sister Anna who may also have come over at this time, but a younger brother, Philip,[24] had to wait until after the Revolutionary War to migrate, and also claim a daughter of the Rosenbergers. Other Mennonites like George Delp and Isaac Derstine took in young children as servants, paying about ten pounds to the ship captains.[25] The "masters" had to promise to see that their charges were taught "to read the Bible and write with a legible hand." The term for such a child might be from nine to fourteen years. Soon all this immigration would once again be cut off by the approach of war, but before that happened, Johannes Herstein arrived on September 27, 1773.[26] He was one of the last local Mennonites to come from Europe. He married Catherine Schantz and had to take up land in Limerick Township where there were few Mennonites.

Now, if Mennonite farmers wanted to expand or move, it often had to be beyond the original settlements. The Episcopal minister at the St. James Church near Skippack reported to London in 1763 that his congregation

Gravestone of Barbara Kolb at Deep Run. Barbara was the widow of Minister Henry Kolb who died at Skippack in 1730. (Photo by Jay Ruth)

The 1770 Germantown Mennonite meetinghouse, built by Jacob Knorr, as it appeared after the Civil War. (John F. Funk Collection, Archives of the Mennonite Church)

was declining, "as the Dutch buy out the English and settle in their room."[27] Some Mennonites were pushing even farther. Nicholas and Elizabeth Haldeman of Salford moved to Charlestown Township in Chester County, and some years later Mathias Pannebecker, living on the Skippack a mile from the Episcopal Church, also crossed the Schuylkill to operate a mill on the Pickering Creek (below present-day Phoenixville). Before long miller Mathias would be ordained minister and then bishop of the Schuylkill district. Another local move, in 1774, was that of the fluent preacher Jacob Funk of Franconia, who bought a farm from Jacob Keyser in Cheltenham near Germantown, and transferred his minister's office to the congregation there. Others went even farther, as Henry and Arnold Van Fossen of Providence, who in 1766 had land laid out for them "near the Great Juniata River."[28]

The picture we have been assembling of the "Skippack" Mennonites up to this point would certainly be much sketchier, were it not for the survival of their replies to two European requests for information. The first came in 1771 from a wealthy Mennonite businessman in Hamburg, Gysbert van der Smissen, who was trying to construct a genealogy of his mother's family (De Voss). He lacked information on the descendants of two of his grandfather's cousins—Cornelia van Sintern and Adriana Karsdorp—who had migrated from Hamburg to Germantown before he was born. Van der Smissen's contact in Pennsylvania was apparently the recent emigrant from Hamburg, Hendrick Roosen, now a "sugarbaker" in Philadelphia. But the person who had the desired data was Izaak van Sintern's oldest daughter, the aged widow of Minister Martin Kolb, stil living at Skippack. Magdalena Kolb, now in her mid-eighties, apparently knew not only her own descendants but those of her sister Sara, who had married Deacon Jacob Kolb. Of the family of a third sister, Adriana, wife of Hendrick Sellen, who had moved to York, she was less certain—some of the grandchildren were in the Swamp community. But in supplying van der Smissen with the names of 202 American descendants of the immigrant van Sintern family, Magdalena Kolb put together the first known Mennonite genealogy outside of Europe. This early record ties together Kolbs, Bechtels, Detweilers, Rittenhouses, and others in such a way as to make it an indispensable historical reference.[29]

But even more important was the other request from Europe, sent a year or two later by four leaders at Krefeld and Utrecht. They sent along a copy of the Dutch "Name List of the Mennonite Preachers." In a future issue of the list they wished to include American information. They were interested specifically in such questions as how the Pennsylvania communities were settled, why the people had left Europe, how many congrega-

Auger marked "1770 RL." Probably owned by Rudolph Landes of Deep Run. (Harrison Landis)

tions there were, who the ministers were, how the people made their living, and whether they had books. The letter, which must have been in the Dutch language, was answered in German on March 1, 1773, by three bishops: the brothers-in-law Izaak Kolb and Andrew Ziegler, and the younger Christian Funk.[30] The latter probably did the writing. The bishops protest briefly that they are "unlearned people" and so "deficient in writing" that it is all they can do to keep proper records. Their "forefathers," furthermore, "left little or nothing in writing" regarding their Pennsylvania beginnings. They had come "poor into the country," and had been forced to use all their time to make a living. Even the preachers, who might have been thought to care about such things, had had to use "every unoccupied hour" to do both their economic and spiritual work, and so they had left nothing either. Only a page or so from the pen of the first bishop, Jacob Gaetschalck (then of Germantown), remained in the community to describe the early days, and that named specifics only for the period from 1698 to

1712. After transcribing this, the three bishops have only three sentences to sum up what has happened in the previous sixty years. Their estimate is that there are now at least eighteen bishops "and fifty communities" of Mennonites in America, but distance makes them uncertain: "We dwell, so to speak, at one end of the land." The reasons they give for the original migration are the "great freedom" of conscience promised by Penn, and the desire to escape heavy taxes.

No poverty, they report, afflicts Pennsylvania's Mennonites; "There are among us even people who are rich." In matters of civil requirements, "we enjoy unlimited freedom. We have never been compelled to bear weapons." Testimony can be given before the good magistrates "with yea and nay" rather than an oath. Members refrain from holding government offices because in performing them "force is used." If a person marries out of the church, he or she is excluded from the kiss of peace and the Lord's supper until "expiation" has been made "to the community." Mennonite books are available in Dutch, German, and English. "For the present," preaching is in German in all the congregations.

While they were writing, the three American leaders thought of a few questions of their own. They wished to know whether the Dutch had the same marriage requirement as the Pennsylvania Mennonites; how the bread was shared at communion; whether the Dutch were keeping up "the observance of footwashing"; and what process was used to choose preachers. Doubtless these four topics were issues of significance at Skippack or Rockhill. In conclusion, the "unlearned" ministers wondered rather pointedly what the letters "A.L.M. & Ph.D." and "Emeritus" meant with a picture of a Mennonite leader the Dutch had sent over. And these Americans knew enough of the Dutch scene (perhaps from reading books on church unity by Joost Hendricks) to ask how the "Waterlanders" and "Frisians" or "United Flemish" parties had been getting along with each other, "and if there is a division whether they seek to bear themselves toward each other with love?"

A postscript lists the present "communities" of Mennonites as these leaders know them. North of Philadelphia, in their own region which is "at one end of the land," are five basic communities, each with at least one bishop, and having together eighteen other ministers. Included are intriguing names of congregations such as "Hosensak" (Upper Milford), "Lehay" (Lehigh—"Siegfried's"?), and "Term" (Durham—Springfield?). The bishops' knowledge of the Conestoga scene is much less definite; they name seven bishops but only five ministers, and guess that "meetings are held in more than forty places." That would mean that they regard the Conestoga Fellowship as about twice the size of their own "Skippack" district.

This letter breathes a spirit of good will and peacefulness; it even reminds its sophisticated Dutch readers that "love is not the least but the greatest command" of God. It is ironic, in retrospect, to see that the writers themselves were unable, in the difficult atmosphere of the American Revolution just ahead, to maintain their own peace. In the "Stamp Act" controversies of a few years before the letter was written, when Great Britain had tried to demonstrate that she, rather than her colonies, would dictate laws, the noncommercial Mennonites had not been involved. But as American dissatisfactions would widen, and a new government would set itself up in defiance of the king, Andrew Ziegler and Christian Funk would find themselves greatly at odds over which Caesar to render unto.

The early stages of the conflict did not, apparently, precipitate controversy among the Mennonites. What did they care about a tax on tea? But then the newspapers told of farmers firing on British soldiers in Massachusetts, and angry handbills began appearing from groups of citizens calling themselves "Committees of Observation." Three Mennonite preachers called on the Quakers of Gwynedd to take counsel on the growing militarization. A fever for "drilling" swept the countryside—even little boys made marching their game. By June 1775, when the "Battle of Bunker Hill" took place at Boston, teams and wagons had been requisitioned from local farms to haul supplies for the soldiers. At least that is what was later claimed by members of the Fretz family. They told stories of how seventeen-year-old Abraham Fretz of Deep Run went along with his father's horses, carting a load of gunpowder from Trenton to Boston.[31]

Inflation made prices bounce alarmingly, and new paper money was afloat. A strange new "tax" or fine of three pounds ten shillings was announced as payable by those men who for one reason or another did not wish to "drill" in the new militia. Of course no Mennonite could join the militia, but the Mennonite ministers also felt "unanimously" that this "tax" should not be paid to the rump government, which they viewed as "rebellious" and hostile to the king.[32] Unanimously, that is, except for Christian Funk, bishop at Indianfield. He pointed out that Mennonites were using the "Continental" paper money put out by the new government to pay their bills. In that, he argued, they had already acknowledged it as a government.

Collection of taxes and fines for not drilling were at first disorganized, and apparently ignored by country people. Many, after all, viewed the trouble as a kind of civil war; only a third of the population was in favor of overthrowing the king. The Mennonites had a deeply ingrained tradition of confessing themselves the ruler's "most devoted subjects"; it was an article of faith to them to respect public authority when it did not contravene their

scriptural beliefs. So when the question of "independence" from Great
Britain was raised, the Mennonite conscience was jolted. A discussion of this
topic brought "nearly the whole township" of Franconia to a meeting. Attending a township meeting for the first time, Christian Funk agreed with
the two thirds of the audience that he estimated was Mennonite, that "a defenceless People" could neither "institute" nor "destroy" any government.
Since the English king was the rightful "head or protector of Pennsylvania," it would be wrong to tear away from his authority.[33] But when
Pennsylvania shortly went ahead and drew up its own Constitution, Christian got himself a copy and was pleased to discover that the cherished
exemption from military service for the sake of conscience was still allowed,
as long as the draftee made a monetary payment. This "caused much
reflection in me," wrote Funk. It was like the "liberty which William Penn
had guaranteed our fathers in Europe." But the other ministers still
regarded Congress as "rebels." Why must this be? asked Funk, maintaining
that "there were other republics—perhaps America might become
another." What was, after all, the basis of national legitimacy? On this
question Funk could think rationally rather than traditionally. He was obviously more widely read than his colleagues. "The English," he reasoned,
"had taken America from the Spanish: and the Americans were about to
wrest it from them." Such logic, however, struck Christian's fellow-
ministers as "foolishness," and he began to sink in their estimation.[34]

As new laws setting up a regular draft and even a loyalty oath were
passed, the atmosphere became heated. Soldiers roamed the community
taking horses, feed, and cloth for military use. In some cases horses would
be "taken out of the plough" for the military "waggons." Guns were confiscated from people who would not take the "Test" oath. Up at Hosensack,
Henry Funk, Jr., was the victim of a citizen's arrest by neighbors who said
his principles, which kept him from taking the oath, were inimical to the
United States.[35] The magistrates of this community seemed more unsympathetic than others.

Real excitement set in when the British army landed in Maryland.
"Whig" (Revolution-favoring) families streamed out of Philadelphia toward
Lancaster, some of them on wagons impressed from Mennonites of both
"Skippack" and "Conestoga." After a fierce battle at Brandywine in
Quaker country of Chester County, the British moved north on the west
side of the Schuylkill River, foraging as they went. Washington's troops did
the same thing, withdrawing to protect their supplies in Berks County.
Minister Mathias Pannebecker had his grain and flour taken, and his milling machinery broken up, as British troops camped on his property.[36] Then
the British surprised the strategically retreating Washington by crossing to

the east side of the Schuylkill, and marching triumphantly down to Philadelphia, where they occupied the capital. Stung, Washington immediately moved closer. On September 26, 1777, his army of 10,000 men arrived with drums beating at the mill of another Mennonite, Samuel Pannebecker. This cousin of Mathias Pannebecker lived along the Perkiomen Creek (site of present-day Schwenksville). By nightfall all his fences had been burned, and in the few days the army remained, all grain, hay, fodder, and even poultry had disappeared, except for one hen trying to hatch a late brood. Samuel described it in a note on the margin of the family Bible "For those who come after me," estimating the number of troops at three times the true amount.[37]

Down near Germantown Minister Jacob Funk was perhaps regretting his move there from Franconia Township: he lost all his livestock to the occupying British, and saw much of his property ruined. Soon to be hidden in his house was the furniture of a "Loyalist," or non-Whig, which would later bring him trouble of another sort when it would be discovered by the Americans. Jacob would have to buy a yoke of oxen to start farming again.[38] But first, on a foggy Saturday morning in October, there was a surprise attack on Germantown by Washington's troops. Fierce, confused fighting swirled around the Chew mansion and the Mennonite meetinghouse itself. A British general was killed by a shot from behind the graveyard fence. American General Francis Nash had his horse killed under him, and his thigh gravely mangled by a cannon ball. He was carried out of Towamencin Township on a litter of poles, where he bled through two featherbeds in the house of Mennonite farmer Adam Gotwals.[39] Washington's troops, after thinking they had won the battle, panicked and fled, dragging along wagonloads of their wounded over bloody roads all the way back to Pennypacker's Mills.

Here at "Camp Perkiomen," a chagrined Washington shared his "mortification" the next morning at breakfast with Tom Paine, the propagandist of the Revolution. It was time to reorganize. A group of Quakers came up from Philadelphia to present their convictions against involvement in war, and protest the imprisonment of some of their leaders. Washington wrote a letter to the main British general, now comfortably established in Philadelphia, stating that the American Army's destruction of mills was "a procedure fully authorized by the common practice of armies," and not without precedent among the British themselves.[40] This strange (to us) practice of corresponding with an enemy, debating protocol and points of ethics, was crowned by an even more intriguing gesture. During a meal in the mill itself, a dog wandered in "to ask for its dinner." On its collar was the name of the British General William Howe. Perhaps it had run along out with the retreating American troops from the battle of Germantown. In any case, General Washington sent along with the carrier of his other letter, bearing a flag of truce, the stray dog and a note: "General Washington's compliments to General Howe—does himself the pleasure to return to him a dog, which accidentally fell into his hands and by the inscription on the collar, appears to belong to General Howe." The delighted recipient sent back from Philadelphia "A warm letter of thanks."[41] And having spared the dog, Washington prepared to hang a human deserter from his army.

That execution would take place several miles closer to Philadelphia, in the vicinity of the Towamencin Mennonite Meetinghouse, to which Washington now moved his army. But first came the burial of General Nash and several other officers who had been mortally wounded at Germantown. This occurred on a rainy day, in the cemetery at the edge of Bishop Jacob Gaetschalck's Towamencin homestead. General Washington had thousands of troops drawn up in parade; an oration was given and cannon were fired, alarming the quiet countryside for miles around.[42] From the meetinghouse grounds the soldiers went back to their ragged camps, chopping down acres of old oaks for firewood, so that in the week of their encampment the old forest vanished. Local farms were visited again and again by the undisciplined soldiers, who drove their officers to distraction by the unnecessary firing of guns through the camp. All the local people— Schwenkfelders, Mennonites, Lutheran, Reformed—were affected. Seventy wounded or sick soldiers were taken to the Jacob Geissinger farm along the Lehigh River. Fifty-six "Dragoons" stayed at the farm of a Reformed family at Perkasie, where all food stores disappeared, except the smoked meat which the family had buried. One gang of soldiers reportedly went up to the "Butter Valley" or Hereford Mennonite community, where they helped themselves to a wedding feast and brought home wagonloads of other food and supplies.[43] Fever spread from the camp, and one of the victims was minister Jacob Moyer of the "Perkasie" (later Blooming Glen) congregation. Horses were hidden in woods and back country areas, and market produce was taken past American encampments to Philadelphia where there was "real" instead of paper money.

When Washington, looking for a chance to attack the British at Philadelphia, shifted his troops back across the Schuylkill to "Valley Forge," and snow started to fall, he ordered guards placed on all roads into Philadelphia, to keep market people and spies from going back and forth. Many of his nearly starving and poorly clothed soldiers ranged, officially or not, in a wide radius from Valley Forge, looking for food and clothing. The closer people lived to Valley Forge, the more likely they were to be visited. Miller Mathias Pannebecker, so conscientious that he would not lock his

doors, now saw his orchard used as a parade ground, and his barn surrounded by a constant guard of American soldiers. Inside were kegs and
barrels of gunpowder for Washington's army.[44] Before January 1778 was
over, there was no more fodder in the neighborhood. A local farmer became
so enraged that he shot a soldier caught in the act of milking a cow.

Mennonites, among others, found it hard to take the guard around
Philadelphia seriously. It was not their war, and they did not care to wait
until it was over to sell their produce. Abraham Hunsberger managed to get

Gravestone for a Yellis Cassel, and monument for Brigadier General Francis Nash of North
Carolina, in the Towamencin Mennonite burial ground. The monument was erected without
ceremony in 1844 by patriots John Fanning Watson and Mathias Holstein, aided by contributions of people from Germantown and Norristown. (Photo by Jay Ruth)

into the city with his marketing, but was locked up by the British, who thought he might be a spy. A man who was known to sing while at his work, Abraham apparently sang his way out of the lockup after a one-night stay.[45] Others, like John Souder and Isaac Benner, were summoned to account for their selling supplies to "the Enemy"—the British.[46] From Bedminster Township came Mathias Tyson, who was caught trying to ride past the American guard with a packsaddle of butter and eggs. Mathias was court-martialed and found guilty of "supplying the Enemy with provisions." General Washington approved his sentence: "to be put in the Provost at night while working at Camp Fatigue during the day." But this decree was apparently modified to one of briefer duration. He was "stripped to the waist, tied to a tree with a dozen soldiers placed ten paces away each sup-plied bountifully with eggs, and at the word 'fire,' his . . . body was reduced to an eggnog, his gray horse was confiscated and he was allowed to depart, with the assurance, if he ever came down that way again, that he would be shot." A hundred years later the tree in question would still be pointed out as the place of the Mennonite marketman's punishment.[47]

This spring of 1778, so miserable for the shivering soldiers at Valley Forge, saw the breaking out of the worst ill-feeling so far in the community, not excluding the Mennonites. After two armies have contended in a com-munity, each seeking the support of the local populace, there are inevitably scores to settle among the civilians. Abraham Gehman, minister at Rockhill, wrote that his family had been disturbed and even robbed, apparently by foragers, but had not suffered want.[48] But there was another very trou-blesome problem. Abraham's congregation, and the one at Franconia, were unhappy with the behavior of their bishop, Christian Funk. Abraham's wife and her mother, the wife of the other Rockhill preacher, Samuel Bechtel, were adamantly claiming that Bishop Funk had taken the Test Oath or at least an "Affirmation" that would serve the same function: disclaiming loyalty to the king.[49] This was a matter of the utmost concern to the Men-nonites in general. It was a case of conscience. Although, when they had been naturalized, they had not been willing to *swear* loyalty to the king, as their neighbors had, they had given their *word*. They had affirmed "in their own way and manner," along with Quakers, Dunkers, and other "scrupu-lous" people for whom the Sermon on the Mount was the binding code of behavior. To make an opposite affirmation now, even though another "government" was requiring it under threat of serious punishment, would be disobedience to Christ's clear teaching: "Let your yea be yea." But here was a new law demanding that this "Test" be taken by June 1, 1778; those refusing would not be allowed to make or administrate wills, and would be liable to double taxation, fines, and even expulsion from the state.

Mrs. Gehman and Mrs. Bechtel said they had it on good authority from their Reformed neighbors, and others also reported hearing, that Christian Funk had signed the Test himself, and advised at least three local young men to sign it and save themselves the fine. Funk denied these rumors vigorously. Nevertheless, when communion time came around he found that his deacon (and uncle) Christian Meyer, Jr., and several other "servants" in his bishop district were not "at peace"—the necessary requirement for the celebration of the Lord's Supper. The congregation at "Clemens' " (Salford) and Plains were ready to proceed as usual, but Franconia and Rockhill were not. Harsh words flew, as Christian investigated the problem, between his neighbor and co-minister Jacob Oberholtzer and Christian's wife, Barbara. But after apologies were made, and tears shed, the district's communion observances were held with good attendance.

However, the disturbing report that Christian had advised people to yield on the "Test" was spreading beyond his district. Apparently the whole conference was discussing the question. Christian Meyer and Skippack Bishop Andrew Ziegler went up to "Goschenhoppen," where Funk's brother Henry had been a preacher, and "proposed" to the congregation there "that no person should pay" the special tax of three pounds ten shillings. Soon the old blind bishop at Deep Run, Abraham Schwartz, was also meeting to discuss the issue with Funk, Ziegler, and Meyer, illustrating the close and binding tie felt across the wider Mennonite community. Bishop Ziegler, outspoken and unbending, brought "six ministers" to meet with Christian at his home. Withholding the ordinary "kiss of peace," Ziegler announced that they had come to see "whether, according to the gospel, we might pay the tax or not."

"You already knew my opinion," replied the accused bishop. Caesar was not "considered by the Jews as their legitimate sovereign," and yet Christ had told them to pay the tribute. "Were Christ here," reasoned Christian, "he would say, 'Give to congress that which belongs to congress, and to God what is God's.' "

Something in this statement deeply angered Bishop Ziegler. Rising, he snapped that he would "as soon go into the war, as to pay the three pounds ten shillings,"[50] if the first option were not so dangerous. He seems to have meant to convey the thought that paying the new tax would be as serious a sin as breaking Christ's commandment to love one's enemy. Historians have variously interpreted this to mean that Andrew was (1) objecting to paying the Congress *any* tax (since Congress was considered rebellious rather than legitimate), or (2) rejecting this tax because it was for military purposes. In view of the long-standing willingness of prior generations of Mennonites to pay special taxes even when they were levied with obvious reference to war situations, the present writer accepts the first interpretation. The dominant factor in the thinking seems to have been the instinct for respecting traditional government as "ordained of God"; the new Revolutionary setup was thus perceived as something sinful. This seems also to be the way Bishop Funk interpreted the understanding of his opponents, who were by far in the majority.[51]

Around this time the British army abandoned Philadelphia, and Revolutionary authorities turned their attention toward punishing those who had either helped the British or shown resistance to the new government. Such were to suffer forfeiture of their goods (with a few even hanged). Hardest hit of the Mennonites was one John Overholt, a miller of Tinicum Township, who was "attainted of treason," and apparently fled to British-controlled Staten Island, where he shortly died. His widow appealed, apparently in vain, for relief.[53] A Martin Overholt, it would later be claimed, spent time during the Revolution in Canada, and within a decade, several Overholts, including one "States" or "Statts" Overholt, would settle on the Niagara peninsula.[53]

Another frightening case of forfeiture occurred in the Saucon community, whose local officials had earlier seemed bent on baiting the pacifist Moravians. Here twelve adult Mennonite men, apparently the basic congregational unit at Saucon, were jailed for not taking the Test Oath by June 1. Shortly, inventories were made of their movable goods. Sentenced "to be banished out of the State within thirty days," the men appealed the Easton Court's decision to the "Supreme Executive Council of Pennsylvania," stating "in all humility" that they had "always been peaceable subjects." They had always been "ready and willing to contribute" their "full proportion" to the "State or Government we lived under . . . except going into the military service, it being contrary to our religious principles to bear arms in any case whatsoever, and if we are found guilty of anything contrary . . . may we suffer the severest penalties. . . ." Relief was asked from the harshness of the local officials' interpretation of the law. Twelve neighbors signed a supporting petition, stating that the prisoners, though blinded by "an unhappy bias in their Education," were not disaffected to the present government. They were, rather, "men of unblemished reputation for uprightness and integrity . . . in their dealings. . . ."[54]

The appeal was in vain. Agents receiving a 5 percent commission seized, and Sheriff John Siegfried, himself of Mennonite heritage, sold the goods of the Mennonite community. Forty thousand pounds' worth of tools, cattle, grain, furniture, bedding, and even books were sold, with the justice of the peace and the sheriff both joining in the bidding. Clocks, spinning wheels, chests, stoves, and even a looking glass were redistributed through the community. A few of the goods, at the first auctions, were bought back by some Mennonites.

Shortly after the last auction, two of the prisoners' wives—Eve Yoder and Esther Bachman—filed a petition to the Assembly in Philadelphia. Signing by marks (neither could write), they protested that their husbands had never made any trouble, "but paid their taxes and fines, furnished horses and teams for the continental service, whenever demanded, and some of them have gone with their teams as drivers to carry provisions to the army of the United States, for which service they have . . . received no pay. . . ." Now that their property had been taken, including even stoves that had been bolted to the floor, there was not "a morsel of bread" left even for the children. Some of the women "were pregnant," and have "to lye on the floor without any beds." In sum, "ten of the respectful and considerable Familys in the . . . County of Northhampton" were "becoming destitute."[55] This appeal brought a rather quick and favorable response from the Assembly, who authorized relief "by a draught on the State Treasurer." All the families seem to have recovered and stayed in the area. Doubtless helped by other Mennonites, they seem in a few years to have regained their normal economic status.

The firmness of these men in refraining from the "Test" because it appeared to them "like joining our hands to the military service," while they nevertheless claimed to be "peaceable and useful subjects to the State," was a clear restatement of the special Mennonite ethos.

Down at Franconia, the Test was also causing trouble, but within rather than from outside the fellowship. Our record of this controversy is all in a written account by its aggressive central figure Christian Funk, who produced it to appeal for understanding first to the "Conestoga" Mennonites, and then to the general public. He recalls that "after harvest" in 1778 his functioning as bishop broke down.[56] This "great calamity" first became evident when no deacon would cooperate with him in a baptismal service. He went ahead anyway, getting his blacksmith brother John, of Perkasie, to "bring water." This independent action brought immediate response. There were visits from other ministers, and Christian was told he was considered "unfit" to serve until he sincerely repented. He asked for specific accusations, and when some were offered, called them "rotten untruths." When a meeting of ministers was held without him, he accused them of bypassing "evangelical" or "gospel" procedure according to "Matthew 18." Bishops Schwartz and Ziegler then called an open meeting with the Franconia congregation, to which Christian was invited. Ziegler, acting as moderator, began by saying that anyone who had taken the "Test" could not participate in the discussion. Jacob Oberholtzer responded to a request for clarification of the issue by describing "Christian Funk and his children" as "very proud and obstinate" people. "They laugh and ridicule" the other two ministers at Franconia, he said. Some twenty other persons had also "complained against" Funk. He was now asked to "submit" his will to the "Council"—later, in English, to be called the "Conference."

The embattled bishop, after some reflection and counsel with friends, went before the assembly and asked everyone's forgiveness in anything whereby he might have offended them.

"That is not the thing," came the reply. "You must oppose the taking of the allegiance."

When Funk would do no more than reply ambiguously, "Of that I am clear," he was promptly "silenced" not only as bishop but as preacher. Looking for support, he went to see Bishop Martin Bechtel at the western end of the conference, and Minister Jacob Knorr at Germantown, but neither would take his part. Then the final blow fell. All the other bishops, including Jacob Meyer and Philip Geissinger of the northern district, excommunicated Christian from the "Christian congregation" in general. He could no longer participate in the Lord's supper even as a layman. Two factors had apparently made this step mandatory: there was increasing gossip that Funk had cheated in business deals, and he would not "submit himself to the Council." Without such submission, or willingness to acknowledge the binding authority of the church, most traditional Mennonites would not know how to "keep house," or "maintain the right fellowship" as they had learned it from their forbears. It is interesting to observe that Christian's brother at Hosensack, the silenced minister Henry Funk, had suffered much the same fate, having been accused of showing a domineering spirit, being a "horse-swapper," and not sticking to the truth in legal testimony. One of the specific charges against Christian, the area's leading miller, was that he had cheated Franconia Township in a horse deal. "Christian Funk is a township thief and a congress cheat!"[57] was one public accusation, the tone of which illustrates how a spiritual feud can degenerate into common name-calling, especially in a tightly interwoven community.

It is impossible to review this situation, of course, with complete fairness, given our fragmentary and one-sided access to its characters and events. There seems to have been little counterpart to it in the Conestoga, Maryland, and Virginia Mennonite settlements, or anywhere else in "Skippack" than where Christian Funk and his relatives lived. We are thus probably safe in concluding that he did not represent any major opinion among the Mennonites, and that his abrasive personality was a considerable factor in the friction. A Conestoga minister regarded his published account as "scandalous." At Franconia, after his neighbor George Delp locked the meetinghouse against Funk's new congregation of relatives and friends, they worshiped in barns or under the open sky.[58] For about half a century after this there would be small groups of "Funkites" meeting in perhaps four locations: Franconia, "Fricks," Towamencin, and Evansburg. The affair was the first of three dramatic divisions that would produce confrontations in the meetinghouse at Franconia over the first three centuries in America. There would be another in 1847, with much greater consequence, and one in 1956.

It is worthy of note that Christian's very detailed account of the fuss makes very little reference to Scripture—a distinct difference from usual Mennonite writing. He does candidly quote the various insults offered him, making the reader wonder why so many of his neighbors in the church found him obnoxious. His statement that his colleagues opposed him "for no other reason but because they supposed the king would subdue America" seems less than balanced or insightful. He exercises no self-criticism; his theme is that he was right, and that he had received the traditional treatment of a prophet with unwelcome foresight. What he does not dwell on with any sympathy is what others keep bringing up in the dealings—the necessity of "submitting to the Council" of the wider church. The willingness to do that was after all what held the community from Saucon to Germantown together in a covenanted body in Christ. When this became secondary to being personally proven right, the bonds of conference would loosen. In almost every subsequent generation there would be members who would take this option.

For over four more years the war continued, but the battlegrounds, except for several Indian flareups, were in other states. It was a generally contentious time, with constant militia fines and substitute fees. Henry Funk, Jr., now active again as a minister in the Funkite circle, began to claim exemptions from militia fines, causing local authorities to call for a hearing on his actual status with the Mennonites.[59] There was guerrilla outlaw activity by a small gang of bandits in the Deep Run area, sometimes involving hiding on a Mennonite farm, and even counterfeit "British prisoner" escapees who were really Americans testing whether anyone would help the British. Among the persons caught giving a meal to such was elderly Susanna Longacre of Coventry. Her sentence was to be a fine of 150 pounds or "to receive one hundred and seventeen lashes on her bareback at the public post." She protested that she had always made it her practice to feed "the needy traveler" who turned aside from the road in front of her house and knocked at her door. What she did was simply "an act of hospitality corresponding with her general conduct for many years past." Threatened with her was a neighbor, Dunker Bishop Martin Urner, who had also entertained such false guests.[60] A much more pleasant wartime encounter was that of Elizabeth Fretz of Bucks County, who fell in love with a Philadelphia soldier campaigning in her community in 1779.[61] Twenty-seven years after their marriage, John Kephart would be ordained a nonresistant Mennonite minister—the first resident one for the Doylestown congregation.

The Treaty of Peace which brought this troubled chapter of American history to a close came just a month short of the 100th anniversary of the arrival of the *Concord* at Philadelphia, carrying Jan and Mercken Lensen, the first Mennonite couple of the Pennsylvania experiment. Now there were already fourth-generation Mennonites in the land, with only a vague knowledge of their great-grandparents' transatlantic crossing, and what lay before that. Already some of the present generation, like the famous David Rittenhouse of Philadelphia, had become part of the macroculture (his cousins belonged to the Methacton congregation). How would the heritage be transmitted and maintained? Those who were taken into the church received only a few special hours of instruction from an unlearned bishop, before a day of fasting and prayer, followed by their baptism. There were some devotional books, of course, and schoolteachers rewarded their pupils with beautifully inscribed hymns and Bible verses as writing samples. The hymns cited were seldom if ever written by either teacher or pupil, but came from the great Pietist school of writers in Germany. "Humility is the weapon / Against the Devil's power," one stated,[62] and another, "How brightly shines the morning star!"[63] Or a student in the school at Franconia might copy the verse, "Enter in through the narrow gate...."[64] At Deep Run, Johannes Mayer admonished his pupil Abraham Landes on September 21, 1779, "*Mit Gott fang alles an! Mit Gott auch alles ende!*" (Begin everything with God! And finish all things with God!).[65]

But the real carrier of the particular Mennonite vision was the Sunday sermon. To someone from another culture, it would have seemed an unpolished, sleepy thing, preached, in the plainest of meetinghouses, in a melancholy chant, strung together with endless scriptural quotations, and resonant with a sadness deriving from a deep-settled conviction that the "world," or conventional society, is not at heart friendly to Christ or his people. There are two kinds of people, flatly stated Christian Halteman of Salford, as he sat down to "write something on the human life and walk" on Easter, March 31, 1782.[66] Already in the book of Genesis we are told of the "children of God" and the "children of men." The distinction pervades the entire Old Testament. God takes special care of "his own," and they know who they are. This thought rings a bell in the Mennonite mind; Christian

Funk too commented that "we Mennonists collectively consider ourselves" what the Bible called Israel: "the people of God." There is an intense feeling of family-hood, rooting back into the original covenanting "under the cross" which occurred in the 16th century. Its continuance is motivated not so much by any wish to exclude other people, as by a vivid sense of what it means to belong to a defenseless Christian family whose spirituality is authenticated by sharing in the suffering and rejection of their Lord.

This creates a continuous issue for a church committed to "maintaining the right fellowship." After all, "most people" in European or American society are baptized and profess Christ publicly. Unfortunately, many of them "still lead heathen lives." It was in trying to come to grips with this confusing situation that the Anabaptist fellowship had been born. We must reckon with false as well as true Christians, discerning "antichrists" as well as disciples. Certainly the recent war years had revealed, among Christians, plenty of behavior that bore no resemblance to the example of Christ. True Christians, writes the Salford farmer-preacher, are those who accept "the seal of obedience and of following Jesus, and confess themselves to be under his cross and suffering," and, unlike false Christians, do not stop at confessing. They actually "walk in the path . . . of Jesus, which is love, joy, peace, chastity, gentleness, goodness, faith, meekness, being compassionate . . . not vengeful, not proud, but lowly, meek, not seeking wealth and honor or high office. . . ." Here is the old Mennonite ideal of a humble, obedient, and suffering church. Others may "claim to be good Christians" even though their behavior is "greedy, wrathful, unfriendly, disobedient," but those who truly "name the name of Jesus Christ separate themselves from the unrighteous."

Such sermons, ranging the Scriptures from Genesis to Revelation, were not intended to entertain or please. They were meant to sound a continual warning against a loss of vigilance and the encroachment of self-assurance. They were valued according to how readily they drew on the Scriptures. Christian Halteman, though considered not as fluent a preacher as his son Abraham would be, would nevertheless be remembered for one particularly apt choice of a text. An enthusiastic hunter (so goes a varying local legend),[67] he was walking one morning toward the Salford (or Herstein) meetinghouse, when he became engrossed in following the trail of a fox in a new-fallen snow. Having finally traced the tracks to a lair, he hurried to the meetinghouse to find his congregation already seated, wondering what had happened to him. Stepping into the "preacher's bench," he took a text that brought together both a hunter's pleasure and the Mennonite sadness at the world's rejection of the true Christ: "Foxes have holes, and the birds of the air have nests; but the Son of man hath not where to lay his head."

Chapter 6

"We Will Keep House as We Understand It"

1787-1819

There had been no room left for pioneering among the "Skippack" Mennonites already before the Revolution. By 1783, even in Bedminster Township, which had been a later settlement, only a half-dozen little corners of "vacant" land were scattered among the Mennonite plantations.[1] Families with a tradition of moving once a generation since they had left Switzerland a century earlier now looked for a place to start again. There was a strong crop of young people. Schoolmaster Johannes Mayer from "Tohecke" (Tohickon), and his successor at the Deep Run school, Lutheran Hans Adam Eyer, had nearly fifty children enrolled. They met in one end of the stone Mennonite meetinghouse, built two decades earlier. At "Perkasie" (later Blooming Glen) Eyer had another fine school, with six children from the Jacob Kolb family (grandchildren of Bishop "Strong Izaak" Kolb). And at Eyer's third school, organized by two Mennonite and Reformed families straddling the Hilltown-Rockhill township line, he had a crop of young Biehns, Dersteins, Detweilers, Gehmans, and Haldimanns.[2] With such a sizable new generation, there could not be a farm for each oncoming son.

Some families were looking north, across the Lehigh River, into Northampton County, an area much of which had been taken from the Indians by the infamous "Walking Purchase." As this region filled in with white settlers, there was a small Mennonite component. A congregation and even several meetinghouses appeared in the Mount Bethel area (later Bangor). Names such as Ackerman, Delp, Godschalk, Kappes, Oberholtzer, Rothrock, and Ruth became common.[3] But like most other Mennonite communities that were either isolated or on the far fringes of the larger "family," these congregations would never thrive, and would finally be

158

absorbed by Lutherans or the strongly evangelical movements of a generation or two later.

There was a good bit more moving around than would be remembered, a century later, by the descendants of families who stayed put. Farmer Abraham Moyer of Upper Hanover, for instance, had three daughters living on the home place, all married. But when he wrote his will in 1786 he listed four other children then living in other states. Two sons were in North Carolina, a third in Georgia, and a daughter lived in Maryland.[4]

Another region drawing Pennsylvania Germans was Virginia's Shenandoah Valley, where local Mennonites had settled well before the Revolution. Henry Funk, Jr., the Funkite Mennonite preacher and miller at Hosensack, took this option. He sold his mill to a Schwenkfelder, and took the younger members of his family to the Virginia frontier. His youngest son, Joseph, would become a well-known music teacher and publisher there (at "Singer's Glen"). Another son, Henry, would marry Susan Geil, daughter of Jacob, who was moving to Virginia from Chester County, Pennsylvania, just when the Funks came. Geil (in Europe spelled Galle) had come to America as a boy some three decades earlier and first settled in the Springfield area of Bucks County.[5] His fourth wife was a Drissel from that general region. In the Swamp district, the eastern meetinghouse was built near a burying ground at "Drissel's." Now a "Trissel's" Mennonite congregation emerged near Jacob Geil's new home in Virginia, suggesting to us that relatives of his wife had also joined the migration. And a few years later a contingent of Showalters—in-laws of Henry Funk—began arriving. Daniel Showalter had moved down from the Lehigh area to Chester County (site of present-day Devon) before the war, and now (1788) migrated to the Shenandoah Valley. Before long his brothers John, Henry, and Ulrich would come too.[6]

Even before this latest Virginia migration, contacts were in the making for a much larger outward flow of eastern Mennonites—to Canada, on and just north of the "Niagara Peninsula." The very beginnings of this move are poorly documented, but some interesting hints can be gleaned among records and recollections of the Oberholtzer clan of the greater "Deep Run" settlement.[7] Martin and Jacob Oberholtzer, sons of 1709 immigrant Marcus who had settled at Schuylkill, had been among the earliest settlers at Deep Run, with Jacob Wismar, Jr., who had come up from Carolina. Some of the Overholts, as they were often called, also lived across the Tohickon Creek in Tinicum Township. This hilly and more sparsely settled area, next to the Delaware River and an island on which still lived the fierce Indian-hater Edward Marshall, had been a center of Loyalist sympathy during the war.

A number of small incidents suggest that some of the local Mennonites sympathized with their Loyalist neighbors, or at least did not oppose their views. The Scotch-Irish of the community were strong Whigs, and this tended to make the polarization sharp. Five muscular sons of the Quaker Joseph Doane, who prior to the war had been respected local citizens, reacted in anger to what they considered unjust levies and confiscations made against some of the seventy-six Bucks Countians who were suspected of Loyalist leaning. The Doanes' resentment turned them into a gang of Robin Hood-like robbers, plundering here and there to recover what they felt had been unfairly taken by the new government. Their exploits and escapes became legendary, reaching as far as Chester County. Among the farms they hid on were those of the Mennonite Meyer and Wismer families, sometimes, at least, with the owners' knowledge and cooperation. Joseph Doane, who escaped death by opening his jail door with a key he made of lead, fled to Canada before the war was over.

It had been in this Loyalist-leaning neighborhood, on the Tinicum side of the Tohickon Creek a mile or two west of the Delaware, that John Overholt had had a mill (there were actually at least three mills in the family). This enterprising grandson of immigrant Marcus Oberholtzer (1709) had been among the at least fifteen Bucks Countians attainted of treason after the British army had moved out of Pennsylvania. By 1779 Overholt had fled after the British when his mill was confiscated by Revolutionary officials, and had died on Staten Island, then under British control. His wife Elizabeth made a series of vain appeals for relief, one of them in June, 1781. The records are too skimpy to reveal the precise charges against the Loyalist miller, but it seems suggestive that his cousin Martin Overholt was later claimed to have spent time in Canada during the war years, "with others of the family."[8]

There are records stating that Martin's "estate" in Pennsylvania was being taxed in his absence. The Canadian weather being not to his liking, runs the family tradition, he returned to Bucks County, and we shall later find him moving to western Pennsylvania. There are other hints in the lore of Overholt descendants of early migrations to Canada and Nova Scotia. An Overholt family in Sweden in the 1980's claims that its ancestor John Overholt was born in Canada in 1779.

Slightly more accessible is the experience of the attainted Tinicum miller's son Abraham. It suggests a fairly serious involvement in Loyalist circles by the Mennonite families closest to the Delaware River, on the other side of which the British army had for some time been in control. Kulps as well as Overholts farmed to the very western bank of the River. Doubtless outraged by the confiscation of the family property by American authorities, and the lack of their official response to his mother's repeated pleas, young Abraham Overholt was said to have joined "Butler's Rangers"—an organization of Loyalist fighting men who made telling raids on American positions in the area between British-controlled Canada and Pennsylvania. Their commander, John Butler, had his headquarters at Fort Niagara, and after the war his followers were given extensive land-grants nearby. In the uneasy years after peace was declared in 1783, Abraham Overholt remained active in his home region, somewhat in the vein of the notorious Tory "Doane Boys" of the same neighborhood. In 1786 he was arrested for stealing horses, but as the constable led him toward the Bucks County seat of Newtown, he escaped (he had failed to deliver his mother's third appeal for clemency). In the following year he applied, as a Loyalist, for a grant of land in "Upper Canada" near Niagara. When his request was turned down on the grounds that he had been a stealer of horses, he protested that he had done this only on behalf of the British.[9]

Abraham had doubtless considered his chances for a grant good, since some of his Mennonite cousins and neighbors had found their claims of being "United Empire Loyalists" accepted by the British authorities. Four families had received a total of nearly 2,000 acres at the "Twenty Mile Creek" on the Niagara Peninsula when they had moved there in the spring of 1786. This is the date historians usually mention as the beginning of the Mennonite communities in Canada. The claim has rested on the rather vague account by a Bucks County historian in 1876.[10] As the bicentennial of this migration approached, several family historians looked more closely at official records in both Ontario and Pennsylvania, and at last established the fact that the first stages of the "Mennonite migration" had indeed resulted directly from Loyalist motives.[11]

From the Deep Run family of a cousin of the deceased miller Overholt went a letter[12] to relatives in the Palatinate, in the year 1787, containing the comment that considerable "indignation" was being felt in Pennsylvania. It was directed at "those who use the name of the Lord," wrote elderly Rudolph Landes, "to greedily fill their hands and pockets with the farmer's possessions. . . ." Rudolph himself felt that although Christians might "plead with the offender," they must give to the "King"—which now in the United States was the Congress—what was demanded. But some of Rudolph's wife's Overholt cousins were not so complacent. With the news that there was free Canadian land for people who had suffered for their British loyalties, a group of Bucks Countians undertook to emigrate (one report placed their number at 185). Among them were several Mennonite families, each of whom made a successful appeal for land as "United Empire Loyalists."

	Father's Name	Age	Children	Acres Granted
	Jacob Kulp	56	3	560
	Tilman Kulp	42	4	468
	Staats Overholt	43	6	536
	John Han	25	1	302
(In 1787)	Franklin Albright	25	1	302[13]

The key persons in this cluster of at least twenty-eight people of known Mennonite background seem to be the Kulps and the Overholts. The Kulp brothers were sons of immigrants (1729) Dielman and Judith Kolb, and grandsons of the well-known bishop Peter Kolb of the Palatinate. Their sister Molly had married another miller on the Tohickon, John Fretz, a man remembered for resisting the confiscation of his gun by American collectors in the Revolutionary War era. Moving from the Delaware to the much larger acreage of their British grants on the southern shore of Lake Ontario, the two Kulp families retained their "nonresistant" convictions but not their Mennonite fellowship; they were drawn before long into the "River Brethren" group, called "Tunkers" in that region. They never went beyond meeting for worship in their own homes, in their so-called "Culp Settlement," to the building of a meetinghouse, and in the course of generations their families became members of the "Disciples" or "Christian" denomination. The Christopher and Frances Kulp family which arrived three years later than Jacob and Tilman, and are sometimes erroneously claimed to be of the same family, were actually from the Strasburg area of Lancaster County, Pennsylvania.[14] The "Stoffel" (nickname for Christopher) Kulp home in Canada became a center of Methodist activity.

Staats Overholt of Tinicum Township had married his first cousin Susan Hunsberger; they were second cousins of Tinicum's Abraham Overholt who had been arrested for horse-stealing. In their new settlement the Overholt family became the nucleus of a Baptist fellowship, but, like the Kulps, retained their nonresistant convictions for a generation. As late as the War of 1812 the Baptist congregation noted that Staats (named for his mother Elizabeth Staats) and Susanna Overholt "could not walk with us because we bore arms." Less is recorded about the John Hans and Frank Albrights, though Albright is known later to have married a widow from Bucks County, Annie Wismer Ruth. Her two sons, after coming to Canada, became Baptists as well, one of them a deacon.

This earliest grouping of Mennonites on Lake Ontario thus founded no Mennonite community, although they did serve as a reference point for relatives who would join them thirteen years later. When that would occur, the earlier settlement would actually share a small portion of their land with the later group, who had to acquire their farms by purchase rather than government grant. The adjacent farms of the Kulps and Overholts lay near the Twenty Mile Creek on the Niagara Peninsula between Lake Erie to the South and Lake Ontario to the north. After 1783 surveyors had not been able to "lay out the land fast enough for the multitude of settlers who came in" as the recipients of grants. Yet it still had the appearance of empty country; travelers on the Iroquois Trail running parallel to Lake Ontario across the settlement of Kulps and Overholts would encounter only an occasional inn. Locations were identified by their nearness to one of the creeks flowing north into the Lake. These creeks were named by their distance in miles west from the Niagara. Thus the Kulp-Overholt settlement was at "The Twenty," while Christopher Kulp of Lancaster County lived near "The Thirty."[15]

Back home in Pennsylvania some of the Mennonite ministers were still "uneasy" about the recent war. According to outcast Bishop Christian Funk, they were still saying in 1784 "that there is no peace, and . . . that if congress is a government, they have been in an error these seven years."[16] Burdensome fines for nonparticipation in the militia continued, and there were new state and federal taxes. Some Pennsylvanians, according to Rudolph Landes's letter, could not "become reconciled" to these taxes. "Little warfares" or rebellions were breaking out here and there. There was an awkward adjustment to be made as the Mennonites had to recognize, with everybody else in the new nation, that the king had been replaced by a Congress they had regarded as unlawful, and that this situation had become permanent. It galled Christian Funk that his former co-ministers did not now acknowledge the correctness of his political predictions in 1777. He continued to agitate for vindication and reinstatement. In 1784 two of his supporters sent his written account of the long dispute "To the Ministers" among their "Opponents," stating that unless these ministers were now reconciled with those of Funk's following, the document would be spread before the public.[17] Funk seems to have had about fifty adult male members in his four congregations, including some of the Rosenberger and Meyer families that had originally opposed him at Franconia.

Where the Mennonites lived in this era, there were no towns. The closest thing to even a village would have been the cluster of buildings around an inn on a road linking Philadelphia and the Lehigh area. There were no bridges over creeks or rivers. The top of Philadelphia County was cut off and renamed Montgomery in 1784, with resultant political wrangles over where to put the county seat. Bucks would not move its seat to Doyle's Tavern until 1812. People went down the trails and roads to market on horseback, although an occasional wagon, or string of wagons, took grain to the city. Young Abraham Allebach of Hatfield Township died of the yellow fever he caught in the city. Anna, the aging wife of Michael Ziegler, Jr., of Lower Salford, was killed in a wagon accident while on the way to Philadelphia in 1790. In these years most of the German-speaking people considered vehicles built merely for riding to be unnecessary convenience. It was, of course, all right to ride if a wagon was going anyway, as teacher Andreas Kolb did in 1792, catching a ride from his school at Franconia (Ro-

Fraktur wedding certificate, undated, by Mennonite schoolteacher Andreas Kolb. A somewhat similar wedding certificate was made in 1784 for a Deep Run Mennonite couple by Lutheran schoolteacher J. A. Eyer. The closing lines are: "*Disz Wunscht dir brautigam, / Und auch dir Braut, / auch Jedem ders Wohl Meint / und Gott vertraut / Ein Treuer freund / Der euch ist Hold, / Sein [Name] ist und heiszt / A[ndreas] K[olb].*" (The Schwenkfelder Library)

senberger's) to another one in the Mennonite community at Saucon.[18]

The last wolf would not be caught in Bucks County until about 1800. Game and fish were still in meaningful supply. Incredibly large flocks of passenger pigeons, sometimes over a mile long and a half-mile wide, dimmed the sky. When they "encamped," as many as twenty nests could be seen on one tree, and people standing among these trees could hardly hear each other talk. In the spring and fall the birds could be caught in nets. Henry Wismer of Bedminster was particularly good at this sport, "frequently" catching enough "to fill two or three barrels before breakfast." Some were salted for future consumption, some sold at twenty-five cents a dozen in the neighborhood, and others sent by horse and wagon to the Philadelphia market.[19]

The nearly simultaneous deaths of perhaps the two oldest Mennonites of the whole region, caught the notice of the Germantown newspaper. On February 4, 1787, Jacob Wismar, Jr., of Plumstead, already beyond his 102nd birthday, finally passed on. We will remember him as having sailed to Carolina some seventy-eight years earlier. Now the progenitor of 170 descendants, he had been able to "walk out and undress himself until within two weeks of his death."[20] More remarkable was the aged Franz Latschar of Colebrookdale (Boyertown area), at the opposite end of the Mennonite community. He had come to Pennsylvania about the time Wismar had taken up his land at Plumstead. Sixty years later, in his 102nd year, he frequently walked twenty to twenty-five miles a day. He died two days after Wismar did, shortly after walking "twenty miles to visit a sick relative."[21] Surpassing even these stories was that of the Reformed Gabriel Schuler of Lower Salford who, according to local legend, single-handedly felled the thickest oak in the neighborhood on his 100th birthday, and asked his friends to let it lie where it had fallen as a memorial to him.[22]

It is from such vignettes that we must gather our impressions of this era: Christian Overholt of Bedminster, who had no children, leaving half his estate for the "use of the poor" of the Deep Run congregation.[23] The children of John Clymer, telling their children the amazing story of their own father's late marriage. When John had "already reached middle age," they claimed,

> he was visiting at a house where a child was lying in the cradle. As he rocked the little girl, he said, "Perhaps I may yet marry her." Sure enough he did, when past sixty.... From this late marriage he raised a family of nine children, five sons and four daughters. Indeed one of his sons must have been born when he was eighty years of age.[24]

An Indian squaw living with the Andrew Ziegler family in Lower Salford, telling the children, when it thundered, that the Great Spirit was angry. Bishop Henry Hunsicker of Skippack conducting her funeral, when her body was buried in the Lederach family plot.[25] Christian Meyer and Maria Landis of Deep Run receiving from the Lutheran schoolmaster a sparkling Fraktur wedding certificate (1784).[26]

A word more might be said here about the schoolmaster of this era. Part of his role was to teach singing. Bachelor Hans Adam Eyer, also an organist, was making rewards and booklets for his pupils, including many Mennonite children, as early as the fall of 1779. One "Harmonic Melody Booklet of the Best-known Hymns in the Marburg Hymnbook" is dated April 12, 1780, and given to Heinrich Honsberger at "Birkenseh"[27]—Eyer's Germanization of Perkasie. At first only one staff and one melodic line are given, but some years later the schoolmasters would provide three and then four-part harmony. Eyer also made inscriptions on the flyleaves of his pupils' books, such as the newly printed Mennonite catechisms of 1790, the *Christliches Gemuetsgespraech* by Gerhard Roosen, with this edition containing two of Christopher Dock's hymns.[28] One type of Fraktur the Mennonites did not need, of course, was the baptismal certificate so important to Lutherans and Reformed. The Mennonite records of birth were more likely to be kept on the flyleaves of Bibles. In 1801 John Detweiler of Skippack gave special instructions in his will that his "large Dutch Book of the Sufferings of the true and faith in Christ shall be . . . the only Property of my Son-in-law [Bishop] Henery Hunsicker. . . . So that my children may at any time see their age as they are all entered therein."[29] Eyer also made some Mennonite family registers, and many gorgeous *Vorschriften*, or writing samples, such as had been used among the Mennonites at Skippack since Christopher Dock's time. Sometimes Eyer handed out exquisite little pupil's rewards.

Found among his papers was an extremely fine and imaginatively designed Fraktur on the pictorial and scriptural theme of eagles, and signed by another bachelor schoolteacher, the Mennonite Andreas Kolb (1749-1811). At this point only speculation can connect these two Dock-like figures. Andreas, born at Skippack as a grandson of immigrants Martin Kolb and Andreas Schwartz, taught at the Franconia school, probably at Salford, at Saucon, and doubtless at other places. The effortless creativity of his many Frakturs, and the aptness of his linking pictorial motif with the meanings of hymnic or scriptural texts are parallel with yet recognizably distinct from the style of his contemporary Eyer.[30] There were actually quite a few Mennonites among the schoolteachers who practiced this art, often imitated on pieces by their pupils. We even find a Fraktur-decorated "Little Writing-chest" with a hidden lower drawer, from the hand of John

Drissel, for Jacob Rohr in 1795.[31] A similar box was found to contain letters by Andreas Kolb and his relatives.[32]

It should be kept clear that Mennonite Fraktur is only a modest part of a much broader cultural phenomenon. What is interesting is that this is one of the few folk-arts that was affectionately espoused by Mennonites, and found useful for religious purposes. In Johannes Mayer, Andreas Kolb, Hupert Cassel, the later Martin and Samuel Gottschall, and a few other unidentified artists, it was even brought to an impressive delicacy. There was afloat in Pennsylvania, and, one gathers, particularly in the region served by such people as Dock, Mayer, Eyer, and Kolb, a folk conception of the schoolmaster as having a saintly vocation, one that transcended practicality. A folk song appearing now and then in the local manuscript singing-school books, and printed in broadside by a Mennonite teacher as late as the 1850s, has the schoolmaster asserting that he is well pleased with the single life. His joy is in carrying out his calling:

> Preceptor, they title me,
> Because I teach the children;
> And if I truly please my God,
> This is my highest honor,
> And this is my desire,
> And this is my delight.

"Schreibkistlein" (little writing chest) made by John Drissel, dated January 31, 1795, for Jacob Rohr of New Britain Township. Preserved in the Rohr family for generations, donated in 1983 to the Mennonite Heritage Center of Souderton by Dr. George Gaugler. (Mennonite Heritage Center, Souderton, Pennsylvania)

> Although I may not please all men,
> If I may only please my God—
> This is my true desire,
> And this is my delight.[33]

As late as 1877, a conservative former Mennonite schoolteacher from Deep
Run would publish a modified version of this poem, and even quote with
warm approval a poem by a schoolteacher who was also an organist:

> Wann ich dann die Orgel spiele,
> Gemüths von göttlichen Gefühl,
> Und die Gemeinde mit mir singt,
> O, wohl es mir im Herzen klingt![34]

One also finds several of Christopher Dock's hymns used in writing samples
or practice books as late as sixty years after his death.[35]

    We have seen that Mennonite children were learning tunes to hymns
in the Lutheran hymnal, but they also used the *Ausbund,* and the
Reformed Lobwasser's *Psalms.* In 1875 we find Andreas Kolb at Franconia
designing a bookplate for Sarah Rosenberger's new *Ausbund.*[36] A few years
later there would be a call for the Mennonites to publish a new selection of
hymns. Another publishing venture of this era seems to have been at the
personal initiative of John Herrstein of Limerick Township, a remote extension of the Skippack district. Herrstein traveled back to Europe, where he
had printed, at the expense of himself and a Palatine Mennonite named
John Schmutz, 500 copies of a fat collection of *Meditations* by an immer-
sionist pietistic minister at Hamburg-Altona, Jacob Denner. Herrstein and
Schmutz arrived in Philadelphia on September 22, 1792.[37] A related folk
story claims that the two entrepreneurs then went out to sell their respective
halves of the inventory. Herrstein, so goes the story preserved in a neighboring Gottschall family, did quite well in Montgomery and Bucks counties
(*i.e.,* "Skippack"), quickly finding customers for his share, but Schmutz
came back from "Lancaster" much disgusted, with most of his books, saying that the thing for which there was a demand among the Mennonites
there was oxen, not books.[38] However, the significant number of Denner's
books still being found among the "Lancaster" Mennonites makes this story
seem of questionable authenticity. Herrstein, having lived in America
before, knew the neighborhood much better than Schmutz.

    By the 1790s the once primary Germantown congregation was increas-
ingly isolated from the larger Mennonite community, losing some of its
spiritual members to the neighboring Dunker congregation, and embroiled
in internal difficulties[39] from which it would seemingly never recover. The

parents of bachelor schoolteacher Andreas Kolb, who had moved to that community from Skippack, were highly critical of the two ministers at Germantown, Jacob Funk and contractor Jacob Knorr. Andreas, presently teaching at Franconia, went to see Bishop Henry Hunsicker at Skippack, who had the oversight of the Germantown congregation, to express his parents' concerns. The bishop had already asked the Germantowners by letter to try to become reconciled, promising, if this effort failed, "to take counsel among us and our fellow ministers to hand down a decision. . . ." Bishop Andrew Ziegler, in "Middling Good Health" but now in his eighties, no longer wished to be involved. Jacob Funk turned out to be as difficult to deal with as his father's cousin Christian Funk had been. When "the Hunsickers" said that he could not "serve" in their pulpit at Skippack while he was not at peace with his own congregation, Funk lost his temper, and said that Bishop Hunsicker could "not see more than an inch in front of his nose." A "council" was then called, enlisting Bishops Jacob Gross of Deep Run and David Ruth of New Britain, but Funk refused all cooperation, insisting in front of six ministers that he alone would be the "housekeeper" at Germantown. Finally a letter by some of the Germantown members stated that they would no longer "appear" in services led by Jacob Funk or Jacob Knorr. "Our desire," they wrote, apparently to Bishop Hunsicker, "is that you would cleanse the pulpit and occupy it yourself." The behavior of the two Germantown ministers would otherwise bring shame to the other Mennonite leaders. This request was apparently favorably acted upon, and the ministers silenced. A schedule of visiting preachers was drawn up, which supplied the Germantown pulpit every four weeks. Preachers from as far away as Coventry and Deep Run were involved. Bishops Gross and Ruth and Mathias Pannebecker, of Chester County, would each take a turn. The latter had just (1795) overseen the forming of a small congregation in Charlestown Township, Chester County, involving Preacher Joseph Schowalter and trustees George Clemens, Abraham Haldeman, Jacob Johnson, and Christian Wisler.

Perhaps Jacob Funk was eventually reconciled; we find a man by that name participating in a ministers' conference at Franconia in 1806. Regarding the winning of several Germantown members to the Dunkers, there survives an interesting letter from Elder Alexander Mack. Writing to a friend in Maryland in about 1785, Elder Mack, who had at least one Mennonite son-in-law, reveals how the Mennonites appeared to him. He calls local Mennonite John Keyser "an obstinate man," who will not permit his wife, Elizabeth, to be baptized by the Dunkers, even though she had "applied" for this when she was sick. Finally she had been "baptized . . . with the ceremony used today by the Mennonites. This ceremony they performed in her bed, and tried to persuade her that she was now baptized." After her recovery she became "frivolous and vain," but when her daughter, also a Mennonite, received immersion from the Dunkers "in the true faith in the Son of God and found refuge in Jesus," Elizabeth again "blamed herself for not being baptized." Mack had heard of all this, but discreetly stayed away "in order to prevent the strange attitude of the Mennonites from increasing her distress." Mack asks the prayers of his Dunker correspondent on behalf of the "weak-in-faith" Elizabeth, and requests the strictest confidentiality for the information he has passed along.[40]

But the most consequential action of the postwar story is the new migration. Of inflow there was little. Young Philip Schwerdle of Eppingen, east of the Rhine, did come, probably as an indentured servant, in about 1782.[41] In 1792 arrived carpenter Jacob Schutt, with wife, Elizabeth, and infant daughter, on a ship sailing from Hamburg.[42] He lived first in the Towamencin area, then bought land in New Britain (near Doylestown), and his daughter married an Overholt. Two other new "immigrants" to this community were sons of the Jacob Geil who had gone to Virginia twelve or thirteen years earlier. John, now about eighteen, had disliked his apprentice-work at a tannery in Virginia, and had reportedly run away after his father died.[43] In another fifteen years this tall and impressive young man would be ordained as a minister at New Britain (Line Lexington), where he would be held in respect and appreciation for half a century.

In 1797, it seems, a new outflow began in both westerly and northerly directions. Although we have seen that the very first moves to Canada, in the 1780s, had to do with Loyalist feeling, that could not have been the motive for going over to "Jacob's Creek" in the recently erected Westmoreland County. Martin Overholt, who had not been satisfied with Canada's weather, was one of the first to move from the Deep Run area in this westward "wave," with Henry Rosenberger, Adam Tinstman, and Henry Wideman and their families (1797). Martin and wife took along their fourteen children, and apparently sent home such a good report that in 1800 his brother Henry, living next to the Deep Run meetinghouse, also came, with his twelve children, half of whom were already married. This emigration must have made a stir in the Bedminster community, where Henry and his son-in-law lived on adjacent farms. Henry sold his 175 acres for 1500 pounds to Andrew Loux on April 25, and two days later his colony of at least thirty-four souls set out on a string of covered wagons for his brother's territory nearly 300 miles west. Once in that new community, Henry's family settled in a clump around him—Durstines, Fretzes, and Louxes. Son-in-law Peter Loux owned much of the land on which the town of Scottdale would be built. Son Abraham Overholt would become rich as the distiller of "Old Overholt" whiskey. And there were other families in this new settlement from the same home region: Funks, •Ruths, and Yothers. These settled mostly north of Jacob's Creek, while emigrants from the Lancaster Mennonite communities took up land south of the creek.[44]

A solitary emigration seems to be that of Christian Clemens, son of John, earlier a zither-playing miller along the Branch Creek in Lower Salford. Christian, it has been claimed, moved to the Clinton River near Detroit in 1798, where he was said to have founded the town of Mt. Clemens. Here he served as a colonel in the militia, justice of the peace, and judge, apparently abandoning his Mennonite teachings.[45] At home he would not have been allowed to be a church-member while performing such duties, as was the case with Ralph Stover, son-in-law of Miller Abraham Funk at Springtown. Stover, also a justice of the peace, served in the Pennsylvania Legislature from 1793 to 1799. Though he and his wife attended the Deep Run Mennonite meeting with their relatives, he was not a member.[46]

Whereas the Westmoreland County emigration had drawn on the Deep Run area, a larger group of families mostly from Hilltown (the "Perkasie" congregation) and Tinicum was considering Canada. With the Kulps, Albrechts, and Overholts, already there for over a decade, some information must have been coming by letter to such as the Kulps' sister Mary (Molly), elderly wife of miller John Fretz on the Tohickon Creek. Families such as the Fretzes had more grown children than farms could be found for them in the Deep Run area. We recall as well that Mrs. Staats Overholt was a Hunsberger. In 1798 Abraham Hunsberger and his two oldest sons went up to investigate "The Twenty." Germans from Pennsylvania were welcome in this country, because they had cash to buy land that had been granted to veterans of the British military who were themselves not serious farmers. The Hunsbergers chose land beside the Overholt and Kulp community at The Twenty. The farming situation here was made attractive by an unusual topographical feature: running the length of the east-west "Peninsula" a few miles south of the Indian trail was the crooked spine of a continuous hill or mountain named "The Niagara Escarpment." This protected the strip of fertile land between it and Lake Ontario from the chill of winds blowing off Lake Erie. Thus fruit-growing was as possible here as in Pennsylvania. Well-pleased, Amos Albright and Abraham and Jacob Meyer, another prospecting party in the summer of 1799, left a deposit of $40.00 before walking back to Pennsylvania.[47]

That fall, a collection of "Perkasie" and "Deep Run" families[48] formed a wagon train to found what would become the first permanent Mennonite community in Canada. Involved were the families of Amos Albright (doubtless a relative of the Franklin Albright who had come in 1786); Abraham Hunsberger and his brother "Deaf John," a tailor; Valentine Kratz and his neighbors Dilman, Jacob, and Abraham Meyer; George Althouse, a driver; and the bachelor Moses Fretz, who had a large family of parents and siblings at home waiting for a report. The memory of this trek lingered,[49] though with occasionally contradicting details. There were said to be oxen-drawn covered wagons, and each family had a four-horse team. Cows as well as horses were shod, and at least one cow provided fresh milk. What was left over from drinking went into a churn on one of the wagons; as this bounced over holes and ruts, "It churned them a little butter." The travelers, including the children, walked most of the way, taking an occasional ride if their feet became sore. A ten-year-old boy, Jacob Albright, was a cow driver. At night they built a campfire, and occasionally baked bread. Once a calf was killed for fresh veal. After nearly twelve weeks, they came to the greatest of their crossings—the Niagara River. Here the cow and oxen had to swim, and the wagons were pushed over by hand. The children remembered getting their bare feet wet as water crept into the "wagon boxes" during the crossing. Fortunately, the Fraktur keepsakes they had gotten in school (a certificate for the "first singer" at Perkasie given to Jacob Meyer by Hans Adam Eyer, and a hymn given to Jacob's future wife, Magdalena Bechtel by Andreas Kolb)[50] were not soaked. They were probably between the leaves of the carefully stowed family Bibles.

In addition to this group, two young brothers from Plumstead who also came to Canada that year joined the adjacent settlement of Overholts and Kulps. The brothers were Henry and Jacob Ruth, whose widowed mother had married Franklin Albright, who had been in Canada since 1787. Settling as neighbors to Staats Overholt, Henry Ruth shortly married the Overholts' daughter Mary. Before long he would become, like Overholt, a Baptist, and in the ensuing War of 1812 his twelve- or fourteen-year-old son would enlist as a drummer boy.[51] Having come without spiritual leadership, these earliest Mennonite arrivals of 1786-7 had almost immediately shifted their spiritual identity, while nevertheless retaining strong religious interest.

On the other hand, the groups of Mennonites who came in 1799 and even more numerously in 1800 had every intention of preserving their spiritual identity. Their move was rapidly becoming considerably more than a Bucks County affair. People from Montgomery and Chester, and even Lancaster and Franklin counties were on the migration trail. There were Dunkers and Moravians as well, pouring onto half a dozen tracts both on and north of the Niagara peninsula. Sixty-three-year-old John Biehn of Montgomery County with sons-in-law named Rosenberger and Stauffer, bought 3,600 acres just south of the future site of Kitchener in Waterloo County. Next to the Biehn tract fifty-four-year-old George Bechtel took

2,160 acres. Also in their new community was Abraham Bechtel, and they were shortly joined by young George Clemens of Chester County, and Joseph Wismer of Bucks.[52]

Joseph's brother John had also migrated, but was staying with another group arriving at "The Twenty" down at Niagara, this same summer (1800). The largest subgroup in this party was the clan of seventy-year-old John Fretz, a former miller on the Tohickon Creek in Haycock Township, and brother-in-law of the Kulps of the 1786 migration. His descendants would remember the churn of white cedar Fretz had made for his daughter Elizabeth, wife of Abraham Grobb, a few years before the migration. Doubtless it too made its share of butter on the trek. Other children of Fretz in the group were the family of son Manasseh Fretz, and those of daughters Diana Rittenhouse and Sarah Hipple. Sarah, about twenty-eight years old, walked all the way carrying her latest baby. Still others in the large traveling party were Daniel High (Hoch) and sons Abraham, Daniel, and Philip, as well as Jacob High, Christian Hunsberger, Jacob Hauser (son-in-law of "Strong Izaak" Kolb), Jacob Frey, Isaac Kolb, John Wismer, and David and Samuel Meyer.

Thirty-three-year-old Samuel, a cousin of the Jacob Meyer in the previous year's group, had two four-horse teams. David Meyer's horses were "poor bony nags." For the whole party of about sixty persons there was a total of eleven teams, "four horses to a wagon being the rule." Daniel High had the best animals: one two-horse and two four-horse teams, one of which consisted of "four magnificent stallions . . . decked with splendid new harness, ornamented with belts." It seemed ironic that when a falling tree crashed into the camp, it killed three of High's best horses, leaving David Meyer's "poor bony nags." Sam Hauser "drove the first team all the way" through "mud, mud, mud." As one evening approached, a wagon-part broke, forcing the party to stop while one of the boys rode back twenty miles on horseback to the nearest blacksmith. He returned with the mended iron part at dawn the next morning, when the journey was at once resumed. Such pressing forward brought them to their new home in little more than half the time taken by the previous year's party.[53]

This colony at the Twenty, with about two dozen families and more on the way, was not able to buy its land all in one piece. They would have preferred to do so. And there were concerns about the danger of going too long "without any regular Christian organized meetings." Perhaps they had in mind developments among their relatives, the Niagara immigrants of 1786, who apparently had already become Methodists or Baptists. Two natural leaders in the more recently arrived Mennonite group were Jacob and Samuel Meyer, cousins from Hilltown, both preacher's sons, and both

in their early thirties. Within half a year of his coming, Samuel wrote back
to the bishop of the Deep Run-Perkasie district, Jacob Gross, asking for
some Pennsylvania leaders to come and oversee the ordination of ministers
and deacons in Canada. It is interesting to recall that it was exactly a
century earlier that recent immigrants to Germantown had written back to
established Mennonite leaders in Europe with the same request. The results
were also the same.

Bishop Gross replied the following September (1801), to "our little
Mennonite brotherhood in Upper Canada." He had read Samuel's letter
before the local conference "of ministers and deacons," and asked their
counsel. He had also written out to "Conestoga," telling them that this Canadian request involved them as well as the "Skippack" people. The Conestoga leaders had written back, however, after discussing it at their own
conference, that for the present year they had all they could do to visit their
remoter communities and isolated families in Pennsylvania.

Back East, as well, there was no one among the elderly bishops who
felt "armed with courage and strength" to "venture" the 300-mile trip,
which was usually made on foot. "And if someone would venture without
the spiritual armament," wrote Gross, "What that you need could he ac-
complish?" Yet the Canadian request was considered to be very much in
order. The bishop advised the new community to go ahead itself, prayer-
fully, with nominations followed by casting of lots, to select both ministers
and deacons. If all the votes fell on one person, and he were willing, he
might be considered properly chosen, whether for minister or deacon. Such
a person would have a true calling, "whether preachers are there" to assist
with the ordination "or not." "Certainly, human support and procedure are
also from God, and not to be rejected," as long as they are available, "but
the Lord is not tied to that." The Scriptures show that the Lord sends
people into his manifold service both with and without human mediation.
"As long as it is of the Lord, it will have good consequences, unless the one
called does not remain true and in humility, which is what the Lord demands of all his servants."

The bishop's closing remarks give us a brief look into how an elderly
shepherd of this era viewed his flock. "Dear friends," he wrote, "we think of
you often."

The wish of your true brothers is that in the new land you may lead a
new life, in holiness and righteousness, as is pleasing to God. . . . Oh
see to it, each one, that he fears and loves God from the heart. If that is
not your desire, preachers and meetings will help nothing, but [your
spiritual life] will again become . . . an old, power-lacking and insipid
thing, as among us there are too many such souls.[54]

Such expressions had been typical of Gross well before he had been chosen
a minister. As a young man in the Palatinate he had imbibed a strong
pietism and stress on emotional warmth from the Mennonite revivalist
preacher Peter Weber. He would sound the same note on his deathbed.
Closing his present letter with the hope that the Canadian brotherhood
would accept its disappointing parts in love, he asserted that the leaders
from Deep Run and Perkasie were willing "to try to serve" the infant community, "as best we can, with counsel through letters." Four other ministers
and a deacon showed their approval by signing beneath their bishop's
name.

Within months, the Canadians accepted this advice and permission.
For the role of minister they selected forty-year-old Valentine Kratz, and for
the deacon's work, the elderly John Fretz. A year later a second minister
was added—Jacob Meyer; by 1807 he would also be confirmed as bishop.
This man, son of one of the ministers who had signed Gross's letter, would
become, like his father at Perkasie, a highly respected leader. Something of
a "home doctor," he "earned the reputation of peacemaker in the neighborhood" around the Twenty. He stayed in contact with the Pennsylvania
Mennonite community, and would actually die there, in his mid-sixties,
while home for a visit.[55]

These migrating people had left behind in Bucks County a fairly
domesticated agricultural landscape. We can get a feel of its daily scenes by
dipping into the will of Abraham Overholt, an elderly farmer whose land
spread across the Bedminster-Plumstead township line. Abraham left very
little to chance in describing how his children should provide for their
mother after he was gone. "Week in body but of perfect mind," he spelled
out his wishes on October 23, 1802, in an English so roughly spelled that it
is presented here corrected for readability:

> ... My sons Abraham and Isaac shall maintain my wife, Madlin, and
> she shall have a right to live in any house where my son Abraham lives
> in. It is my will that she shall live in the back room of the house and
> have it all to herself, and she shall have the liberty to open the shutter
> when she pleases. And she shall have liberty to pass ... through the
> old room into the kitchen to make fire and cook what she pleases. And
> she shall have two chairs and the armchair. It is my will that she shall
> have the dresser and all what is in it and on it, and she shall have the
> frying pan and three iron pots and a big iron kettle and a little kettle,
> and she shall have the big brass kettle and ladles and skimmers what
> there is there, and she shall have one pot rack and iron tongs and the
> fire shovel, and she shall have earthenware as much as she pleases, and
> wooden ware. She shall have the cooking tub and a peeler and the
> turning churn and two buckets and a pail. And it is my will that she
> shall have the chest and all what is in it, and she shall have books as

many as she pleases. And it is my will that my widow and my son Isaac shall have the pipe stove and the clock between them, and after my widow's decease my son Isaac shall have the clock and the stove. . . . It is my will that my widow shall have three hens. It is my will that my son Abraham shall give to my widow one barrel of cider and one gallon of whiskey yearly if the apples hits as long as she remains my widow. And she shall have the eight gallon keg and the bake plate and the big skittel. And it is my will that my son Abraham and Isaac shall give to my widow ten pound of flax and ten pound of tow and six pound of wool and ten bushel of buckwheat and four bushel of Indian corn yearly as long as she remains my widow. And it is my will that my son Abraham and Isaac shall let my widow have a horse to ride when she pleases and shall have her saddle and bridle, and she shall have a cow which she pleases of mind, and Abraham and Isaac shall find pasture for her in the summer . . . and feed her in the winter as they feed their own. And she shall have apples out of the orchard for house use when she pleases to take them, and she shall have a piece in the garden . . . and two hives of bees as long as she shall remain my widow. . . .[56]

Such particularity was no more nor less common in Mennonite wills than in those of other rural Pennsylvanians. John Fretz, also of Bedminster Township, had stipulated three decades earlier that "my wife shall have a row of apple trees in my orchard, the fourth row from the barn." Perhaps Magdalene (Detweiler) Overholt was sitting beside the scrivener, supplying her stricken husband with specific details.

"She shall have books," directed Abraham, "as many as she pleases." There was indeed a variety of devotional materials, especially in psalm and hymnbooks, in the eastern Pennsylvania Mennonite homes of 1802. Among the eleven books listed in the inventory of the possessions of Philip Hoch of Hilltown in 1802, are at least three and probably four different psalm and hymnbooks:

Family Bible	Do. called the Golden Apple
Book called Martyrology	Psalm Book
Do. containing sermons	Switzer song Book *[Ausbund]*
[probably by Jacob Denner]	Book called the Childrens Bible
Do. called the wandering soul	Do. Switzer Testament [Froschower]
Psalm Book	Do. Songs[57]

This variety made for some confusion when people brought "two or three" differing psalm and hymnbooks to meeting. The singing-school books which teachers and pupils carefully filled with tunes referred, on their title pages, to the Lutheran, or "Marburg" hymnal. The Reformed Ambrosius Lobwasser's *Psalms* were also around, and of course the old *Ausbund*, which had last been reprinted in 1785, but was no longer favored among the "Skippack" Mennonites. The acutest need of all was probably felt on the western Pennsylvania frontier, from which the newly arrived Mennonites apparently made a strong request for hymnbooks to their eastern relatives.

Both "Conestoga" and "Skippack" called together committees to gather hymns for a new Mennonite-sponsored collection.[57] This joint undertaking assumed a general unity throughout Pennsylvania Mennonite communities. The Skippackers, considered "well trained in singing" by the Conestogans, rapidly collected over 400 hymns and subscriptions for 3,000 books. "Conestoga" moved more deliberately. "After a time two Skippack brethren" arrived with their list of selections at a meeting in the house of Deacon Martin Mellinger with "two leading bishops." To the chagrin of both groups, they found their lists of hymns more widely divergent than they had foreseen. The Skippackers wanted only thirty of the Psalms, while the Conestogans wanted twice that many. Requests that did not match those of Skippack had come in from Virginia and "Jacob's Creek" (Westmoreland County). The "Fort Pitters," originators of the whole project, in Deacon Mellinger's opinion, doubtless had no singing schools available as at Skippack, and they were adamant that notes should be printed throughout the book, even if this cut down on the number of hymns. Further, the Conestogans were ready to include nearly half of the *Ausbund*, whereas the Skippackers chose only two of its songs. Could this mean that the "Swiss" heritage of the Palatines who came to "Skippack" had been effectively altered by views of the earlier Dutch, unshared by the "Conestoga" churches?

A "lengthy discussion" took place in Deacon Mellinger's house. Perhaps the two "Skippack" brethren present were Minister Jacob Oberholtzer of Franconia and his son-in-law Samuel Gehman, preacher at Rockhill. They are mentioned in Mellinger's correspondence about the book. On the second day of the joint committee meeting, the Skippackers reluctantly stated that they were not authorized to change the selections their people had made, in order to fit both sets of selections between two covers. They now "saw no other way than to have their book printed in Germantown," where they had convenient access to a printer, and the Conestogans could go ahead with one of their own. Deacon Mellinger felt this was "a pity"; it would have been better if both communities could have been united in the use of one book. "It is not to their liking either," he wrote, "but they are at fault as well as we. . . ." His hope was that perhaps the Conestogans, after actually seeing copies of the new "Skippack" book, might decide to use it after all.

In the summer of 1803 the new hymnal was taking form on the Germantown press of Michael Billmeyer. "Is all going well?" wrote Deacon Jacob Kolb anxiously near the end of the harvest season. He enclosed "two additional hymns of comfort for young people who are very sick or at the verge of death, that were taken from . . . an old Lutheran hymnal."[58] Other last-minute submissions accumulated into an "Appendix" of fifty-one hymns, in addition to the 424 already included under forty-two devotional headings. By September 18, Jacob Oberholtzer was showing the completed book to his people in meeting at Franconia, and reporting that they considered it a beautiful book, well-printed. Deacon Mellinger hurriedly ordered several copies to show at the Conestoga fall conference a few weeks later. There, however, he was sorry to find the sentiment of the western "Vorpiters" swaying the more moderate majority. The new Skippack book, without musical notations except for twenty-two psalms at the beginning, was "not at all the book" which the Fort Pitters wanted. And so in the following year another Mennonite collection, *An Undenominational Songbook*, was published in the town of Lancaster.

Thus "Skippack" or "Franconia" had the honor of issuing the first American Mennonite hymnbook, but only by a year. Its title was *The Little Spiritual Harp of the Children of Zion (Die Kleine Geistliche Harfe der Kinder Zions)*,[59] put out "at the order of the Mennonite Congregations." A second title page, after the thirty Psalms, announces simply a *Collection of Old and New Spiritually Rich Songs*, issued "at the desire of good friends." Neither in the very brief "Introduction" nor in the contents of the hymns is there evidence of Mennonite identity, as might be found in the Conestoga collection, which even contained a hymn on "Footwashing." There is much more Lutheran material in the Skippack *Harp* than in the Conestoga *Songbook*, even though the latter is specifically called *Undenominational*. The Conestoga book has more songs under such headings as "The Christian Walk," "The True Congregation of God," and "Love of God and Neighbor." The Skippack book has many more on "Death and Burial" and "Morning Songs." Both books include songs by Christopher Dock, the *Harp* having three and the *Songbook* two. The Conestoga "Introduction" is considerably longer, referring specifically to weaknesses in the Pennsylvania Mennonite scene, whereas the Skippack writer mentions only the "critical condition of the Christian communities" of the moment. Whereas the Conestoga book scatters printed tunes throughout its pages, the *Harp*, in its main section, has words only. Otherwise the books have virtually the same size and format. The fact that there were two hymnals instead of one ultimately made no hard feelings, "for we love one another," wrote Deacon Mellinger to Europe, "and we visit them and they visit us every year."[60]

The appearance of the new hymnal was a sign of some spiritual energy. Probably no one was more grateful than farmer Abraham Hunsberger of Limerick Township, near "Herstein's." Both he and his family would be remembered for their skill and enjoyment in singing, not only locally but at Coventry and in western Pennsylvania. Eventually two of the Hunsberger daughters would marry the brothers Henry and John Keeler, local Lutheran boys,[61] and thus bring another new name into the Mennonite "family." Now, in about 1800, "Herstein's" seems to have gotten a building for school and meeting, as there was another not far from the home of another Hunsberger daughter, Magdalena (Mrs. William Z.) Gottschall (later Eden Mennonite congregation). She, it would be said, knew every hymn in the new book.[62] Still another, Hannah, became the leading singer in the singing school held at "Herstein's."[63]

Similar patterns can be seen, in this first decade of the new century, at the opposite end of the "Conference"—the "Deep Run" area. There it was Mary Anna Fretz who would marry (1808) a young man who had been raised by two Fretz families—Jacob Bischofsberger—and make "Bishop" too a "Mennonite name."[64] And just as Herstein's had been the growing outward edge of the Skippack district, where Henry Hunsicker was bishop, so here where Jacob Gross had that office the Deep Run congregation erected a small meetinghouse in the next township of Plumstead (1806). Similar growth occurred in nearby New Britain, where Doylestown's congregation built a stone meetinghouse, and the one at Line Lexington doubled the capacity of theirs.

The bishop of this latter congregation was David Ruth. He, Jacob Gross, and Henry Hunsicker were now drawn into the last stages of the painful dealings with Christian Funk.[65] The estranged bishop had been out of the church for over a quarter of a century. He seems to have been living with his son John, also a Funkite minister, near the lower end of the Skippack creek (present-day Evansburg), in the "district" of bishop Henry Hunsicker. The latter, valued for his genial and broad-minded attitude at both "Skippack" and "Conestoga," seems at first not to have had spiritual dealings with Funk, though his sons were marrying Funk's granddaughters. An initiative came rather from Jacob Gross, apparently now the senior bishop, who led the discussions at the conference at Franconia. It is possible to see the three bishops just named in their role of "keeping house" and peacemaking in the wider fellowship, by reading the latter pages of Christian Funk's sharply worded narrative.

In 1804 Funk received word from the elderly shoemaker-bishop Gross and his colleague, farmer David Ruth, that they would be willing to meet with Funk to try to "promote a peace" between the main body and Funk's small separated flock. Christian took two of his men to the home of David Rosenberger, where the bishops met him and said a reconciliation would make them "glad." Funk replied that he had been grievously transgressed against, in having had to live for decades under the accusation of "thief." He begged, as he had at the beginning when the issue was his Whig sympathies, for a churchly inquest into the specific charges against him. But then, having called the bishops into the kitchen, he promised privately that if his former colleagues at Franconia, Minister Jacob Oberholtzer and Deacon Henry Rosenberger, would "acknowledge their transgressions" against him (*i.e.*, state that their accusations had been false), he would "give up every other consideration." What he longed for was less reconciliation than vindication.

The bishops, without replying, walked out of the house to confer. Then they called Funk and made their own proposal: if he would allow himself to be "received" back into the fellowship of the church "by the hand," they would see to it that the stale charges of theft would be publicly pronounced false. This was partly welcome news to Funk. But to admit even by implication, that is, in coming back into the fellowship by accepting the right "hand" of a bishop, that the church had had a right to exclude him, was what he could not, or would not, do. At least not unless the church would conduct the inquest he had demanded nearly three decades earlier.

Since the reconciliation that Gross and Ruth had sought seemed blocked, half a year later Funk took an initiative of his own, and appealed to Henry Hunsicker of Skippack. This bishop at first gave his caller "but little for an answer," but soon sent word that he would bring the matter up at the approaching spring council at Franconia if Funk desired it. Christian did, but Hunsicker first tried to work with his fellow-bishops for a more private resolution. When nothing was said at council, one of the ministers remarked, "I thought Christian Funk's affair was to have come before us." Moderator Gross tried to lay the matter aside by replying that it would be brought to the Council for approval after the reconciliation had been privately arranged for. But now the topic was on the floor, and easygoing Bishop Hunsicker felt obliged to tell the group that the estranged bishop had offered to come back if his old critic Jacob Oberholtzer would simply "make an acknowledgement" in front of the conference. This "gave much pleasure" to the assembled group of some thirty ministers, "except for about four." Old Deacon Rosenberger said that if Christian were taken back as a member, he could not keep his bishop's role. This was immediately "contradicted" by Hunsicker and the other bishops, who were followed by Jacob Oberholtzer saying that he had not repeated his original charge of theft against his former bishop.

This gave Bishop Hunsicker some hope, and he called on Christian Funk with what he believed was acceptable "advice." "If you will allow yourself," he said, "to be received by the hand, then we will state to the congregation [the whole Mennonite community] that the charge of theft is nothing but a fiction...." Hunsicker pressed his case home: "What a pleasure," he urged, it would give if Funk could only consent to that symbolic authority of the church. After all, it was not a matter of who had been right, the Whigs or the Tories. It was a matter of what it meant to be a brotherhood in Christ. But Funk was unbending, "I could not," he replied, "put my soul under the ban." His thought here seems to have been that being received "by the hand" would be admitting a guilt he did not feel for himself or his people, so that it would falsely reflect on his and their integrity.

"No ban shall touch you," pleaded Bishop Hunsicker. Punishment was not the point. It was rather that the church's authority to "keep house" could not be compromised. But Funk stood his ground. It definitely was the ban, he said, since it was "not customary . . . to receive any one by the hand unless he [had been] under the ban." Were the Mennonites of Skippack, Funk continued, going to allow a ban to lie on the Funkite "defenceless congregation" in a way similar to the ban between the Mennonites and Amish for the past eighty years?

"No," replied the disappointed Bishop Hunsicker, and left his stubborn neighbor. Thus ended the second attempt to reconciliation.

A third try a year later (1806) began with Funk's own deacons talking to Hunsicker, asking for a reconciliation in view of the "uneasiness" the split was causing among their young people who were marrying into the main body. This time Hunsicker invited Funk to come himself to the upcoming "meeting of ministers" at Indian Field (Franconia). Funk's account of this episode takes us directly into a spring session of Franconia Conference. He and five other Funkites found themselves seated with thirty ordained men from the main body. His mind went back twenty-eight years, to when he had stood just outside "this door in the night," deciding whether to go back in and "make an acknowledgment." He recollected how he had done so, but had found his speech considered insufficient, and how he had then been both "silenced" and excommunicated. Ten of the "established ministers" who had either participated in that decision or helped to apply it later were now gone; there were six new faces in the group, who might be appealed to. One of them was Jacob Gross, now the moderator, and telling Funk, "You are at liberty to speak."

The controversy-scarred veteran arose and rehearsed his twenty-eight-year story in emotional detail. Some of his audience had been small children when it had all begun. He might have accepted a reconciliation by this time, he stated, had it not been for the condition of his "laying the ban" upon his own soul by seeming to accept the church's earlier discipline. What a price had been paid for the schism! "Brother ministers, know ye not how our Menonist congregation hath been disturbed these twenty-eight years in Connestago as well as in Skippack?" If we ask some of our members why they are inactive in their church covenant, they reply, "Where shall we go to? You ministers are not in union yourselves." It was doubtless a long, impassioned talk, but Christian ended it by saying, "You may now decide what answer you will give me," and walking "quietly out" with his supporters so that the Council could deliberate.

When the Funkites were called back in, the Council first knelt for prayer. Bishop Gross then informed Christian that they were "satisfied" with what he had said to them, but that since the earlier bishops had now passed on, the present ones would "not readily say that the ban was quite right, nor that it was wholly wrong." The "deceased brethren . . . kept house according to their judgment, and we will keep house as we understand it." What the present Council wished was to get a new start, without rehearsing the whole controversy. If Christian could promise to accept whatever the "Indian Field congregation" would "impose" as conditions for his reinstatement, it would all be over. This looked so promising to a relative of Christian's, Minister Jacob Funk, that he said "it would be settled in a quarter of an hour" if it was his to do.

But Christian flatly refused any such conditions. "I cannot give myself up," he retorted, "to the people who proclaimed me these twenty-eight years the man under the ban, and these twenty years a great thief and cheat." He, not the Franconia congregation or the Council (Conference), would set the terms of his reconciliation. And when Bishop Gross raised another topic—the status of the ordinations Funk had performed when he had made his son John a minister and his son-in-law John Detweiler a deacon, Christian was completely unyielding.

"They are two upright men," he stated; "if you reinstate peace with me, you must receive us all." If the Council felt that the Funkite leaders had not "kept house" well enough since the schism, that would have to be overlooked.

Then, to the "astonishment of all," a breakthrough occurred. Old Minister Jacob Oberholtzer, an original opponent of Funk when they had been neighbors and fellow preachers at Franconia, went quietly up to the seventy-five-year-old outcast and, in evident sincerity, asked his "forgiveness" for his past actions. Christian "met him" in the same spirit, and they then "gave each other the hand accompanied with the salutation of a kiss."

Seizing the moment, Moderator Gross said that if he himself had done wrong against Funk or his followers, he would also ask forgiveness. Then came eighty-one-year-old Deacon Henry Rosenberger, likewise a former arch-critic. Finally, "all the rest who were present" followed suit, and the Council "parted in peace" from what they must have felt was a historic session. Reconciliation had come after twenty-eight bitter years!

But on the following Sundays, as the bishops announced the new accord in several meetings, they heard expressions of dissatisfaction. Apparently a number of people could not agree with what their ministers were trying to do in relation to this old, scandalous feud. Bishop David Ruth, having come over from New Britain to declare the peace at Franconia, Funk's old congregation, found his message "rejected" there, and went home "dissatisfied." Some of the Franconians also severely criticized their aged deacon Henry Rosenberger for the new move. He then traveled to Deep Run, bypassing his own Bishop Ruth, to talk to Conference Moderator Gross, and attempted to organize a congregational meeting at Franconia. Funk was invited to this, but arrived only to find it called off at the last minute. Still trying, the bishops polled the five congregations which made up the district around Franconia, and found that only forty-five out of 163 members were ready to accept Funk back without requiring him to give his "hand," thus recognizing the church's discipline.

This set the stage for the final attempt at reconciliation—a meeting in the home of Funk's son-in-law John Reiff, in Towamencin Township. Bishop David Ruth was there with his deacon, Markus Fretz, to bring a report on the recent poll. One hundred and eighteen out of 163, Ruth said, would require Funk's acceptance of "the hand" before he could return. At this one of the Funkites asked what the status of John Funk and John Detweiler would be, if their leader consented to the terms offered.

"John Funk dare not to preach," replied Ruth, "nor can John Detweiler [now a miller on the Funk homestead at Indian Creek] be a deacon."

The questioner then asked what would be required of those people who had married into the Funkite fold. The answer was that they too would have to publically accept "the hand."

"Do it!" urged Bishop Ruth fervently; "it will give great pleasure."

But Christian Funk protested that this being received "by the hand" was a step backward. The Council had already given him their hands at the Spring Conference. Why must there be another step?

"The congregation determined so," replied Ruth, once again standing by the collective rather than individual preference. So Christian tried that tack too. He asked Ruth to add the "thirty" ministers who had given him their hands at conference to the "forty-five" out of 163 voters who were not requiring "the hand." This made seventy-five who, in effect, experienced "peace" with Funk as things now stood. In his own flock were fifty. Adding them to the seventy-five made 125 who needed no further reconciliation—a slightly higher total than the 118 who had voted to require "the hand."

"If you do not agree," said Bishop Ruth, "you will break the peace."

"No," countered Funk, "the 118 will break the peace [which] the thirty [ministers] concluded with me."

As a last effort, and surely with considerable sadness, Ruth proposed that Funk take four weeks to reflect, before making a complete refusal.

"You need not give me a single day," was the crushing reply. What the "thirty ministers" had concluded at conference was already "a perfect peace," and Christian Funk would accept no more requirements. Ruth, with such a disappointing report to take back, felt that even the "forty-five" might now no longer stay in "peace." Funk replied that he couldn't help it if they "broke" it. Ruth said he himself would keep it, and Funk testing what he meant, asked if he could share with him in celebrating the Lord's supper the following Sunday. When Ruth predictably would not consent, the meeting was at an end.

It was also the end of attempts to conclude a peace, though Funk still proclaimed that he had hopes. Three years later, in his late seventies, he was again writing a narrative of the troubles, "out of love and encouragement" to his little "defenceless evangelical congregation."[66] But before long he died with the schism unhealed, leaving his mantle of leadership to his son John. The latter was not of his father's caliber, except in political contentiousness. His family would recall that he "took to speculating" in the boom times a few years after his father had died, and, having been "sold out to the walls," moved out of Montgomery County. The advice his sons ironically remembered was commercial: "Buy land, boys, buy land!"[67] Others of the Funkites now presented their founder's writings to the public in both German and English (1813, 1814), under the title, *A Mirror for All Mankind,* and erected at least four small meetinghouses, at Franconia, Fricks, Towamencin, and Evansburg. But they remained a tiny and spiritless minority, lasting only a generation before transferring to the Dunkers or a new splinter group, the "Reformed Mennonites," spreading out of Lancaster County. The very last to remain in the Funkite fold would be several sons of Deacon Jacob Moyer of Lower Salford, on whose farm one of the meetinghouses was built. Local people nicknamed them the "Moyer People."[68] The Towamencin meetinghouse was given to the Dunkers, and the one at Evansburg eventually disappeared, leaving a forsaken graveyard to intrigue local antiquarians.

What justification is there for the disproportionate attention we have given this painful story, coming as it does through the distorting lens of one of its main partisans? One reason is that Funk's narrative, slanted as it may be, is unique in giving us detailed access to the personalities of the community we are considering. Another equally valid reason is that the dynamics of a schism are a commentary on what a community finds important (even though the survival rather than the difficulties of the community are the main story). This particular controversy, ironic in a group stressing "love," both reveals weakness and allows us to observe how the community functioned to remain faithful under threat. It failed in keeping an aggressive, independent thinker in a constructive relation to the main body. Unable to "contain" him and his gifts, or to win him to yield his will to the congregation or "Council" (conference), it felt constrained to deny him leadership, and then membership. His attitude was seen to be a fundamental threat to the essence of the fellowship, less, ultimately, in his political leanings than in his insistence on following his own lights whether or not the brotherhood consented. Undoubtedly he was smarter than most, if not all of his fellow members. Certainly his opponents were merciless and exaggerated in their gossipy criticism, which the church was later ready to pronounce as based on "a fiction." Surely resentment over his self-assertive manner became uncharitable anger.

But "keeping house" in the community of Christ, or "maintaining the right fellowship" which reflected the humility of Christ, was almost the original theme—the basic identity—of this spiritual family that had such difficulty with Christian Funk. When we are considering this topic, we are as close as we can get to the central thread of our story. The requirement of mutual yieldedness, considered by the majority to be a primary feature of their spiritual heritage, could not be suspended when convenient. Funk himself charged the church, not without grounds, with not using the literal procedure of "Matthew 18," which was to deal with an erring brother personally before involving the church. This order, claimed Christian, had been violated in his case, and in that consisted a great wrong. But the main community, on the other hand, was concerned more with symbolic attitude than technicalities of procedure. Its leaders held to the authority of the assembled body to discern and declare that one of its members was out of order and out of fellowship. Without this prerogative, the old deeply felt brotherhood would have had to change something of its essence.

When an individual, however superior in insight, could challenge the authority of the church to define what reconciliation would require, one would have another dynamic than had been worked out two and a half centuries earlier. When the Anabaptist fellowship had first covenanted into a church, it had spoken of the concept of "the rule of Christ," an "order" that depended on mutual recognition of the church's authority and submission to it. This had become a recognizable tradition, and the special "feel" of it was still predominant in the central district of the "Skippack" Mennonites. Nearly three quarters of the members of five congregations polled felt that Christian Funk could be reinstated only after publicly recognizing the authority of the church to call him to account. This shows where the center of gravity lay in the community. It was not even superseded by the "authority" of the ministers. Eventually more room would be made for individualist initiative. A newer model of democratic procedure would supervene on the older ideal of mutual resignation. But that too would not come about without strong resistance, and an even greater schism.

All through this era, Canada, western Pennsylvania, and now Ohio were continuing to lure emigrants from the filled-up farmlands of eastern Pennsylvania. The David Histands of the Vincent area felt that not all of their ten children, born between 1785 and 1809, could "stay near home." Two sons moved to Northampton County, two daughters married Lancaster men, and one son, David, rode horseback to Canada in 1816. Upon his arrival he "planted" the willow whip he had brought from home. Other emigrants, having walked up to Canada behind Conestoga wagons, now walked back to visit relatives, and Bucks County Mennonites did the same in the opposite direction. Sometimes such trips were in quest of marriage partners. Henry Oberholtzer, who came back from Westmoreland County to claim a bride from a Meyer family at Deep Run, was kicked by a horse and died shortly before what was to have been his wedding day.[69] Emigrating to Canada in the half-decade 1806-11 were families from all across the "conference" area, such as (in the order of their departure) Philip and Esther Bliehm, John and Anna Schowalter, Abraham and Magdalena Clemens, Bishop Jacob Gross's son Jacob, Cornelius Pannebecker, and Abraham and Alice Schantz.[70]

The last-named family pronounced Canada too cold, and moved back in 1811 to their home community near Coventry. A few years later they would join a new Mennonite colony north of Pittsburgh. News from the latter region could travel back and forth with people like Isaac Fretz of Tinicum Township, who had teams on the road carrying freight north and west from Philadelphia. One westward disappearance is recorded in a humorous notation in a Bible owned by Abraham Ziegler: "In 1809 in May, Betz moved to the Juniata with Bill Ziegler, and the Lord knows when they will come back again. It doesn't matter, either."[71] Another western traveler was forty-eight-year-old Minister Jacob Nold of the Swamp congregation, who traveled as a visiting preacher through Lancaster County in the fall of 1813, accompanied by Deacon Abraham Wismer of Deep Run. Nold, at least, also looked into the frontier settlements across the Pennsylvania border in Ohio.[72]

The biggest Mennonite land purchaser in western Pennsylvania was probably Abraham Ziegler, who in 1814 formed a land company that included three of his brothers, his brother-in-law Preacher John Boyer of the Hereford congregation, Henry Buckle, and David and Jacob Stouffer. They bought some 9,000 acres north of Pittsburgh from a Christian community named the "Harmony Society," a group of hardworking German mystics under the leadership of "Father" George Rapp. Although the Rappites had already built three villages with sturdy homes, shops, and a church, they had been inspired to move on to the Ohio frontier and get another, purer start. In 1818 Abraham wrote back to his parents that a Lutheran pastor, "to whom we sold the town of Harmonia, is bankrupt and has run away because of debts, and I have taken back the land and the town."[73] Preacher, later Bishop, Boyer got 1,088 acres, with his sons and son-in-law, and they were able to get established. Boyer would later be remembered walking barefooted to meeting, to preach. Other Mennonites moving to this settlement included the Abraham Schantzes of Coventry and two Yoder families from the Saucon congregation. Soon a significant cluster of Easterners would make "Harmony" a recognizable name in Mennonite awareness.

Preacher Jacob Nold, of Swamp, also moved west, but went forty miles farther into Ohio, where he had earlier visited. He remained in touch with proprietor Ziegler, who wrote home that "Old Noll is quite satisfied in this country." At least four of Ziegler's Mennonite colony built stone houses at once, and, by 1825, they had erected a substantial meetinghouse after the Eastern pattern. Ironically, though their church would eventually die out under the leadership of Abraham Ziegler's elderly son Joseph, this building would survive as one of the finest remaining examples of an early "Skippack"-type meetinghouse. Its historic graveyard would contain stones carved with names basic to Montgomery, Bucks, Berks, and Lehigh counties.

Abraham Ziegler, trying hard to lure settlers to his community, engaged a German tailor. From him Abraham ordered a coat to be made in "Mennonite" style (1819).[74] This meant that its collars were not to be so full that they would lap over, as the modern fashion was. At this time Pennsylvania's Mennonites were apparently not receiving young men into membership except with the older, less fashionable style of collar. About a decade later this would be given up as a requirement for baptism.[75] The line would rather be drawn for new ministers, who would be required to wear the older pattern, with standing collar. Elderly men in the community wore the old breeches as well, at least into the mid 1830s. The coat question was also an issue for Dunkers and many Quakers. In the 1840s it would figure importantly in a major division in the Franconia Conference.

Relations with the civil government were another continuing topic of concern. The persistent fines for nonparticipation in the militia might feel burdensome, but it was simple to draw that line; no one would be tempted to call himself a Mennonite and a bearer of arms. Nor would a Mennonite be allowed to serve as justice of the peace, which required the administering of oaths. Those sons of Mennonite families who did so serve, such as David Kulp, storekeeper of Towamencin, or Ralph Stover of near Deep Run, did not join the Mennonite fellowship. Not so well defined was the township office of "constable," which seems to have been passed around reluctantly among local farmers, and need not, in these years, involve forcible arrests. Thus we find Abraham Alderfer of the Salford congregation sharing this office in 1811 with his "Irish" neighbor Neddy Flynn.[76] Also not forbidden was serving as representative to the Pennsylvania legislature, as did Henry Funk of the Springfield congregation in 1808-9, and other Mennonites in subsequent decades.

The neighboring Dunkers were perhaps even more scrupulous on such points in these years. At their annual meeting at Coventry in 1813, when the newspapers were full of "gloomy" news "in the kingdom of this world" and political vitriol, they decried the "party spirit" of American society. The printing shop of one of their own former ministers had been vandalized in Norristown.[77] Since there was such ill feeling between political factions, they decided "it would be much better not to vote at all for such offices, for as long as there is such a division, we will render ourselves obnoxious . . . on one side, we may vote on whatever side we will." With the same emphasis on being a "defenceless" people as the Mennonites had, they felt "electioneering" and even voting might be an inconsistency: "We might, perhaps, help to elect such as would afterwards oppress us with war." The Christian's role is in another sphere. "To pray diligently for our government we believe to be our duty and most pleasing to the Lord."[78] Such a statement seems identical to what the Mennonites of "Skippack" generally believed. It surely would have been embarrassing for them to be identified with the Funkite minister (John, son of Bishop Christian) who in 1817 was rebuked by a Norristown newspaper for "one of his political sermons"—apparently a harangue in a local house. He "had the boldness and impudence to say," reported his critic, "that no man but Federalists, Tories, and Vagabonds would vote for Joseph Hiester. We would advise him to pay more attention to his religious duties. . . ."[79] In this sentiment most local Mennonite ministers would have heartily concurred.

The culture of "the world" impinged only lightly on the completely rural Mennonites of these decades. Commercial noises were heard at both geographic extremes of the community, along the Schuylkill and Delaware rivers, as canal fever gripped some investors, and created new villages. But the proliferation of newspapers, academies, factories, and railroads was still several decades in the future. The only printed materials to appear from the Mennonites were another edition of their *Confession of Faith* in English at Doylestown in 1814, and two new editions of the 1803 hymnbook, *Die Kleine Geistliche Harfe* (1811 and 1820).

The first stirrings of a new kind of religious activism, involving "Temperance," Sunday schools, and missions, hardly touched the main Mennonite fellowship, culturally isolated as it was. One exception to this was the affluent and generous Bishop Mathias Pannebecker, miller along the Pickering Creek near Phoenixville. Not only did he subscribe to a local English lending library, and memorize the New Testament in both German and English; he actually anticipated the first Temperance organization of the neighborhood. This group, gathered mainly from Quakers and Dunkers in the Green Tree School House across the Schuylkill from Mathias's home (1817), protested the time-honored practice of supplying liquor to farm laborers, especially in the haying and harvest season. Bishop Pannebecker had been known to espouse the anti-liquor position before his death a decade earlier.[80] Also illustrative of new tendencies to organize Christian concern or activity, crossing denominational lines freely, was the first Sunday School in Norristown (1817). A year later emerged a Baptist missionary society in Hilltown (1818). It was typical of such groups to begin by drawing up a constitution, which gave impressive structure and protocol to the group's functioning. The sense of rationality and spelling out of organization would not reach into the folk-mind of the Mennonite fellowship for another quarter-century.

Nor would there be any significant change in the schooling patterns until a new state law would begin its standardizing, English-based work in 1834. Boys, and to a lesser extent girls, attended school for several months in the winter. Two simple types of school sponsorship continued. Either the school was held in the meetinghouse itself, or families at a distance from such a building joined to erect their own schoolhouse and hire a teacher. The former pattern still held at Salford, and in 1818 the congregation at Swamp decided, by a vote of fifteen to eleven, to have "a new meetinghouse and schoolhouse" rather than "only a meetinghouse."[81] The private trustee association is illustrated in a school built in Hilltown in 1816, with two Mennonites—John Hunsberger and Michael Derstine— joining two Welsh Baptists as trustees.[82] In Franconia Township Minister Jacob Gottshall built a schoolhouse on his farm, and apparently supple-

mented his weaving and shoemaking occupation by teaching. His bent
toward Fraktur, in which his sons also excelled, was expressed even in
carved designs of birds on the partition of his barn's threshing floor.[83]

One of the most interesting Fraktur pieces of this era is by Deacon Rudolph Landes of Deep Run, in February of 1814.[84] Gracefully crowned and
framed by a symmetrical pair of carefully feathered birds and sinuous-
stemmed flowers leaving a vaselike central space, is an original poem of
seven stanzas. It turns out to be an acrostic on Rudolph's name, each succeeding stanza beginning with the next letter, until "Rudolph L" has been
spelled. The very first stanza, set in the "neck" of the vase, has one more
line than the other six. This poem must have been cherished not only by the
deacon (who may also have been a schoolmaster), but by others in the community, for we find it added to the appendix in the 1820 edition of the
Kleine Geistliche Harfe.[85] Here it has grown to thirteen stanzas, enough to
spell out the rest of "Landes." Each of the stanzas after the first one has
been expanded with a refrain, "*Und lasz mich dir stets leben*" (And let me
live faithfully to thee). The final stanza announces that the author has now
reached or passed his sixty-fifth year. This is the familiar parting or sum-
ming-up-of-life poem, as from the hand of Christopher Dock, or the later
Bishop Christian Herr of Lancaster County. Forgiveness is asked from
friends and family, and admonition given, especially to children. Rudolph's
version plays on the time-eternity, earth-heaven, "here-there" theme; it is a
developing petition, giving account of his life to God. The final stanza
changes the key word in the refrain from *leben* to *sterben* (live, die). The
poem begins, "*Rath, Hilf und Trost, O Herr mein Gott*":

> Aid, comfort, counsel, Lord my God,
> Alone in thee I'm finding;
> O help me out of all my need,
> Shine down with grace abounding.
> Here in my great anxiety,
> 'Mid foes so unforgiving,
> O let me by thy grace be free,
> And firm in thee be living....
>
> Sixty and five are now my years—
> How soon has time removed them!
> To thee, my Lord, it now appears
> How well I have improved them.
> Forgive me, Lord, the sins so sore
> Upon my record lying;
> I would be faithful to thee here,
> And firm in thee be dying.

The insertion in the hymnbook of such a poem, so conscientiously composed and embellished by an elderly deacon, suggests that beneath the practical, culturally unpolished surface of the Mennonite community, ran a potential, usually untapped vein of sensitivity and modest spirituality. Further quite persuasive evidence is the survival, in families all over the Franconia Conference area, of dozens of beautifully designed name-plates on the flyleaves of all the early editions of the new hymnbook (1803, 1811, 1820, 1848). Of course the younger generation for whom these books were so lovingly inscribed would be thereby reminded of a mind-set that, after the 1830s and the increasing presence of English newspapers, would seem quaint. Yet the Frakturs were not discarded. It is food for thought that the fragile paper on which these hearts, flowers, and birds were penned has tended to survive at a higher rate than the thick stone walls of the houses and barns being built, at the very same time, by these no-nonsense farmers and weavers.

We may observe in Rudolph Landes's hymn that there has been a decided shift away from the atmosphere of the Anabaptist songs of a previous century. In the peaceful 19th-century farm community the "enemies" are spiritual, and the struggle is seen as entirely inward. The prayer is not for the courage to endure opposition, but for forgiveness, and for assurance of a blessed death. The tendency to reflect the pietistic mood of Lutheran devotional literature is also visible in other parts of the additions to the hymnal. The very first hymn added (in 1811) stresses the love that is felt in the "newborn mind" for other Christians. It ends with a prayer that God will give peace, and an admonition: "Let us hear nothing of the quarrels and strife among brethren." Such a song was appropriate for a fellowship that had been dealing with a decades-long schism such as the one that had produced the Funkites.

Others of the hymns now speak of finding security of faith in "the wounds of Jesus," or address Jesus as the "sweet light of grace." Perhaps most significant is a hymn, not used in the Conestoga book, addressing people who are slow to come to communion. Various excuses for this are refuted. "Ach komm doch!" urges the writer,[86] suggesting that in this era there might have been felt a lack of enthusiasm for the church by some of its potential members. The "Preface" to the 1804 Conestoga hymnal had stated openly that "many of our youth" regarded the command of Christ to be baptized "very lightly," and did not submit themselves to this ordinance.

One intelligent young boy of this period, destined to become an important Mennonite leader, would never forget the pious songs of his parents' new hymnal, the *Kleine Geistliche Harfe*. Seventy years later he would recall how his "father and mother arose early in the morning, and he

made fire in the stove, and she then brought over the spinning wheel and
spun awhile yet before day, and together sang in unison, while we children
still lay in bed."[87] Two of the songs which rang in memory seven decades
later delighted in renouncing ordinary pleasures. The first asked Jesus to
"call me from the world," and the second became earnestly graphic:

Say, what help's the world	What is the golden shine
With all its goods and gold?	Of ornaments so fine?
To disappear it's doomed,	Gold is but ruddy earth,
As smoke by wind consumed.	The earth is not much worth.
What help are features rare,	What is the dye so famed,
Fair as the angels are?	That "purple" has been named?
Beauty goes to the grave;	From snails amid the sea
The roses none can save.	This purple comes to be. . . .
What help is golden hair,	Away, O world, away!
Eyes that are crystal clear?	From you there's no true pay.
Lips that are coral-red?	Th' eternal you don't fear;
Soon all of them are dead.	All your reward is here.[88]

The modern reader must be careful to realize that such sentiments, doubtless a means of coping with unpredictable death from disease, are not
particularly Mennonite. The above-quoted song appears, in fact, in the
earlier Lutheran hymnal from which many of the hymns in the *Kleine
Geistliche Harfe* were taken.

Yet world-forsaking and sad thoughts were also standard fare in Mennonite sermons. Notes of discouragement and alarm are heard in the farewell letter of Bishop Jacob Gross to his congregations at "Deep Run,
Perkasie, and New Britain" in December of 1810. This was, to be sure, written "five days before his death, when he was weak and quite wasted," but
the language of his passionate youthful letters was still at his command.
After stating his "regret" that his departure was occurring amid signs of
Christ's prophecy that "the love of many shall wax cold," he utters a melancholy cry:

> O love! O indispensable love to God and His Word, how little room
> findest thou in the human heart towards Thee and Thy Word, towards
> friend and foe! O love of the world! O lust of the eye, and lust of the
> flesh! O pride of life, how high hast thou risen up![89]

There was a special admonition to "come diligently to the public meeting
and hear the word of God . . . if not, the candlestick shall be taken away
altogether." Such pessimism, it might be observed, was sometimes a

conventionally expected note from elderly preachers. In the long series of ordained men from the Gross family at Deep Run and Doylestown it was eventually considered a recognizable trait, and produced a local phrase, "die grummliche Grosze."

But the same years which to some threatened disintegration of the "old foundation" of the Mennonite fellowship produced a crop of conscientious new leadership. The Line Lexington congregation got an impressive minister of "an uncommon power of mind"[90] during the last decade of Bishop David Ruth's life. It was John Geil, who as a young man had run away from his apprenticeship in Virginia and found a wife—Elizabeth Fretz—in Bucks County. "Six feet tall and straight as an arrow," this modest and neighborly farmer would lead his own congregation well and play a memorable role in conference affairs for half a century. Of only six weeks schooling, he had an "extraordinary retentive memory" for the contents of the books he read, in German and English. He was able to rise before an audience "without embarrassment," and bring out of his treasure "things new and old." His preaching was not the customary chanting of Scripture; it "was logical, largely explanatory, and abounded with historical facts." His calm eloquence was remembered decades after his death. As a young fellow he had been lively. Family lore claimed that he had even, while passing by the Three Tuns Tavern, accepted a dare to dance on a mirror, and left the glass unbroken. Hitching his thumbs in his trouser pockets as he talked, he would display an entertaining wit. He had a reputation for helping neighbors with their mortgage papers, German letters, or financial needs, and he would help to settle quarrels out of court. His characteristic good humor ran over in a constant tendency to be singing—as he came down the stairs in the morning, walked along the road, or even, quietly, when he fell into a lull in conversation. A good manager himself, he found himself in a position to make loans, for which he would not accept more than 4 percent interest even when the going rate went higher. Tenants liked to have him as landlord; when they paid the rent, he always met them with a discount. In matters of church controversy he would be remembered for his mildness and deliberateness.

A year or two after Geil's ordination, schoolteacher, shoemaker, and weaver Jacob Gottshall, namesake great-grandson of the first American Mennonite bishop, was placed in the same role at Franconia (1813). Though having grown up near Doylestown, he would serve as the main leader in the center of the conference area for three decades, following a similar career by Henry Hunsicker. Jacob's counsel would be sought from all sides of the conference. In 1819 we find him earnestly invited by his brother, Preacher Herman Gottshall, to visit among the Mennonites of

Northampton County.[91] A brother-in-law was a minister in western Pennsylvania, and another brother a Presbyterian elder in Doylestown. Eventually Jacob would be seen as the central authority figure in the Franconia Conference.

Over at Doylestown the Mennonite congregation got a new minister in 1818. Jacob Kulp had had his name placed in nomination by his own wife. Having grown up in Lower Salford and Hilltown, she claimed a lack of knowledge of the local men's abilities, but she was sure that Jacob would be able to preach.[92]

Most influential of all in the century's second decade was Bishop Henry Hunsicker of Skippack, which was still the leading congregation. There was by 1812 a three-generation tradition of Hunsicker leadership here. Immigrant Valentine Hunsicker, who had helped to build the first meetinghouse, had become a deacon; his sons Isaac and Henry Hunsicker had been ordained, respectively, deacon and minister, and now Henry's son John was also an increasingly respected minister of forty. People spoke of "the Hunsickers" at Skippack with respect. Another of Henry's sons, Abraham (perhaps the most impressive of all), would be ordained later, as well as one of his nine namesake grandsons, Henry Bertolet. By 1812 Henry had been a bishop for at least three decades. His fair-mindedness, his wit, his fluency in both German and English, his impressive large family of materially successful children (all of whom were staying aloof from the emigration going on around them), and his location at Skippack—the "supream court" of the conference, as one local man remarked—all underscored the authority of Henry's leadership. Even out at Conestoga, where his great-grandfather Valentine Klemmer had died on a visit, Henry's counsel was cherished, one family saving some fifty letters from him and his son John. In 1816 the last of the nine Hunsicker children had been established on a farm or in business in the community. The youngest and brightest, Abraham, that year married Elizabeth Alderfer of Salford, and they moved to a farm near the famous Perkiomen Bridge. Before long, they would present Bishop Henry with the youngest of the nine grandsons with his given name. Henry had a way with these children, delighting them with mint-drops from a cupboard near his chair in a corner, or giving a namesake two silver dollars.[93]

Still vigorous in his mid-sixties, the bishop confessed to having "few unoccupied days." Traveling to preach at a lonely schoolhouse at the northern edge of his district (later Schwenksville), saddling up with his wife at three o'clock on a Sunday morning for a communion visit to Germantown, dealing with the quarrelsome Funkites, ordaining four men in two weeks, baptizing a class of nine here and another of thirty-three there, preaching the funeral sermon for the last local Indian squaw, writing letters of spiritual counsel—such was his busy shepherd's life. All this was expected to be done in addition to overseeing a normal farm's activity. Now, of course, Henry's son Garrett had taken over the farm on which his parents still lived. A relative once said to the bishop that it was hard to see how he could afford all this time for church work. "Why don't you pay me then?" was the humorously challenging reply.[94]

One of his acquaintances out in "Lancaster" was a thirty-six-year-old farmer, Christian Herr, one of those promising young people who had never joined the church. There had been dissatisfaction in the Pequea-area fellowship since about the time Christian had married (1800), when a vocal neighbor and cousin, Francis Herr, had been expelled from the church. The gossip was that it had been because of a shady horse deal, a charge which we might be cautious to accept, remembering the ambiguity surrounding a similar accusation in the Funkite controversy. Herr himself, and a son John, charged their Mennonite neighbors with having deviated from the teachings of Menno Simons and having become spiritually dead. The Herrs met for worship in private homes, and a spirit of animosity toward the "old" church festered with an intensity that many decades would not heal. In 1812 a separate church was organized, with John Herr as bishop, and a meetinghouse was erected. In 1815 John published the first of a number of books, which appeared the following year in English as *The True and Blessed Way Which Leadeth Beneath the Cross to Heaven....* The key words here are *Beneath the Cross.* Herr painted a very critical picture of the contemporary Mennonite fellowship, asking his readers to "view their fleshly life, their proud arrogant deportment, and their careless, cold hearts, in Divine things; their insatiable world spirit; their dealing and their way, how sensual it is in every point, almost throughout the whole of them."[95] Some of the Mennonites, he wrote, had been involved in lawsuits, contrary to immemorial Mennonite teaching. Others had served on juries, and still others had frequented taverns and race tracks. The "old foundation" of Menno Simons and a consistently "defenceless" church were being lost.

Such charges planted seeds of lifelong controversy for some, and many were challenged to examine their assumptions. It was just at this time that Christian Herr at long last became serious about his own spiritual standing. Impressed by Bishop Henry Hunsicker of Skippack, who had recently passed through the Lancaster community, Christian wrote a letter asking the older man's opinion of the Herrite charges, and his definition of "the principal doctrines of the Christian Church." The busy leader found time to answer within a few days.[96] Anxious to see Christian's recent awakening come to full flower, Henry informed his correspondent that "in spirit" and in prayers he had "often" been with him since their recent visit. Because of the seriousness of the Herrite (pronounced "Harraleit" in "Dutch") issue, Henry promised to "open [his] heart" to his "dear brother." He then listed six fallacies he saw in the Herrite, or "Reformed Mennonite" approach: (1) they rebaptize people who falsely claim that their first baptism was without repentance; (2) they forbid members even to hear other preachers, which is "sectarianism"; (3) they lack charity, which the Bible says is essential; (4) they apparently claim that Christ will imminently return, which fails to allow for the fact that the gospel must first be preached to the whole world—something which has not yet been done; (5) they falsely claim that the "old" Mennonite Church does not preach repentance and regeneration; (6) they erroneously regard the first Christian church as faultless, and seem to expect that one can have a church without spot or blemish.

Then, as the Skippack bishop comes to defining the "principal doctrines of the Christian Church," he reveals a traditional concept of the "old foundation." (1) Christ, the author of our faith, and sent by God into the world to save sinners, "reaches all who believe in him." (2) He "will be with his church," which is defined as "those who have learned meekness and humility" in his "school." (Here is the old Mennonite teaching that faith must be visible in behavior.) (3) The mandate for the church may be understood from "Matthew 5:1-12, and also the 18th Chapter." There it was again— the Mennonite reference to the Sermon on the Mount and "Matthew 18." This felt so basic, so taken for granted by the bishop, that he broke off, asking himself why he should "thus write to one who himself is taught of God." And indeed Christian Herr was on a serious quest to relate himself authentically to the covenanted Christian church. Bishop Hunsicker had not used the word "Mennonite" in his letter, had not referred, as many did, to the "pious martyrs" of earlier centuries, or even urged baptism. Yet, two years later, after "due deliberation" and "instruction," Herr would finally espouse the Mennonite church of his parents, and eventually be ordained, in sequence, deacon, minister, and bishop. He would one day fill the role in his own community comparable to Henry Hunsicker's at Skippack.

The Herrite challenge was soon felt at "Skippack" as well as throughout "Conestoga." By the summer of 1819 John Herr had traveled east to preach in Henry Hunsicker's region, and drawn "large crowds from all denominations."[97] The local Mennonite leaders, while perhaps advising against attendance, did not prohibit it. "If we did this," wrote minister John Hunsicker, "how could we blame John Herr's people for party spirit?" The meetings did raise considerable discussion, and "many" regular Mennonites in the Skippack region copied and passed around an account of a conversation between the two Herrs, John and Christian (the latter of whom had only been baptized the year before). "On the whole," reported John Hunsicker to Christian Herr, he did not think it had been "damaging to let [John Herr] come among the people." Still, he was "going to be careful in the future."[98]

The main result, as it turned out, was that a number of the Funkites, wishing to keep their Mennonite identity but filled with family-bred resentments toward the main body, found in the vigorous "Reformed Mennonite" or "Herrite" movement a new supportive structure and hope of survival. The emotional depth to which this intramural Mennonite struggle penetrated would be revealed in the surprising survival of Herrite remnants in Montgomery County at least 160 years later. They refused ever to hear any preachers but their own, and their narrowly focused Mennonite loyalties would often remind the main body, with alarm, of its own temptations to an exclusivist mentality that could contemplate a heaven to which only their own little group would be admitted. The gradually shrinking Herrite fellowship lived quietly and peacefully with the larger group it held was apostate. Old grudges were transmitted in family patterns whose origins were lost to the children who felt them, and as a result opted for membership in other denominations.

Simple as life remained in this preindustrial countryside, there were multiple spiritual currents to keep a Mennonite bishop alert. Not far from the Providence meetinghouse a Dunker preacher occasionally held forth on a Sunday afternoon in Mennonite George Brower's meadow, and a future revival would produce a Dunker congregation there. Bishop Jacob Gottschall, his predecessor David Ruth having just passed on, was asked by his brother, Minister Herman Gottshall of Northampton County, to find him devotional reading by Christian Hoburg and Caspar Schwenkfeld. Herman's greeting would have satisfied any warmhearted evangelical, with its wish that the Holy Spirit would "find in my and all your hearts a right reception and that we thereby come to a true inner recognition of our Savior."[99] Such words were of course most welcome as long as they were not accompanied by the discovery that the writer was preparing, in pursuit of an inner piety, to give up Christ's teaching on "defencelessness," or the practice of "Matthew 18."

As for Bishop Hunsicker, he was hardy enough at the age of sixty-six to make his way on a cold winter morning to his remote preaching outpost at the northern edge of his district. Not far from the farm of William Gottschall, in the hills around the former Perkiomen copper mines, was a school and meetinghouse which the Mennonites used every four weeks. Here, as at a number of other places, Lutherans and Reformed shared facilities with smaller communities of Mennonites. But at this point the local relationship was about to change. As Henry arrived, and the stove was fired up, smoke filled the small room. Someone then discovered that the pipe had been stuffed shut with wet tow. It was an unsubtle signal that someone did not want them using the building, or at least it was taken to mean that. The little congregation of Gottschalls, Hunsbergers, and Zieglers meekly withdrew, and seven men shortly accepted from William Gottschall the deed to a small plot of land on Mine Hill.[100] During that same year (1818) they selected William as their first deacon, and the little congregation was thereafter called "Gottschalls' " or "Zieglers' " (today, Eden Mennonite). Bishop Hunsicker now had four small congregations in addition to his main one at Skippack, which met every two weeks "with a full house."

Chapter 7

"The Subject of Assurance" vs.
"The Plain Duties of a Christian"
1820-1839

It was usual to hear spinning wheels humming or singing in almost every farmer's house," wrote a nostalgic Amishman of 1860, recalling his youth. "The women and daughters spent the winter spinning . . . and where this was not the practice, it would be remarked of as people who did not do their duty."[1] By 1810 Montgomery County had counted 9,987 spinning wheels in its homes, and for every thirty-one of these, a loom; 38,800 yards of woolen cloth were produced one year "in families," in this time before the cotton gin and cheap, store-bought clothing.[2] One nearly incredible report from the family of Martin Fretz in Hilltown Township calls the spinning wheel "one of the fixtures of the family." Among the ten daughters were six spinning wheels in motion at once, "commencing at 5 o'clock in the morning, and continuing until 10 and 11 P.M."[3] Hardly less impressive was the family of farmer, sawyer, and weaver Samuel Wismer, of the Deep Run congregation. His six daughters kept five spinning wheels going "while the 6th daughter done the reeling." In the summer all of them "made full hands in the hay and grain fields, and some of them assisted at the saw mill."[4]

The same industrious scene was the milieu of little Abraham Cassel, growing up in a low-ceilinged farmhouse over in Towamencin Township. "Whole families followed spinning," he would remember. It was at the feet of an older sister at her wheel that he learned his ABC's. Then, as he taught himself to read, he would sit as near as he could to the flickering tallow lamp suspended from the ceiling. In its inexpensive light (sometimes even dog or horse fat would be used) his mother and sisters plied their "three or four spinning wheels." Sometimes his father, sitting up close to the light where it was suspended from the ceiling, would pore over the Bible—the only book he ever read. This left young Abraham, nearly desperate to read, straining his eyes "in the shadow."[5]

Recalling his boyhood as an old man, Abraham could not remember a house in his Towamencin neighborhood that was two full stories high. He had been born in 1820, and had seen a generation of young people courting before there were parlors. His father Yellis Cassel had married a Dunker girl, and had moved into a house with two rooms on the first floor: the kitchen, containing the huge fireplace, and "the room," where the parents slept and the "milk cupboard" stood. Here is where everything centered, and where the women spun. The girls had to take their "beaus" into the kitchen, to the "chimney corner by the fire." When bitter winter nights found them too cold even there, the couples would sometimes crawl into bed fully clothed. Abraham's oldest sister refused, but his cousins Rachel and Catherine, daughters of Deacon Hupert Cassel of the "Plains" congregation, consented more than once. Abraham was sure of that, because when the fire had gone out on the hearth during the night, he had been sent over to Uncle Hupert's to bring back fire in an iron pot. Arriving before dawn, he had seen Rachel's and Catherine's beaus emerging from the house with their clothes full of down from the feather beds. "I knew a great many girls," Abraham would reminisce, who kept warm during courting in this manner as a "regular habit . . . and they all preserved their good moral character, their reputation."[6]

In these last decades before railroads would shock the countryside into a new consciousness of progress, the only continuously rapid movements were the swift gestures of repetitive hard work. Almost no "implements" or machinery other than wagon and plow lightened farm labor as yet. Henry Fretz of Bedminster had been nicknamed "Hurrying Hen" because of his habit of hurrying and "urging his men."[7] His niece Susanna, eighth of Martin and Anna Fretz's daughters, was remembered in her family to have "generally spun eighteen cuts of flax per day [making over three miles of yarn], and one day she spun twenty cuts."[8] Though Susanna had become, literally, a spinster, she was taken by Jacob Funk as his second wife, after his first had been killed by a neighbor's savage boar. Diligence marked a girl as desirable. Bishop Henry Hunsicker's grandson, born in 1825, remembered that "it was considered praiseworthy for girls to be on their knees scrubbing and rubbing to whiten the floors, for the whiter the floor, the greater the credit of the housekeeper. . . . Even the stone-laid paths leading to the oven and the spring came in for a share of scrubbing," and "the roadway to the barn—especially on Saturdays—had to be swept."[9]

Such a work-oriented society, only infrequently visited by newspaper or other distraction, was open to the temptations of narrowness and materialism. What persecution could not do to weaken the faithfulness of these Mennonites, peace and prosperity might. Already in 1770 a local Mennonite writer had complained that some people worked even at night, and out in "Lancaster" the talk among some Mennonites was supposed to be all "of buying and selling, planting and building . . . all day Sunday, until at and in the meetinghouse, before and after the sermon."[10] Fine three-story houses of stone were increasingly being erected higher up the slope from the earlier and smaller ones built over springs. There was still woods to clear, as original farms were subdivided among oncoming sons who did not want to go north or west.

But in all this labor Mennonites felt corrective scruples as well. Deacon Abraham Fretz of Deep Run thought that he had charged too much for a cow, and went after the buyer to refund half of the price. "I wouldn't want to be damned for a cow," he explained.[11] A vein of piety did run in some members of this family. His brother Martin took special pains to keep his children from leaving the church services before the benediction had been pronounced, as some must have done.

> Wer naus geht vor dem segen,
> Geht dem fluch entgegen,

he would repeat (whoever goes out before the blessing goes in the face of a curse).[12] Minister John Geil of New Britain was also of an exemplary spirit. Twice his cellar was robbed by poor neighbors of the "bread, pies and other provisions" his wife, Elizabeth, had put there. Once this happened on a Saturday night, so that the Geils had nothing left for Sunday morning breakfast. The minister was almost certain who had been in his cellar, but when that neighbor became ill, the Geils sent over "a good supply of provisions," leaving word that the neighbors should come and get more when they needed it.[13] A similar ethos among the Swamp-area Mennonites was remembered by one son of the West Swamp congregation who joined the Reformed Church. His people, he commented, were characterized by "sobriety, industry, non-resistance and shunning of debt. Not to pay one's debts was considered a marked disgrace, and to sue, unrighteous."[14]

A helpful corrective of possible distortion in this benevolent view may be gained by glancing into the docket book of Justice of the Peace Jacob Clymer of Lower Milford Township.[15] Our observer's own father, a miller and later a minister among a liberal branch, is listed time after time as having engaged in small civil suits. The fact is that Mennonites, or children of Mennonites, did occasionally sue. To be sure, this act brought swift church censure and even, when there was no confession, excommunication, but there was a persistent minority who felt that using the local justice of the

Yarn-winding reel made by
Henry O. Alderfer of Upper Salford in 1840. (Arlene Ziegler)

peace to collect debts was only common sense. In the next few decades
there would develop a definite grouping of such Mennonites—particularly
around the edges of the "conference" area—who would prefer to employ
this option when they felt it necessary. To the main body, on the other
hand, this was an impossible concession for a "nonresistant" people. A
certain amount of civil arbitration seemed to be allowed: Abraham Hunsicker of Perkiomen submitted a case involving the water rights to a mill he
owned, and sat as arbitrator himself when two local pastors—Lutheran and
Reformed—sued each other over the Temperance issue. But this too was
considered, by most Mennonites, a worldly business.

   For centuries the teaching had been that there were two kingdoms—
Christ's and what was "outside the perfection of Christ." Only love, or
"Matthew 18," could be used in the first kingdom. In the second, a person
had recourse to legal or civil rights, but using them meant that one had
given up on the ultimacy of the first. This is what John Rosenberger of the
Swamp area had apparently done. Having been accused of stealing flax, he
sued Abraham Sell for "assaulting abusing and thretning" him. In another

case in 1838, Abraham Shelly charged Jacob Detweiler with "falsely affirming," already in 1825, certain information "in taking the benefit of the in-
solvent laws of the state." Anna Taylor, in another kind of case common to
local dockets, accused John High of Bedminster of having had "carnal
knowledge of her body, whereby she . . . is now big with Child. . . ."[16] In
1836 the brothers John and Jacob Leatherman, also of Bedminster, could
not agree as to how close to Jacob's mill race John could plow and sow. John
cut down the willows their father had planted along the race. An attempt at
mediation failed. After Ulrich Hockman and John Overholt were also
drawn into the dispute, it was taken to a justice of the peace, who settled it
by law.[17] In all such cases, any Mennonites involved were required to make
confession or "acknowledgment" to the church before they could again
partake of the Lord's supper.

Of course, a number of young men simply joined other churches, if
they were inclined toward the political or civil arena. Mathias Pannebecker,
Jr., miller at Phoenixville and son of a Mennonite bishop, was a member in
1826 of the Pennsylvania Legislature, as was John Stauffer of Boyertown a
few years later. Stauffer was a son of the family on which the first meetinghouse of the Boyertown Mennonite congregation would be built. The
children of both the Pannebecker and Stauffer families would recall a
strong piety in their parents' character, but no teaching of a distinct,
nonresistant covenant that expressed the Christian faith in a special
"order." One of the Pannebecker sons would be burgess of West Chester,
and another of Phoenixville. Their grandfather, Bishop Mathias, had
spoken Dutch, English, and German, but they could understand only
English; the family's devotional books, now curiosities, were stored in the
springhouse, where one of the sons cut the pictures out of the old Bible.[18]
Less affected by "English" was Skippack, where members of the Tyson
family still conversed in Holland Dutch as late as 1820, as did Metzes and
Godshalks of Towamencin.[19]

An issue that proved sensitive for many conservatives was the coming
of carriages—personal travel vehicles, as opposed to the rough, springless
and white-topped farm or market wagons that had been good enough for
previous generations. At Bedminister, Martin Fretz had been among the
first to get a "Dearborn," complete with "bows" which could be fastened in
place to hold on the black top when weather made it necessary. This was
probably about the time (1824) when Abraham Krupp, Dunker brother of a
Mennonite preacher at Plains, advertised for a wheelwright "who under-
stands making Dearborn waggons."[20] At Perkiomen, Abraham Hunsicker's
new Dearborn and elliptical spring would bring the deacons to protest. John
Geil, the gentle minister of New Britain, would have been ready to get a

carriage, but kept his white-covered vehicle several decades longer in order not to offend "some weak brother's conscience."[21] In the Lower Salford of 1834, only one family had a carriage—that of Michael Alderfer—and they were of the worldly inclined generation not joining the church even after marriage. Fifty years later, Sunday morning would find the Salford meetinghouse still surrounded by white-covered wagons.

The financial depression following the War of 1812 lingered on into the 1820s. "There was no demand for anything then," remembered a Tyson from Skippack. Wheat brought less than 15 percent of what it had been worth in the boom years. The Tyson clan in particular was so hard hit by sickness and death that one of its young widows and her three little daughters had to be supported by the Skippack congregation. Another family lived on the meetinghouse farm.[22] Records of aid to helpless people were kept in the alms books of both the Skippack and Franconia-Salford-Plains-Rockhill clusters of congregations. One interesting notation in the Skippack Alms Book of 1825 is the first appearance of the German word *Vorsteher* for deacon.[23] Prior to this the term *Ältester* had been used.

The difficult times seem to have increased the frequency of emigration to a veritable stream. From all over the Franconia Conference area families—both young and middle-aged—hitched up their teams and headed north. In Perkiomen Township the family of Benjamin and Elizabeth (Detweiler) Hallman were finding it difficult to get ahead on their hillside farm. Their oldest son, seventeen-year-old Jacob, set out for Canada on foot in 1822, without any money, and carrying "only a little bundle of clothes." During the same year a forty-four-year-old miller and Funkite minister, Jacob Detweiler, who had been preaching at "Fricks," moved to a "bush" farm in Canada.[24] Two years later Jacob Hallman returned to Pennsylvania and persuaded his parents to go back with him. Though still limited financially, they were able to bring along five horses. After crossing the Niagara River on a large flat boat, they visited three days with a Joseph Rosenberger family. Later they bought 200 acres of land, nearly all forest.[25] Jacob Shoemaker, leaving the Hersteins' area for a new start in Canada, would be ordained a Mennonite minister in his new country, and live past his 100th birthday. Also moving from Franconia Township in 1822 were Daniel Hagey, who had recently declared bankruptcy, and Henry and Sarah Clemmer, who had been farming on what would later become the Mopac beef-packing plant.[26]

The years 1825 and 1826 also saw heavy traffic on the trail to Canada. Two young women, Catherine and Elizabeth Funk of Bucks County, went to visit friends at "The Twenty," and found husbands. Elizabeth married John Rittenhouse, and they made their wedding trip to Bucks County on horseback.[27] A set of three grandsons of Preacher Jacob Oberholtzer of Franconia also migrated north. Their father had been a cattle dealer who, according to varying local traditions, had died before his family had grown up. This John C. Oberholtzer had either refused to be a minister, or been ordained and then silenced for drunkenness. Having had only ten acres of land, he had left behind little economic opportunity for his sons, who now became Canadians. The oldest, Jacob, would be ordained a minister while still young.[28] Other family groups moving to Canada in 1825-26 included those of George (a "woolen manufacturer") and Maria Shoemaker and their son John (a shoemaker) and his wife; and the families of Jacob Clemens, Solomon Gehman, Jacob Kolb, and Henry Moyer.

Continuous communication flowed between the Canadian and Pennsylvania communities. Bishop Jacob Moyer at "The Twenty" sent to Bishop Henry Hunsberger of Hilltown several letters from European Mennonites that had been passed to him by Bishop Benjamin Eby. Jacob felt that the Pennsylvania Mennonites ought to respond to this rare voice from abroad.[29] In a kind of pastoral address to "all believing brothers and sisters in Jesus Christ who read or hear this, and especially all co-workers and co-ministers of the Gospel," the Canadian bishop recalled to his Pennsylvania relatives the parting admonitions of Bishop Jacob Gross of Deep Run a decade and a half earlier. "Have we followed this scriptural counsel of our old servant?" he asked. Then he reported the coming of several Amish families of Bavarian origin, who had been in Bucks County in the summer of 1826. Their leader Christian Nafziger had first been in Waterloo County in Canada in 1822, to scout out a place for settlement, and had subsequently spoken personally with King George IV in England, to ensure proper title to land for his people. Then he had come back to North America with a family or two, landing at the port of Philadelphia in the spring of 1826. A family of Bucks County Mennonites "took them into their home and gave them money, a team and a wagon for their journey to Canada." Jacob Moyer wrote that the Amish party had arrived at his place near "The Twenty" with their horses in good condition, and enough money to get to Waterloo, with a little left over. "They told me of much good that you have shown them, and seemed to be so thankful for the love that you had shown them and the leading of God that it moved me ... to tears...."[30]

Still another contact was a visit to Canada by a group including Preacher Christian Gross of the Deep Run congregation in 1827. On the return, Bishop Jacob Moyer accompanied them at least until he had seen them safely across the Niagara River.[31] The benevolent spirit of this shepherd, born in Bucks County and destined to die there on a visit in 1833, would be long remembered. "His very countenance had something unusually attractive about it," wrote a German Mennonite immigrant. "I count it as of great value to myself to have know this worthy preacher in his lifetime."[32]

The Ohio frontier too was calling dozens of Franconia Conference families. Over 500 covered wagons of emigrants bound for Ohio were counted passing through Easton in the five weeks between September 19 and October 24, 1817. Christian and Sarah (Holdeman) Wisler moved to Columbiana County from Bucks County in 1820. Several years later young Daniel and Elizabeth Tyson followed. At least four ministers joined the migration. Peter Longenecker, born in Montgomery County and ordained in 1802, and Jacob Kulp of Doylestown, ordained in 1818, moved to Holmes County, Ohio, around 1831. Within a few years both a "Longenecker's" and a "Kulp's" congregation emerged there. And from a new settlement in Medina County, Ohio, came Henry Geisinger, born in Northampton County, Pennsylvania, but later of Ontario, to fetch his uncle, Preacher William Oberholtzer of Mount Bethel, back to Ohio. A number of other Mount Bethel Mennonite families moved out around this time, including members of the Weiss and Delp families, and Minister Jacob Kappes. The three Northampton County congregations (Oberholtzer's, Mount Bethel, and Rothrock's) never thrived after this loss.

From Bedminster Township in Bucks County to Medina County in Ohio went Jacob (nicknamed "Dick Check"—Fat Jake) and Margaret Leatherman with three small children. Margaret's older sister, Sarah Leatherman, who had just become a widow after planning to come along to Ohio with her husband, decided to make the move anyway, and brought seven children, including twin baby girls. She fed them along the way with milk from a cow they were driving. Fat Jake's twenty-one-year-old cousin, Abraham Leatherman, also walked out to Ohio, bought 108 acres, a wagon and a team of horses, and built a two-room cabin. Then he drove back to Bucks County to marry Hannah Landis, and bring her back to his clearing along with her parents and their children. Abraham, whose brother Sam would be ordained minister at Line Lexington, would walk back and forth between Medina County and Bedminster six times in the following years.[33]

There were now Bergeys, Moyers, and Freeds in Holmes County, Ohio. Catherine (Mrs. Martin) Kindig of Upper Salford Township, a sister-in-law to Bishop Jacob Gottschall, moved out to Medina County with her younger children after her husband died in 1830. Before long John and Veronica Fretz of Tinicum Township migrated first to Wayne County and then Putnam County, Ohio, where they lived in a "dense wilderness" thirty miles from the nearest mill, ate corn bread, wore wooden shoes, and helped to build a Mennonite meetinghouse. In 1839 Johannes and Anna Detweiler and their two little girls headed west from Bedminster Township with two wagons pulled by three horses. The two-horse wagon carried a bed for sleeping en route. While they were crossing the Alleghenys, whose height made them feel "wierd" and "sad at heart," one of the old farm horses foundered and had to be killed. At Bedford they lost their "little yaller dog." Finally they arrived in the "wilds of Ohio," where they were greeted with a hearty supper and rest in the cabin of "Uncle Michael Myers," who had preceded them by a year or two.

Another group of families was headed northward, in these early 1830s,[34] to the Genessee County area of New York State, recently made accessible by the Erie Canal. Henry Derstine, son of Deacon Isaac at Rockhill, moved up in about 1831, and by 1835 we find Beidlers, Lapps, and Wislers there as well. John Lapp wrote back to his "Dere frends and relations one and all" with a glowing report. "A man can do better here with a lettel mony than with you with a heap." There was plenty of work "at high wages and generly cash." John already owned 165 acres of river bottom land along the Tonawanda River, with a "Fine long frame barn" and "new house part log and part frame." Visitors could get to the region "by way of Canall cheap. . . . If any of you go to Canada I hope you will give us a call."[35] In this report, Lapp makes no spiritual reference.

All through this era, as well as throughout the next century, there were ministerial visits between the "Conestoga" and "Skippack" communities (as well as to the scattered homesteading communities now pushing ever farther west). When a pair of ministers would travel, preaching appointments would be set up for them, and a series of meetings (always in the daytime) would mark their progress. These meetings were cherished by congregations for the variety they brought to the local "preachers' bench," and ordinary work would be suspended when they occurred. We may follow one such tour, a round-trip of about 200 miles in the last week and a half of October 1824. The simple records of the bishop at Franconia, weaver and shoemaker Jacob Gottshall, show him stopping first at the home of minister Johannes Hunsicker near Perkiomen (very possibly Johannes went along on the rest of the trip, although the records make no mention of this). Then the party traveled forty miles to the home of one Jacob Rutt in the Weaverland area in Lancaster County. After five visits in this neighborhood, they went on to Groffdale, then west, stopping at congregations as far as Donegal Township. There were at least twelve visits in the first week. On the way back there were stops at "Mellinger's" and a visit with Bishop "Henner" Martin at Weaverland.[36]

Certainly one topic of discussion among the visiting ministers and their hosts must have been the emerging "Herrite" or "Reformed Mennonite"

Der evangelische Botschafter

Eine monatliche Erbauungsschrift für den christlichen Landmann,

Herausgegeben

von

Heinrich Bertolet,

Prediger an den menonistischen Gemeinden in Skippack ⚹

Motto: Ein Säemann soll der christliche Prediger sein; aber sein Acker liegt in den Herzen seiner Gemeinde; Sein Same ist Gottes Wort.

Part of the title page of "the first Mennonite periodical in the world," *Der Evangelische Botschafter*, dated July 1, 1836. "The Evangelical Messenger," a monthly devotional magazine for
the Christian farmer, was published only one time, by Heinrich Bertolet, "Preacher at the
Mennonite Congregation in Skippack." (Author's Collection)

communion. A family of Swartleys living next to the Franconia meetinghouse was moving into the Herrite fellowship at this time. One of their
sons-in-law, John George Ernst, moved into the Franconia community from
"Lancaster," as a Herrite minister. After his wife, Anna Swartley, died (she
was buried at Fricks in 1838), he would for some reason be expelled from
the Herrites, and move back to Lancaster.[37] Jacob Gottshall's own brother-
in-law Martin Kindig seems also to have followed the Herrite emphases;
before his death he had sent the bishop a long, mournful, hymn-quoting
epistle largely drawn from John Herr's writings, alleging that the "Old"
Mennonite Church was spiritually dead. "Ach Gott Ach Gott!" he expostulated, accusing Jacob of dereliction in his spiritual oversight.[38]

The charge that Mennonites lacked "inner religion" could come from
a variety of angles in these years. Jacob Gottshall had a nephew in Ohio,
Minister John Funk, who was beginning to preach too much like a Methodist to please some of his congregation. In Virginia a schism threatened
over the preaching of Frederick Rhodes who, under the influence of the
"United Brethren," had become passionate and loud in his sermons. In
Bucks County an evangelist named Frederick Plummer gained a large
following who called themselves "Christians."[39] Philip Fretz, of Mennonite
parentage, was one of the trustees who helped to build one of their new
meetinghouses, at Carversville. In addition, Methodists and Baptists began

to hold woods and camp meetings, or "protracted" evangelistic meetings in churches. There was a Methodist meeting place on the Allentown Road in Towamencin Township, next to the Rittenhouse farm. Here and there a Custer or an Allebach or a Rosenberger learned to testify in the emotional manner of the revivalists. All such joined the new evangelical movements. And the Dunkers too had a revival near Providence, drawing in descendants of Mennonites.[40] Back at Franconia, George Delp, the Mennonite song leader, transferred to the Dunker congregation at Indian Creek. A new Dunker meetinghouse ("Klein's") was then built at an old Dunker grave-yard near Delp's farm. One person representing a move in the opposite direction, from Dunker ancestry to Mennonite, was the eloquent preacher at Plains, John Krupp.

We must not think that the Mennonites were alone in dealing with such challenges to their inner unity. The local Reformed churches split decisively (though not permanently) over the question of a seminary. The Lutherans at Pottstown divided over whether or not to use English in church. The Quakers split too, in 1827, and the Schwenkfelders expelled members who grew so "evangelical" as to kneel to pray in public. Literature from mission and tract societies in both English and German began to appear, bringing, at first, sharp reaction among Lutheran and Reformed traditionalists. Few Mennonites were reading this material at the moment. Sunday schools were attacked as mere proselyting ventures.

These decades produced a number of good leaders in the "Franconia Conference." An unusually thoughtful young farmer and weaver, Abraham Gottschall, was ordained in 1824 at Doylestown. A nephew of Bishop Jacob Gottschall, he would prove capable of articulating the essential Mennonite views of such favorite "evangelical" topics as "justification" and "regeneration." Another young minister, Henry Bean of Skippack, "soon went far ahead" of his fellow preachers, and was enthusiastically praised by his younger hearers.[41] Abraham Halteman was a forceful new leader at Vincent, a more ready speaker than his aged father at Salford. John Geil, whose illustrative materials ranged easily through the Scriptures and ancient history, was in his prime at Line Lexington.

But there were troubling disappointments, too. At Hereford, a man refused to pass through the casting of lots, and when it then "fell" on John Z. Gehman, the new minister felt he had not been God's true choice. On occasion he would read to the congregation out of Jacob Denner's *Betrachtungen*. And before many years had elapsed Henry Bean of Skippack, proud of his abilities (according to his critics), had fallen into what the bishops called "gross sin," and was "silenced." His replacement, Elias Landes, proved a poor speaker,[42] and a sizable part of the congregation was resentful that it could not have Bean back. The fact that all was not well in the congregation seems to be reflected in an experience of the Tyson family. A little girl had died of scalding while John Hunsicker was away—probably on one of his tours through Lancaster County. The Schuylkill River was too swollen to cross, and there was no bridge closer than Pottstown for the "Chester County ministers" to use. At the funeral, probably at the Providence meetinghouse, there seemed to be no leader present who could give an audible prayer. Deacon John Gotwals did "read a chapter in the meetinghouse," but there was nobody to "pray or sing or exhort."[43] Though the bereaved young parents did soon join the Mennonites with their relatives, they eventually opted for a group with a more expressive religion—the "River Brethren."

A revolution in transportation patterns was already underway in the 1830s. The resounding blasts of boatmen's horns had been heard along the twisting Schuylkill Canal for little more than a decade when a more important invention—the railroad—began to creep northward from Philadelphia. The first "train" of nine cars, each pulled by a horse, got as far as Germantown in June of 1832. A crowd of 30,000 people watched this epoch-defining procession. In five years a tunnel had been bored at Phoenixville, not far from the home of Mathias Pannebecker, Jr., wealthy Mennonite miller and one of the main agitators in an unsuccessful attempt to get the railroad on the west side of the Schuylkill. Before the end of the decade a spark-belching steam locomotive was hauling a train a day all the way from Philadelphia to Reading and back, at a top speed of twelve miles an hour. It was the phenomenon, the myth of the age; travel was now a thrill instead of a chore. When the horses of a Mennonite family gave out on their way from Canada to Bucks County for a visit, in 1839, they were able to pursue their journey by a sequence of facilities that would have seemed luxuries or dreams when they had first emigrated: "railroad, canal steamboat and the mail coach."[44] In only fifteen more years the "Franconia Conference" area would be penetrated through its geographic center by a north-south railroad that would create a string of new villages, and expand stagecoach stops into towns. But as yet, where a depot and then a town named "Souderton" was destined to appear, there were only a cluster of farms and a sawmill, called by the historic name of "Welshtown."

Railroads, turnpikes, and bridges might be generally welcomed, but cultural changes, such as in language and education, were more sensitive to Pennsylvania's Mennonites. They had not previously needed to develop new strategies to transmit their covenant-teachings. That transmission had been taken care of by the principle of *Handel und Wandel*—the simple observance by the children of their parents' labor, manners, and beliefs. But this worked only when the community could "have the children to themselves." This protecting distance had been provided earlier by persecution, and more recently by rural isolation. The only sources of children's awareness beyond the home were church and school, and these were all one—extensions of each other. The school was often held in the meetinghouse (as was the case in the 1830s at Franconia, Salford, and West Swamp), and the teachers were local, German-speaking men who taught hymns, prayers, and Scripture in German, as the basis of the curriculum.

Even this could be felt as superfluous, or a threat, by the most conservative "plain people." Yellis Cassel of Towamencin, who never read a newspaper in his life, was severely frightened by his son Abraham's fascination with books and reading. If allowed to run its course, he felt, it would only make Abraham an infidel, and he tried whippings, depriving Abraham of candles, and giving him extra work.[45] Less spiritual was old Benjamin Alderfer of Lower Salford. The *Vorschrift* he had received from his schoolteacher at Salford in the 1790s had begun with a hymn stanza, "Humility is the weapon/Against the Devil's Power." But Benjamin's concern about schooling was that too much of it, or reading, represented time "cheated" from work. At least that was the way his grandson interpreted his stern talk.

Benjamin's son-in-law Abraham Hunsicker was of another opinion; he saw education as a blessing rather than a curse, and dreamed of sending the rising generation of Mennonites to school. This well-to-do butcher, marketman, farmer, and general community leader was a progressive in every sense of the word. In 1832 he tore down the "low and squatty" old schoolhouse across the Turnpike in front of his house near "Perkiomen Bridge" (later Collegeville), and joined his neighbors in erecting one more pleasant for the children. His son Henry's disparaging recollection of the older facility provides us with a valuable historical picture of the early Pennsylvania schoolhouse. Surrounded by woods (on the site of present-day Ursinus College), the fifteen by twenty-five foot log building measured "from 7 to 8 feet from the floor to the loft beams."

> The interstices daubed with clay; low, narrow sash with 8 × 10 panes fixed tightly in the body of the logs, served as windows. The desks were hung to the logs around the dingy room; the benches of rough hewn slabs of oak with no backs. No provision for ventilation except as the door opened or perchance through chinks or crevices of the logs.[46]

Young Henry Hunsicker learned his ABCs here, from 1830 to 1832. In the latter year his father transferred him, at the age of ten, to a new academy in the nearby village of Trap.

Abraham Hunsicker kept abreast of educational developments on the wider scene by taking two of the many new local newspapers—one in German and one in English. He was recognized as a man generally proficient, whether in helping the pastor in the nearby Lutheran Church by "giving out the words of the hymn," "bleeding" neighborhood people without charge, or allowing two men from New England to manufacture a new device called a "threshing machine" on his property. He developed a surprisingly fluent English writing style, without parallel among other Mennonites. In 1835 he erected a stylish house along the turnpike, and by the time his youngest son was born in 1843 he was ready to name him for the great Massachusetts educator, Horace Mann.[47] Eventually Abraham would fulfill a dream of building a "seminary" or academy for young Mennonite men, and another for young women. Before that would happen, he would have helped to lead the progressive wing of the Mennonite fellowship in parting ways decisively from the more traditional majority.

The other main proponent of progress who would figure in the forthcoming drama of division could be found, in 1824, teaching in a one-room school in Berks County, several miles up the road from the Hereford meetinghouse. John Hunsberger Oberholtzer, a few months short of his sixteenth birthday, had his hands full with a set of unruly sons of a local farmer, John Ritter. The latter had tried the money-saving experiment of building a schoolroom as a second story of a pigpen on his farm. Pupils other than his own children also attended, paying tuition in accordance with the old "subscription" arrangement. The bright young schoolmaster was frustrated, from time to time, by the wiles of the Ritter boys. When displeased with their teacher's discipline, they would go down to the pigs and stir up the "swill-barrel." The resulting storm of grunts and squeals would force Oberholtzer to suspend classes. Dissatisfied with the prospect of a lifetime of schoolteaching, Oberholtzer learned the crafts of a "blacksmith and locksmith" as well, and for a time earned his living in a combination of endeavors.[48]

The name of this schoolteacher was destined to be as widely known as that of any other American Mennonite in the first two centuries after 1683. With Abraham Hunsicker, who would leave the Mennonite fellowship a few years after being ordained as a minister, John Oberholtzer was one of the more fluent in English of American Mennonite leaders up to his time. Even in German he had a way of speaking that sounded different from the traditional Mennonite preaching. Short of stature, he was ambidextrous, and his family would remember him as so adept with a pen that he could write two different sentences simultaneously, one with each hand.[49] He had little knowledge of nor interest in the past. He would later imagine that the reason his forefathers had not taken interest in education, as he hoped his present generation would, had been trouble caused by neighboring Indians. But he did not know what his grandparents' life had been like, or even his grandmother Oberholtzer's given name. As an old man he realized that he had never learned how the Oberholtzer family had come to Berks County (his great-grandfather had immigrated from the Palatinate sixty-seven years before he was born).[50] In this John Oberholtzer, who kept very much abreast of trends in his own day, was probably representative of people in his era.

After teaching school for nine years, at the age of twenty-four John married a woman five years older than he, Mary Biehn of the "Flatland" area just east of Quakertown. When the Mennonites of Swamp and Springfield built a meetinghouse there a few years later, he provided the locks and shutterbolts. By this time Mary had given birth to both of their two children. The older, a son named "Davy," was a bright boy, with many of his father's best qualities, but also destined to bring his parents disappointment and grief. John later characterized his wife, Mary's, lot as one of "unendingly many illnesses and sufferings, along with manifold difficulties and woes. . . ."[51] Their other child Anna was born in 1836. About this time John gave up schoolteaching entirely in favor of the work of a blacksmith and locksmith in Lower Milford Township, where his family attended the West Swamp church. The longtime leaders here were Bishop Samuel Musselman and Minister "Christel" Zetty, both nearly seventy. Recently, in 1832, help had been sought for the aging leadership team, and the lot had fallen on a forty-year-old newcomer to the congregation, Jacob Hiestand. A native of Vincent in Chester County, Hiestand had moved up to the small Mennonite community at Mt. Bethel in Northampton County, farmed there for a decade, and then, as the Mennonite community eroded, started again in the Swamp area. Here too, however, he would not find a permanent home, and when he would move on to Doylestown a decade after being ordained at Swamp, the latter congregation would need to have another ordination. That one would change the life of John Oberholtzer, his congregation, and the Franconia Conference.

Another Mennonite schoolteacher of the 1830s was the son-in-law of Bishop Jacob Godshall at Franconia, Henry Neiss, or Nice. Five years older than John Oberholtzer, Nice represented, with his three or four Godshall brothers-in-law who were also schoolteachers, attitudes more common to the central districts of the conference, where the Mennonites were more thickly settled. He would still be teaching German enthusiastically, and evoking lusty German singing from local pupils, as an old man. Both he and Oberholtzer would be ordained ministers in their thirties, and each would

become the key spiritual leader in his district. There would be correspondence between the two men over basic differences in the way they
viewed the Mennonite fellowship. Whereas Oberholtzer would seek to in-
novate, Nice, also a miller and farmer, would work at preserving elements
of an older ethos. His bachelor brothers-in-law Martin and Samuel Gottschall would perpetuate the art of Fraktur with particular zest and delicacy.
A painted drawing of Adam and Eve attributed to Martin, apparently done
in the 1830s, would be considered by collectors of the 20th century to be
one of the finest known examples of the art. A stunningly decorative piece
of Fraktur which either Martin or Samuel apparently gave as a reward to a
pupil contained a lovely verse, expressing in Blake-like simplicity a
confession of aesthetic and theological stirrings in the heart of the traditional Mennonite schoolmaster. The verse's affectionate air seems appropriate to the family of Bishop Jacob Gottschall, whose descendants kept
alive until well in the 20th century the local schoolmaster's song, "Preceptor They Title Me."

> Wenn Mir ein schönes Kind begegnet
> Dasz Gott Mit schönheit hat gesegnet,
> So fallen mir Gedanken ein
> der gott der so viel schöne sachen
> Aus einem blosen nichts kont machen,
> der mag wohl noch viel gröser sein.
>
> (When I a beauteous child may meet,
> Whom God has blessed with beauty sweet,
> Thoughts come that I can not forget:
> The God who from nothing at all
> Such teeming beauty forth can call—
> He must be so much greater yet.)

This piece of folk art, so modestly done and presented, was given the lavish
honor of a magnified reproduction on the large poster announcing an
exhibition in the Philadelphia Museum of Art, October 17, 1982, through
January 9, 1983: "The Pennsylvania Germans: A Celebration of Their
Art."[52]

Into the quiet scene of these church-controlled or parental association-
administered schools came, in 1834, a new Pennsylvania law, making
schools free, tax-supported, and directed by a state-wide, legislated
philosophy. It was part of a nationwide trend. Fostered most fervently in its
beginning stages in Pennsylvania by two politicians who had been born in
New England, it was a severe jolt to many German-speaking citizens, and
certainly to the "majority" of the Mennonites. A comprehensive system of

county divisions and township districts was designed. A fund of some $2,000,000 was held by the state in escrow, from which the new "Free School" legislation promised substantial subsidy to those townships which would provide for election of directors, and a local school tax.

The purpose of the law was to make certain that "the poorest child of the poorest inhabitant of the meanest hut" in Pennsylvania would not be deprived of a basic education. But its taking the initiative away from parents and church brought a storm of protest. At first only one township in Montgomery County approved the new system. All of the townships with large Mennonite population dragged their feet, and heated discussions arose. Although a progressive like Abraham Hunsicker appreciated the promise of enlightenment, his fellow-member of the Skippack congregation, George Detweiler, sternly disapproved. The Hunsickers even thought it would be good for ministers—Mennonite ministers—to have some education. George Detweiler insisted that God, in his sovereign power, needed no such human assistance. If God willed, he could "make a post preach."[53] The Hunsickers never got over that statement, nor the spelling on the ballots of some of the local people who voted "No School": "Now Skule." What better proof could there be that there ought to be school now, free and state-supported? Yet it would be eight years before Upper Providence Township accepted the state subsidy slowly accruing in escrow, and Salford and Franconia Townships, where almost everyone was German-speaking, were two of the very last to capitulate, sixteen and seventeen years after the law had been passed. This was finally acceptable to the Franconians in part because three of the newly erected "directors" were Mennonites, and the curriculum could include what had always been most important. In the words of the Franconia directors hiring a new teacher, he was to offer "Die Zwäy Ersten monat die Deutsche übung als Singen bäten lesen Buchstabieren und schreiben u.a.w. [The two first months the German practice, such as singing, praying, reading, spelling and writing, etc.] and the two Last Month the Inglish Branches all Common books."[54]

German-speaking people as a whole felt uneasy about the trend to English-dominated schools. Delegates from a dozen townships in Montgomery County came together in protest meetings at Skippack demanding that all state laws be printed in German as well as English. In solidly German sections, they held, only German should be permitted as the language of the courts, and where the population was mixed, the officials should be persons who could understand German. Many of the Germans in Pennsylvania, they argued, had come there for freedom of conscience. They should be recognized as valuable to the country and deserving of the right to their own cultural choices. It is "to their endurance, their industry, their activity, we, their descendants, owe the flourishing condition of agriculture, which distinguished Pennsylvania so favorably from so many of her sister states." Among the delegates to the gathering which issued these statements were some Mennonites: Christian Souder, later a public school director in Franconia Township, as well as Isaac Fried of the same community; schoolteacher Henry Johnson and his friend, song leader Henry Kolb, both of the Skippack congregation; and Jacob Kolb, farmer of Towamencin Township, soon to be ordained a minister at Plains.[55] The resolutions were reported favorably in a German newspaper from the village of Sumneytown, where a German-language academy would be organized, and be publicly endorsed by Minister Jacob Kolb of Plains.[56]

These mid-1830s brought with the encroaching English language a growing political ferment which inspired a set of new newspapers in the expanding villages and county seats. From Doylestown, already the source of a number of short-lived papers, came a new German one, *Der Bauer*. It appealed directly to the interest of the German-speaking farmer concerned for his way of life. Its editor was twenty-year-old Joseph Jung from Lehigh County, where the descendants of Mennonite immigrant Valentine Jung were numerous. Later, *Der Bauer* would be renamed *Der Morgenstern*, be edited (1848-84) by a Bavarian Jewish immigrant named Moritz Loeb, and become a great favorite of Mennonite readers across the Franconia Conference area. This and a new paper at Skippack, the *Freiheits Waechter*, took up the current Anti-Masonic party label—a sign that political ideology was penetrating the rural districts with new force. The Skippack paper also campaigned for the benefits of education. Up at Hereford, a culturally isolated Mennonite farmer like Abraham Gehman reached out rather eagerly toward such sources of information. From time to time he subscribed to the *Friedensbote* or the *Lecha Patriot*, both from Allentown; and the *Bauernfreund* from Sumneytown. In addition to these, he tried an English newspaper, and a publication called the *Christlich Zeitschrift*. Also widely read in his community was the Reading *Adler*.

In another decade or so, sons of a growing wing of liberal Mennonites would actually publish English newspapers at Doylestown. The distant cousins Samuel and Edwin Fretz, neither a member of his parents' church at Deep Run, would edit, respectively, the *Bucks County Intelligencer* and the *Bucks County Express*.[57] But before that, already in 1836, one of the ministers in the Skippack circuit made an abortive attempt to found a Mennonite paper—perhaps the first such attempt in the world. The forty-year-old publisher was one of the nine namesake grandsons of Bishop Henry Hunsicker, who died in his eighty-fifth year, in the very month the new paper appeared from the press a mile or two from his farmhouse. Henry

Four tunes with three-part harmony from the singing school *Notenbuch*, dated 1826, of schoolteacher Henry Johnson of Skippack. Whereas the texts are familiar German hymns and spiritual songs (e.g., *"O Wie seelig sind die Seelen!"* and *"Schwing dich auf zu deinem Gott"*), the tunes are obviously named with local reference. Johnson's books contain at least one tune designated as "composed" by Skippack song leader Henry Kolb. (R. Walton Johnson)

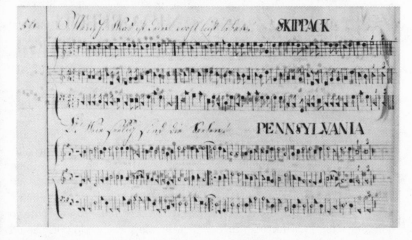

Bertolet came from a family of Huguenot background which had earlier "leaned toward" the Mennonites, but not joined them until his father Abraham had married a daughter of Bishop Hunsicker. Now Henry, listed as a farmer and drover in New Hanover Township, had apparently been ordained for the preaching point at "Herstein's." With no backing or sanction from the Mennonite community, he responded to the new tendency to publish with a sixteen-page paper, *Der Evangelische Botschafter* (*"The Evangelical Messenger"*), which he informed his readers was especially intended for Mennonite readership. He wished to bring together the themes of faith and agriculture, and subtitled his paper, "A monthly Devotional for the Christian Farmer." Printed in the office of the new *Freiheits Waechter*[58] at Skippackville, this magazine-like periodical had two sections. In the first would be "general discourses on godly things" and news on the affairs of the Mennonite congregations. The publisher expected future issues to contain notes of marriages and deaths in the Mennonite community. The second section would have articles on gardening and farming; instructions for vine, silk, and tobacco culture (there was a silk-craze at the moment); and—a sign of the time—news of "inventions and improvements in industry and agriculture." Bertolet hoped to have as agents "all of the preachers and deacons of the Mennonite congregations in the whole Union."

But the first sample printing of 2500 copies was the last. The paper fell so soundlessly into oblivion as to suggest a complete lack of Mennonite appreciation or approval.[59] This was 1836, and even in 1852, when still another *Botschafter* would appear and survive for a few years, it would be produced by a person who was not in the old framework of the "Franconia Conference." Henry Bertolet left no other trace of his interests on Mennonite records, and thus did not represent any real readiness by his people to have their own paper. Personal initiative such as he had taken was doubtless interpreted as mere forwardness. We hear almost nothing again of the Bertolet family until 1847, when a Mennonite meetinghouse was built for and by them in Frederick Township.

Also affecting some liberal Mennonites was the heightened political campaigning of these years. John Hunsicker, who followed his father in the bishop's office at Skippack, had an oldest son, Joseph, in the lumber and coal business at Black Rock, along the Schuylkill River below Phoenixville. Joseph's political involvements grew until, in about 1835, he was appointed an associate judge, sitting at court in Norristown—an activity that would have required his father to exclude him from the Mennonite communion. Shortly thereafter a severe economic depression occurred, causing banks to fail, and some local factories to pay their employees in scrip, nicknamed "shin-plasters." Just then a Constitutional Convention was being held in Harrisburg, where miller Mathias Pannebecker, Jr., among many other delegates, sought to modernize Pennsylvania's legal charter. This convention dragged on for months, and was eventually complicated by a controversy that began with the election of a Bucks County Mennonite as county commissioner.[60]

The man in question was forty-four-year-old Abraham O. Fretz, an "extensive" weaver of coverlets and a farmer, then or later from the Perkasie or western Hilltown area, and a member of the Rockhill congregation. In the hotly contested elections of October 1837, when Abraham Hunsicker of Perkiomen also was a candidate (for director of the poor) but lost, Abraham Fretz won by a margin of twenty-five votes out of a total of 6,547 cast. He had run for the office of commissioner of Bucks County, on the "Federal, Shin-Plaster, Abolitionist ticket." His opponents, of the "Democrat" party, complained bitterly that at least thirty-nine of Abraham's votes had come from "Negroes" in Bucks County. Had these Negroes been denied the vote, Abraham would have lost by fifteen votes. Negroes had no legal right to vote, argued the "Democrats," and their doing so constituted an "invasion" of the "sacred rights" of the white citizens. This they felt they could prove "in a court of Justice." Abraham was called before the Bucks County Court of Quarter Sessions, where he denied that he had been illegally elected, but the president judge of the district ruled that Negroes had no voting status in the state of Pennsylvania. This issue was then heatedly discussed at the Constitutional Convention going on out at Harrisburg, and to the shame of that body, it finally voted to insert a new adjective in the wording of the old 1790 document: the word "white" was to be added between the words "every" and "freeman," in the original sentence, " . . . Every freeman of the age of twenty-one years . . . shall enjoy the rights of an election." Mathias Pannebecker, Jr., was one of those arguing against this racist restriction.[61]

Abraham Fretz, whose tenure as county commissioner seems to have lasted only two months, would be ordained, four years later, as a Mennonite minister in the Rockhill congregation. After briefly resisting some of the requirements of the nonconformist, nonpolitical Mennonite tradition, the new minister would be won over to a strong advocacy of them. (The claim that he later was Bucks County treasurer has no support in fact.) On the other hand, Abraham Hunsicker, a man of the same age, and who had been a candidate in the same public election season, would also be ordained a Mennonite minister, but would be led more deeply into political activity, and out of the Mennonite covenant-community.

We may note that although Mennonites disapproved of slavery (certainly Abraham Fretz welcomed Negro voting), they did not become involved, like the Quakers and a few Dunkers near the Schuylkill, in the fiery abolition agitation. An actual station on the "Underground Railroad" was set up by the Quaker Lukens family on their Towamencin homestead (near the present-day Christopher Dock High School). But the only record of even token involvement of the Mennonites in this kind of activity was their not forbidding the use of the Providence meetinghouse for a lecture on abolition by the young orator Salmon P. Chase, "the attorney general for runaway negroes," in the winter of 1838 or 1839.[62] Bishop John Hunsicker's son Joseph, the judge who was no longer a Mennonite, "opposed abolition" in favor of colonizing the Negroes back in Africa. It would be nearly a century before there would be black members of the local Mennonite congregations.

These political issues and involvements were in a sense not hard for the Franconia Conference leadership to warn against. Noisy "county meetings" prior to election time had a worldly spirit easy to point out and condemn. What was more of a challenge was for a spiritual shepherd to declare why his people should not accept the logic of the various religious revivals playing across Pennsylvania's general populace. When, in centuries past, the danger had been cruel persecutors, Mennonites had known how to persevere in their faith, and help each other. But in an era of no persecution, when a variety of impassioned and persistent preachers, making no reference to the Mennonite sense of a covenanted community based on "Matthew 18," told the Mennonites that their religion was "dead" and "cold," another kind of response was needed. "Evangelicals," followers of the Lutheran revivalist preacher Jacob Albright of Berks County, reaped a harvest of conversions in the Upper Milford area in 1833 and following years. These people were a kind of German Methodists, though without that name. "Christians" or "Campbellites," Baptists and Methodists held meetings, indoors and out, all over the countryside. Only in the geographic center of the Franconia Conference, where Mennonites were in some places almost a majority, were they not much affected, and even there the Dunkers played a modest version of the same "evangelical" role.

In this generation, as in every subsequent one, there would be preachers pointing to the undemonstrative, tradition-flavored, family-bound and work-oriented Mennonites, and telling them that they lacked the vital spirit, an inward passion, a warmth of heart, a personal assurance of salvation, or a particular and narratable conversion "experience." In congregations which had spiritual leaders like John Geil, John Krupp, or Henry Nice, such evangelical allegations seem to have had little permanent effect. Controversy over the subject of baptism arose in these years, and another edition of Bishop Henry Funk's 1744 book, *Ein Spiegel Der Tauffe* (A Mirror of Baptism) appeared in 1834, again without a publisher's name. John Geil listened to the growing discussions, but remained silent for a long time, before taking a regular Sunday morning service to "set forth the teaching of the Gospel and the views of the Church" on this topic, in a calm and convincing manner.[63] But around the edges of the conference area the logic of the evangelicals took firmer hold. A John Rosenberger joined a Methodist Class in Upper Providence,[64] and a John Rosenberry of the Skippack area was named a preacher by the Evangelical Association.[65] Hannah Custer, also of Upper Providence, "related to the [Baptist] church the dealings of God with her Soul,"[66] and was immersed in the Skippack. At Doylestown the Mennonite minister Abraham Gottshalk began to ponder the themes of "justification" and "regeneration," as constantly raised in camp meeting preaching. In Ontario, too, camp meetings were drawing Mennonites to gatherings of 600 to 800 people.

We may catch an echo of the neighborhood discussions in a talk between two converted Schwenkfelders of the Upper Milford area, where a part of the Mennonite congregation too would be won over to "evangelical" logic two decades later. The two Schwenkfelders were returning from an evangelical meeting one night, when

> they came to a large chestnut tree . . . at which their ways diverged. There they stood, at said tree, all night discussing the subject of assurance until the day dawned in the East. They quoted Scripture passages, the Catechism, old spiritual hymns, passages from Tersteegen, Schwenkfeld, A Kempis, and others and discussed them. Finally Daniel Kriebel made the declaration that if one's religion is genuine and Scriptural, he must know it and feel it, for the Psalmist has said,—O taste and see that the Lord is good—Psalm 34:8. And thus this important matter was decisively settled by these two men.[67]

This emphasis on "experiential" or "experimental" religion, and the set of pietistic sources quoted, were not the program Mennonites had originally started with: following Christ and carrying his cross, sharing with the brother and sister, and maintaining the right fellowship. The very fact that the narrator of this incident relates that something "important" was transacted under the chestnut tree shows the difference of conception between his outlook and an Anabaptist one. From the latter point of view, something of equal importance still lay in the future: the behavior which would provide the evidence that something important had indeed happened. Nostalgic accounts of "glorious conversions" and talk of how one knew and felt the sensation of regeneration still left undiscussed crucial areas of obedience, in which the presence of the kingdom of God was acknowledged. It was in the mutual yielding to Christ within a disciplined covenant that the Mennonites "felt" their religion. It hardly occurred to them to discuss the emotional states that accompanied this yielding and mutuality, as subjects in themselves.

But the evangelicals continued to preach and sing about conversion, and there were indeed Mennonites who needed it. Some had only inarticulate or reluctant ministers, with little guide but tradition. Preacher Christian Gross of Deep Run worked in a continuing somewhat pessimistic mode. As he wrote a letter of counsel to his recently ordained brother in Ontario in 1839, he bemoaned the spiritual condition of his congregation. He felt his calling was "a hard office and duty, especially here at this time because with many the mark of a true Christian is extinguished. . . . It seems that up to now all advising, effort and labor was fruitless. The adversary has gained the upper hand. . . ."[68] At the same time another Gross brother, Johannes, recently ordained minister at Doylestown, was finding preaching a difficult task.

But Johannes's fellow pastor at Doylestown, Abraham Godshalk, was just in these years uttering a clear Mennonite challenge to the encircling evangelicals. This weaver and farmer, now in his middle forties, was the father of six children. In apparently poor health, he had "often" turned over in his mind a conviction that the "rather generally accepted teaching on faith and justification" that one heard in revivalistic sermons "might not have the desired outcome of making the person righteous." Eventually Abraham found himself so strongly "motivated to express the light" that he felt he had "on this matter," that he gave his thought "over to the judgment" of the public in 1837, in a sixteen-page pamphlet entitled *Wahre Gerechtigkeit Vertheidigt* (True Righteousness Defended, or a Demonstration of How One Is Really Justified by Faith).[69]

In these pages, comprising the first spiritual essay published in the Franconia Conference since before the Revolution, we meet a mind that is both open to the logic of the New Testament and bound to the Anabaptist view of world and church. Abraham Godshalk could hold in his imagination, as a collection of threats common to the Christian Church, European persecution, Herrite exclusiveness, and pietist emotionalism. A person must "marvel," he exclaims, at the strange "ways and means" that are used to "win people and keep them together" in a church: "Force, withholding of the Holy Scriptures . . . the rejection of reason," and "the prohibition of listening to others."[70] Abraham's own wish was "to win or hold no one except through the conviction of the truth." What he wanted to do was present a balanced view of the Scriptures, which contained, as he understood them, "the most reasonable teachings in the world." Dramatic preaching on the mystique of "assurance," or fine-tuned exegesis on "justification" that did not involve a call for righteous living made the question of holiness more complicated than it really was. After all, according to Christ's simple teaching,

> If you see a person who, in all his words and works, doing and behavior is holy, you may know that this person has the Holy Spirit. For by the fruit one learns to recognize the tree. Again, if you feel in yourself a sor-

row for your sins, yes an abhorrence of evil, and a longing for what is good and holy, you have a measure of the Holy Spirit.[71]

Obedience as a way of knowing and testing the truth, rather than savoring inner emotional discoveries, is what interests Abraham as the essence of "real" faith.

Unfortunately, as a Virginia Mennonite minister also observed in this decade, a certain kind of "glorying in conversion and repentance" is too often unaccompanied by certain necessary "good fruits." Such "evangelical" teaching, Abraham feared, might even have the effect of holding "the person back from true righteousness."[72] It is not enough to stress faith. "Faith must bring forth good works. . . . Justification by faith means a true justification, a true repentance, yes a true rebirth, and not simply an imputing of the righteousness of Christ, without a change in the sinner."

In Abraham's "Pocket Book of Memorandums" is a prayer which further expresses essential attitudes of his Mennonite tradition. Much like his first cousin John Geil, who "in his public prayers . . . never forgot to pray for the young people,"[73] Abraham expresses to God a "special petition . . . for the youth" of the land. While he does not ask that they receive a glorious conviction of the reality of their conversion, his prayer is "evangelical" in its own way.

> Give unto them the Holy Spirit and a true and living faith in the power of thy word, so that they may all be formed into a church which shall be a light in the world and salt of the earth, and that all may finally have eternal life. . . .

"That they may be formed into a church": the body is as important as the individual, in Abraham's conception, and the character of that body is a part of the gospel witness. And then, adapting a prayer from the closing page of the *Martyrs Mirror,* Abraham mingles the nonresistant, quietist faith of his Mennonite teaching with a kind of American patriotism.

> We also pray for those who bear rule in our country, this glorious America, the people of which enjoy liberty of conscience and of worshipping God according to the dictates of their conscience. Bless these thy servants with wisdom and with the desire to glorify thee in their official life.
> Grant that thy church which is without external weapons, may have the protection of the government so that she may fulfill her mission among the people, leading men who sit in the darkness of sin and unbelief into the light as it is in Christ Jesus. Lead us in the path of righteousness so that we may be no offence to them, cherishing fully the liberty which is guaranteed to us. May this liberty be also the heritage of our children, and grant that none of these that bear rule may be

eternally lost but that all may come into life, through Jesus Christ, thy
beloved Son, to whom be praise and glory, now and in all eternity.
Amen![74]

As his illness grew serious, the forty-five-year-old preacher continued
to meditate diligently on the current evangelical challenge, and worked out,
partly on his deathbed, one of the clearest statements of American Mennonites on this topic in the first two centuries of their witness. This time his
thoughts filled a small book published in both German and English, in
separate volumes, entitled *A Description of the New Creature*.[75] His aim
was to describe *true* spiritual rebirth. He did not label his teaching Mennonite, nor even mention that name in his argument. One thing regeneration is not—and here he shows his cautious Mennonite attitude—is
"fanaticism." It is rather "a most sober and rational thing, and he that has it
will show [it] in all his conversation." As in his previous pamphlet, he
defines regeneration not in terms of emotions accompanying it, but as "a
change in man" that involves "putting on Christ by faith." This "is not
merely to believe that he is, but to receive him" in "doctrine" and
"example," as well as in accepting his "merits." If we do this we will certainly repent and then "pattern" ourselves after Jesus. Anyone who has
"truly put on Christ cannot otherwise than love God, and his brothers...."
And a person who has this true love, which he shows by keeping God's
"commandments," is "indeed a New Creature."[76]

The belief that Jesus is the Christ is now preached everywhere in the
land, observes Abraham, "and we are brought up to it from infancy." But
this by itself is "a kind of a dead thing." A "true and living faith embraces
Christ whole"—that is, by identifying with Christ in his behavior as well as
his "merits." So many preachers are talking "against" the "moralist, equat-
ing him with the self-righteous Pharisee, that I honestly fear many are
thereby hindered from being moral, and made so fearful of self-righteousness, as not to become righteous at all."[77]

Before he is finished, Abraham comes to "such truths as some will not
readily receive...." These are truths one will not hear preached by the
soul-stirring revivalists, or taught in their instruction classes, but they are
truths right out of Jesus' teaching. Some readers, Abraham writes, may find
his little book "very rigorous, and a poor comforter.... I say my sincere
aim [is] to make it just as much so as the holy word of God is in itself, when
fairly brought together, and no more...."[78] Thus when it comes to discussing "one of the hardest commandments of Christ, namely, love your
enemies," the Doylestown preacher speaks candidly and firmly. No amount
of rejoicing in conversion can replace obedience to this plain commandment.

It will not do to plead too great a degree of ignorance, for if we have not yet learned the plain duties of a Christian, we are not yet grown up . . . in Christ, for knowledge is wherein the Christian grows as much as in anything: neither will it do to plead too much weakness, for the young man in Christ is strong, and the word of God abideth in him . . . . [79]

Preacher Gottshalk's description of a truly regenerated young Christian spells out the Scriptural logic behind Mennonite attitudes toward the government:

. . . The young man in Christ, or the completed child of God, doth not resist evil: but if any one smite him on the right cheek, he turns to him thy cloak also [sic] . . . . He loveth his enemies.

He is subject unto the higher powers . . . or the government under which he lives. In all things that are not against the law of God. But if his government should require him to do that which his God prohibits, he cannot yield absolute obedience, knowing that "the powers that be are ordained of God:" and consequently not equal or superior, but inferior to God; wherefore he most rationally concludes, that the law of God is paramount to all human laws, and therefore finds himself bound to obey God first; and if the government under which he lives should be offended at this his conscientious course, he will fly to a milder region if he can, and that by permission of [Jesus] . . . . And though he cannot always yield absolute obedience to his government, yet he passively submits to all grievances, without rebellion, or violent resistance; and is therefore least to be dreaded by a government, of all men. [80]

"I am a farmer," Abraham had written in his introduction, "who was at a pretty early day [age thirty-three] called to be a preacher of the gospel, and who has not even had the advantage of a good common education, and have therefore not the power of writing in a polished style . . . ."[81] His book was written, according to its printer, when Abraham was "bound to a sickbed" with "only a faint glimmer of life" remaining[82]—a condition which may suggest to us a tradition including Minister Hinrich Kassel of the Palatinate in 1681, and a deacon at Deep Run as late as 1969-70. Nothing of his illness is mentioned by Abraham Godshalk himself in his book. He wrote his will on June 15, 1838, and died two months later, shortly before the book was published. He left a wife and six children, three of whom were under fourteen years of age. The oldest, Samuel, who had just turned twenty-one, was appointed an executor of the will. He would be a well-known schoolteacher, song leader, and minister at Deep Run. The dying Preacher Godshalk requested that each of the children receive, from the proceeds of his estate, "a new suit of clothes, not overly costly or gay." The crowd at his funeral arrived in a procession of wagons that stretched from his house at Doylestown to the meetinghouse, a mile away. The meetinghouse being "entirely too small for the assembled congregation," the services were held under a large walnut tree.[83]

Perhaps some in the crowd remembered that the last preacher whose body had been interred in this cemetery had been David Evans, who died in the year that Abraham had been ordained, 1824. Evans was an aged Universalist minister, the first and only one of his persuasion in Bucks County, who had gathered a small congregation in New Britain.[84] We may speculate that his death, at the age of eighty-six, had found him a pauper, and that it was this that had motivated the Mennonites to allow his burial in their cemetery. We certainly find, among the Mennonites themselves, little echo of Universalist ideas. Yet they could not have been entirely absent in the persistent discussions of the times. In 1838 we find a thirty-two-year-old Skippack man writing to his "Friend in the Lord," schoolteacher Henry G. Johnson of the Skippack congregation, a request for his "Opinion About the future Ixistence of our souls.... You know the Universalist creed and ground is that all as soon as Removed Enjoy Eternal happiness."[85] Others, writes Garrett Bean, promise "Universal Salvation" after some preliminary punishment. And the

> 3rd and last class say If they do not die in peace with god and man and as a Christian aught to die then hell will be his Portion he will be cast in Everlasting and Unquenchable fire and there remain Yea 1 week 1 Year 1000 Years Millions of Years and again millions &c &c Now Your Candid and Cool Opinion is what I would like to Receive And Also about the Baptism how it is to be performed & how far Salvation can be obtained by it & whether it has to be Obeyed Strictly—

This is not only a different language than that of the old "Preachers' Bench" at Skippack, but a different intellectual agenda as well. From here on the guardians of the "Old Mennonite Foundation" would discover that simple reiteration would not capture the imaginations of the whole of the oncoming younger generation.

Bean's letter had opened with the request that Henry Johnson, local music teacher, send back "with the Bearer ... the Bass of the hymn Commencing 'In the dark woods no Indian nigh' " (a currently popular revival song purporting to be the conversion testimony of an American Indian). The request for the "Bass" line shows that in 1838 the use of "part singing" was an accepted enjoyment. In fact, one of Henry Johnson's own beautifully decorated singing school books had been sketched out already by 1826. Another contained at least one anthem with a bass line composed by

Henry Kolb, song leader at Skippack, and also a schoolmaster and maker of fine grain cradles. Other three-part compositions bore titles like "Perkiomen," "Pennsylvania," "Skippack," and "Hilltown." In 1830 Kolb, the *Vorsinger* of the Skippack Mennonites, had a small organ made for him by John Ziegler, also of Skippack. Kolb used the organ at home, rather than at meeting, where singing was still in unison rather than in multiple voices. But he also led the singing at a nearby Reformed church, and his son Garret would be an occasional organist there. Something of the intense interest taken in singing in these years can be detected in the recollection that Garret Hunsicker, youngest son of Bishop-John, could "sing by note any piece of music by sight."[87] This six-foot-two singing schoolteacher married a local Baptist girl in 1839, a sign that Bishop John Hunsicker's family was not inclined strongly to Mennonite loyalties. A cousin of the Hunsickers, inn-keeper Henry Longaker of nearby Perkiomen Bridge, who never joined any church, had been elected sheriff of Montgomery County.

The camera had not yet begun its documentary work in Pennsylvania by the time this chapter must close. But the memory of schoolteacher John Oberholtzer informs us that the young Mennonite men who were candidates for baptism were no longer required to wear the old shadbelly coat.[88] Quakers at the new Haverford College were stricter than this. Their catalog stated crisply that the student's "body-coat, round jacket and waistcoat shall be single-breasted and without lapels or falling collars."[89] Coats were no issue at all when Mennonites came to Sunday meeting on a hot summer day. Here our picture is painted by the memory of Squire John Boorse of Towamencin. Nearly everyone came walking along the roads or "in single file on paths across the fields," "the entire family always . . . together." All of the clothing was homespun and handmade. None of the men wore coats, and all of the fifty to a hundred people, except "a few old women," were barefoot. Gathering in the meetinghouse yard, they would wait until the minister arrived "in a white-covered wagon." After the service, as the men came back out into the yard, "the first remark would be, 'Who can strike fire?'" After someone had produced "flint steel and punk . . . the men would light their pipes and cigars . . . and have a general social talk."[90] This post-meeting picture would remain unchanged in basic outline for another century.

Other quick glimpses come to us from a visiting minister who preached at Skippack in the spring of 1839—Jacob Krehbiel of upstate New York near Buffalo. Bishop John Hunsicker, who had "made the opening" (given the first pre-sermon meditation), sat next to the speaker in the pulpit in the old stone meetinghouse, which was doubtless crowded. At the close of the meeting Hunsicker said to his guest, "You have spoken a few minutes less than an hour." Surprised, Krehbiel asked the bishop how he knew this. Hunsicker replied that he had checked his watch, and that preachers at Skippack "usually spoke about this length."[91] Krehbiel, an immigrant eight years earlier from the Palatinate, had other friendly visits in the community, with elderly leaders from Salford, Franconia, and Rockhill. One topic of conversation that particularly intrigued him was the beginning of the Mennonite fellowship in Pennsylvania a century and a half earlier. The old ministers, and especially Deacon John Lederach of Salford, could still tell stories of this. They claimed that "the first preacher of the Mennonites in America was chosen [by casting lots] several thousand miles distant from the congregation," in Europe. Deacon Lederach even told his visitor that "the documents dealing with this matter were still preserved in Germantown." Lederach had often thought that he should ask for these papers, to be kept for historical reasons "in one of our congregations in Montgomery County." The Germantown congregation seemed at this time (1839) to be on the point of "dissolution," and "without any particular connection with the congregations in the neighboring counties." Krehbiel asked whether the remaining members at Germantown would give up such historic papers. "Without hesitation," replied Deacon Lederach.[92] Unfortunately, there is no record of any such transaction ever occurring.

Jacob Krehbiel, who became a bishop this year in the Ontario Mennonite Conference, was pleased with what he observed in his visit in Montgomery County. After returning to his home he wrote back to John Lederach and "all the Brethren at Salford, Franconia and Rockhill," commending them for the "harmony" and "brotherly love" which seemed evident among them, "as much as I could see."[93] Krehbiel had good reason to find the topic of harmony important. His own people in New York were disturbed at the moment by the Herrite controversy, and the European Mennonite community he had left eight years earlier was also tense with a continuing polarization. In 1836 Palatine Mennonites had experienced a kind of schism when some congregations had substituted a new catechism for the older *Christian Conversion on Saving Faith* by Gerrit Roosen (still in use in Pennsylvania). There were other issues involved, some of long standing. What is of interest to us is that these same issues would agitate the Franconia Conference, and produce, within the next decade, an even more decisive schism than the one in the Palatinate, where so many second cousins of Pennsylvania's Mennonites still lived.

Already in 1775 a Palatine leader had complained about men refusing to take their place in the casting of lots for ordinations. This "disobedience," he asserted, was "making serious inroads in the Palatinate."[94] The conservative bishop Johannes Galle (first cousin to the Geils and Kolbs of Pennsylvania), led the traditional side. He blamed the troubles on a lack of submissiveness to the discipline of the church. The people "marry where they want to," he said, "and walk on the broad road."[95] There was also in these decades a movement away from the original practice of nonresistance, which had been affirmed by concerned leaders meeting at Ibersheim in 1803, but was increasingly not accepted by the younger men. One Mennonite historian from the Palatinate would later observe that around and after 1800 "Mennonitism" in the Palatinate "underwent a radical change." In one important Mennonite village a "prayer-house" was built, modeled on a Baptist chapel in England, where the new pastor had studied for the ministry.

A new desire for academically trained preachers, as opposed to members called out from the ranks of the local congregation, was a sign of this substantial change of mood. The debates tended to be between people like Johannes Galle, who vigorously opposed the new "prayer-house" as an expression of pride and style, and progressive-pietist men who nicknamed the affluent old bishop "Rich Galle," and said it was time to stress inner devotion and let the outer form take care of itself. By 1848 there were "mission meetings," fostered by ministers like Jacob Ellenberger of Friedelsheim. He not only encouraged his members to subscribe to the *Evangelical Messenger to the Heathen,* but kept a tin box for mission contributions.[96] Another voice on the progressive-pietist side came from North Germany, where a young pastor who had recently studied at a university and a pietist *"Missionhaus"* in Basel wrote a letter of inquiry to Canadian Mennonites. Expressing deep concern over the state of their fellowship, Carl Justus van der Smissen asked about the quality of their spiritual life. His longest question dealt with the opposition between faith and works. In an ensuing letter, he wrote sadly that he had heard that American Mennonites were superficial in their catechetical instruction, and put great stress on the "external."[97] He asked no questions about the traditional Mennonite concerns of nonresistance, separation from the world, or church discipline. His letters have importance for our story in that they eventually caught the attention and disturbed the feelings of John H. Oberholtzer, who would write back to the European Mennonites in terms of almost precisely the set of concerns of this pastor. Van der Smissen's 1840 letter seems, indeed, to lay down an agenda which Oberholtzer would translate into far-reaching results.

Jacob Krehbiel, the recent visitor in the Franconia Conference, was much more sympathetic to the traditional Pennsylvania outlook, and wrote a rather complimentary account back to Europe. But had he looked more closely, he might have seen already in 1839 signs of the same differences as had taken shape in his home Palatinate. Jacob had visited in the "central" bishop district; the signs of unrest were more visible nearer the fringes. At Deep Run, in the bishop district of Henry Hunsberger of Hilltown, there was a growing group of young men who felt the old Mennonite way was too strict, and who were not a part of the communicant congregation. Two sons of Isaac Fretz, Abraham and Mahlon, may serve as examples of this group. Abraham had married a Reformed girl from Lower Salford in 1820, and as a result had been "excluded" from the Deep Run congregation. Instead of coming back with a "confession," as many such younger people did, he remained outside with his wife. Only when a liberal wing of the congregation would be organized a quarter of a century after their marriage, would they become Mennonite communicants.[98] Abraham's younger brother, Mahlon, never joined any church, having what his family historian termed "a military tendency." But he, too, when the more liberal congregation was founded at Deep Run, would help to build their new meetinghouse.[99] Others who were excommunicated for one reason or another became a part of this grouping. At the opposite end of the conference, at Hereford, there were similar feelings. Minister John Gehman made a note of concern in his diary in December 1838. His son-in-law Christian Clemmer and another of the congregation's promising young men, Ephraim Hunsberger, were "opposed to the Conference."[100]

What objections to the conference might be entertained by these two men in their mid-twenties, both to be ordained Mennonite ministers within a decade? What did it mean that John Gehman recorded them as opposed not to the "church," or parents, or Christ, but to "Conference"? Did it have to do with Christian's personal feeling of a "call to the preacher's office," which must wait until the "lot" would fall on him?[101]

These were not the first voices from an outlying congregation to challenge the "housekeeping" of the bishops, whose authority was central in the deliberations of the twice-yearly conference in the Franconia meetinghouse. Over two years earlier, in May 1836, a preacher nearly three times their age—Michael Landis of Saucon—had gone home from conference dissatisfied. Bishop Jacob Gottshall of Franconia, apparently the moderator, had said that he did "not like to serve where there is disunity," and where he heard "complaints." It would be better, he seems to have told Preacher Landis, for a person to complain about himself than about others. But Michael shortly wrote a letter to Bishop Gottshall stating that his conscience could not be "submitted to human judgment" ("*beugten zur Mensch*"). He felt surrounded daily by disunity. There was very little humility and meekness that he could see, "as learned from the Savior." Michael recommended that the Bishop take an example from the biblical story of Jethro, the father-in-law of Moses, whose advice was that Moses delegate authority rather than try to run everything himself. Some "elders" might be elected in the local districts. Michael felt that he knew several good candidates for such an office, from Saucon and Swamp. There was one person who should prove acceptable to Samuel Musselman, the elderly local bishop. Then there ought to be a *Vorschrift*, a written order or constitution, by which congregational arrangements and procedures could be regulated, in regard to all "outward" matters. Had there been such a *Vorschrift* earlier, there would not have come about as much disunity as Michael said existed.

There were actually two ministers at Saucon, a relatively small congregation at the far north edge of the conference. The other one, Valentine Young, was also in his sixties, and had been ordained about the same time as Michael, over three decades earlier. Where Michael wished for change, Valentine was conservative. "My punishment is with me morning and night," wrote Michael, and his mention of the sister Swamp congregation suggests that the "disunity" was felt there too, already in 1836. Michael speaks of a *"Gegenpartei"*—an "opposing faction." But he vigorously wards off any opinion that he himself is making trouble, or that he lacks humility. Quoting the inevitable Gerhard Tersteegen, the great proponent of inward spirituality, Michael says that what seems humility is often a false-front for pride. "The mouth can indeed say much, but God alone knows the heart." [102]

Thus by the end of the 1830s there was an undercurrent of questioning of the "order" and authority of the Franconia Conference. It was audible not so much in the central district, where Bishop Jacob Gottshall's thirty-five-year-old son-in-law, schoolteacher Henry Nice, was now ordained as a minister, but nearer the edges—at Skippack with its unskillful preacher Elias Landes, at Phoenixville, Deep Run, Hereford, Swamp, and Saucon. This questioning would not die; within a decade it would grow into pressure for more congregationalism, less emphasis on "externals," more openness to the surrounding culture, a constitution, and a new independent body. There would be two versions of the local Mennonite family, rather than one. A debate would smoulder between those who cherished "the old nonresistant Mennonite foundation," and those who felt that the church needed more life, more freedom, mission, and education. It would be a difficult time.

Chapter 8

"I Thought I Had a Perfect Right"

1840-1846

In 1840 a Schwenkfelder from Worcester Township, David Heebner, made and sold a threshing machine to a neighbor, Joseph Allebach.[1] Power was provided by horses moving a "sweep" around in a circle. This first machine took Heebner six weeks to make, but a swiftly accelerating procession of threshers and horsepowers from his expanding works would service, in a few decades, a worldwide market. The force of the mechanical revolution in the Western world was such that already by 1846, the closing year of this chapter, a smaller local competitor of Heebner's could advertise not only steam engines, but "Cornstalk Cutters and Crushers, Corn Shellers, Clover machines, Churns and Churn Powers; two, three and four Horse Powers," and even the kind of "woollen and cotton machinery"[2] that would shortly silence for good the fireside hum of the spinning wheel.

The compression of time by mechanical improvements changes our feelings and modifies our beliefs. When, in 1844, a message first flashed instantaneously across formerly time-consuming distance, its own sender asked, "What hath God wrought?" When our very bodies are swept in comfortable, distance-annulling trajectories, we feel a mythic pleasure. When tireless machines take over brute work borne immemorially by straining human flesh, we sense a kind of deliverance. We read the advertisements for these machines with strange attention. Preacher John Gehman of Hereford, who recorded only the most basic data of his life in a simple diary, had included in 1833 his beginning to "cut grain with cradles";[3] only thirteen years later he "Cut cornfodder with the machine for the first time." Halfway between those progress-marking dates had come John's worried notation that his promising son-in-law was "opposed to Conference."

Listening to Pennsylvania's voices from these years, we hear excited and celebratory language. The entire Schuylkill Valley feted the grand opening of its completed railroad in 1842. "An immense procession of seventy-five passenger cars" nearly a quarter of a mile long carried over 2,000 passengers to the tune of three "bands of music."[4] Locomotives on this new Philadelphia and Reading Railroad, at the western edge of the Franconia Conference, carried names that were both mythic—"Spitfire" and "Dragon"—and cosmic: "Rocket," "Planet," and "Comet." A Lower Salford schoolmaster, born in 1829, needed epic language to express his sense of majesty: "It seemed as if the Titans were aroused from slumber, and came forth to put the giant Steam into harness...." The "ancients" may have had their gilded chariots, "But now we have the iron horse to go snorting and thundering along as far in one hour as they went in a day.... To chisel a hole through a mountain to drive through with their chariots they never dreamed of. So much are we ahead of the ancients."[5] In the same vein was a newspaper account of the first setting up of the "Magnetic Telegraph" between Philadelphia and Norristown in 1846: "This wonderful instrument," marveled the writer, has "a velocity infinitely much more rapid than thought itself."[6]

When a changed relation to time or a feeling of "improvement" makes people feel that they are transcending old limits, they may be merely amused by issues which their parents wrestled with or even wept over. If their community tends to maintain its older manners in the new and faster era, those who admire progress may feel disturbed. In terms of our present story, a difference arose over what was the essence of the Mennonite community. One side, attentive to voices carried by tradition, struggled to preserve its unique "old foundation"; the other side, its eyes shining with reflections of current "progress" and "efficiency," offered a revision, in up-to-date terminology, of the group's reason for being.

The early 1840s were, roughly, the midpoint between the introduction of the "Common School System" legislation and its complete acceptance. By 1842, half of the townships in Montgomery County had adopted the system; the others were mostly German-speaking. But change was coming; by 1844 the only township in the county that had not elected directors was Franconia, and the next year it too had a set, though these men did not accept the new system for another seven years. In the meantime, the older voluntary or "subscription" schools held on, as also at Salford and Deep Run. Here teachers found "no uniformity in books. The pupils came with any kind ... that their fathers or grandfathers used...." One teacher who lived in Lower Salford remembered that he had to "teach out of about a dozen different arithmetics."[7] The Salford Mennonite school had finally hired someone to teach English in 1841—a Mr. Calendar of Doylestown who indeed seemed to the community "quite English." In 1842 the trustees built one of the popular "Octagon shaped schoolhouses. There was another near Doylestown, and still another across the road from the recently (1835) built meetinghouse at Diamond Rock in Chester County, in a little Mennonite community centering on a family of Beidlers, who had migrated from Bucks County. At Salford, classes now moved out of the meetinghouse itself for the first time since the days of Christopher Dock (d. 1771). A similar move had occurred at the West Swamp meetinghouse in 1839.

Apparently, conservatives in the Salford community feared the use of English less than the loss of authority over their own educational concerns. At nearby Lederachville, three Mennonite trustees of another school (also German and English) were charged by the donor of the land not to allow the building to be used under the Common School System, even if this "should be accepted" by the township. Singing school, for some reason, was also not to be held in this house.[8]

Singing school was still very much in vogue. Two of the more popular teachers of the 1840s were Martin Hunsberger of Coventry,[9] son of the musical Abraham of "Hersteins," and Samuel Godshalk,[10] son of the deceased Preacher Abraham of Doylestown. Whereas the former apparently joined another denomination, the latter was to become a well-known minister at Deep Run. Although behavior was sometimes a problem at these evening singing schools, they made learning music a socially enjoyable experience, and thus strengthened church singing in general. It was one interdenominational exercise that Mennonites could enjoy.

A little-remembered product of this musical interest is a book called *Die Neue Choral Harmonie* by Samuel M. Musselman, a schoolteacher and gravestone-cutter of Lower Salford. Appearing in 1844, the book offered instruction in reading music in both German and English.[11] Three-part harmony (trebel/tenor, counter, and bass) accompanied texts for each of 190 songs. The compiler stated that thirty-five of his "choral melodies," and a large number of the "music pieces," had never appeared in print before. Indeed, he claimed on the title page to have "composed" as well as "collected" the materials in the book. Among many well-known tune-names appear such intriguing ones as "Hilltown," "Franconia," "Milford," and "Upper Saucon." The last-mentioned, misspelled by the printer into "Alpper Saucon," turns out to be a close adaptation of the popular tune, "Home, Sweet Home." Other pieces, including "fuguing tunes" enjoyed in singing schools, seem more original, and evince gusto and charm. The book's transitional nature is evident in its supplying English as well as German words for most of the songs. Over at Deep Run, Samuel Godshalk too had a growing collection of music in his manuscript notebook, but it never approached the proportions of Musselman's work.

Regarding the musical scene of this era, the contrast between two communities helps us to understand the tension between tradition and modern cultural influences. In a growing village like Trap, the neighborhood of the affluent Abraham Hunsicker family, "English" was increasingly dominant. The Hunsickers had access to the library of a new literary society based at an academy for boys, and even Bishop John Hunsicker, of the nearby Skippack congregation, availed himself of its borrowing privileges. There was also a vigorous debating society which prided itself on its *au courant* topics. No wonder that the teenage Henry Hunsicker, participant in all these modish cultural activities, boarded with the local doctor, an anti-slavery activist, rather than with his own Mennonite cousins whose children attended his school at the Salford meetinghouse. It was with pride that Henry later recalled the superior musical life of his home village. "No less a personage than the distinguished musical composer, Lowell Mason, of Boston, gave instruction . . . and assistance in some of the musical concerts" held in the academy at Trap.[12]

By contrast, a rural Mennonite community like Deep Run was able to hold much longer to some of the German folk arts. A colorful Fraktur bookplate for Barbara Meyer's singing-school book at "The Octagon School" near Doylestown is dated as late as May 3, 1843,[13] and one boy from the High family in Bedminister would be producing Fraktur in the 1880s, long after the art had died off almost everywhere else. And scattered among Deep Run Mennonite homes were "*Zitters*" (zithers)—remnants of an ancient European folk tradition that stretched from Switzerland to Scandinavia. These long, narrow instruments, with anywhere from three to a dozen strings, were simple enough to be played by a child. They were placed on the player's lap, or on a table. One or two strings were pressed down on a series of frets, making a melody playable, and the rest would be strummed or bowed in an accompanying drone. Mennonite families of both "Conestoga" and "Skippack" had used these zithers prior to the American Revolution. Among them were two neighbors of the Salford congregation. John Clemens, miller along the Branch Creek, was remembered a century after his death as having "spent much of his time" playing a "zitter,"[14] and among the household effects of Henrich Ruth, on whose first farm the Salford meetinghouse had been built, was found an object which a Welsh neighbor called a "dulcimar" (1757).[15] The haunting medieval whine of these homemade ancestors of the so-called "Appalachian dulcimer" drew listeners back in time, rather than forward. Yet Deep Run and Doylestown Mennonites—of the Gross, Lapp, Leatherman, Meyers, and Overholt families—made and played them in their homes or at spelling bees until long past the Civil War. When the folk music enthusiasm of the 1960s had borne its fruit and thousands of Americans learned to play "dulcimers," musicologists had rediscovered the Pennsylvania Dutch *Zitter* as a late survival of the ancient European *Scheitholt* tradition, and people in the Alsace were vigorously reviving their own version, the *Epinette des Vosges*. It was to the memory of the Lapp and Overholt families of Deep Run and Doylestown that these scholars owed their best access to knowledge of how this instrument had had its amazing survival, accompanying singing of the old slow hymns in the homes of Pennsylvania Dutch people.[16]

Since Abraham Hunsicker of "Perkiomen Bridge" would shortly take a leading role in trying to "reform" or enlighten his Mennonite community, a further glance at the influences in his neighborhood will be to the point. At the 100th anniversary (1843) celebration of the nearby Lutheran Church of Trap, which Abraham doubtless attended, the pastor offered a nutshell account of noteworthy activities in his denomination. The Lutherans of America now had a college, four "classical schools," and four "Theological Seminaries." (Before long Abraham would build an academy himself, which he hoped Mennonite young men would attend.) The Lutherans even had a "Parent Education Society." A "Book Establishment" and periodicals in both German and English helped to keep Lutherans up to date with religious progress. Mission societies—both domestic and foreign—were active. Right there in Trap there was a "Muhlenberg Missionary Society," but not with the intention of drawing people from other denominations into the church. On this point Pastor John Richards could not withhold a crack at the busy Evangelicals, Methodists, and Baptists, those "proselyting vipers that crawl into our houses."[17] The local Lutheran Society was interested rather in the foreign heathen, and saddler Mathias Haldeman led the "excellent choir" in a currently popular mission hymn:

> Wake the song of Jubilee!
> Let it echo o'er the sea.

As Abraham Hunsicker pondered such a series of enlightened activities, he must have wished for some of it among his own culturally sluggish Mennonite community. It was a year later that he would name his youngest son Horace Mann. Even the new Lutheran Sunday school, giving out red and blue tickets for Scripture memorization, doubtless numbered among its "110 scholars" some of Abraham's children. Another set of progressive Mennonite parents who were already allowing their children to attend a community Sunday school were the parents of John Fretz Funk, of the Line Lexington congregation. By the following year nine-year-old "Fretz" would have memorized 1,600 Bible verses.[18]

These 1840s were also years of "Temperance" agitation, with denunciations, cow-hidings, church splits, and feuds between neighboring pastors. Abraham Hunsicker himself gave up providing spirits for the men who came to work in the fields (much to their chagrin), but he was a moderate in the debates. He was chosen as chairman of a public meeting in Trap "to consider the violent and abusive measures of the advocates of teetotalism." Resolutions passed at the meeting approved the cause of Temperance "if properly conducted," but protested against abuse and insults, especially by clergymen.[19] Over near Doylestown Daniel Gross, soon to be ordained deacon, and the only son of Bishop Jacob Gross who was not a minister, sent an extremely long and finely written letter of concern on Temperance to his Canadian Mennonite friends and relatives. He had noticed printed in the Bucks County *Bauer* a resolution of the Canadian Mennonites not to participate in the Temperance movement. ". . . I and . . . many of our brethren," he wrote, "deeply regret" this statement. His father (died 1810) had already in his day called drinking one of the greatest evils of mankind.[20] This anti-liquor feeling would continue particularly strongly in the Gross families of the Doylestown congregation until finally, in the 20th century, they would be among the very first in the Franconia Conference to substitute grape juice for wine at communion.

On the other hand, most of the conservative Mennonite leaders were very suspicious about joining any organized group other than the church itself. Even affiliations in good causes were felt to be potentially erosive of the specifically focused spiritual accountability that had always characterized the Mennonite family. Still more strenuously forbidden, of course, was membership in the lodges now springing up in local towns. These were read by church leaders as ways of bypassing the brotherly processes of the church, and finding security (in death benefits) outside the covenanted fellowship of Christ. Yet on this point Abraham Hunsicker took a very liberal view.

But it was in Abraham's growing political involvement that we may find, to use his son Henry's words, the real "beginning" of his "church troubles."[21] The presidential election in the fall of 1840 created an almost unprecedented excitement. Hard financial times put an edge on the issues, and feelings became so intense that even schoolchildren had demonstrations, with either log cabins, on the Whig side, or hickory poles on the Democrat. The Whigs, of whose ranks Abraham Hunsicker was an "ardent" member, supported the hero of military campaigns against the Indians, William Henry Harrison. Over at Deep Run Joseph Fretz, a leader among the most liberal of the lay members, named his new son Henry Harrison Fretz. Abraham Hunsicker took part in both township primaries and "county conventions that framed the tickets." The local enthusiasm was unprecedented. In Lower Salford young John Boorse of the Towamencin congregation saw his first American flag, and his "first colored man," at a Harrison mass meeting at the White Horse Hotel (later called Mainland). Almost all members of the community, "old and young," were there; Boorse distinctly remembered that "there was no restriction on account of religion." This, he recalled, would later be changed (doubtless particularly among Mennonites). A log cabin built on a locally owned wagon was pulled along by eight white horses, while the black man played a violin from the window. After the speeches a gang of the men rode their horses down to the flat land along the Skippack, and sang a song seven-year-old John Boorse would never forget:

> Ye jolly young Whigs of Ohio,
>   And all ye sick Democrats too,
> Come out from among the foul party
>   And vote for old Tippecanoe.
>
> And if you [are] anywise thirsty,
>   We can tell you what you can do:
> We can bring down a keg of hard cider,
>   And drink to Old Tippecanoe.[22]

The speeches that accompanied such festivities were filled with invective. Jacob Pennypacker, who attended the Phoenixville Mennonite meeting, was particularly struck with a remark from one orator at a mass meeting at Valley Forge, where a group of old veterans of the Revolutionary War sat on the stage. "Beware of [Martin Van Buren]," ranted the speaker, "He would dig up the bones of his Mother and sell them."[23]

Such a scene was considered foreign to the nature of Christ by the Mennonite ministers. Although possibly taken off their guard by the unexpected political excitement, they knew their duty. Minister Elias Landes and Deacon John Gotwals came to talk to Abraham Hunsicker, objecting to his political activities, and "warning him of having offended the rules of the meeting, assuming that such was the duty only of the people of the world." And other matters came up, such as the requirement that Abraham's daughters (though apparently not yet members at the Skippack congregation) "wear caps at meeting," and Abraham's attitude toward "resorting to processes of law to recover lost property," or toward "liberal education."[24]

This churchly concern seemed to have little effect. When the next presidential election (1844) created new fervor, the Abraham Hunsicker family got into the thick of the campaign. Nineteen-year-old Henry joined

the "Henry Clay Club, No. 1, of Montgomery County," and traveled with
it to Washington on a canal boat to compete for "a prize banner." Hettie
Hunsicker, Henry's sister, was on a committee to present "an elegant satin
banner," which Henry carried at a mass meeting supporting Henry Clay at
Valley Forge. Recalling "that gala day" as an old man, and "the glory of appearing at the head" of the Upper Providence delegation, Henry called it
"the proudest day of my life." One reason for this was that sitting in the
stands watching it all was the famous Daniel Webster, speaker of the day.
That night Webster was the guest of Isaac Pennypacker, who had grown up
attending the Phoenixville Mennonite Meeting. The Pennypackers had become socially prominent, and politically so successful that Isaac's one-year-
old son, Samuel, would one day be elected governor of Pennsylvania.[25]

Invention, education, and political excitement, then, surrounded the
Mennonites of the 1840s with slogans of speed, enlightenment, and
democracy. The persistent Evangelicals, with repeated camp meetings and
altar calls, located the center of importance in the experience of personal
conversion, leaving speed, progress, and democracy generally uncritiqued.
As we have seen in Abraham Godschalk's book, Mennonites too found
regeneration a fundamental necessity, but they missed, in much talk of it, a
carrying through of certain practical conclusions. There was an instinct
among these culturally insulated farm families—a barely articulatable
sense, an "Old Foundation"—that Christianity consists as much in accepting and maintaining a "right fellowship" as in sensing an inner drama. In
bearing testimony to the grace of God, the church must make that cosmic
reconciliation visible in terms of a human *order*, a "colony of heaven" that
will stand over against as well as within national, technological, and cultural
patterns. This order, or "right fellowship," once resisted the punishments of
state-enforced religion. Now, with persecution gone, its leaders had to
"keep house" in the face of more ambiguous challenges: evangelicalism,
progress, and democracy.

The five bishops, traditionally the "housekeepers" of the Mennonite
fellowship, averaged seventy years of age in 1840. There were twenty-seven
other ministers, according to a list drawn up that year by Deacon David
Allebach of Towamencin. This list, not even mentioning the Germantown,
Phoenixville, Boyertown, Plumstead, Flatland, or Northampton County
meetinghouses, doubtless reflects the understanding of someone in the
central districts of the conference. But Deacon Allebach's German spelling
and his relating of preachers to meetinghouses are so interesting that they
will be presented here, with the addition of ages and identification of
bishops. The list was supplied to a correspondent from Lancaster, and dated
May 16, 1840.[26]

Cawendrie & Winsen	Abraham Haldeman (60), Johannes (36) & Jacob Latschar (44)
Schibbach, Ziglers, Upper Brawidens, Mardetsche	(Bishop) Johannes Hunsecker (67), Abraham Wismer (43), Elias Landes (44)
Domensen, Solford	Isaac Alderfer (67), Johannes Berge (57)
New Britain	Johannes Krob (61), Johannes Geil (62)
Auf der Blen	Jacob Kolb (42)
Deils daun	Johannes Gros (54), Isaac Gottschall (53)
Dib Ronn	Christian Gross (64), Abraham Kolb (69), Daniel Landes (71)
Schwammer Versammlunghaus	(Bishop) Samuel Musselman (76), Christian Zetty (74), Jacob Hiestand (49)
Hereford	(Bishop) Johannes Bechtel (61), Johannes Gehman (47)
Frencone	(Bishop) Jacob Gottschall (71), Henri Neis (36)
Rockhill	Samuel Gehman (70), Jacob Detweiler (45)
Bergese	Jacob Hunsicker (70), (Bishop) Henrich Hunsperger (72)
Springfield	Jacob Meier (49), Abraham Geissinger (51)
Sakene	Falendin Jung (67)
Goschenhoppen, Hosen Sack Versammlunghaus	Johannes Geman (69), Johannes Schantz (66)

The average age of these thirty-two men was fifty-six—not particularly promising at a moment of cultural challenge. There was, to be sure, some strong leadership here and there. Coventry and Vincent had a good speaker in sixty-year-old Abraham Halteman, Skippack had the broad-minded John Hunsicker, Plains had both the vigorous Jacob Kolb and a preacher of whom one local historian used the adjective "celebrated": John Krupp. No one was more highly respected than Line Lexington's quietly eloquent John Geil. Franconia had in its "preachers' bench" a fine schoolmaster-miller, the youngest minister in the conference at thirty-six, Henry Neiss.

But the overall picture included quite a few more discouraging facts. Abraham Halteman was about to move away from Vincent to Juniata because of "faction" in his congregation. The majority of John Hunsicker's large congregation at Skippack was unsatisfied with his colleague Elias Landes's slow-tongued, old-fashioned preaching. Salford, Deep Run, Line Lexington, Perkasie (Blooming Glen), and Upper Milford all needed younger preachers. Rockhill had just ordained one—Jacob Detweiler—to help seventy-year-old Samuel Gehman, but the new minister had proved incapable of preaching more than a few minutes. This must have been particularly disappointing to some, in view of the fact that the bishops had removed from the "lot" the nomination of a more capable man, Abraham

Fretz. This had been done because of Fretz's recent involvement in Bucks County politics. But because of the poor results with Jacob Detweiler, apparently, another ordination was held in the following year (1841).[27] This time the name of Abraham Fretz was allowed to remain, and the lot fell on him. Difficulty nevertheless loomed when Abraham seemed determined not to yield to the older ministers' request that he wear the older "round" coat when his present coat wore out.

The results of ordinations over the next four years continued to emphasize the issue of effective versus weak speakers in the pulpit. John Gehman of Hereford never pretended to be able to preach; when the lot was cast for an assistant in 1842, it fell on Gehman's son-in-law Christian Clemmer—a strong leader, but, as we have seen, with feelings "opposed to Conference." For years before he was chosen, he had felt a "call." It took Deep Run two and a half years after the death of elderly Preacher Daniel Landis before they cast lots, and ordained Daniel's nephew Isaac Meyer. Later it would be remembered that young Meyer had hesitated at length over which side of his polarizing congregation to take up with.[28] His choice of the "older" side left the considerable group of liberals without ordained leadership (in contrast to the situation at Swamp, Hereford, and Skippack).

An ordination at Salford also produced a younger minister—Jacob Kolb—but it turned out that he simply could not preach. Perhaps this was the time when a fluent younger liberal from the congregation, David Bergey, had fled to the Towamencin congregation to escape the risk of passing through the lot at Salford, and possibly being ordained.[29] Many men dreaded this possibility, with its life-changing consequences, and its requirement that they henceforth exemplify the sober Mennonite ideal.

John Geil too, at Line Lexington, got a younger assistant—Sam Leatherman. Sam was a devout man, and later chosen bishop, but he spoke in a voice so low that many in the audience could not hear. Perkasie (Blooming Glen) got a twenty-six-year-old preacher in 1844, when Henry Moyer decided to move back from Westmoreland County where he had just been ordained. But he too never preached a full sermon, or prayed audibly. A final example comes from the Franconia congregation, where the death of Bishop Jacob Gottshall in 1845 created a need for assistance for the bishop's son-in-law, Henry Neiss. An obvious candidate in the minds of the congregation was the forthright, capable, and musical Herman Gottshall, son of the deceased bishop. Yet no less than thirteen other names were also placed in the lot. Of the twenty-six votes that had been accepted, ten were for Herman, twice as many as for the next highest. Eight men had received only one nomination each. Yet when the lot was cast, it was one of these eight—farmer Jacob P. Landes—who was chosen, and Herman Gottshall,

242

the outgoing somewhat forward song leader would become a well-known local miller, and never be ordained.[30]

While the results of casting lots thus disappointed some members, others understood this as God's inscrutable and benevolent way of keeping his people humbly obedient. Listening faithfully to a poor speaker, while less enjoyable, was nevertheless an expression of one's submission both to the will of God and the brotherhood. In contrast to the dynamics of American democracy, in which leaders sold themselves to their followers in self-celebratory rhetoric, or maneuvered for position and influence, the key to "the right fellowship" was non-self-assertive humility and faithfulness. Only this "gospel order" was Christ's true nature visible in human society.

That, indeed, was the traditional logic, but no longer was the whole Mennonite fellowship satisfied with it. Among the persons who were not, the outstanding figure was the schoolteacher-smith John H. Oberholtzer. His "whole lifetime," as he put it, had been "an unbroken chain of learning . . . and teaching."[31] Since before his sixteenth birthday he had been teaching nearly every winter, but he also was what he called a "*Grobschmidt*" and "*Schlosser*"[32] (blacksmith and locksmith). His opinion of the leadership may be heard in his later comment that "a large number of the ministers" had "sunk to a low state of ignorance," and that, as speakers, "four out of five were failures."[33] In 1842 we find Oberholtzer making a quite modest living in Lower Milford Township, where he resided less than a mile from the West Swamp meetinghouse. His small family consisted of his sickly wife, Mary, and their two children Davy and Anna, now eight and six years old, respectively.

The only minister at Swamp younger than seventy-six years old, Jacob Hiestand, moved to the Doylestown area in 1842, where he would build a mill and help with the preaching at the congregation there. This left a serious gap in the Swamp leadership, and the seventy-eight-year-old Bishop Musselman moved quickly to ordain a younger minister to help him and his aged colleague, "Christel" Zetty. From among the families who attended both "West" and "East" Swamp, and probably "Flatland," as well, no less than fifteen men were nominated for the lot. It "fell" on thirty-three-year-old John Oberholtzer, and in accordance with "ancient usage" he was ordained on the spot.

The suddenness of such a calling usually produced a strong emotional response, both from those who heard the welcome words of the bishop who had just opened their books, "You may go free," and from the one on whom the solemn responsibility now came. Strong impressions were often left by comments at this life-defining moment. Such was the case with John Oberholtzer. Two or three Sundays after the ordination, before he had done

Jacob Wismer Bergey (b. 1818) and his first wife, Susannah Leatherman (1824-55), of the Doylestown congregation. If, by appearance, their ages are judged to be about thirty and twenty-five, these daguerreotypes would have been made at about the time of the 1847 division in the Franconia Conference. (Paul M. Mininger)

any preaching, he received, to his "greatest joy," his very first visit from a fellow minister in the Franconia Conference.[34] The "lower congregations," as he called the districts south of the wooded Ridge at the edge of the "Swamp" area, were not particularly well-known to him at this time. Some years later the "lower" areas were nicknamed *"Menishteland"* ("Mennonite-country") by Swamp-area people, because of the density of the Mennonite population in the central districts of the conference. The whole notion of the conference itself—its meaning and background—was not at all clear in Oberholtzer's mind. He would later define the "Franconia Conference" as a "body of preachers and deacons" which had been "founded by Henry Hunsicker" and "Jacob Gross of Franconia—approximately in the year 1799."[35] Here a lack of interest in the past seems evident. He must have vaguely believed that the "conference" as such had originated only a decade or two before his own birth.

In any case, the new minister was delighted with the visit of forty-nine-year-old weaver Abraham Fretz, the former Bucks County politician who had a year earlier been ordained at Rockhill, and had yet to get a "plain coat." As John later recalled their conversation, Abraham remarked that "the old preachers soon begin, after a man is chosen for the preacher's office, to observe him and bring pressure on such newly chosen servants to change [the style of] their coats." Both Oberholtzer and Fretz realized, of course, that the new preachers were allowed first to wear out the coats they had at the point of ordination. But Fretz now made a proposal to his younger colleague: "Since some [people] keep having this strange opinion, let us stay as we are with our coats, and see what they do." Oberholtzer, already of the same opinion, felt greatly strengthened in it by Fretz's advice, and gave it his enthusiastic "Ja und Amen."[36] Many years later, as he pondered the unforeseen rift that had soon thereafter opened up in the Franconia Conference, he wondered whether he might not have been easily led to soften his stance on his coat, if he had not been confirmed in it by Fretz at this crucial time. It was certainly an impressionable moment for him, a capable young minister looking forward to his first sermon. The advice of a friendly and respected older man to disregard the counsel of the bishops and ministers would have consequences far beyond what Fretz foresaw. Years later, when Oberholtzer was asked what other ministers beside himself had refused to get a plain coat, he would reply that Abraham Fretz was the only one he could remember. Ironically, as Oberholtzer would become ever more unyielding on this point, Fretz himself would opt for the submission of his will to the brotherhood, and become one of Oberholtzer's "hardest opponents."

After another two or three weeks the new minister's first opportunity to preach occurred without warning. As he arrived at the meetinghouse and met Preacher Zetty and Bishop Musselman, the aged bishop's first word of greeting was, "Today you must preach the sermon." Oberholtzer did the standard thing expected of a properly humble new minister; he "excused" himself. The Bishop then responded with the customary approach: "You try it, and if it doesn't go, we will take it over from you." What followed was an experience that in later years Oberholtzer recounted almost as a litany. During the silent, kneeling prayer after one of the old ministers had "made the opening," the new preacher felt shaken by the solemn task before him. His prayer was that he would not be found "dumb" before the waiting flock. "Then a verse," he would recall, "came into my mind as lifelike and as distinctly as if someone had called it to me out loud": "I will not leave you nor forsake you." Heartened, he rose and took his text from Ephesians 2:8-9: "By grace are ye saved through faith; and that not of yourselves: it is the gift of God: not of works, lest any man should boast." The sermon then flowed so easily that some in the audience felt their new schoolteacher-preacher must have come prepared to preach.

"That was a studied sermon," was "the first thing" Oberholtzer heard by way of response.[37] Unfortunately, this was meant not as a compliment, but as an objection to his impressive and unusually structured style of speaking. But if some carped, others were delighted. In John's own words, he had become "somewhat popular in the community generally" by his

"Schoolteaching at different places, and among many different classes of people." Now he received frequent invitations "to preach amongst [his] old Schoolfriends, in their Churches and Schoolhouses, without any denominational distinction. . . ."[38] This was a service he performed with relish; one of his very first sermons was preached at a funeral in the nearby Lutheran Church.

A limited amount of such interchange of ministers had occurred among Mennonites from time to time at least since 1749, and would continue. When the Rockhill congregation had inaugurated the use of its new meetinghouse in 1838, the main sermon had been preached by the Reformed Pastor John Andrew Strassburger, who jointly conducted many funeral services with his Mennonite friend Samuel Gehman.[39] Pastor Strassburger would be the speaker "in the house" at the death of Perkasie's beloved Deacon Samuel Meyer in 1847. On Christmas Day in 1843, the speakers at the dedication of a new Dunker meetinghouse at the Salford edge of Franconia Township were Mennonites Henry Neiss and John Bergey of the Franconia and Salford congregations. But the sheer frequency of John Oberholtzer's preaching among other communions, "principally on weekdays, or on Sundays when [he] was not engaged . . . at home," was out of scale with its more modest precedents. A time of "testing" and criticism now set in; conservatives complained that John did new things: he "took money" for his services, went up into the high pulpits of other churches, and "called people" with whose doctrines the Mennonites had traditionally disagreed "brothers and sisters in Christ."[40] Comment also increased on his failure to conform to the other ministers by getting the older style of coat.

Considering his critics at Swamp to be "ignorant and restless members," John later stated that he "did not consult with flesh and blood" on merely human opinions. "I had other things to take care of that were a hundred times more important than to chatter about changing my coat." To wear his usual coat was something, he observed, that "I thought I had a perfect right to do." When it was suggested that his coat should not have the modern collar or buttons, he felt he need not "pay any attention to such queer and in fact Superstitious notions."[41]

At conference in the fall of 1842 the subject of John's coat (and probably Abraham Fretz's) was briefly referred to. At the following session, in May 1843, when it was seen that John had still not made the expected change, it was "more spoken of." By now John was traveling in the wider conference-area, as to Deep Run, where his capable preaching stayed in the mind of Isaac Meyer, a new preacher just a few years younger than Oberholtzer. In his visits the Swamp preacher also got to Skippack, where he had an enthusiastic reception. To his surprise, Abraham Fretz now gave in to their fellow-ministers' advice, and after saying he could not afford a new coat, accepted one as a gift. From thenceforth Oberholtzer found increasing support among the Skippack congregation, with its elderly, well-to-do, and liberal bishop, John Hunsicker.

But although Hunsicker, carrying on the long tradition of his father, Bishop Henry, had considerable influence in the conference, he was unable to prevent the conference from putting strong pressure on the eloquent new minister from Swamp. By the May 1844 session, two year's after Oberholtzer's ordination, the conference was no longer willing to let the coat issue in the air. During the deliberations "They tried to persuade Mr. Oberholtzer to conform," remember Isaac Meyer, "but without success."[42] Oberholtzer replied that he would not be willing to change his coat "until convinced from scriptural points." As he later put it, "The creed"—perhaps referring to his understanding of Mennonite belief in general, or the writings of Menno Simons—"allowed us to dress as we wished, and did not prescribe any form...."[43] Isaac Meyer, of the other persuasion, agreed with that in principle, observing, "There was nothing in the cut of the coat...." Conference rather gave as its reason "why they desired him to conform to the rules in the matter of dress," their concern "that the people would have confidence in him," as "it would appear he was disobedient to the rules." The "cut of the coat," said Meyer, was "nothing ... except that it showed disobedience."[44]

The matter of "rules" was particularly aggravating to forward-looking John Oberholtzer. What were they, and where, other than in people's evolving memories, were they recorded? The rules he wished for were those of a parliamentary, rational procedure, so that the informal, nonstructured discussions at conference could be subjected to common sense when necessary. As it now was, the meanings seemed to leap from mouth to mouth in impulsive, nonrational patterns. Some bishops had disproportionate influence, some ministers who knew better would submit their wills for the sake of "unity," and members often voted together in a group mentality rather than allowing each man to think things through rationally in his own mind. If only minutes could be kept, and a parliamentary, rather than an improvisatory, traditional procedure be invoked! Then perhaps a more acceptable order could be maintained.

As a matter of fact, John had been able to put his own congregation at Swamp on a constitutional basis just five weeks before conference. Though this was probably an act unprecedented in the American Mennonite fellowship, Preacher Michael Landis had asked Bishop Jacob Gottschall for something like it eight years earlier. Oberholtzer had drawn up a document much like the constitutions of current Sunday schools and mission societies, with twenty-one rules governing procedure and organization. It aimed at efficiency rather than doctrine. Fifty-three men—including eighteen Shellys—had signed the document,[45] among whom was the aged Bishop Musselman himself, now a follower rather than a leader.

What was at stake here—at least as the conservatives viewed it—was the conception of church order. John Oberholtzer felt that shaping the dealings of the church proceedings by rational rather than traditional patterns had nothing to do with the essence of the church. The majority of the ministers, on the other hand, regarded the coherence of the community as more important than the advantages to be gained from listening to individual insight as fast as it came. The drama for them was not in streamlining the church or bringing it in line with current improvements, but in making sure that a unique and difficult set of Christian motifs was not blurred. Yet these conservatives seemed more complacent about watching promising young people leave the church than was John Oberholtzer. And we hear of no older minister, whom Oberholtzer might have respected, taking him kindly and reasonably aside to develop the rationale of the older way in his mind. His ministerial colleague at Swamp, Christian Zetty, was now dead, and his bishop, Samuel Musselman, at eighty, enfeebled.

At any rate, the May 1844 conference, having resisted Oberholtzer's objections, passed a decisive resolution that those members of its ranks who continued to be disobedient (in this case, refusing to wear a plain coat) would not have the right to share in the deliberations of the conference.[46] On the one hand, this was an expression of the basic logic of the Mennonite fellowship: without an acknowledgment of the authority of the church over the individual volition in some points, there was no mutual yieldedness; the "gospel order" itself would go out of focus. On the other hand, by this action the conference took from John Oberholtzer his most valued means of working: the power of persuasive speech. In bitterness of soul, he dubbed their resolution "a coat law ... an absolutely human commandment," foreign to the spirit of the New Testament.[47]

Returning indignantly to Swamp, John determined that two thirds of the ministers and members of the "Swamp Bishopric"—the Swamps, Flatland, and Springfield—were opposed to the conference's action. Their thinking was more and more taking the stamp of his "reformation." This included a new emphasis on the instruction of children. The regularizing and enlivening of pre-baptismal instruction was, in his mind, long overdue. Religious content was being less emphasized in the local day schools as the new Common School System was taking over. Here was a historic vacuum which the church should be alert to fill. So Oberholtzer had Joseph Jung, the youthful German publisher at Doylestown, reprint the so-called "Waldeck Catechism,"[48] which had been reprinted for Canadian Mennonites two decades earlier, and had figured, since then, in a schism among Mennonites in the Palatinate.

Oberholtzer's unsigned prefatory remarks show him conscious of a possible wider role in the church. He addresses "all bishops, teachers and servants, together with the other members of our Mennonite congregations." While assuring the reader that this book comes as the result of "manifold desire," he states, "But nothing new is involved here ... only the ancient teaching which Christ and his apostles taught." This was apparently unconvincing to more conservative leaders, one of whom later stated that the "questions" in the catechism differed from those in the old *Christliches Gemuethsgespraech*, on important subjects such as "going to law, marrying outside the church and some other points...." Oberholtzer goes on to stress that "our dear youth must be taught discipleship of Christ our Savior in their tender childhood." His reading of the spiritual condition of the Mennonite community is evident in his statement that his catechism could "also serve many adults, who are still children in understanding."[49]

To be so earnestly at work as to challenge the church's time-honored custom of using Gerrit Roosen's *Christliche Gemuethsgespraech* for instruction—and then not to be allowed a voice in the *Rath*—the council or conference—itself! Oberholtzer realized that he was not only partially "silenced" as a minister, but "excluded from Council," and so did not attend the next several sessions. Instead, the troubled Swamp congregation, now divided into distinct factions, sent a committee of three to the October 1844 session. They too were not allowed to speak. It is perhaps from this moment that there drifted down in the Oberholtzer family the tradition that he had once stood on a stump outside the Franconia meetinghouse at conference-time, and declared that if he were not allowed to address the council itself, he would speak outside.[50]

There apparently was some sentiment toward providing the disaffected minister with a way back into conference acceptance. An undated scrap of paper surviving in the Nyce family contains a twice-written statement suggesting the view of the Oberholtzer situation as held by the Franconia Conference.

> According to the regulations *[Ordnungen]* of the forefathers, resolved that if Oberholtzer comes and [is] obedient to the regulations of the forefathers and promises to uphold and accept for his own rule our nonresistant foundation and reconciles himself with the Council which has been offended by him, he shall [be] welcome and be taken up and accepted in love as a fellow-brother and fellow-minister.[51]

The real distance between Oberholtzer's and the majority's perceptions is evident in the fact that this statement makes no reference to the coat issue, which for Oberholtzer seemed to be paramount. For him it was the intolerable sign of legalism. For the traditional majority, the coat issue was a subdivision of the issue of covenant loyalty to a "nonresistant" heritage.

This had been the summer (1844) when Skippack—the leading congregation in the conference—had finally resolved to get a new meetinghouse. In July the original stone building—oldest and for long the largest in the conference—had been "broken down,"[52] and a larger one, fifty by sixty feet, erected. There had been differences of opinion over this change. The new building was kept traditionally simple, with the usual long "preachers' bench" running along the longer side. Doubtless the same attitudes guided the builders as were articulated in these years by Deacon Henry Clemens at Salford, where a new meetinghouse was also being planned. "There is no intention," wrote Clemens, "to erect a splendid temple, in accordance with ornament and pride; no superfluities are intended—rather only what is serviceable, orderly, becoming and enduring."[53] While the Skippack building was going up, Bishop Christian Herr and three other ministers from "Lancaster" came through, and preached in the woods on the meetinghouse farm.[54] Herr had a warm spot in his heart for the Hunsicker family, whose father Henry had meant so much to him, spiritually, nearly thirty years earlier. Now he was one of the main leaders in the Lancaster Conference.

The 1844 Skippack Mennonite meetinghouse, referred to after the 1847 division as "Lower Skippack." (Alan G. Keyser)

On October 6, the Sunday following the fall conference, Skippack's new building was finally "consecrated," with "about one thousand people there."[55] Perhaps it was around this time that one of the preachers remarked, on a Sunday morning of large attendance, "This church blooms like the rose."[56] John Oberholtzer, though not a participant at conference, had many admirers at Skippack. In the months following the opening of the new building he preached both in the meetinghouse itself and at "Henry Allebach's." "I was there," noted young Garrett Kolb the organist, "& he did preach first rate."[57]

Sixteen months after having been silenced at conference, Oberholtzer was uneasy at heart. He had read criticisms of the spiritual condition of American Mennonites in European correspondence, as published in Canada. He felt a continuing urge to write back to Europe.[58]

A week after Oberholtzer preached yet again at Skippack, in September 1845, occurred the death of Jacob Gottschall, for years the senior bishop of the conference. Later in the same week, his colleague Samuel Gehman, preacher for nearly half a century at neighboring Rockhill, also passed on. Bishop Gottschall had been born only six years after the death of the first bishop of the conference, his own great-grandfather Jacob Gaetschalck. Minister Gehman had been the fourth in an unbroken pedigree of Gehman preachers dating back to the 1717 migration. Such a significant double passing called for reflection.

It is revealing that the person chosen to preach Bishop Gottschall's funeral sermon was not another bishop, though there were four such available. Not John Hunsicker (the new conference moderator), or elderly Henry Hunsberger of Hilltown, or Bishop Gottschall's younger replacement, Jacob Kolb of Plains—none of these was chosen. Rather, it was the venerable preacher John Geil of Line Lexington who was given this significant role.[59] Now in his late sixties, Geil spoke on the text considered particularly apt for ministers: "I have fought a good fight. I have finished my course. I have kept the faith." The old preacher could well have been speaking for himself. Yet he would survive—and preach—for another two decades, and be remembered sitting "behind the preacher's desk, an old man with long white hair and a yellowish, white overcoat, with a cape, or several capes, as was the customary style with the plain people in those days."[60] He was probably the most respected leader in the conference, and the most approachable from either side of the ominous growing polarization.

His voice was heard again at Franconia less than two weeks later, as the fall conference convened. With Bishop Gottshall gone, the liberal John Hunsicker was moderator, and a new chemistry seemed to affect the proceedings. Two important "resolutions" were passed, both surprisingly favorable and heartening to the liberal part of the body. The first called for the testing of all proceedings and rules against one criterion and one only: "the Gospel." Of course no one could object to such a standard; it remained to be seen what this resolution meant in practice. As the progressive minority saw it, it meant that only such "rules and usages of the forefathers" as were found to be "based on gospel truth" would be kept. And just as "acceptable" to them was a proposal of John Geil: that "everything which would in the future be discussed in Conference should be written up." Perhaps now, at the first session after the passing of longtime leaders Gottshall and Gehman, was the time to make this improvement. John Oberholtzer, of course, had been asking for this before he was silenced. Anything he asked for had seemed suspect to the conservative majority, but coming from John Geil himself, there could be no real objection. The resolution was "accepted unanimously."[61]

"Inspired with new hopes" by reports of these liberal-sounding sentiments, John Oberholtzer and his colleagues from the Swamp district who had been silenced two years earlier turned up at spring conference in 1846. They anticipated "a reconciliation." Conference had not heard Oberholtzer's voice for the past two sessions. In the previous fall, the assemblage had seemed content to welcome some new emphases. But either there had been second thoughts since then, or the presence of John Oberholtzer, still without a plain coat, catalyzed a negative reaction. Perhaps a growing rift in the congregation at Skippack had also cast its shadow on the conference itself. Conference members seemed to sense that at their previous session they might have been too incautious. The tone was now protective rather than expansive. Instead of reaffirming their recent resolution that all practices would have to be corrected by "the Gospel" alone, they now "decided . . . that we shall continue to labor on the foundation and customs of our forefathers, turning neither to the right nor to the left." It also seemed that most conference members "did not want to hear anything about record-keeping," in spite of John Geil's resolution in its favor at the last session.[62]

This was not, certainly, an auspicious atmosphere for a proposal made by John Oberholtzer, who not only attended, but now apparently spoke whether he was "permitted" or not. In the interest of "peace," he offered to "sacrifice" his "privileges," and get "another coat," if the conference would revoke its earlier resolution silencing him for disobedience. But he had misread the mood of the conference. His plea was not granted, and he thereupon retracted his offer. Testing the direction of the body, someone asked whether the conference could show by a rising vote whether they were still in harmony with their previous resolution "to go with the Gospel" alone, rather than with custom. Moderator Hunsicker, apparently eager for a reaffirmation of this principle, trying repeatedly to call for the vote, found himself stymied by persistent objections. An older minister finally expressed doubt as to whether "going by the gospel alone" was really a safe course—a statement that seemed unfortunately revealing to the liberal opposition. But it was evident that something basic was wrong; John Hunsicker's leadership was not being accepted by a large part of the body—doubtless those who had appreciated Franconia's Bishop Gottshall in the moderator's role. The conference "broke up" in a "confusion"[63] probably unparalleled since the days of Christian Funk, seven decades earlier.

In the uncertain months following, the liberal Bishop Hunsicker and John Oberholtzer had increasing contacts. When Oberholtzer preached at Skippack on a Tuesday morning in July, the large meetinghouse was "overwhelmed" with listeners.[64] In turn, the seventy-three-year-old Skippack bishop came to Swamp, supported by his affluent brother Abraham. Together they visited all the congregations in the Swamp "bishop district," trying to woo back into unity the conservative minority upset by John Oberholtzer's actions. The Hunsickers called for a meeting of all the ordained men in the Swamp district—a kind of subconference session—at which peace might be reestablished. But when the appointed day arrived, it became starkly clear that several of the ministers had stayed away without explanation. Deeply disappointed, "the old bishop" Hunsicker dismissed this meeting, and nothing was done.[65] The disunity in Oberholtzer's congregation, now considerably more acute than at Skippack, was possibly beyond repair.

It was a time—this summer of 1846—full of talk of war between the United States and Mexico. No draft was levied during this controversial campaign, but one congregation—Towamencin—nevertheless breathed a whiff of gunpowder. A much-publicized encampment of "volunteers" was held in August as "Camp Washington," the site of the Revolutionary Army's week-long bivouac in Towamencin Township in October 1777. An enormous crowd of spectators gathered—one person guessed there were 10,000—to watch the maneuvers of a mere 200 soldiers. In the midst of the surrounding "quarreling, gambling and drunkenness," the soldiers planned to honor the memory of the patriot General Francis Nash, whose cannon-mangled body Commander-in-Chief George Washington had buried with full military pomp beside the Towamencin Mennonite meetinghouse. Only two years before the present encampment, patriotic citizens of Norristown and Germantown had erected, without ceremony, a ten-foot marble obelisk in memory of Nash, for whom the City of Nashville, Tennessee, had been named. Here, where this monument towered over the simple gravestones of Gottschalks, Hendrickses, and Boorses, the soldiers wished to fire a memorial salute. The Towamencin congregation did not favor permitting this, but before the encampment was over, John Boorse remembered, "their objections were finally withdrawn."[66]

One further incident of the fall of 1846 merits a page in our story: the birth of the last new congregation in the Franconia Conference area, while that conference was still a single entity. It took place in hilly and wooded Frederick Township, not far from where Hans Neus, one of the first Mennonite ministers at Germantown, had purchased land after forsaking his ministry. Here the devout, Huguenot-deriving Bertolet family had been farming for generations. At least half a dozen had married Mennonite spouses, and one—Henry—had even become a Mennonite minister in the greater Skippack circuit. On a rainy day in September, Samuel Bertolet met in his mill with his brother Daniel, Daniel's son Benjamin, and a neighbor, John Hunsberger. They agreed that there ought to be a Mennonite meetinghouse in this venerable but thinly populated countryside. All three of the grown men pledged $100, and later three more men, including a third Bertolet brother, Johannes, contributed the same amount.[67] Johannes would have a grandson, Nathaniel Bertolet Grubb, who would become a strong Mennonite leader, and preach at "Bertolet's." He would find it "strange" that his "deeply spiritual" grandfather, who spent most of his last years reading the Bible and Johannes Arndt's *True Christianity*, and helped to build the Bertolet's Mennonite meetinghouse near his home, would seldom attend public worship, and never unite with the Christian Church.[68]

The Bertolet homestead in Frederick Township. (The Schwenkfelder Library)

Chapter 9

"This Is Not Christian"
1847

Seldom could there have been so dramatic a moment in the memory of the Skippack Mennonite congregation as the one that unfolded in their packed and hushed meetinghouse on the morning of Tuesday, New Year's Day, 1847. In the absence of detailed records, our imagination must fill in for us what tradition must have prescribed for them: the long pulpit lined with ordained men, among whom stood the venerable Bishop John Hunsicker, now in his mid-seventies, and in need of more assistance than his two conservative younger ministers, Elias Landes and Abraham Wismer, could provide.

Though parts of the Franconia Conference itself were now at the point of being "divided into factions," the Skippack congregation had somehow stayed peaceful enough to hold its last communion in September, and plans for an ordination could be made. Age had indeed crept up on Bishop Hunsicker—he and his father had now held the leading role in the district for a combined total of fifty-five years—but his mind was crystal clear, and his health so dependable that he had not bothered to make a will. Now he stood before a "class" of ministerial nominees that included, as its most interesting member, none other than his youngest brother Abraham, at fifty-four the most outstanding member of the congregation: financially in a class by himself, widely read, fluent in English, politically involved, and with a modern passion for education. But sitting beside John in the pulpit, slow-tongued Elias Landes must have entertained serious misgivings. His worldly Hunsicker cousins had already caused him considerable spiritual concern, perhaps grief. How unpleasant it had been to accompany Deacon John Gotwals to the aristocratic, turnpike-fronting new house at Perkiomen Bridge, to ask the wealthy Abraham to account for his electioneering, his modish carriage, and his daughters' attending meeting without caps! Abraham, of course, could talk circles around Elias, and the fancy Hunsickers would doubtless trade many a private joke about their solemn investigators on their errand of "keeping house" in the church. The two families, indeed, were increasingly living in different cultural milieus. Abraham's son Henry, ready to begin teaching school, had been getting an advanced education in a Baptist-run seminary in nearby Norristown, and Abraham had a nephew Joseph, grandson of bishop John himself, who was about to graduate from Union College in Schenectady.[1]

So perhaps it may have been difficult for cautious Preacher Elias Landes to take equably the presence, in the row of ministerial candidates at the front of the Skippack meetinghouse, of politician Abraham Hunsicker. Could it be, Elias may well have thought, that someone so worldly wise as Abraham had been considered an acceptable candidate for an office requiring such humility? Yet when the massive hand of the tall and ruddy-faced Abraham had placed in his bishop-brother's grasp the book he had chosen from the lot, that very book was found to contain the slip of paper which revealed the chosen one. The century-old Hunsicker dynasty at Skippack had a future.

But did "the old Mennonite foundation"? Never had the Franconia Conference had a minister of such cultural savior faire and worldly stature as displayed by wealthy farmer Abraham Hunsicker. How had the old tradition of casting lots, considered in need of correction by the liberal group, ironically made possible the ordination of two such outspoken progressives? The other one was, of course, John Oberholtzer of Swamp, a friend of Abraham's. To Oberholtzer, this new ordination must have been as heartening as it was alarming to Elias Landes.

The contrasting impact was felt in the Skippack congregation almost immediately. Before the winter was out, Abraham had already begun to exert a strong role, taking it upon himself to address the most influential spokesmen of the Franconia Conference, in several letters. One went to longtime Bishop Henry Hunsberger of the "Perkasie" [later Blooming Glen] congregation, apparently next in seniority as a bishop to John Hunsicker of Skippack, and another to the noble-spirited John Geil of New Britain. Co-signed by Abraham's brother, the "aged" bishop of Skippack, the letters stated that it seemed "necessary," since the conference had already "divided into factions," that the two sides should each "choose four or five ministers" to attend a special meeting on the day before the next conference in May, for a "prayerful" review of their "misunderstandings." Such a gathering would surely, in Abraham's opinion, enhance "the welfare of the church."[2]

But the energetic new leader at Skippack soon found that one could

Abraham Detweiler Hunsicker (1793-1872) and his wife, Elizabeth Alderfer (1798-1898), of "Perkiomen Bridge" (present-day Collegeville). Ordained a minister at Lower Skippack on New Year's Day, 1847, Abraham Hunsicker founded Freeland Seminary a year and a half later. (Henry A. Hunsicker, *A Genealogical History of the Hunsicker Family*)

not adjust the traditional conference methods as easily as one could call a meeting on township issues. If the conference itself could not settle dissension, how could a private pre-conference meeting do it? John Geil replied tactfully that although he believed the suggestion of a special meeting "was good," he had found, on taking "counsel," that "others had not thought so." Preacher Geil, for all his intelligence, did have a reputation for submitting his own ego to the wishes of the brotherhood. Bishop Henry

Hunsberger, to whom Abraham Hunsicker's other letter had gone, was less diplomatic. The proposed consultation, he replied pointedly, "would be too much like a county meeting."[3] Let the world do things its way, and let us keep our humbler tradition in which God, not our designs, controls the procedure.

This rebuff to the politician-minister was accompanied by another, on his home ground. Grave criticisms of Abraham's worldly behavior were coming from his co-laborer, the slow-tongued Elias Landes. He was obviously speaking for others in the congregation who could not identify with Abraham's attitudes, and a major rift was rapidly taking shape. In response to Elias's cutting remarks, the liberal majority (what one observer called "the younger people") swiftly had him placed "on the repentance bench" (*an die Busz Bank*), his ministry suspended "until the church calls for him."[4] For the first time in years Elias's name was not signed to the annual audit of the deacon's fund.

This was serious trouble, making necessary a congregational "*Umfrage*" (inquiry meeting). Since the local bishop, John Hunsicker, was a part of the Skippack congregation itself, outside assistance was sought. Old Bishop Henry Hunsberger of Perkasie, who seems to have been next in seniority in the conference to John Hunsicker, did not himself attend the *Umfrage* (perhaps because of his age), but did send his written "Opinion" of the principles of "housekeeping" that would govern this case. Schoolteacher-minister Henry Nice of Franconia was in charge of the proceedings. He began by announcing the absent Bishop Hunsberger's opinion that all those "at peace with the congregation" had a "right to a voice in this case." Further, the congregation indeed had the authority to silence one of its ministers, but only for "gross sins" (as had earlier been done in Henry Bean's case). If, on the other hand, a minister had remained silent on his own volition, he need not have the congregation's permission to begin preaching again, as long as he explained his actions.[5] The necessity for such carefully drawn statements shows that the two factions at Skippack were actually contending over basic understandings of church authority.

As the *Umfrage* discussion waxed warm, the new minister Hunsicker bluntly stated his opinions of Elias Landes' criticisms. They had been so general, Abraham said, that he had not realized they were aimed at him; half of them, furthermore, were not true, and there were no witnesses—no one had "testified" to the reports. This surprised Elias, who had considered Hunsicker's failure to respond earlier to his complaints an acknowledgment of their truth, thus making "witnesses unnecessary." Although the liberal majority was blaming the unrest on Elias's sharp criticisms, he stubbornly insisted that he could not take back what he had said "as long as he lived."

If witnesses were needed, he asked if he could then and there call people out to bring "testimony" to the truth of his complaints.[6] When this request was refused by the majority present, Elias and his supporters felt unfairly blocked.

It seemed to be a matter of whether, in the sharpness of his criticisms, Elias had committed a "gross sin." Members of the progressive wing, resentful of the dismissal of their earlier favorite Henry Bean, reasoned that Elias's sin was also a major one, and that they could prove it. But such proof, according to their opponents, never materialized. "They *never* did it," was the opinion of David Allebach, deacon at neighboring Towamencin and husband of a Hunsicker; "that turned me against them."[7] And before long, the other Skippack minister, pleasant Abraham Wismer, began to feel that Abraham Hunsicker's attitude was as questionable as Elias's. One man was, he stated, "as deeply at fault" as the other. Hearing of this, the new minister went to Wismer twice, demanding that he too "take back" his comment; it was an injustice, Hunsicker argued, and unless it were withdrawn, Wismer would be silenced by the congregation as Elias had been.[8]

But by now Wismer had become as firm as Elias in their criticism of their stylish co-pastor, and insisted that he would wait for the opinion of the regular "Big Conference" at Franconia. Provoked by this, the Skippack progressives demanded "a confession before the congregation." But Wismer stood his ground, asserting that he would make up his mind only after an impartial investigation from outside the congregation had been overseen by the conference. In this crisis it began to appear that the liberal Skippack majority was now beginning to view conference efforts at "housekeeping" as an intrusion into their internal affairs, while the smaller group of conservatives looked to conference as a more dependable keeper of the "Old Foundation."

In mid-April, with conference drawing near, a half dozen supporters of Elias Landes drew up an unusual appeal directly to "the Conference," asking this body to "choose unbiased men to investigate the case and settle it." These conservatives, including Elias's wife, his sister and several neighbors, felt that Abraham Hunsicker was getting the best of the struggle by bypassing traditional authority. They themselves were "willing," they wrote, "to yield to the Conference"; they desired "to continue according to the old ground and . . . to have such a committee as are at one with the old foundation. . . ."[9]

But their old bishop, John Hunsicker, also looking ahead to spring conference, was taking an opposite direction. With his younger brother Abraham, he was now ready for actual changes of long-held requirements that his liberal wing was finding more and more distasteful. He wrote a letter to the preacher at Swamp who, though only half his own age, had been the best articulator of the idea of a "Reform." The bishop's letter invited John Oberholtzer to a special meeting (refused, as we have seen, by John Geil and Henry Hunsberger), to be held the day before conference. In the Skippack meetinghouse the gathered ministers would discuss the "prevailing derangement among the congregations," and "measures" for a possible "settlement." The bishop asked his young colleague at Swamp "to write some project to that effect."[10]

Only two or three weeks were left until conference, but in his smithy near the West Swamp meetinghouse Oberholtzer had been thinking, since about New Year, of a possible "Constitution" to regulate conference proceedings. Such a document would also be an opportunity to disassociate, on record, the Mennonite ideals from what Abraham Hunsicker called "servile reverence . . . for antiquated forms, and traditional customs." It was time, in Abraham's words, to give a due role to the God-given "faculty of thought—the privilege of reason—that great prerogative of the soul." The leadership should pass from people who wished to "cling tenaciously to . . . their ancient Church discipline." The "enlightened government" of the United States, and "the free and liberal spirit of our many good institutions" were bringing Americans of all sects and ethnic origins "to mingle more freely with each other, as neighbors. . . ." Mennonites who held to "mere external forms and ceremonies" of Menno Simons' day were inconsistent. They had "long ago bid adieu" to "log houses and cumbrous implements" for farming. In getting their "brick houses" and "modern implements" there had been "no sacrifice of principle, or irreverence." Why then could they not see that modernization in church life was, likewise, not "a matter of fancy or mere utility," but a "necessity"?[11]

Oberholtzer, in constant contact with Abraham and John Hunsicker, had broached to the bishop, around the time of Abraham's ordination, his idea of a conference *"Ordnung"* or constitution. To this Bishop Hunsicker had responded "cordially."[12] Now, if ever, with a bishop's direct invitation to present a "written project" to settle the confusion "among the congregations," was the time to test the Mennonite community's receptivity to the new idea, so common among church organizations of other communions. At least there was more to gain, for John Oberholtzer, in linking up with progressives at Skippack and Hereford than in trying on his own to pacify the adamant conservatives at Swamp. For here, too, as at Skippack, a minority was bypassing their ministers and appealing directly to the conference body. They had asked, in fact, for another minister, and were on the verge of building a separate meetinghouse.

In haste, with barely two weeks left until conference, the locksmith-

John Hunsberger Oberholtzer
(1809-1895), whom Abraham
Hunsicker called "the ac-
knowledged pioneer of our
... reform." (H. P. Krehbiel,
*History of the Mennonite
General Conference*)

preacher drew up a sequence of seventy "articles"[13] for "the guidance and
government" of the Mennonite "brotherhood." Their purpose, he wrote,
was to see that the "purity of the teaching of Jesus," and a "discipline"
consistent with that teaching, would be "cultivated and maintained." The
"articles" reveal a new blend of motifs from both the "Old Mennonite
Foundation" and contemporary cultural ideals. Great interest is shown in
organization and defining the roles of leaders. Individual congregations are
given more freedom from the monolithic authority of the conference. Effective instruction of children and baptismal applicants is stressed. There is less
restriction on "going to law."

Starting on the topic of "Offices" and "Officers" (*Vorgesetzte*), by
which he means bishops, ministers, and deacons, Oberholtzer uses the
words *fähig* and *Fähigkeit* (capable, capability) four times. "It is particularly necessary, when choosing a minister," to "consider [his] capability,"
since he may later become a candidate for bishop. Throughout the
"Gospel," writes the reformer, great stress is laid on "choosing none but
such as are capable of teaching others," or at least have "teaching gifts"
that can be developed: "a clear distinct voice" and "natural fluency." Even
more important, however, is "a blameless life." Then Oberholtzer in-
troduces a new procedure in the choosing of ministers: after the congrega-

tion has, as traditionally prescribed, handed in its "nominations" for the ministerial office, a special "vote" is to be taken, to determine which two men are considered the best candidates. Only between these two is the lot to be cast.[14] (John himself had been one of fifteen nominees.) Here the reformer is de-emphasizing the former blind trust in God's overruling power, and strengthening the democratic element. Although he retains the use of the lot itself, this change would be immediately lifted out by conservative critics, not only because they saw it as "a dangerous encroachment on the right of the congregation" to have all their candidates presented to God, but because in such a procedure the "Lord's choice would . . . be interfered with."[15]

Even more striking are the young organizer's directions for the process of voting at conference. "There shall be a chairman and a secretary . . . elected annually by a majority vote." This, said by conservatives to be "imitating the world exactly," would nevertheless solve the problem of the superannuated moderator with inherited authority. The chairman must "be seriously concerned with orderliness," and the secretary "shall keep an exact record" in which "all decisions," even those "of the least significance are . . . promptly recorded, so that one can always see what has been decided and settled."[16] With such a procedure one could at least pin down capricious leaders who contradicted their own earlier statements in the supposed interests of the brotherhood. Yet conservatives condemned this, saying "the Gospel is record enough to keep the Conference and the church in order."[17]

And when matters came to a vote, there was to be no more mere group-thinking. No vote on a matter of importance would be considered valid "if the whole Conference" stood up "all at once." Rather, it was here "ordered that everyone who is entitled to a vote rise individually, and conscientiously answer for himself Yea or Nay, for or against it." That would prevent the triumph of such reasoning as John Geil's who deferred his personal tastes to the voice of the brotherhood. Abraham Hunsicker disliked that attitude intensely, saying it was resigning one's "power" to "the governing will of man" rather than to Christ. To protect conference-procedure against this old failing, Oberholtzer included a clause that carried a parliamentary, if not outright political ring: "Every member has a right to demand that every member answer for himself alone, and thus it must accordingly be done."[18] The contrast with the old "voting," with its reflexive group-impulses, sideways-glancing, and appeals to precedent and solidarity, was here complete. There was a new definition of how the Spirit would work in the discerning body.

Yet in the section on "Discipline in the Congregation," Oberholtzer clearly evokes the "Old Foundation": "The impenitent sinner shall be dealt with according to the rule of Jesus, Matthew 18." If he shows no repentance, he is to be "excluded" or "banned"—"separated from the congregation." An interesting list of exclusion-deserving offenses includes both "contentiousness" and "quarrelsomeness," "unrighteous seeking for financial gain," "impudent mockery, cruelty to subjects, and the like."[19] But strict as these rules may seem, when it came to the Christian's relation to the government, a topic important to the "old nonresistant ground," there is more permissive language. Whereas "taking the sword to wage war" is still flatly "forbidden in the Mennonite brotherhood," the statement regarding the swearing of civil oaths is a milder "we do not approve...."[20] For conservatives jealously guarding the "old foundation," that would have been a major deflection. And the article stating that members might "call upon the government," if necessary, "to protect and save our honor and our property"[21] was an outright challenge to Mennonite teaching since the days of the Anabaptists. Preacher Isaac Meyer of Deep Run read this as "a fundamental difference" from what he had been taught.[22] Yet Oberholtzer felt his statement was more honest than the church's usual position. The "old" body merely "pretended," he later observed, not "to use the law for redress of wrongs." He and his more liberal supporters were "not opposed to go to law in a just cause. Every man determines whether his cause is just for himself, but it may be considered by the church."[23]

Another major change suggested in this fascinating document is that "permission" is granted, under proper conditions, for members to marry persons outside the fellowship.[24] Doubtless this had reference to the sizable number of people who remained excluded from communion in the Franconia Conference area because they had never "confessed" to the church after marrying nonmembers. And we may finally notice what some "old" Mennonites seemed to find most threatening of all: a statement that people transferring into the Mennonite fellowship from other denominations which had baptized them as infants need not be "baptized again," if they were "satisfied" with their first baptism.[25] This would draw from several bishops of Lancaster total alarm; it "would at once," they reacted, "destroy at the root our old evangelical ground of faith and confession which has been confirmed by thousands of martyrs because it would open the door for infant baptism...."[26] As it turned out, this statement, important to Abraham Hunsicker, was considered too liberal by some of Oberholtzer's other followers.

A topic of prime concern to the "old" wing that is completely absent in this "Constitution" is separation from the world, or "nonconformity." This does not seem to have been a category of Oberholtzer's thought. In the fact that his document "contained nothing about [the plain coat]," he observed thirty years later, could be seen his "plan of getting rid of the coat regulation." Since "There would be no written regulation . . . everybody had his choice."[27] Surprisingly, he himself changed his choice during the very days he was at work on his new "project," and consulting on its themes with Abraham Hunsicker. With conference only a week away, Hunsicker "prevailed on me," remembered John, "to change my mind." Hunsicker certainly recognized, experienced as he was in "framing tickets" and arbitration, that it would be traumatic enough for the elderly ministers at conference to be confronted with an unprecedented written basis for their functioning, without having it read to them by a person whose very appearance symbolized a rejection of their authority to order the church. Convinced of Hunsicker's logic, the younger minister managed to have "a new round coat made to order yet" in the week before conference "came off."[28]

At least he considered it a plain coat, and wore it to a specially called preparatory meeting at Skippack. Here, as he "presided in the chair" before seven other ministers and five deacons who had responded to Bishop Hunsicker's invitation, John sensed no one regarding his new coat as anything but "a right good one, of the kind."[29] He read his "project for a constitution" twice to his little audience, who came from about ten different congregations. From the local Skippack congregation had come the Hunsicker brothers; the cousins Israel and Jesse Beidler represented the little Phoenixville and Diamond Rock congregations; and the other three ministers represented three congregations from the northern borders of the conference area: "Bill" Landis from Saucon (whose father had challenged the authority of Bishop Jacob Gottshall eleven years earlier), Joseph Schantz from Upper Milford, and Christian Clemmer from Hereford. Each of the latter three had left at home a conservative fellow minister. Israel Beidler, Christian Clemmer, John Oberholtzer, and Joseph Schantz were all in their thirties.[30] All the men now present at Skippack approved the plan of reading the constitution in a similar fashion on the following day, May 7, at the Franconia Conference.

It was spring. From the Skippack to Butter Valley people were planting potatoes and hauling manure. While Christian Clemmer had been sitting in the Skippack meetinghouse, his father-in-law, Hereford Preacher John Gehman, had been planting "corn with machine for the first time." But Gehman was not looking for innovations, when it came to the conference at Franconia. More likely he dreaded what might become of the growing differences in his family, his Hereford congregation, and throughout the conference. People were talking, and word had gotten around that something major was likely to happen at Franconia. Thursday morning dawned crisply, but warmed steadily as a crowd of not less than 200 swarmed into the meetinghouse at the edge of Preacher Henry Nice's farm. Many more lay-members than ordained men were in the audience. As seventy-five-year-old John Hunsicker took his seat near the front, he was firmly committed to seeing that now, at the end of a half-century of his and his father Henry's leadership, a new and better basis for conference procedure be introduced. His sense of ownership was so strong that John Oberholtzer had formed the impression that the conference itself had been "founded" by his father Henry. Now, self-consciously wearing his brand-new "round collar," Oberholtzer was seated, manuscript in hand, among the closely packed ministers.

First came other matters, particularly the trouble at Skippack between Elias Landes and Abraham Hunsicker. "Only the breadth of a nail," Abra-ham Hunsicker rose to say, in this his first conference since he had become a minister, stood between him and Elias. If Elias would only "take back his untruths as error," the problem would be resolved. "But Landes," reported one of Abraham's backers, "said every time he could not do that." The con-servative majority at conference seemed to feel that the Skippack congrega-tion was being "too hard on Landes," and they produced a resolution of at-tempted evenhandedness: if Elias "would make a sincere confession before the congregation, and the majority of the congregation would request him to serve [again], the conference would recognize him "as a brother" in its deliberative process.[31]

It was an inauspicious preparation for the more difficult topic to follow. Everyone was keenly aware of the impending presentation of the constitution (two of the men signing it at Skippack the day before had also attended, that evening, a meeting of ministers in a home, probably Preacher Henry Nice's, near the Franconia meetinghouse). John Hunsicker doubtless took over his role as moderator as soon as the discussion of his own particular congregation had led to the "decision" on his junior minister, Elias Landes. He then brought up the topic of the new constitution, and in "due time," John Oberholtzer himself "arose" to call for a reading of it. First, however, he asked the assemblage to take note of the fact that he had now gotten the new coat they had formally resolved, three years earlier, that he should accept. No sensation seemed to sweep over the audience, nor was there any expression of gratification. To John's surprise there was only one dubious response. An "old member" stood up, glanced over at him, and observed to the crowd, "He now has another coat, but I think it is yet worse than the other one." This left Oberholtzer feeling, in his own words, "very much mortified."[32] Forging ahead nevertheless, he requested permis-sion, in the name of the thirteen signers, to read his manuscript before the entire body, with the recommendation that it then be voted on as a basis for future conference life and procedure.

The actual spoken request to hear read in their traditional gathering so modern a thing as a *constitution* must have registered a kind of breathless shock, a sharp knocking at the door of a new era. It certainly was "ebbes neues"—"something new"—and had come on too fast for most of the group to have gotten used to the idea. The mere length of it—seventy articles (later making a booklet of twenty-one pages)—may have seemed overwhelming. Had there indeed been a secretary to keep regular minutes of the discussion, our picture of the reaction would be much clearer. As it is, we must piece it together from the varying memories of polarized participants.

All witnesses agree, of course, that as soon as the reading was proposed, there were "objections." But they disagree on the mechanics of the conference's response. The progressives would claim heatedly and repeatedly that a *vote* was taken on the request for a reading, in which vote the conservative majority turned down the request. Preacher Henry Nice, something of a spokesman for the majority, would later deny this version of the procedure. The constitution, he would write, was in point of fact "not voted on at all—either for or against." What happened, as he understood it, was that it was merely "left lying," without a definite action as desired by its proponents.[33] Perhaps this means that most of the conference-members found the proposal a maneuver so out of line that it did not merit a response. On the other hand, John Detweiler, deacon at Rockhill and brother-in-law of Moderator Hunsicker, had said, "Let it be read."[34]

Whatever did in fact happen was, in the eyes of the progressives, a form of rejecting the document itself. And John Oberholtzer had not taken all this trouble only to have his efforts ignored. He or someone in his party then made a request as to whether those who favored the constitution might, at least, have it printed, so that all members of the conference might read it at home by the next session, and so come to their own ideas as to its worth. To this request came a response from aged Bishop Henry Hunsberger of Perkasie. "It would be absurd," he said, to permit to be printed, in the name of the conference, a document whose content was unknown. This put the minority in a double-bind: they could not make the content of their document known, and because it was unknown, they could not print it. At length Moderator Hunsicker was able to call for a vote on the question of printing. The results were crushing; a "large majority" rose to vote it down. Apparently sensing a breakdown of fellowship, and "deeply hurt in his feeling," the aged moderator startled the assemblage with an accusation: "This is party spirit. It will be printed anyway."[35]

There had been strained moments in conference for at least the past three years, but such an expression from the moderator himself meant that coherence was fast eroding. Observing the session drifting toward an indeterminate close, one of those who opposed the proposed constitution, in an apparent reconciling mood, asked whether it might not be reasonable to appoint a special committee to read the document privately, and render a report to the larger body. But "no hearing" was given even to this moderate suggestion. The vote to deny the printing was turning out to be the "last business" of the session,[36] and had already left with the progressives a profound impression of rejection. Bishop Hunsicker, sensing that his leadership had been compromised, remarked with discouragement that by now there was insufficient time left to read the document even if this were desired. And, in any case, everyone would have a personal copy before long.

"It will be printed anyway." The bishop's shocking reaction, defying the authority of the conference to regulate the behavior of its members, had now pronounced the polarization acute. His growing anger, and that of his colleagues, was taken back to their home congregations at Skippack, Hereford, and Swamp, where it simmered throughout the summer of 1847. John Oberholtzer, determined that the "*Constitution*," or "*Ordnung*," be read across the conference, placed an order for a thousand copies with a printer in Allentown. It may be that, hearing of this bold action, his opponents looked for an opportunity to defeat it. Oberholtzer left instructions with the printer to have a box of the twenty-one-page pamphlets shipped by stagecoach down to his home at Milford Square. At Coopersburg, where stage and baggage were ordinarily "changed," lived William Oberholtzer, John's older brother, in a house next to the Saucon meetinghouse. He was told to meet the stagecoach and take out of the box enough copies for the Saucon congregation. He took fifty (an indication that every family, at least, was to get a copy), and sent the rest on. But when the stage arrived at Milford Square there was neither box nor pamphlet to be found. The commonest theory around Coopersburg was that the box had been "intercepted and destroyed" by a thief looking for valuables. But there was also suspicion as to possible collusion by opponents of Oberholtzer.[37] Though the mystery was never cleared up, it turned out that there remained enough copies, in addition to those in the box, "to satisfy the congregation." Deacon Abraham Wismer of Deep Run had his own copy by June, and noted that it had cost him "6¼ Cts."[38]

It was perhaps alarming to read, on the title page of a published pamphlet, the words, *Ordnung der Mennonitischen Gemeinschaft* (Constitution of the Mennonites). Alarming, that is, to someone who read in this a kind of claim to official status. While it doubtless was read in this manner by those who opposed Oberholtzer, he himself intended the publication as a proposal, not a *fait accompli*. However, no editorial words to that effect appeared in the booklet. The issue seemed so grave that Minister Henry Nice both sent a hand-carried copy of the booklet to the bishops of the Lancaster Conference, and went out for a visit himself.[39] After the Lancaster leaders had read the constitution, they wrote (August 29) their opinions back to Nice. Observing first that although the Lancaster and Franconia Conference procedures were not identical, they were "the same in principle," they objected to "the new proposals" of Oberholtzer under five headings: choosing ministers, supporting ministers, calling on the government to protect honor and property, marrying outside of the faith, and receiving members with only infant baptism. The writers of these objections were deeply perturbed by what they read in Oberholtzer's "printed booklet." Saying they were speaking "from the depth of our hearts," they called on their "esteemed Brother Nice" to hold to the "old Ground." "We feel convinced and believe firmly"—the words are probably those of the Hunsickers' old friend, Bishop Christian Herr—"that if the old faith is so torn down, as the new constitution shows, the days of the nonresistant Mennonite Church would be numbered."[40] This letter was copied and circulated widely in the Franconia Conference.

Tempers ran high on both sides, and there were outbursts of ill feeling. A month before the Lancaster letter was written, there had been a dramatic "occurrence" at the West Swamp meetinghouse. As John Oberholtzer told the story, the alienated conservatives in his congregation had received permission from the conference to have "other ministers" to "preach for them in one of the congregation's [two] meetinghouses" ("East" or "West Swamp"), if the congregation agreed. But when "this question" was "presented to a regular meeting of the Congregation," it was decided "nearly by common consent," according to Oberholtzer, to allow "no alteration in their meetings and no division in the congregation."[41]

Outside of this "common consent" were at least seven local families who were by this time so at odds with their progressive preacher that they were ready to contribute substantially for a meetinghouse of their own. This minority decided "privately" to disregard the prohibition by the congregational majority, and invited Henry Nice of Franconia, by now recognized as a central leader among the conference majority, to come up and preach them a sermon. They planned to go to the meetinghouse which for the day would be empty, while the main congregation met in the other one. It happened that it was the Sunday for the congregation to meet at the East Swamp meetinghouse, a mile and a quarter from the western one. News of the conservatives' plan got out in the neighborhood, however, and the trustees—members of the liberal majority—decided they would not give out the West Swamp key for that purpose. Since the congregation would be having its regular Sunday meeting at East Swamp, anybody who wished to worship could attend there. This refusal left the conservatives in an embarrassing position, since they had already engaged a preacher and invited their sympathizers. One of them, on the Saturday before the meeting was to come off, tried the key to his own house on the lock of the meetinghouse, and found that it worked.

But the next morning, as Franconia Preacher Henry Nice, his deacon Abraham Clemmer, and "quite a number" of other people collected outside the door, the key could not be made to work. The trustees, having doubtless noticed traffic to the meetinghouse, also came. They refused to open the door, "informing the meeting," according to Oberholtzer, that "under the present circumstances" the house "would not be opened." Oberholtzer's version of the story was that this had been done "in a decent and brotherly way." The conservatives' tradition claimed that they had been driven off with "sticks"[42] or "clubs."[43] In any case, the gathering had been invited to the East Swamp meetinghouse, where, if they would come, John Oberholtzer had promised not to preach that day. But the gathering refused this offer, and "dispersed," regathering, according to one family's tradition, in a house. Oberholtzer called their attempt to meet by themselves an "extraordinary" and "irregular experiment." One certainly could not expect a minister to approve a part of his congregation meeting by themselves. Years later Oberholtzer remarked indignantly that these conservatives at Swamp "made great alarm pretty much the world over, that their meetinghouses were taken from them and locked against them . . . and without any further ceremony seceded out of the Swamp Congregation. . . ."[44]

It was probably the following Friday when those members at Swamp who, as they put it, favored "the old rules and customs of the Mennonite Church," met "to consult with one another, whether it is proper or advisable, or . . . really necessary to build a meetinghouse." "We believe," recorded the secretary, "that we have a specific reason with which nearly everyone is familiar." The group voted unanimously to build, and, since "the congregation [was] weak," to ask "sympathetic members of other congregations for voluntary contributions."[45] The new house was to be built of stone about midway between the other two meetinghouses, on land donated by township auditor Philip Geissinger.

Geissinger's $125 was the largest of a total of seventy-nine contributions from people of Swamp and six other congregations, including "Perkasie" (Blooming Glen), Deep Run, and Doylestown. The range of the

others was from $50 by Abraham Schantz, one of the "builders," to a mite
of "10¢" from the "Widow Shelly." The list shows which of the ministers in
the wider Swamp district supported the conservative side: old John Schantz
of Upper Milford (whose son had signed the constitution); the even older
Valentine Young, minister at Saucon for over four decades; and two
preachers at Springfield, Abraham Geissinger and Jacob Meyer. The latter
was shortly (or perhaps already?) ordained bishop of the Swamp district by
the "old" Mennonites to fill the place of Samuel Musselman. This older
bishop died less than two months after the conservative dissidents in his
congregation had begun to build a third meetinghouse.[46] It was perhaps the
saddest time of his long ministry. He had chosen for his funeral text the
apostle Paul's farewell at Ephesus (Acts 20:25-32): "Take heed . . . unto
yourselves, and to all the flock. . . . For I know . . . that after my departing
shall grievous wolves enter in. . . . Therefore watch, and remember, that
. . . I ceased not to warn every one. . . . And now, brethren, I commend
you to God. . . ." Within eight months, we find the name of Minister Jacob
Meyer of Springfield listed among the other bishops of the Franconia Conference. Among the liberal majority in the Swamp district, John
Oberholtzer, the new bishop, received as a fellow-minister the enthusiastic
William N. Shelly.

Down at Skippack, tensions had certainly not abated during the summer. In accordance with the conference "decision," Preacher Elias Landes
had spoken words of "confession" in a congregational meeting, but his
statement contained no acknowledgment that in his criticisms of Abraham
Hunsicker he had said more than was true. It was this that Abraham was
demanding. Elias does seem to have admitted that he might have said more
than was called for, but he refused to retract the truth of what he had said.
When Abraham Hunsicker specifically asked him to "take back" his
criticisms, Elias stubbornly shook his head and said, "The Conference did
not require that of me; old [moderator Henry] Hunsberger said I would not
need to do that." The same response came from the other minister, Abraham Wismer. When Hunsicker challenged him, he too "shook his head a
little and said, 'Ich halt mich am Rath' " ("I hold to the Conference").[47]

This summer of discontent was a time of destiny—the last interval
before the Franconia Conference would find itself permanently and officially divided. The national news was still of conflict with Mexico, and
there were protests in Norristown that the war had "been brought about
without the knowledge of Congress." The first postage stamps appeared on
American letters in July. Daguerreotypists were recording American faces
with a new, uncanny specificity. A group of men organized to turn the
North Wales Road, running through Harleysville to Sumneytown, into a

turnpike, complete with arched stone bridges. The new meetinghouse at "Bertolet's" was dedicated, with sermons by John Oberholtzer and Abraham Hunsicker. The latter had education on his mind; it had "already for a long time engrossed [his] most serious attention."[48] Soon he and Oberholtzer would again collaborate by speaking together at the dedication of a new building for "The Skippack Association for the Promotion of Useful Knowledge," where they were included in a list of worthies advertised as "capable speakers."[49] Now in his mid-fifties, and already worth over $100,000, Abraham had developed into an apostle of improvement. "Man being a progressive creature," he had come to believe, "must rise gradually; nor is there a limit this side of infinity, to which the perseverance of man . . . may not attain."[50]

In general the Hunsickers were in a cultural transition. Bishop John Hunsicker had a grandson Joseph about to become principal of an academy in Trappe (formerly spelled "Trap," but now elevated even, on occasion, to a spurious "La Trappe"). Joseph, whose grandmother could not even write her own name, had just graduated Phi Beta Kappa from Union College at Schenectady, where he gave the Hebrew oration to a class including a future president of the United States. Abraham Hunsicker's bright son Henry, teaching summers at the school at the Salford Mennonite meetinghouse, won a debate at Trappe on the positive side of the question, "Was Congress justified in removing the Indians beyond the River Mississippi?"[51] And out beyond that river, a month after the debate, there arrived at the Great Salt Lake a family from Trappe who had joined the Mormons. The wife and mother, Eleanor Beidler Bringhurst, was a sister of Mennonite preacher Jesse Beidler of the Diamond Rock congregation. Her oldest son William, now aged eight, would grow up to be a Mormon bishop in Salt Lake City, and father, with three wives and twenty-five children, who had Mennonite cousins scattered through Bucks, Montgomery, and Chester counties.[52]

It was also an ordinary time, with baptisms and communions and harvest home services. Reformed Pastor John Andrew Strassburger, friendly with many Mennonite neighbors, married three Mennonite couples in one day in September. Henry Alderfer of Upper Salford made spinning reels. In Lower Salford, Polly and Nancy Alderfer, unmarried sisters living with their widowed mother, sewed caps, never charging more than a dollar a week. And Simeon Kratz, of the Perkasie congregation, was running unsuccessfully on the Whig ticket for Commissioner of Bucks County.[53]

In the midst of such a scene, then, came "that memorable October 7, 1847," and the fall conference at Franconia. "A great crowd" assembled on this cloudy, somewhat rainy Thursday, with laymen, such as twenty-five-year-old Jacob Bechtel of Boyertown, far outnumbering the sixty or so ordained members of the conference. Sixteen men—the same number as had cumulatively signed the proposed constitution half a year earlier—sat dramatically apart from the other members. Among them was the former moderator, elderly John Hunsicker. His role had now been taken over by Bishop Henry Hunsberger of Hilltown, who was, at seventy-nine, the oldest man in the body, outside of eighty-two-year-old Deacon John Lederach of Salford.

Hunsberger was in no mood to conciliate. He was faced with a group of ministers and deacons who had openly defied the authority of the "Council" *(Rath)*, and who were now expressing a defiant solidarity by having "seated themselves apart." As Hunsberger allowed the discussion to get under way, Bishop John Hunsicker "blamed the Conference," remembered Jacob Bechtel, "that they did not desire to have the little book read."[54] Moderator Hunsberger countered this by saying that Hunsicker himself had remarked, at one point in the previous session, "that it could not be read, it would take too much time." For whatever reason, neither Hunsicker nor any of his fifteen supporters responded to this. But John Oberholtzer made another attempt to have his constitution considered by conference. The sixteen men who had subscribed, he suggested, could choose six of their number, "And you, the Council, will appoint six on the other side." This joint committee could "examine the document thoroughly, and reject any point ... which should be found wanting." When no response came to this speech, Bishop Hunsicker tried another variation, proposing that all sixteen of his group stand, and sixteen of the other group stand with them; this would comprise a committee to discuss the constitution (with equal support on both sides of the question). Here Hunsicker apparently appealed directly to the seated conference, paralleling the role of the moderator, Henry Hunsberger. But again there was no response whatever; "the Council remained silent."[55] The process of forming "sides" was already finished.

There was a more fundamental question. On what basis could this unusual discussion be prolonged? Moderator Hunsberger, representing the conservative majority, set it before the conference. Was it proper that those who denied the conference's authority to control their behavior participate in its "house-keeping"? Should they, Hunsberger put it, "have anything to say in the proceedings?" The majority then rose "unanimously" to vote in the negative.[56]

Two models of church order were here contending for the future of this Mennonite community. The newer one had rationality, democracy, and clarity on its side, as well as a different definition of piety. The traditional one represented the submission of the individual initiative, even when it might be more enlightened, to the authority of the larger brotherhood. That mutual surrender was a key to their self-understanding. But in the midst of a rapid flexing in the cultural framework—the new role of reading, the consciousness of the larger political currents, the prodding by evangelical movements, the opportunities of professional careers—the traditional leaders were unable or unready to speak of their precious "old nonresistant ground" of *Gelassenheit* in accents that would charm the imaginations and emotions of those eager for reform, progress, and positive change. For the latter, too, it was a question of conscience. The conservative leaders seemed to value inaction or a kind of ignoring of issues precipitated by changes in the surrounding culture. At the same time, John Oberholtzer and Abraham Hunsicker were de-emphasizing the covenantal dimension of the Christian fellowship, formerly a central motif in their Mennonite heritage. Their reaction to an intolerable cultural stagnation had modified their vision and sympathies.

And now they and their fourteen colleagues who had proposed considering a new basis of organization had been roundly rebuffed, and informed that their voices no longer counted at all in the proceedings. To a person looking for democratic procedure, a person searching his own conscience for what seemed right, such a denial of parliamentary "rights" had a clear and simple meaning. John Hunsicker himself, seated among his indignant fellow progressives, articulated it for them, in another crisp comment. "We are done," he is quoted variously; "we have nothing [to look for] here. We won't be heard."[57]

"We will not put you back," replied the elderly moderator, "any further than you put yourselves back. [But] Until you come and are reconciled with the Conference and with your proposition, that is, the new ordinance, we will have nothing to do [with each other in Conference discussion]."[58]

At this point the thin thread between the two polarized wings of the Franconia Conference snapped in full view of the crowd. Wealthy old Bishop John Hunsicker, in what must have been the saddest and most traumatic moment of his long career as minister and bishop, rose and led his colleagues out of the meetinghouse and out of the conference. They walked through the Franconia meetinghouse door feeling that they had been expelled by a vote of conference. It was the twilight of John Hunsicker's and the Hunsicker dynasty's half-century of Mennonite leadership. The next time many of those present would again be in his presence would be six weeks later at his own funeral, the largest one that could be remembered at Skippack. As with John Oberholtzer's bishop, who had died only a week or two before the conference, John Hunsicker's sensitive personality had doubtless received a greater shock than it would tolerate.

After Hunsicker and his group had made their agitated departure from the Franconia meetinghouse, the discussion persisted for about an hour. What would the conference do, someone asked, "if any" of the dissidents "would return"? A resolution was offered and passed by vote: "That if the brethren who have subscribed that little book entitled 'ordinance of the Mennonite Congregation' come and make a recall and declare the same as being in contradiction to the Evangelical ordinance of the said community, and conciliate themselves with the Council and the congregation over which they are set as ministers, bring a minister or lay brother along as a witness that they [have] performed as above said, then they shall be received as members and deacons in love."[59] This statement was signed by three elderly men who were, in effect, the most influential leaders at the moment: the two eastern bishops Henry Hunsberger and Isaac Gottschall (Doylestown), and Minister John Geil. It was apparently sent to someone among the dissident group.

Consternation and turmoil now swept the congregations around the outer edges of the conference—Skippack circuit, Hereford, Upper Milford, Swamp, Saucon, Springfield, and Deep Run. In the geographic center or at Doylestown very little dissension seemed to appear, except at Rockhill, where the deacon interrupted Abraham Fretz in a meeting to read a document of some sort. Ten or eleven of the sixteen progressive leaders convened within three weeks at Skippack, where, as at Swamp, they had a majority of the congregation. There they elected as chairman the admired Abraham Hunsicker, and as secretary, John Oberholtzer. Reviewing their experience at conference, they agreed that they had been driven out, and that this "expulsion" was "in the highest degree unjust." They had, after all, only proposed, not adopted, their constitution. And could they now, someone asked, "make a recall" of a document which, they had believed, "was throughout in all important points clearly based on Bible truths"? As for "minor points," the assembled group felt, "common sense" could be the guide. And what of the invitation of the Franconia Conference to return by confession? "Bill" Landis of Saucon put it plainly: "I cannot see how a Christian person could comply with that demand with a true conscience." Put to a vote, the "demand" was unanimously rejected.[60]

Turning back, now, and restudying their constitution, the eleven men made a few modifications. Regarding the new method of narrowing to two the number of men in the "lot" when ministers were to be ordained (severely criticized by the Lancaster bishops), the new conference made this optional rather than required. They also amended the article on receiving members with prior baptisms, stating that such baptisms must have been on "confession of faith" (*i.e.*, not in infancy) to be considered valid. The statement allowing members to "call on the government" to protect honor and property must also have met considerable objection, as the assembled men now pronounced it not in force until further consideration could be given it. As it turned out, these topics would continue to cause debate, and disunity, for the next decade or two.

The little new conference then made a special declaration: congregations could elect ministers and deacons "at any time" they would "deem it necessary." This was of special urgency to congregations such as at "Gottschall's," or the struggling group at Deep Run, where no ministers had been among those favoring the constitution. The new council also made a gesture toward the considerable body of people who were not at present communing with the Mennonite fellowship, because of some church disciplinary action against them, perhaps years in the past. Such people were now issued a general invitation to return, and promised reception as long as it could "not be shown that they had sinned against the teachings of Jesus." This would at last open the door to members of "mixed marriages," who did not care to acknowledge that they had offended the church by marrying outside its covenant. In general, "persons who have been excommunicated" were now "welcome" to request "restoration";[61] if no serious objections came from the newly organized congregations, they too could come to the Lord's supper. It was definitely a new atmosphere for local Mennonites—a scandalous breakdown of order, when viewed by the conservatives, and a heartening breakthrough of Christian liberty and rejuvenation, as felt by the younger group.

"Since the memorable 28th day of October, 1847," testified John Oberholtzer, "we have acted as a distinct body from the Franconia Conference."[62] The new group called itself "The Eastern Conference of the Mennonite Church of North America."

Abraham Hunsicker, chairman of the new conference, lost three close relatives to death in the following three weeks: a six-month-old granddaughter, a twenty-seven-year-old son-in-law, and his elderly brother, the bishop. Perhaps a highly contagious virus had taken this toll, and found John Hunsicker with defenses weakened by the stress of unprecedented church trouble. The immense crowd at his funeral on November 20 included people like Preacher John Gehman of Hereford, though he himself adhered to the conservative body. (It was still uncertain as to what might be the final result of the recent dramatic separation at conference.) Gehman noted in his diary the selection of the text, once again the apostle Paul's "I have finished my course. I have kept the faith."[63]

In addition to this major loss there was a general lack of ordained

Deacon William Z. Gottschall (1784-1825) and his wife, Magdalena Hunsberger (1787-1864), the parents of the widely known Eastern District preacher "Mose" Gottschall, of the "Gottschalls'" (later Eden) congregation. Deacon Gottschall is wearing the old plain coat and vest, with the traditional *Halstuch* (neckcloth). Magdalena, an accomplished singer, was the daughter of Abraham Hunsberger, who was said to have sung his way out of prison in Philadelphia during the Revolutionary War. (Alan G. Keyser)

leaders in the majority group at Skippack. Two ministers and both deacons had stayed with the conservative group. But within two weeks of John Hunsicker's funeral, these gaps were filled by new ordinations, allowed by the liberty of the new constitution. On the same day, December 2, forty-one-year-old Henry G. Johnson, the schoolteacher, was ordained minister at Skippack itself, and at the small "Gottschall's" congregation, Deacon William Z. Gottschall's son Moses was likewise called. The latter soon amazed audiences with his forceful sermons. On the following day, December 3, a new bishop—Abraham Hunsicker himself—was ordained, along with his rather strange young nephew, Abraham Grater, as deacon. The latter would eventually prove something of an embarrassment to all concerned.

Over at Deep Run there was no ordained person at all to lead the sizable minority who would join the new conference, though Abraham Hunsicker reported being present at three "well-filled" meetings in "Bucks County," during the fall. On the day before Christmas, no less than fifty-one men, including a number who had never joined the church though they were already past fifty years old, signed a petition requesting the use of the Deep Run meetinghouse "every 4th Sabbath for Public Worship."[64] This was considered something of a threat, since the congregation there ordinarily met every Sunday. Considerable ill feeling was expressed. "We were all angry," remembered the "old" Mennonite preacher.[65] The petition stated that if the request were not granted the petitioners would "feel under the necessity of building another house for Public Worship on the same Premises." Before this issue would be resolved, there would be appeals to the Bucks County Court, insults, and even talk of opening the door with axes. In warm weather, the younger men of the liberal side would sit on the fence outside the meetinghouse and disturb the worship, while Isaac Meyer, a preacher their own age who, after some hesitation, had cast his lot with the majority, would thunder against them from the pulpit.

At Skippack there was a dramatic struggle over the property of the congregation. Since both deacons were with the conservative group, this faction had in their possession the ancient alms book and the pewter baptismal basin. They also assumed that they, rather than the innovating liberal majority, were the rightful custodians of the meetinghouse and the 100-acre meetinghouse farm—the symbolic original church property at the center of conference life. When it became clear that the Hunsicker-led majority was just as determined that the property belonged to them, some conservatives bolted the door shut from the inside, using straightened wagon wheel rims as reinforcement. Their outraged opponents then persuaded one of their own young men to break in. He "bored a large hole" in the three-year-old door, "and secured a strong steel saw and sawed until the bolt was sawed through." Then, recalled the man years later, "we went in to hold services."[66]

The conservatives appointed a committee—"Godshall, Keyser and Landis"—to request from the trustees the use of the meetinghouse every other Sunday. This, they later claimed, was "positively refused,"[67] and there were, apparently, further confrontations. One folk story handed down among the "old" Mennonites claimed that as their people drove up to the meetinghouse in their wagons, persons standing behind trees threw stones at the horses to keep them from halting. Forty years later a minister among the "old" Mennonites would write of his congregation's attitude toward the current occupants of the meetinghouse, "We feel that they unjustly possess property which, according to the Gospel as well as to the law, belongs to the old Mennonite Church."[68]

Up at Hereford, though feelings were also intense, a more gentlemanly process was used for the time being. Both liberal and conservative parties met in the same building, with their respective ministers—Christian

Clemmer and his father-in-law John Gehman—in charge of the meetings. The same method was used at the congregation's smaller wing at Boyertown. Each "side," at least for a while, seems to have listened to the preaching of the other, but separate communions were held. At the other important center of the "new" Mennonites, Swamp, the struggle was already over, since the conservatives had built a separate meetinghouse in the summer before the final break at conference.

What shall be our final glimpse at this agonizing year of 1847, when a three-century-old Mennonite fellowship could no longer maintain itself within one covenant? Foregoing analysis and even comment, we might watch the new Bishop Abraham Hunsicker going through his deceased brother's house and barn, taking inventory.[69] There had been no will to guide the executors—Abraham and his brother Garrett—who now found among the old bishop's papers bonds and notes worth over $30,000. Many neighbors had been among the borrowers. In the barn, Abraham and Garrett checked over John's horses, carriage, sleigh, harness, sidesaddle, and saddlebags. In the house they appraised the aged widow's spinning wheel and reel, and her husband's desk, bookcase, and "library." Then there were the "spectacles" with which John had doubtless read his friend Oberholtzer's new "Ordnung," and the "silver watch" by which he had checked the duration of a visiting preacher's sermon. Would that Abraham and Garret had then saved the many letters they must have found among the bishop's things from the Lancaster Mennonite leaders! At this very moment, in fact, Abraham was wondering why Bishop Christian Herr, who had over fifty letters from the Hunsickers in his own collection, had not replied to Abraham's latest one.

Or we might listen, via folk memory, to the conversation of two Skippack women—sisters, it was said. Soon after their congregation had split, their families had come together at a Sunday dinner. Now one asked the other, "Welli sin' recht?" (Which side is right?).

"Ja well," replied the other, "du wit sehne. Selli wie zunehme, selli sin' recht" (Yes well, you'll see. Those who grow are the ones that are right).[70]

A later comment by Preacher Henry Johnson, Abraham Hunsicker's newly ordained colleague at Skippack, is more poignant. Someone in his family eventually asked how, after all, this whole division had really begun. To tell the truth, Henry replied, it had all started when two Skippack families were "standing in market," and one of them looked across the aisle at the other family, and called them "lange Nase" (long noses).[71]

Perhaps William Johnson of the Colebrookdale area put it best. Gathering his family around him as the controversy progressed, he said to them, "Children, this is not Christian."[72]

Chapter 10

"Our Reform" and "Our People"

1848-1860

There were now two official ways of understanding the Mennonite fellowship in southeastern Pennsylvania—two different spiritual landscapes. Leaders of the "new" congregations rejoiced in a "reformation" and "improvement" that they saw "spreading like a forest fire in dry woods." John Oberholtzer wrote to Europe, "My heart is confident when I at times reflect on the happy prospect."[1] His friend Abraham Hunsicker likewise wrote to Bishop Christian Herr of Lancaster, whom he addressed as his "Dear Brother in Christ," that the newly ordained "young ministers are getting along so splendidly that it causes admiration." The Skippack congregation, though all the other ministers and deacons had "stayed back," was in the process of receiving sixty-seven new members in a series of baptisms. "Oh, Brother," wrote Hunsicker, "we have the strongest hope that God is with us, for the factions cannot both be right. We surely do not suppose that we are both wrong. Whichever work then is from God will endure."[2]

Abraham's optimism led him to overstate somewhat the size of the new conference. Of the existing meetinghouses, he informed Bishop Herr, "we have 16, and at most of them nearly all the members." In actuality, about a fourth of the Franconia Conference members were in the process of adhering to the new grouping. Reading a copy of Hunsicker's letter, Minister Henry Nice of Franconia concluded that there were also among the new conference some "frail human beings."[3]

John Oberholtzer later remembered these first heady months of the Eastern Conference as a time when "some thirteen congregations from the Franconia Conference organized themselves." There was evidence, he wrote, especially at the very beginning,

278

that many were awakened from spiritual slumber, and transposed into a spiritual life; worship meetings were attended more zealously and diligently by young and old; the preached Word sounded at all places with earnestness, power and reception; sleeping ceased in many meetings and reverence and quiet increased, yes, people began to search the Holy Scripture and pray more diligently at home; in a word it gave the impression as though many were asking, "What must I do to be saved?"

The heartiest love was mutually manifested among those who believed that they had been delivered from human fetters and useless fables.... People were inclined everywhere to put their hands to the work. Congregations were organized; new meetinghouses were erected; more ministers and deacons had to be installed in office....

Members who had been set back [from communion] for long years for the sake of trivial human opinions rejoined these congregations; young people came in numbers to instruction, and joined in this with fathers and mothers, yes even grandfathers and grandmothers who still stood outside the fellowship, so that for quite a time there appeared a mighty awakening among our east Pennsylvania Mennonites ... and made much talk near and far, not only among the Mennonites but also among neighbors of other persuasions; and not only this, but in a large area of eastern Pennsylvania nearly all church and schoolhouse doors of other denominations were joyfully opened for the free service of the efforts of this new Mennonite direction on Sundays and weekdays, which the preachers driven out of their own conference humbly accepted from their brothers in the faith who differed in some points, yet [were] likeminded in Christ.... Yet here be it also observed, regarding the behavior of our old brothers in the faith, that everywhere here in the East where they had the majority in the congregation, they kept the doors of their meetinghouses locked against the service of all preachers who stand under the written Constitution....[4]

A particularly important feature of the "awakening" was Oberholtzer's new "*Kinderlehre*," the instruction of children in the catechism. "Grown" as well as small children attended the sessions every second Sunday afternoon during the summer. In some congregations as many as "60 or 70 children" were involved in this activity, which was a kind of substitute for and forerunner of Sunday school among Mennonites. Sunday school itself would not be accepted for another decade. After a half or three-quarter hour "practice in singing," the minister led in prayer, and the children recited what they had memorized at home. The book used was the "Waldeck" catechism which Oberholtzer had gotten printed already in 1844, and which the second session of the new conference (May 4, 1848) decided should be reissued in both English and German, along with a slightly revised version of the new constitution. At the *Kinderlehre*, "older members" helped the minister listen to the recitations. Oberholtzer reported this activity with gratification to European Mennonites, the topic having been one of the main concerns of letters he had seen from them. He also expressed "deep sorrow" that some "old" Mennonite "opponents" of the "improvement" had said that they would prefer to have their children "go fishing or to the tavern on Sunday rather than to catechetical instruction." Such Mennonites, wrote the reformer, "who find externals so important declare themselves to be archenemies of any reformation by which sinners may be awakened." As for the leaders of the struggling new conference, "Our comfort is," wrote Oberholtzer, "that we have a clear conscience and strive to live honestly in all things."[5]

And what of the feelings on the other side of the division in these first years? "You wonder what we rely on," wrote Preacher Henry Nice of Franconia in reply to a letter from brash young Abraham Grater. "We rely on this, that we want to keep what we have undertaken, and our forefathers before us, and on the great grace of God and on the merit of Jesus Christ. That is the reliance on which we rely and not on our good works...." So far in his letter, Nice had used the "high German" word for "we"—*wir*— but as he got to his most deeply felt point he lapsed repeatedly into the Palatine or Pennsylvania Dutch *mir:*

> ...as you are no longer at one with us and are going on according to what you think is good, do leave us in peace. We [wir] want to do the same and we [mir] ought to be trying all together to prepare ourselves for eternity, which we [mir] must all soon enter.[6]

Nice, although not a bishop, was the person to whom the "new" Mennonites looked as a spokesman for the "old." The third session of the new conference (October 5, 1848), appointed a committee of two to take to Henry Nice, in writing, an invitation to a public discussion of the differences (there was no response). It was Nice, apparently, who wrote up a brief statement presented to the spring 1848 Franconia Conference, which tried to set the record straight as to what procedure had been followed a year earlier (May 1847). The New Mennonites were claiming that the Franconia Conference had voted not to read the constitution. This, claimed Nice, was incorrect. "... We know that at no time was a vote taken, whether it should be read—and John Hunsicker said that it could not be read on the said day, it would require too much time. This we attest with our own hand."[7] Thirty ministers and deacons present at the May 1847 conference signed this three-sentence statement, and there the matter was apparently dropped. Strangely, though it would be forgotten for seventeen years, it would suddenly come to the attention of the new conference, and cause fresh controversy, in the midst of the Civil War era.

Out in Lancaster, Bishop Christian Herr took his letter from the new Bishop of Skippack, Abraham Hunsicker, to a meeting of a dozen bishops and ministers. The oldest of these, apparently conference moderator Jacob Hostetter of Manheim, abruptly refused even to write back to Hunsicker. Another questioned how Christian, an old family friend of the Hunsickers, could still call Abraham "brother," when adopting a constitution such as the latter was fostering "would confuse and destroy our congregations." The assembled leaders were "unanimous" in the opinion that "those who devised the new standards and constitution" and then proceeded "thereby to claim and confiscate the church houses" had committed "an injustice which cannot be well-pleasing to the Lord."

Bishop Herr accordingly wrote back, addressing his letter to "Friend Abraham Hunsicker," with "a heavy heart."[8] He challenged Hunsicker's statement "that it was not the printed constitution that divided the congregations." In the eyes of the Lancaster bishops, if this had not technically started the disunity in the first place, it had become "the chief basis and conclusion of the division, and also a division between us and you if you keep on with it." Why, asks Herr, "did you act so rashly and erect such a bulwark for a split?" Why not rather follow "Matthew 18 . . . and keep house accordingly?"

Abraham had stated that, for as long as he could remember, there had been around Skippack the widespread opinion that certain "customs" of the Mennonites "ought to be dropped." This, responded Bishop Herr,

> seems strange to me, for it has now been well onto thirty years that I learned to know your father, and a great support he was to me. And many strengthening conversations as well as sermons have I heard from him. Also I still have in my possession more than fifty letters from your father and your brother John. And to the best of my knowledge [I have] never heard a word out of their mouths or read in their letters that they wanted to change the ground and discipline of their Conference. Also neither you nor any other man could make me believe that, if your dear old father were still alive and had his physical and mental strength as he had, he would accept Oberholtzer's standards and constitution or join in with him in his course.

The schism that had now occurred, prophesied Bishop Herr, would produce "extremely great harm" unless Abraham could turn "back again to become an instrument in the hand of the Lord as your father was," in caring for "the great congregation on the Skippack."

Hunsicker, the chairman of the new conference, himself felt personal "sorrow" that the long-standing "bond of love" between him and the Herr family should be broken. But he felt there really was no "sufficient reason" for this. And with his new Mennonite liberty, he was at the point of realizing, at last, his dream of making provision for the "general diffusion" of education "among all ranks of society," including "the youth of both sexes." In the spring following his election as leader of the Eastern Conference, he laid out twelve acres of the land he had recently purchased across the Perkiomen Turnpike from his stylish house, and engaged a carpenter from Trappe to erect a new building for a "seminary" or academy-type boarding school. By fall it stood imposingly where months before there had been a mere woods—four stories topped by a captain's walk and cupola, from which one could look down to Perkiomen Bridge a mile distant and see the stagecoach approaching from Norristown. Abraham's unmarried and unbaptized twenty-one-year-old son Henry, recently a teacher at the octagon schoolhouse beside the Salford Mennonite meetinghouse, was engaged as the principal. Henry placed an advertisement in a Philadelphia newspaper, and found thereby a Professor Warren Sunderland. A waitress, chambermaid, and cook completed the staff.[9]

It was, in these years, something of a fad to build academies. Montgomery County already had three. John Stauffer, whose father had given the land for the Colebrookdale (Boyertown) Mennonite meetinghouse, would build one in 1850, and another would bloom briefly among the Bertolets of Frederick Township in 1857. The name Abraham Hunsicker chose for his school was likewise a sign of the times. As "a very ardent free-soiler and anti-slavery advocate, and being imbued with the spirit of the times which demanded free soil, free schools and Fremont," he "gave the school a liberty ring—'Freeland.' "[10]

After launching the first term on election day in November 1848, with only four pupils, young Principal Hunsicker saw his enrollment mount to seventy-nine by the end of the school-year, and before long Freeland was as popular as any school of its kind in the state. From all over Montgomery and Bucks counties came young Pennsylvania Dutchmen—Beans, Hunsickers, and Kulps from Skippack; Bechtels and Schultzes from Colebrookdale in Berks; a Frick from Line Lexington; Stauffers from Milford; an Allebach and a Tyson from Lower Salford; a Funk from Hilltown. But although such names signified Mennonite background, the Mennonite response in general proved a disappointingly small percentage of the whole. This was a temporary letdown to Abraham Hunsicker, who had "spared no expense" to provide the school "very largely for the benefit of the young men and boys" of the Mennonite community. Nevertheless, the school prospered until it shortly became "the pride of the surrounding country," and such a good investment that in a few years young Henry was allowed to buy it for himself. Incredibly, in 1851, the faculty spawned another seminary, this one for girls, somewhat farther down the Turnpike across from the Perkiomen Bridge. Both schools would thrive until the Civil War, a decade later, would disrupt the pool of students from which they drew, and alienate a southern clientele which had sent daughters north for an education.

While Abraham was absorbed in these projects, the churches in his new conference were undergoing a difficult process of reorganizing. At Hereford, Preacher John Gehman "laid down his office for awhile,"[11] as his divided congregation determined, by vote, which people would follow Gehman's son-in-law Christian Clemmer into the new group, and which would cling to the Franconia Conference. The "new" group ordained Clemmer bishop on August 3, 1848, and on November 28 the "old" fellowship chose John Bechtel as minister. Doubtless each side witnessed the other's ordination, as they both continued to meet alternately in the old meetinghouse at the edge of the road. The new group soon decided, however, that they wanted a new building. Some ill feeling was evident, at least to John Bechtel, who wrote that Christian Clemmer "publicly denounces us from the pulpit as trouble makers and good-for-nothings."[12] Yet when trees were cut down for the new meetinghouse at the other end of the church lot, the new group scrupulously gave exactly half the worth of the timber to the members remaining in the old building.

At Phoenixville, where the membership was small, a new Presbyterian congregation used the Mennonite meetinghouse for its organizational gathering. Jesse Beidler, the preacher at nearby Diamond Rock who had at

Freeland Seminary, built by Abraham Hunsicker in 1848, across the Perkiomen Turnpike from his house. Abraham's son Henry was principal. The boarding house on the right was built by another son, Benjamin, and managed by Benjamin's widow Hannah. (Henry A. Hunsicker, *A Genealogical History of the Hunsicker Family*)

first signed the new constitution, now decided to return to the Franconia Conference.[13] That left his younger cousin Israel Beidler in charge of the local "new" Mennonites. Farther up the Schuylkill, at Vincent, there was no real following for the new group. We find Bishop John Latshaw performing a significant marriage on February 7, 1850—that of Jonathan Kolb and Elizabeth Funk. From this couple and the future family of a young man coming in from Bowmansville looking for work—Joel Good— would largely stem the future of the Vincent congregation.[14]

Up at Saucon (present-day Coopersburg) the liberal majority must have been shocked by the untimely death of their outspoken fifty-year-old preacher, "Bill" Landis, in the summer of 1848. The Upper Milford congregation got an unusual new minister to help Joseph Schantz in 1849, when the lot fell on twenty-two-year-old William Gehman. He was a devout young man who had been raised Lutheran, influenced by the local "Evangelicals," and then baptized by the Mennonites. In the next few years he would become unhappy with the Mennonite reluctance to condone the lively Evangelical type of prayer meeting.

A gesture toward the Franconia Conference was made at the third session of the new Eastern Conference, held at the Skippack meetinghouse on October 5, 1848. At this session John Oberholtzer replaced Abraham Hunsicker as chairman. The gathering drew up an "offer to make peace" with their "opponents"—the Franconia Conference. This "offer" was accompanied by a "demand": that the Franconia Conference leaders "publicly prove" their statement that the members of the new conference had "departed from the old defenceless ground" by printing the constitution and signing it. The new conference declared itself "ready to meet" with their "opponents, and discuss the matter," pledging "to relinquish any point that will not stand the test of right and the Word of God. But we also insist that our opponents shall make the same willing and honest effort to establish peace." William Schelly and Moses Gottschall were appointed a committee to see that this "offer and demand" reached, in writing, Preacher Henry Nice of the Franconia congregation. The offer was to remain good between October 15, 1848, and January 1, 1849. No response was received; the Franconia Conference leaders doubtless read the "offer and demand" as containing no change in the opposed conceptions of what constituted a basis for "binding and loosing" or "keeping house" in the gospel fellowship. The Eastern Conference then "printed and made public" the proposed procedure, "so that all may know what we have asked and demanded of them,"[15] and declared itself ready, at some later time, "to meet publicly with our opponents, to seek an honorable peace."

The two most volatile Mennonite communities of the new group—

called "Oberholtzer people" by the old group—were at Skippack and Deep Run. Whereas the northern Hereford and Swamp, two of the most basic congregational "pillars" of the new conference, would remain stable in these crucial early years, Skippack and Deep Run would be wracked by dissension that would leave long-lasting scars. Skippack began more smoothly under the leadership of the admired Abraham Hunsicker. The conservatives withdrew, though aggrievedly, built another meetinghouse not much smaller than the one the whole congregation had erected four years earlier, and ordained the education-criticizing George Detweiler as their third minister. Probably at least some of the materials for the new meetinghouse were bought from the "Holz und Brett-Hof" (lumber-yard) of Henry Souder in Franconia Township. Souder, whose barn would be removed a few years later to make way for a new railroad from Philadelphia to Bethlehem, and around whose sawmill "Souderton" would be built, was advertising boards, rails, and shingles in the Skippack *Neutralist*.

In the liberal wing of the Skippack congregation, young Principal Henry Hunsicker was baptized a few months after the start of his new career, and in August 1849 Bishop John Oberholtzer performed Henry's wedding to a young woman from the Swamp congregation, Mary Weinberger. On the following New Year's Day, in a notable double ordination among the new wing at Skippack, Henry and his cousin, Deacon Abraham Grater, were selected for the ministry. Neither of these two grandsons of Bishop Henry Hunsicker had much respect for the "old" Mennonite convictions, and it would shortly appear that they were also impatient with their own colleagues in the new conference. Much as in schoolteacher John Oberholtzer's case, Henry Hunsicker found himself with "frequent invita-

The 1848 "Upper Skippack" meetinghouse, as it appeared in the 1930s. (Photo by John D. Souder, The Schwenkfelder Library)

tions" from admiring people in "neighboring churches to preach for them," and he gladly accepted. This itself made no problem, but when he even "shared communion with them," people like his co-minister Henry Johnson disapproved. By communing with "people who [took] up arms" and baptized babies, Henry was seeming to "sanction" the very practices in protest against which the Mennonite fellowship had originally been gathered. "I was warned," remembered Henry, "as going too fast. It was even suggested by some good members that as a Mennonite preacher I had better shave off my whiskers and comb my hair down straight." His ministry in the new conference would, in fact, last little more than one year before he would be "silenced" by his fellow-reformers.[16]

Over at the eastern end of the Mennonite community, excitement of an evangelical nature arrived in the person of a young, self-appointed preacher from Canada. It was Jacob Meyer, grandson of the deceased bishop of the Twenty, of the same name. He had been recently converted in an exuberant revival that was sweeping his community under "Evangelical" and Methodist leadership, and that was even affecting his Minister Daniel Hoch and Bishop Jacob Gross. Gross actually gave up his role to serve as a minister with the Evangelicals, while Hoch, holding at first to his Mennonite background, made contact with the new liberal group in Pennsylvania, and, like them, drew up and published a "Constitution." The Mennonite community at The Twenty, largely consisting of emigrants from Deep Run and Hilltown and their children, would never recover its first-generation stability and unity. Now young Jacob Meyer, arriving among his cousins in Bucks County to share the fruits of his awakening, looked up Deacon Daniel Gross of Doylestown, brother of the Bishop Jacob Gross of Canada who was throwing his lot in with the Evangelicals. Meyer asked Deacon Gross for permission to preach, on the Sunday two days later, in the Doylestown congregation. It was a classic case of the person who felt an inward call confronting the more deliberate and conference-invoking process of discernment. The Doylestown ministers being divided in their opinion, Bishop Isaac Gottschall gave his reluctant permission. But "Perkasie" (Blooming Glen) and Deep Run refused, and Franconia, Salford, and "The Plain" were also opposed to the idea. "The excitement in our community is great," reported one Bucks County Mennonite, apparently one of young Jacob Meyer's relatives. "Some allowed him to preach in their houses here and there, and he preached at least once among the Methodists. . . ."

Looking for support, the youthful visitor consulted with John Oberholtzer, and on the following day in a sermon at a schoolhouse seemed to express unity with "the Oberholtzers." What amazed one "old" Mennonite observer was that Meyer seemed "so sure in himself that he is called by God to work in these matters that he will take counsel with absolutely no human being.... He always says the Lord would show him what he should do." Some people felt that there was "something wild and stormy" about Meyer, and that he was "not quite right," but others felt he meant everything well. By the time he preached at the Plumstead meetinghouse the excitement had become unusually high. The "old" Mennonite observer, quoting Gerhard Tersteegen's devotional poetry, felt that nothing with such an air of self-will could be quite right.

> *Fasten, lesen, singen, bäten,*
> *Und mit engelzungen reden—*
> *Alles dieses acht ich nicht*
> *Wann mann nicht den Willen bricht.*
>
> (Fasting, reading, singing, praying,
> And with tongues of angels speaking—
> All of this I disregard
> If one's will has not been broken.)[17]

Whatever young Meyer's intentions, there seems to have been no permanent fruit of his preaching. He soon dropped out of sight, and died shortly before his twenty-fifth birthday in early 1851.

A longer-lasting issue was the controversy at Deep Run over whether the more liberal group, which at first had no minister, would be allowed to use the meetinghouse. "The members of this new Sect," as the Deep Run ordained men put it, "in proportion to the old is about as 60 in two hundred." Nine men of this new group, ranging in age from forty to sixty-five, applied to the Bucks County Court for a charter. Their request of January 4, 1849, was published in the Doylestown newspapers, and triggered from the old congregation a counter appeal. The persons signing the application, wrote the ministers, were "not members of our religious society." Three had been disowned for violation of the "long established" discipline of the congregation; one, sixty-five-year-old John Leatherman, had withdrawn; and the other five had never been members. (The latter group included Philip Kratz, father-in-law of Deep Run Preacher Isaac Meyer.) "The old congregation," which met for worship every Sunday, now believed that the new group was legally incorporating "for the purpose of claiming by some means the property and Real Estate at Deep Run belonging to the old Society." The ministers hoped the court would "perceive that this fragment is not the true and genuine Mennonite Society," and not allow it to be "incorporated under" the Mennonite name, and thus be "clothed with legal privilege" to "deprive" the old congregation of their property. The new group had already "made several efforts to obtain possession of the meetinghouse for the purpose of holding their meetings therein...." With both contradictory appeals before it, the court granted a charter to the new congregation, "no sufficient reason being shown to the contrary."[18]

The new group chose for minister forty-year-old farmer Martin Fretz, son-in-law of conservative Skippack Deacon Johannes Kratz, and for deacon the blacksmith Samuel Atherholt. They appealed to the spring 1849 session of the Eastern Conference to allow them to be included in John Oberholtzer's Swamp bishop district. Next, armed with their legal charter, they served notice on the "old" congregation at Deep Run that they had "appointed a Meeting for the worship of God on the 3rd day of June and on every second Sabbath thereafter...." A proposition was sent along: the meetinghouse and grounds were to be sold at public auction to the highest bidder. Half of the proceeds would then be given to the group which did not own the property. Each "society" would use the property, but on alternate Sundays. Then came a statement showing how strong the feelings had become:

> Provided the above proposition is accepted by you, you need not fear any ill will, malice or disturbance from us hereafter. But if the same is not accepted by you we will be compelled to try and obtain our just rights in another way....

The five Deep Run ministers and deacons of the "old" congregation, after consulting with other ministers and leaders "of the Lancaster Conference," resolved that they could not "permit such proposals," nor another group holding meetings in their facilities. "You will therefore," stated their blunt written reply,

> have the courtesy not to come since no permission shall be given you. We ask you for your own good to cause us no further trouble. We will let you alone in peace and quietness, but we also ask the same from you. And all that you have spent on the dwelling house we will refund to you when you will withdraw peaceably. We shall no more concern ourselves with this matter unless you should again enter into agreement with the resolution passed by the [Franconia] Conference [after the sixteen men had left on November 7, 1847]. Furthermore, we are willing also that you bury your dead here at any time and on such occasions to have full rights to the house.
> As it has been done so shall it continue to be.[19]

The first signature under this tradition-invoking reply was that of Minister Christian Gross, now in his seventies. The day after he signed this document his younger brother Jacob, the bishop in Ontario, would be put "under the ban" by Bishop Benjamin Eby for his "evangelical" activities and disregard of Mennonite "house-keeping." Such departures caused old Christian Gross "much sorrow of heart." Events had "an appearance as though our fellowship would be destroyed," he wrote to his brother Jacob. "I am of the opinion that a door has been opened, for the oncoming youth, by which the defenseless foundation will be lost or disregarded...." Gross quotes the *Martyrs Mirror*, and asks his "Evangelical" brother, "Where should we find a better evangelical foundation than we were instructed in and accepted in our youth, the foundation which was laid by our forbears, under cross, tribulation and heavy persecution, on which ... we were instructed and baptized...?"[20]

The refusal of the "old" leaders at Deep Run seemed to take from the new group any more interest in gaining the use of the meetinghouse. In less than two weeks a committee met in the home of miller Isaac Fretz of Tinicum Township, and decided to buy a lot of their own from a sympathetic member of the "old" congregation, directly across from the old graveyard. Subscriptions were taken, and money flowed in briskly, including a contribution from the Jewish printer in Doylestown, Moritz Loeb, partner in *Der Morgenstern*. A 55' × 40' meetinghouse was completed in the next five months, built, as the recent "Bertolets" and the forthcoming new house at "Gottschall's," of brick. It had a "gallery" (balcony) over a *Küch* (anteroom), and a pulpit raised so high (four feet from the floor) that a later minister would request that it be lowered. The building was dedicated on December 1 and 2, 1849.[21]

The Deep Run Mennonite community, though split in two, now seemed to be at peace, but before long the new congregation would wrestle with serious internal divisions, and not really get on a solid footing for two decades. In less than a year they would request that they be transferred from John Oberholtzer's bishop district to the one at Skippack, and would be under the tutelage of a bishop from the opposite edge of the conference for over forty years. Early in 1851 Deacon Atherholt was accused of improperly charging the congregation for supplies from his blacksmith shop, and both he and Minister Martin Fretz left the congregation, refusing to turn over the original membership book. A new minister, Samuel Weinberger of Swamp background, seems to have been involved in the general unhappiness, and by the end of 1852 some ten families had withdrawn, eventually rejoining the old congregation, or a variety of other denominations. Those remaining committed themselves to refund the contributions that had come from the members now leaving, and congregations throughout the conference helped to pay off this substantial debt.

The Deep Run Mennonite meetinghouse, built in 1766 and enlarged in 1795, photographed by Samuel F. DuBois on April 26, 1872, a week before it was razed and replaced with a new building. (Library of the Bucks County Historical Society)

The "Brick meetinghouse" at Deep Run, built in 1849 by the new congregation that affiliated with the Eastern District. Later this was referred to as "Deep Run West." (Author's Collection)

Soon after withdrawing, Martin Fretz seemed to have experienced difficulties in his family. A seventeen-year-old unmarried daughter gave birth to a child and died some months later. The family moved permanently to New Jersey, where Martin became a Presbyterian elder.[22] More significant for our story than anything else in his life was the contribution made by his son Abraham. The latter, an itinerant Methodist minister, found himself nostalgically drawn to his ancestral Mennonite community at Deep Run, and in his latter years compiled an astonishing series of thick genealogies of Mennonite families. To this historian, though himself not a Mennonite, American Mennonite genealogists stand permanently in debt.

Without the ballast of a body of traditionalists, the new eastern Pennsylvania conference struggled with one controversy or another throughout the 1850s. John Oberholtzer, who had replaced Abraham Hunsicker as chairman by the third session (October 1848), reached out by letter and visit to Europe and Canada, hoping for a new unity that would help the progressive Mennonite element, and make possible educational and mission activities. One favorable response came from an unexpected direction—Lancaster County, where the "free school" question was agitating the citizenry of the Bowmansville area in Brecknock Township. Although the Pennsylvania "school war," begun in 1834, had pretty much been decided by 1850 (Franconia Township itself yielded in the following year), a few German-speaking communities held out. At Bowmansville there were Mennonites on both sides of the question. A "free school" was finally opened in the first week of the New Year, 1850, by Samuel Hertz, son of a local Reformed pastor. But a few days later three angry men invaded his classroom—two opponents and one supporter of the free school plan. One of the opponents held a fist under the supporter's nose, and the teacher, pale with fright, picked up his books and left. The former teacher then came back on the old "subscription" basis. This so displeased the free school supporters, led by Mennonite farmer Daniel Sensenig, that they brought criminal charges against the "anti-school" rioters, and had them bound to appear at the approaching Quarter Sessions Court at Lancaster. Those charged walked the twenty miles to Lancaster on foot. Their progressive critics, who had been subpoenaed as witnesses, came by carriage. As the latter group caught up and passed the walkers, an angry exchange occurred. The rioters were required by the court to pay the costs of the proceedings, and to show no further malice. Nevertheless, from then on there was an economic boycott of Daniel Sensenig and storekeeper Samuel Bowman. Further, the Mennonite congregation at Bowmansville excommunicated Sensenig and others who had gone to law in the quarrel. Eventually Sensenig, three Bowmans, and two Musselmans withdrew or were expelled from the Bowmansville congregation (local Reformed people too were divided).[23]

The ousted Mennonites set up a little congregation of their own, and appealed for support to the liberal Eastern Conference. By 1854 they had built a new meetinghouse in a grove of pines just south of Bowmansville. Some of the wives remained in the old congregation. William Shelly, co-pastor at Swamp with John Oberholtzer, moved out to serve as minister and bishop of the small group which was without organizational relationship to the thousands of other Mennonites in Lancaster County. With Shelly came his young Reformed hired man, Solomon Ott of Bedminster Township. Later Ott would marry in the community, become a Mennonite himself, and serve for many years as the pastor of the isolated congregation. Thus the Eastern Conference gained its first outpost west of its original borders, one that for its first century would never be large, but would endure.

In the very months following the outbreak of the Bowmansville "school war," the Eastern Conference was discovering that a clearly drawn constitution was no guarantee against the breakdown of fellowship. It was becoming evident that educators Abraham and Henry Hunsicker and their Skippack colleague Abraham Grater did not share the traditional Mennonite conception of "maintaining the right fellowship." They advocated and practiced a new freedom: the sharing of communion with Christians of other denominations. This touched a sensitive nerve in the Mennonite fellowship. Taking communion with people affiliated with "secret societies" or who favored going to war at the call of their government or who had been baptized as infants was a striking innovation. It seemed to call into question the essential covenantal bond, the "old foundation" or "ground" of the Mennonite fellowship. The "lodge" question, in particular, was just at this time engaging the attention of the whole community. Fraternal and beneficial organizations were springing up in towns of any size, as American society became less church-dominated and more factory related. Most important was the Independent Order of Odd Fellows, originally imported from England in 1819, but suddenly becoming very widespread in about 1846. No less than fifteen chapters appeared in Montgomery County alone in the next three or four years. Some people only listless in their church affiliation became enthusiastic promoters of this new type of association.

Most conservative Christians, and Mennonites in particular, objected to the very principle of "secrecy" in the various new "orders." Further, the idea of "combin[ing] outside the teachings of Christ and his Apostles and put[ting] their faith and trust in the arts of man," as Joseph F. Freed of Towamencin wrote, was a basic undermining of that all-focussing loyalty Christians should have to the church.[24] This modern fragmenting of one's "belonging" into sacred and secular compartments was to be resisted. "Beneficial societies" were seen as a bypassing of dependence on the Christian brotherhood in times of crisis. The new Eastern Conference, meeting at Swamp on May 2, 1850, was unequivocal: "Resolved that we not permit any to become members of our Church, who belong to Secret Societies, nor permit any to become members of our Society already belonging, to commune with us."[25]

This forthright statement was ratified, however, against the strong wishes of Bishop Abraham Hunsicker. He "expostulated" with the conference he had originally chaired for what he considered an "imprudent step." They should at least not have taken it, he argued, until they were able to "substitute something as good or better than Secret Societies." The essence of Christianity, in his opinion, was charity, and that was what beneficial societies were designed for. The founder of Freeland Seminary was a Mennonite, he wrote, insofar as he "understood the doctrines of Menno to coincide with the general spirit of Christ," which he understood to be "the spirit of charity and benevolence." Charity is "the soul of our social and religious life," and it is not merely "a speculative idea of general benevolence floating in the head." The real reason for the proliferation of benevolent societies throughout the country was "a woeful neglect on the part of the Christian Church."[26]

The depth of Hunsicker's concern on this point is evident in his proposing a "Fund" for the "honest and industrious poor, who labor hard," but by "misfortune and disease" are made unable to provide "an honorable competency." Hunsicker apparently felt that the old alms fund of his Skippack congregation was an inadequate method. A plan to aid the "poor and suffering members of the Christian community," dated October 26, 1850, remains among the papers of the West Swamp congregation. East Swamp also adopted a new plan, and a meeting on the topic was held at Skippack. But Preacher Henry Johnson did not favor an organization of what was traditionally done by simple brotherly impulse, and others, Hunsicker reported, "ridiculed" his fund as "an insolent pretention to improve on the good old Mennonite ground."

One "old" Mennonite from Upper Salford wrote to a friend in Canada that the "Oberholtzers" wanted to set up a fund from which to give a wedding present of $25.00 to any young couples getting married with "less than 300 dollars worth of property" to their names. Abraham Grater had been preaching on this theme at Skippack while his older colleagues Henry G. Johnson and Abraham Hunsicker sat on the bench beside him. Grater announced that he had had an important dream: "I dreamed I was in a great courtyard with a beautiful gate that led out to a beautiful, pleasant road, and in this courtyard was a fine herd of sheep. And as we wished to drive the herd out to this beautiful, pleasant road, one sheep stood right in front of the gate, so that the rest, rather than going out onto the . . . road, sprang against the wall." Then Grater turned around to where Henry Johnson was sitting and said, "That is you, brother" (referring to the uncooperative sheep). "Yet," remarked the letter-writer, "they serve with each other and call each other brother as before."[27]

This brotherly relation was not to continue long. By Christmas (1850) Henry Johnson had had enough of Grater's ideas and eccentricities. When Grater, in another sermon, actually "advocated . . . free-communion," and said that those who did not agree were like "Pharisees," Johnson called a meeting at the nearby schoolhouse. Grater stuck to his position, with the apparent tacit agreement of Bishop Abraham Hunsicker. This led to a meeting of the congregation a few weeks later, which resolved that any minister maintaining that people with only infant baptism and people belonging to secret societies could "commune at the Lord's Table" with them would "not be allowed to preach" in the Skippack congregation. The announcement of the action, made just before the benediction at a service, caught Grater by surprise. The strong action received the hearty approval of William Shelly, still serving with John Oberholtzer at Swamp, when soon after the decision he was a visiting preacher at Skippack. Lifting his hands high in emotion, he said it had made him truly happy to hear how Skippack had taken a stand against open communion, "for it is here, as it were, that the 'head' of our whole Society is."[28] It was not only the "old" Mennonites, at this point, who were concerned to "maintain the right fellowship" by proper "housekeeping" in the church of Christ.

The Skippack congregation now had a major problem of authority on its hands, since their own bishop, Abraham Hunsicker, was calling the preservation of "the forms, and usages peculiar to the Mennonite Creed" (the term had never been used among the old Mennonites) "a narrow and selfish policy." So they called a committee of seven preachers and deacons from other churches in the new conference, to hold an *Umfrage* (counsel meeting or investigation), and report to conference. This struck Hunsicker as underhanded. "Without consulting me," he complained, they "assumed the authority . . . to do that, which was *constitutionally* mine to do. . . ."[29] In any case the committee of seven, meeting at Skippack on February 24 and 25, 1851, sanctioned the congregational decision against Grater, and took notice that Bishop Hunsicker supported Grater against the discernment of the congregation. The earlier conference decision rejecting secret society membership was confirmed. The committee wished to leave other denominations in peace, but did not consider it advisable "to make communion too free, since out of the Gospel we recognize that there must be unity in doctrine and life if this is to be of the right kind" *(eine Einigkeit in Lehr und Leben stattfinden musz, wenn es rechter Art seyn soll)*. However, if a minister was called on in some kind of emergency *(in Fall der Noth)* he might discern himself whether to give communion to nonmembers. Moses Gottschall had apparently done this for one Odd Fellow who had requested communion while in "a declining state of health," even though the man had said Moses could call for Bishop Hunsicker in case he himself (Gottschall) had a conscience against it.

The committee then made a recommendation that John Oberholtzer himself might not have subscribed to in his own struggles with the Franconia Conference four years earlier: "We beg the whole body of ministers of the whole Skippack District, as well as the whole membership of the said District, to have patience with all the ministers and members.... However, it is herewith made the duty of each minister of the District to make themselves willingly subject to the fellowship *[Gemeinde]* ... and to accept, for the sake of peace, what the fellowship lays, with good grounds, on each one."[30] Oberholtzer, who seems to have hesitated on how firm to make the ruling, was for some reason replaced by Christian Clemmer as chairman of the next two sessions of conference.

The Committee duly submitted its "Report" at a controversial conference which met on May 1, 1851, at the "Branch" or "Gehman's" meetinghouse (Rockhill). Abraham Hunsicker and several other ministers refused to concur. In response, a meeting of the congregation at Skippack resolved that their bishop could no longer preach there. A special session of conference then convened at Skippack (May 23), and this time John Oberholtzer, doubtless with reluctance because of his friendship with the Hunsickers, also voted to back the Skippack congregation's decision. Bishop Hunsicker, brilliant, affluent, and influential in the community though he might be, was pronounced to be "erring," and forbidden to preach or participate in conference. John Oberholtzer, even with the help of a secretary and a constitution, had to do what he had earlier condemned the Franconia Conference for doing to him.

Now it was Hunsicker's turn to feel outraged. He published "A Statement of Facts" in both English and German, giving his version of what had happened. John Oberholtzer, he wrote, "the acknowledged pioneer of our late Reform ... disowned me as a brother in Christ ... by his vote.... And wherefore? why, simply because I could not in conscience call that *right* which my heart called *wrong*." Not only had "their intolerance ... driven me from their society," but "fain would close and did close the doors and shutters of one of the Meeting Houses against me and my hearers...."

Further, Abraham complained, "never ... has a single member of that Synod which suspended me and declared me *in error,* been to see me or to converse with me on the subject...."[31] It would, of course, hardly be surprising that ordinary Pennsylvania Dutchmen, even of liberal leanings, would hesitate to debate an educator who was capable of writing that "the tide and current of improvement are mightily flowing onward and upward, until knowledge shall assimilate man with his Maker...."[32] Though not communicating directly with their former bishop, the Eastern Conference did issue a large German broadside, "*An das Publikum*" (To the Public), setting forth their actions and declaring any other versions the public might have heard to be "basically false."[33]

While the new conference, having lost one of its main leaders, was thus struggling for equilibrium, the Franconia Conference had become "quite calm in comparison to what it was a while ago." This was the report of a Hilltown Mennonite writing to Canada in January 1851. "Some have quieted down and have reconciled with the old ones. The meetings are fuller than they were before." Over 200 people communed at both "Perkasie" and Deep Run. There seemed to be no "Oberholtzer People" at all at Doylestown.[34] One recollection placed the number of communicants at the Franconia congregation about 1850 at seventy-one; this, however, seems strangely low in view of the fact that sixty-seven new members were reported as having been received between 1847 and 1854.[35]

An encouraging note for the Eastern Conference was the interest shown by some Canadian Mennonites, among whom John Oberholtzer (and apparently Abraham Hunsicker) had visited. Reacting against a newly ordained conservative bishop, Dilman Moyer, several dozen Canadian families organized a fellowship much like the Eastern Conference among their relatives in Pennsylvania. The latter conference entered the Canadian group's rules on their own minutes. Soon Daniel Hoch was selected as the new bishop of the liberal Ontario Mennonites, and by November 15, 1851, John H. Oberholtzer had ordained him to that office. For several years Hoch would remain in close contact with the Eastern Conference, but then be drawn away in the "Evangelical" direction.

The Skippack Mennonites, once the source of much of John Ober-holtzer's support, were now in an extended process of fragmentation. The silenced Bishop Hunsicker and his followers, feeling that they had a right to use the meetinghouse, found themselves legally charged by the group loyal to Henry Johnson with having "committed a trespass."[36] The case was heard before three bemused arbitrators in May 1852. Their verdict favored the Hunsicker group, but assessed the Johnson group damages of only six cents. They did direct that the Hunsickers be allowed back in the meetinghouse. Some remuneration, they noted, should also be made to the "old" Mennonites who had built their own meetinghouse four years earlier.[37] It was probably at this time that the pastor of the Reformed Church of Trappe, A. B. Shenkle, allowed the Hunsicker faction to gather in his congregation's building. Two years after the arbitration, a group of about thirty-five persons organized a "Christian Society of Montgomery County," for which a meetinghouse was built in 1855 next to the home of Abraham Hunsicker. By this time one of their ministers, Abraham Grater, considered a local eccentric, had purchased the hall of the defunct literary society in Skippackville. Here he held forth independently for twelve years, in sermons on the book of Revelation, designating Menno Simons as "The Beast" of that vision.[38] Sometimes audiences came to hear Grater for the apparent purpose of amusement. Young people would laugh when he said, "Let us bray." He was reported to have produced an unsuccessful invention: a chair on which, he fondly hoped, a rather sedentary and amply-bodied daughter of his would be able to hatch eggs.

On January 1, 1852, the "new" Mennonites at Skippack sought a replacement for Bishop Hunsicker by casting lots between Henry Johnson and Moses Gottschall. The choice fell on Johnson, but in May the conference granted the district's request to ordain Moses Gottschall to the same office. Another ministerial ordination at Skippack saw the lot fall on David Bergey, who had earlier escaped ordination twice, according to family traditions, by moving from the Salford congregation to the one at Towamencin, and from there to the "new" Mennonites at Skippack.[39] It turned out that Bergey could not get along with Henry Johnson, and the latter eventually "laid the ban" on Bergey. A small group of the Skippack congregation then formed a separate congregation meeting at Skippackville, under Bergey's leadership, but there too he had difficulty with the bishop to whom he was assigned—Moses Gottschall. Finally Bergey himself was made a bishop. His little congregations at Rockhill (called "Branch") and Skippackville (the latter meeting in the facilities of another church) lingered until the 1880s, when both finally expired. Meanwhile the other "new" Mennonites at Skippack had subgroups meeting in the Providence and Methacton meetinghouses, alternating with "old" Mennonite congregations. Before the splitting process was finished at Skippack (by 1855) there had emerged at least five factions where in 1847 there had been one major congregation, considered the leading one in the oldest Mennonite community in North America. In addition, new Brethren (Dunker) and Brethren in Christ congregations in the community each drew off a number of members. Henry Hunsicker, the bishop who died in 1836, would not have recognized his once-blooming congregation, could he have revisited it two decades later.

Having lost the powerful support of the Hunsickers, John Oberholtzer continued to press in conference a topic he had been raising since 1849: a printing press for the church. Most other active denominations benefited from their own printing activity, he argued, and the conference seemed generally favorable to his sentiment. But nothing happened until Oberholtzer himself, about the time of the Johnson-Hunsicker arbitration in the early summer of 1852, bought a handpress and arranged his smithy near Milford Square into a printshop. Having only a slender income, a sickly wife, and a bright but unpredictable teenage son, Oberholtzer felt the weight of his venture rather heavily. But, eager for the benefits he knew would accrue to the Mennonite fellowship, he issued, on June 9, 1852, a prospectus for a little spiritual paper he entitled *Der Religiöse Botschafter* (The Religious Messenger).[39] On the following August 23 appeared the first issue. For the next two and a half years, until he ran out of health and money, the energetic reformer labored heroically and late into the night, writing, editing, and printing his biweekly German *Messenger*.

It was the first Mennonite paper in the New World to last beyond one issue. In it Oberholtzer worked at linking Mennonites of scattered communities in a new manner of denominational consciousness, especially in relation to topics like missions, education, and benevolent projects. In his first issue he invited European Mennonites concerned about compulsory military service to come to America. He reported news of missions and tract societies in other denominations, and offered to channel contributions for such efforts. He called attention to forthcoming sessions of the Eastern Conference, or attacked a tract by Abraham Grater as an "Abominable Mishmash." He published notices of deaths and marriages, wondering now and then why more ministers did not submit such items. Some subscriptions eventually came from recent Mennonite settlements in the Midwest, and there were Canadian and a few European subscribers. Mostly ignored by "old" Mennonites, the paper attained a circulation of over 700, though not all subscribers kept paid up. In its pages appeared the first challenge to Mennonites to form a nationwide conference.

Debates on tobacco, temperance, prayer meetings, foot washing, and the relation of Christians to government office appeared from time to time. Ephraim Hunsberger, formerly a minister at Hereford, but ordained by Oberholtzer in 1852 to serve as bishop of a small congregation in Medina County, Ohio, was a frequent correspondent. He told of his congregation of Bergeys, Nices, and Alderfers at the little town of Wadsworth. Another minister of the same congregation, Henry Nice, wrote to Skippack asking for contributions for a new meetinghouse. In April 1853 editor Oberholtzer published an admonition by Ephraim Hunsberger that Mennonites should consider it their most serious duty to do mission work. "It would bring me hearty joy," wrote the Ohio bishop, "if you could deal with this matter somewhat at your Conference."[40]

Spring conference of 1853 was made memorable for the New Mennonites by the presence of two visiting bishops: Daniel Hoch of Canada and George Leiter of the "Juniata" area in central Pennsylvania. Representing liberal factions in their respective home congregations, the visitors each gave encouraging admonitions. Leiter was leader of a group that shared a meetinghouse with a Lancaster Conference congregation in which Abraham Halteman, formerly of Vincent, was a preacher. In Halteman's part of the congregation were families with "Franconia" names such as Bergey, Landis, and Myers. George Leiter would continue a special friendly relation with the "Johnson Mennonites" of Skippack for several decades. After Abraham Halteman's death, Leiter's congregation would mostly be reabsorbed (though not permanently) by the Lancaster Conference. As for Daniel Hoch (who would form a temporary new small conference with Ephraim Hunsberger's people in Ohio), he now preached as a visitor at Swamp, and among his "blood-relatives" at Deep Run. John Oberholtzer enthusiastically encouraged the somewhat emotional Canadian bishop, and even issued a German publication in his defense. It was the first book from Oberholtzer's Milford Square press, a 108-page *Disclosure of the Persecution Against Daniel Hoch, Preacher of the Mennonite Fellowship in Upper Canada.*[41] In this highly argumentative and rather unspecific work, Oberholtzer drew a brief parallel between his own difficulties with the Old Mennonites and the criticisms Hoch had encountered in Canada.

Consciousness of relatives in Ontario remained strong in Montgomery and Bucks County Mennonites until the end of the 19th century. The flavor of friendly correspondence can be sampled in a letter from Old Mennonite John O. Clemens, a young married man in Lower Salford, to his friends Tobias and Magdalena Kolb of Breslau. After the standard commentary on weather, health, and prices, Clemens closes with a bit of friendly banter that mingles "Dutch" and English idioms.

> *Mr Kolb mach eich auf u. kommt einmal noch alt Pennsylvania and besucht uns einmal. Es wird euch nicht reuen wann ihr einmal hier ware wann deine Frau noch mal getreibt fur nach Pennsylvania zu gehen Dan halt nicht zuruck dann sag kom on ich bin Rede Lasst uns gehen Mette Dann mach dich Rede und Beck nicht aus . . . vergiss dein Hans nich Er denket allen tag an euch . . . .*

Mr Kolb, make up your mind and come once to old Pennsylvania and visit us once. You will not regret it once you are here. If your wife urges a journey to Pennsylvania then do not hold back. Then say, "Come on, I'm ready, let's go, Mattie." Then get ready and don't back out.... Don't forget your John. He thinks of you every day.... [42]

In another such letter Clemens humorously warns that if Kolb doesn't soon reply he will throw Kolb "out of the *Freundschaft*" (clan of relatives).[43]

John H. Oberholtzer too had friends in Ontario, both *an der Zwanzig* (at the Twenty) and in Waterloo County to the northwest. He took up their invitation to visit the independent group led by David Hoch for their little "Conference" session and communion in June 1854. Leaving his *Botschafter* in the hands of his twenty-year-old son, Davy, the typesetter, he also looked up Mennonites in rural New York and Cleveland on his tour. He especially enjoyed visiting an "Evangelical Printing establishment" in Cleveland with a liberal Mennonite of German origin, Daniel Krehbiel. Together they gazed out from the "dome" of the printing house over "the shining waters of Lake Erie," and talked of improvement, outreach, and unity among the scattered American Mennonite settlements.[44] Krehbiel gave his Pennsylvania guest the names of recent German immigrants as far west as Iowa. This made it possible for Oberholtzer to send out sample copies of the *Botschafter,* with the quick result of eighteen new subscriptions. A link was thus forged between East and West. After five years of news from the West in the columns of the short-lived *Botschafter* and its sequel, there would be a mutual awareness which would make it possible to call for a "General Conference" of Mennonites.

While his father was in Canada, Davy Oberholtzer found it impossible to get the *Botschafter* into the mail on time, since he had "had to help at the hay on the day of publication." Just below his apology in the June 26, 1854, issue, appeared a commentary on a current political phenomenon, the "Know-Nothings." This secretive, anti-Catholic and anti-foreign party had recently been gaining strength and holding conventions. Before the year was out (and before John Oberholtzer's return from Canada?) Davy was issuing from the converted Oberholtzer smithy a Know-Nothing newspaper, in cooperation with one Rynear T. Donatt. Entitled *The Star-Spangled Banner,* it folded after a very brief run, having had, in John Oberholtzer's later words, very shallow rootage.[45] Davy himself, soon after being married by Bishop Moses Gottschall to Sarah Schimmel at the age of twenty-one, abandoned his father's shop at a time of family "sickliness," forcing the demise of the *Botschafter* itself. In its final issue, dated December 31, 1855, the elder Oberholtzer proposes that a new start be made on a broader basis—an association of stockholders. No matter which way we look, he writes, we may see Christian presses of all denominations pouring out periodicals and tracts for the salvation of "poor souls." "Oh, who can be diligent enough in this?"[46]

The appearance of the *Botschafter* from time to time was an important thread of continuity for the "New Mennonites," since their conference life was in a very difficult condition. Congregations themselves may have been less troubled. But after the issues of foot washing and prayer meetings had been raised at the spring 1853 conference session, no substantial resolutions were recorded by the secretary for three or four years (there would be no real peace in conference until 1860 or 1861). Henry Johnson, the foot washing-fostering secretary, injected a poignant note in the spring 1855 minutes: although God "is a God of order," "we poor weak human beings often differ concerning the best method by which this or that may be accomplished."[47] The Eastern Conference, even with its clear constitution, was facing the old problem of how to proceed when sentiment was divided. So they were reminded by the secretary's résumé of the discussion that "Should the majority not favor taking up the matter it is to be considered disposed of for the time . . . ."[48]

Matters were apparently so difficult that there was no fall conference in 1855, and the next spring session acted only to ask the bishops to "investigate and act upon certain matters of misunderstanding."[49] Finally, on May 2, 1856, at a meeting in the home of Deacon William Z. Gottschall, the five bishops recalled the resolution which had allowed prayer meetings (May 1853). Although William Shelly was one of the five signers, after "riper reflection" he withdrew his signature from the decision by an "open protest."[50] And before long Henry Johnson was equally distressed to see the other bishops also rescind their earlier permission of foot washing. Now Shelly of Bowmansville and Johnson of Skippack no longer came to conference. Shelly and minister William Gehman of the Upper Milford congregation called the bishops' ruling that meetings specifically for prayer need not be held "unevangelical." But when a vote on prayer meetings was taken at the October 1857 conference session, only three voted favorably, as opposed to twenty-four opposed.[51] Minister David Henning of Mt. Bethel, at that point, must have been the only person beside Shelly and Gehman who voted with the minority.

There was now another small schism in the Eastern Conference. The names of eight ministers and deacons were "stricken from the list" in 1858 and 1859. William Shelly, formerly John Oberholtzer's colleague at Swamp but later bishop at the little Bowmansville congregation, was not sorry. He had already written to Daniel Hoch of Canada as a kindred spirit, asking for a look at Hoch's recent constitution as a possible model. The Eastern Conference had been "pharisaic" in its attitude toward prayer meetings, Shelly claimed, and furthermore, most of its members would have to "repent" before they could be taken into the Christian fellowship. There were even "some souls," Shelly dared to write, "who were baptized by Oberholtzer in unbelief." If such people should now prove unsatisfied with that baptism, Shelly as bishop was ready to go with them "into Jordan,"[52] *i.e.*, baptize them by immersion, as the "Evangelical Association" did. William Gehman, the younger but stronger leader of the Mennonite Evangelicals at Upper Milford, was now refused the use of the meetinghouse where he had been preaching since 1844, by a congregational vote of twenty-five to twenty-four.[53] For some months he met with his followers in a room on the second floor of his brother David Gehman's store building in the tiny village of Hosensack. The old congregation consented to pay the sum of $300 to the new group, and by 1859 the latter had a new building of their own. Interestingly, when they dedicated this facility they referred to it not as a *Versammlunghaus* (meetinghouse) but a *Kirche* (church), perhaps reflecting William Gehman's Lutheran background.

The "Evangelical Mennonites" were full of devotional fervor. Neighbors later sometimes nicknamed them "Holy Rollers," and went to their meetings to be entertained with the "shouting," occasional leaping, and actual rolling on the floor that transpired. Johannes Schantz of Hosensack wrote that "Gehman's People," as he called them, felt they were "the closest to Menno's teaching" among the Mennonites. They claimed that Menno had fostered baptism by immersion, an assertion for which Schantz could find no convincing evidence in Menno's writings. "It seems to me," wrote Schantz, "too much as though people always want to be better than the next person . . . ." But he wanted "to wish them all well."[54] Less charitable was an anonymous writer to a local newspaper, who disputed the new group's claim to the name Mennonite. They were really, he asserted, a kind of Baptists. A better name for them would be the "Hosensack Fanatics."

Eventually the Evangelical Mennonites found adherents at places like Saucon, Skippack, Hatfield, and Vincent, as well as close associates under other names in Canada and the Midwest. In a series of mergers, they adopted the name "Mennonite Brethren in Christ." Although the Mennonite stress on separation from the world, as well as a sense of close fellowship lingered for a century, sometimes producing very plain clothing, the motifs from the Evangelical tradition eventually proved more definitive. Central to the newer identity were the emotional conversion after dramatic scenes around the "Mourner's Bench," and the frequent use of the term "saved," meaning a once-for-all experience. By the 1960s many had forgotten the more "charismatic" beginnings, and in Pennsylvania had dropped any reference to the original name Mennonite in favor of "Bible Fellowship Church." Even this name, however, gave a contemporary witness to the power of fundamental emphases in the original Anabaptist movement: the centrality of the Scriptures, and the living of the Christian life in an accountable society.

In order to distinguish among the "old," "new," and "Evangelical" Mennonites in the Upper Milford area, neighbors sometimes spoke, respectively, of congregations "Number One," "Number Two," and "Number Three." A similar situation was calling for nicknames among the splintered parts of the Skippack congregation. Here Bishop Henry Johnson was independently leading the group that was left after three other parts of the original fellowship had left. Johnson's group was larger than that of his alienated assistant minister David Bergey, but smaller than the "old" Mennonite group who had built another meetinghouse. Johnson's congregation, in possession of the spacious 1844 meetinghouse, was now free to practice foot washing, an ordinance which even a large part of the Franconia Conference did not keep. Now there was still another name to reckon with—the "Johnson Mennonites." This nickname lasted longer than "Gehman" or "Oberholtzer" Mennonites, because the group stayed independent for over a century, and because for three generations the main leaders—father, son, and grandson—had the same name: Henry G., Henry H., and Henry M. Johnson. Sometimes, to distinguish between the "old" and "Johnson" Mennonites, "Upper" and "Lower Skippack" were used respectively.

These 1850s, then, were a stormy and sometimes discouraging period for the East Pennsylvania Conference, testing to the limit and beyond its ability to cohere. The Franconia Conference, by contrast, having lost many of its dissatisfied members, had much less of a struggle to maintain its "order." John Oberholtzer's continuing problems goaded him to look for a more stable frame of reference, one less entirely dependent on the *zersplittert* local Mennonite membership. His own unpopularity among "old" Mennonites was reaching almost mythic levels. The Evangelical Mennonites questioned his spiritual integrity. Even in his own district of the "new" Mennonites there was a serious challenge, as Minister Jacob Meyer of Saucon brought a "charge" against him that seemed to call for the reformer's "silencing." But when this reached the "High Council" or conference floor itself, the conference voted, "with the exception of a few members . . . that nothing more could be done with regard to the petition of the Saucon congregation."[55] Jacob Meyer then returned to the Franconia Conference, with a part of the congregation. Before long, having made an "acknowledgment," he was allowed to function again as a minister in the old conference.

Yet John Oberholtzer, harassed as he was by persistent conference dissension and family problems, never gave up or looked back. Two young men from his community—John Stauffer and Andrew Shelly—caught something of his vision in these years for a renewed Mennonite church. They became involved in the printing venture Oberholtzer had begun. In 1856 a "Mennonite Printing Union" was formed from interested supporters. This gave stable support to a new periodical, *Das Christliche Volksblatt* (The Christian People's Paper). Apparently the subscribers to the earlier *Botschafter* followed the replacement, since the subscription list continued to number about 700. Now even when John Oberholtzer would be away in church visitation, his devout young cousin John Gehman Stauffer would keep the *Volksblatt* going. Much more dependable than Davy Oberholtzer, Stauffer would set type for an occasional small book, or even do job work for the public. Eventually he would take over the shop as his own business. The printery was moved to a fine new brick building at Milford Square. Here Stauffer founded a number of magazines and newspapers, both religious and general. After a quarter century in this neighborhood he would move the business into nearby Quakertown.[56]

During the interval between the issuing of the *Botschafter* and the *Volksblatt* Oberholtzer's shop had been occupied in the reprinting of a sizable book Oberholtzer felt valuable for devotional reading: Gottfried Arnold's *Geistliche Erfarungs-Lehre*. There was also a translation of a long, tract-like invitation for sinners, *Komm zu Jesu*. But the most interesting title from this printery at Milford Square was a little book by Oberholtzer himself in 1860, *Der Wahre Charakter von J. H. Oberholtzer (The True Character of J. H. Oberholtzer, Preacher and Bishop of Several Congregations in East Pennsylvania, With Insight and Understanding of various Situations and Other Conditions of the Christian Church in General, Which Especially Relate to the Mennonite Fellowship)*. This 115-page volume contains a spirited essay expressing the reformer's church philosophy. It appeals in turn to his own conference people, the Evangelical Mennonites, the "Old" Mennonites, and Christians in general, candidly discussing all the points of contention among the Mennonites, both doctrinal and organizational.

But readers led by the title to expect autobiographical information will be disappointed. Such insight as is to be gained into "My Real Character" (one of the chapter titles) must be inferred from an apologia lacking any specific data, and with only the briefest of narrative touches. A few excerpts may suggest something of Oberholtzer's zeal and directness, while at the same time they fail to dispel a certain psychological mystery or ambiguity in the manners of this intelligent and aggressive man:

Have I not, in many places, brought about Children's Instructions and established them in order to counter the stream of evils among the youth, especially on the Sabbath?... Have I not also introduced in many of our congregations a deep and basic instruction, which to a great degree here in our fellowship in this country has been lost and neglected? Have I not brought together the first evangelical Constitution *[Zuchtordnung]* for the American Mennonite fellowship, systematically and according to the content of Gospel teaching, which, when rightly understood, fosters and maintains right and righteousness in all general cases? Have I not, throughout my whole time in office usually had to stand where the battle was hottest, and the testing was heaviest and most dangerous?

... And finally, have I not set up the first—so far as I know— printing press in the Mennonite fellowship since Menno Simons' time, taking up as an unsponsored individual heavy costs? Was it not I who spent whole nights without sleep at the press and in the preparation of evangelical truth for the people? And all this in order to be useful to my dear fellow human beings and to win souls for Christ, and while my foes lay softly, restfully, securely, unconcernedly and indifferent to their soul's salvation sleeping on their beds, or perhaps may have been awake and making plans whereby they wished, in spite of all my efforts for their and others' salvation, to undermine, destroy and ruin me.[57]

I must freely acknowledge that, because of the endless attacks, slanders and defamations, I have stood different times at the threshold of the secular government—in which I am not completely unaware of what, with the greatest certainty, I could do—in order to hand over to the secular government for their punishment several perverse and malicious people; I have also ... been strongly encouraged thereto by many of my friends, who, I certainly believe, meant it faithfully and in good counsel; but every time God and his Word came between ... as well as many other witnesses out of God's Word....[58]

... I have, by nature, a somewhat sharp and hasty disposition. Yes, just this has perhaps sometimes led me to all too hasty speech and action, and thereby made me guilty of many imprudent mistakes; and my disposition itself is one of my most dangerous spiritual enemies for me to overcome.... Dear reader, consider here your own temperament.[59]

Now I ask quite simply: why are many people fearful of me? Why have I had to bear so much hate and scoffing? Why are many people frightened if they only see me, or hear my name mentioned? etc. Oh, here is no basis for fear and mistrust; it must therefore come because I seek to honor my Lord and Master, who will someday, certainly punish the evil for their wickedness.[60]

The book's themes are recapitulated in a passionate closing prayer. The harassed reformer sees himself in the train of those "in all ages" who, having sincerely sought to "hold fast" to God, had thereby incurred scorn

and slander. He prays for his critics, "Oh spare them if it is still possible."
His ambivalence between patient suffering and the desire for vindication is
evident when he includes in a book written for publication the prayer to
God that he "must complain to Thee and Thee alone." The accents of
deeply felt piety and spiritual longing are there, coexisting with an equally
strong claim of being in the right.[61] The responsibility for the 1847 division,
he reminds his "old brethren," rests on the majority at the October 1847
conference, and "nevermore on the minority."[62] This was a claim
Oberholtzer would energetically state again in 1863, 1870, and 1884, always
expressing hope that the "old brethren" would once more extend the peaceful hand of fellowship.

Although, in comparison with Oberholtzer's innovations, the Franconia Conference hardly seemed to be in motion, one of its congregations
had a young man—John Fretz Funk—who would, in another decade, establish a magazine with a larger circulation than the *Volksblatt*. The congregation was the one meeting at "Trewig's" (Line Lexington), past which
stagecoaches rumbled daily on the Bethlehem Road. Its venerable minister
John Geil had already felt, in 1852, that his work was nearly finished. At the
age of seventy-four, having preached for four decades, he was as clear-
minded and impressive as ever. He wrote to his congregation a "Departing
Word" which was distributed as a broadside. "Beloved in the Lord," he
admonished his people, "We have come upon critical times in which many
sects and denominations have already arisen. . . ." The tenor of Geil's
fatherly counsel was not, as John Oberholtzer's, to look around to see what
advances other Christians were making. It was rather to inquire into what
one had been originally taught.

> . . . We are in danger of being turned from ourselves, to look abroad
> and seek the kingdom of God [outside of] ourselves, while it is to be es-
> tablished in us. . . . This is the hope of our blessedness, to build on
> Jesus, the Rock of our salvation; and this you will do if you hear his
> words, and believe and do them.[63]

The elderly minister, who could be heard singing quietly as he rode along
the road by himself, closed his admonition with a stanza of the parting
hymn by schoolmaster Christopher Dock. But he also seems to have
inserted two stanzas of his own, expressing a deep and calm Christian faith:

Ach Gott, durch deine Liebeshaende	(O God, by thy dear loving hand,
Mach' du mich jetzo noch bereit,	Make me to be in readiness,
Dasz ich an meinem letzten Ende	That when at life's last end I stand,
In deinem Heil getrost abscheid.	My parting trust be in thy grace.
Dein Will' sei mir in Ewigkeit,	May thy will be, eternally,
Ein Centrum der Zufriedenheit.[64]	My center of felicity.)

Against his own expectations, Geil lived and preached for another thirteen years, during which his nonactivist piety paradoxically captured the imagination of the bright young man in his congregation who was consumed with desire for a larger sphere of action.

John Fretz Funk, born in 1835, had grown up on the farm of his parents, Jacob and Susanna, some three or four miles east of Geil's meetinghouse, just inside the Hilltown Township border. He had gone to the "Chestnut Hill" schoolhouse on land his father had donated, where at eighteen he had turned from scholar to teacher. From the solemn, untaught eloquence of John Geil's sermons young "Fretz" was internalizing, without realizing it, a strong ideal of the traditional Mennonite sense of Christianity. From his mother he learned faithfulness and industry, and from his father an independence of mind, and a will to succeed. Farmer Jacob Funk was a great-grandson of Bishop Henrich Funck, pioneer author and bishop at Franconia. Jacob read an English paper from Doylestown, followed political trends, read *Uncle Tom's Cabin* in spite of the deacon's objections, and laughed off churchly criticisms of his daughters' ribbons. On their fourteenth birthdays, he gave each of his sons a silk hat and a swallow-tailed coat. He refused to provide liquor for farm laborers; Susanna made a kind of root-beer instead. Jacob wanted to see his children become wealthy, and must have been quite pleased when a son-in-law, Jacob Beidler, began to prosper greatly as a lumber dealer in Chicago. The *Tribune*, mailed east from that new city, was also a part of the Funk household reading.[65]

The children were allowed to attend a nearby Baptist Sunday school, and revival meetings by the same group. Much more "happened" in such meetings than at those under Mennonite auspices. In his mid and later teens John watched others "weeping, weeping, weeping" at those revivals, but confided to his diary that he himself felt cold and unmoved. After teaching for a while, he wanted more training. Bypassing several newly opened Bucks County academies, he enrolled at Freeland Seminary in the week of his twentieth birthday (April 1855). Here the formerly Mennonite Hunsicker proprieters were just finishing a new meetinghouse, across the turnpike from the seminary grounds, for their independent "Christian Society of Montgomery County." The bright new student signed up for the "Common English Course," and attended the dedication of what he called the "Hunsickerite" meetinghouse. On a Sunday afternoon he took a little ferry across the Perkiomen Creek to look up his relative, Preacher Abraham Wismer of Skippack.[66] Attending Dunker services at "Green Tree," he was strongly impressed by the practice of foot washing.

Several months at the seminary proved "pleasant," but when John Funk got back to his bucolic home farm in Hilltown, and gazed around, he

thought he "had never seen or ever would see anything more beautiful."[67]
It would be characteristic of this young man, both culturally and spiritually,
that he would venture out into the world, but discover, after the initial
thrill, fundamental inner loyalties. The texts from which he heard John Geil
preach were basic to Mennonite attitudes: "Ye are my friends, if ye do
whatsoever I command you." "Seek ye first the kingdom of God." Forty
years later John Funk would find that he had not forgotten these sermons,
some of them preached in a local schoolhouse called "Sylvandale." John
Geil was not narrow, but he showed a respect for people with more conservative feelings than his own. When the German Bible in the schoolhouse
was missing, he simply read his text from an English one, and without fuss
launched into his sermon in German.

Though John Funk had been in "higher" circles at Freeland, he took
his home scene seriously. One Sunday he was unable to get inside the
crowded Line Lexington meetinghouse; Bishop Jacob Kulp (Kolb) of Plains
was baptizing eighteen applicants, with Abraham Wismer of Skippack
preaching the sermon.[68] In the same summer John arrived late at the
"Perkasie" (Blooming Glen) meetinghouse one Sunday morning, and stood
outside listening for a while. Wondering "who it was that could preach so
well," he went in and "saw it was a young man of earnest humble appearance, who evidently felt the deep responsibility resting upon him . . . ."
Later John heard it was thirty-year-old Isaac Rickert, just ordained at
Doylestown, and here making his second attempt at preaching. Funk's
comment to his diary suggests some identification with what he interprets
young Rickert as representing: "If he advances as he has commenced he
will make a very excellent preacher."[69] Funk's linking of the values of
earnestness and humility with excellence in preaching shows the ideals he
had learned to value even before he himself had opted to be a Mennonite.

Both thoughtfulness and activity characterized this future leader of his
people. When he met, while out on a walk, a black man named Isaiah, he
was fascinated. He had doubtless read *Uncle Tom's Cabin* about the time
his father had, and now "scanned" Isaiah, a former slave, "over and over
again, from head to foot," as if to discover in him a mystery that could be
discovered nowhere else. How ironic, he felt, that "four million human beings . . . bearing the image of God" should be "dragging the chains of
slavery . . . under the shades of that banner whose stars and stripes declare
that *all* men are free."[70] In his second year at Freeland, Funk threw himself
into his work, also teaching Sunday school at the "Christian Meeting
House" of the Hunsickers, along with Henry Hunsicker, principal and
preacher of the new church, and a decade older than Funk. Back home in
the fall of 1856 Funk taught school again, but was restless. "The narrow

John Fretz Funk, before joining the Mennonite Church, with some of his Sunday school boys in Chicago. (John F. Funk Collection, Archives of the Mennonite Church)

confines of the school room are far too limited for me now," he wrote to Jacob Beidler, his brother-in-law at Chicago, "I have determined to see the West. . . ." He thought of raising beef cattle in Missouri, but decided to accept Beidler's offer of a position in the lumber firm.[71]

In April 1857 the handsome young bachelor joined the great American western wave, taking the train via Ontario, where he visited relatives. He arrived in Chicago with two suits, $60 in cash, and a dream of future wealth. The next day he went to church with Beidler and immediately enrolled in a Sunday school. He knew of no nearby Mennonite congregation, though other younger men from Mennonite backgrounds were in the city involved in the same economic ventures. Before long Funk was attending three Sunday schools and two church services every Sunday. He attended a "Commercial College," and revival meetings at Third Presbyterian Church, where other up-and-coming business people were involved. And early in the following January, as a major revival swept the city, he surrendered his will to God when alone on the sidewalk. Though part of a larger spiritual movement, he made his decision while communing with himself.[72]

Now came a significant moment in his spiritual career. Almost as a matter of course he had joined a class of instruction in the Presbyterian church, of which his brother-in-law was then or later a member. He appreciated his circle of Christian friends there, and had been blessed by the powerful preaching, on a level far beyond anything he would have heard at Line Lexington. He had been to Chicago prayer meetings of 5,000 persons. But the boy who had grown up worshiping in simple meetinghouses in Bucks County now found himself strangely restless in the new $60,000 Presbyterian church building. "Why is all this pomp and show?" he asked himself. How could people so taken up with "pride" claim to follow the Christ "who had nowhere to lay his head?" What he found himself longing for was "the simple, plain, and untarnished" faith he had known at home. "My mind revolts," he wrote in his diary.[73] In an apparent attempt to get his spiritual bearings, he seems at this time to have been reading the two simple, Scripture-filled books his great-grandfather Henrich Funck had written a century earlier at Franconia, *A Mirror of Baptism* and *Restitution.* Their antique German phrasings must have sounded a strange note in the midst of the roaring commerce of Chicago. But they rang a bell in his spiritual memory. If only, he wished, he could "be where those who worship God as I do would open their arms to receive me."[74] It was, as events would prove, an irrepressible yearning for the experience of faith as mediated by fellowship in the traditional, nonresistant Mennonite family.

This memory won out. Less than ten months after arriving in Chicago, Funk determined to make a spiritual pilgrimage back to his home and be baptized there. The long train ride completed, he went to Preacher John Geil, now eighty years old, for pre-baptismal instruction. On the first Sunday after Funk's return, Geil preached one of his now infrequent sermons. The text was the same one Funk had heard the old man preach on two and a half years earlier: "Ye are my friends, if ye do whatsoever I command you." This was the kind of teaching Funk had come back to hear. Conversion itself was absolutely necessary, but the continuing drama of seeing God's will realized in one's life and the life of a family of God was what now occupied Funk's mind. Geil's sermon was "a good sound one," noted the young businessman,

> full of life and animation, love and hope; one that told well the duty we owe to God and the way we must attain his friendship, his love, and his protection; one that inspired the soul with hope and rejoicing in the blessed promises of Jesus Christ.[75]

Here there was no Presbyterian predestination to filter out, nor condoning of war when "necessary." Funk was at home. Three weeks later he was baptized in the Line Lexington meetinghouse by Bishop Jacob Kulp. He had also ridden on the bay mare to see one of his former pupils, his demure second cousin Salome, daughter of Jacob Kratz.

Returning to Chicago as a member of the Line Lexington congregation, the young lumber merchant had not fully resolved an inner dialogue. He was still very much on the make, and drawn toward the excitement of political campaigns. But a month after his baptism he was viewing his fellow Chicagoans as a vain set who "love to make a show, cut a high swell, wear the finest clothes, drive the fastest horse, do the largest business, make the most money. . . ." Running roughshod over family and spiritual obligations, Chicagoans seemed ready to "give themselves over body and soul to the pursuit of wealth. . . ."[76] But probably the reason Funk said this to himself in his diary was that he himself was fighting the same temptations. He had two potential selves: the one that wanted to be like his brother-in-law and a cousin, both of whom were becoming millionaires in Chicago and affiliating with "popular" churches, and the one that looked to his Mennonite teaching for another definition of life's meaning.

Back home, father Jacob Funk wrote a letter asking his son to return and take over the farm. John was dubious, asking in return, "How much do you generally make out of the old farm in a year?" Before long he had made up his mind to stay in the Chicago he had recently hated for its impersonality and greed. He even borrowed $1,000 from his disappointed father in order to become partner in the lumber business. Recognizing his son's direction, Jacob confirmed it: "Now try to make money and get rich." John wrote back promising to "omit no exertion," but to avoid dishonest dealings.[77]

And yet this attitude would last only a year or two before the themes of his spiritual heritage would haunt him and drive him to work rather for the revival of his church than for the accumulation of a personal fortune. Gradually he was becoming able to put down in words—at first only in his diary—what was really important to him. He would define the quiet Mennonite ideal in the midst of an expansive age that mocked it or found it uninteresting.

> Our religion is more a practical religion—not much high, studied theology, not many learned men, not many great things. [Mennonites are] mostly identified with the poor, the humble, the low, the meek, the common people. This is our religion, this was the religion of Jesus. . . . Our people are a humble, simple people.[78]

Preacher John Geil's teaching had taken hold.

The community Funk left behind had its own fortune-making fever in the late fifties. The North Penn Railroad, linking Philadelphia and Bethlehem, was completed in 1857, when a locomotive prophetically named "Civilizer" pulled the first train the length of the tracks through the heart of the Mennonite community. Younger men from both Montgomery and Bucks counties now moved to the new villages springing up, such as Franconia Station (later Souderton) and Lansdale. Henry Souder's sons all went into business around their father's lumberyard at Franconia Station, and across the tracks Jonathan Hunsberger's boys matched them with a store, feed store and hotel. Herman Gottshall moved in from Franconia

The 1838 meetinghouse of the Rockhill congregation, showing the proximity of the North Penn Railroad, completed in 1857. The small "Branch" congregation of the Eastern District, led by Bishop David Bergey, also met here until it was disbanded about 1888. (Author's Collection)

Township to erect a new mill where the Souders' barn had been torn down to make way for the railroad, and Milton Bergey came from tiny Harleysville to join the Souders in the store business. Henry R. Derstine, earlier a schoolteacher at Rockhill and now a Gwynedd farmer, built the first new house and a feed store at Lansdale, named for the engineer of the new railroad. Young John Clemmer, son of the deacon at Franconia, moved next to the Derstines. It was the biggest change the landscape had seen since the white man had come.

The railroad took a toll both symbolic and literal. The country's worst railroad wreck had occurred on July 17, 1856, near what would later be called Ambler, before the project was even completed. The tracks grazed one end of the old Derstine family burial plot near the Rockhill meetinghouse. "Quite a few" victims of accidents, fights and disease among the Irish laborers who built the railroad were interred in this plot, which served as a kind of potter's field, and was then left unmarked and forgotten. For the next century worshipers at Rockhill would be interrupted by passing trains just outside the windows (in 1925 a new building would be placed a little more distant). One young man paid a personal price: Jacob Erb, living on his grandfather's farm, the Hagey homestead in Franconia Township. When a bunch of boys with whom he was walking along the tracks "got the idea to see who could walk nearest a passing train," Jacob proved the boldest. He also had, from then on, an arm that "hung useless by his side."[79]

Franconia remained the most conservative of townships. In 1856, when less than 5 percent of the schoolchildren in Montgomery County still received German instruction, half of them were in Franconia.[80] Immigration to the West continued, with Detweilers and Nices now moving all the way to Illinois. At Coventry, a "class" of thirty applicants was baptized, seeming to promise a renewed future for this old congregation. This promise was destined to be unfulfilled; the Dunkers would reap a substantial harvest among the Coventry membership, and in another half-century the Mennonite congregation would disappear.

The Eastern District, in May 1858, registered another advance: its first regular and official Sunday school. The Franconia Conference would not get its first one until 1870. Out in Ohio, Ephraim Hunsberger had started one in 1854, and before that there had been community-sponsored Sunday schools at "Bertolet's" and Flatland. The Mennonites of West Swamp had begun by cooperating with the local Reformed people in a Sunday school at Steinsburg in 1857, not far from the West Swamp meetinghouse. John Oberholtzer's children's instruction sessions on Sunday afternoons seem to have ceased. Now the young school and singing schoolteacher, Andrew B.

Shelly, was picked as the first superintendent of the forty-nine pupil school at West Swamp.[81] Soon there was another Sunday school at East Swamp, and before long others began to appear throughout the Eastern Conference District.

In the last years of the decade, when division darkened on the national political horizon, a light of unity seemed at last to be kindling for the more liberal Mennonites scattered in pockets from Pennsylvania to Iowa. John Oberholtzer had been carrying a torch for this possibility both in his earlier *Botschafter* and now in the *Volksblatt*. The issue for February 22, 1860, included some interesting "Correspondence from Iowa." It was from Oberholtzer's friend Daniel Krehbiel, who, after ten years as a businessman in Cleveland, had moved among his relatives in Iowa to keep up his church fellowship. Here Krehbiel had come to the disturbing realization that the recent Mennonite immigrants had their churches on a kind of mere congregational basis. They were not accountable to or unified into any conference. Krehbiel himself had strong convictions; he had come to North America to escape military service in Europe. Already in 1859 he had helped to bring about a preliminary meeting between two Iowa congregations. These people did not see themselves in sympathy with the largest group of Mennonites, who kept their distance from the culture of the "world," and who even tended to dress plainly, and recognizably as Mennonites. So Krehbiel threw out a general appeal, via the *Volksblatt*, for a "general conference" of Mennonites who would be interested not only in fellowship, but mission outreach and education.[82]

The invitation, which seemed to have no effect whatsoever among the "old" Mennonites, was to a meeting at West Point, Iowa, on "the second day of Pentecost" in the spring of 1860. John Oberholtzer enthusiastically supported the idea, and his Eastern Conference endorsed it on the first Thursday of May. An article in the *Volksblatt* following an editorial recommending the idea also promoted the publication of tracts, and threw down a challenge: "Brethren, what shall we do!? Shall we remain inactive, or shall we stride forward?"[83] Perhaps these words were written by young editorial assistant Andrew B. Shelly, who was contributing articles in favor of a general conference from behind a pen name, "*Freimuth*."

John Oberholtzer, now fifty-one, was anxious to go to Iowa, but had no means to pay for the trip, nor provision to care for his wife while he would be away. Not everyone felt it was a necessary trip. Minister Enos Loux, the widower who had recently sold his mill in Hilltown and moved to another one at Swamp, was willing to go along. But as the date approached and no door seemed to open, Oberholtzer sadly gave up his plans. This moved the minister at East Swamp, Levi Schimmel (whose relatives in the next years would have considerable wealth), to solicit the needed money and make arrangements for the support of Mary, Oberholtzer's elderly wife, while the bishop was gone for six weeks. Encouraged, Oberholtzer and Loux took their leave by train, stopping to visit Bishop Ephraim Hunsberger at Wadsworth, Ohio, on the way. Hunsberger, himself an enthusiast of missions and Mennonite unification, had already joined Bishop Daniel Hoch in a small Canada-Ohio Conference.

An all-night train ride brought Oberholtzer and his short, stocky colleague, miller Loux, to the banks of the Mississippi, twenty miles from their destination, West Point, Iowa. The two travelers, eagerly hoped-for by those who had called the "General Conference," turned out to be the only non-Iowans who attended. But there was nevertheless an air of expectant excitement in the Methodist church borrowed for the meeting, and crowded not only by local Mennonites but by neighbors who sensed an unusual happening. The next day was Pentecost Sunday; communion was celebrated, with the eastern visitors participating. On Monday, after three more sermons, the first business was to elect a chairman. The unanimous choice was the visiting editor of the *Volksblatt*. Then a committee of five was chosen to draw up a plan of union for "all Mennonites of North America." Again Oberholtzer was included.[84]

That night the eastern printer and the four Iowa farmer-preachers drew up six resolutions on the topic of union. It was "humiliating," they observed, that though "there are about 128,000 Mennonites" in the United States and Canada, "they have never been raised to the position of a church" (*noch nie zu einen wirklich kirchlichen Standpunkte erhoben ward*).[85] It was time to take a new stance. "All branches" were now called on, in the very first resolution, to "extend to each other the hand of fellowship." No accusation of "heresy" or "transgression" should be considered "valid" unless it was "established on unequivocal scriptural evidence."

Such expressions would have struck the "old" Mennonites, had they read them, as amazing. How could a little group of ministers representing five widely scattered congregations presume to speak in the name of Mennonitism in North America? How could people who were themselves unwilling to cooperate with the main body of Mennonites put out a call for unity? But this was not the only perception of this meeting. To some Mennonites, especially those of more recent immigration than those in Pennsylvania, it brought hope. Within the next five or six years, in the midst of a terrible national crisis, there would indeed arise a gathering and organization of progressive Mennonites from various states and from Canada. There would be yearly "General Conferences," mostly at Wadsworth, Ohio, which was more central than Iowa or Pennsylvania. This "Conference" would employ the *Volksblatt* as a basic mode of intercommunication. Further, it would incite both mission work and the creation of a school for future ministers. When a massive wave of Mennonites would arrive from Russia in the mid-seventies, it would be to this organizational umbrella, rather than to "old" Mennonitism, that they would look for affiliation.

On the way back from Iowa, John Oberholtzer sat down to start writing his impressions of the conference for the *Volksblatt.* So much that he had hoped for had been enthusiastically approved at West Point. He had been given the welcome of a faith-hero and valuable brother, in contrast with the criticism he so often endured around home. He had met old friends. A mission treasury had been set up, with two collection points—one in Iowa and one at the office of the Mennonite Printing Union at Milford Square. Memories of the 2600-mile train and steamboat journey, the visits, meetings, and farewells surged across his mind. "Even now," wrote the happy homebound leader, "my eyes become moist with tears so that I am unable to write...."[86]

Chapter 11

"Warfare: Its Evils, Our Duty"

1861-1865

An excited crowd gathered in front of the courthouse in Norristown on Monday evening, April 15, 1861. A well-known local judge orated fervently to them of an insult to their country's flag. Southern states which had been withdrawing from the "Union" had now gone beyond the tolerable. Their "Rebels" had fired on and taken captive the Federal soldiers guarding Fort Sumter in South Carolina. President Lincoln, inaugurated less than six weeks earlier, had immediately called for the rusty state militias to muster 75,000 men. In a three-month term, they would teach the Rebels a lesson. Governor Curtin of Pennsylvania had passed on the order to his militia. With the North from Philadelphia to Chicago aflame with outrage, it was time, urged Judge Daniel Smyser, to throw away the scabbard.

The crowd applauded, a band struck up "Yankee Doodle," and other speakers took turns, several offering large monetary gifts to the Montgomery County militia. Then a handsome lawyer in his mid-twenties, soon to run successfully for the office of district attorney, stepped forward and pledged to march in defense of the Union on two days' notice. It was a grandson of the Mennonite bishop John Hunsicker of Skippack, an alumnus of Freeland Seminary and Union College. "I follow," shouted Charles Hunsicker, "the fortunes of the flag." The newspaper picked up the speech approvingly: "It is not time to talk; we want men—we want money. I shall go wherever called out by the Governor, and will not return unless honorably."

By Saturday morning the war-fever had brought 600 volunteers, including Hunsicker's older brother, Davis, to line up in front of the courthouse. The whole local population, swelled by hundreds of people from the countryside, roared their support. Again the "impassioned and eloquent words" of Judge Daniel Smyser electrified the crowd, giving hearers a deeper sense of "the word *country*" than they had ever felt before. Flags were presented to the drawn-up volunteers from "the ladies of the county." Then as the band played a stirring march, church bells rang and thousands cheered, the recruits "wheeled into column" and carried their flags in quick time across the Schuylkill bridge to the Bridgeport train station. By two in the afternoon they were at "Camp Curtin" near Harrisburg.[1]

These volunteers did not dream that a long and incredibly bloody civil war lay ahead. Many of them, having seen only a skirmish or two in Maryland, refused to stay in their regiment a day longer than the three months they had promised, even though their general, expecting an imminent battle, "requested" them to continue. On the other hand, Charles Hunsicker, appointed adjutant (assistant to the commanding office), did stay longer, as did his brother Davis. Davis even considered raising a company by himself, later enlisted for three years, and was made a lieutenant. He would come back, he wrote to an older brother, "with honor to *myself* and *friends* and *to the name* I bear, or not at all. I want to do that which on my return will make those who know me feel proud of me, and make others anxious for my companionship and fellowship...."[2]

The name he bore had not, in previous generations, been honored in military terms. How had these Hunsickers of Skippack (specifically the Providence congregation) learned to talk war instead of the centuries-old Christian nonresistance of their grandparents? The answer lies in their father's generation. Joseph Hunsicker, son of Bishop John, had cashed in on the lumber trade on the Schuylkill Canal, and sent several of his five promising sons to Freeland and to college. They were becoming attorneys, justices of the peace, and one would even be sheriff. Though Joseph had become a man of means and an "Associate Judge" of Montgomery County, now that the railroad was replacing the canal traffic he was about to lose both business and the home farm. In the midst of this "humiliation" two of his brightest sons were talking of enlisting for three years. He began to think of his spiritual heritage. He visited and wrote letters to his sons as they drilled in a camp near Washington, D.C., but could not convey to them the logic of his nonresistant heritage.

"Pap don't understand this war business," observed Davis to another brother, also an attorney. "It is new to him and contrary to his early teaching."[3] Apparently Davis himself had grown up without absorbing such teaching. He did know that "the first lessons taught" to his father by Bishop John Hunsicker's generation at Skippack had been "for peace and to war under no circumstances," but Davis felt no such conviction. In this "Strange world," he thought, "we must leave all to the guidance of an overruling and wise Providence," and let the matter at that. He had not internalized a sense of a faithfully covenanted Christian community. The "troops of friends" his father had had as a successful local businessman had all "deserted" when economic "adversity" struck. Perhaps, Davis thought, he should go back to Providence and "make a tremendous effort to redeem" the Hunsicker farm of his childhood.[4] Instead, he enlisted. A year and a half later, as his regiment defended a bridge near Antietam, Maryland, he was wounded in a fierce bayonet battle in a cornfield, and died two days later.[5] His body, shipped back from Hagerstown to Providence, was buried beside the little Mennonite meetinghouse, where his family raised among the plain rows of gravestones a towering obelisk.

One hundred and twenty years earlier, when war had threatened the local Mennonites, they had arranged the translation and printing of their nonresistant story, *The Martyrs Mirror.* This time, no such preparation seems to have been made. True, Abraham Godshalk's 1838 book on *Regeneration* had shown a Mennonite minister teaching nonresistance as an integral and firmly held part of Christian conversion. But no special effort seems to have been put forth by the church to prepare the younger generation on this topic. The progressive Eastern Pennsylvania Conference Mennonites, having reorganized in part for the very purpose of getting better instruction for the youth, had made no provision for this emergency either. Though they had introduced a printing press, a magazine, children's instructions, and now Sunday schools, it became evident as soon as the war broke out that something had changed in their understanding of nonresistance. Whereas they had refused any tolerance to lodge membership or foot washing, it now appeared impossible for them to agree about requiring abstinence from warfare, as their ancestors had done since the founding of their church. "The matter of the present war was considered," wrote the conference secretary in October 1861, "but no action was taken."[6] There would be similar statements in the minutes for the duration of the war.

Unbaptized young men from both "old" and "new" Mennonite families were among the enlistees in 1861. Over a dozen "traditionally Mennonite" names, such as Buckwalter, Clemmer, Detweiler, Kulp, or Moyer, were on the roster of the 600 volunteers making up Charles Hunsicker's Montgomery County regiment.[7] Among Bucks County Mennonites it was no different. At least four sons of Joseph Fretz, who had been expelled by the old Deep Run congregation and then become a lay leader in the new one, got into the Union Army. One—William—had poor eyesight, but managed to be hired as a civilian quartermaster.[8] Two sons of Mahlon Fretz—never a member but an active sympathizer with the New Mennonites—also joined.[9] But so, from Old Mennonite families, did a grandson of Preacher John Geil,[10] and a son of Preacher Abraham Godshalk.[11] The Mennonites were swept up by the general indignation among local "Republicans" against the southern seceders and northern Democrats, soon to be nicknamed "Copperheads." "The war excitement is verry Great at the present time," wrote aging farmer Jacob Funk to his son John in Chicago, "as there is still traters among the people. . . . But they Must keep very quiet or recive a Coat of tar and feathers."[12] Another son, Jacob, Jr., wrote to John that he had been involved in a horseback rally at Sellersville, in an attempt to intimidate the local Copperheads.

John himself was finding Chicago "all excitement" over the war, and he became so involved in patriotic rallies and marches that he had no time for his diary. On July 4, though he had been out until three in the morning at a "fair," he got up at four, and before breakfast hoisted a flag and fired a "salute of six shots" over it with his revolver.[13] Perhaps this was the same national holiday that saw an unfortunate "excitement" back in Pennsylvania near Funk's alma mater, Freeland Seminary. The Pennsylvania Female College, which the Hunsickers had also founded, was being decorated by northern girls for the occasion, when some southern belles in the student body spit on the flag. One of the southerners also delighted in waving a photograph of Jefferson Davis, president of the Confederacy, in front of the northern girls, and kissing it. The school never really recovered from this general crisis, since the southern girls, an important segment of the student body, were called home.[14] Freeland Seminary itself received a nearly mortal blow. When an actual draft occurred, "twenty-six students left for their homes in one day." Henry Hunsicker docked the salaries of his demoralized faculty without taking counsel with them, and found rebellion on his hands. Students had their minds on the draft and military training. Before long Abraham Hunsicker, ordained fifteen years earlier as a Mennonite preacher at Skippack, could look out the front windows of his fine house and see his teachers drilling their students in military maneuvers. The local villagers "hugely enjoyed" this spectacle, and "Right about face, left about face, forward, march were words in the mouth of the youngest students." Principal Hunsicker's brother-in-law, who had grown up in the West Swamp congregation, remembered it all as though "a West Point academy was right in the little village" built around Preacher Abraham Hunsicker's farm.[15]

The Skippack church Hunsicker had left was having its own severe problem in 1861. Bishop Henry Johnson, who was finally ruled to be outside the Eastern Conference in May, had just replaced his co-minister David Bergey by holding an ordination on his own authority. But the new minister, Christian Detweiler, though chosen by the casting of lots, was deeply troubled, and eight months later was found drowned in a well. The "old" Mennonites took this as an indication that Detweiler had doubted the rightness of his church.[16] In fact, many Mennonite ministers found ordination a difficult experience. John Walters of the Line Lexington congregation, who had been ordained some months before Detweiler, had "made but little progress in preaching" a year and a half later. He had yet to attempt a sermon. "All he has done," wrote a young man in the congregation who had grown up listening to John Geil's sermons, "is to read a chapter sometimes and make the initiatory address. At first he could not speak words enough to make an address, he would commence and utter a few sentences when he would stand mute 3 minutes perhaps, before he could think of anything to say."[17] A fear of such difficulty may have been behind the refusal of a man from the "old" Mennonites of Upper Skippack to join fourteen others in submitting to "the lot" for a new minister in July 1862. But so strong was the old teaching on this that young John Clemens of Lederach, reporting to a Canadian friend the resultant ordination of John Hunsberry, referred to the man who had declined the lot as "disobedient."[18]

In the early months of the Civil War, John Oberholtzer was occupied with the budding "General Conference" of Mennonite churches. In May 1861 he led a delegation of six from the Eastern Conference to its second session, at Wadsworth, Ohio. They joined delegates from five non-Pennsylvania congregations in signing "articles of union." At this gathering Oberholtzer led in a strong rejection of membership in "secret societies," and in plans for a new church-sponsored school.[19] Ephraim Hunsberger, formerly of Hereford but now the local minister at Wadsworth, would be charged with finding a location; five years later the school would be built across the road from his own house. First someone would have to go around to stir up support and collect contributions in Iowa, Illinois, Ohio, Canada, and Pennsylvania. A zealous young preacher from Summerfield, Illinois—Daniel Hege—was appointed to this work, and during the following year he began his rounds. His unprecedented visits through the Eastern Conference netted contributions of $2522.50, 44 percent of the total amount subscribed.[20] In addition to this, John Oberholtzer raised a collection to help the congregation at West Point, Iowa, erect its own building.

The northern mood took a downward turn after the first "Battle of Bull Run" near Washington, D.C., on July 21, 1861. President Lincoln soon called for a national day of humiliation and prayer. Bounties were offered for enlisting. In Worcester Township William Freed, who had gathered a group of workers to enlarge his house, came back from the sawmill with boards only to find that his whole crew had gone off and enlisted.[21] Over at Doylestown young Henry Derstine, fascinated by a visit of "the Ringold

Regiment," waited until his Mennonite father had gone to Philadelphia, and got himself "sworn in as an Artilleryman." The elder Derstine then set out to get his son back, reported Jacob Funk, Jr., to his brother in Chicago, and "after spending about forty or fifty dollars, succeeded."[22] A similar story would be told of former Freeland Seminary student Benjamin Alderfer of Lower Salford, whose wealthy father Michael was a member of Bishop Moses Gottschall's congregation at Schwenksville. Though he had two small children at home, went the report, Benjamin had enlisted in Philadelphia. But his wife, born in a Dunker family, had wept so incessantly that her health was despaired of, and Benjamin had been somehow extricated to save her.[23]

In August 1862 President Lincoln called for 300,000 volunteers, and for a draft of 300,000 additional men through the state militias. The latter was a new and ominous sensation for millions of Americans. Every county was given a quota, and as assessors came around to register the young men there was an unprecedented feeling of panic. Rather than face this draft, a sizable group left for Canada or western territory. A gang of at least thirteen was known to have gone north from the general area of Bedminster and Plumstead townships.[24] In the Franconia-Lower Salford area, Henry Derstine, Jacob Landes, and Abraham Moyer were among the "skedaddlers."[25] On the other hand, twenty-one-year-old Joseph Hagey, from a Mennonite farm along the Allentown Road, enlisted.[26] Most people were hoping that there would be enough such enlistees to satisfy the county quota, but in areas like Lower Salford where the Mennonite concentration was heavy, there was little chance of this occurring. A "War Committee" was formed in Lower Salford "to pay bounties to those who voluntarily enlist to the credit of our township." Michael Alderfer contributed $100 and his wealthy old uncle from the Salford congregation, Abraham Alderfer, gave $125.[27] Groups of draft-age men pooled their funds, pledging to give the amounts necessary to find "substitutes" for those in their pool whom the draft might strike. "Union Leagues" sprang up for this purpose. At Trappe, Principal Henry Hunsicker was elected the local president.[28]

It was just in the weeks of this excitement that David Hege of Illinois came around looking for contributions for the prospective Mennonite "educational institute." John Oberholtzer wrote several delightfully tangy Pennsylvania Dutch dialogues on the subject, between two fictional eastern Pennsylvania Mennonite farmers. But some readers of the *Volksblatt* were offended, and so Oberholtzer dropped publication after only two conversations had appeared.[29] Hege, having been directed to look up Mennonites living in the city of Philadelphia, found there "a goodly number," and preached for them.[30] After he left, these scattered recent migrants to the city were called together again by preachers from the Eastern Conference, and for the next two years services were held for them "as regularly as circumstances would permit." Then a Baptist meetinghouse on Diamond Street was rented for these services, and before long, purchased. From this group would come, in another decade, the first urban Mennonite congregation in America, and for some years the largest one in the Eastern Conference. John Oberholtzer gave the credit for its beginnings to visitor Daniel Hege.

All men from eighteen to forty-five were now being "enrolled." There was an allowance, rather lenient by later standards, for exemptions, which could be claimed for health, family, and certain occupational reasons. More important for the Mennonites, one could claim exemption for reasons of conscience, though sentiment in the neighborhood made it clear that some price would have to be paid so that the conscientious would bear an equal share of the burdens of the crisis. To claim an exemption, the potential draftee had to appear before a justice of the peace, be sworn or affirmed, and state his case. He could also avoid military service by finding a "substitute" to go in his place, making whatever financial payment the substitute would settle for. Among those who would be automatically exempted were mail carriers, schoolteachers, and ministers.

An anxious crowd of 900 men seeking exemptions could be seen in Doylestown in the second week of September 1861. "I have never seen harder pressing and crowding in all the days of my life," wrote one Mennonite man who was present; "everyone had to push with good earnest and all his might to get his name registered in the forenoon."[31] Apparently Mennonites who had already claimed exemptions for physical reasons also declared conscientious exemption. There was a good deal of confusion. In some townships, dozens of men were trying to ignore the whole issue. One Mennonite who applied for a conscientious exemption, John Overholt of Bedminster, claimed that his conscience would not allow him to make even the normally required "affirmation." He was refused an exemption.[32] More than 250 other Mennonites from Bucks County were classified as exempted, however, and when a Doylestown newspaper published a list of some 312, it turned out that two thirds of them had "Mennonite" names. Among the ninety-eight Mennonite names from Bedminster and Plumstead, an Eastern Conference pastor later was able to find seven from the "new" Mennonite congregation at Deep Run.

The Doylestown *Democrat* rather pointedly stated that future readers would find the long list of "conscientious" men very interesting, and would compare their profession with the kind of life these men went on to live. The newspapers also expressed considerable skepticism over the variety of

324   *Maintaining the Right Fellowship*

the ailments reported. We may find a sampling of Mennonite cases suggestive of the scene that summer:

Abraham Kulp	Bedminster	Perfect Dwarf, 4 ft. 6 in. 61 lbs.
Samuel Souder	New Britain	Becomes nervous when frightened....
Henry B. Moyer	Hilltown	Minister, hearing poor
Tobias W. Myers	Hilltown	Arm fractured once; useless now cannot reach in pantaloon pocket
John Schantz	Milford	Nearly blind in left eye
Jacob Rosenberger	Rockhill	hernia for fifteen years
Joseph Leatherman	Plumstead	cripple[33]

"It is truly astonishing," wrote one correspondent, "what a number of sick
and decrepit men we have among us."[34] Of course, many non-Mennonite
names were also on the list.

As the Bucks County draft kept being delayed by the great number of
"examinations," young men who were from Mennonite families but were
not church members were looking around for substitutes. Some believed
that every man who was exempted as conscientious would still have to pay a
fine, perhaps quite heavy, when legislation was completed. In general the
Mennonite leaders were ready to accept this. There was much discussion
among both the "old" and "new" Mennonites. What should the church be
doing? The Eastern Conference, meeting in its fall session at Bertolet's with
the draft still not taken, was not sure how to respond. "There were numerous opinions expressed concerning non resistance," noted the secretary,
"but the Council decided that it would be best to refrain from action at this
date."[35]

But on another topic there could be unified action: the critical comments aimed toward them by the "old" Mennonites. It seems likely that in
the neighborhood discussions of the conscientious exemption question
brought the issue of what constituted Mennonite identity to the surface.
"Old" Mennonites may have pointed out that there were two groups, and
that in their opinion the "new" Mennonites were no longer characterized
by all the original scruples, especially relating to nonresistance. To ground
this distinction on an official action, they apparently referred to a statement
adopted at the May 1848 Franconia Conference, which denied that an
actual vote against the Oberholtzer constitution had been taken. The effect
of this was to place the blame for the split on the "new" Mennonites, and
undermine their historic claim to the nonresistant tradition. Although Abraham Grater of Skippack had immediately reacted to this "statement" in
1848, the Eastern Conference of 1862, struggling for internal stability, now
reported that they had never heard of it before. To hear it under the present

circumstances rankled deeply. Since the "old" Mennonites had thus "continued incessantly to malign them falsely," and "continued to use their [May 1848] resolution," the Eastern Conference now asked for the setting up of a committee of six—three from each conference—"to settle the differences between [the two] brotherhoods *fraternally*, on the basis of witnesses."[36]

But as before, there was no reply from the Franconia Conference. Instead of the larger body helping the younger one in this time of crisis, the older group felt there could be no basis of discussion other than repentance on the part of the other group. When the Franconia Conference met the following May, they had "for this time not much to do." One of the Franconia preachers reported to Canada that "Everything seemed to be at peace in the congregations (God be thanked)."[37] Angered by this lack of response, the Eastern Conference issued to the public a German broadside entitled *History of the Division Among the Mennonites in 1847-1848*. Appearing after the spring 1863 conference, it made no reference whatever to the discussions on the nonresistance question, but tried to set the record straight on why there had arisen a new conference. "All justice and reason" had been "suppressed by the majority" at the 1847 Franconia Conference sessions, stated the *History*, and at the October 1847 session, when the sixteen men had left, the conference had passed its motion to invite them back on the basis of repentance "far too fast," in a manner that was "utterly unjust." The Franconia resolution of the following May, furthermore, denying that a vote against the constitution had been taken, was, "in a word— *untrue*." The Eastern Conference had now resolved that this 1848 Franconia statement put "the truth into a perverted light," and that they were "ready to prove" it.[38]

Six leaders signed this angry broadside, with regrets that this "old story" had still not been laid to rest. They were hereby reversing, they stated, the "ban" under which they felt themselves to have been placed "back since 1847." They would now return the ban on the "old" ministers and deacons who had "placed it on innocent brethren on that memorable October 7, 1847; they shall now remain bound by it until they free themselves of it by scriptural means...." This seems to have been the last official expression from either group in relation to the other, though from time to time an individual writer to the press would take pains to dissociate his group from the other one in the public mind. Generally, the Eastern Conference people reacted against being identified with cultural conservatism, and Franconia Conference people raised the issue of the "nonresistant ground."

The nervous weeks just before the October 1862 draft, testing young

men's convictions deeply, were a time of spiritual destiny for John Funk. It
was going on four years, now, since this rising young Chicago businessman
had been baptized at old Line Lexington, and he had yet to participate in a
communion service. In a life filled with commerce and war rallies, and surrounded by young friends of strong military leaning, Funk had written to
Abraham Detweiler, preacher in Illinois, asking when the Mennonites there
would celebrate communion. Detweiler, whose people were not in a state of
unity, referred Funk instead to the Mennonite community around Elkhart,
Indiana. So it was that the stylish "young fellow from Chicago" arrived at
Deacon David Good's house, a few miles southwest of Goshen, on a Thursday night in October 1862. There had just been "Conference" at the Yellow
Creek meetinghouse, and nearly fifty young people, mostly young men
about to pass through the unprecedented draft, had applied for baptism. It
was a definitive emotional moment. The "grand sight," on Saturday, of
these young recruits to the nonresistant church of their forbears, moved
John Funk deeply. It was a vision of another order than the one he was surrounded with in commercial and patriotic Chicago. It was the largest Mennonite baptismal class to be received in this part of the country in the 19th
century. It gave Funk, he remembered, "a very favorable and encouraging
idea of the Mennonite Church in Indiana." There were also present many
ex-"Bucks Countians" to greet and identify via the network of relatives.

    But Sunday morning, October 10, was the climactic point of the
weekend. "I shall never forget that meeting," wrote Funk many years later.
The forty by sixty foot Yellow Creek meetinghouse was jammed with an
immense crowd that included many standing outside. A third cousin of
Funk, Bishop John Brenneman of Elida, Ohio, who had baptized the young
men, preached again. "Over 600 brethren and sisters" then took part in the
communion and foot washing. John Funk felt surrounded by a vital Christian family in this his first communion. Writing back to his parents of his
solemn feelings, he remarked that he especially appreciated the foot washing, "one thing which I think our people in too many places in Pennsylvania have either forgotten or neglected."[39] When he got back to his
"lumber office" in Chicago, Funk's life had a different tone. News of war
and politics, formerly so much a part of his diary, now all but disappeared
from its pages, and the lonely bachelor, finding his identity crystallizing,
began to pine sharply for his sweetheart back in Hilltown, "the prettiest . . .
girl in Bucks County," Salome Kratz.

    By the time the draft came off a week later, the Mennonites in the East
were still not ready. Some of them had asked Bucks County officials for advice, "but they had none for us," remarked Preacher Jacob Beidler of the
Old Mennonite Church at Swamp. "But then some of our preachers arose

and again went to our governor and once more petitioned."[40] Among these leaders, apparently, were elderly Deacon Abraham Clemmer of Franconia, and Bishop Jacob Kulp of Plains, now sixty-four. The group, helpfully accompanied by the Jewish editor of their favorite German newspaper, Doylestown's *Der Morgenstern*, managed to see Governor Curtin at Harrisburg. Here Bishop Kulp's "earnest pleading and humble deportment"[41] seemed to communicate the Mennonite concerns effectively. "We propose," wrote Beidler, "that the brethren who are caught by the draft be released, that they not be compelled to go, yet that they not be released from paying a fine." Congregations such as Line Lexington received contributions to pay for these trips to Harrisburg.[42] Editor Loeb let the Canadian Mennonites, slow to pay their subscription money, know that he had been "of assistance" to their Pennsylvania relatives during "the drafts."[43]

"Tomorrow morning, the 16th of October," editorialized John Oberholtzer in the *Volksblatt*, "is the appointed day declared by our Governor." If this draft really came off, which Oberholtzer "sorrowfully" expected, it would "draw hot tears from many."[44] And indeed the following morning, in both Doylestown and Norristown, cylindrical "tin wheels" crammed with tightly folded bits of paper each containing a man's name were spun while officials watched. A blind or blindfolded man picked out slips until the quota was met, and all day clerks wrote out draft notices for the names on the slips pulled out. As messengers carrying the notices arrived at the homes of draftees, as at the "peaceful little town" of Milford Square, "robust men" could be seen weeping with the women. "Everyone ran toward the messenger," reported Oberholtzer, to see "whether . . . the destroying angel had passed them by." Now some who had been "struck" decided to apply for conscientious exemption. John and Andreas Mack of near Hereford went out to Harrisburg, and a few days later applied for the exemption at Norristown.[45] There they were joined by other Mennonites like Jacob Moyer of Salford, Jacob Stover of Towamencin (both future preachers), Jacob Rittenhouse of Towamencin, and Abraham Benner of Hatfield.[46] Schoolteacher Joel Bower of Douglass Township walked the eighteen miles to Norristown. On the way down, he stayed overnight with the Samuel and Tobias Swartleys of Franconia. But when he discovered at Norristown that schoolteachers were indeed exempt, he "felt enabled through joy to walk right home, and did so."[47]

Young men who had not joined the Mennonite Church of their parents were in no position to claim conscientious exemption. For them the only way to escape military duty (as did most of their non-Mennonite neighbors as well) was to hire substitutes to fill their places in the draft. A hurried traffic in substitutes sprang up in the four days between draft and mustering-in time. In these dealings there was considerable variation of amounts paid; they ranged from $100 to $1000. Gideon Stover of Hilltown found "a German" for $600, but Christian Myers of Plumstead had to pay out $1000 for his substitute, Asher Collum of nearby Danboro.[48] This money had to be raised rapidly, and brokers appeared on the scene. One was none other than Michael Alderfer of Lower Salford, a member at "Gottschall's," who had not been baptized until the months following the 1847 division. These brokers seem to have been resented for profiting from their young neighbors' fears, and later community tradition attributed a troubled conscience to wealthy Michael Alderfer.[49] A great many young men with Mennonite names, who had not applied for conscientious exemption, used the substitute method. No records exist of the deliberations of the Franconia Conference in this period, but the Conference apparently allowed this way of meeting government requests. The Eastern Conference was not in internal agreement on the topic of nonresistance itself.

At least two Mennonite drafted men had a conscience on the matter of substitutes. Middle-aged Jacob S. Overholt of the Lexington congregation apparently did not take the exemption, and he felt that he would be responsible for the life of a substitute if he engaged one. Perhaps he was too conscientious even to claim an exemption for his health or his large family; in any case he was sent to camp with the drafted soldiers. There as he was working one day none other than the President of the United States came by, and struck up a conversation. Learning that Overholt was forty-six years old and had a family of twelve children back home, the kindly Abraham Lincoln wrote out a note ordering Overholt's release.[50] The other man, Frank Moyer of Lower Salford, who had paid $1000 for his substitute, was greatly shocked when the latter was killed. Standing beside the grave, the saddened Moyer looked down saying that it was really himself who had died.[51]

The draft fell far short of producing its goal of 335,000 soldiers, and that was the last time the state militias were used for this purpose. Now Congress began working on a new law for a Federally administered draft. Young men became anxious all over again, but one probable improvement was welcome to the Mennonites: there would be a "commutation fee" by which drafted men could pay off their obligation to the government, and which would be used to help the wounded. Schoolteacher Abraham Funk of Hilltown, younger brother of John in Chicago, watched the papers closely, feeling he could probably finish his spring term in 1863 and still move to Chicago in time to escape the local draft and its commutation fee.[52] The Samuel Lapps, also of the Lexington congregation, got a letter from Abraham Leatherman of Ohio, telling of his community's anxiety about

John F. Funk, businessman of Chicago, after joining the Mennonite Church. Note the absence of his mustache. (John F. Funk Collection, Archives of the Mennonite Church)

"another draft." Already the Leathermans' son Jacob had paid "$205 of his earnings to get clear." But Abraham commented that he "would rather see my children carried to their graves [than] to see them forced into the war...."[53] Letters from Jacob Nold also described the situation among Mennonites in Ohio.

Samuel Lapp was able to prosper in these years making shoes. The need for soldiers' boots and uniforms gave a boost to local industry. In the Harleysville area John Binder (not a Mennonite) took large contracts for making soldiers' clothing, parceling out the work to local women, to whom he also sold sewing machines "by the car-load." Apparently Mennonites participated in this, as many of them did in the new cigar-making cottage industry of these years. In general there was a business boom in towns like "Souder's" and Lansdale, where Mennonites were building new mills, stores and homes along with their ambitious neighbors.

A prosperous but sober John Funk, still a bachelor at twenty-eight, came home from Chicago for a visit at New Year of 1863. Amazingly, eighty-four-year-old John Geil had the sermon at Line Lexington on the first Sunday Funk attended. Still intellectually sharp, the old preacher was memorizing two long German hymns that winter. His admonition in the chilly Lexington meetinghouse was not long that morning, but he spoke, Funk marveled to his diary, "with the same force and strength that he has these many years. . . ." No one could "listen to the aged man without the deepest feeling." His "solemn, measured tones" seemed to reach from "the shores of Eternity." After the service the young businessman and the old minister met around the stove in the middle of the meetinghouse, where Geil had come to warm his hands and light his pipe (even the old Mennonite women frequently smoked white clay pipes). Geil called Funk by name, asking him if he lived in Chicago. Funk replied affirmatively.

"Have they made a soldier of you?" Geil wanted to know (his own grandson had enlisted).

"No," replied the visitor. "I would make a poor soldier—I would not fight."

"Yes, that has always been our privilege," commented the old minister; "and we shall probably always retain it."[54]

Funk hated to see the aged preacher leave, feeling that it might be the last time they would meet. Then, having vainly "begged and begged and begged" his Salome to marry him and come to Chicago, he returned himself, and spent many evenings translating into English Abraham Godshalk's book on "Regeneration,"[55] written at nearby Doylestown when Funk was only three years old. Funk liked the book's teaching so much that he sent parts of it to Mennonite ministers in Indiana. He was thinking about doing some writing on spiritual themes himself. He was particularly concerned that "so many of our Mennonite boys had already and were still enlisting."[56] In these years he was very active in several Sunday schools, cooperating at times with a young Christian worker named Dwight L. Moody, who shared his unusual Christian convictions against participating in war. And in midsummer of 1863 Funk received an interesting visitor at one of his meetings, another bachelor from Bucks County with strong Mennonite loyalties and an interest in publishing. It was twenty-six-year-old John Gehman Stauffer of Milford Square, John Oberholtzer's cousin and right-hand man in the *Volksblatt* office. Funk himself was one of the most enthusiastic of the *Volksblatt's* 700 subscribers. Stauffer had become weary with an overload of work; he had served, he later claimed, not only as "compositor, printer, foreman" and "in part bookkeeper," but for "the last year as editor" of the *Volksblatt*. He was now on a seven-month "western tour." In a Michigan railroad station house in Chicago he observed John Funk and his younger brother Abraham, a recent arrival, at a "Teachers' Prayer Meeting." As Funk spoke his convictions, tears trickled down his cheeks, making "a deep impression" on the visiting Stauffer.[57] The decades ahead would see both of these young men trying to advance the nonresistant Mennonite teaching through editorial projects—one in Chicago and the other in Milford Square and Quakertown. But whereas Funk would gradually find reception among his Old Mennonite constituency, the more marginal Stauffer would feel less and less support among his, until he would give up in frustration.

As Stauffer came through Chicago, Funk was at work on an essay for the times, boldly "addressed to the Mennonite Churches throughout the United States." It came off the press in July as a sixteen-page pamphlet, *Warfare. Its Evils, Our Duty.* In its clear articulation of the old nonresistant teaching, it struck a favorable chord among the old Mennonites, among whom this issue was a kind of litmus test of loyalty to the church.

On the day this booklet appeared, the new Federal draft was held at Doylestown. It was the only topic of local conversation. Since the "commutation fee" had been set at $300, the price of substitutes stayed below that figure, but brokers again did a brisk trade. Many more of the drafted men engaged substitutes than paid the fee.[58] In Milford Township thirty-five men got substitutes, and none at all paid the fee. Quite a few drafted men did not even respond. There were, in fact, "skulkers," or draft-dodgers all around. Attempts to bring them in triggered little riots, and a tragedy in Upper Hanover Township. Abraham Bartolet, son of the deceased Mennonite minister Henry Bertolet who had tried to publish a magazine in 1836, was trying, as a local officer, to "enroll" a "skulker," when the latter shot out of a window and killed him. There was no nonresistance left in this formerly Mennonite family. Abraham's brother Henry wrote to President Lincoln demanding the murderer's execution, and in August 1864 the latter was publicly hanged at Fort Mifflin near Philadelphia. Considerable demand developed for "tickets" to this occasion.[59]

Andreas Mack (pronounced "Mock"), a young farmer and song-leader of the Hereford congregation, was drafted twice before the war was over. On September 15, 1863, the lot fell on him and he was ordained a minister of the Old Mennonites in their low, pent-eaved Hereford meetinghouse at the very edge of the road leading to Boyertown. Bishop Jacob Kulp, who had come up from "Plains," performed the ordination. At the close of the service Andreas himself announced the hymn "What God Hath Done Is Done Aright."[60] On the following day the new minister walked and took the train to Norristown, possibly to register his change of draft status because of his new calling. By the time he had walked home again through the night, his wife had given birth to twin babies.[61] Wresting a living from his stony little farm on the "Mocke Barrick" (Mack Hill), Andreas was to

Andrew Bauer Shelly (1834-
1913), successor to John H.
Oberholtzer at Swamp, and
outstanding leader in both the
Eastern District and the
General Conference for half a
century. (Mennonite Library
and Archives of Eastern Pennsylvania)

become a bishop and the respected moderator of the Franconia Conference. Two months after his ordination, preacher Abel Horning was chosen
at Rockhill. He would be known for his numerous funeral sermons for
people of all local denominations. Both Horning and Mack would have a
friendly spirit toward their counterparts in the Eastern Conference.

In the Eastern Conference, too, there was an ordination of an Andrew
which would have far-reaching consequences. It was for the West Swamp
congregation, where John Oberholtzer, now fifty-five, needed help. On
March 25, 1864, the lot was cast between plow-maker Aaron Moyer and
thirty-year-old farmer, schoolteacher, singing schoolteacher and Sunday
school superintendent Andrew Bauer Shelly.[62] The lot fell on the latter. His
leadership had been also recognized shortly after the first draft, when he
had been elected secretary of a "Relief Board" in Milford Township, to help
cushion the financial shock of families whose breadwinners had been
drafted. A physically short but impressive-mannered man, Shelly became
an invaluable complement to his mentor Oberholtzer. Where the older man
was bluff, Shelly was smooth, and fully as committed to the cause of the
church. His writing style was clearer. Where Oberholtzer had broken the
way, Shelly would work to give stable form. Nearly half a century of
leadership in the most important offices of both the Eastern Conference
and the General Conference lay ahead of him. Eventually he would person-
ify, to the western General Conference churches, the best qualities of his

own eastern fellowship. As he would gradually and without controversy take over the aging Oberholtzer's mantle and offices, the Eastern Conference would acquire a permanent organizational equilibrium.

Abraham Hunsicker's group was also seeking stability and expansion during the war years. Tired of meeting in contentious Abraham Grater's little hall, the Skippackville wing of the Freeland "Christian Society" erected its own church, with Abraham Hunsicker footing much of the bill.[63] This and the mother church at Freeland were now to be referred to as "Trinity Christian." Grater, once a preacher of this group, was displeased, and unleashed in both German and English a tract full of comments on the "beast" Menno Simons and the errors of the Hunsickerites.[64] At around the same time (November 1863) the little remnant at Germantown, loyal to the Hunsicker group, reorganized as a "Reformed Mennonite Church" in the old meetinghouse. Guided by a new preacher, F. R. S. Hunsicker, they drew up a constitution which showed how far the Hunsickers had moved from the traditional Mennonite position in the sixteen years since the 1847 division. "It shall be the privilege of our Ministers," stated the document, "to baptize infants if desired...."[65] A good deal of patriotic rhetoric also came from this congregation and the three or four others that made up the "Conference" of Trinity Christian and Reformed Mennonite churches. A few years later F. R. S. Hunsicker left and became a Presbyterian, but the Germantown congregation continued to send out delegates. The conference, influenced chiefly by Abraham Hunsicker, even tried to expand during the war years, with little congregations or chapels at Mingo and Ironbridge (Rahns) as well as the older congregation at Phoenixville, led by Israel Beidler. The latter urged the conference on March 18, 1864, to have each pastor preach a sermon on "patriotism" on Sunday, July 3.[66]

The Eastern Conference, meeting in October 1863, tried to address "the present War situation," but could only come up with an ambiguous "recommendation": "that when members of our congregations bear arms, each congregation is to handle such a brother according to circumstances, but in a way that the Council is respected." The secretary, H. O. Stauffer, also recorded an "opinion," that members who had not been affected by the draft owed it "as a duty not a charity" to help those who had been drafted.[67] But there was disunity behind these comments. Conference did not meet the following May, and when it reconvened in October 1864, the secretary was instructed that he had "no right to ... execute a document in the name of the Council except as directed by the Council."[68] From then on there was no more reference to the war in the minutes. It was much more unifying, and pleasant, to discuss the forthcoming school at Wadsworth, Ohio.

John Funk had begun to dream of a forthrightly nonresistant periodical for the Old Mennonites. His plans reached fruition on the bitterly cold New Year's Day of 1864. His first issue of a paper called *Herald of Truth* (in both English and German versions) was by this date ready for shipment, although the weather was so bad that even the trains stopped for several days. Having mailed out the issue, Funk headed once more for Bucks County, and this time claimed his Salome, having promised her she might visit her home every year. They were married on January 19 in the home of Isaac Meyer, minister at Salome's Deep Run congregation.[69] The appearance of the young publisher's periodical would prove to be a watershed in the life of his Old Mennonite fellowship. He wrote a letter of cheery fraternal greeting to the *Volksblatt*, whose circulation his own paper would quickly exceed.

It had been in the previous summer that Pennsylvania had been touched to the quick by the war. Advancing southern troops had been halted only by the burning of a bridge across the Susquehanna River west of Lancaster. The city of Chambersburg had been burned, and the East Swamp congregation sent its Harvest Home service offering, in August, for the homeless. In the great three-day slaughter at Gettysburg, boys from Mennonite families were scattered among the Union ranks. John Hagey of Franconia Township lay mortally wounded, as his brother Joseph fixed his canteen at a place where the enemy could not find him.[70] Joseph went on to serve under General Sherman. The General's purported definition of war as "hell" came home personally to Joseph a year later during the battle at Petersburg, Virginia, where he left a leg "amputated five inches above the knee." He returned to become a shoemaker in Hatfield Township.[71]

In a further attempt to keep the war from turning into a remembered abstraction, we may recall John Fretz, son of the first minister of the Deep Run New Mennonite congregation. While his regiment was being nearly annihilated around him at Spottsylvania, he himself expired "from a bayonet wound in the mouth and a rifle ball which entered his right eye."[72] Or we might listen to Abraham Godshalk, Jr., son of the preacher at Doylestown who had written, when Abraham, Jr., was a little boy, that the new person in Christ "loveth his enemies." Abraham, Jr., left a leg at the Battle of Chickamauga. As the surgeons, having chloroformed him, were working on his leg, Rebel troops charged close up to the house they were using, and the doctors "ran away," leaving their patient "in an unfinished condition." After the danger had subsided, and they had dosed Abraham again with chloroform, a barrage of shells made them retreat again. Finally, in a third attempt, they were able to finish the excruciating operation. That night, as Abraham awoke from his stupor, all was a blank. "I wondered who and where I was," he recalled. "I could not have told my name, or that I had ever lived before...."[73] And so we might go on through a list of

wounded and killed from Mennonite background, including Bugler James
Landis, Sergeant Jacob Moyer, Corporal Josiah Godshall, or a dozen other
such names from Montgomery County alone.[74]

It was doubtless a severe disappointment to Bishop John Oberholtzer
and his wife, Mary, to see their only son Davy leave his wife and two little
daughters in Upper Saucon Township, to enlist in the Union Army on
September 3, 1864.[75] Had he been attracted by the high bounties offered to
volunteers? Davy too was wounded slightly in action, but this was the lesser
of his dangers. The short, brown-haired recruit who gave his occupation as
"printer" was like his father in mind but not in heart. Falling into bad company, he eventually disappeared. Contradictory family traditions placed
him in New York, or at the bottom of a river at Baltimore, from which city
he had written home about the "Johnny Rebs." He was rumored to be the
victim of gambling ventures. His widow claimed never to have seen him
after September 1867, and a great-granddaughter would hear that a sad
John Oberholtzer had gone down to Baltimore to identify his son's body,
after which the family kept the story quiet. Years later, Davy's daughter
Mary, on visiting West Point and seeing General Ulysses Grant's uniform,
would remark that her father had probably sewn on the buttons.[76]

As the year 1864 began, Mennonites were in a state of concern lest
new legislation would not include the option of a commutation fee, such as
had been permitted in the 1863 draft. In Bucks County 221 men, almost all
Mennonites, signed petitions against any "repeal" of the commutation option.[77] It may strike a modern observer as strange that these nonresistants
were anxious to have the privilege of paying the government what
amounted to a monetary equivalent to military service. But on this point the
Mennonites were not like the Quakers, nor had they been, in the Palatinate
and Pennsylvania, for the past two centuries. When Congress passed its
new act on February 24, 1864, it did include the commutation option, but
strictly limited its use to members of pacifist churches. Many Mennonites
seem to have regarded this as a wonderful privilege, afforded by a benevolent government. It was certainly less expensive than the bargains being
driven by some substitutes. As late as March 1865, with Lee's surrender
only three weeks in the future, the Swiss-born hired man of the Tyson Detweilers in Franconia charged a "Mr. Price" of Lower Salford $750 to take
his place in the Army.[78] This was more than the total paid by several local
Mennonites who paid the commutation fee twice, after two consecutive
drafts had caught them.

We have seen evidence that significant numbers of Mennonite
families in both conferences had sons in military service in the Civil War,
but that the majority chose to avoid such service. The proportion choosing

the military option would seem to be higher than ever before in the family lines of these Mennonites. Lacking specific records, we cannot learn how many soldiers "came back" to the Mennonite fold. It is certain that entrance was not granted to the Old Mennonite fellowship without a public acknowledgment that the applicant had transgressed against the teachings of Christ by taking up the gun. This was also required by Bishop Christian Clemmer of the "new" congregation at Hereford. However, according to John G. Stauffer, Bishop John Oberholtzer did not require this of two West Swamp men, Henry Oberholtzer and Samuel Weiss, who had been drafted into the Army.[79] The Old Mennonites felt confirmed in their opinion that their New counterparts had not maintained a definitive nonresistant stand. To the Old, making this choice an individual rather than a covenanted one was a change of the essential conception of their church, and unprecedented in their community's history. Thus the issue remained a sore point over the next century. Old Mennonites resented seeing their denominational name connected in public with churches condoning individual military involvement; New Mennonite pastors, struggling to uphold the nonresistant ideal but not feeling able to make it a test of membership, resented what they felt was a pharisaic harsh criticism from the Old wing.

Two interesting visitors to the local Mennonites came in November 1864, one because of the war, and the other hardly aware of it. They came from two opposite directions. One was a minister from Virginia, Christian Brunk, who had been among the people driven from their farms in the Shenandoah Valley.[80] A sixteen-mile-long wagon train containing many Mennonites had moved north from Harrisonburg toward Pennsylvania a few months earlier, leaving behind a pall of black smoke from barns and houses fired by Yankee troops. One of the latter was Samuel Hunsberger of Souder's Station in Franconia Township. One of the Union officers involved in the destruction was George Armstrong Custer, a descendant of the original Mennonite Custer family at Germantown and Skippack, and later to be famous as an Indian fighter.

A few days after Preacher Christian Brunk gave a sermon for the Old Mennonites at Deep Run, the other visitor sat down at nearby "Bridgetown" (Perkasie) to write an explanation to his relatives at home as to why he had been away so long. It was schoolteacher Isaac Z. Hunsicker of Ontario, but originally of Skippack. Already an unusually accomplished Fraktur artist when he had migrated three decades earlier, he had continued to make certificates and inscribe family records in Bibles for his Ontario pupils and friends. Now, on his visit among his Pennsylvania relatives, he found himself in strong demand to fill out their own family registers, either in the pages between the two Testaments in the large Bibles popular at the time, or "on writing paper." Hard-of-hearing Preacher Henry Moyer of Hilltown, a recent visitor to Canada himself, was one of those who wanted a family register, and after making it, Hunsicker would find it necessary to travel on to Deep Run and back to Skippack to satisfy his many customers. The demand must have been considerable, as Hunsicker had already been in Pennsylvania for two months, and was longing to get back to Canada. Concerned about his supply of ink at home as the winter months approached, he wrote back asking friends to get it out of his bureau-drawer to keep it from freezing before he returned.[81]

Throughout the war years, the Mennonites had continued to vote at election time. Their identification with the recently formed Republican Party was so complete that the *Bucks County Intelligencer* viewed them as rallying "almost as a single man on the side of the Union and Freedom."[82] In the election of November 1864, although Montgomery County gave an overall plurality to President Lincoln's opponent General McClellan, those townships with strong Mennonite settlements went heavily for Lincoln. It was a Mennonite rather than a merely German-speaking vote. The three "most Mennonite" townships voted 68% for Lincoln, while the three equally "German" but "least Mennonite" townships voted 88% against the Emancipater.[83] The isolated Mennonite Bechtel family living near Greshville in Berks County felt strong resentment from their "Democrat" German neighbors against their own pro-Lincoln stand. Although their new minister Andrew Mack had favored Lincoln too, he had been glad he had not voted, when Lincoln had declared war.[84]

But pro-Union sentiments among the Mennonites struck the editor of the *Intelligencer* as patriotic in a good sense. It meant that although the Mennonites were "on principle opposed to the use of violence," they had not been completely indifferent to "the present struggle." They had "given to the Union cause the powerful support of approving words and liberal contributions." No one had paid their taxes "more cheerfully," and they had given "liberally toward the payment of local bounties" (used to pay local enlistees in the Army). Though they would not themselves participate in military service, they had proven "willing to pay whatever may be necessary toward the support of the army."

Reading this commentary out in Chicago, publisher and lumber merchant John Funk became somewhat disturbed. The editor of his hometown newspaper was viewing Mennonite attitudes through Republican spectacles, and praising them for their willingness to support the army. The closing paragraphs of the article, entitled "Patriotism of the Mennonites," sent Funk quickly to his desk to write a letter of disagreement. The editor of the *Intelligencer* had picked up and here reprinted a set of "resolutions" issued by a "Mennonite conference" at Germantown in March 1865. The editor offered them as an exhibit of Mennonite patriotism. He could hardly be blamed, of course, for not knowing that the sponsors of the resolutions represented only a tiny group, barely clinging to congregational existence in Germantown, and with a minister about to join the Presbyterians. The likely author of the actual phrasing of these resolutions was Minister Francis R. S. Hunsicker, son-in-law of Abraham Hunsicker, founder of the annual "Conference of the Trinity Christian Churches of Freeland and Skippackville and the Reformed Mennonite Churches of Germantown and Phoenixville."

"Whereas," began the statement, "the cruel and causeless civil war ... has not yet ended, but is still ... baptizing the cause of liberty and eternal truth with the best blood of our countrymen; and whereas, this rebellion ... is now being rapidly shorn of its power,"

> *Resolved,* That the success of our arms on sea and land ... calls aloud for thanksgiving and praise to Almighty God....

> *Resolved,* That the present war is a struggle between truth and error, right and wrong, freedom and bondage....

> *Resolved,* That we pledge [to the president] our undivided support and most ardent prayers in his efforts to maintain our national honor untarnished, and crush out the last vestige of this slaveholders' foul rebellion.

> *Resolved,* That ... he who in the hour of his country's travail stands not up manfully to vindicate her cause, or withholds his support from the government whose fostering care has guaranteed him all the rights and immunities of citizenship, is recreant to God and false to the highest principles of truth and justice, and unworthy the name of an American citizen.[85]

No Baptist or Presbyterian could have been more roundly in favor of the Northern cause.

But these statements, protested John Funk in his immediate letter to the editor, were "entirely erroneous as setting forth the views of the Mennonite Church in general...." There might be "several branches ... who are less strict" in their attitude toward war, but they would have "deviated from the maintenance of [the] peaceful principles which Jesus taught [and] which Menno Simons ... earnestly sought to promulgate and for which many in the past ages have suffered the most severe persecutions...." The largest part of the church, "known as the 'Old Mennonites,'" still believe that "no Christian, according to the gospel, the teachings of Christ and his apostles, and their examples, can advocate war, or under any circumstances take up arms, or engage in the destruction of his fellow men." Those adhering to this religion "cannot rejoice in those terrible victories which cause human blood to flow in streams...." Rather, they must mourn, humble themselves before God, and "pray and labor" to the end "that the fierce conflict of blood may be stayed." As disciples of the Christ who "left us an example," we are to "show forth that love, that meekness of spirit which ever distinguished Him who we profess to follow...."[86]

Thus did the former Hilltown schoolteacher spread on the public record in his home community the traditional Mennonite understanding of his "non-resistant faith." That his feelings were so congruent in spirit to the teaching of his people helps to explain why he was allowed, even by conservative Mennonites, to publish a paper on their behalf. Already he had 500 more subscribers than the *Volksblatt* had, and in the very month of his letter to the *Intelligencer*, he was ordained a Mennonite minister. Then, although his wealthy Presbyterian brother-in-law and partner Jacob Beidler thought it was a great mistake, John Funk sold his share of the lumber business. From then on the Mennonite Church was his life.

When news of Lee's surrender came to little "Souder's Station" in Franconia Township, someone rang the old dinner bell on neighbor John Hunsberger's farm for an hour. Five days later came the shock of Lincoln's assassination. Jacob S. Overholt, who had been personally released from an army camp by the president, was now in the last stages of a fatal illness. He wept as his son brought him a copy of the *Morgenstern* carrying the news of his benefactor's death.[87] Jacob's old minister at Line Lexington, John Geil, preached "a memorable sermon" on Lincoln's passing, though he had just turned eighty-seven.

But his days, too, were numbered. As he tried to get to the Line Lexington meetinghouse several months later to hear two visiting preachers from Virginia, his strength failed, and in the following January the old saint passed on. The special quality of his life was observed in the placing of an original verse on his gravestone:

> Hier ruht der treue Hirt in dieser Gruft,
>   Aus Mennos klein zerstreuter Herde,
> Bis der Herr dereinst ihn wieder ruft
>   Zu sich aus dem Staub der Erde.
>
> Er leitete durch Kummer und Beschwerde,
>   Die Schafe zu der bessern Lebensquell—
> Vereinige ihn, Jesus, mit seiner Herde,
>   Wo die Verklarungssonne strahlet hell.[88]

(Here rests the pastor true, within this tomb,
    From Menno's small and scattered flock,
Until the Lord recalls him once again,
    Unto Himself, from out the dust of earth.

He led, through grief and difficulty,
    The sheep unto the better fount of life—
Unite him, Jesus, with his flock beloved,
    Where the Transfiguration blazes bright.)

Three decades later John Funk could still visualize his boyhood pastor, "commanding and serene," preaching in "the plain old church of stone" at Line Lexington.[89]

As the Mennonite community thus lost an influential leader, it was, as we have seen, gaining new ones. Bishop Moses Gottschall, the most forceful preacher of either conference, baptized a boy not yet fifteen in the month the war ended. No one could realize that bright young Nathaniel Bertolet Grubb, coming from a farm near the little brick "Bertolet's" meetinghouse in Frederick Township, would turn out to be one of the Eastern Conference's foremost leaders for half a century. Grubb's progressive eloquence would be much more "English" than that of another type of preacher who was ordained that fall for the Old Mennonite congregation at Salford. This was twenty-nine-year-old farmer Henry Bower, who had been baptized with his wife, Anne, at a more traditional age than Nathaniel Grubb's—twenty-two. Though born at Coventry, Henry had moved with his parents and sister to a farm at Skippack. There he had grown up on a farm next to the one owned by Preacher Henry G. Johnson of the "Johnson Mennonites," who practiced foot washing. Though the Bowers belonged to the Old Mennonites, young Henry was convinced that the church should practice this rite.

Henry and Anne experienced a tragedy in their little family in the summer of 1864, when two of their three children died suddenly of scarlet fever. Henry, as an only son, would now seem to have been about to inherit the family farm. His father was already fifty-nine. Yet in the spring of 1865 the young Bower family moved to another farm on the edge of Harleysville, about a mile from the Salford meetinghouse. The reason for this surprising move, according to people who knew Henry, was that he had had a "vision" that he was to be a preacher in the Salford congregation.[90] Stories of such foresight, sometimes in dreams, were not uncommon among people who passed through the "lot."

Salford's need, certainly, was obvious. Of the three ministers, the youngest was fifty-two and the oldest, devout John Bergey, eighty-two. For several years Bergey, a sufferer from asthma for a quarter century, had been unable to attend meeting. Jacob Kulp, the next in age, was sixty-six, and "never could preach." Even distiller Isaac Clemens who lived next to the meetinghouse, was mocked by the wealthy local Binders as being "finished" with his sermon almost as soon as he had begun, filling in the spaces between words with a kind of chant. So in the spring of 1865 it was clear that an ordination was not far off. Another loud voice spoke to the Bower family, newly arrived at Harleysville, that summer. Their three-year-old daughter Barbary, "well and hardy," was running past a bucket of boiling water when she slipped and fell into it. After severe suffering, she died the next day, leaving Henry and Anne with one three-month-old child.[91]

Five months later, with John Bergey on his deathbed, the expected ordination was finally held (for both a minister and a deacon). Of the eight men nominated the lot fell on newcomer Henry Bower, still not thirty years old. For the next four decades this farmer and clockmaker and repairer of Harleysville would make an imprint on the community, the Salford congregation, and the Franconia Conference. Like his only brother-in-law Jacob Mensch, also born in the Coventry congregation and shortly to be ordained at Upper Skippack, Henry Bower was of strong opinion and conviction, and blunt in his expressions of both. He could tell his congregation that nonresistant people should not have turkeys, since they wandered onto neighbors' property and caused quarrels. He could tell them not to nominate marketmen—"hucksters"—for ministers, since the occupation of middle-man was not conducive to honest dealing. He could debate baptism strenuously with the local Brethren preacher. Always beginning his sermons, his eyes half-closed, with the same formulaic words (*"Die Güte Gottes und die Wahrheit und 's Lewe...."*) he would chant or "sing" his admonitions in the traditional manner. His stentorian voice, appreciated by the hard-of-hearing, was sometimes aimed directly at a corner in the rear of the meetinghouse where the young fellows sat. His boldness in addressing them, as they straggled in or out to their place on the fence where they would have a social smoke, sometimes brought mockery. He was called a "Repentance Preacher," in distinction from the other main type among the Old Mennonites: the "Scripture Preacher." The former type tended to challenge his hearers, and the latter to teach them. Among the New Mennonites Moses Gottschall of Schwenksville was of legendary fearlessness in confronting sin from the pulpit. But Henry Bower's main legacy to the Franconia Conference was his advocacy of foot washing. The acceptance of this rite, apparently not practiced at the time he began preaching it (though discussed as early as 1735 in conference), now crept eastward across the Franconia Conference until eventually, years after Bower's death in 1909, even Deep Run, over the protest of one of its ministers, would begin to take up the towel and basin with the rest of the conference.

Henry Bower was old-fashioned; he walked to and from Philadelphia to get supplies for his clockmaking, even though there was a railroad. He and his brother-in-law Jacob Mensch, who took over the Bower farm, would be pillars of the group seeking to maintain without much change a traditional folk ethos. Their counterparts in the Eastern Conference were looking rather for improvement and expansion. At the October 5, 1865, session this conference chose two ministers to visit each of their congregations and bring back a report from their *"Rundreise."* This was devising a new procedure to make sure that old concerns were not left to individual impulse. And a third of a century before the Franconia Conference, they called for the support of "missions." A final resolution of improvement was aimed at the worship service itself. From now on the congregations were asked to be more responsive to what was going on in the pulpit. Unlike previous practice in Pennsylvania, the people should rise to receive the benediction.[92]

As the year 1865 ended, John Oberholtzer and his editorial assistant John G. Stauffer had a pleasant surprise. Christmas had fallen on a Monday, and "Second Christmas," when families sometimes completed their visiting, on Tuesday. As the editors came to the *Volksblatt* office on Wednesday morning they found a little package which had been mailed from Germany half a year earlier. Marked "Emden," it contained a gift of eighteen manuscript sermons by a preacher at Ibersheim along the Rhine. The accompanying letter was from an unusual Mennonite woman, the wife of a successful East Frisian merchant and government official. Anna Brons was a contributor to the German Mennonite periodical started a year or two later than Oberholtzer's *Botschafter,* the *Mennonitische Blätter.* Reading Mennonite history to her weak-eyed husband, this intellectually vigorous and largehearted woman had developed a strong love for the Mennonite heritage and testimony. Eventually she would write the first important Mennonite history in Europe. Perusing the pages of the little *Volksblatt* from Pennsylvania, she had rejoiced in the news it brought of plans for renewal through building a school for Mennonite preachers. Her letter expressed concern for the American Mennonites during the tensions of the Civil War, and advocated the spirit of *"Wehrlosigkeit"* (defenselessness) as taught by Menno Simons. Oberholtzer, who had earlier yearned to visit Europe himself, must have been especially delighted to find in this surprise package a large portrait of Menno Simons, which Frau Brons wrote was to be given to the new school the General Conference Mennonites were about to build in Ohio.[93]

Chapter 12

Faithfulness: Covenant or Mission?

1866-1890

It was all in one square, flat-roofed, three-storied brick building, sitting bald and un-ivied in a field across from Preacher Ephraim Hunsberger's house in Wadsworth, Ohio. But it was stately and beautiful in the eyes of its eager supporters. The long prayed-for Educational Institute—the first post-elementary school Mennonites had been able to produce, as an official project, in nearly two centuries in America! And now, on this morning of October 13, 1866, the bell in the tall cupola was calling together the first assembly, to inaugurate two days of dedicational exercises.

Among the guests crowding up the stairs to the hall on the middle floor were at least eight Pennsylvanians from six congregations in the Eastern District. They were delegates to the fourth session of the General Conference, which would convene on the day following the dedication. Only seven other congregations, from Illinois, Iowa, Ohio, and Canada, were represented. At the head of the eastern delegation was fifty-seven-year-old president of both the Eastern and General conferences, John H. Oberholtzer. It was he who rose, after the choir's anthem, and made the opening remarks. It was to his dream of young preachers educated for mission work, and to his initiative in editorial agitation and raising contributions, as much as to his friend Daniel Krehbiel's initiative, that the school owed its promising, if precarious existence.

Among the speakers was Samuel Clemmer, minister at Hereford where Ephraim Hunsberger had once preached: Clemmer took the text, "Come, for all things are ready." A. B. Shelly, younger colleague of Oberholtzer both as minister and editorial assistant on the *Volksblatt*, used "The master is come and calleth for thee" (both, of course, preached in German). And it was Oberholtzer who, on the following day, focused the dedication in its closing moments by proposing as a motto for the school so

343

cherished in his dreams, the words of Christ: "He that believeth on me, as the scripture hath said, out of his belly shall flow rivers of living water." Then, asking the densely packed audience to stand, he himself fell on his knees and dedicated his beloved *Bildungs Anstalt* to God, in "a powerful and beautiful prayer."[1]

It was typical of John Oberholtzer to envision considerably more than his people might be ready for. The new school would last, debt-ridden, for only eleven years, making an important symbolic beginning, but struggling constantly with a constituency neither large nor unified enough to serve as a stable base. The dream itself was noble. Recognizing their aging chairman's historic role of leadership among them, the ensuing session of the General Conference presented Oberholtzer with the highly unusual gift of $100. But this gesture also had a slight feel of valediction, since the conference discussed giving the editorship of the *Volksblatt* to younger hands. Some even wanted the press transferred from Milford Square to Ohio, which would be more central to the widely scattered readership among the 1,000 or more members of the General Conference.

Before long, as it turned out, the rising A. B. Shelly, now thirty-three, would take over the editorial role officially. The name of the *Volksblatt* was changed to *Mennonitische Friedensbote* (Mennonite Messenger of Peace), and the Eastern Conference itself finally took over the sponsorship of the struggling paper.[2] In five more years Shelly would also succeed his senior pastor as chairman of both the Eastern and the General conferences. Soon after the editorial change, the printer, John G. Stauffer, also a member at Swamp, launched out of the same building the first of his newspapers, a German one entitled *Der Bucks County Patriot*, later the *Patriot and Reformer*.

In a shop on South Main Street of nearby Quakertown, worked a youthful cobbler, Jacob S. Moyer, son of Preacher Samuel Moyer of the Eastern Conference congregation at Springfield. As he stitched and hammered, he felt a call to become a minister. There was no precedent, in either the Franconia or the Eastern Conference, for a person to announce himself as a potential minister. But this call came at about the time of the dedication of the new school at Wadsworth, which was a kind of invitation to a change in the ancient method of choosing ministers by casting lots. The Eastern District would employ this practice, as a matter of fact, for only a decade after the school actually began (the Franconia Conference keeping it another eighty years). Sensing the new liberty, devout young bachelor Jacob Moyer left his cobbler's bench to join the first class at Wadsworth,[3] when the school finally managed to gather a faculty and begin classes in January 1868.

Printing Office of John Gehman Stauffer of Milford Square about 1877. In 1871 Stauffer had purchased the establishment from the "Mennonite Publishing Union" which issued the *Mennonitische Friedensbote*. His son Berend, standing beside him on the porch, was born on April 4, 1872. In 1881 Stauffer moved his business to Quakertown. (Marvin Rosenberger)

In the whole Mennonite denomination no person had been found adequate to teach the "English" curriculum. The theological courses would be handled by an elderly, learned Mennonite pastor from Friedrichstadt in northern Germany, Carl Justus van der Smissen. Unfortunately, he could not get along with the principal, Christian Schowalter of Iowa, and the bewildered student body was sometimes polarized bitterly.[4] In 1869 the preacher at East Swamp, Levi Schimmel, also received a call from Wadsworth to move out and serve as steward while he took some theological training. This he accepted. In the nearby Saucon congregation William H. Oberholtzer, brother of John, was one of the trustees of the Wadsworth school. And from Hereford, Swamp, Deep Run, Springfield, and Schwenksville there trickled out to Ohio with Jacob Moyer a stream of as many as two dozen young men a year, mixing names like Fretz, Geissinger, Gottschall, and Shelly with the young Haurys, Galles, Sommers and Sprungers of the more recent German Mennonite immigrants of Ohio, Illinois, and Iowa. Included was even Abraham Fretz, son of the alienated first minister of the Deep Run congregation, now a Presbyterian in New Jersey. Among teachers at the institute who came from the East were Schwenkfelder Jonas Schultz and "steady, clear-headed" Manasseh Moyer.[5]

Jacob Moyer, somewhat older than the other students, came home in 1871, after about three and a half years of training. Without hesitation, the Springfield congregation ordained him to assist his father. The Deep Run congregation, too, had a serious need; its pastor Joseph Rosenberger had recently resigned and joined the Franconia Conference. Bachelor Jacob Moyer was now asked by this congregation to include them in his charge. In another year he was ordained elder (bishop), though still unmarried.[6] In these moves the Deep Run New Mennonite or "West" congregation gained the first strong and continuing leadership it had known in its quarter-century of existence. One of its own teenagers who had recently been to Wadsworth, Allen M. Fretz, would later serve as a strong leader for over half a century both at Deep Run and throughout the conference. The brief role of Wadsworth in thus preparing future ministers was often given considerable credit by grateful Eastern conference leaders.

As for the Franconia Conference, the sponsoring of such a school would have been, in 1867, unthinkable. It would only introduce a prideful copying of methods invented by the world, in which technique overshadowed content. What ministers in the "old, defenseless" fellowship needed was an attitude of humility and faithfulness. This attitude was held to be, not as some critics claimed, a "human work," but a gift of God. God would supply the strength, understanding, and leading, as called for by the needs of the church. Of course, older ministers must give fatherly advice to newly ordained ones. Such informal education, rather than curricular studies rewarded by a diploma, was the proper type. Thus, soon after thirty-two-year-old farmer Jacob Mensch, a newcomer in the Old Mennonite congregation at Skippack, was chosen for ordination (from a "class" or "lot" of thirteen), Bishop Abraham Wismer of the same congregation sent the new minister a letter of counsel. It contained admonition regarding the essential Mennonite emphasis, in the same vein as the book by Preacher Abraham Godshalk of Doylestown, three decades earlier. The minister, Wismer wrote, must not consider his work to be an effort of his own will. He must pray that God will strengthen his faith daily. But this in itself is not enough. Even though he earns no credit with God for his effort, he must also see to the "appearance" of his faith; there must be visible "good works," or the whole notion of faith is academic. Wismer quoted a German hymn warning against "empty" faith.[7]

Where cultural change came most slowly, as in Franconia Township, this special emphasis survived most vigorously. The Franconia congregation, growing toward a position of the strongest church, numerically, in either conference, ordained a dependable and conscientious bishop in December of 1867—forty-year-old farmer Josiah Clemmer. This left the respected Henry Nice, now sixty-three, as a valuable elder statesman in the same congregation. Clemmer's stable leadership, and that of Andrew Mack of Hereford, ordained bishop in 1875, would last into the 20th century. "Perkasie" (Blooming Glen) also had a bishop, Isaac Oberholtzer, of rare gentleness and lengthy span of office. At Deep Run and Doylestown the Gross family continued to produce conservative leadership. One daughter, Sarah (Mrs. Sam Lapp), of this Gross *Freundschaft* took the unusual step for a woman of that time, especially a Mennonite woman, of studying some aspects of medicine with a doctor in Harleysville. Later she would put her knowledge to good use in the frontier community in Nebraska.[8] Deep Run, particularly, had strong leadership in this era, in Isaac Meyer, and his younger colleague Sam Godshalk, son of author-preacher Abraham of Doylestown. Sam was an enthusiastic singing-school teacher and traveler, at home in the English language. In 1869 he took an extensive "Mennoniting" tour of Canada and the Midwest, in the course of which he saw the new Wadsworth Institute,[9] and he visited churches in Virginia five times.

In the Eastern Conference, where tradition played a less definitive role and there were fewer "solidly Mennonite" settlements, there was a greater element of experimentation. At Schwenksville, Bishop Moses Gottschall was ready for a younger assistant in 1868. His congregation had increased under his leadership of two decades. This musical (like his mother Magdalena Hunsberger), conscientious, Bible-steeped pastor was an overpowering orator. "He was one of your straight up-and-down men," remarked a fellow minister. "There is no man among us that can match him" was the comment of his close friend John H. Oberholtzer. People of all ages loved to hear him preach or converse, quoting his fearless tirades from the pulpit, or laughing over his bout with angry wasps stirred to action by his pounding on the seldom-used rostrum at the "Settlement" meetinghouse north of Allentown.

A grandson's memories[10] of this Schwenksville preacher remained vivid two decades after his death:

> He spared no one in his fiery zeal for righteousness against iniquity. I well remember ... the significant nods and glances that were exchanged between pews after some besetting sins of the day and locality had received the most merciless flaying and excoriation.... It was a judgment day in miniature.
>
> His pulpit manner was intensely dramatic. He repeated conversations between men, mimicking their attitudes and expressions, conventions and mannerisms, and emphasized the realism of the scene by making use of the Pennsylvania German dialect.
>
> ... His earnestness gained momentum, his eyes flashed fire, his delivery doubled its speed, his voice awakened reverberating echoes

throughout the building, and his right hand, raised above his head and trembling ominously like the dreaded lull before the storm, presently came down with terrific force into his left palm, or upon the pulpit or the Bible. Every eye was winking in anticipation of the crash.

After the services he would pack up the melodeon he had brought along from home, and head back through the little valley to his farm, followed by a dozen carriages full of his hearers, "all rolling along as if in funeral procession." People loved to hear him talk at home, even though "He preached in his ordinary conversation. It was the only thing he could do." Similarly, when he sat in a rocker and sang a hymn, he threw his whole heart into the performance.

> The preacher's home on a Sunday afternoon would ... be bustling with life and cheerfulness. Dishes rattled, children ran in and out, men were gathered in knots, singing accompanied by the organ filled the air by fits and starts.... The table groaned under the load of ... farm-produce, and usually there were several tables. After dinner all gathered in the parlor and prepared for religious discussions. The preacher furnished the theme, as every one expected. Then sometimes for hours together he poured out ... the richness and fulness of his experience....
>   He generally had more than one [child] upon his knee while at work edifying the parents. Often he would interrupt the serious part of the program to sing some amusing ditty to the little one or dance it to and fro or up and down.

Of course there were times as well when Moses Gottschall's blunt expressions were considered too harsh; when his richest member committed suicide, his dramatic funeral sermon was "severely criticized."

Now fifty-three, the Schwenksville bishop arranged for the ordination of a younger assistant. In accordance with the Eastern Conference constitution, the congregation chose only two men for the lot: blacksmith William Blanchford, a Civil War enlistee who had married a niece of Moses, and Samuel Longaker, son of a local miller. When the lot fell on the latter, he dutifully moved out to Wadsworth to study. But after only two years of classes and attempts to preach, the intended follower of Moses Gottschall was discouraged enough to submit an "earnest request" to be released from his office, since he felt "he was not a public speaker."[11] There was another Schwenksville youth studying at Wadsworth, Bishop Gottschall's oldest son Heinrich. But in 1871 he became ill and died. By this time a third young man, Nathaniel Bertolet Grubb, also an employee in the local mill, had shown unusual promise as a leader. This fiancé of another niece of Bishop Gottschall had been elected superintendent of the "Gottschall's" Sunday school at nineteen. Two years later the congregation was so unanimously in favor of his being their assistant minister that Bishop Gottschall, overriding scattered concerns, ordained him (May 9, 1872) without casting lots.[12] The following winter Grubb too went to Wadsworth for several sessions, and on his return he became a devoted, imposing, and increasingly visible young preacher in the Perkiomen valley. His home base was the little Bertolet's congregation, but he shortly began to cut a figure in the larger conference deliberations. Before long he took the opportunity to establish a little English newspaper, *The Item*, in the railroad-stop town of Schwenksville, now boasting a new bank. Up at Milford Square, Editor John G. Stauffer of the German *Reformer* commented favorably on the Christian tone of the new paper.

Two strings of railroad towns now boomed with mills, factories, and houses along the new Perkiomen line (1869) as well as the older North Penn (1857). The old stagecoach stop villages like Franconiaville (Elroy), Kulpsville, and Steinsburg were left behind in a quiescent stasis. Mennonite entrepreneurs moved not only to Souderton, Lansdale, North Wales, Norristown, and Royersford, but to Allentown, Bethlehem, and Philadelphia as well. Where open fields had spread in 1847, by 1867 neat, tree-shaded blocks of recently built homes made for a pleasant life along Diamond Street near Germantown Avenue at the northern edge of Philadelphia. Here visiting preachers of the Eastern Conference, following the beginnings of Preacher Daniel Hege in 1862, gathered groups for worship in various homes, and Moses Gottschall helped them organize, in a rented chapel, a congregation of about thirty members.[13] The population was much more shifting than that of the communities rural Mennonites were used to, but when elderly Deacon David Taylor (Anglicized from Schneider) of East Swamp also moved down to the city, it seemed the congregation was about to find permanent form. It was the first "mission" of the Eastern Conference, although all its original members were baptized Mennonites originally from the country. Here at the growing edge of the city their children were fast becoming English.

In 1868 the thirty-three members received permission from the conference to call a pastor—Samuel Clemmer, son of Bishop Christian at Hereford. He died in a year or two at forty-eight, and in 1872 Levi Schimmel, formerly of East Swamp but recently steward at the Wadsworth school, was called to come and preach at Philadelphia. His pastorate too was short, as half of the still unstable congregation was already demanding some English services, and Bishop Moses Gottschall was resisting. A "Second" Mennonite congregation abruptly emerged, amid considerable controversy, causing the Eastern Conference leaders embarrassment and regret for the reputation of Mennonites "before the world." Eventually this second congregation disbanded and a large percentage of its members joined a nearby Moravian congregation.[14] Still another Wadsworth student, Albert Funk, son of an Evangelical-leaning deacon near Boyertown, was then called, but he too would eventually join a new denomination. Not until N. B. Grubb would be called away from the Schwenksville congregation in 1882 would the first Mennonite Church of Philadelphia begin its swift rise to the status of the largest (and fanciest) congregation in the Eastern Conference.

The topic of mission work, dear to the hearts of John Oberholtzer and his successor A. B. Shelly, had figured in the discussions of the Eastern Conference since its very inception in 1847. Oberholtzer had written to Europe with questions on this theme. It had been central in the formation of the General Conference in 1860. The first actual organizational move in Pennsylvania had occurred in the Swamp congregation in 1866, when the "Pennsylvania Mennonite Mission Society" had been set up, with seventy-two members.[15] It was once again a case of getting something going before there was widespread support. Just as the constitution idea itself had first been given a trial in the West Swamp congregation, and then was realized at the conference level, so the entire Eastern Conference took over from Swamp, in 1873, its Mission Society, and requested all its congregations to hold special meetings and take mission offerings at least once a year.[16] The willingness to support missions was seen by both Oberholtzer and Shelly as a basic indicator of spiritual vitality in their churches. Lack of interest in this meant they were still in the traditional sleep and deadness. At each session of General Conference this was a main theme, generating a wistful excitement both there and in the columns of the *Friedensbote*.

The closest the "old" Mennonites in the Franconia Conference came to missions in this era was in their visiting of scattered relatives on midwestern homesteads. They perceived missions, when they thought of them at all, as unnecessary efforts of churches who saw themselves wrongly in an Apostolic role. This would begin to change as the columns of John Funk's Indiana-based *Herald* kept hinting cautiously at the necessity of witness and outreach.

The hardened breach between the two conferences still stabbed John Oberholtzer with sharp pain whenever he considered it. Having just passed his sixty-first birthday, he wrote a friendly letter[16] to Preacher Henry Nice of Franconia, now also in his mid-sixties, and the person to whom the Eastern Conference had directed earlier communications on the topic of reconciliation. The aging reformer now asked afresh about "the ban" which he claimed the Franconia Conference had laid on the "New" Mennonites, and was delighted to receive what struck him as an "open-hearted" reply. He responded with a long, detailed letter, rehearsing his own original calling and appealing to Nice to see it as coming from God. He recalled the progress of the coat-controversy, and the differences over the constitution, leading to what Oberholtzer considered the "gross injustice" of the Franconia Conference's call for repentance on the part of those who had subscribed to it. He then described the General Conference he had helped to organize, and asked why all Mennonites of North America could not join it, taking up more of the attitude of the disparate European Mennonites who managed to have a "loose brotherly" fellowship.

Henry Nice had written that he didn't see the "New Mennonites" as literally banned by the Franconia Conference. This brought an intense response from Oberholtzer:

> If no ban lies on us, where then does the fellowship of the Old Brothers stand in relation to us? Why can our Old Brothers allow none of our members to serve among them? Why cannot our members go to communion among the Old without making an acknowledgment? Why do the Old exclude their young members if such marry among our members?

As he warmed to the topic, Oberholtzer pulled himself into a little dialogue almost confusing in its haste.

> There stands thus a ban, in fact a very terrifying one, between the Old Brothers and us. And who laid it and confirmed it? Why, the Old Brothers, and what was the reason for it, why, these did not want to follow us, the old, in their opinion! namely, it had been demanded of them, through a law, that they wear plain coats, and because they were not willing, they were excluded.

After eight long pages, Oberholtzer confessed that he could hardly stop writing, especially since both he and Nice were now "standing on the threshold between time and eternity."

Although in this letter Oberholtzer was definitely reaching toward Nice out of a strong regret for the breach, he also made a number of statements that could only have made it seem more necessary, from Henry's point of view. Oberholtzer questioned the universal validity of the "Dortrecht Confession" for Mennonites, by pointing out that not all European Mennonites accepted it. This must have seemed a very willful attitude to Henry, for whose conference the Dortrecht Confession stood next to the Bible itself. Oberholtzer further affirmed "sincerely and solemnly" that he had never "sought or desired a division in 1847." And when it came to Nice's question as to whether Oberholtzer didn't consider Abraham Hunsicker "banned" by the Eastern Conference, the old debater said he found this a downright "amusing observation," showing a complete misunderstanding of the Hunsicker separation. Hunsicker's treatment had been quite different from that accorded to Oberholtzer by the Franconia Conference. "He was given all opportunity to defend himself before he was excluded, because it was believed that there were errors in his teaching. Where, even in part, was this opportunity given to me by the Old Conference?" Hunsicker's members "may come to communion with us if they wish without making an acknowledgment...." And so on for ten long pages, before Oberholtzer signed off "with respect and love" as "Your fellow-minister in Christ bound together in the Lord."

It seems doubtful that Nice replied to this epistle. Seven years later at a court trial in Boyertown, Oberholtzer would once again tell the story of the 1847 division in detail, and again in 1884, at the age of seventy-five, he would write the longest account of all, apparently hoping for the publication of a small book appealing the "injustice" done to his fellowship by the Franconia Conference. There is no evidence that the leaders of the old group took any of these statements seriously. Their attitude was perceived by Eastern Conference leaders as one of "silent contempt."

While John Oberholtzer was absent from the October 1871 session of the Eastern Conference at Bowmansville because of the serious illness of his wife, full editorial responsibility for the *Friedensbote* was finally transferred to A. B. Shelly. Two days later Mary died, after a life her husband described as containing "unending miseries." Now Oberholtzer was seen by the Eastern Conference he had founded as having completed his main work of leadership, and at the following spring session, though he was only sixty-three, he was replaced in the chairman's office, again by his younger colleague Shelly. This meeting took place in a Lutheran-Reformed church in Boyertown, since the local Mennonite meetinghouse had proved too small for the conference session. In a respectfully and carefully worded address to the retiring pioneer who had been either Secretary or Chairman for all but four of the sessions in a quarter century, Shelly spoke of the many "dark and troublesome years" through which Oberholtzer had been "severely tried." "How often," asked the new Chairman rhetorically, "has the enemy pressed you from the side of the world, yes, even from the side of the Conference and the brethren?" But "you have remained true and firm and God protected you from harm."[17]

A similar transaction occurred half a year later, at a session of the General Conference at Wadsworth, Ohio. A. B. Shelly was also voted into the chief executive office of this body, and once again, after chairing the election, John Oberholtzer stepped down. A month after this session Oberholtzer married a widow from the Upper Milford congregation, Susanna Moyer. They later moved to her home in Philadelphia, a setting he did not particularly enjoy. Here he helped in the ministry of the First Mennonite Church. His daughter-in-law, widow of Davy, and granddaughter "Ellie" were also in the neighborhood. But his marriage turned out to be unsuccessful; the aging partners separated permanently, each living for a while on a different block near the Mennonite chapel. Eventually the old pioneer would move back up to Perkasie to live with his only daughter, and then, when there was no one left to claim him, on to the home of a niece at Saucon. Yet his counsel, preaching visits, and presence in conference were respectfully recorded. Some critics, including Old Mennonites, saw scandal in the failed marriage. But from time to time the Eastern Conference leaders recalled with appreciation his unique and original contributions to their church life. For two decades after A. B. Shelly had taken over his three important editorial and executive roles, Oberholtzer's mind and handwriting remained sharp, and he would always attend Conference sessions.

While he had still been editor and chairman of the General Conference, Oberholtzer had received a letter directed to the deceased Daniel Hege at an address in Pennsylvania, from a Mennonite in Prussia. Feeling that his friends of recent immigration at Summerfield, Illinois, understood the European situation better, Oberholtzer sent the letter to Christian Krehbiel, one of the most active leaders there.[18] It turned out to be the opening inquiry in a correspondence that would lead, by the end of the 1870s, to a mass migration of some 18,000 Prussian, "Polish," and Russian Mennonites to the North American continent. Political unrest in Prussia, and above all, a decree by the Czar revoking for Mennonites in Russia their original exemptions from military service, had made them extremely interested in the American frontier as a possible new home. By 1872 little scouting parties had begun to arrive at New York. Taking the trains west, they consulted with leaders like Christian Krehbiel and John F. Funk. One elder from Volhynia in East Russia, Tobias Unruh, along with two Hutterites, actually sat down with President Ulysses Grant on Long Island in August 1873, asking what chances there were for military exemption in the United States. In his annual message to Congress several months later, the President, without mentioning the Mennonites by name, said that it spoke well for his country that "an industrious, intelligent and wealthy people, desirous of enjoying civil and religious liberty," would want to settle in it.[19]

An emigration of German-speaking people out of Russia, of which Mennonites constituted only a fraction, got underway in earnest in 1874. In that year alone, 1275 Mennonite families arrived by steamer in New York and Philadelphia. Although nearly all got on the train immediately for the West, both the Eastern and the Franconia conferences were drawn into helping the refugees by monetary contributions and occasionally providing temporary housing. Both the *Friedensbote* of Milford Square and John Funk's *Herald* of Elkhart, Indiana, especially the latter, hammered on the theme of aiding the immigrants. The emergency produced, in the Midwest, a "Mennonite Board of Guardians" that joined Old and New Mennonites in the work, and in Pennsylvania, a "Mennonite Executive Aid Committee" in which, possibly for the first time since 1847, an Eastern Conference person, Deacon Casper Hett of the Philadelphia congregation, had official spiritual dealings with a Franconia Conference Mennonite, former miller Herman K. Gottshall of Souder's Station.[20] Primary initiative for this committee had arisen in Lancaster County.

The instinct of mutual aid was still very strong in the Franconia Conference. In January of that year (1874), Preacher Jacob Beidler of Swamp had died suddenly while walking to the morning train at Shelly, which he had wanted to take down to "Menishteland." "Mennonite-land" was the nickname for the thickly settled Mennonite region running from Skippack to Hilltown and beyond.[21] Preacher Beidler had intended to collect money for rebuilding the just-burned barn of Isaac Longacre. By that April, the largest congregation in "Mennonite-land," Franconia, had raised a collection of $1600 for a wider cause, the "Russian Relief Fund," with another $1170 ready "to be loaned."[22] Vincent and Coventry too were listed as donors in the *Herald*. This was in the months when a debate was going on in Congress over whether to grant military exemptions to the new Mennonite immigrants. "Have we not enough of the fighting element in America?" wondered one senator. "If there is any portion of the world that can send us a few advocates of peace, in God's name let us bid them welcome."[23]

In May the Executive Aid Committee of Pennsylvania sent a printed letter to Mennonites who had not yet left Russia, recommending a Quaker-owned steamship line that would bring them to the port of Philadelphia and the Pennsylvania Railroad.[24] The midwestern "Board of Guardians" felt that the easterners were unnecessarily distrustful and competitive in having their separate committee make its own arrangements for transportation. But the easterners wrote to Russia that "Philadelphia is in our neighborhood, and we can easily reach it to receive our arriving brethren...."[25] At the moment, the Eastern Conference was wrestling with the split in its Philadelphia congregation. Herman Gottschall, local treasurer of the Aid Committee, seemed to take the greatest initiative on the Russian matter.

Gottschall, son of the longtime bishop at Franconia, was a former schoolteacher and financially successful miller now living across the Main' Street from the mill he had built in Souder's Station. Having sold it to hardworking young Christian Moyer, Herman had time to think of more than business. Considered a somewhat domineering person (his grandson nicknamed him "the Governor"), he had not been able to pass on his business, as he would have preferred, to his ne'er-do-well only son-in-law. Now he became involved in local affairs such as the Harleysville-Souder's Station Turnpike, a new bank, German school in the schoolhouse beside the Franconia meetinghouse, and a new Mennonite meetinghouse for Souder's Station, soon to be called Souderton. As he agitated the Russian relief issue, and brought immigrants for visits, he was dubbed by some local critics, the "Russian King."[26]

A manner like Herman's, of somewhat dictatorial righteousness, was one of the features of some Old Mennonite communities that most annoyed members of other denominations that did not make their ethical claims as absolute. This manner was perhaps a commonly found one among country Christians, but it became more ironic when seen in people who set forth the "defenseless" doctrine. A vignette from Skippack in August 1874 provides an example. A young Philadelphia lawyer, Samuel Pennypacker, wished to explore his roots among the Mennonites in the community (his grandfather had been the bishop at Phoenixville). Meeting the scythe-carrying deacon of the Old Mennonites of Skippack, Pennypacker inquired, "Is this Mr. Tyson?"

"My name is Tyson but not Mister," retorted the deacon, but then helpfully brought out the ancient Skippack "alms book" for his guest's examination. Minister George Detweiler, on the other hand, was harder to deal with. When Pennypacker met him at his barn, to which he had just returned from a little fishing expedition, the old preacher "turned to his son to talk to him about the oats in Dutch." After fifteen minutes of being left waiting, the young lawyer suggested that they might talk in the house. There, however, when he explained that he would like to see some deeds of the neighborhood for historical reason, Detweiler seemed somewhat distrustful and uncooperative, and Pennypacker left "in disgust."[27]

Yet bossy people are sometimes extremely conscientious in responding to cries of need. And appeals were coming to Pennsylvania Mennonites from two directions, East and West, in the summer of 1874. Three "pitiful and lamentable" letters arrived from the church of Tobias Unruh in "Polish Russia," where Mennonites of Swiss as well as Prussian origin had been living for several generations. John Shenk, one of the Lancaster members of the Executive Aid Committee, took the letters to both his own and the

Elder Tobias A. Unruh (1819-1875) of Karolswalde in Volhynia or "Polish Russia." Having made a preliminary visit to America in 1873, he arrived with the last of his people at Philadelphia on January 28, 1875. After preaching in local Mennonite congregations, he moved to South Dakota, where he soon died of typhoid fever. (John F. Funk Collection, Archives of the Mennonite Church)

Franconia Conference sessions, asking for help.[28] Eventually $20,000 would be raised among Pennsylvanians for this particular Volhynian group of immigrants, who were generally poorer and less well organized than other incoming groups. But other "pitiful" letters were also coming from Dakota, where earlier immigrants, trying to settle in, lacked necessary food and shelter. The Eastern Conference, having wrestled long and hard in its October 1874 session with its Philadelphia church-split, turned its attention to the new immigrants, and passed a resolution to request each of its congregations "to collect money to assist our Russian Brethren in the West in the present need." The Franconia Conference too wanted its representative, Herman Gottshall, to go to Dakota with the Executive Aid Committee and observe personally how bad the conditions really were. Having traveled out by train, he found the refugees in a "truly pitiful" state. He could also report to suspicious Franconians that there was no visible *Hochmuth* (pride) among the Russians (*"Hochmuth fanden wir keinen unter ihnen"*).[29]

But it was the actual arrival in Philadelphia of the storm-tossed Volhynian immigrants that was the nearby Mennonite community's closest brush with the movement. There had been trouble on the journey—a boat collision, delays, several deaths followed by burials in a London cemetery, smallpox, and fearful storms. The group had been separated into at least four parts, and was in a discouraged state. Tobias Unruh, their vigorous elder, had stayed in England to accompany the very last contingent of the closely related fellowship. The Pennsylvania "Aid Committee," which had

had to pay out $7000 by the time the refugees had reached Belgium, had people waiting at the docks in Philadelphia. A total of 265 families came on at least four separate steamers from November 30 to January 28, 1874-75. The Pennsylvanians expected to keep them over the winter in homes and empty buildings in both the eastern and Lancaster communities. But to their surprise they "could not get a single family" of the large group arriving on Christmas Day to stay with them. "We gave them a dinner and a supper at Philadelphia," wrote John Shenk, "and gave them provision" for the journey they insisted on making immediately to Kansas. Arriving on the prairies, they stepped out into twelve-below-zero weather, and found no one ready to help them. The eastern committee was then criticized for "sending" them out, and so more contributions had to be raised quickly. Two of the families who did remain behind, the Julius Nachtigalls and Johnathan Flickingers, stayed with the Samuel Wismers in Bucks County, but were anxious to learn the precise whereabouts of their westward-disappearing relatives.[30]

The last two groups of Volhynians arrived at the Philadelphia docks on January 9 and 28. On the second boat, the *S. S. Illinois*, was elder Tobias Unruh himself. Among the ninety-three in his group was a baby, Susanna, who had been born four days before the landing, to Anna (Schmidt) and John Dirks—their second child. "We were met," noted Unruh, "by many American brethren," including some ministers. "People had come from . . . 20 miles to welcome our arrival; it was indeed a warm, friendly, charitable reception. . . . Everything was arranged well. . . . We all had nice warm rooms and enjoyed the rest after a rough stormy voyage." Two days later, all the newly arrived families "were distributed and given temporary homes."[31] The John Dirks family, with their new daughter named for the ship, Susanna Freudenport Illinois Dirks, were placed at the farm of Abraham K. Nice a mile or two west of Souder's Station (close to the present-day Penn View Christian School). Others were lodged in a former clothing factory on the Main Street of Souder's Station, where local citizens gaped at their bulky overcoats and large fur caps. Herman Gottshall was in charge of the project. Ten-year-old John D. Souder of a farm near Telford helped to clear a house for the immigrants' use, "in reply," as he later put it, "to what others had done for our parents when they came 200 years ago."[32]

Fifteen of the families were taken to homes in Bucks County, where Tobias Unruh preached for the Deep Run Old Mennonites in February.[33] Most had plans to move on either to Kansas or South Dakota, whither twelve families went already in March. Tobias Unruh was one who chose the South Dakota location, but he had hardly more than reached his new home before he was stricken fatally by typhoid fever.[34] The rest of the fifty families in the Bucks-Montgomery County area had to earn money before they could travel west. An unrelated group of Mennonites—550 in one boatload—arrived in Philadelphia on July 31, and had the means to take the Pennsylvania Railroad west immediately.[35]

Two sad deaths among the Volhynian group left markers in the Franconia Mennonite graveyard. Two-year-old Benjamin, son of Jacob and Susanna Jahns who were staying in Franconia Township, was gored to death by a bull. His funeral occurred on a Sunday afternoon; one of the preachers participating was John F. Funk, who had been brought to Franconia in the morning as a visiting preacher by Henry Ruth of Line Lexington. Funk was in the community to attend the funeral of his own father, Jacob.[36] In the following summer, John Dirks, still on the Abraham Nice farm, died of "consumption," leaving beside his widow Annie a little Peter and Susie, the baby born on the *S.S. Illinois*. Annie then scrubbed floors for the recently widowed Isaac Gross of Plumstead Township. A few years later she rejoined her relatives in Kansas, but Isaac soon called her back to be his second wife. Her daughter Susie, having grown up in the Doylestown area, was to marry "Butcher Dan" Myers.[37]

A century after these events, almost no one in the Eastern or Franconia conferences knew anything of the story of their ancestors' helping the immigrant Russians. Many of the Volhynians who went to Kansas were gathered into the piously conservative flock of Preacher John Holdeman, originally of Ohio, but stemming from the pioneer Halteman family of the Salford congregation. His followers called themselves the "Church of God in Christ,

Susanna Freudenport Illinois Dirks, born on January 24, 1875, on the ship for which she was named, four days before landing in Philadelphia. A daughter of Volhynian immigrants John and Anna Dirks, she eventually married "Butcher Dan" Myers of Doylestown. (John L. Swartley)

Mennonite," and others called them "Holdeman Mennonites." Others of
the Volhynians got a foothold in Turner County, South Dakota. When their
grateful descendants sent a commemorative plaque to the eastern Pennsylvania Mennonites in 1974, no one in the East knew what it was for.[38] Even
the grandchildren of Susie Dirks knew little more than that their grandmother had been "born on the boat" just before reaching Philadelphia.
Only a few scattered records, such as those kept by Preacher Henry Bower
of his Salford congregation, remained to show how the hearts of the Mennonite family had expanded to bear the burdens of their hitherto unknown
friends from Russia. Even the Schwenkfelders and Dunkers of the neighborhood contributed, as well as a few other neighbors. Some of the money
was lent, and some "Given . . . as a Present." A few examples from Bower's
records will show the variety of gifts from Lower Salford:

Hannah Groff	20.--	Dunkard Meeting	53.--
Gerret Clemens	50.--	Jacob Groff	10.--
Jacob C. Moyer	40.--	Henry Bower	5.--
Samuel Landis	10.--	John Wasser	2.--
Widow Mary Alderfer	2.--	Jacob Moyer (old)	1.--
Nancy Alderfer	20.--	Garret Delp	75.--
Jacob N. Clemens	5.--	Widow H. Detweiler	1.--
Margaret Keely		Widow Minninginger	3.--[39]
(for her family)	40.--		

The loaned money came back slowly, because of difficult farming conditions on the frontier, and occasionally there were expressions of impatience.
As late as the years of World War I, Herman Gottshall's successor as
treasurer, Deacon Henry Krupp of the Souderton congregation, would
continue to channel back payments to the congregations who had lent
money over forty years earlier,[40] and it was believed that most of the obligations were eventually kept.

Probably no other cause linked the Eastern and Franconia conferences
as noncontroversially as this one did, until the needs of Mennonites in
Russia after World War I would elicit a guarded cooperation through
another "central committee." "Russian" Mennonite ministers from Kansas,
Nebraska, or Dakota made many visits in Montgomery and Bucks counties
for the next quarter century, sometimes preaching in congregations of
either conference. A later small group of immigrants from "Galicia" lived
for a while near the West Swamp congregation, before moving to Minnesota.[41] As it became evident that most of the "Russian" Mennonites were
being drawn toward the General Conference, Herman Gottshall would give
vent to an irritable disappointment felt by some "old" Mennonites.

This expansion of the General Conference moved the Eastern Conference into a much less central role in the larger body. A. B. Shelly continued to be president, as well as secretary of the (foreign) Mission Board, but the center of gravity in terms of population now shifted farther west. A new periodical dealing with immigration concerns, *Zur Heimath* (To the Homeland), subsidized by a steamship company hoping for Mennonite business, sprang up almost with the birth of the new Mennonite community in Kansas. In a few years (1882) this merged with the always struggling *Friedensbote* of Milford Square, under the name *Der Christliche Bundesbote* (The Christian Union-Messenger).

In the midst of the Russian immigration, the General Conference had met for an unprecedentedly long and difficult session of twelve days, in the Sunday school hall of the fine new, two-leveled church building at West Swamp. Nine congregations from outside the Eastern Conference had sent delegates. Mounting troubles at the deeply indebted Wadsworth Institute, including faculty disunity and student rowdiness that had reached the point of local scandal, called for a special committee to meet while the conference recessed, and determine what was the root of the problem. There was friction between Pennsylvania and midwestern members over the personnel of the faculty, and the indebtedness. The Canadian members from "The Twenty" had withdrawn from the conference. It is helpful to remember that at this point the whole General Conference was probably no larger in membership than the Franconia Conference, though with the new "Russian" influx, this was about to change dramatically. John Oberholtzer himself, now sixty-five, was asked to reply to letters of inquiry about membership in the conference from two large "Russian" congregations in Kansas. Oberholtzer's brother William, a year earlier, had raised the ire of "western" conference members by his actions as a trustee of the Wadsworth School, where he had lived for several months while investigating its problems.[42] The Institute would endure, in fact, only a few more years, even though a new English teacher, amiable young Anthony S. Shelly, nephew of A. B. Shelly, would effectively rejuvenate the English curriculum. There simply were not enough Mennonite students continuing to show interest.

Four ordinations in the Franconia Conference which took place within a nine-month period in the midst of the Russian immigration, provide a window on Old Mennonite life in this decade. Preacher Andreas Mack of Hereford, now thirty-nine, was the unanimous nominee of his "Schuylkill" district for the office of bishop, and so the rare phenomenon of an ordination with no casting of lots occurred in the Franconia Conference. No longer would elderly Bishop Latshaw of Coventry have to ford the Schuylkill (once, it was said, his carriage began to float) to serve com-

The 1873 West Swamp Mennonite Church, location of the seventh session of the General Conference in November 1875. (James J. Gerhart)

munion at Hereford. But at first the slender though strong Mack experienced a kind of nervous reaction that kept him from preaching for a year.[43] Later he was to be remembered for the strength and forthrightness of his leadership, as well as his broad-mindedness. He would even attend a session of the Eastern Conference, when that body convened in its Hereford church, and offer a few friendly spiritual remarks.

At Rockhill, Preacher John Allebach, who had reached seventy, and his younger colleague Abel Horning wanted assistance. John's affable carriagemaker son Christian, a man who expressed himself easily, had moved over to the Towamencin area after marriage, in order to be in a congregation where his wife could realize her desire of practicing foot washing (on the advice of Bishop Jacob Kulp of Plains). This also allowed Christian not to be placed "in the lot" at Rockhill, which surely would have happened, because of his gifts, had he stayed. As a boy, he had "preached" so effectively, while sitting on a fence, that tears had come to his listeners' eyes. At Towamencin, he would seem to have been safe from "the lot," since this congregation had always been served by ministers ordained at other meetings. Back at Rockhill, when the lot was cast in the spring of 1876, it fell on a thirty-five-year-old farmer—Sam Detweiler—who could not even read, let alone speak in public. When he made his first attempt to preach, in the Franconia meetinghouse, no words came. He stood in the pulpit paging through the Bible, tears running down his cheeks, until he finally said, "I give it up," and sat down.[44] It was just the kind of situation John

Christian B. Allebach (1841-1917), who at the age of thirty-five found himself unexpectedly ordained as the first minister specifically for the Towamencin congregation. (Alpheus C. Allebach)

Oberholtzer's constitution had sought to avoid. But Sam Detweiler's wife, Annie, then managed to teach him to read, and twenty years later he would be advanced to the office of bishop.

Two other ordinations followed in rapid succession, at Line Lexington and at Towamencin. The first made Sam Leatherman, the extremely quiet-spoken minister, into a bishop, to serve along with Josiah Clemmer of Franconia. Sam had been a particularly appreciated visitor, the previous summer, at the bedside of the dying father of John Funk, a member at Line Lexington.[45] The second ordination saw the lot fall on former Rockhill-member Christian Allebach. Having chosen to transfer to Towamencin for entirely other reasons than this, Christian complained bitterly, at first, about the irony of his move. But he recovered his spirits, and in the following decades "Grisht" Allebach became a memorable and beloved figure in his adopted congregation. Unafraid to correct the erring, he inspired hope in the troubled, and became not only a very stabilizing influence in the congregation, but, in the words of a young member, *"Jedermans Freund"* (everybody's friend) throughout the community. In a remarkable coincidence, Allebach, Andrew Mack, and Sam Detweiler—all ordained in the same half year, would preach for over forty more years, and die within a month of each other at the end of the German-preaching era, in 1917.

As the nation's centennial arrived, the spread of English was gaining momentum even in the "Dutch" townships, making the conservative older leaders somewhat sad. German was no longer taught in the public schools; at Franconia old Minister Henry Nice and miller Herman Gottshalk, also a former schoolteacher, led the young people to the meetinghouse school on Saturdays for the lusty practice of German hymns. Occasionally Herman hauled a few boys out to the sessions from Souder's Station.[46] Whereas, in 1873, twenty-one-year-old Deborah Bergey of Franconia Township would write her "Love Song" in "Dutch,"[47] a half decade later Henry Godshalk, son of Preacher Sam at Deep Run, would write crude poems and songs in English.[48] J. G. Stauffer, now the sole proprietor of the printshop at Milford Square which had been built for the earlier *Volksblatt*, began publishing a profitable German Sunday school leaflet, *Himmelsmanna* (Heavenly Manna) in the centennial year, but only three years later, when he also issued an English version, he found that it soon outsold the German. By 1881 he would pack up both printing business and his family and move a few miles east and found an English newspaper, the *Quakertown Free Press*, to complement his other German one, the *Patriot and Reformer.*[49] Schwenksville, of course, had had its English *Item* since 1877. Thus members of the Eastern Conference were in the forefront of the changing communications network of their neighborhoods, while the Old Mennonites took no leading roles.

It was a Lutheran who brought the largely Old Mennonite town of Souderton a German newspaper by 1878, but even there an English paper, the *Independent*, replaced the German one in a mere three years. The rapid transition produced in the May 1878 session of the Franconia Conference, expressions of alarm over the possibility of losing the German language. The Vincent congregation, which had had an English preacher (David Buckwalter) already in 1854, was going entirely English in its services this year(1878)[50], and the Eastern Conference began using English in its sessions. Within the decade the language switch would occur in the minutes themselves. When young Henry Godshalk of Deep Run, having recently emigrated west, was found lifeless on the Kansas prairie in 1879, his minister father collected some of the young man's poetry and had John

Funk of Elkhart publish it with other materials in an English booklet in 1880, *Encouragement to Early Piety*.[51] Anthony Shelly, having grown up in the "Dutch"-speaking West Swamp congregation, would become principal, before long, of a public school in Lower Bucks County. The change was now accelerating.

The Eastern Conference adjusted more quickly, of course, having leaders fluent in both languages who would inaugurate an English publication, *The Mennonite*, as early as 1885. By this time, some of the Old Mennonites were just getting into the debate. From farther west, they had available John Funk's *Herald*, in either language. Every so often John Funk came back to visit his Bucks County relatives, urging new subscriptions, but humbly fitting in to the old ways as well, helping to make hay if his visit came in that season,[52] and preaching in German in various pulpits. The only English Old Mennonite heard from their pulpits came from a visiting preacher from Virginia, or Quakers. The novelty of the latter was great, since the Quakers surrounded their remarks with the unfamiliar procedure of waiting in long silences. A young Souderton observer interpreted this as visibly annoying to Bishop Josiah Clemmer.[53]

The language change would be so protracted in the Franconia Conference that a century after David Buckwalter had been ordained, the Franconia congregation would still be able to sing German hymns vigorously from its own special supplement in the back of its hymnbook. Some of the feelings engendered by the first weakening of the German were expressed by farmer-poet William Gross of Fountainville, near the Doylestown meetinghouse. When a case of what he believed was hydrophobia kept him in a darkened room for nineteen days in 1882, the conviction grew in him that he should address the parents of his people in regard to their passing on the faith to their children. How could the children be nourished through the preaching they heard in meeting, he asked, when they could not understand the only language the preacher, chosen by God, was able to use? It seemed that even parents who themselves could not speak English properly were conversing with their children, out of prideful motives, only in that language. A potentially serious gap of spiritual communication was threatening. "Perhaps you answer," wrote Gross, " 'Yes, the time is soon coming when church services will generally be held in the English language.' I answer, 'If that comes, it will not hurt our children if they are practised in their mother-tongue.' "[54]

Five years earlier than Gross's essay, in 1877, there had appeared from the press of John G. Stauffer a little black book of 111 pages that expressed an even greater pathos.[55] Written in the language that Bucks County Mennonite youth were now in the initial process of forgetting, it was something of a voice from an earlier age. It was the testament of aged Abraham Meyer of Deep Run, born in 1794, and earlier a schoolteacher, when Fraktur and zithers were current. In the sleepless nights of his final months and years, Meyer had composed poems in the manner and sometimes the very phrasings of Christopher Dock, who had died a century earlier. Among his effusions was a traditional acrostic poem based on his name (such as the one Deacon Rudolph Landes of the same congregation had produced in 1814), an "Admonition to Young and Old," hymns for "You brothers and sisters" and "the youth," and an example of the familiar "farewell hymn." The only internal evidence that there had been a cultural change since the days of his youth is in Abraham's references to the splintered congregation, and the modern spirit of individuality. "Strong-minded people" were now regarding themselves as more intelligent than their spiritual forebears. In a poem referring to his congregation, he asks God to restore this flock "which is the smallest on earth," so that there may again be "one shepherd and one flock." This tiny volume of poems, some reprinted from other sources, must have struck the younger readers to whom it was directed as hopelessly quaint. Yet Henry Godshalk, who had tried his hand at poetry himself in English, had taken as his theme on one occasion the saintliness of the now departed old schoolmaster Meyer.[56]

Sunday schools were so well organized in the Eastern Conference that during the nation's centennial year the Conference inaugurated a durable tradition of "Sunday School Conventions" without copying anyone else's model.[57] The meetings served as a pleasurable knitting together of the conference family as well as a continuing seminar of methods of Christian education. The location was shifted from congregation to congregation, sending visitors from one end of the conference to another. In the Franconia Conference, the Sunday school came much more haltingly and sporadically, starting at the western extreme of Vincent in 1870, as well as in the form of community schools that gathered in schoolhouses or in Mennonite meetinghouses but were taught by members of a variety of denominations. One such began at Doylestown in 1882, and another in the new meetinghouse in Souderton, led by Herman Gottshall.[58] However, when the latter conservatively suggested that the Bible, rather than quarterlies should be used, his non-Mennonite helpers lost interest.[59] At the worship services in the new (1879) Souderton meetinghouse, a short walk behind Herman's house, all denominations came and filled all the benches. There was little else of a social nature to do in this village of mills, factories, hay houses, and stores. In less than a decade the Eastern Conference, too, would begin to hold services there, at first in the hall of a hotel a few blocks away from the Old Mennonite meetinghouse.

Relations between the two conferences in this era remained fairly sullen. At Saucon the death of Old Mennonite Preacher Samuel Moyer in 1877 effectively ended the separate life of the remaining "Franconia" element. The Eastern Conference congregation too was weak. At neighboring Springfield, where Samuel Moyer had also preached to an "Old" congregation of about twenty members, the group held on, served by visiting preachers from "Mennonite-land," and using the meetinghouse alternately with the Eastern Conference congregation of about 100 members, led by Elder Jacob S. Moyer.

But a similar arrangement at Boyertown, where the "Old" element was in the majority broke down about this time.[60] Each congregation had used the meetinghouse in turn, leaving the key afterward at a nearby tavern. Now the "Old" congregation, apparently considering itself the owner, determined that the building must be replaced with a better one, and sent the "New" congregation a notification of this intent. The "New" was welcome to continue to use the building as before, but was informed that nothing new, such as musical instruments, might be brought in. This proceeding was not pleasing to the "New" congregation, and its trustees secured a court injunction halting the work of demolition until there could be a hearing. Quite a few witnesses were called, on both sides of the issue, including John Oberholtzer himself, now living in Philadelphia, and Preacher Isaac Meyer from the "Old" congregation at distant Deep Run. Both were able to recall the history of the 1847 division from their own experience. A "Master" was appointed by a Berks County judge to try to untangle the conceptual problems related to the competing claims to legitimacy of the two conference groups. There was interesting testimony and revealing cross-examination, the transcript of which later became a valuable source of information to historians. But not until at least two years after the legal process began, in March 1879, was a decision handed down.

During this time the building project at the main crossroad in Boyertown remained stalled. Nor was the master's decision accepted as final. Finding that the ruling was against their claim, the New Mennonites appealed, and the judge appointed a new master. This jurist, after recalling several witnesses and waiting another year, ruled in the opposite direction, and required the Old Mennonites to pay the costs. Now the latter group filed legal exceptions. Five years after the controversy had become public, Berks County Judge J. Hagenman, chiding the Mennonites for not being able to settle their own differences in line with their "world-wide" renown for peacefulness, ruled that the Old Mennonite position was wrong. But even this was not the end. Joel Bower and Henry Gabel, of the Old Mennonite building committee, now instructed their attorneys to appeal the case to the Pennsylvania Supreme Court. On this final round the ruling was again reversed in favor of the Old Mennonites, nearly six years after the trouble had begun.

Each side, of course, took the other's behavior as evidence of malicious motives. The long legal process reopened old wounds, evoked letters to newspapers, and kept the new meetinghouse unbuilt (though in 1879 a cornerstone had been dated). Out of the whole discussion the truest words may have been those of Judge Hagenman, as he reminded the Mennonites that "The Court is the last place to which they should resort." In legal proceedings, no matter which verdict is rendered, feelings are engendered "That many years will not allay." The Old Mennonites had an internal debate as to when the line of "nonresistance" was crossed, while moving from answering charges in court to asking for continued legal process. The Franconia Conference, meeting in the fall of 1883 after the Supreme Court had rendered its verdict, required trustees Bower and Gabel to confess that they had gone too far (in seeking legal rulings), both to the conference and to the Boyertown congregation. But now the building project could at last be completed, and some Old Mennonites could not completely conceal their gratification with what they felt was a justification of their side by the Supreme Court decision. Not to be denied their own claim to Mennonite identity, the little Eastern Conference congregation at Boyertown erected a building of their own and named it, pointedly, the "Menno Simons Mennonite Church."

One specific issue in the controversy may very well have been the requirement by the Old Mennonites that no musical instrument be allowed in the forthcoming meetinghouse. In these very years organs were being installed by congregations such as Gottschall's and the musically strong West Swamp. A new building at Upper Milford, dedicated in 1877 just when the Boyertown controversy erupted, had a raised platform for an organ. But the congregation here was not yet ready for another advance in a "church"-like direction—a bell. Though William Moyer bought one and tried to donate it to the church, he was turned down. The congregation did accept his gift of a reed organ. He hung up the bell on his own farm across the fields from the tall new brick "Kirche," and rang it there on Sunday mornings before going to church.

It was in these late 1870s that two Mennonite congregations, at the southwestern and northeastern extremes of the traditional community, expired or were absorbed by Lutheran congregations meeting in their facilities. Industrialization and urban development, less of a threat to the larger denominations, took this toll. In English-speaking Phoenixville, where Buckwalters, Haltemans, Pennypackers, and Showalters had once worshiped in a schoolhouse, and where the Hunsicker "Reformed" Mennonites had taken over in 1851, no leadership was left after Israel Beidler died in 1876. His uncle Jacob Beidler, builder of a Mennonite meetinghouse at Diamond Rock, several miles south of Phoenixville in the rural Chester County hills, had also died, and no congregation met there. Bishop Mathias Pennypacker's grandchildren were wealthy, involved in politics and the professions, and "popular" denominations.

Henry Hunsicker, now the main leader of the Reformed Mennonites, watched a set of glittering new stores and shops crowd the little old meetinghouse on its square of "the most valuable ground in the borough." He decided that a more modern church-house was needed if the congregation was to survive, sold off part of the cemetery to raise money, and built a new church in 1873. But a debt of $2,000 remained, and the congregation was dwindling. At the same time, a Lutheran congregation, which held its organization meeting in December 1875 in the new Mennonite building, was growing rapidly. Hunsicker, who had sold Freeland Seminary a decade earlier and was deeply involved in the lumber business, was unable to inspire the following his father Abraham had commanded. Before long he himself would be a Presbyterian. He allowed the Lutheran congregation at Phoenixville to take over the new building, with its debt, and with a promise of keeping the old Mennonite cemetery. Eventually the Lutherans replaced Hunsicker's building with a large church of their own, and buried the old grave markers in their lawn.[61]

A similar process occurred in the same years in Northampton County at Mt. Bethel, where the borough of Bangor was organized in 1875.[62] In this vicinity a community of Mennonite farmers with names like Ackerman, Delp, Godshalk, Oberholtzer, and Ruth, having been there since well before 1800, had erected a little brick meetinghouse in 1822. Emigration westward had claimed key leadership, and the slate industry, founded on some of the Mennonite-owned land, had attracted a new, nonagricultural population. The once visible Mennonite presence, producing villages named Ackermanville and Delpsburg, was now almost completely gone. A few miles south of the Mt. Bethel meetinghouse, another one, nicknamed "Rothrock's," was also empty. The last pastor and deacon at Mt. Bethel, David Henning and Jacob Godshalk, had joined first the "New" and then the "Evangelical" Mennonites, but there had been no subsequent growth. By 1870 there were only Preacher Henning and his wife and one other widow.

On the hill behind the little meetinghouse were scattered the graves of dozens of Mennonite families, "nearly all" of whose children had joined the Lutheran Church. Lutheran Pastor B. F. Apple, of nearby Centerville, was in charge of most of the current funerals at the meetinghouse. His ministry at Mt. Bethel was a kind of Lutheran "mission." Reformed and other ministers conducted meetings there too, as the sense of the local Mennonite "family" atrophied. Only where a minimal density of Mennonite population held, it seemed, could the feeling of "peoplehood" operate as an effective expression of spiritual energy. Without this minimum, only the stringency of the Mennonite tradition remained, without the necessary warmth. A non-Mennonite neighbor girl remembered the last local Mennonites as quarrelsome.

A few months before the Phoenixville Lutherans had organized in the Mennonite church there, the Lutherans in the new borough of Bangor set up a Sunday school in the old brick Mennonite meetinghouse. Pastor David Henning, now past seventy, decided to offer them ownership, if they would take care of the cemetery. When they hesitated, he found the Lutheran custodian at work in a slate quarry and gave him a month to accept, since the same offer was being made to the Reformed people. This prompted the Lutherans to take over, and on April 6, 1878, they organized what became the Trinity Lutheran Church at Bangor. For five years they met in the Mennonite meetinghouse, and then built beside it a large brick edifice. For a time the two buildings stood side by side, in mute witness to the contrast between the two fellowships that had produced them. Only the hillside gravestones, and names in the Lutheran congregation such as Ackerman, Godshalk, and Ruth remained to witness of the earlier Mennonite community. But as late as the end of the century, Mennonite visitors from Canada still took the train to Bangor to see relatives.[63]

Pastor Henning, though his own congregation had now dissolved, had the joy of seeing his Evangelical Mennonite denomination increased by a merger with a group of similarly minded Mennonites from Canada and the Midwest, in November 1879. It transpired at a special conference at Upper Milford, home church of founder William Gehman. Among the Evangelical Mennonite ministers was Joel Rosenberger of a little congregation at Hatfield. Rosenberger had been ordained by Henry Johnson in the Lower Skippack Mennonite congregation, after the untimely death of Christian Detweiler, but now Johnson, who had also seen four other ministers leave his congregation via schism, had to lose still another, this time to a more expressive fellowship. The newly merged group, accepting the name "Evangelical United Mennonites," "went down on their knees" in the Upper Milford Church in thanks for this gift of unity with their emotion-loving friends of Mennonite background. "There was shouting," wrote the secretary of the conference, "leaping and clapping of hands, to the honor and glory of the great Head of the Church."[64] Although most other local

Mennonites, both "Old" and "New," considered these "Methodistic" outbursts of feeling inappropriate and even ridiculous, some felt the attraction. For two years Deacon John Funk of the nearby Hereford "New" Mennonite congregation had been holding emotional prayer meetings, though these were opposed by the pastor Abraham Gottshall (brother of the well-known Moses.) In 1880 Funk and several others in the congregation left and joined an Evangelical Association church, where he served as an ardent exhorter and class leader. His children followed, and even as his son Albert, presently pastor at the First Mennonite Church in Philadelphia, would eventually leave the Mennonite fellowship and help to found a new denomination, the Christian and Missionary Alliance churches.[65]

The rapid appearance of banks in the railroad-spawned towns of these changeful seventies precipitated from the Franconia Conference a "housekeeping" response. When towns like Lansdale, Schwenksville, East Greenville, and Souderton organized banking associations, affluent Mennonite men from these communities were among those asked to "stand for director." Half the directors at Souderton were Mennonites, including Herman Gottshall and his "dear friend" Charles Z. Godshall. At East Greenville the president himself was a member of Gottschall's Mennonite congregation: Michael Alderfer, wealthiest man in Lower Salford. His Eastern Conference seemed to raise no questions, but it was otherwise in the Franconia Conference. Already in 1867, when Herman Gottshall had been nominated for director at Lansdale, he had talked to a Mennonite who held such an office. This man had told Herman that before he had accepted the appointment, Bishop Jacob Kulp of Plains (d. 1875) had given his opinion that a nonresistant person could consistently serve as a bank trustee.[66]

Bishop Kulp, though affluent himself, would be remembered for his exemplification of a rare antique spirit of mutual aid. As an unofficial scrivener, he would occasionally visit the courthouse in Norristown to do some minor legal business for a local family, staying overnight with storekeeper David Funk, one of the few Mennonites then living in Norristown. Though he could well afford a wagon or carriage, Kulp would make the trip on foot. His family recalled that when, on one occasion, the driver of a passing vehicle stopped to offer him a ride, he declined, saying, "Ich hab's a'genumma fa laufa" (I had made up my mind to walk). As one of the more well-to-do people of his neighborhood, he was approached from time to time for personal loans, in those days before banks. His informal records of the amounts owed him, it would be claimed, were written on the whitewashed wall of a small washhouse between the house and the barn.

When it came time for the periodic whitewashing, the children responsible for the job asked what should be done about these records of still unpaid debts. The bishop instructed them to go ahead with the work.[67] His implication was taken to be that God had the records, and that it was our duty to give whether a return was certain or not. It was in the context of respect for his generosity as well as his intelligence that Bishop Kulp's informal comment (that there was no prohibition against a nonresistant brother's serving as a bank director) had been received.

Herman Gottshall, unlike a very prosperous cousin in Lansdale, Andrew G. Godshall, wished to remain a Mennonite. Herman and his bachelor brother Sam (the largest shareholder in the new Souderton bank) were strong supporters of the congregation emerging in the new meetinghouse a block back from Herman's house on Main Street. But trouble arose when the bank, a few steps from Herman's front door, foreclosed on a loan, and "sold a man out." Complaints were heard at the next Franconia Conference session. The Mennonite Church, it was argued, had become responsible for using civil force, through the actions of the bank directors. The conference then passed a "regulation," without an official written record, of course, that members should not be bank directors.[68] This seems to have brought a significant change of personnel on the board of the Souderton bank. But at least two of the men whom the ruling affected took serious offense.

One was Herman Gottshall, song leader at Franconia, Sunday school enthusiast, booster of the new Souderton meetinghouse, treasurer of the Russian funds, and successful investor. The bank had become a hobby of his. He spent so much time sitting in its back room discussing current topics with other businessmen that one wag called him, in a Perkasie newspaper column, "Our worthy bank president." If he did not enjoy this joke, he was downright indignant over the action of the conference. Stung by what he took as a somewhat personal rebuke, he argued, though usually a conservative, in a way that would have been natural for John Oberholtzer. "I always count it dangerous to make too many new regulations," he wrote to minister Jacob Mensch at Skippack. "There are now already [more] regulations by our large Council than are being kept...." For years the church had "borne in love" with those who had been serving on juries; why should it now hold Herman and Charles Godshall accountable for a bank foreclosure they may not even have wanted? "The question," after all, "comes up, who is the bank[?] ... some think the directors, but basically the shareholders are the bank ... everything is tied together, and still the penalty was placed on the directors." The word "penalty" suggests that part of the conference action had been to require an "acknowledgment" or confession for the Mennonite directors' involvement in "selling a man out."

Although Herman and Charles left the Board, they both reacted so strongly to this "ruling of the bishops at the Council" that it was years before Herman would go to communion again, and Charles would never go back. "We have no brotherhood way," complained Herman, regarding conference procedure in "house-keeping." "We just have to submit to their decrees, be they just or unjust, or we must look for something else." It was a statement one might have expected rather from someone in the Eastern Conference. Herman was especially hurt over the withdrawal of Charles Godshall from the church, along with the latter's son-in-law Samuel Swartley. Herman did not claim that the conference action was the only cause of Charles' leaving, "but it had a lot do with it. . . ." Herman himself even pondered the possibility of uniting "with another denomination," but realized that even if he were to do so, he would never be able to "discard the basis of our . . . faith," which was "good if . . . handled properly."[69]

The strength of his identification with the nonresistant church of his forebears was such, however, that he could not leave. Before long he would be turning the severity of his criticisms just as bluntly toward the General Conference Mennonites, for their innovations on "the old ground." He was drawn back into the Franconia Conference by a solicitous caring on the part of leaders like Jacob Mensch, and even Bishop Andrew Mack, who wrote from Bally asking how Jacob was doing in mollifying Herman's feelings. "I rejoiced," Herman wrote to Jacob, "that you held such love toward me."[70] For another quarter of a century Herman and his brother Sam would be centrally involved in the growing Old Mennonite congregation in Souderton.

In contrast, Charles Godshall remained alienated. A young bank teller who waited on him thought he seemed "very queer" and "melancholy," but not crazy, as some were gossiping.[71] Now the families of Godshall and his son-in-law Abraham Swartley of Franconia, with a few other people, began to gather for worship in private homes. Their first preacher was a former minister among the Evangelical Mennonites who had come to disapprove of their liveliness in worship: Samuel Landis of Quakertown. A man who lived with Landis for many years, Jonas Schultz, also began to preach at the meetings. Of Schwenkfelder ancestry, Schultz had earlier served as a teacher at the Wadsworth Institute among the General Conference Mennonites, and now worked with John G. Stauffer, helping to produce lesson commentary for the prospering *Himmelsmanna*. Other preachers followed, but the Godshall group remained small. In 1887 they were holding services every four weeks among the remnants of the old Mennonite community at Settlement, in the countryside north of

Samuel W. Lapp, ordained deacon at Line Lexington in 1870, married Sarah, daughter of Doylestown minister John K. Gross, in 1856. In 1878 the Lapps moved to Ayr, Nebraska. Their eleven children included four Mennonite bishops. (Mennonite Library and Archives of Eastern Pennsylvania)

Allentown. Beside the little meetinghouse, where a strenuous sermon by Mose Gottshall had been interrupted by a nest of wasps it had activated, was a neat graveyard filled with stones bearing names like Baer, Hiestand, Landis, and Ziegler. Though this upper outpost of the main Mennonite area, with the Blue Mountain on its northern horizon, could not be revived, the Godshall fellowship itself clung to life in the Quakertown or Telford areas, with remarkably tenacity. Sometimes also nicknamed "Landis" or "Swartley People," they referred to themselves simply as belonging to the Christian church. A century after its beginning, the group was still holding services in a tiny "Diamond Street Chapel" in the town of Hatfield. A grandson of Charles Godshall, Paul Swartley, eventually joined the mid-western-based "Holdeman Mennonites," and became a minister of that group, though living in Souderton until his death exactly a century after the Franconia Conference session that had offended his grandfather.[72]

The bicentennial (1883) of the founding of Germantown brought some visitors to the Germantown Mennonite services, where Samuel Penny-packer, and John H. Oberholtzer spoke. The congregation at this time was quite weak. The last "Hunsickerite" or "Reformed Mennonite" minister, Israel Beidler, had died in 1875, and a number of members had drifted away. The remnant of thirteen members had then appealed to the Eastern Conference for affiliation and aid. N. B. Grubb of Schwenksville and John

M. Holdeman, a silenced Franconia Conference minister who had been accepted by the Eastern Conference, preached for them on alternate Sundays. A bright young convert named Henry A. Fredericks preached for two years, but then left for a Methodist pulpit. N. B. Grubb never forgot one humorous moment from the summer of the national centennial. On a Sunday morning in July he announced a hymn to a large audience that had been drawn to the historic Germantown meetinghouse by the anniversary. The old organist, one "father Heilig," became flustered when his instrument could not be made to work, though he "pumped and pumped . . . and pressed the keys." He burst out in an audible expression of irritation, realized he had embarrassed himself before a sizable audience of strangers, and strode quickly out of the meetinghouse, never to return.[73] During the next eight decades, as minister after minister tried to revive it, this premier Mennonite congregation of North America would sometimes barely survive.

The deacon at John Holdeman's former congregation, Line Lexington, had fallen into economic difficulty in these years, as the market for his shoemaking business declined after the Civil War. By 1878 Samuel Lapp's troubles were acute; his deacon's account is blank for that year. When he and his medically trained wife Sarah (Gross) took their family to a homestead near Hastings, Nebraska, questions were even raised at the Franconia Conference about the alms funds he had kept. His sons vowed to repay all their family's debts (and kept the vow); four of them became Mennonite bishops, and two of these were missionaries. When ministers from the Franconia Conference traveled west to visit their acquaintances among the "Russian" Mennonites of South Dakota, Nebraska, and Kansas, they looked up the Lapp family as well. There was also a Henry Yothers family near Hastings, and several hundred miles south in Kansas, families of Alderfers, Prices, Moyers, and Swartleys from Franconia and Lower Salford who had moved out at about the same time as the Lapps. Young Henry Godshall's unexplained death on the Kansas prairie was a shock to the group. One rather eccentric emigrant to Kansas from Montgomery County, a John Landis, could find no one in the new community properly qualified to give him the true baptism. He arranged for several of his friends to support him as he stood in a stream, whereupon he immersed himself. Before long he returned to Montgomery County, where for many years he behaved as a kind of free-lance prophet. This powerfully built community character wandered into villages, towns, and even churches, denouncing such errors as selling milk on Sunday, or unnecessary architectural frills.[75]

When Bishop Andrew Mack of the Old Mennonites at Hereford was visiting among his "Russian" friends around Beatrice, Nebraska, in 1881, they challenged him on a subject of great current interest to them: missions. The General Conference had had, for the past three years, a mission magazine called *Die Nachrichten aus der Heidenwelt* (News from the Heathen World), and in 1880 the first missionaries, the Samuel Haury family, had been sent to Indian Territory in what would become Oklahoma. When Andrew Mack was asked where he stood on the question of missions, he replied only, "A minister dare not engage in mission work when the laity do not back him."[76] In the Eastern Conference, by contrast, there was considerable enthusiasm for the "great cause." The chairman, A. B. Shelly, was also the secretary of the General Conference Mission Board, which had sent Samuel Haury to the Arapahoe Indians. This young pioneer had personal acquaintances in the Eastern District, having studied with them at the former Wadsworth Institute. Later he had gone to a missionary school in Europe, and then enrolled at the Jefferson Medical College in Philadelphia. Here the pastor of the First Mennonite Church was his Wadsworth classmate, Albert E. Funk, originally of the Hereford congregation. While a student at Jefferson in 1876, Haury began to write seven "letters" articulating the potential importance of missions for Mennonites. In February the first of the letters appeared in the *Friedensbote*, and in the next year they would be gathered into a published booklet.[77] Under A. B. Shelly's leadership, much discussion of the first mission venture of the General Conference took place at the Eastern Conference sessions. It was hoped that this cherished work would be the source of spiritual revival and unity to Mennonites in general. It was time, as Haury had written, for Mennonites to turn away from debating and banning each other to "the fundamental facets of Christianity"—"being born again" and "the spread of the kingdom of Christ."[78] Before the decade would be out, A. B. Shelly, on one of his many western trips, would himself baptize the very first convert, a seventeen-year-old half-Indian girl named Maggie Leonard.[79] In the meantime many a mission sermon was preached in the Eastern Conference, occasional "Mission Festivals" were held, and many mission offerings received.

Continuing reports from the western mission appeared in a new (1882) General Conference periodical, *Der Christliche Bundesbote* (The Christian Union-Messenger), since into this paper had been merged not only the *Friedensbote* published at Milford Square, but the two western Mennonite papers representing immigration and missions interests. By its sixth month, the *Bundesbote* heard from Souderton's Herman Godshall, still smarting over the discipline the Old Mennonites had given him, but ready now to correct the New. "I read much in the *Bundesbote* about mission," he began. He acknowledged that it had indeed been "commanded" to the apostles, originally, "to go into all the world and preach the gospel," and they had been "faithful." But what scriptural evidence was there, inquired the crusty Old Mennonite, that once this task had been carried out, which the Scriptures indicate was the case, the bishops and ministers in the churches the apostles had founded were also to go out with the gospel, where the apostles "had already preached to all peoples and creatures"?[80] This Old Mennonite jab and its dubious exegesis was followed in the *Bundesbote* by a tactful if lengthy answer by the Indiana editor, S. F. Sprunger.[81] Later, Godshall would not be let off so mildly. Nor did he speak for all the Old Mennonites, for they too had their mission enthusiasts. That same year (1882), out in Elkhart, Indiana, John F. Funk was instigating the organization of a "Mennonite Evangelizing Committee." Aware that it would be criticized as an imitation of "worldly" denominations' activities, its members at first announced only the aim of collecting offerings to help ministers visiting "scattered members of churches." But within a few months the purpose was broadened: "to preach the Gospel where our church and doctrines are not known."[82]

Simply to follow with preaching those who drifted out of the home community would have been mission work enough to tax the capacities of the Eastern and Franconia Conferences. Here the Eastern Conference was conscientious. During the 1880s they held services in Brooklyn, Philadelphia, and Delaware, as well as in more local communities like Springtown, Ridge Valley, Chalfont, Souderton, and Harleysville. Of the latter, only Souderton would take root. The Franconia Conference too had members in Norristown and Philadelphia, where employment was to be had, but showed little apparent interest as yet, in forming congregations in such surroundings. Sometimes they met in a Dunker chapel in Norristown. Occasionally Preacher Jacob Loux of Plains, whose son Hiram was becoming a well-known physician but not a Mennonite, preached in the Reformed congregation growing in the industry-based town of Lansdale. Here, some gossiped, Loux could preach to former Old Mennonites, such as Andrew C. Godshall, whose modern roller mills were making him rich.[83]

Keeping in touch with marginal members, whether living at the edges of the conference area, or in frontier settlements a thousand miles west, was a matter of conscience for the Old Mennonites. Observers in a later century might fail to observe behind the apparent informality of this "family"-type activity a deeply serious intention. Without being overtly religious, it was a form of maintaining the fellowship. Narrow as it often became, the old Mennonite sense of "our people" produced journeys of visits that had a pastoral effect on many homes. A significant number of Franconia Conference preachers took the trains and "Mennonited their way" from Pennsylvania to Kansas, Nebraska, and South Dakota (even Manitoba) and back before 1890. Hundreds of letters were written, intertwining social and spiritual themes. When Jacob Mensch of Skippack made up his mind to take a western trip, editor John Funk, who had lost nothing of the feel for old-fashioned writing, laid down for him a detailed itinerary. In addition to specific commentary on former easterners now living in other states, Funk mentioned "Russian Mennonites" known in the East, and even suggested that Mensch stop in at a Hutterite colony.[84] When Funk was in his eastern home community for a visit and "Russian Mennonite immigration" business in the summer of 1877, he recorded in his diary more than sixty-five individual visits among Mennonite homes in less than three weeks.[85] It was an unsophisticated, unstructured, but fundamentally important way of nurturing the sense of peoplehood, which for Mennonites had become a means of grace. Doubtless Funk was also interested in getting contributions and subscriptions to his *Herald*. Ranging from Doylestown to Coventry, he did not miss the rather weak Mennonite community at Worcester. Here he visited a daughter of John Metz, Catherine, who had been "confined to her bed for over 20 years—pale as a shadow." The busy editor, bringing into the sickroom the aura of the larger peoplehood, prayed and sang with Catherine.[86] He also went to Norristown, where he visited with storekeeper David Funk.

The Eastern Conference characteristically took a more structured approach to such needs. It had a Home Missions Committee, and continued to commission one or two ministers to make a *Rund Reise*, a definite itinerary among the conference congregations, and bring back a report to the next session. New York City was discussed as a possible location for a new congregation. From the Springfield congregation Owen Schimmel and his brilliant young nephew, Joseph Taylor (originally Schneider) had gone to New York for business and educational reasons, respectively. As a lonely student, Joseph dropped in at "The Church of the Strangers," where he was warmly welcomed by the Reverend Mr. Deems. Both Taylor and Schimmel joined this church, though Taylor also frequently wrote to and visited the Mennonites of the Eastern Conference back home. Later Taylor received a "Doctor of Pedagogy" degree from New York University, and became an executive in the public school system of the city. He named a son for the pastor whose welcome had charmed him into his adopted church, and Deems Taylor eventually became a nationally known music critic.[87]

Also going to New York in these years (1881-1887), under other auspices, were no less than six children of former Deacon John Funk of the Hereford New Mennonites.[88] Influenced by their "Evangelical" friends, they got into city mission and training work. Even Albert, pastor of the First

Philadelphia Church until 1881, brought his new wife along to New York in 1885, having surprised the Eastern Conference by writing them that he had "united with the membership of another denomination." The conference noted this "with regret and sorrow," finding in his letter "no substantial . . . reason for the step he has taken. . . ."[89] It had been under the youthful Funk's leadership as both minister and bishop that the First Mennonite Church of Philadelphia had built on Diamond Street a rather large brick church, and dedicated it a few months before his resignation. Funk had gone through the Eastern Conference congregations, and raised over $1,000, but the project had cost at least $9,000, and there remained the discouraging debt of $5,000. Though the membership had grown to over 100, attendance was "very small," with "a great part of the membership . . . scattered."[90] After Funk's sudden resignation, which had raised questions both in the *Friedensbote* and at conference, he had gone to help his schoolmate Samuel Haury for a year among the Indians of Oklahoma.

Moses Gottshall of Schwenksville, now in his late sixties, was reappointed as bishop of the troubled Philadelphia congregation. The Perkiomen Railroad provided convenient connection. But when the city congregation cast eyes on Moses' handsome young assistant preacher, Nathaniel Grubb, Moses was unhappy. Forty-two members had been baptized in his congregation in the past two years, as Grubb, the vigorous founder and editor of the town's newspaper, had been coming into his own as a leader. He had been helping to fill the pulpits at the "Herstein," Bertolet and Skippackville outposts. He was of such caliber that the Eastern Conference was about to elect him as their thirty-three-year-old chairman, in place of the respected A. B. Shelly. There was another promising son of Moses Gottshall coming on—Willie—but he was a mere seventeen years old. It had been in editor Grubb's printing shop that Willie had not been able to resist "a desire to turn the cylinder," which then caught and badly mangled his left hand.[91]

In spite of his senior pastor's reservations, Grubb decided to give the Philadelphia work a try. He cautiously leased his *Item* to a friend for a year. Finding only twenty-five to thirty Philadelphia Mennonites attending services in their stately but debt-ridden building, he declined to promise to stay permanently. But as he got into the work, preaching impressively in both German and English, and also on Sunday afternoons at the nearly helpless Germantown meeting, he seemed to come into his own element. Here the Mennonites had someone who could take on and enjoy the more complicated urban life. Tall, dignified, and wearing a fashionable beard, he made an imposing figure. Almost from the moment of his coming, the congregation began to grow. After some years it would become usual to take in as high as thirty and forty members a year, as Mennonites, particularly from the "upper" areas of Bucks County, streamed into the city and got involved in a broad spectrum of commerce. Sometimes there were more transferrals from other denominations than baptisms of Mennonite "ethnics." Quick to print a program or brochure, or organize a new activity, N. B. Grubb would invite visitors of other denominations to communion, and gather hundreds of newly arriving Mennonites into a congregation that need envy no Baptist or Presbyterian neighbors their style. Within a year and a half of his coming he would be ordained bishop of the congregation, his mentor Mose Gottshall preaching at the service in German, and A. B. Shelly giving the charge in English.[92] Living near the church was aging John Oberholtzer, separated from his wife, but still active as an elder statesman in the conference and congregation.

The Eastern Conference had taken a new step in regard to leadership in 1881, when the Upper Milford congregation, its more "evangelical" members having left for their own fellowship, called in a pastor from outside the community. It would be seventy years before this would begin to occur in the Franconia Conference. Carl Heinrich Anton van der Smissen, thirty-year-old son of the former German teacher at Wadsworth, had studied at the universities of Basel and Tübingen, and thus was a unique phenomenon among his Eastern Conference colleagues. New developments occurred at Upper Milford during his decade-long pastorate. A Ladies' Aid Society appeared during the very first year (soon Philadelphia, Deep Run, and West Swamp each got one too). More importantly, the new pastor shortly began the practice of dedicating infants (observed also in the Philadelphia church). He even brought to conference the disturbing report that his Upper Milford congregation had voted unanimously not to require baptism of a new member who had been baptized as an infant. Other "exceptions" to the constitution, similar to this, stated their petition for approval, had already occurred, and "no harm came of it." The conference replied that it could not "with a clear conscience grant the petition," lest there be "disquieting results" among members who did not have the same "convictions." Nevertheless, "the present case" was left to the "conscience of the Upper Milford congregation."[93] Shortly thereafter, in 1885, Pastor Van der Smissen was asked to preach also for the Hereford congregation, which had been wracked with dissension in recent years. He consented, but there was a strong party supporting the other pastor, Abraham Gottshall, and as van der Smissen prepared to leave home one morning for Hereford, he found his front carriage-wheels missing. Not to be stopped, he rode down across the Hosensack hills to Hereford on horseback, causing considerable comment. The wheels were found widely separated.[94] At Hereford (also called Bally and Churchville), he preached and taught in both German and English. Here, in 1887, van der Smissen introduced among the young people the first Mennonite chapter of the Christian Endeavor Society, strongly favored by miller James B. Funk.[95]

Another significant addition to the ministerial leadership of the Eastern Conference occurred in October 1883, when the Deep Run fellowship, still pastored by Bishop Jacob S. Moyer of Springfield, finally found among its own ranks an "educated" but warmhearted leader—Allen Myers Fretz. Having attended Wadsworth Seminary, as well as an institute in Bucks County, Fretz had been teaching public school and serving as the congregation's Sunday school superintendent since the age of nineteen. Soon after the death of his wife and infant son in childbirth, he had run unsuccessfully for the state legislature. Not quite thirty, the lonely widower was away on a trip to the Midwest and Ontario (where he found another wife), when his Deep Run congregation took nominations for a new minister. All but two of forty-seven were for Allen Fretz. On Saturday, October 13, 1883, old Bishop Moses Gottshall ordained him without casting lots.[96] For the next fifty-seven years he would be a pastor at Deep Run and a series of supplementary charges, one of the main leaders of the Eastern Conference.

Bishop Gottshall, elderly but still vigorous in the pulpit, was now (1884) forced to find a replacement for his departed assistant N. B. Grubb. Both of the candidates selected for the lot by his Schwenksville congregation were his own sons: nineteen-year-old William and thirty-one-year old Moses, Jr. The lot fell on William, who was later to claim that he was the last minister to be so chosen in the Eastern Conference.[97] It would be another eighty years before the Franconia Conference would abandon this method. Two weeks after this talked-about ordination at Schwenksville, when the Old Mennonite congregation at Franconia cast lots for a deacon among a class of thirteen men, three of them carried the same name, Abraham Moyer.[98]

Now past seventy, balding, and with a sunken mouth suggesting the loss of teeth, Mose Gotshall nevertheless delivered his most notable sermon of all in May 1885, at the largest funeral ever seen in Lower Salford.[99] Eighty-one-year-old widower Michael Alderfer, wealthiest man in the community, bank president, owner of properties in Norristown and elsewhere, benefactor, and the oldest member of "Gottshall's" congregation, had been found hanging from a halter in his son's new wagon shed. Rumor had it that Michael had been a troubled man, and had made the strange statement that anyone taking his own life ought to be buried in a manure pile. His dealings as a substitute-broker in the Civil War were remembered. He had been sickly for several years, the more compassionate recalled; depressed and "much plagued with sleeplessness," he had, at the doctor's advice, taken to morphine. The local newspapers recounted his reputation for generosity in helping young entrepreneurs get a start. Among people gossiping in the Souderton bank, the liberal opinion was that "no one woud hang himself who was in his right mind," whereas a Lower Salford Mennonite "held that no Christian could commit suicide."

On the day of the funeral, N. B. Grubb came up from Philadelphia to assist with the customary preliminary service at the house of mourning. From Freeland came ex-minister Henry A. Hunsicker, nephew of the deceased. At the nearby Salford Mennonite meetinghouse, beside which four generations of Alderfers had been buried, a crowd of well over a thousand people pressed hard on the pallbearers, as they approached the door with the casket. Recently the Franconia Conference had ruled that at funerals the corpse should not be taken into the meetinghouse. Since many non-church-members attended funerals, they became occasions for frequent infractions of Mennonite standards, and thus conference continued to discuss behavior at them. But this was a rainy day, and as the pallbearers hesitated, someone in the crowd called out, "In with him!" The casket was then placed in front of the long pulpit, in which were seated both Bishop Gottshall and his twenty-year-old son, William, along with a Brethren preacher and a Schwenkfelder preacher.

Mose Gottshall's voice rose to its familiar high pitch as he launched into a lengthy and unforgettable tirade. Outside, waiting to use the meetinghouse for their own service, waited the family of a drunkard who had just been killed on a nearby railroad. Slamming his spectacles down on the "predigerstuhl," Mose Gottshall addressed the casket in front of him rhetorically. "Mike, Mike, Mike!" he called out to his old friend, "*Was husht du gedu?* What have you done? Thirty-two times I handed you the communion! God didn't do this! You didn't do it! The devil did it! And out there lies another man [in the same condition] ready to be buried!" On and on he preached, angering some in the audience by his severity. But there was general expectation that preachers would call suicide a sin. Conservatives were not pleased to hear a preacher say, "We hope the Lord will be gracious." And from time to time, of course, suicide would occur, as in 1889, when sixty-three-year-old farmer John Landis of Franconia hanged himself in the woods. Unlike Michael Alderfer, John had been an Old Mennonite, and his melancholia seemed linked with his overstress on humility. Constantly admonishing against the onslaught of pride, he had walked around for some time with drooping head.[100]

Now Mose Gottshall looked for assistance in his bishop role. Once

The eloquent Bishop Moses
Hunsberger Gottschall (1815-
1888), ordained for "Gottschalls" congregation (Eden,
at Schwenksville) in 1847, five
weeks after the founding of
the "East Pennsylvania Mennonite Conference." He was
the son of Deacon William
and Hannah Gottschall. (N.
B. Grubb, *A Genealogical
History of the Gottshall
Family*)

again the lot was to be cast, but between which two candidates? Among
those nominated were Mose's brother Abraham, the cantankerous minister
at Hereford, and Solomon Ott, faithful minister at the small, isolated
Bowmansville congregation. Most suitable of all, doubtless, was the thirty-
three-year-old Allen Fretz of Deep Run; and he, with the twenty-one-year-
old William Gottshall, were the two left in the lot. On November 24, 1886,
in the Schwenksville meetinghouse, A. B. Shelly preached a sermon, and
seventy-seven-year-old John Oberholtzer led in "a fervent prayer." Then
William Gottshall and Allen Fretz each picked up a book containing a slip
of paper. The one in William's contained the word, "Bishop." Father
Oberholtzer then laid hands on the youthful bishop and kissed him.[101] Allen
Fretz was left to carry his thoughts back to Deep Run (though six years
later, the use of the lot having ceased, he too would be ordained bishop).
Young William Gottshall, now Allen Fretz's bishop, went on to study at the
seminary at the nearby Ursinus College (a Reformed school that had been
founded in the original Freeland Seminary facilities). He would serve for
many years, both at Schwenksville and other congregations, as a more
polished, if slightly less memorable version of his sonorous preacher-father.

Moses Gottshall's last sermon was at the fall communion at Deep Run two years later (1888), where A. M. Fretz had his hands full with a Temperance-controversy in the congregation. A subgroup was calling for the use of grapejuice instead of wine at the Lord's supper. This would become an issue among Old Mennonites thirty years later. A. M. Fretz's congregation was soon to lose about forty members over this problem, though some would return.[102] Preaching to the divided congregation with his old vigor, Moses may have overextended himself, for he was stricken shortly afterward. He died later that week, having been the foremost preacher in the Eastern District for forty-one years. No longer would audiences watch him mopping his brow with a handkerchief, then placing the handkerchief in his Bible rather than his pocket, because he would shortly need it again. No longer would a certain old man in the audience need to get his own handkerchief out as soon as Moses rose to preach, in view of the certainty that he would be wiping his eyes before long. At the funeral John Oberholtzer, one of twenty-seven ministers present, "melted all hearts . . . by indulging in a flood of personal reminiscences, revealing the David and Jonathan friendship that had existed between them so long."[103]

It was with diverging assumptions that the two conferences worked at the task of maintaining a right fellowship. The emphasis in the Eastern Conference was on awakening the members to activity, rather than on discipline. Mention of public confession ceases in the West Swamp records around 1881, although the *Umfrage* (counsel meeting) continued to be held before communion.[104] A few years earlier, publisher John G. Stauffer, longtime associate of Pastors Oberholtzer and Shelly, had stopped going to communion, being apparently unsatisfied with what he perceived as a drift from strict standards of nonresistance. Though he kept a friendly demeanor in his relations with Oberholtzer and Shelly, they stayed clear of each other on spiritual topics, and Stauffer never returned to the Swamp congregation.[105]

One way in which the Eastern Conference strengthened its fellowship, in the mid-eighties, was by inaugurating a periodic meeting for ministers, at which pastoral topics of theology, homiletics, or church administration would be discussed. Another significant interlinking occurred when three of the leading pastors—N. B. Grubb, A. B. Shelly, and Allen M. Fretz—gained the backing of the conference for a new monthly periodical in English. Its name was succinct and forthright: *The Mennonite*, an indication that these leaders considered their specific heritage important. Aimed at the younger and more progressive element, but intended to draw all readers into this category, the magazine replaced the "Eastern Depart-

ment," a section in the German *Bundesbote* which had been specially
edited by A. B. Shelly. Now marriages and deaths were reported in English;
summaries of talks at conference, Sunday school conventions, and mission
festivals appeared; and the manifold activities of the advancing congregations of N. B. Grubb and C. H. A. van der Smissen were spread on the
pages of the new magazine.

It was in drawing people into involvement with such activity that A. B.
Shelly's hopes for revival lay. He himself traveled persistently to the West in
his offices of chairman of the General Conference and secretary of its
Mission Board. On one occasion he officiated, "in the presence of a great
multitude," at the cornerstone-laying of an impressive stone building for a
new Mennonite college in Kansas—Bethel.[106] Half a year earlier he had
presided over a meeting of the General Conference at his own West
Swamp. From thirty-five congregations across the country had come both
"Russian" and "German" Mennonites, who had fanned out, after the
sessions, to preach in various Eastern Conference congregations, and enjoy
"the romantic hilly landscape" so different from their prairies.[107] But as
Chairman Shelly, through such wide contacts, and through his reading of
literature from other denominations, learned of increasing mission activity,
he was moved to sadness when he compared the involvement of his own
Mennonite family. Observing "conditions . . . so little changed," with "so
little effort . . . made to keep and cherish our teaching and fellowship," he
felt "deep . . . regret and sorrow. . . ." When, he wondered in 1886, would
Mennonites "demonstrate a greater measure of activity in building up the
Kingdom of God"?[108]

N. B. Grubb, on the other hand, stressed the positive change he saw
coming "since the Missionary spirit" had been "revived" among Mennonites in the early 1880s. He was like John Oberholtzer in his tendency to
try to inspire loyalty by holding in front of his people vistas of progress.
Another writer in *The Mennonite* insisted that "our church is no more a dying church, but one that awakens from a deadly slumber and resolves to
take its place in the ranks. . . . Our principles and the distinctive features of
our denomination are too little known, but will inspire . . . as soon as our
. . . members . . . fully understand them, all with a zeal like that of our
fathers. . . ."[109]

In the Franconia Conference the emphasis, in this era of the growth of
railroad villages into towns, was on fighting off worldliness. The witness
consisted in keeping a distinct peoplehood. At session after session the topic
of fashion was discussed, sometimes in a tone of mild despair. "Pride rules
everywhere," was the feeling.[110] Even Old Mennonite women were wearing bustles, ruffles, lace and hats, and many had their "caps" on only in

Susanna Fretz Funk (1802-1890), capable spinster in her youth and mother of John Fretz Funk. (John F. Funk Collection, Archives of the Mennonite Church)

church services, placing them in "cap-boxes" in the "*Küch*" (anteroom) before going home. At Vincent and Hereford, in Bishop Andrew Mack's district, women were received into membership "with their hats and without coverings" (the term "covering" appeared later in the discussion). The issues with men were hair—beards and mustaches—and vehicles. For three decades the conference would struggle to ward off what it felt was a threatening loss of identity and a loosening of the covenantal bond, until finally, a decade into the 20th century, resolutions on clothing would be made a test of membership, and the tide of "worldliness" would actually be checked, and even reversed.[111] Wearisome and forbidding as these discussions would appear in retrospect, they were evidence of a deep caring. They represented an attempt, frequently unlovely in tone, to "maintain the right fellowship." From John Oberholtzer's point of view, it was such a "harsh" holding of the line on merely "external matters," that drove many of the most forward-looking people out of the fellowship. But had no love been contained in the center, this fellowship would have disintegrated.

As always, there was difficult "housekeeping" to do, such as the silencing of Preacher Abraham Young at the Old Mennonite Swamp congregation, for ill-advised behavior (the Eastern Conference similarly found that Enos Loux had lost the confidence of his congregation). Young unrepentantly challenged the bishops to find a proper replacement,[112] and this too brought difficulty. When, after a five-year interval, the lot was cast again, the man it fell on proved unwilling to accept his office. The shocked fifty-one-year-old Enos Beidler, remembered the community, went out into the woods, and sat on a stump to grieve over his situation. His claim was that his name had not really belonged in the lot, since it had been submitted, he understood, by a somewhat retarded woman in the congregation. Perhaps he had felt that the Lord would not allow the lot to fall on him. In any case, he steadfastly refused to function as minister, though this cost him the sharp disapproval of the congregation. He was considered a man of some teaching ability. When three of his grown children died of disease in a short time, he was especially hurt that some people interpreted this as divine punishment for his refusal.[113] But he always maintained that his ordination had been a mistake. After the conference had vainly sent two deacons to try to persuade him to relent, the congregation waited over three decades before ordaining another minister. The fact that it could survive at all in such circumstances was an indication that progressive leadership was not the only factor in the health of a Mennonite congregation.

The Blooming Glen congregation (formerly called "Perkasie") went through a seven-year controversy (1886-1893) that once again saw Mennonites going to court. Deacon David Fretz felt that his brother had been unfairly treated in a disagreement over a right-of-way through land next to the meetinghouse property. The trustees, in the process of erecting extra horse sheds, had resorted to stretching a chain across the disputed path. Unfortunately, that chain rattled for years, as meetings were held. Deacon Fretz traveled to take his case to other bishops in the conference, and conference sessions repeatedly heard accounts of the simmering dispute. Once again, as at Boyertown a few years earlier, the quarrel was taken to the Pennsylvania Supreme Court, and once again the trustees had to "make an acknowledgment," for letting the matter go on in the courts. When the silenced Deacon Fretz, frustrated because conference would no longer hear his complaints, actually sued Bishop Samuel Gross, he was excommunicated, and before long joined the Eastern Conference Mennonites. Such a move on his part tended to confirm the opinions of the Old Mennonites regarding the New. Both Fretz and the Blooming Glen trustees, convinced of the rightness of their positions, kept detailed notebook accounts of the controversy.[114]

It was in these 1880s, after the national centennial and the bicentennial of Germantown had borne their fruit, that a new interest in history affected even the Mennonites. It was not an overwhelming or popular impulse, but it appeared at many levels simultaneously. Some of it began in the European Mennonite community. One of the first American persons it struck was John G. Stauffer, whose first major publication after taking over the printing business in Milford Square in 1871 had been a biography of Menno Simons by a German Mennonite minister, Berend Roosen of Hamburg. A year later Stauffer had named his only son "Berend." Increasingly dissatisfied with the direction of his West Swamp congregation, the devout printer had established himself in Quakertown. At the age of forty-eight, with his Sunday school paper, the *Himmelsmanna*, doing nicely, he was fired with enthusiasm by another European book. It was written, he announced to his Mennonite readership, by "an old grandmother [Anna Brons] and member of the Taufgesinnten at Emden in Holland [*sic*]." This warmhearted author, who had written encouragingly to the publishers at Milford Square two decades earlier, had now followed another German historian, Dr. Ludwig Keller, in an effort to recapture the spiritual vision of the original Anabaptists. Her book, the first German overview of all European Mennonite history, was entitled *Ursprung, Entwicklung und Schicksale der Taufgesinnten oder Mennoniten* (Origin, Development and Destiny of the Anabaptists or Mennonites).

This access to the heritage, thought J. G. Stauffer, was just what had "long been needed" by the American Mennonite fellowship. Who could deny, two centuries after Germantown had been founded, "that this fellowship has departed, in many respects, from the *ground of our salvation in Christ*, and the goal, *Jesus Christ* too much lost to our sight?" "*Grace* and *duty*, or faith and works, must not be separated; however, not works but Jesus Christ is the scale in which every denomination will be weighed." It seemed to Stauffer that one reason why "so many" were "indifferent" to the "religion of their fathers" was their ignorance of its derivation. What did Mennonite young people "know about the origin and development of their fellowship? Little or nothing!"[115] In response to this need Stauffer would help to make the new history book available. He sent out sample reprints of parts of it, asking for subscriptions. The local response was disappointing. Only "here and there was an individual willing to contribute a few cents to support such an undertaking; it even seemed that many were ashamed of the history of their fellowship...." Yet from "the West" came some encouraging letters asking that the Brons book indeed be published on a subscription basis, in German.

Stauffer decided to issue it in a sixteen-page pamphlet-sequence, under the title, *Die Kirche Unterm Kreuz* (The Church Under the Cross), with a subtitle, *Botschafter des Heils in Christo* (Messenger of Salvation in Christ), to show that the purpose was not "merely historical." The former title was a rare testimony from outside the Old Mennonite fellowship to the original Anabaptist concept of the "suffering church." Before long the series had achieved the surprising circulation of 2000, nearly three times that of the old *Volksblatt*, and even the Franconia Conference took favorable notice of its nonresistant orientation. Such a publication, they observed, could legitimately be considered a witness to the world.[116] After some issues Stauffer corrected the title to *Gemeinde* (Fellowship) rather than *Kirche* (Church) *Unterm Kreuz*, showing a more precise sympathy with the Anabaptist view. But the response from A. B. Shelly, who was just then helping to found the English periodical *The Mennonite*, was cool. The West Swamp congregation, wrote Stauffer to John F. Funk, supported his magazine "less than the other congregations." "It seems to irritate them when someone offers them my paper...."[117] After the Brons material was used up, Stauffer gave the periodical still another name, *Zeichen Dieser Zeit* (Signs of These Times), and then seemed to move away from interest in maintaining a particularly Mennonite heritage toward a more conventional pietism.[118] Eventually he joined the Souderton Old Mennonite congregation.

John Oberholtzer, too, was writing history in 1884. He produced a carefully written manuscript of seventy-three pages entitled "Licht Über Die Mennoniten Trennungs-Geschichte und Ihrer Folgen in Ostpennsylvanien in 1847" (Light on the History of the Mennonite Separation and Its Results in East Pennsylvania in 1847). It was a response to the Pennsylvania Supreme Court decision on the Boyertown meetinghouse case, which had been a disappointment to the Eastern Conference. Had the court seen the facts in their true light, wrote Oberholtzer, particularly respecting the basic intention of Menno Simons, and the spurious "right" of the Franconia Conference to establish a human law and expel members on the basis of it—the decision would have been reversed. It was simply false, and very injurious, wrote the seventy-seven-year-old retired leader, for the Old Mennonites to continue referring to the New as not being real Mennonites. For whatever reason, this lengthy manuscript was never completed, but broke off shortly after the story of the division had been taken up to the founding of the General Conference in 1860.[119] Surely, the pathos of this old man's feelings has deserved a closer look than the fellowship he founded has felt motivated to give.

In Franconia Township, twenty-one-year-old, not yet married John Derstine Souder was stirred by the sight of an old graveyard, moldering into oblivion near the Souder homestead. He sought out old neighbors both on farms and in the bustling mills of little Souderton, to gather material for a 102-page *History of Franconia Township,* which appeared first in the new *Weekly News* of Harleysville in 1886.[120] As he continued on what would be a lifelong quest for the story of his local Mennonite past, Souder was sobered by the fact that the largest Mennonite congregation in the region, Franconia, though having over 500 members, had almost no records for a historian to consult. After a half-century of collecting information, Souder would see his materials for a history of the Franconia Conference gathered effectively into a book he himself lacked the education to write.

A year or two later a Methodist pastor of West Milford, New Jersey, Abraham J. Fretz, went to work in earnest on a genealogy of his Fretz ancestry. As a young man he had spent a year of study among his Mennonite cousins at Wadsworth, Ohio, after he had already been licensed by the Methodists. Shortly thereafter he had visited his Fretz relatives both in Ontario and Bucks County, and been seized with the desire to compile the record of this family. In 1888, at the age of nearly forty, he concluded that his genealogical research should have begun years earlier, "While there were yet living those of the third generation ... Already ... many ... were unable to trace their lineage farther than to their grandfather...."[121] (This was the case with John Oberholtzer, who began in his eighties to try to pull together some account of his own family line.) Pastor Fretz, whose father had been the first minister of the Deep Run New Mennonites, but had died as a Presbyterian in New Jersey, found his task of tabulating the Fretz family to be of "gigantic proportions," and finally produced a 607-page book. Consumed by a genealogical passion his wife did not share (though he researched her family too), this impecunious, bewhiskered schoolteacher-pastor went on to publish a book of his mother's (Kratz) family a year or two later, and at least thirteen more such genealogies over the following three decades. Other Mennonite families blessed by his efforts included those with the names of Beidler, Funk, Moyer, Nash, Oberholtzer, Rosenberger, Stover (Stauffer), Swartley, and Wismer. At least one book was nearly 900 pages long, and one family (Moyer) was treated in two volumes. Fretz's very last work, written in the closing year of his life (1912) in the Bedminster Township to which he had nostalgically returned, was a valuable little *Brief History of the Old and New Mennonite Churches at Deep Run.*[122] To a later observer of this herculean, Bucks County-centered genealogical quest, there is irony in its being pursued not by the Mennonites themselves, for whom it rendered an important historical service, but by a person who was longingly drawn, from outside, toward a sense of family the Mennonites took so much for granted that they themselves were leaving only the scantiest records of it for their children.

Promise of another Mennonite-related history—regrettably unfulfilled—appeared in the *Providence Independent* late in 1888, when a
controversy burst out at Freeland (later Collegeville) over a change in the
status of the "Trinity Christian Church" established there in 1854 by
Abraham Hunsicker. Freeland Seminary had become, under the auspices of
Reformed purchasers, Ursinus College, and now the Trinity congregation,
pastored by Abraham Hunsicker's jovial, long-bearded and well-fed son-in-
law Joseph Hendricks, was on the verge of joining the Reformed denomination as well. But this roused the ire of several members, most notably
Hendricks's older brother-in-law, ordained a Mennonite minister in 1850,
once principal of Freeland, and one of the original ministers of the Trinity
Church. At a public meeting called to discuss the proposed transfer of affiliation, Henry Hunsicker raised ill feelings with several "pointed and
severely personal remarks" directed at his brother-in-law. "I appear," Hunsicker read from a prepared paper,

> as the eldest living son of my father Abraham Hunsicker [died sixteen
> years earlier], who was his closest confident all through that arduous
> struggle that resulted in securing for us religious toleration, and
> freedom from the arbitrary demands of denominational prejudice and
> bigotry . . . to firmly protest against any change of established policy
> inaugurated during his and my connection with this church. To change
> the policy of the Church for mere convenience sake is a flagrant perver-
> sion of the intention of the founder, and a violation of the trust reposed
> in his successors, and wholly unworthy of that spirit of self-sacrificing
> devotion in its founder to a principle that surmounted the trammels of
> denominational hedges and dogmatical creeds.[123]

The real legacy of Abraham Hunsicker's church, felt the ex-principal
Henry, was its "deeply cherished principle" of nondenominationalism. It
seemed outrageous to Henry that after "the brighter light of the nineteenth
century had dispelled the murky mists of superstition and bigotry," the
church his father had founded was being pulled back toward "man-made
creeds and hide-bound dogmatic theories. . . ."

Calling for a "truce" in the proceedings, Hunsicker proposed to the
editor of the *Independent* "a series of brief letters" containing "some history governing the period of our church's existence—and a time slightly an-
terior to it." Letters from his pen did indeed ensue, but the promised history was not included. Twenty years later, as a retired Presbyterian businessman in Germantown, he would contribute a series of pleasant
"Sketches" of earlier days at Perkiomen Bridge,[124] but then too he would
not quite get to the story of the division he again promised. On Monday
evening, February 11, 1889, the church his father founded was transferred

into the local Reformed Classis, with two denominational representatives from Philadelphia "welcoming the members of the Trinity church," many of whom had had Mennonite parents, "to the bosom of the Reformed Church." Sitting in the "Trustees' corner" was aged Abraham Grater, ordained by Abraham Hunsicker forty years earlier at Skippack, and for years something of a local character around Freeland. As the Reformed preacher predicted a time when "the churches of all denominations would be united," the old "Parson" Grater remarked "above a whisper," "Why not begin now?"[125]

Perhaps the most significant historical project among the Mennonites in these years was a book in English written by a retired schoolteacher. Formerly from Salford, Daniel Kolb Cassel was one of four schoolteacher-brothers. Now he was deacon of the little Germantown congregation. In May 1887 he received a copyright for his *History of the Mennonites*, which, he promised, would contain "Over 500 pages," but came out to 450, with index. Among the leaders from whom he claimed endorsement were his brother-in-law, Bishop Josiah Clemmer of Franconia, Editor John Funk of Elkhart, Indiana, and a committee of members from Cassel's own Eastern Conference.[126] The book's contents were made possible by the recent appearance of research by Philadelphia lawyer Samuel Pennypacker (who for years was mistakenly convinced that the Pennypackers were originally Mennonites in Europe), and the German writers Ludwig Keller and Anna Brons. Cassel also solicited material from writers like A. B. Shelly, John G. Stauffer, and Henry Johnson. Somewhat of a miscellany, the book nevertheless deserves appreciation for its presentation of specific data unrecorded elsewhere, and for its status as the first published survey of Mennonite history in the United States. However, the major fact of the 1847 division among the east Pennsylvania Mennonites is virtually ignored. By 1890 Cassel had also produced an expanded German version of the book, with a section collected out of Frau Brons's writings as published by J. G. Stauffer.[127] Both volumes, published by the author, contained likenesses of Cassel as frontispieces, an indication that he had strayed from the old Mennonite conviction of humility.

And still other pens, including that of Pastor C. H. A. van der Smissen of Upper Milford, were scratching out Mennonite history in 1888. Van der Smissen's series (in German) on "The Origin of Our Fellowship" began to run in the *Bundesbote* in March. Five years later, after he had left Upper Milford for a church in Ohio, would appear his book, *Kurzgefasste Geschichte und Glaubenslehre der Altevangelische Taufgesinnten oder Mennoniten* (Concise History and Doctrine of the Old Evangelical Anabaptists or Mennonites).[128]

Soon after he had begun this project at Upper Milford, van der Smissen traveled out to Berne, Indiana, with N. B. Grubb, to work on a revision of the General Conference hymnal that would add musical notes, as well as some additional hymns. Grubb was president, and van der Smissen secretary of the committee, which was trying to bring East and West together in this new *Gesangbuch mit Noten*. In one tune-selecting session they sang melodies until midnight, as D. C. Neuenschwander led and Joel Welty played the organ.[129] Yet the language change was coming on so rapidly in the East that in a very few more years a new English hymnal would be necessary. In the Eastern Conference, Flatland held its first English service in March 1889, and among the Old Mennonites the transition could be seen coming when, in the summer of 1890, Deacon Jacob K. Overholt changed languages in his personal record of burials at Deep Run. Among the Hereford New Mennonites, there were Sunday school classes in both languages.

The appearance of all this history in a half decade just when the language question was acute suggests a crystallizing of feeling. The impact of modern machinery, railroads, and telegraph had made reflection on the past almost involuntary. Both youthful John Souder of Franconia and elderly Dunker historian James Heckler, of Lower Salford, mused at length over the stunning reordering of life in their community. No one of the new generation, they liked to say in the 1880s, would believe how previous generations had "plagued themselves." They saw old sociality and neighborliness as threatened by urbanization—and yet it was obvious that everybody in the small railroad towns still knew everybody else. Divorce became more frequent (though there had always been some, since Colonial days). N. B. Grubb, acting on his own authority as bishop married a divorced woman whose previous husband, one Abel S. Gehman, then sued her for bigamy.[130] Grubb's action showed that there was a continuing move away from conference authority toward congregational. In contrast, the whole Franconia Conference assembly two years later (May 1887) deliberated a divorce issue involving the Towamencin congregation. A man who had married a divorced woman was applying for membership. The conference decided that they might be admitted, "if his congregation votes unanimously in favor of receiving him."[131]

The Eastern Conference was accepting various features of modernization between thirty and forty years earlier than the Franconia Conference. On some sensitive points of visible identity and "worldliness" the interval would be longer. One of the most outstanding differences by the later 1880s was the preaching. All the major Eastern Conference congregations had "educated" preachers, whose manner contrasted sharply with the Old

Mennonite ones who chanted their sermons rather than using the tone of a lecture or oration. In Souderton, where the only meetinghouse was Old Mennonite, people of other denominations attended even when one of the old-fashioned preachers came, although a visiting preacher from Virginia who spoke in English brought unusual enjoyment. All the Franconia young fellows came in after the meetings had started, "in a long line, bound every one of them for the back bench." One bright young grandson of town-founder Henry Souder found the preaching of a Salford minister "very unfortunate." Christian Allebach struck him as sincere, Samuel Godshalk seemed more at home in English than German, and Andrew Mack was especially admired. Once, when no minister showed, Deacon Abraham Clemmer of Franconia "made a short speech" without standing up, and surprised the young observer by preaching "pretty well."[132]

It was just at this time that Mrs. Amanda Leber of Souderton, who was a member of N. B. Grubb's First Church in Philadelphia, "whispered" to her pastor that it would be nice to hear him preach in Souderton. Grubb obliged, in the rented hall of a hotel, in January 1887. From then on there were biweekly services, and when a new Reformed church was built (with N. B. Grubb speaking at the cornerstone-laying), the little New Mennonite congregation rented this facility,[133] even though the Old Mennonite meetinghouse often stood unused on the Sundays involved.

This was the year (1887) when a new turnpike was laid between Souderton and Dublin, and Souderton became a borough. On the newly elected school board were members of both the Old and New Mennonites. Young John D. Moyer, also the town assessor, had just been received as one of the first members of the new congregation meeting in the Reformed Church. Serving with him on the school board was Herman K. Gottshall, Sunday school superintendent of the Old Mennonites. Herman was watching the New Mennonite developments, as he perused the *Bundesbote,* with increasing dismay. Writing to the editor again, he called it "regrettable" that people "who want to own the name Mennonite" were departing from "what the Mennonites in America were years ago." Though he had agreed with the New Mennonite bank cashier that a visiting Mennonite from Lancaster County had preached "mostly old fogeyism" (John Landis had held "that the outer actions, garb &c are and ought to be a type of the inner person" and "laid much stress on the defenceless character of their sect"),[134] yet Herman was deeply disturbed about the recent General Conference innovations. He considered it his "duty," he informed the editor, "to write something" for the *Bundesbote.*[135]

Herman had probably been surprised and disappointed to see the recent Russian immigrants taking up with the new Mennonites. Now that they were building a college in Kansas, things had gone too far. Not only was such a school out of character with the tradition of the American Mennonites; money was going for it that was still owed to Eastern Mennonite lenders. This "important and unfortunate" development had offended Easterners, to whom Gottshall felt accountable. "I must observe," he now wrote, "that much that is new is in our country since the Russians have immigrated." Were these people not

> taken up in a friendly and brotherly manner? Was not everything done for them that could be asked? Did not they pay for the passage of their poor...? Now they take their own way, [and] ask little about the old ground of the defenceless Mennonites ... or one would not hear so much of unfamiliar things among the Mennonites.
>
> ... We are to be separated people. Are we not in great danger that we will no longer be recognized by the government as a nonresistant people, if we continually take up new things which are not in harmony with the order of our forefathers and the Gospel?
>
> ... Is it not believable that ... God ... would be more honored if you had sought first to do righteousness with your benefactors by paying the debts of your poor, [rather] than collecting and using money for such things as are not known among the Old Mennonites?
>
> ... There is more than $20,000 in travel money to be paid, beside what they borrowed. They let nothing be heard from them. Is that Mennonite or Gospel sense?

In these sharp words Herman was doubtless expressing the thoughts of his relatives in the Franconia Conference, although few of them might have expressed themselves so bluntly. In these very weeks a letter criticizing New Mennonites for going to court appeared anonymously in the Skippack *Neutralist*, and suggested that people who did such things were not really to be called Mennonite.[136]

Gottshall's letter brought an angry "Protest" from Bishop N. B. Grubb of Philadelphia, who, with A. B. Shelly, was especially sensitive to the Old Mennonite claim that the New Mennonites were weak on nonresistance. There was "not the least breath of the Christian spirit" in the letter, wrote Grubb, who recognized Herman Gottshall behind the initials with which it was signed, and accused him of cowardice for not signing his full name. "Judgmentalism, self-righteousness ... and orthodox Phariseeism" were all that was there. Whoever knew the author as well as Grubb did would "agree with me that such [could] only come from a spiteful disposition." Then Grubb paid back the Old Mennonites in kind, writing that where attitudes such as Herman's prevailed there was only "Dead formalism" and "heathen darkness."[137]

The constant questioning of the nonresistance of the New Mennonites got on their nerves. A. B. Shelly rejected the accusations "decisively" in the *Bundesbote,* even while his son-in-law's business associate, J. G. Stauffer, was supplying evidence to the contrary to young John Horsch, one of the editors of John Funk's *Herald of Truth.*[138] N. B. Grubb found a public forum to make a rather fashionable statement on the topic at a convention of the "Pennsylvania Peace Society" in Philadelphia. "A Mennonite," he orated, reading from a "handbook for church and school,"

> after having made a public vow, sealed by the rite of baptism, is under no conditions, whatever, allowed to bear arms nor render any military service.
>   This is the platform on which the Mennonite Church of this country stands today, 250,000 strong, and I rejoice that I am permitted to bear testimony in their behalf.[139]

In a quieter vein, a similar confession was made by Preacher Henry Johnson of Lower Skippack, as he contributed an article to Daniel K. Cassel's new book. "Generally we are called 'Johnson Mennonites,' " he commented; "we hold firmly to the nonresistant confession of faith, and the membership stands at 75 or 80."[140]

It was around this time that the only fraternal group the "Johnson Mennonites" had was being organized. It was the former "Leiter's" congregation, near Richfield, out in Juniata County. On May 24, 1883, one hundred twenty-five members, with a bishop, two ministers, and two deacons, withdrew from Lancaster Conference. In 1886 they erected their own building, and a special friendship continued with the distant Johnson Mennonites, involving reciprocal visits by the preachers. Jacob Mensch, the Skippack Old Mennonite minister who, it seems, corresponded with every other Old Mennonite community, wrote out to a ministerial friend in Juniata County to "try to prevail on Herman Snyder" and others not to "go after" the seceders from the Lancaster Conference.[141] After four decades of independence, the Richfield congregation would finally (1928) become a western outpost of the Eastern Conference.

As we take our leave of this quarter-century of Mennonite life after the Civil War, we are pursued by the question, what is the true history of a family of faith, even a divided Mennonite family? Should it not include a sample of the little topics of its Sunday afternoon conversations? Christian Landes, strongest man in Towamencin, single-handedly lifting up a horse-power (treadmill) with the horse standing on it, to set it at a better angle; Abraham Delp of Line Lexington being baptized on his deathbed at the age of fifty-five by the Herrites; seventy-five-year-old Preacher John Alle-

Abraham G. Ruth (1855-1919) and his third wife, Amelia Nice (1867-1948), members of the Line Lexington congregation, in front of their farmhouse near Newville in New Britain Township. A few years after this picture was taken, Abraham's brother "Joe" was ordained minister at Line Lexington. (J. Russell Bishop)

bach of Rockhill breaking a colt, and then outliving it; Henry Krupp of Franconia engaging twenty men for a barn-raising; Betsy Bean of Souderton serving the Old Mennonite demand for bonnets; preacher Jacob Moyer of Salford hearing a thrice-repeated voice outside his farmhouse window, a harbinger of his father's death at exactly the same time during the following night; super-conscientious Jonas Landis of Worcester, catching a torpid rabbit bare-handedly and giving it to a sick neighbor, only to be overcome with guilt when realizing he had done this out of hunting season, turning himself in to a justice of the peace and paying the fine, then going back again to pay another fine for his neighbor who, by accepting the rabbit, had also technically broken the law.[142]

Or we might look in on a pleasant visit taking place on the farm of "Father Joel Good" of the Vincent congregation, in the last summer of the decade. The guests were the family of New Mennonite Preacher N. B. Grubb of Philadelphia, out for a "Mid-Summer Ramble" in the country.[143] "How instructive and elevating" it was, wrote Grubb for his New Mennonite readers, "to be in company with such a goodly man of whom every one speaks so highly. He . . . has a kind word for all; free from bigotry and prejudice. . . ." Perhaps the conversation turned to the new meetinghouse the Vincent congregation had built the year before, with its steep roof like the one on the Phoenixville meetinghouse, now filled with Lutherans. It was gossiped that the reason the roof on the new Vincent meetinghouse was so fancily steep was that this would make it easier to sell to another denomination in case, as it was feared, the Mennonite congregation would die off.

Speaking of such a possibility, the visitors may have mentioned the name of Annie Stauffer. "Aunt Annie" was "a very spiritual woman," remembered an old man some eighty years later. One spring "they didn't open the Sunday School" at Vincent—the first congregation to have countenanced a Sunday school in the Franconia Conference. Annie, who was not afraid to confront even a minister or bishop with her convictions, then went around with "another sister . . . and saw pretty near every brother, and they said, why, they daresn't stop the Sunday School. And it started up [in 1890], and soon after that we had it all year round." Vincent's sister congregation, Coventry, had earlier been the larger, but there Sunday school was not accepted. Vincent's future did not look particularly bright; its bishop, Andrew Mack, could preach only in German, which often disappointed younger people who could not understand him. But he invited bishops from Lancaster who could preach in English at communion and baptisms. Then in about 1896 a spirit of revival caught on at Vincent, and the congregation solidified, while Coventry died. A later bishop at Vincent gave credit to Aunt Annie Stauffer. "If that woman wouldn't have been there," he mused, "and the Sunday School had stopped, the church might have been like at Coventry. Just standing there."[144]

Thus Annie Stauffer, like hundreds of her unrecorded sisters in both wings of the divided Mennonite family, played an indispensable role in maintaining the fellowship. Great are the ironies of male-written history, Mennonite as well as any other! And great are the ironies of the story of maintaining the right fellowship! What would the N. B. Grubbs and their hosts, the Joel Good family, have thought, could a voice from the future have entered their conversation there in the quiet Mennonite countryside, telling them that ninety years later Pastor Grubb's lively congregation in Philadelphia, after becoming the leading church in the Eastern Conference, would be reduced to a handful of members; that instead, the little congregation he had just begun in Souderton would be the largest; and that the quiet Vincent congregation, having found new life and outworn its tall-roofed meetinghouse, would build a new one, as a thriving 20th-century fellowship, on land next to the farm of Father Joel Good?

Chapter 13

Two Paths into a New Century
1891-1920

John Oberholtzer, ordained before the telegraph was invented, lived into the decade that discovered electrons. Though without a specific pastoral responsibility, and past his eightieth year, he still preached at least every two weeks, and kept a clear memory. Surrounded by younger Eastern Conference ministers with neatly trimmed beards, he had, noted a newspaper correspondent, "a clean shaven face" and a full head of "long grey hair." His hearing remained "as sharp as ever, and his eyesight good."[1] Somewhat weakened in his back and limbs, he nevertheless made annual visits to friends and relatives in Berks County, where he had been born. In 1890, residing at the home of his only living child, Anna Nase of Perkasie, he was pleased to receive a letter from his friend N. B. Grubb, asking for facts from his memory relating to the founding of the First Mennonite Church of Philadelphia a quarter century earlier. "I take it for granted," he wrote back in English, that "if our General Conference never would have been organized ... no Mennonite congregation ... might exist in the City of Philadelphia."[2]

It was in such reflection on how, through the efforts of "our Eastern Reform Conference," the local Mennonites had been roused "from their death-slumber," that the aged pioneer found his greatest satisfaction. He reviewed for his visitor his work with the constitution, the *Botschafter*, Sunday school, General Conference, the Wadsworth Institute, and his introduction of organ music at Swamp. Oberholtzer felt "especially gratified," recorded the correspondent, that he had been spared "to see the extent and the good work" of the General Conference mission societies. A. B. Shelly, his successor at Swamp, was secretary of the Committee for Foreign Missions. So different in manner, these two veteran ministers occasionally shared the pulpit, with Oberholtzer at least once causing the younger man

398

concern as he tilted back on his chair, eyes closed, while nevertheless following the sermon. The older leader, who smoked cigars as did most of the Old
Mennonite ministers, and in his aged loneliness was not particularly well
kept in dress, was not the favorite of the younger people, it would be
remembered. On the other hand, the conference itself asked him to preach
the "Conference Sermon" when the session was held at West Swamp in
May 1892, and passed a resolution honoring its eighty-three-year-old
founder with a vote of thanks to God for "these fifty years of grace." Two
years later "Dear old Brother" Oberholtzer gave some touching words of
encouragement at the conference.[3]

His personal life was touched with sadness. He signed an application
for a Civil War pension for his daughter-in-law Sarah on March 9, 1891, on
which she stated that she had last seen her husband, Davy, nearly twenty-
four years earlier[4] (yet several months later the Reading *Eagle* would say,
"He has . . . a son and a daughter"). Oberholtzer sometimes visited his
niece Susan Landis, near the Saucon meetinghouse, where, it would be
remembered, he would call for fire in the central room so that he would be
able to write.[5] One of his last efforts to have been preserved was his
manuscript entitled "Short History of the Oberholtzer Family" (in
German),[6] which he wanted to leave for his handful of "descendants."
Here, in referring to his deceased and present wives, the latter of which was
living separately in Philadelphia, he was pensive: "Both spouses had sickliness through unendingly much illness and sufferings together with manifold difficulties and woes that this family had to bear, here and there, for
the most part of more than 60 years." Reflecting on the character of his
Oberholtzer clan, which he characterized as "unassuming" and "generally
used to sitting below rather than above," he was led into observing that no
one can predict with certainty, on the basis of one's preference, how things
will turn out (presumably in a family). Many a person had experienced this,
in both the spiritual and the worldly realms, "with bitter disappointment."

When his daughter Anna died in 1893 (and was buried in the Lutheran cemetery at Sellersville), and his brother William also passed on in the
same year, there was concern in the conference as to how to keep the old
man without a family. Two houses in his name were both mortgaged for
their entire worth, and his widowed daughter-in-law had few means. He finally made a will at the age of eighty-five, designating N. B. Grubb and his
old printshop helper John G. Stauffer (who was not in sympathy with him)
as "agents."[7] Two years earlier the conference had appointed a committee
to provide for "such persons who cannot care for themselves," and now the
original pioneer had become one of them. While he was living with his
niece Susan Landis, sentiment was gathering that an old people's home

should be founded, but he died a year before this occurred.

Ten days before his passing there had been a ministers' meeting at the nearby Saucon meetinghouse. The old leader, who had missed the last conference, requested that the group come to see him. They had prayer and a hymn of parting. On the morning of February 16, 1895, his mind still alert, he read from the commonly used devotional book, Johan Arndt's *Wahres Christentum*, and remarked that it helped him to understand a certain Scripture better. Somewhat later, as he sat on a couch conversing with several callers, he called for a drink of water. Having received it with thanks, he laid his head on a pillow with the final words, "*Siehe, Ich sterbe*" (See, I'm dying). At the next session of conference, the assembled delegates took special note of this "peaceful passing" of one of their "founders," who had been for them "a wise counsellor." They thanked God for his "useful life," "his Christian character," and "his unwavering faith in Jesus Christ and his merits." His memory, wrote the secretary, would remain "a benediction."[8] N. B. Grubb then attempted to sell the real estate at auction, but it did not bring a price sufficient to cover outstanding notes.[9]

Our view of such happenings must be pieced together, regrettably, from odd newspaper clippings, a legal document here, or a family memory there. Rare indeed is our access, by the pen of a firsthand observer, to the original flavor of the scenes we are trying to recall. So perhaps we should not leave out of our story the description of a funeral in the Deep Run Old Mennonite congregation as preserved by a connoisseur of Pennsylvania Dutch culture.[10] In the last weeks of the year 1892 the Bedminster-Plumstead community had been stunned by an unsolved murder. Sam Detweiler had found the body of his uncle, farmer Jacob Detweiler, face down in a little tributary of the Deep Run flowing through his farm along Applebutter Road. Bruises on Jacob's head suggested foul play, and his missing purse seemed to prove it. He had been carrying money to a neighboring bank-messenger. Neighbors strongly suspected Jacob's son-in-law, and even Sam Detweiler who had found the body, but no evidence was ever confirmed (many years later the deed was privately confessed by Moses Landis, a neighbor's hired man). Curious people swarmed around the spot where the body had been found, and over three hundred teams converged on the farmhouse for the first part of the funeral. Among those attending was a future professor of English at the University of Pennsylvania, in whose memory the scene would remain sharply etched over thirty-five years later.

Knots of people stood "near the house, by the barn, and along the road," conversing "in low tones." Then the concourse made a long, slow procession, containing "everything from a market wagon to, literally, a one-horse shay," moving solemnly in the direction of the meetinghouse. Two hours were consumed in this process, though the distance covered was hardly more than five miles. It was a cold, gray day, with patches of snow on the frozen ground. A welcome smell of coffee boiling greeted the arriving mourners. "Great copper kettles" hung by chains from saplings laid across the lower limbs of oaks and hickories in the meetinghouse grove. The kettles were still boiling after the burial, with "coffee for all" to go with the "doughnuts and sandwiches and cakes" brought along by "many of the people." The academic observer (perhaps here in the role of a newspaper reporter) remembered the scene for its picturesqueness and atmosphere: the plain-dressed people with "bonnets and broad-brims" standing about in groups as the afternoon darkened; the bracing smell of coffee "mingled . . . with the friendly smell of horses"; the carefully blanketed animals filling and overflowing "the many sheds of the meetinghouse yard"; the reluctance of the people to disperse; the animation and "bustle and confusion and loud talking" when the gathering finally began to break up. It was, of course, not a usual kind of funeral.

"Father" John Oberholtzer could observe, in his last few years, a substantial outburst of "home missions" in the Eastern Conference. Souderton had been the first (after Philadelphia), and Oberholtzer attended his last conference session, and had the closing prayer, in the new chapel of the "Zion" congregation, built along the "Blooming Glen pike only about a square from the railroad depot." Of the twenty-six charter members, six came from the defunct "Branch" (Rockhill) congregation.[11] The choice of a special name, Zion, anticipated similar names (Eden, Bethany) in the next few years by other Eastern Conference congregations. The dedication of the chapel building brought an "immense audience" on Pentecost Sunday, May 21, 1893. Souderton was "full of visitors" from places like Hereford and Schwenksville. "About one hundred" came from Philadelphia alone, now by far the largest congregation in the conference, and the railroad dispatched a special train to take them home late in the evening. Their pastor, N. B. Grubb, "with great solemnity performed the solemn rite of consecration" (no one could match him at this kind of thing). All day on Pentecost Monday the services went on, with a missions festival capped by an inspiring sermon by Souderton's own Methodist missionary hero, H. G. (Appie) Appenzeller, eventually to become famous as a great mission organizer and martyr in Korea, and now home on his first furlough.[12]

This year 1893 was a time when local denominations in general were establishing missions in growing towns. The Methodists came to Telford, the Reformed organized their congregation in Souderton, and the Lutherans there were also holding services (before long storekeeper Jonas Landis, from a Mennonite home in Franconia, would donate land for a

Lutheran church). The Old Mennonites, with about seventy members, began to hold evening meetings in their Souderton meetinghouse. Before the year was out, the Home Missions Committee of the Eastern Conference had fostered the beginning of services in Allentown, Norristown, Pottstown, and Quakertown, a move that came a quarter century earlier than a similar one by the Franconia Conference. However, the core of those attending were less nonchurchgoers than Mennonites who had retired or gone into business in these towns. First in homes, then in rented halls, the meetings eventually attracted congregations in all but Norristown (where the Franconia Conference Mennonites would finally organize in 1919). Even at Schwenksville, where the meetinghouse had stood on a hill in the countryside, N. B. Grubb announced that the "new church shall be built in the heart of the rapidly growing town."[13] In Philadelphia, where N. B. Grubb's two advancing sons expected to be preachers, a mission was begun on February 9, 1894, that would become the "Second Mennonite Church." The earlier Second Church had disappeared soon after its beginning in the mid-1870s. It was said that N. B. Grubb wanted a place for his son Silas to preach. When a permanent chapel was built in 1899, there were pasture and rail fence across the street, but in a few years all would be built up.[14] Such a church was actually more than what would later be called a mission; it served a continually growing group of Mennonites moving to the city. By the end of the decade, when the membership of the First Church had passed 400, even the Franconia Conference would acknowledge that there

The family of N. B. Grubb (1850-1938), minister of the First Mennonite Church of Philadelphia, around 1900. L. to r.: William Henry Grubb, Wallace Bertolet Grubb, Catharine Roth (Mrs. Silas) Grubb, Salome Gottschall (Mrs. N. B.), Grubb, Nathaniel Bertolet Grubb, Silas Manasses Grubb. (The Schwenkfelder Library)

were "about forty Mennonites" (of its own group) living in Philadelphia.[15]

N. B. Grubb had a way with publicity. He would be remembered by some as "the big cheese." His dignified pictures appeared over and over in the papers, and he gladly supplied reporters with information about his expanding church. Those who had been "added by letter" to the membership, he stated in 1894, had come from no less than "eighteen different denominations, among them ... the Presbyterian, Baptist, United Brethren, Episcopal, Methodist, Lutheran, Reformed, Amish and Old Mennonite...."[16] He was a great enthusiast for Christian Endeavor Societies, becoming a national board member, attending conventions, and bringing back glowing accounts of their inspiration. He gave illustrated talks, dedicated churches, exchanged pulpits with other denominations, brought out a *Mennonite Yearbook and Almanac* (1895 ff.) containing good historical material, and served as president of the Eastern Conference and chairman of the Publication Board of the General Conference. He reported 1400 pastoral calls in one year (he was constantly citing statistics), wrote letters to his members at the end of the summer telling them he expected to see them in church, and managed to secure the body of one Jacob Kratz, who had died in "the Philadelphia almshouse," from the pickling vat before it could be used as a cadaver in a medical college. He had promised the fearful Kratz a regular burial, which then took place at Lower Skippack, and the body was pronounced as still "in a good condition and the face was easily recognized."[17]

The former editor of the Schwenksville *Item* "was methodical in all his endeavors," remarked a close friend. He used to say that he "was never late and never missed an appointment."[18] He was not a man to be brushed off or trifled with, and his enthusiasm for historical Mennonite teaching had not eradicated a certain combativeness. He once recognized a confidence man who had been "borrowing" several dollars from a series of helpful clergymen, and decided to make a citizen's arrest. A scuffle ensued, and the petty swindler, who had recently spent time in the state hospital, broke out of Grubb's grasp several times. The indignant minister pursued his quarry for five or six blocks in the vicinity of First Mennonite, "and the spectacle of two large, fine looking and well-dressed gentlemen who had been walking quietly along the street suddenly, as it appeared, getting into a fight caused no end of astonishment and attracted a great crowd of spectators."[19] A well-orchestrated campaign in the First Church, complete with printed flyers, placed the pastor among ten Philadelphia clergymen whose congregations had done the most shopping at Snellenburg & Co.'s department store, and he received thereby a free trip to Europe in the summer of 1900. He diligently sought out Mennonite churches on his tour. While he was away the congregation installed a new pipe organ, and played it for the first time at his welcome home.[20]

It was to Grubb that the Eastern Conference owed the location of its "Home for the Aged and Indigent" in his native Frederick Township. As a young fellow he had been one of the last six students of the failing "Frederick Institute," in the spring of 1868. Still standing tall and cupola-capped on the elevation above the Bertolet and Nice homesteads, it went up for sale when its Bertolet owner died. Grubb attended the auction, and found himself the high bidder at the price of $765. The executor of the estate refused to sell at this figure, but Grubb, who was on the recently appointed Eastern Conference committee to make provision for the aged, said he would stick by his bid. When the executor later said he would sell for $1150, a special session of conference was called (February 1896). Fourteen men met at the home of Benjamin Bertolet, just across the road from the building. They approved this bargain-purchase, and empowered Grubb to solicit the conference congregations. He was not hesitant to approach people. One of the very first contributions came from a man who owned a string of cigar-factories in the Perkiomen and North Penn railroad towns, Otto Eisenlohr of Philadelphia. Listening to Grubb describe the new project as they rode the train between Philadelphia and the Perkiomen Valley, the industrialist handed the pastor $15.00. From all over the conference began to come gifts in kind—apple butter from Swamp or cabbage from Deep Run—which inaugurated the durable tradition of an annual "Donation Day." Sarah Overholt of Philadelphia, her father-in-law John H. Oberholtzer now deceased, was engaged as temporary matron. (The first two guests were the elderly Joseph Schimmel of Deep Run and George Baringer of Flatland.) On the day of dedication, September 1, 1896, group after group of visitors "ascended the tower of the building to take in the grand view" of the surrounding Frederick farm and hill country. N. B. Grubb, as usual, gave the dedicatory address.[21]

It would be only two decades until the Franconia Conference too would have such a "Home"—in a more central location and with heavier financial backing. This interval would be shorter than the ones following some of the Eastern Conference's other new steps. And there was also occurring, in these 1890s, an old Mennonite mission trend similar to the one among the New Mennonites, but at the more distant midwestern center of Elkhart, Indiana. This had its ripple-effect on younger people back in the Franconia Conference, who could not yet have opportunities for service such as the Eastern Conference offered. At Elkhart, a general "Mennonite Evangelizing Board" emerged in 1892, then an independent "Chicago Home Mission" which the Board soon adopted, and a "Benevolent Organization" in 1894, which shortly merged with the Evangelizing Board and its committee on "Home and Foreign Relief" (1897). The latter was a response to famine in India, which stirred widespread compassion; at Hereford Andrew Mack's wife was drying apples for Indian relief. In 1898 members of the General Conference Foreign Mission Board met at Elkhart with their newly organized Old Mennonite counterparts to explore the possibility of working together. But the old Mennonite "people back home" were not ready to support such cooperation, and before long the country of India would see double and separate Mennonite organizations—and churches. Both the Eastern and Franconia conferences eventually sent personal representatives, though neither got involved immediately. The Eastern Con-

The former Frederick Institute of Frederick Township soon after it had been purchased by the Eastern District Conference in 1896 and converted into an old people's home. (The Schwenkfelder Library)

ference occasionally had a younger volunteer in the work among the
Arapahoes and Cheyennes in their missions in Oklahoma.

The new activity in Elkhart also produced, for the first time, an Old
Mennonite academy or "Institute" in 1894. There were calls among the
more scattered western churches for an Old Mennonite version of a General
Conference, which would offer support and unity to member conferences.
But although men like Preachers Jacob Mensch and Isaac Rickert (of
Doylestown), and Bishops Andrew Mack and Josiah Clemmer traveled out
west in traditional visiting-circuits, a majority of their people felt there was
more purity to be lost than strength to be gained in affiliating with a
"general" Mennonite organization. This put Andrew Mack, who saw the
value in such a joining, in a difficult spot, and elicited from him a
memorable speech. It occurred on November 11, 1897, at the Pike Old
Mennonite meetinghouse near Elida, Ohio. Fifteen "Old Mennonite" conferences were represented either officially or unofficially, as "the great
question" of whether or not there should be a General Conference was debated. Fervent support came from westerners, but "not a few" expressed
the more "hostile attitude of the large and far more populous districts of the
east." In anxiety lest there might be a church division, many seemed
"afraid to vote."

Andrew Mack arose, "at this critical moment," and made his long-
remembered "earnest address in German." In the words of an eye-witness,

> He made it clear to all that the attitude of the eastern conferences was
> not hostile to the General Conference movement as it applied to the
> west; that the passive attitude prevailed among them because there
> was no condition there that suggested a need for General Conference
> action. If the congregations in the west were in such circumstances that
> they needed a General Conference, he said, we are ready to let them
> have it, and no one need fear a division or separation in fellowship from
> us because you vote for something that you stand so much in need of.
> We know that you need it, and why not vote for it?[22]

These last sentences seemed to calm the meeting, which went into a session
of silent prayer without further speaking. The vote which followed was almost unanimous in favor of "a General Conference." Ironically, the Franconia Conference would never affiliate with the organization their German-
speaking bishop had helped to make possible (though in 1971, after the
General Conference had been replaced by the Mennonite General
Assembly, the Franconia Conference did participate).

The new generation was at home in English, but here and there, especially among the Old Mennonites, the German remained primary. When
Henry Krupp was ordained as the first deacon for the Old Mennonites at

Souderton in 1891, someone wrote him a long German poem, presenting a very serious view of the deacon's office.[23] In the Doylestown congregation was prolific poet William G. Gross, identical twin of Bishop Samuel Gross of the same congregation, and brother of home-doctor Sarah Lapp in Nebraska. As devout as any in the long line of pioneer Bishop Jacob Gross's descendants, farmer William rhymed extemporaneously, even when nearly delirious with smallpox. He had quite a few devotional poems printed in broadside, many only identified with the closing tag, "Fountainville, Pa." His manuscript book of poems, submitted after his death to the new publishing house at Scottdale, seems to have disappeared after a fire had occurred there. But among the pages of many a German family Bible between the Delaware and the Schuylkill would be found, for the next fifty or sixty years, his long "New Year's" or "Good Friday" hymns, written around the turn of the century.[24]

William's earlier admonition to teach the children German so that they would understand the preachers took on a different light when, in 1895, the lot fell on a thirty-three-year-old farmer at Deep Run—Jacob Rush—who could not preach in German. This provoked a crisis, since Jacob's grandfather, Preacher Isaac Meyer, was quite old, and in fact died several months after the ordination. There were also two other preachers in this large congregation. One, John Gross, was almost as old as Isaac Meyer had been, and so conservative that no Sunday school could be started. He wept as the young people insisted on singing an English hymn at the end of the services, and refused, it was said, to lean on the backrests that were added to the benches. The third preacher, John Leatherman, had been ordained a few years earlier at the age of forty-four, but he too "sang" his sermons in the old manner, always beginning with the same formulaic opening words: "*Viel geliebte, theure gekaufte Seele in Jesu Christi*" (Much beloved, dearly bought souls in Jesus Christ).[25] The newly ordained Jacob Rush had to come to the meetinghouse early on Sunday mornings to be taught German, first by his grandfather Meyer, and also by others.[26] Eventually he himself would be known as a real Deep Run conservative, albeit a witty one, and not afraid to object, even from the pulpit, to his congregation's gradual acceptance of foot washing.

Other new ordinations that were bringing in preachers capable of speaking in English were those of Abraham O. Histand at Doylestown (1896), Warren Bean at Skippack (1897), and Clayton Kolb at Coventry (1899). A number of their friends in the Franconia Conference were quite aware that there was an awakening at Elkhart. Young Abraham Leatherman of Plumstead wrote to John Funk and asked about educational possibilities for a Mennonite. Funk's reply showed a proper caution:

> M. S. Steiner belongs to the Old Mennonite Church and is a good solid member, and holds very closely to the doctrine. He is studying Bible doctrine, but not for the ministry, unless God should some time Call him to that work. You know in our church the ministers are chosen by lot, so a man cannot study for the ministry, but he can study to know the bible and when he knows the bible he will be able to preach if ever called to do so. Steiner . . . is in the theological department, because he can go there cheaper than in any other. Oberlin is for classical studies as well. . . .[27]

Later Leatherman also studied at Oberlin. And the neighboring Doylestown congregation had a young member interested in education: Hetty Kulp, daughter of marketman Isaac Kulp who had grown up at Deep Run, but was now impatient for a chance to do spiritual work. In a consultation with the bishop—probably the just-ordained Henry Rosenberger of the Blooming Glen congregation—it was suggested that it would probably be safest for Hetty to attend the only Mennonite school, at Elkhart, rather than a Quaker school closer to home. She took a year at Elkhart in about 1898-1899, probably the first woman in the Franconia Conference to have this kind of training.[28]

It was somewhat easier for young men. Warren Bean of Skippack had been at Ursinus. Yet no clear vision lay before bright young would-be ministers. It would have been a shame, almost, for a person in the Franconia Conference to admit that he wished for such a calling. Jacob D. Mininger of the Rockhill congregation, embarrassed and hurt by being farmed out to other families as a child while his father stayed in several mental hospitals, was "profoundly converted" in a Methodist camp meeting near Sellersville, went to the local high school, and determined to be a Christian worker, but definitely not a Mennonite.[29] Mahlon Gross of Doylestown, the son of an independent-thinking father, studied to be a teacher at Millersville, and was also converted at a Methodist evangelistic meeting. He married a Baptist girl, and actually found a role as Methodist preacher in New Jersey. His nonresistant heritage, however, remained on his conscience, and he would eventually return to the Doylestown Mennonite congregation and even be ordained there.[30]

The Gross family were strong advocates of "Temperance," and would finally see themselves vindicated by the switch to "unfermented wine" at communion at Doylestown. It was often a heated issue. Deacon William Moyer of the Deep Run New Mennonites would protest, almost in his dying words, that the doctor was to give him no medicinal liquor. "*Ich bin arg gehe brande*" (I am strongly against brandy), his family heard his whisper. The new Bishop Henry Rosenberger, on the other hand, kept the older attitude, and would be remembered by his nieces to have customarily offered

Hettie B. Kulp of the Doylestown congregation, as a student at the Elkhart, Indiana, Institute around 1898. On July 27, 1904, Hettie married Jacob Detweiler Mininger, and they moved from Philadelphia, where they had been doing mission work, to Marshallville, Ohio, where they superintended a Mennonite old people's home. (Paul M. Mininger)

a couple he had just married glasses of his wife's rose-petal wine.[31] Rosenberger, who had once been one of John F. Funk's pupils in Hilltown, was a liberal-hearted man. He preached effectively in a clear voice, and occasionally argued at conference against the strictness of the rules held by congregations west of Blooming Glen.

The spring 1894 session of this body heard about the liquor issue from a son of Preacher John Gross, but was not favorably inclined toward his urging that Mennonites should take the Temperance Pledge (Jacob Mensch, in his private German diary of Conference proceedings, spelled this, "Temberance pletch"). Those who took the pledge, and thus joined a temperance society, were "set back from the breaking of bread until they give up the pledge, then nothing will be required of them" (i.e., a confession). The old stress on a nonsubdivided covenant was evident in the conference thinking, as Jacob Mensch recorded it for himself:

> It seemed to the Council that in our baptismal covenant we make a pledge, and promise God no more to live for ourselves, and deny all Satan's things, and when we do this, we need to take up no other pledge or Society.[32]

The man who wrote these words was a person who could clearly hear voices from the past, while having difficulty listening to the current concerns of progressives, and getting along with his own son. He could take his wife, Mary, to Samuel Musselman, "the pow wow doctor," and have himself treated as well (for a donation of $4.00) with a clear conscience, but he was heartily worried about a group of applicants for baptism at Vincent who needed to be instructed about wearing "caps" in church services.[33] He traveled around in his Skippack district, collecting money for Mennonite families suffering from hard times in Nebraska and Manitoba (1895), and walked out of a social gathering when someone began playing an organ. Through it all he stayed in epistolary contact with the widespread North American Old Mennonite family, writing 939 letters to 187 different persons in the decade beginning in 1894.[34] He scrupulously saved the many hundreds of letters he received in return, thus providing for Mennonites all across the country a historical window on his era. He also kept an unofficial record of the Franconia Conference deliberations. Where else might his descendants learn that at the funeral of Preacher Jacob Funk of Vincent on June 22, 1894, four Mennonite preachers—Andrew Mack and John Ehst (Hereford), Henry Wismer (Skippack), and Henry Godshall (Plains)—had been pallbearers? Or that the Franconia Conference had offered the advice, at its next session, "that when a preacher dies the pallbearers should not be only preachers, as that is the custom among higher people"?[35]

It would take a strong inthrust of activism from midwestern visitors before the old Franconia fellowship would give its eager young people more latitude. In the Eastern Conference, by contrast, there was encouragement to study for service. A conference committee was working in 1895 (the year after which there were only annual, rather than twice-yearly sessions), on "a plan to aid young men preparing for the ministry." The conference also received "with gladness" an invitation from the Schwenkfelders to participate in the work of their recently acquired academy, the Perkiomen Seminary, at Pennsburg. N. B. Grubb became a board member. W. S. Gottshall had studied there earlier, as had Bishop Andrew Mack's son Noah. Old Mennonite Jacob N. Clemens had attended Brunner's Seminary at North Wales around the time of the Civil War, and his son Jacob C. Clemens attended the Sumneytown Academy as well as Perkiomen Seminary. Now there came to the latter institution a little wave of young success-bound Mennonites—a budding intelligentsia. Towamencin Old Mennonite Elias Kulp came in 1898, but many more of the influx were New Mennonites: Samuel M. Musselman and Elwood Shelly of Swamp, Andrew S. Bechtel of Boyertown, John W. Schantz of Macungie, Harvey Gottshall and Maxwell Kratz of the Schwenksville area, Florence Shelly, Herbert and Oswin Berky of Hereford. Perkiomen prided itself on being a "feeder" school for Princeton, and thus Musselman and Kratz also studied at the latter institution, as did Aaron Willauer, brought up in the Old Mennonite congregation at Salford. Others attended the West Chester state normal school: Alvin C. Alderfer of Harleysville, Seward Rosenberger of Swamp, Annie Funk of Hereford, Jacob Kirk Leatherman of Bedminster, and Old Mennonites Abraham Mensch of Skippack and Elvin Souder of Franconia. Nearly all of these people became deeply involved in the life of their churches.

Then there were the intellectual half-siblings Harvey and Ann Jemima Allebach, children of storekeeper-banker Jacob Allebach of Green Lane, and members of Eden Mennonite Church at Schwenksville. Harvey was said by "Dean Kline of Ursinus" to have had "the most brilliant mind" he had encountered in his teaching career.[36] Hampered by weak health (his mother, stepmother, and brother had all died when he was young), Harvey was not only, as Jacob C. Clemens, an accomplished botanist, but also the best poet in English in the Mennonite Church of any branch. Although while studying at the University of Pennsylvania he wrote a witty poem entitled "My Methodist Girl," he was destined to find a Mennonite wife in Iowa. While still a student, he was given an evangelist's license, and helped N. B. Grubb in the pulpit of First Mennonite in Philadelphia. At the age of twenty-five he took up the pastorate of the Emmanuel Church in Noble, Iowa—a recent addition to the General Conference. Later Samuel ("S. M.") Musselman from West Swamp would serve this church for many years. In 1901 Harvey would be appointed editor of *The Mennonite* (in a new format, and from then on to be a weekly). In this position he would reside at Berne, Indiana, where he would publish nineteen poems in a booklet entitled *Echoes from Parnassus*.[37] His longest poem, "May Flowers," was impressive evidence of genuine literary powers. This grandson of Moses Gottschall, so different from him (or the vociferous W. S. Gottschall) in style, would later be called "the best preacher in the [Eastern] Conference," and a man of rare spirituality. His last years were marked by pathos, when he returned east to serve as a beloved pastor in the "Swamp Charge," while his wife remained in her native Midwest. The forced retirement, for reasons of health, of this lanky, intellectual and devout preacher, left his congregation in tears. He died of tuberculosis at the age of fifty-one.

His half-sister Ann Jemima was even more outstanding.[38] Neither of her parents had been raised as Mennonites, and unlike Harvey, she had not had Mose Gottschall as a grandfather. Her mother, second wife of her father, had actually been a founder of the Lutheran church in Schwenksville, and her father had been Reformed until his first marriage, to one of Mose Gottschall's daughters. Annie took after her Lutheran mother, who had been a businesswoman, but had died when Annie was seven. At the age of seventeen Annie began to teach school in her home community, quickly

Annie C. Funk (1874-1912) of the Hereford congregation in the Eastern District, missionary to India from 1906-1912. She drowned while returning from England on the famed *Titanic*, April 15, 1912. (Mennonite Library and Archives of Eastern Pennsylvania)

establishing extraordinary control over a large roomful of mischievous pupils. After being baptized at Eden in Schwenksville, she studied elocution in Philadelphia, and began to teach it at Perkiomen Seminary, and then as Principal of a "Collegiate School" in East Orange, New Jersey (her brother Harvey taught there too). In nearby New York City she became heavily involved in a wide range of benevolent church work in Episcopalian chapels, winning admiring commendations for her outstanding aggressiveness and Christian faithfulness. This remarkable woman also studied extensively toward a doctorate in pedagogy and philosophy. Finally, she would transfer her Mennonite membership from Schwenksville to First Church of Philadelphia. In 1911 she asked Pastor Grubb to ordain her as a minister. His performance of this historic act would not be representative, at that moment, of the feelings of the Eastern Conference as a whole, nor of a particular sense of Mennonite heritage. Her preaching, on the rare occasions when it occurred in the Mennonite Churches of Eden or Zion or at the Harleysville Chapel, drew large crowds, but seems to have been regarded by most local people more as a novelty than as an option for other congregations. Her ordination had resulted, rather, from her own strong convictions, and those of N. B. Grubb and the pastor at Eden, John Wenger Schantz, a graduate of the Lutheran Mt. Airy Seminary, that Christians should be at the growing edge of social awareness, and that Mennonites should not lag behind. Schantz's eloquent sermon at Ann's ordination in Philadelphia ranged over the Scriptures, drawing from them an interpretation that rose above "local, national and therefore transient" elements:

> Paul's words [on women keeping silent in church] were addressed to the Greeks. To the Greek churches only were there such limitations of woman's rights and privileges. . . .
> What would the Greek think if he were told that woman studies music, poetry, art and philosophy? What if he were to behold the Christian meetings today and see the unveiled faces, hear her voice in song and prayer? He would ask, Is this Christianity?
> What was good for Greek customs does not harmonize with ours.
> Shall we take a peculiar interpretation in one Province of the globe and make it the criterion for judging of woman's position and instruction everywhere?[39]

Some of Schantz's members at Zion found this interpretation far too liberal, and reprimanded their pastor sharply.

Another Annie, daughter of miller James B. Funk, deacon of the New Mennonites at Hereford, likewise could not wait for her Mennonite fellowship to employ her own talents. As her counterpart of the same age at Green Lane, she was an enthusiastic participant in the Christian Endeavor Society of her home church (her father had initiated it—the first in the conference).[40] Annie Funk studied missions in a "training school" at Northfield, Massachusetts. Again, as had Annie Allebach, she went to the New York City area, where she got to work with the Young Women's Christian Association, officially with the Methodists. Finally, after she had passed thirty, she was called by the General Conference Mission Board, of which A. B. Shelly at West Swamp was secretary, to work in the new Mennonite mission field in India.

On November 15, 1907, Annie Funk, who had grown up at her father's mill along the Perkiomen, was bade farewell by her Mennonite friends at Bally. When another woman who intended to travel with her was prevented by illness, Annie chose to embark for India by herself. Here she traveled on a bicycle donated by Eastern Conference young people of the Quakertown and Philadelphia congregations, founded a school for girls, and wrote enthusiastic letters home. In 1912, when she planned to have her first furlough, she chose at the last minute to take passage on the famed *Titanic* on its maiden voyage. The electrifying fate of this enormous ship was brought home in great grief to the people of Bally and the Eastern Conference. It was reported that Annie had given up her place in a lifeboat to a young mother with her child. The girls' school in India was named in Annie's honor. After what was probably the largest memorial service in the history of the Hereford Mennonites, the congregation raised a monument to Annie C. Funk in the cemetery they shared with the Old Mennonites.

Among Annie's fellow passengers on the *Titanic* had been members of the wealthy George Widener family of the Elkins Park area of Philadelphia. The Wideners had already entered a lifeboat when George and his son Harry gave up their seats to a mother with her baby. As it happened, the Wideners had earlier employed, for the erection of their opulent family mansion, a Mennonite masonry contractor. He was Joseph Bechtel, a member of the Old Mennonite congregation at Hereford, but for forty years a resident of Philadelphia. When the surviving Mrs. Widener decided to build a new library for Harvard University in memory of her son Harry Elkins Widener, Joseph Bliem Bechtel was chosen to do the masonry construction. In the summer of 1913 the Bechtel family rented a house near the ocean at Lynn, Massachusetts, as Joseph oversaw the brickwork of the massive Widener Memorial Library in "Harvard Yard" at nearby Cambridge. It was only the latest of many large building jobs Joseph Bechtel, now approaching sixty, had taken on; others included the State Capitol at Harrisburg, the Campbell Soup building in Camden, New Jersey, a lavish summer home for the Wideners at Newport, Rhode Island, and campus buildings at State College in central Pennsylvania. The size of even these projects would be dwarfed, in later generations, by the worldwide exploits of construction carried out by the children of Joseph's first cousins who had migrated to Kansas when farmland had been taken up in Berks County after the Civil War (the Bechtel Corporation).[41]

It had been in Annie Funk's home church at Hereford that the Mennonite General Conference, convening in October 1899 had voted to found its first foreign mission in India, and to create an "Emergency Relief Commission" to gather funds for famine-stricken people in that country. Harrison Landis of First Mennonite in Philadelphia was named treasurer. Serving as president of the General Conference at this session was Hereford's own pastor, Anthony S. Shelly. This tall, thin ex-teacher, a better writer than a preacher, and serving Upper Milford as well as Hereford, was something of a scholar. It was he who would shortly translate into English the Cornelius Rys "Confession of Faith" for the consideration of the General Conference, and he would be the only person in Pennsylvania who would subscribe to the new German Mennonite *Lexikon* (Encyclopedia).[42] It was his conviction that Mennonites of his community lacked a sufficient sense of their spiritual heritage.

Less than two years after this General Conference mission to India had been organized, a former Franconia Conference boy who had grown up in Nebraska, Mahlon Lapp, was appointed missionary to India under Old Mennonite auspices in the Midwest. No such activity was as yet possible in the Franconia Conference itself, but the Lapp family had already been instrumental in bringing the spirit of mission activity eastward. Mahlon's older brother, Dan, had been preaching around Doylestown before February 1895; in that month he penned a kind of pastoral follow-up letter. "I have been thinking a great deal about you," he wrote to "the converts at Doylestown." Now that they had "made a start in the Christian life," Lapp wished to encourage them to a new activity and a new piety. This significant blend would characterize the spiritual growing edge of the Franconia Conference for the next six decades. It was a change of atmosphere, and it did not occur immediately all over the conference area. It would bring to the next two generations a series of new outlets for pent-up energy, and revivify, as a set of puzzled bishops tried cautiously to control it, the tradition of plain clothes in a way that made them less a sign of humility than a uniform of piety and evangelism. "We have each a work to do a grand noble mighty work," urged evangelist Lapp. But this was not to be seen as in conflict with being an Old Mennonite.

> Attend regularly all the services at the church have your family prayers read your bibles Faithfully & above all have your private Prayers their is a wonderful power in Private prayer that can only be realized by those who practice it. Keep yourself from worldly amusements & worldly associates they will have a powerful influence upon you for evil.[43]

Back at Doylestown, Sunday school-minded persons like butcher Isaac L. Kulp of Danboro gratefully accepted such awakening admonitions.

By the time Dan Lapp came back for another preaching tour in 1897, when a full house heard him at Line Lexington and he helped to start a Sunday school teachers' meeting there, the excitement of eloquent English preaching from western visitors had been twice relived. In 1896 bachelor A. D. Wenger, not quite thirty, had filled thirty-five preaching appointments in the Franconia Conference area. Having been ordained at Versailles, Missouri, this traveling preacher averaged more than a sermon a day, and elicited confessions of Christ from "a number of souls." Yet he found "Franconia" less ripe for such a harvest than "Lancaster." He had attended the Moody Bible Institute two summers previously, and brought with him some influence of premillennial teaching.[44] This was new to the Franconia Conference, and would increasingly become an issue over the following

decades. In the Eastern Conference too this teaching would have its consequences, especially through Moody-enthusiast W. S. Gottshall, occasioning
sometimes strenuous debates and alignments.

Next to make an itinerary through Franconia Conference congregations was John S. Coffman of Elkhart, right-hand-man of publisher John
Funk, one of the main supporters of the Elkhart Institute, writer of Sunday
school materials in English, and for years already a very successful evangelist among Mennonites west of Pennsylvania and Virginia. His usual caution lest he offend conservative leaders was heightened in the Franconia
Conference area of 1896. "In one place in Bucks [County]," he reported, "I
was not wanted by one dear aged brother.... Appointments have been
made at all the other principal places...." The disapproval of evening
meetings was a hindrance, and Coffman found the seating arrangement in
the meetinghouses unhelpful. Apparently the young people sat in a far
corner. "You can hardly see the young people at all," observed Coffman,
who had found it "almost impossible to speak a word to them at
church...."[45] As for the conference prohibition of having visiting
preachers for more than two consecutive services (the point was to avoid
"protracted meetings" such as the Methodists and Baptists used to win
converts), Coffman's supporters evaded this by having him preach at one
end of the conference area and then, after he had been absent for several
weeks while preaching in another part of the conference, inviting him back
for two more services. "He spoke in any little church he could," remembered Amos Kolb of Vincent, who stayed home from school to hear the welcome and graceful speaker. After the sermon, sixteen-year-old Amos went
up to Coffman and told him he wished to be a Christian.[46] This was a key
moment in the life of the Vincent congregation, which seemed henceforth
to gain new strength. Two years later it benefited from another "western"
visitor, the twenty-seven-year-old schoolteacher-preacher S. G. Shetler of
Johnstown, Pennsylvania. Soon to become a widely effective evangelist,
Shetler preached his first sermon outside of his home conference at Vincent
on August 20, 1898.

Both the western and the eastern areas of the Franconia Conference
thus witnessed, in these closing years of the century, the most vivid
"awakening" in their history. This time it increased, rather than diminished
their membership. Some forty young people joined the Blooming Glen congregation after John S. Coffman's evangelistic visit. He had purposely refrained from talking about "school," but Hetty Kulp of the Doylestown
congregation went out to the Elkhart Institute (class of 1900). And the visit
of still another western preacher—Daniel Kauffman of Versailles, Missouri,
saved for the Mennonite fellowship a young man from Rockhill whose

name—J. D. Mininger—would before long become a symbol of a new spirit of indefatigable mission activity. Jacob Mininger was deeply impressed by Kauffman's preaching at Doylestown. If a preacher like that could be a Mennonite, Jacob decided, he would be one too. Though yet unmarried, he presented himself to Bishop Josiah Clemmer and Deacon Henry Krupp as a candidate for church membership, and heard the elderly Deacon say, as he left, "If it will only hold out."[47] It was customary for Old Mennonites at that time not to join the church until after marriage (though there were exceptions).

While Daniel Kauffman was in the East he looked up a new mission in Philadelphia, just established under the supervision of contractor Joseph B. Bechtel. As it happened, there was also a Joseph B. Bechtel in the First Mennonite Church of Philadelphia, a prosperous and influential jeweler. The two businessmen with the same name sometimes referred to each other humorously as "the rich Joseph Bechtel" (eventually the Old Mennonite contractor dropped his middle initial to avoid confusion). There were now two Mennonite "missions" in the city—one pastored by N. B. Grubb's son Silas, and the other, more oriented toward bringing in children of "outsiders," serviced mainly by visiting preachers from the Franconia Conference. Daniel Kauffman wrote back to Jacob Mensch encouraging the Franconia Conference leaders to get behind the new mission, which was being organizationally backed by the more mission-minded Lancaster Conference.[48] The Franconia Conference session a few months later (November 1, 1899) permitted its ministers to preach in the new mission with the proviso that the meetings were to be conducted "as at home." This resulted, over the next decade or two, in a number of ministers taking the train to Philadelphia to do the preaching, while Joseph Bechtel, the leader of the program, served as an initially hesitant but faithful superintendent. Two Lancaster Conference women—Amanda Musselman and Mary Denlinger—energetically carried out the real day-to-day work of a city mission.[49] Other lay-workers were the family of butcher and grocer Isaac Kulp, who had moved down to Philadelphia from Danboro and opened a store. His daughter Hetty, having come back from her studies at Elkhart, worked in the store and helped in the mission activities,[50] dressing in the new plainness as modeled by the midwestern Old Mennonite activists.

Also moving to the city in order to be involved in this outreach was young Jacob D. Mininger of Rockhill. For four years he hardly missed a Sunday morning at the mission. Then, when Menno S. Steiner, one of the leading mission-promoters of the Midwest, asked Mininger to serve as the superintendent of a new Old People's Home at Rittman, Ohio, Jacob was eager for the job. A later generation would hardly be able to understand the

power of the mystique of Christian "activity" for an ambitious young
person of Jacob's Old Mennonite generation. When Steiner observed that
the superintendent should be a married person, Jacob replied that this
could soon be arranged. He was even willing to find another fiancée, if
necessary. But when he proposed to fellow mission worker Hetty Kulp,
though six years older, she agreed, and they were married a few months
later (1904).[51] Their assignment in Ohio was the first of a series of western
moves by younger members of the Franconia Conference eager for Christian service, but frustrated by the prospect of waiting until there might be a
casting of lots in their home congregations. The mood caught on first in the
congregations of Doylestown and Vincent, but soon appeared in the center
of the Conference area, Souderton. Here another "teachers' meeting"
began to meet in private homes in 1902.

A "Mennonite Printer" named Joseph B. Steiner appeared in the
midst of this new activity, and set up shop first in Skippack and then
Doylestown. He advertised years of experience in bookbinding, and issued
proposals for an English translation of the old Mennonite devotional book,
the *Meditations* of Jacob Denner, first printed in Hamburg, Germany.
Steiner got the written endorsement of five Franconia bishops, and
promised to use excess profits "for helping the poor widow Sisters." By
January 1901 he was under instruction for church membership. In 1902 he
published a sizable book for evangelist A. D. Wenger, just back from a
world tour, entitled, *Six Months in Bible Lands and Around the World in
Fourteen Months.* Wenger and Steiner seem to have sold this Doylestown
printed book in visits throughout the conference; it would turn up at countless auctions of household goods over the next sixty years. Its usual unworn
appearance indicates that the book must have regarded as a curiosity
by most of its seldom-reading purchasers, but as something that a Mennonite probably ought to buy. Before long publisher Steiner, who had no
hesitation in calling himself "Brother" in print, seems to have absconded
with the subscription money raised for the printing of the Denner book.[52]

Arriving in the 20th century, the Franconia Conference was finally
experiencing an "awakening" to the kind of "activity" John Oberholtzer
had agitated for six decades earlier. But this time the young proponents of
the new ideas did not try to evade the authority of the bishops or the conference. Even the western evangelists, as they came through, were not only
respectful and cooperative, but, amazingly, openly supportive of distinctive,
plain clothing. It would take only a decade or two until these exciting
preachers would be considered valuable even by conservatives. Surely no
preacher in the home ranks could cause the English-speaking young people
to flock so willingly to hear a sermon.

There were, of course, some objections. J. Clayton Kolb, recently ordained minister for Vincent and Coventry, followed his conservative father's opinion that Sunday schools, having no specific scriptural precedent, were "idolatry." He caused a stir at Vincent by accusing a visiting western minister of preaching less than the truth on the subject. As the conference moved to discipline him, old Bishop Josiah Clemmer counseled moderation, but later observed, "Mit so'n Kerl kann ma gor nix du" (You can't do anything at all with a fellow like that).[53] Kolb eventually moved to Lancaster County and affiliated with the Old Order Mennonites. And in the geographic heart of the Franconia Conference people were also slow to endorse the new ideas. The Franconia Congregation, whose membership constituted over a sixth of the entire conference, changed the most slowly of all, in language, custom, and attitudes.

A key set of ordinations occurred in the years 1904-1906, in the "central" bishop district of the Franconia Conference, setting a tone for the first third of the century. In 1904 Abraham G. Clemmer, slight of build but impressive in speech and manner, was chosen as a minister at Franconia. By the time a new bishop was to be ordained a year and a half later, he had filled his role so well that he received twenty-two nominations for this office, seven more than the total received by the other six nominees. But the lot fell on the less refined, blunt-spoken Jonas Mininger of "The Plain" near Lansdale (he had received three nominations). This colorful-mannered, blunt-spoken, powerfully built man was traditional enough to suit conservatives—he had opposed foot washing until he had been told by Deacon Henry Krupp, after collections had been taken to pay off Jonas's farm, that he should now support this ordinance along with the rest of the conference. When he had originally been placed "in the lot for minister," he had paced the barn floor all night before he could "give himself up" to this call of the church. He was not at ease in the English language of the young people. His old-fashioned habits of smoking and chewing tobacco would eventually be objected to by the new wave of Christian workers. Known for his sociality (he "always noticed the children," and if he saw someone walking along the road he would stop his buggy to learn who it might be) and his physical strength (he took two piles of hay on one forkload, and singlehandedly held up an automobile while a tire was being changed), he would be remembered as a conscientious but sometimes culturally naive leader. He "always preached the same sermon—from one end of the Bible to the other." He was effective in his manner of quoting various appropriate Scriptures or thoughts relating to the Lord's supper as he walked among the congregation, handing out the bread and wine. But young people would giggle over his English mispronunciations and his monotone singing, or tell stories about how the horse blanket on his carriage seat sent up spirals of smoke from a lighted cigar hidden underneath it. Not that Jonas was different from many other Mennonite men in this. Spittoons still stood behind some of the pulpits, and at Salford a woman even slipped and hurt herself on a spot of tobacco juice on the meetinghouse floor. As late as the 1930s the porches of Old Mennonite meetinghouses in the central district of the conference might be filled with smoking men, after the meeting had dismissed. Often the young fellows would wait outside until well after the worship had begun. One of them would listen at the door at Franconia, it was said, and when he sensed that the preacher had gone far enough in his sermon, would announce, "Come on, boys, he has Zaccheus up in the tree now. Time to go in."[54]

Many young people among the Old Mennonites of these years did not become spiritually serious until well after marriage. Instead of being drawn toward church loyalty by becoming involved in "activity," they would eventually feel a cumulative consciousness of an embracing spiritual "family." The mnemonic repetitions of the droning, sad-sounding preachers had been recorded in their memories while they were only half-listening, and a sense of a spiritual continuum arose in their minds when their youthful mischievousness died down. Repentance was the process of acknowledging that one had not been serious, surrendering one's will, and taking on a humble attitude of obedience. The sense of peoplehood was fostered by countless "Sunday dinner" visits among relatives and friends from home and neighboring congregations. People from Vincent traveled "cross country" toward Franconia or all the way to Doylestown; young men from Bally found wives down at Salford, or vice versa; a Franconia girl would marry a boy from Deep Run. This pattern held longer in the more old-fashioned Franconia Conference than in the Eastern Conference, though it often worked there too. People who felt their social needs fulfilled in this interchange sometimes found it hard to understand the restlessness of others who needed the excitement of the new preaching and evangelism. The latter, in turn, saw the older types as resisting a movement of the Spirit.

Bishop Jonas Mininger had an unpleasant responsibility shortly after his ordination. His elderly fellow-minister at Plains, Henry Godshall, though capable of preaching so earnestly that crowds who came to hear him at Franconia on Good Friday were moved to tears, had been accused of unbecoming speech and behavior in the neighborhood. Before long Jonas silenced him, and moved, in the fall of 1906, to ordain a younger man. There was gossip that Godshall had been chosen through an improper use of "the lot." Now a new set of nominees was sought, and toward the end of this process, the name of a fancy young violin-playing banker in the con-

Schoolteacher Jacob Clemens (1874-1965) and his future (1899) wife, Hanna Clemens Rittenhouse (1880-1977). "J. C." Clemens was ordained for the ministry at the Plains congregation in 1906. (J. C. and Hanna Clemens Family)

gregation, Jacob Cassel Clemens, was also handed in. Bishop Mininger was somewhat dubious, but let the nomination stand. Clemens himself had just received a job he very much looked forward to accepting, that of cashier in a Norristown bank. But it was he on whom the lot fell, stunning both him and his wife, Hanna, and the congregation as well. He would have realized immediately that this was the end of his bank position, and the beginning of a humbler mode of life. He and Hanna had to be helped out of the meetinghouse by friends. "I've never seen anything like it since," remarked a man who was present, over sixty years later.[55]

Yet in this dramatic calling of a noble-spirited younger man who did not want the role, the Franconia Conference ironically gained one of its most inspiring preachers. Without the use of the lot, it would never have happened. Jacob could speak equally well in English or German. A former schoolteacher, he read history, and spoke with a range of contemporary reference unique in the Franconia Conference of that time. With his friend, the newly ordained Amos Kolb of Vincent, he traveled to western Pennsylvania to acquaint himself with the Old Mennonite publishing house recently established at Scottdale. Within eight years of his ordination he would be receiving calls to hold series of evangelistic meetings in the Lancaster Conference and farther west. He read the *Enchiridion* (Handbook) of Christian doctrine by the Dutch Anabaptist Dirk Philips, and took a stand for traditional Mennonite teaching in the face of a gathering influx of doctrines from other sources. He found particularly threatening the new challenge of "premillennialism" or, as it was often called by its critics, the "literal reign" view of eschatology. With this often came a Calvinistic view of "eternal security," fostered by visiting evangelists who had learned their theology at recently founded Bible institutes, and used the new C. I. Scofield edition of the Bible.

As devout and "evangelical" as any of those he debated with (sometimes by letter), J. C. Clemens struggled to keep the difficult balance of "nonconformity to the world" along with a natural zest for observing the natural world and gaining the benefits of "progress." With Minister Joe Ruth, ordained about the same time at Line Lexington, Clemens could make an audience feel that they were hearing something interesting when he spoke. It was not the old melancholy chanting. He was an open-minded person, and so preached a sermon by invitation for the "Johnson Mennonites" at Skippack (for which he was sharply corrected by Bishop Mininger). In his prime, he was the conference's most memorable and gracious preacher. After obediently giving up his bank position, he supported himself on a small farm along the Allentown Road near the birthplace of his wife (and former pupil), Hanna Rittenhouse.

For the "Dutch"-speaking, more traditional people in the center of the Franconia Conference, the most influential leader from 1904 to 1937 was the somewhat older Abraham G. Clemmer. Studying his Bible and dictionary, this deliberate-thinking man, impressively articulate in "high German," found his opinions increasingly respected. In 1913 he was ordained bishop to assist Jonas Mininger, and though not the conference moderator, probably wielded more influence than anyone else in the conference after Andrew Mack died in 1917. As the authority of the bishops seemed to become more and more definite in the era leading up to the middle of the century (it was even more final in the Lancaster Conference), Abraham was one of its most respected exemplars. Vivid in the memory of the community lay the tragic death by drowning of his two young sons in the summer of 1906, while he and his wife had been on a preaching trip to Bally.[56] Slight of build, he and the muscular Jonas Mininger made an unusual, contrastive pair, but they seemed to work harmoniously. As the use of English began to predominate at about the time automobiles became common (1914 and following), it was also helpful to have new bishops such as A. O. Histand of Doylestown and Warren Bean of Skippack, who were more English than Dutch, and could meaningfully conduct baptisms and communion in the eastern and western districts where German was fading more rapidly. J. C. Clemens of "the Plain" was nominated for the lot three times, when a new bishop was to be called, but always, as he put it, "got free."

Of course there was no one in the Franconia Conference who could muster the pulpit-presence of an N. B. Grubb, the intellect and literary allu-

Pastor Allen M. Fretz (1853-1943), in the recently remodeled (1908) chapel of the Zion congregation in Souderton. (Zion Mennonite Church)

siveness of a Harvey Allebach, or the oratorical flourish of a John Wenger Schantz—the latter ordained for Schwenksville in 1907. After growing up at Upper Milford, Schantz had attended Muhlenberg College and the Mt. Airy Lutheran Seminary. In 1910 he would be invited to add to his recently received Schwenksville charge the young Zion congregation at Souderton, which had somewhat abruptly parted ways with A. M. Fretz soon after expanding its church building in 1908. A man of "almost boundless energy," J. W. Schantz would lead the Zion congregation in a spurt of growth from 150 to 264 members in the six years of his ministry there. His life was then swiftly cut short by cancer.[57] Another polished speaker from the Eden congregation was Maxwell Hillegass Kratz, instructor at the Perkiomen Seminary and then law student at the University of Pennsylvania. He moved his membership to the Second Mennonite Church in Philadelphia. But no one equaled the pulpit flourish of N. B. Grubb, pastor of the congregation which now had over twice as many members as the next largest one in the Eastern Conference. Grubb was constantly quoted in the papers. Strongly interested in Mennonite history and its nonresistant themes, he had sought out as many Mennonites as he could find on his recent European trip, and brought back materials which he edited into the annual *Mennonite Yearbook and Almanac.* He and Anthony ("A. S.") Shelly of Bally translated a significant number of old Mennonite documents or German-written history for the pages of this family publication. But Grubb could also be swept by the momentum of his crowd-pleasing rhetoric into the popular mood of the hour. His Thanksgiving sermon in November of 1906, printed in *The Mennonite,* was hardly representative of the Mennonite conscience regarding the kingdoms of this world:

> ... Behold now, let us say it with modesty and with gratitude, the
> most honored, most powerful and most resourceful nation. The stars
> and stripes that now float over the land of the good and the brave is the
> ensign of liberty and righteousness among all nations. No one has yet
> dared to even approximate the wealth, the influence, the possibilities,
> the expanse or the limit where to the American people it will be said,
> thus far and no farther. . . .[58]

Apparently this most visible Mennonite minister in the Delaware Valley
was untouched by a sense of the ironies of American imperialism. He liked
to portray Mennonites as early proponents of ideas that were becoming accepted in modern times. He passed this enthusiastic view of Mennonite history on to his two preacher sons, Silas and Bill.

Several of the "missions" of the Eastern Conference took firm root in
the century's first decade: Allentown, Second Church in Philadelphia, and
Quakertown (Bethany). A surprising contribution for the new building at
Allentown came from the Hamburg Mennonite congregation in Germany.
Its pastor had recently been visiting in Pennsylvania, and now sent over,
from a fund in his congregation, the sum of 200 marks.[59] This recalled the
early connection between the Germantown and Hamburg Mennonites.
The young congregation at Quakertown initially drew some members from
East Swamp, making that congregation's hold on life temporarily
precarious. Perkasie could not raise its membership above thirty-six, and
before it would receive a permanent building the Old Mennonites of the
town would have their own new meetinghouse. Pottstown, though it had a
recently built chapel, kept dwindling in membership, and would disin-
tegrate after Pastor Harvey Allebach would be called away in 1915. Barely
hanging on were Boyertown and Germantown. The latter congregation
made more gains after 1905 than at any time in the previous century, when
an elderly Methodist carpenter-preacher, John W. Bayley, took it on as a
kind of project. He stirred up interest, roofed and refurbished the historic
meetinghouse, added a stone Sunday school annex, and raised the money to
pay for it all. An appreciative Eastern Conference accepted him as a Mennonite minister and even elected him president of the conference. Yet the
little Germantown congregation would not see its membership grow beyond forty-one. In contrast, the young Second Church, with slow-speaking
Silas Grubb in charge, grew to 150 members by 1909. The two Grubb-pas-
tored city churches constituted, by 1905, a quarter of the total membership
of the Eastern Conference.[60]

The fact that membership figures exist for both conferences for the
year 1905[61] makes it possible to reflect on the comparative growth they had
experienced in the six decades since their division. Without the 637 mem-

bers listed in the Eastern Conference as missions (except Souderton), the conference membership would have numbered 1355. In the Franconia Conference, where the only new congregation that had been formed since 1847 was among people already members in Souderton, the membership now stood at 3452. Thus by founding missions in other towns and cities, the Eastern Conference had added or saved enough members to maintain or slightly improve its original proportion of the eastern Mennonite population. With 1992 members in 1905, the Eastern Conference had 36 percent of the total—probably a little better ratio than it had begun with. On the other hand, it is interesting to note that the Franconia Conference had evidently kept a higher ratio of its own children, since it had apparently nearly maintained its percentage of the total Mennonite population without drawing in new people through missions.

The Franconia Conference was now, however, edging closer to the point of having missions too. Minister Henry Wismer of Skippack left $50 in his will in 1903 to the Philadelphia mission of "the old school of Mennonites,"[62] and when the Lancaster Mission Board bought a home in Philadelphia for this work, Joseph Bechtel (the Old Mennonite builder) contributed the first $4,000 of the $11,000 cost.[63] The May 1908 session of the Franconia Conference invited other contributions from its members, noting that "we are also interested in the [Lancaster-sponsored] mission at Philadelphia." But other issues of a "housekeeping" nature tended to dominate the conference sessions. "Aunt Annie" Stauffer, who had earlier saved the Sunday school and perhaps the congregation at Vincent, was protesting the use of wine at communion, and she was only the first of a forthcoming bloc. Bishop Jonas Mininger insisted at conference that the proper celebration of the Lord's supper should include wine, "the stronger the better." Moderator Andrew Mack reacted sternly, saying he never wanted to hear an expression like that at conference again.[64] Others protested against the taking of pictures of people. Portraits were only made, they said, for reasons of personal pride. Ministers were to ask their people to rid themselves of these ego-flattering mementos. And at every conference session the question of the woman's covering was belabored. Fancy hats were more and more common among the younger women.

The years 1909-1911 proved to be a kind of watershed on the dress issue in the Franconia Conference. But they also saw a breakthrough of the urge among lay people to move beyond the traditional limits of weekly meetings for worship. Young "workers" were beginning to hold meetings for Bible study at Blooming Glen, Line Lexington, and Souderton, where eager would-be ministers could stand up and address a group, even if it was only in a home. A "gang" of five such young men in the Souderton area included Jacob M. Moyer, Clayton Derstine, and Rhine Benner of Telford.[65] Even conservative older people like Elizabeth Clemens of Lower Salford (mother of J. C. Clemens), went eagerly to more meetings than were offered in their home congregations. Elizabeth recorded in her diary attendance at four harvest home services in the nine days between July 18 and 27 in 1903: at Towamencin, Plains, Salford, and the Lower Salford "Swingfelter" meetinghouse.[66]

Less traditional but equally pious was a member of the Blooming Glen congregation, Mrs. Abram Hunsicker. While praying in January 1909 she "had a vision," and sent her husband to talk to marketman William Moyer to see what could be done about getting a meetinghouse for Old Mennonites in the growing town of Perkasie. Moyer, who had become acquainted with the Philadelphia Old Mennonite mission as he did his market business in the city a year or two earlier, quickly called together Bishop Henry Rosenberger and other Blooming Glen leaders, and within eight days they had purchased a lot.[67] By August of the same year Bishop Andrew Mack of Bally was preaching the first sermon in a new building fronted by columns unprecedented in a local Mennonite meetinghouse. No congregation as such formed here, and it was not really a mission. It was a facility for a town wing of the Blooming Glen congregation. Interestingly, many of the Perkasie Old Mennonites preferred to keep on driving over to the main meetinghouse for worship. But the new Perkasie meetinghouse became a rallying point for young people eager for new kinds of meetings and preaching. Sometimes it was crowded all out of proportion, as when, in 1914, the first "Young People's Meetings" were allowed by the conference to take place there.

There were continual stirrings at Doylestown, too. A small group there wanted foot washing, and it was recalled years later that members of the Godshalk family had observed this rite in their own homes. A special "Bible Instruction" meeting, modeled after the "Bible Conferences" that had been held in other denominations for decades, was arranged by the Doylestown congregation without prior conference permission in 1909. The Franconia bishops, concerned that members not get the notion that such initiative could be taken independently, required a "confession" from the Doylestown sponsors of the meeting, and then allowed them to go ahead "for this one time."[68] That made it clear where the ultimate authority for such things lay, in contrast to the congregationalism of the Eastern Conference. The topics chosen for the visiting speakers—S. G. Shetler of Johnstown and Daniel Kauffman, now of Scottdale—would hardly seem threatening to a conservative attitude. They included "Self-Denial," "Devotional Covering," "Feet Washing" (still controversial in some parts of the

Franconia Conference), "Humilty," and "Worldly Gatherings."

A certain restlessness in the Doylestown congregation was symbolized by Deacon Clayton Bergey's leaving for rural Virginia in a white-topped "covered wagon" in 1910. Detweilers and Shaddingers from Doylestown also went to Virginia, some to return after several years. Moving to Colorado after the death of his wife was mission-activist Isaac Kulp, followed by several of his children's families.

And then in 1910 there was another Bible Instruction Meeting, at the opposite end of the conference—Vincent. This time due conference permission had been received. Vincent needed help. Some members of the congregation were fearful that it might be in its last days, like Coventry, and the calling of this meeting was doubtless an attempt to spark a revival. The announcement tapped a deep vein of interest in the newly awakened throughout the conference. Farmers milked their cows in midafternoon so they could attend the evening series. As many as thirty overnight guests crowded into one farmhouse near the Vincent meetinghouse, some sleeping on the floor on chaff bags. Meals were like picnics, with local women buying boxes of fruit, crackers, and cheese. Without any facilities beyond those designed for the weekly gathering of the congregation, the assembled listeners had a marvelous time, and a new spirit possessed the Vincent congregation, for once the center of attention of the Franconia Conference family. At the focus of it all, again, was the fascinating, even overwhelming preacher S. G. Shetler from the Johnstown area. He taught and preached like the successful schoolteacher he was; "he made everything clear." Nothing could be more enjoyable than to listen, in the pleasantly crowded meetinghouse, to sermon after sermon.[69] The bishops themselves were by now so impressed that they were ready to welcome Shetler back the following summer to Blooming Glen (though here again lay people took the initiative).

By that time two young families from Vincent had gone out in active Christian service—John Stauffers to a mission at Altoona, and Arthur Moyers to the Welsh Mountain Industrial Mission in Lancaster County. It was a wave of the future. When Preacher Shetler returned for the meetings at Blooming Glen in August 1911 he was accompanied, as he had been at Doylestown in 1909, by the persuasive and much-published speaker, Daniel Kauffman (whose Dunker grandfather had emigrated to "Juniata" from the neighborhood near the Saucon meetinghouse). Conservative Deacon Henry Krupp of Souderton, listening to Shetler preach at a preliminary meeting at Skippack, permitted himself an enthusiastic note in his diary: "I have never heard a human being speak like Bro. Shetler. He made himself free regarding conformity to the world."[70] Both conservatives and activists now followed Shetler to the Blooming Glen meetinghouse, where he and Kauffman preached, afternoon and evening, for a week. For some people the sensation of attending a church meeting in a lighted meetinghouse in the evening was itself a pleasant novelty. From all over came buggies and even rented hacks, carrying up to sixteen passengers from Perkasie or Souderton for 25¢ a round-trip. Spirited singing was led by Abram and Leidy Hunsicker from the recently published *Church and Sunday School Hymnal.* There was a printed program in English, old hat to the New Mennonites, but an experience of freshness to the Old. Shetler and Kauffman dealt eloquently with just the topics the bishops were interested in, such as "Non Resistance," "Humility-Pride," "Feet Washing," "Devotional Covering," and "Life Insurance." The final sermon, by Shetler, was on "Conformity to the World."[71]

The favorable excitement of these meetings, placing the older concerns in a context of forward-looking and action-inviting preaching, seems to have prepared for an important move at the Franconia Conference, as it convened for its fall session a month later. After several decades of increasingly persistent complaints regarding worldliness, the conservative leaders sensed that there was a shift in sympathy among concerned lay people. It was the moment to crystallize the new trend toward church loyalty among those who had been stirred to recognize new possibilities in their own Old Mennonite fellowship. The conference resolutions were taken down in English by Jacob Clemens, in the unmistakably crisp accents of a new mood:

> First.—That the Brethren and Sisters be required to submit themselves to the teachings of God's word according to I Timothy 2:8-9 and I Peter 3:3-4 and further that none will be received into the church wearing fasionable clothing or gold for adornment, or women wearing hats.
> Sisters who are accustomed to wear hats are required to dispense with them before spring communion and instead wear the plain protection covering. All complying with the foregoing resolution will be recognized as Brethren and Sisters in the church. Second.—That the Brethren be admonished to wear the plain clothing.[72]

The word went out to the congregations, to Vincent and Bally as well as Doylestown and Skippack. At Vincent four married couples "stayed back from communion" for a while, but later returned. Minister Amos Kolb went to them and said, "Conference made this, and this is what the Bible says." The old pull of the family of faith proved strong. Sure enough, at preparatory services one of the women appeared with a covering, and another one, who died shortly thereafter, had a covering on her head in the coffin, although she had not worn one in life.[73] At Blooming Glen, Doylestown, and

PROGRAM

for the

Bible Instruction

to be held in the

MENNONITE CHURCH

Near Doylestown, Bucks Co., Pa.

——

NOVEMBER 21 TO 27, 1909

Sunday

Morning—Sermon	S. G. Shetler
Evening—Sermon	D. Kauffman

Monday

Evening—Study of God's Word	S. G. Shetler
Evening—Sermon	

Tuesday

Morning—Prayer	D. Kauffman
Morning—Self Denial	S. G. Shetler
Evening—Women's Work in the Church	D. Kauffman
Evening—Sermon	

Wednesday

Morning—Parental Training	S. G. Shetler
Morning—Idolatry of To-day	D. Kauffman
Evening—Devotional Covering	S. G. Shetler
Evening—Sermon.	

Thursday

Morning—Thanksgiving	D. Kauffman
Morning—Giving	S. G. Shetler
Afternoon—Thanksgiving Sermon	2.30
Evening—Spurious Investments	7.30
	S. G. Shetler

Friday

Morning—Feet Washing	S. G. Shetler
Morning—Humility	D. Kauffman
Evening—Worldly Gatherings	S. G. Shetler
Evening—Sermon	

Saturday

Evening—Eternal Punishment	
Evening—Sermon	

NOTE—Morning Sessions open at 9 o'clock. Evening Sessions at 6.30 o'clock. Queries each evening. Song Service at opening of each session. Bring Bibles and Church and Sunday School Hymnal. ALL WELCOME.

PROGRAMME

FOR THE

Bible Instruction Meeting

TO BE HELD IN THE

Blooming Glen Menonite Church

Bucks County, Pa.

~~~~~~~~~~

August 27th, to September 2nd, 1191

NOTES

All are cordially invited to attend this meeting.

Afternoon Sessions open at two o'clock. Evening Sessions at 6.30 o'clock. Queries each evening. Song Service at opening of each session.

Bring your Church and Sunday School Hymnal.

Coaches leave Perkasie Sta. at 1 o'clock p. m. Return leave Blooming Glen at 9 p. m. Round trip 25 cents.

FRICK PRINTERS, FRICK, PA.

Sunday

Morning—Sermon	
Evening—Sermon. Perkasie	

Monday

Evening—Repentance	D. Kauffman
Prov. 16, 25	S. G. Shetler

Tuesday

Afternoon—Home Government and its Effects on the Church	D. Kauffman
Relation of Laity to Ministry	S. G. Shetler
Evening—Non Resistance	D. Kauffman
Sermon	

Wednesday

Afternoon—Humilty--Pride	S. G. Shetler
Brotherly Love	D. Kauffman
Evening—Morality as Compared to Christianity	S. G. S.

Thursday

Afternoon—Feet Washing	D. Kauffman
Devotional Covering	S. G. Shetler

Evening—Baptism	D. Kauffman
Sermon	

Friday

Afternoon—Life Insurance	S. G. Shetler
Self Denial	D. Kauffman
Evening—Idolatry of To-day	S. G. Shetler
Sermon	

Saturday

Afternoon—Extra Session	
Evening—Secret Societies	D. Kauffman
Conformity to the World	S. G. Shetler

Moderator—I. F. Swartz. Blooming Glen, Pa.

Choristers { Abram M. Hunsicker. Perkasie, Pa. / Leidy D. Hunsicker. Perkasie, Pa.

Corresponding Committee { Dr. D. M. Landis, Perkasie, Pa. / Titus K. Moyer, Blooming Glen, Pa.

Programs for the Bible Instruction Meetings at Doylestown in 1909 and at Blooming Glen in 1911. (Mennonite Library and Archives of Eastern Pennsylvania)

Vincent especially, it seemed, plain coats appeared. History seemed to be rolled back. Such coats were not worn by the young men in other parts of the conference (although this would change after the coming World War).

All told, fewer than 100 persons throughout the conference seemed to stay away from communion over this momentous issue, and it was guessed that fewer than twenty-five stayed away permanently. The bonnet was back, and the ladies' hat gone, for members. No confessions were required of those who needed to change—only obedience to the new printed rules. It all worked so well that from then on cumulative lists of conference resolutions would be published (in the manner of the Lancaster Conference), leading to a greater and greater sense of codification. At Franconia a little note on "Apparel" was apparently handed to applicants for membership. "Sisters shall wear bonnets that are plain," it spelled out, "and cannot be mistaken for a hat."[74] The actual prayer coverings should be "of sufficient size with the strings at the proper place for tying." It was a new era, and the emphasis, widespread as well among most other Old Mennonite communities throughout North America, would be vital for nearly half a century in the main body. A remnant of elderly ladies would be devoutly obeying these rules over seventy years later. That the new mood of visible identification with the Mennonite-Christian family was introduced along with the simultaneous breakthrough of lay evangelistic action, and that it would survive as long as this activist outthrust lasted, pose intriguing questions. Was the new emphasis on plain clothes a reaffirmation of Mennonite tradition, or was it a defensive reaction to the threat of erosion of the old covenant family? Or was it a price one paid to the guardians of tradition for the privilege of being allowed to become "active" in the new mode learned from other evangelical Christians? In any case, its occurrence coincided with a revival of spiritual interest that affected the whole conference. Answers to the questions it raises must be sought with reference to similar dynamics throughout the larger Old Mennonite fellowship.

For the next five or six decades the role of the bishop in the Franconia Conference would be increasingly complex and demanding, until the reformulation begun around 1910 would be complete, and the old authoritarian mode superseded. The newly twinned themes of nonconformity and activity would present one challenge after another until the 1960s. Young Clayton F. Derstine, baptized by Bishop Mininger at Souderton a few months after the Blooming Glen Bible Instruction Meeting and the subsequent Franconia Conference resolutions, began teaching Sunday school almost immediately, and spoke at a variety of teachers' and "cottage" meetings in the vicinity. He had a clear case of the "Bredicher Geist" (spirit of preaching), which to the older mentality was not a promising trait.[75] The

Samuel O. and Anna Godshall Landis, married on January 7, 1906. Samuel was a member at Doylestown, and Anna at Blooming Glen. The second picture shows Anna (right) with a friend; the effect of the new stress (1911 and following) on distinct dress in the Franconia Conference is clearly registered. (Author's Collection)

Alpheus Allebach, son of preacher Christian, and Margaret Cassell, daughter of deacon David, at the time of their marriage in 1902, when they were both twenty-eight. Alpheus was a store-clerk and Margaret a seamstress at home. In 1924 Alpheus became a partner with Elvin Souder, Sr., in a store in Souderton, serving the new demand for plain clothes for a generation as the familiarly known "Allebach & Souder." (Alpheus C. Allebach)

following conference session asked that members "be admonished against forwardness"; this may also have had reference to another request from Doylestown for a Bible Instruction Meeting. These were the years when the flamboyant "J. W." Yoder, singing teacher from the "Big Valley" of central Pennsylvania, was beginning to gain an enthusiastic Mennonite following, particularly in the Deep Run Old Mennonite congregation. As no one before him he introduced Mennonite young people to the thrill of a higher type of music, including Haydn's "The Heavens Are Telling" and Handel's "Hallelujah Chorus." Then there were new "Sunday School Meetings," such as the Eastern Conference had begun four decades earlier, and "continued meetings" where the local bishops were in agreement. This stirred the pot in the Franconia Conference, giving people in the more conservative districts new reasons for visiting the communities east and west of them.

The magisterial George Brunk, Sr., of Virginia was invited in 1914 to hold such meetings in an attempt to resuscitate Coventry, but that once-substantial congregation was too far gone. The visit did provide young preacher Amos Kolb, with whom Brunk stayed, a chance to learn theology from a more experienced leader. Amos was intrigued to find Brunk "a great millennium man." As their eschatological discussions waxed warm, Brunk

"set there," remembered Amos, "and laughed as if the joke was on me."[76]
The conference leaders became edgy about such influences, and voted to
"grant to the Bishops alone the privilege to decide which of the visiting
brethren, whose faith is in question, are safe to preach at regular or special
services in their specific districts." They also admonished the Sunday
schools "not to use the large charts in teaching their pupils."[77]

Clayton F. Derstine soon moved on to the Old Mennonite mission in
Altoona where, as Vincent's John L. Stauffer before him, he was ordained
under another conference without the casting of lots. Ordinarily this would
have given him the authority to preach in his home area in the Franconia
Conference as well, when visiting. But the bishops were not to be easily out-
flanked. It was said that Derstine had written to the new minister at Franconia, young schoolteacher Menno Souder, that he should follow his own
rather than the old ministers' leading in matters of progress. The October
1915 session of conference passed a no-nonsense resolution: "If any Brother
leaves the Conference District and is ordained different from our Conference rules, his office is not recognized by this Conference District, except
by consent of Conference." Evangelist and later Bishop Derstine, though
famous as a pulpiteer among most other Old Mennonites except in
Lancaster, was persona non grata in Franconia Conference pulpits for most
of his life. He was considered too self-promotional and insufficiently subject
to conference authority; thus his great gifts of oratory and humor could not
be used. Derstine's youthful fellow-enthusiast for Christian service, Jacob
M. Moyer of the Moyer feed business in Souderton, proved much more
ready to work obediently within the old authority system when he was ordained in the same year Derstine was, but through regular conference-sanc-
tioned procedure at Souderton. The first preacher chosen specifically for
this congregation, he followed Deacon Krupp's instructions to comb his hair
down over his forehead, and held out longer than most other Mennonites
against buying an automobile. He stood somewhat in contrast with his half
brother, accountant Franklin Moyer, an active member of the Eastern Conference Zion congregation of the same town.

The Franconia Conference further protected itself against undue outside influence by declaring that "lay members of the Church are not to
make appointments for visiting Ministers." Anyone from the liberal new
Goshen College in Indiana was similarly forbidden to preach.

The new mood made a change in the little Providence congregation,
where some of the "community" people left and a more definite Mennonite identity was reestablished. In the Bedminster area, too, there were
some readjustments, involving an influx of former Mennonites into the
Lutheran congregation of the Dublin Union Church. Had their Mennonite

heritage been of concern to them, they would have had the option of joining A. M. Fretz's Eastern Conference congregation at Deep Run. At Doylestown the changes were proving attractive enough to draw back into the Mennonite fold the Methodist schoolteacher Mahlon Gross and his formerly Baptist wife, Annie. He had been a preacher and Sunday school teacher among the Methodists, and active, with Annie, in the cause of the Women's Christian Temperance Union. As a Mennonite he could, of course, no longer preach, and sat weeping, on occasion, in the Doylestown meetinghouse after the others had left. But about eight years later, in 1920, the lot was cast and fell on him. The children had also joined, and from then on the issue of wine at communion was strong at Doylestown.[78]

Let the record also show that the eighteen-year-old daughter of Doylestown's deacon began helping mothers care for their new babies on August 20, 1912. Seldom receiving recognition, and noiseless in their humble participation in the community and the household of faith, unmarried "maids" such as Nora Gross made an indispensable contribution. Whereas her brothers such as Titus or Joseph (later a bishop) were much more in the limelight of the congregation's affairs, Nora would work quietly in home after home for the next twenty years, taking care of fifty new babies. They would include such newborn future Mennonites as Walter Hunsberger of Line Lexington, Edgar Clemens of Souderton, Claude Histand of Doylestown, Marvin Allebach of Rockhill, Claude Good of Oley, Lois Bergey of Doylestown, and Sarah Jean Stutzman of Salford.[79]

Though women were expected not to speak in church, those with strong feelings were not without influence in the church's affairs. Annie Gross gave one visiting preacher from Lancaster his comeuppance in her own home. He had stressed in his sermon that women should keep silent. During the post-service visit he happened to ask Annie's opinion on some matter. "She sat up erectly," remembered a son, "with hands folded, head high, and lips pinched tightly." As her husband, Mahlon, laughed, the visiting preacher did too, confessing, "Annie, you are whipping me with my own stick."[80] Just as determined was Barbara, wife of Preacher Aaron Freed at Line Lexington. "I am truly a lover of communion," she wrote to minister Joe Ruth, "but if one will hand it to me that uses filthy stuff tobacco and strong wine, I am not able to take it now.... If I cannot get enything to remember the shed blood but strong wine I will wait till I can drink it new in my Father's kingdom.... Please give me a plain and true answer, if it does cut." Preacher Ruth wrote back to his "Esteemed Sister," agreeing that tobacco was a filthy habit, but stating that there was no specific biblical prohibition of it. "Though it looks as if the word, unclean, would take it in, yet we cannot say for sure that it does." Ruth advised Mrs. Freed to "go

Preacher Christian Allebach of Towamencin (father of Alpheus), shortly before his death on November 1, 1917. At this time he was residing in the new Old People's Home (background) built by the Franconia Conference at the edge of Souderton in 1916. (Alpheus C. Allebach)

slow" in refusing communion, for by so doing she would be "judging God's servant," the bishop. The man in question here was Jonas Mininger. It grieved Barbara, when she was trying to persuade her son not to use tobacco, to be told that the bishop himself did. Joe Ruth reminded her that in doing so "the Bishops violate no Conference rules."[81] But she persisted in her stand, and confronted by her at a Line Lexington Communion service, Jonas Mininger, it was said, reluctantly gave up his habit. Nor was Barbara the only woman who would write the bishops, admonishing them to use their authority to maintain threatened standards of nonconformity.

The accelerated change toward more organized activity produced in one Franconia Conference session (spring 1914) both a committee to buy a

"church property at Norristown" (which led in a few years to the establishment of a Mission Board), and permission to establish "an Old People's
Home in the conference district." The latter project was first delegated to
four capable laymen from four different bishop districts, although it was
also stipulated that the new "Home," if built, was to "be under the supervision of conference." Trustees were selected from among the various deacons, the traditional custodians of charitable work in the church. As in the
recent building project at Perkasie, William M. Moyer was a prime mover
(he and Alvin C. Alderfer of the Eastern District's Eden Congregation
would also lead out in the establishing of the new Grand View Hospital).
After some objections that it was uncompassionate to place older people in
an institution, Franconia Conference members rallied so generously to a so-
licitation that the fifty-occupant building which contractor Joseph Bechtel
insisted should be at the edge of Souderton was finished in 1916, and
shortly out of debt. Bechtel had the same architect for the Home as he had
had in building Harvard University's Widener Library. A mere five years
later a large annex would be added. The planned church building in Norristown, being of a less "practical" nature, took the conference considerably
longer, and the World War would interrupt this project's momentum.

If this was a less crucial era for the Eastern Conference, it was partly
because its members had earlier moved into the activities now being taken
up for the first time by their Old Mennonite counterparts. There was no
Eastern Conference parallel to the new Franconian return to plainness of
dress. Mission board and old people's home had long been established. One
symbol of the New Mennonites' greater readiness to adapt to cultural
changes was the initiation by Alvin C. Alderfer of Harleysville of a new automobile insurance company in 1915 (the Mutual Auto Fire and Theft Association of Harleysville). At first the business was conducted in Alderfer's
home.

A less fixed pattern of leadership was evidenced in the way Eastern
Conference Mennonite ministers shifted from congregation to congregation, or moved in and out of the conference. W. S. Gottschall had gone to
Ohio and A. S. Shelly to California. At Allentown, from whence William
Grubb had also moved to Illinois, a young supply pastor, Lutheran YMCA
worker Victor Boyer was ordained. He became one of the most captivating
preachers in the Eastern Conference for the decade and a half before 1930.
Although enthusiastically endorsing the Mennonite heritage of simplicity
and mutual care, he led the Allentown congregation in getting a new
church "of Gothic style throughout."[82] He also served as conference
president (the position was handed around) before abruptly leaving both
congregation and conference because of personal problems. One pastor of a

younger church who stayed put was Silas Grubb of Second Church in Philadelphia, happy in his assignment by General Conference as editor of *The Mennonite*. He would work at this task from 1915 to the end of his productive years. His well-known father, president of the General Conference Publication Committee, may have influenced this appointment.

Another new minister, the middle-aged Linford Foulke, came from Quaker lineage. He managed to keep the Saucon congregation alive for seventeen years following his ordination there in 1915. Elder A. B. Shelly, who had died in 1913 while still somewhat active at the age of seventy-nine, had reorganized the congregation in 1911, after others had counseled that it were perhaps better given up.

There was vigorous life in the fast-growing Zion congregation at Souderton, which would surpass Philadelphia's First Church in another two decades as the largest in the conference. Bankers, businessmen, and a doctor enthusiastically participated in a campaign by a "Men's Volunteer Bible Class" that gathered as many as 115 men on one Sunday morning. Pastor J. W. Schantz baptized a promising student from Pennsylvania State College, Samuel T. Moyer, son of Dr. Samuel C. Moyer, family physician living near Lansdale.[83] Young Samuel would leave for India in a few years as a missionary. Some of the members of Zion's Men's Bible Class traveled as far as the rural "Rocky Ridge" community, seeking to interest new people. In cottage meetings there they contacted some forty persons, winning several converts.[84] Even when the energetic Pastor Schantz was struck down by disease in 1916, the church continued to grow rapidly under his replacement, Reed Fretz Landis. The latter, well-liked young man from Bucks County, was the grandson of a minister in the old Franconia congregation.

One of the striking developments at Zion, which remodeled to double its seating capacity in 1916, had been a series of evangelistic meetings, shared with the Schwenksville congregation, at which there had been fifty-three "open confessions of Christ" at Zion alone (February 1915). The evangelist was Minister Lee Lantz of Illinois.[85] He had led an even more spectacular revival in the independent Richfield Mennonite congregation of Juniata County a year earlier. No less than sixty-five new members had joined this congregation, which had then been forced to enlarge its meetinghouse.[86] For decades there had been close contacts between Richfield and the "Johnson Mennonites" at Skippack. It had been Bishop Amos K. Bean of Skippack who had performed the ordination of Elmer Graybill, the leading minister at Richfield, in 1902. Now Richfield had on foot a movement to seek affiliation with the Eastern Conference. For various reasons this would not be fulfilled until 1928.

But still farther west, in the Morrison's Cove area north of Bedford, were other Mennonites who were also looking east. The town of Roaring Spring had an unusual Mennonite congregation that was in the process of spawning several others, and in 1912 they all applied for membership in the Eastern Conference. Whereas at Richfield the main leadership was in the Graybill family, the key name at Roaring Spring was Snyder (the family which had earlier given its name to Snyder County). This family had also originally come from the Richfield congregation. In 1895, having moved out from the older Martinsburg congregation to Roaring Spring, Minister Abraham Snyder had bought an old Methodist church and, in a short time, gathered a congregation among people of non-Mennonite background. Abraham's two sons Jacob and Herman, both ordained by him in 1906, were "Sunday School enthusiasts." Having no other contacts with the more traditional Mennonites than the Snyders, the new Roaring Spring congregation voted in 1912 to withdraw from their Old Mennonite conference, and applied to the much more distant but less restrictive Eastern Conference for membership. All three ministers—old Abraham and his two sons Jacob and Herman—kept their plain coats, and at least the sons attended Eastern Conference sessions wearing them, along with black bow ties. In a few years Herman and Jacob had organized little congregations at four locations in their general region: Smith's Corner, Napier, Mann's Choice, and a mission in Altoona. By 1920 all these congregations (and a mission at Barr) had won acceptance into the Eastern Conference,[87] with elders such as Silas and William Grubb traveling out to central Pennsylvania to perform ordinations. One blow to the new congregations was the accidental death of thirty-eight-year-old Pastor Herman Snyder at his work in the Pennsylvania Railroad shops at Altoona, in 1917. He had been preaching at three or four of the new congregations every Sunday. A little nephew was born to him around this time, in the Altoona Mission congregation, who would grow up to be executive secretary of the Mennonite Central Committee—William T. Snyder.

Thus from now on the dual versions of the Mennonite fellowship in the eastern counties would also be available west of Lancaster County. Congregations not content with the cultural aspects or tighter central control of the Old Mennonite way would be added to the roster of the "Eastern District" of the General Conference. Interestingly, it was at the Old Mennonite congregation at Martinsburg, earlier the church of the Snyders, that the ambitious Clayton F. Derstine of Souderton was ordained in 1914. This installed him briefly in the Old Mennonite Mission in Altoona, which worked parallel to the Mission of the Eastern Conference, but with little or no intercommunication. Both Derstine and John L. Stauffer, ordained for the

Altoona Old Mennonite Mission, soon moved on to other assignments, confirming to the dubious Franconia Conference bishops the younger men's impatience with the older procedure of waiting for the lot.

As Europe became increasingly convulsed with war, Americans were under the impression that their nation would stay neutral. President Wilson was reelected in 1916 with the slogan, "He kept us out of the war." Leaders of both the Eastern and Franconia Conferences seem to have made little or no special attempt to prepare their people for a major test of their "nonresistant" faith, Herbert W. Birky, after 1913 a teacher at Bluffton College, but who had grown up under the conscientious preaching of Anthony S. Shelly at Hereford, would later state, "I don't recall ever hearing a pacifist sermon in all my life.... [It] was dormant, excepting in print.... We had no discussions on pacifism that I recall, till the war came."[88] Maxwell Kratz, by now a lawyer in Philadelphia, and like Birky a graduate of Princeton, had concerns for a peace witness, but even he had taught for several years at a military academy. One reminder of the old nonresistant testimony did appear in the 1915 *Mennonite Year Book and Almanac,*[89] edited by N. B. Grubb, Harvey Allebach, and Uriah Stauffer, the Quakertown printer. It was a Revolutionary War petition by Mennonites and Dunkers in Lancaster County, setting forth the old Mennonite feelings about war. The same document was reprinted in one form or another, without comment, in three of the next four issues of the *Year Book.* This seems to be a sign that these Eastern Conference leaders were trying, in the midst of war and rumors of war, to awaken the memory of the nonresistant teaching in their readers' consciousness.

Another concern of the years leading to the war was that of schooling. A group of men meeting in Virginia in 1916 to consider starting a school for Old Mennonites included young Rhine Benner, formerly of Telford, and now a rural mission worker in West Virginia. There was an Old Mennonite college at Goshen, Indiana, but most Franconia Conference leaders considered it too worldly. An exception was William M. Moyer, active promoter of the Perkasie meetinghouse, the Old People's Home, and the new Grand View Hospital. "Lots of our people in Bucks and Montg. Co.," he noted, were "not interested in [Goshen] college as they ought to be." When one of the young fellows in his Sunday school class at Blooming Glen, Clayton Kratz of Hilltown, decided to attend Goshen, William was pleased. Much of the local people's attitude toward Goshen would depend, he wrote to President J. E. Hartzler, on "how Bro. Clayton Kratz will return at the end of his term. I hope that Bro. Kratz will make a success and will stay Christ like. And that more of my class will take a course in the college."[90]

Moyer's attitude was parallel to that of Pastor A. M. Fretz at the Eastern Conference Deep Run congregation, who was pushing Bluffton College among his young people. He went so far as to assert that "The future of our churches depends largely on Bluffton College." He quoted a brother of W. S. Gottschall, who had moved out to Bluffton and was now a leading pastor in the community, as saying that the college's President S. K. Mosiman was "a deeply spiritual-minded man." Further, argued Pastor Fretz, "our boys and girls [ought to go] to Bluffton . . . because there they are taught Mennonite doctrine. How many of our young people in our churches know why they are called Mennonite more than their being called after Menno Simon?"[91] In both Conferences, of course, suspicion of their western schools' orthodoxy persisted. Bethel, the General Conference College in Kansas, was seen as too distant to be an option, and more for the "Russian" Mennonites. The Old Mennonites of the East felt fewer and fewer spiritual connections with the "Russian" westerners whose parents they had helped to immigrate four decades earlier. But they must have been gratified when Deacon Henry Krupp, who had taken over the old loan fund originally administered by Herman Gottshall, received in the fall of 1916 a loan repayment of $7500 via B. F. Buller of Nebraska.[92]

When the United States finally declared war, on April 6, 1917, the burning question for the nonresistant churches was what the forthcoming draft legislation would be like. Within a week a committee of three men representing the General Conference Mennonites was in Washington, interviewing members of Congress and asking that the new law include an exemption for nonresistant people. One of these three men was Philadelphia lawyer Maxwell Kratz, a member of Silas Grubb's Second Mennonite Church and as effective a public speaker as his pastor was weak. This tall, persuasive, resonant-voiced man, who had been raised among relatives in Frederick Township after his father had left his family, was of great service in these years not only to the Eastern Conference, but as one of the founding officers of the Mennonite Central Committee which would appear soon after the War. His committee's goal was fulfilled when the Selective Service Act of May 18 did include an exemption clause. Many Mennonites were not fully satisfied, nevertheless, since the law required at least noncombatant service, and it was not clear whether this would be under military auspices or not.

As might have been expected, the Franconia Conference took a stricter approach to the military issue. Whereas the Eastern Conference held up nonresistance as the ideal, Franconia attempted to require it. No one employed in a factory making ammunition was allowed to commune.[93] "Liberty Bonds" were not to be purchased (at Zion members were en-

couraged to buy them), but this advice was not always lived up to. Since the
Franconia Conference had held aloof when an Old Mennonite General
Conference had been formed two decades earlier, its leaders had no larger
framework, organizationally, as did the Eastern Conference through its
General Conference affiliation. Thus the Franconia bishops and their
English-writing secretary, J. C. Clemens, wrote their own letter to President
Woodrow Wilson. All over the country various groups of Mennonites and
Amish were doing the same thing. The Franconia bishops' letter asked for
more definite exemption—even from noncombatant service—than the new
law seemed to provide for. And as the time for mobilization of the draftees
drew near, four men went down to Washington to speak directly with
Secretary of War Newton Baker. They were Bishop Abraham Clemmer of
Franconia, Minister Joe Ruth of Line Lexington, Deacon Wilson Moyer of
Blooming Glen, and a layman, Sellersville automobile dealer William A.
Derstine of the Rockhill congregation.[94]

A special session of the Franconia Conference was called together two
days after this committee had interviewed Secretary Baker. All persons
interested in the draft issue were invited, and a crowd estimated at 1,000
filled the recently built brick meetinghouse on Chestnut Street, Souderton,
on Monday afternoon, September 3, 1917. Some 350 men from seventeen
Franconia Conference congregations had been drafted, according to a
report in a Philadelphia newspaper. Six of these men had been subsequently baptized at Souderton, being "not willing," as the report went
on, "to go to the camps as non-members of their sect."[95] Abraham G. Clemmer presided at the meeting in German, and schoolteacher-Deacon Wilson
Moyer, "a gently eloquent man," explained the position of the secretary of
war as the committee had heard it firsthand. A newspaper reporter from the
Philadelphia *Public Ledger* was struck by the demeanor of the large
assembly, particularly their lack of protest and bitterness toward the government. The account in the *Ledger*[96] the following morning noted the many
tears, the ministers' greeting each other with kisses, and the general "simplicity almost incredible unless it were seen." The young men were told
that they should report to the "mobilization camps" if drafted, but there
meekly state their belief and decline the uniform. They could then expect to
be sent to "detention camps." They were to be "pleasant" to any who
might harass them.

> "If the drafted brethren have Christ in their hearts," said one
> deacon rising in the meeting, "there will be no need of our going along,
> for He will be with them and be their guide."
> "Christ promised that," agreed Bishop Klemmer.

As though it were impossible longer for them to contain their emotion, virtually every other person in the meeting fell to weeping, the bonnetted women on one side of the auditorium and the scarfless men on the other. The final prayer was also a signal for a flood of silent tears.

The meeting closed with a hymn, "Be Ye Strong in the Lord," and as the crowd left, "several thousand dollars" were placed in the collection boxes at the doors to help the draftees.

The same newspaper also interviewed Bishop N. B. Grubb, chairman of the Eastern Conference's "Draft and Exemption Committee," after this body had met in Philadelphia in the same days.[97] The committee had decided to "send a letter of instruction" to their young men who had been drafted. Bishop Grubb, according to a reporter, "made it plain .that the Mennonites of the eastern district differ from the 'old branch' of the church. . . ." In accordance with "the more liberal interpretation given the Mennonite doctrine," Eastern Conference men could serve in the army, declining to carry arms, but "standing ready to do any other service that the Government may dictate." The bishop said, by way of explaining his own views, that whereas he had heard of Mennonites who made no resistance to burglars, he himself would try to keep a burglar out, but "would not attempt to kill him." His committee, he commented further, had decided "to urge young Mennonites to form units to go to France for hospital and Red Cross work." "So I do not think we can be accused of being disloyal."

Of the "350" drafted Franconia Conference men, only sixteen were actually called to a military camp. Five members were known to have joined the Army.[98] By comparison, in the Zion Mennonite Church alone fifteen men were called, and most opted for military service.[99] From A. M. Fretz's Deep Run three men went to detention camps as conscientious objectors, and two were noncombatants.[100] Springfield had one C.O. Of twenty C.O.s from both the Eastern and Franconia Conferences at Camp Meade in Maryland, eight belonged to the Eastern Conference.[101]

Departures at the train stations tended to be dramatic, with some of the Old Mennonite boys in plain dress. One Deep Run Old Mennonite who held up his girl friend at the train window to kiss her good-bye, would stay in Maryland after the war, and marry a Catholic girl. The Old Mennonite boys received typewritten sheets entitled "Helpful Hints to Our Young Brethren," and were urged to wear "a plain suit and hat," and to meet together to study the Sunday school lessons. At Camp Meade they were at first, under virtual arrest, forced to don army clothing, but after an appeal by church leaders, this requirement was later rescinded. In their barracks they were visited by ministers such as Joseph Ruth, J. C. Clemens, and

Conscientious objectors from the Franconia Conference at Camp Meade, Maryland, in World War I, included (l. to r.) Marcus Lederach of Salford, David Derstine of Franconia, and William Rice of Deep Run (man in back not identified). (J. Russell Bishop)

Visiting at the conscientious objector barracks at Camp Meade, 1917-1918. (J. Russell Bishop)

Wilson Moyer. Some ministers, such as Jacob Moyer of Souderton, wrote encouraging letters. There was some harassment. Abraham Stover at Camp Green in South Carolina had his clothing stolen, and felt that the treatment he received permanently weakened his heart. Abraham had refused to go to a farm as a means of escaping the draft, as he felt this would not be entirely honest. So many other Mennonite young men chose the farm option that Souderton Bank President Allen Reiff, a member of the Indian Creek Reformed Church, was kept up late at night helping them to fill out their exemption forms.

The war issue was felt throughout the community. Old Mennonite James Derstine of the Rockhill congregation reluctantly gave up his mail delivery work, since it required the selling of Liberty Bonds. Warren Smith, one of the young men at Zion who had joined the army, came home from camp at Easter, 1918, and went forward to take communion at Zion while wearing his uniform. Pastor Reed Landis seemed to allow this, but it upset plumber Henry Detwiler, one of the main lay leaders of the congregation. He called Warren aside and rebuked him, saying, "I wouldn't have allowed you to take communion if I were the minister." But three or four weeks later, after Warren had been released from the Army, Henry came to him again and asked his forgiveness for the way he had spoken to him. He had been unable to sleep, he said, thinking about it. When Warren forgave him, Henry said, "Mir wolle grad uff die Knie geh' " (Let's get right down on our knees), and led in a prayer of reconciliation.[102] Another war-related incident was the fining of Rhine Benner, now of Job, West Virginia, for advising his church members that they need not buy war savings stamps. Both he and his bishop were charged penalties of $1,000 by the Federal authorities. Benner was briefly jailed, and soon came back for a stay in Souderton. At State College the youngest son of Pastor A. M. Fretz, Osmund, joined the army that summer. But he found himself unable to obey the orders, in the "student drills," to jam his bayonet into a bundle of sticks while yelling, "You _____ German Hun!"[103]

In the midst of the war excitement, lawyer Maxwell Kratz of Philadelphia precipitated a significant new organization in the Eastern Conference—a men's "Brotherhood." He proposed it a few days after the first draftees had left for camp, at a Sunday school convention at Perkasie. There was, he felt, a "lack of acquaintance among the men" of the Eastern Conference. "The men of the city churches should know their brethren in the country churches, and vice versa." It was Max Kratz's way of getting the men more involved in the church, and of trying to preserve something of the family feeling that had traditionally characterized the Mennonite fellowship. When he gave one of his lawyer-like speeches, with tears streaming down his cheeks, few in the audience could fail to be moved. An impressive group of officers was elected for the new Brotherhood, including Kratz, Deacon Franklin Moyer (a Philadelphia accountant and businessman), Seward Rosenberger (principal of a school in Philadelphia), and John D. Moyer (cashier of the bank in Souderton). The first three, especially, a set of close friends, threw themselves into this work with enthusiasm, helping to raise money for various conference causes (especially war relief), or for the aid of students who lacked sufficient means to prepare for Christian service. The Brotherhood was strongest in its first few years, as the three leaders led the way. But Frank Moyer died unexpectedly in 1922, and the original drive was never fully recovered, as Max Kratz would later acknowledge in another tearful speech.[104] It was an interesting foreshadowing of a similar group appearing later in the Franconia Conference, calling itself the "Clayton Kratz Fellowship." Both groups came from lay initiative, and both found themselves challenged, on occasion, for setting up activities that paralleled those administered by their conferences.

The war months coincided with a turning point in the local funeral customs, brought about also by the increasing use of the automobile. The first afternoon funeral at Franconia, as opposed to the immemorial custom involving the entertaining of relatives and friends at two meals in the home of the deceased, occurred in the just-expanded meetinghouse on February 16, 1918.[105] Less than three months later another significant funeral took place, at the Eden Mennonite Church of Schwenksville. It was for Ann Jemima Allebach, who had died suddenly and unexpectedly after a busy day's work in New York. During the previous summer she had transferred her membership from Eden to the First Mennonite Church of Philadelphia, where her ordination had been performed some seven years earlier. She had been disappointed in the lack of acceptance by Mennonites in her ministerial role, although there had been, on occasion, sizable audiences when she preached at Schwenksville or Souderton. For two years she had been acting pastor of the Sunnyside Reformed Church. Her black-bordered funeral announcement referred to her as "Rev. Ann J. Allebach of New York City." N. B. Grubb and his son William, new pastor at Eden, were in charge of the service.[106]

But a half year later, in October 1918, the most unusual funeral activity in years took place, as eastern Pennsylvania yielded a quota of victims to the worldwide influenza pandemic. Meetinghouses and churches were closed to avoid contagion, and some of the victims had only funerals conducted at the graveside. On October 13 no church services at all were held in the Franconia region. Perhaps these traumatic events were the final blow to the old all-day funeral tradition.

William Derstine and Mennonites of other communities had been going to Washington, asking for agricultural furloughs, or work-releases, for
the conscientious objectors who were merely putting in time at the detention camps. This was granted in the summer of 1918, and all but two of the
sixteen Franconia Conference men were furloughed to farms. Norman
Derstine of Souderton went to a farm in Maryland; David Derstine of Franconia and Marcus Lederach of Salford were sent to farms in Illinois and
Kansas, respectively, after they had first been shipped to Fort Leavenworth
for special interrogation. Mahlon Alderfer of Rockhill worked at a state hospital in Virginia. A month or so after the Armistice (November 11, 1918),
most were discharged.[107] The Franconia Conference asked them to return
to the government any pay that they might have received for their work,
and replaced this with amounts totaling $2,627.18. The spring session of
conference in 1918 sent a letter of thanks to President Wilson "for the care
and regard . . . shown our brethren." Two of the five Franconia Conference
men who had accepted military service were received back into membership by confession. The other three joined Lutheran or Reformed
churches.[108]

Though strong war feelings had been unleashed, as shown by enthusiastic mass "Liberty Sings" here and there, the nonresistant Mennonite
community was not singled out for abuse (in contrast with the experience of
some Mennonites of other communities). An occasional letter to a newspaper questioned agricultural exemptions or the sincerity of "slackers," but
unpleasantness was minimal. In the Eastern Conference, the strongest advocate of the nonresistant stand may have been Robert Stauffer of West
Swamp, who had been sent to Camp Meade in Maryland. A problem did
emerge for some of the families of the Vincent Mennonite congregation, as
a non-Mennonite clergyman of Spring City stirred up the patriotism issue
during and after the war, focussing critical attention on local Mennonites.
The new American Legion organization, too, protested the failure of several
Mennonite children from Vincent to salute the flag during daily school
exercises. The parents in question were Francis Bechtel and John Kolb. The
latter of these two farmers transferred his children Elmer and Dorothy to
the Royersford school, but here too the Legion followed up the issue. So
Elmer dropped out of school (he was high school age) and Dorothy went to
the new school of the Old Mennonites at Harrisonburg, Virginia, where
people like C. F. Derstine, John L. Stauffer, and Warren Kratz had been
studying. The Bechtel family eventually moved to Virginia as well. Before
the affair was over, the Chester County courts had fined both fathers a
token $2.00 and costs, and "ordered them to compel their children to attend
the public schools."[109] This was about twenty-five years before the Fran-

conia Conference Mennonites began to organize their own elementary schools.

Once the war was over, the attention of both conferences turned rapidly toward relief work. Already before the Armistice Harvey Mack of Plains had gone to France with the Red Cross (about fifty other Mennonites were in relief efforts there). William Derstine, who had been indefatigable in traveling to Washington on behalf of the Franconia Conference (at his own expense), had also worked closely with the Quakers, a number of whom visited the morning services at Rockhill in the late summer of 1918. The Franconia Conference took a vote of thanks to Derstine for his valuable help in dealing with a variety of public officials and agencies. And soon after the war ended, in a special session on January 11, 1919, the Conference asked him to represent them in matters relating to congressional pressures for universal military training. But two weeks later this burly automobile dealer and Sunday school superintendent was on his way toward the Middle East aboard a relief ship, the *Pensacola*. He was one of a committee of nine Mennonite men asked to investigate the plight of refugees in Syria and Turkey, and to see whether a "unit" of Mennonite relief workers could be set up there. On reaching a town fifty miles from Constantinople, Derstine and his companion Aaron Loucks of Scottdale found chaotic conditions, and other relief workers who did not seem anxious to have a new unit involved in the work. While Loucks accompanied a train-load of supplies into the interior, Derstine found himself considered "almost indispensable," because of his mechanical knowledge, for overseeing the huge operation of assembling hundreds of trucks to haul relief goods from seaport to countryside. But after a few weeks both Loucks and Derstine returned to the other Mennonite workers in Beirut, and decided to go back to the States with the recommendation that no separate new Mennonite unit be organized.[110]

Both the Eastern and Franconia Conferences held special sessions on the relief question in 1919. The Eastern Conference set a combined goal of $60,000 for relief, reconstruction, missions, and education. The task of raising this considerable amount among a membership of about 2700 that had never been used to a "budget" approach was given to the new Men's Brotherhood, which had begun with about 127 members. A regular campaign was set up, including the use of pledge cards. After a year's efforts $50,000 had been pledged. This was on a scale new to the conference. Eventually $41,663.99 was received.[111] Max Kratz, "the advocate," pleaded for "sacrificial giving," and even though the stated goal was not reached, the campaign was felt by conference members to have been valuable training in giving. One thousand dollars was loaned to the Krefeld Mennonite

Church in Germany, one of the parent churches of the eastern Pennsylvania Mennonites, and twenty-nine bales of clothing went to Russia.

Franconia's regular spring conference session commissioned Bishop Abraham Clemmer and Deacon Wilson Moyer to attend a meeting on relief plans to be held in Iowa. All over North America Mennonites were trying to get involved in meaningful relief efforts. At another special session on November 26 the Franconia Conference decided to send relief to European children via the American Quakers. By the following April about $10,500 had been raised for relief, bringing the total contributed for this cause by the conference since the beginning of the U.S. entry into the war to $49,058.97. From September 1920 to May 1921 another $8487 came in, as well as 139 bales of clothing and shoes.[112]

Although William Derstine and Aaron Loucks had not recommended independent relief work near Constantinople, across the Black Sea from this Turkish port were other people in trouble, Mennonites in Russia. Some of them were starving in the midst of Revolutionary tensions, having seen most of their goods confiscated by roving bands of ruffians. Many were anxious to immigrate to North America, and three of their leaders came to the United States in the summer of 1920 to ask for help in such a move. A historic response occurred: the relief committees of six separate Mennonite groups met and elected a "central committee" as a kind of clearinghouse for their various projects. It was probably the most "ecumenical" act in American Mennonite history. There had already been plans to do something for the Russian Mennonites by both "Old" and "General Conference" Mennonites. The first three workers actually set sail (September 1, 1920), before the new "Mennonite Central Committee" (MCC) had elected an "Executive Committee." And in one of the many parallels of their divided history, both the Eastern and Franconia conferences were represented in the movement by men named Kratz. For when the *Providence* sailed out of New York harbor for Naples on September 1, one of the three Mennonites in this "first independent war relief unit ever sent out by the Mennonite Church" was Goshen college student from the Blooming Glen congregation, Clayton Kratz. Clayton, who had a brother who had served in the Army's Signal Corps, had been chosen for this work by his teacher, Professor Harold Bender. A similar high opinion of him had become evident when the students had just elected him, after his junior year, president of the campus Young People's Christian Association.[113] "Our address," wrote his fellow worker Orie Miller of Lancaster County, will be "c.o. Near East Relief, Constantinople, Turkey."

In the very week of their sailing, the other Kratz—Maxwell—gave one of the most memorable of his "advocate"-like speeches. It occurred during the eight-day General Conference held in a tabernacle in the park of the town of Perkasie, where the Eastern Conference was hosting the twenty-second session of this body which had now grown to nearly 20,000 members. It was an unusual session—the first in history to be conducted in English, and filled, at first, with an unprecedented apprehension of "bitter discussions or even . . . a break in the brotherhood." What should be done, was the question, about the divided response to the recent military draft? The conference delegates arrived amid pouring rain that seemed to symbolize stormy debates. Anthony S. Shelly, formerly pastor at Hereford but now of Bluffton, Ohio, and "the best parliamentarian in the Conference," was president, and he was as concerned as anyone. But as the morning of the first session dawned cloudlessly, frankness turned out to be seasoned with forbearance, and no explosion occurred. "A total of 805 young men," Shelly recorded, had been "in the service during the war" (what the ratio of conscientious objectors was he did not note). The "questions of conscience" they faced had been given, in Shelly's opinion, "too little consideration" in the training the church had earlier given these young men. Now some of the delegates wanted the conference at Perkasie to "take some action or make some pronouncement . . . as a rule or guide for a uniform attitude and practice expressive of our Mennonite teaching." But after discussion the conference declined—"wisely," in President Shelly's words—to call "anyone to account for what had been done under the painful stress of war conditions. . . ." It was not, Shelly wrote, that there was any "thought of receding from the historic position of our Church," but rather that the church's "stand and . . . doctrines" should now be "made better known to the world."[114] So compellingly did some feel this urge that the new Men's Brotherhood of the Eastern Conference promptly passed a resolution to invite essays on the subject of nonresistance, and offer prizes for the three best ones. This idea, however, was not carried out.

The "harmoniousness" of the Perkasie conference session was later credited to Anthony Shelly's "tact and skill," but it may also have owed something to the eloquence of Max Kratz. He gave a long-remembered, lawyerlike plea to the assembled delegates that they not "cast out" the Eastern District because some of its members were beginning to join the Grange, or other organizations known as "secret societies." He himself, however, opposed these societies. He was a rare example of the ability to grow in his appreciation of traditional Mennonite teaching—at least on some subjects—while he grew more sophisticated in the ways of the world. The Eastern Conference had been born, of course, with a strong position against belonging to secret societies, losing as valuable a member as co-founder Abraham Hunsicker in preference to compromising. "We believe," went a statement Maxwell Kratz helped to draw up, "that such outside and temporal associations tend to weaken and destroy the bond of common faith between us, which meant so much to our fore-fathers and ought to mean no less to us." It was for such deeply felt reasons that Max Kratz and Seward Rosenberger had called forth the "Men's Brotherhood" of the Eastern Conference. In a further statement of a committee on which they both served (chaired by A. M. Fretz), they articulated an ideal which showed a strong sense of responsibility for "maintaining a right fellowship":

> We believe that the Christian should find true and complete fellowship only with those to whom faith in Christ is as vital as it is to him and that this association with other men upon terms that profess to be those of the fullest brotherhood, irrespective of their religious beliefs and regardless of the lives they lead, is truly being "unequally yoked together with unbelievers."[115]

There is irony in the fact that such a statement was superior in clarity and grace to the expressions on the same subject by Franconia Conference leaders. But whereas the Eastern Conference would hold up such teaching as a banner, and hope for obedience, the Franconia Conference would demand conformity to its standards on pain of excommunication. These were the two methods, each considered valid by its proponents, of "maintaining the right fellowship" that was the church of Christ. The Franconia Conference was embarked on a campaign for stricter, not more comfortable, order. On October 3, 1918, it had resolved that its "rules," now periodically printed, "should be read to every congregation at least once every year."[116] The fact that this would be done at communion-time, with the intention of maintaining the right fellowship, would eventually create in some younger minds the impression that the Lord's supper was a matter primarily of discipline. The process of growing specificity of regulation would continue for another half century, and then collapse under its own weight. It would not be until 120 years after the 1847 division that the main body of the Old Mennonites in easternmost Pennsylvania would find itself ready to take a culturally less conservative approach, somewhat as John Oberholtzer had fostered. But they worked their way into this position through deliberate processes of consensus and waiting, rather than through the strict parliamentarianism and congregationalism of their Eastern Conference counterparts.

In September 1920 Maxwell Kratz was elected "Third Member" of the Executive Committee of the newly formed Mennonite Central Committee. Two months earlier his distant cousin Clayton Kratz had arrived at Constantinople. Armed with his Bible and money to purchase relief supplies, Clayton embarked with his companion Orie O. Miller for the port of Sevastopol in the Crimea, on the other side of the Black Sea. From there they took the train, and a carriage to Halbstadt, "the most important town in the largest colony [Molotschna] of the Mennonites in Russia." A civil war was raging between "White" Russian forces and revolutionary "Reds." Kratz stayed by himself in Halbstadt, setting up organization for relief-distribution, while Miller went back to Constantinople for supplies. Suddenly the "Reds" began to advance, and local Mennonites urged the twenty-four-year-old Goshen student to flee. Trying to stay until the last possible hour, Kratz was caught by an unexpected overnight arrival of the Reds in Halbstadt. He was immediately arrested, but then released on the plea of the resident Mennonites. Still thinking he could do some good, he refused to go, though a fleet of 105 boats carrying refugees had left for Constantinople, where his colleagues were anxiously waiting for news of his status. Suddenly he was taken into custody again, and this time brutally struck by those arresting him. A local Mennonite who managed to visit him found him "entirely quiet and composed in spirit."

This was the last news of Clayton Kratz that would come back to his fellow seniors at Goshen, his Sunday school teacher William Moyer at Blooming Glen, or his home in Hilltown. Other MCC workers made lengthy but fruitless inquiries of various officials in the chaotic new communist regime. The Russian Mennonites were told that their young American friend had been sent toward Moscow, and would travel from there via Sweden back to the United States. But as time went on they concluded that he had probably died of disease.[118] The name of Clayton Kratz began to mean for the Franconia Conference something of what Annie Funk's symbolized in the Eastern District. For Clayton too, a stone memorial was placed in the graveyard of his home congregation, but with only the simple inscription after his name and birth date, "Went to Russia 1920."

As Mennonite refugees drifted into Constantinople, some were helped by the new MCC to emigrate. Sixty-three younger men arrived in Lancaster County in September 1921, where they were taken up by various Old Mennonite families. Eventually, finding themselves more drawn to the less culturally distinct way of the General Conference Mennonites, some of these immigrants would become part of the little Bowmansville congregation, and still later would form the nucleus of a new congregation called "Emmanuel" near the town of Denver. In late 1923 the last refugee group coming out of Constantinople to Pennsylvania would bring guests to fourteen more homes in Lancaster County, and five in the Franconia Conference. Though the Franconians lent money to, found work for, put plain

ELKHART T

Elkhart's Only Newspaper

ELKHART, INDIANA, TUESDAY, NOVEMBER 16, 1920.

VENIZELOS; C/

RICANS AID JGEES FROM MEAN CRASH

Men, Women and :n Taken on U. S. :ls to Safety in onstantinople.

)POL IS IN A PANIC

Mennonite Student Is Red Captive

That Clayton H. Kratz of Blooming Glen, Pa., aged about 20, had been captured by Bolsheviki, was the word received today by Professor Jacob C. Myers of Goshen college. The message was sent by the Mennonite Relief Commission in Russia, which also added that it knew nothing of his fate. The young man, who was a student at the college, left in September with Orrie Miller of Akron, Pa., and Arthur Slagel of Illinois, for the Russian territory. A letter received at the college about 10 days ago stated that they were all well at the time it was mailed.

GOVERNI ROW WI CO. O/

Western Ur Handle N. on Pr

BREAK 0

Article on the front page of the Elkhart, Indiana, *Truth*, November 16, 1920. (Mennonite Central Committee)

clothes on, and even baptized some of these homeless arrivals at Salford, Franconia, and Line Lexington, the Russians could not feel permanently at home among their benefactors. Salford managed to remove the beard of Henry Dirks, who chopped wood for butcher Henry Clemens' smokehouse and helped to dig out the foundations for a new meetinghouse at Salford.

The workers at the Eastern Mennonite Home drew up Henry's two daughters' hair into buns and placed coverings on their heads. The family hardly recognized each other when they met on Sundays at church. Fifty years later a son of one of these daughters would be executive secretary of the General Conference, and a son of the other, Provost of Temple University.[119]

To share their Christian faith with people beyond their spiritual family was finally becoming important to some of the Franconia Conference Mennonites. Enthusiasts for "witness" had been gathering, especially at the "teachers' meetings" in Souderton homes, where elderly Allen Freed often held forth. In June 1917 he had been elected president of a new "Board of Missions" sanctioned by conference, which was crystallized in part by the long-standing need to have a church in Norristown.[120] Significantly, almost exactly seventy years after John H. Oberholtzer had written his constitution for the Eastern Conference, the new Franconia Conference Mission Board had a seven-page constitution. After nearly fifty years of occasional preaching among the twenty or so members who lived in the Montgomery County seat (gathering in the Dunkard meetinghouse), the Old Mennonites were determined to set up a "mission" there. One of the young participants in the teachers' meetings—former cigar-maker Elmer B. Moyer—was appointed superintendent of the work. A building was purchased on West Marshall Street, in a section of Norristown where there were as yet few black residents, and after several delays the first sermon was finally preached by Bishop Warren Bean of Skippack on April 6, 1919. This was a historic threshold, but nothing moved fast. Of the twenty-three known Mennonites living in Norristown, only five became the original members of this new congregation. One family continued to return to "the Plain" for communion.

Mission work was unfamiliar to the mentality of many conference members, and support was uneven. For those who wanted "activity," it had an air of excitement. But Superintendent Moyer had hardly begun his work, and his wife, Lena, had hardly cleaned the large apartment and hall, when he was asked to "pass through the lot" for the choosing of a minister back in his home congregation at Souderton. It was the traditional community in tension with what was hoped would be a new one. When the lot indeed fell on Elmer, his family had to move back home.[121] On the Souderton "Bench" he became one of the few staunchly premillennial ministers in the conference (along with such as Warren Moyer at Towamencin), differing vigorously but respectfully on this subject with his senior minister Jacob Moyer. The gap at Norristown was voluntarily filled by the aging Allen and Elizabeth Freed, whose willingness was not matched by ability to deal readily with town culture. Mrs. Freed was hardly even able to speak English. Finally, in the month of Clayton Kratz's departure for Russia, Willis and Mary Lederach, a recently married couple from Salford and Skippack, respectively, who had volunteered for mission service in Chicago, were asked by the new Franconia Board to come to Norristown. Willis was a banker and Mary a former teacher at the new Hesston College in Kansas. As superintending couple at Norristown for the next eight years, they arranged for visiting ministers throughout the conference to preach at the Sunday afternoon services, entertained visitors at what became a "Mennonite hotel," invited countless neighbors to the services, or distributed to needy families food contributed by Mennonite marketmen or clothing from recently organized sewing circles in the Franconia Conference.[122]

Mary Mensch Lederach, mother of a growing family as well as what one might call "matron" of the mission work, displayed the firm commitment to the Mennonite heritage that had earlier been evident in her grandfather Jacob Mensch of Skippack. Although a more capable speaker than most of the preachers in the conference, she was of course seldom called on in this capacity in the 1920s and 1930s. Later her speaking gifts would be used somewhat more. Her loyalty to her church was greater than that of her father, who fell somewhat afoul of conference authority through his great eagerness, after about 1921, to begin another mission church in the vicinity of Limerick. Abraham Mensch, along with younger enthusiasts such as Rudy Stauffer of Vincent and a set of Mennonite families who had moved to the Spring City area from Ohio in about 1920, tried repeatedly to get the Limerick "work" under way, but the group was rebuffed by the bishops for its "forwardness." The transition to a mission mentality was not going to be immediate. Eventually Abraham was even excommunicated for running ahead of conference direction. Initiative that in later decades would be gratifyingly appreciated was at this point considered a threat to the proper understanding of church authority. The family of Gabriel Brunk, a preacher who had moved in from Ohio with a group of Mennonites looking for a better economic situation, soon moved back, when it became evident that the bishops would not allow Brunk to preach in the conference.[123] These church fathers did not care to allow the standards of other fellowships to begin to control their own, which they regarded as a sacred trust. "When the call comes to do mission work," resolved the May 5, 1921, conference session, "be sure the call comes from God. Give evidence to prove that the call comes from God. Make it known to the Bishops Wednesday before Conference for their consideration."[124] Whatever happened, "should the question of ordination arise," the bishops would have the prerogative of determining procedure. They were still the "housekeepers," in

Willis K. Lederach (1898-1983) of Salford and his bride (1921) Mary Mensch (1898-1980) of Skippack shortly after their volunteering as mission workers to the Franconia Mennonite Mission Board. (Mary Jane Lederach Hershey)

the old sense, although this term was not surviving the transition to English. It would be another fifteen years before they would feel ready to ordain a minister for their new Norristown mission. Even then they would hesitate to use the traditional method of casting lots, since there was no stable congregational base from which it could rise. Finally they would approve the names of four younger men suggested by the "benches" of several different congregations and then cast lots. [125]

In contrast, the Eastern Conference was happily commissioning one of its educated young men, Samuel T. Moyer, a native of the Lansdale area. As Clayton Kratz was en route to the Near East, "perhaps the greatest service in the history" of the Zion congregation saw the commissioning of Samuel and his wife, Meta (Habegger), as missionaries to India. The growing congregation pledged its support of this son of theirs, who, only a few weeks earlier, had lost his own well-known father, Dr. Samuel C. Moyer, in a tragic railroad-crossing accident near Lansdale. Dr. Moyer, whose wife belonged to the Church of the Brethren, had been a member of the Zion Church Council. His son made the witness to the gospel "the supreme passion" of his life, most of the rest of which he and his wife would spend in India. [126] The Moyers would be joined in that country by another Eastern Conference native, Dr. Harvey Bauman of West Swamp, who also had married a "western" Mennonite wife, Ella Garber. Mrs. Bauman too was a medical doctor.[127]

It was notable that all four partners in these two missionary couples had attended Bluffton College. A sister of Mrs. Moyer was also married to Principal Seward Rosenberger's son Arthur, who would later serve several years as president of Bluffton. And in the year the Moyers left for India (1920), Bluffton got a new treasurer and business manager from Souderton in the person of Henry A. Alderfer, young partner in a store business, Sunday school superintendent, and leader of the "Choral Society" at Zion. A parallel to this in the Franconia Conference, though with a tone of less cultural sophistication, was the growing interest in the new Eastern Mennonite School at Harrisonburg, Virginia. In the same fall, recent Souderton High School graduate Ernest G. Gehman of Chestnut Street enrolled at Harrisonburg. He had been among those involved in the Souderton Old Mennonite teachers' meeting. At the Souderton High School he had been considered bright and entertainingly mischievous. When he returned from Virginia, local young fellows were awed to find him wearing not only a somber plain coat, but soft-toed black shoes as well.[128] Others who went to EMS similarly brought back into conference life the dual notes of the Old Mennonite "awakening": nonconformity and active "witness."

Another Bluffton alumnus became an important part of Eastern Conference life when N. B. Grubb resigned in 1920, after thirty-eight years as pastor of the First Church in Philadelphia. The seventy-year-old leader, now a widower, was feeling lonely, and could already see how population changes in the city were inexorably challenging the old family feeling in his congregation, and altering its long growth curve. Now he was named "Pastor Emeritus," and given a pension for life. What worthy Elisha could be found to follow this Elijah? Two of his deacons traveled out to Trenton, Ohio, to visit a promising young pastor there, Andrew J. Neuenschwander, native of Berne, Indiana, and both graduate and trustee of Bluffton College. Accepting the invitation to serve the 430-member Philadelphia congregation, unique in nature among North American Mennonites, Neuenschwander soon demonstrated the meaning of his nickname, "Speedy."[129] For several years he was able to keep the membership from declining, and it even grew somewhat. Eventually this midwesterner would be recognized as one of the Eastern Conference's most faithful, if nonspectacular, servants. In his and similar cases, the Eastern Conference was thus aggressively beginning to import ministers while the Franconia Conference leaders, ever fearful of the incursion of "pride," were still trying to show their own eager young men that giving public evidence of wanting to be a preacher was not a very good qualification for being one.

New Faces, New Doctrines, New Congregations

1920-1930

One of the many graduates of the Perkiomen Seminary who had gone on to college at Princeton was Dr. Elmer Ellsworth Schultz Johnson. This unusual member of the Schwenkfelder Church at Palm, not far from Bally, had been ordained in 1902 as a Schwenkfelder preacher for a church in Philadelphia, where he also established a new periodical, *The Schwenk-feldian*. But through his father's line he was also of Skippack Mennonite "Jansen" background. From this and his Schultz Schwenkfelder heritage he drew a double enthusiasm for church history. He researched the subject for fifteen years (1904-1919) in Germany, and became custodian of a substantial new Schwenkfelder Historical Library, stored at the Perkiomen Seminary at Pennsburg. The editorship of the multivolumed works of Caspar Schwenkfeld, founder of the denomination in the time of the original Anabaptists, came into his hands as well. Sometimes the wiry little preacher could hardly contain his intellectual excitement, in a sermon, over some historical detail he had discovered.

At the age of about fifty Johnson was appointed professor of church history at the Hartford Theological Seminary in Connecticut, where a few years later a tenth of the student body were somewhat "liberal" Mennonite. The professor grew accustomed to taking the train from the Perkiomen Valley to Hartford every week. In October 1920, at an auction of the book collection of the deceased Governor Samuel Pennypacker, who had last lived on a farm at Schwenksville, Johnson could not help buying some of the remarkable set of Anabaptist-Mennonite books, many in the Dutch language, which Pennypacker had collected from among the oldest Mennonite families in Pennsylvania. Johnson placed these in the new Schwenkfelder

Library—the Mennonites had no such facilities of their own—and asked for help with the cost of his purchase. The Franconia Conference appointed ministers Joseph Ruth, Jacob Moyer, and J. C. Clemens to "examine" the newly acquired materials, and called repeatedly on the congregations to contribute offerings.[1] In the Eastern District, the new Men's Brotherhood set a goal of $500 yearly for the same purpose,[2] but the balance was finally paid through the conference budget.

As this was going on, the Eastern District congregation at Hereford needed someone to preach for them while they looked for a permanent minister. For a quarter of a century they had been led by Anthony S. Shelly, an editor of *The Mennonite*, and five times president of General Conference. Now they decided to hire Dr. E. E. S. Johnson for the interval. They would hardly have foreseen that for the next quarter-century the Schwenkfelder professor would remain in this denomination-straddling role. He gave impassioned speeches on church history and "peace," and tried to protect the Eastern District against the pietism that had once taken a third of the Schwenkfelder membership into "Evangelical" circles. He closed down the declining "Menno Simons" congregation in Boyertown. He built himself a beautiful "English"-style house near Bally, and all the while commuted from Hartford on weekends. "Ach!" whispered one Old Mennonite woman as she heard him orate about Mennonite history, "er war immer 'n Schwinkfelder" (he was always a Schwenkfelder).

Although his congregation at Hereford did not seem as interested in history as he was, Johnson fanned the flame of the Mennonite heritage much as N. B. Grubb did. Editor Silas Grubb, of the Second Church in Philadelphia, likewise with a congregation that knew little of its spiritual ancestry, tried repeatedly to keep historical interest alive. He spoke on "Why I am a Mennonite," attempted a Mennonite novel, and even assembled a set of "magic lantern slides" on the Anabaptist-Mennonite story that kept an audience at one conference session "spellbound for two hours." Along with Elmer Johnson, Grubb hoped to see a Mennonite historical library begun. To the Grubb collection had already come the papers of John H. Oberholtzer himself. Eventually these materials would be given to Bluffton College in Ohio.

In the Franconia Conference too there were a few unquenchable historical enthusiasts, though of less education, particularly people like Preacher J. C. Clemens and farmers John D. Souder and David K. Allebach. At Bally and Boyertown there were Amy Histand Gehman and Mary Latshaw Bower, two of the most careful amateur historians in either conference. Yet on even the most noncontroversial historical topic on which people from the two conferences could converse—their common pre-1847 heritage—there was little if any dialogue, seventy years after the split.

On the other hand, there was no public friction between the two parallel conferences, except perhaps when one felt it was incorrectly identified with the other in the press. It was not gratifying to Eastern District members to be lumped with "the plain people," though Eastern preachers did occasionally speak or write of "simplicity" as a Mennonite value. By 1920, half of Eastern District members gathered in meetinghouses located in towns (if we include Schwenksville but not Bally). This was true for little more than a tenth of the Franconia Conference membership. The latter still had almost no representation among the professions, and the majority lived on farms. In these years when the automobile had become popular, but consolidated schools and radios were still on the horizon, it was quite possible to live a noiseless rural existence with little "worldly" contact.

A look through non-Mennonite eyes at this moment helps to sharpen our picture.[3] "The traveler on the road from Harleysville to Souderton," wrote a Norristown columnist in 1924, "suddenly finds himself amidst an array of old time carriage sheds arranged in tiers on both sides of the road. Hidden behind the unlovely old weatherbeaten sheds is a comparatively new stone building," which the observer found impressive for its size. In the "great room" of this meetinghouse, "one thousand persons can find seats. . . . And it is not rare that the meeting house is crowded." The Salford Meetinghouse is also mentioned as a large one (in fact, four other large Franconia Conference congregations built new or enlarged meetinghouses, 1922-25). Around Harleysville and Franconia, remarked the columnist, one sees "many women and girls wearing . . . white caps and plain dresses." In Souderton too

> are also many Mennonites. But here, as in towns generally, there is not the same disposition to cling to old customs. Zion Mennonite Church . . . has abandoned the ancient style of architecture completely. Instead of having but one large auditorium, numerous rooms are provided for church and Sunday school use. . . . And there are ornamental windows and a tower.

Another "plain" meetinghouse mentioned here is that of the Church of the Brethren at Indian Creek near Harleysville.

An interesting contact with the "world" occurred at the Old Mennonite meetinghouse at Towamencin in the spring of 1923. After a long search, a historian from Upper Darby, Jacob Allen, had found that Washington's General Francis Nash, wounded in the Battle of Germantown, had been buried in the Towamencin Mennonite cemetery. A grand-nephew of

Nash, Colonel Benneville Cameron of North Carolina, came with the Upper Darby patriot to visit his relative's grave. When the two men arrived on
a Sunday morning, they found a communion service in progress. As they sat
among the "common people" in their "plain house of worship," Mr. Allen
surmised that these Mennonites would be "reluctant to permit what
seemed to them a glorification of war." Yet he could not resist passing a
note up to the ministers (Isaac Kulp and Warren Moyer), telling them that
a relative of General Nash was in the audience. Surprisingly, the ministers
invited the white-haired North Carolina colonel to address the congregation. As the old man thanked the people for the 146 years of care given his
grand-uncle's grave, Mr. Allen experienced a "feeling," as he put it, that he
was "unable to describe."[4] But the Towamencin congregation was not
totally permissive. The Daughters of the American Revolution, a few years
later, had to place their bronze commemorative marker across the Forty
Foot Road, and "various efforts ... to remove Nash's remains to
Nashville," Tennessee (named for him), proved "futile."

Still another intriguing view of the "plain people" in "the North Penn
country" is preserved in an anonymous newspaper account of a Saturday
afternoon auction at Franconia Square in early June 1924.[5] The reporter
was bemused by the combination of "plainness" and wealth in "that

Until 1935, the horse-sheds at the Franconia meetinghouse stood on both sides of Route 113
(here, looking toward Franconia Square). (Henry D. Hagey, 1935)

overwhelmingly Mennonite community." The surprising number of "gilt-edged securities" which had been the personal estate of Mary Bechtel were knocked down by the Mennonite auctioneer at "fancy prices." While the women were "plainly dressed in black, gray or other subdued colors," their "undeniably becoming poke bonnets" must have cost as much as a hat-maker's "creation." Their "straight dresses without a solitary relieving touch of color" were draped with "expensive black shawls," and many seemed to arrive at the auction "in large and expensive motor cars." So many "men in their straight coats with collars of clerical cut and straight-brimmed, low-crowned hats" were present that the gathering "suggested a denominational assembly of some import."

It was later that very summer, after a Saturday afternoon Harvest Home Service at Bally, that a "plain clothes store" for the Franconia Conference area was born. Alpheus Allebach, a store clerk and planing mill worker, proposed a partnership to fellow Soudertonian, schoolteacher Elvin Souder, now in his late thirties. The older folks of the community particularly were "starting to buy" the kind of clothes that could be found in special stores "out in Lancaster"—"ginghams and the plain percales, with the plain patterns." "Allebach and Souder," situated just where the trolley turned from Main to Summit Street at the top of the hill in Souderton, became almost an institution in that town for a third of a century, selling "mostly plain things."[6] Plain suits for men could also be bought at several other stores, tailor shops, or factories in Souderton for the next fifty years.

Not only among older people in the Franconia Conference, but particularly where there was emphasis on Christian activity—such as at Doylestown, Blooming Glen, Souderton, and Vincent—did the new kind of plain dress become evident. Quite a few of the older men, when they made the change, kept little bow ties. Women had "strings" on their coverings—whether to tie them or let them hang was for a while a point of no little significance. Somewhat incongruously, stiff celluloid collars were worn under the plain coat, making it undistinguishable, to many non-Mennonite or non-Brethren viewers, from a clerical collar, which was a very non-Mennonite conception. Young people who wanted to be regarded as candidates for church-blessed "activity" were now becoming plain. This tendency was strengthened by the influence of Eastern Mennonite School in Virginia. Yet some of the bishops at the October 4, 1928, Franconia Conference session still found the church in "a deplorable condition in this, that she is drifting to worldliness, especially on the dress question."[7] Ministers Jacob and Elmer Moyer of the Souderton Old Mennonite congregation presented to their people a mimeographed list of specific dress standards, with further comments on the decor of homes and "vehicles" (Jacob Moyer was one of the last ministers to buy a car). The quite detailed rules, after being "explained," were "Accepted by a Rising Vote" of the congregation,[8] certainly with mixed feelings by some. But to "dress plain" became more and more a way of expressing one's full identification with the visible body of Christ in the Franconia Conference.

New notes were being heard in the worship of the Franconia Conference. To be sure, meetings on Sunday mornings remained in the traditional form: the song leaders, glancing from textbook to tunebook, led the congregation without rising to their feet. Two or more ordained men sat on the bench behind the pulpit. There were still two sermons in the Sunday morning services: "the opening," and the longer main address. Silent prayer followed the first talk, and audible, the second, the congregation kneeling for each prayer. But in the Sunday school sessions there was a different atmosphere. A lay brother, often speaking in a flat, unemotional voice, moderated the proceedings, and the song leaders, sometimes two at a time, stood up to lead the singing and even beat time. Most of the classes were in English, with much of the actual teaching and discussion being the quoting of Scriptures. In the class session a driving, multi-toned babble of teachers' voices filled the resonant meeting room. The fact that as many as two dozen teachers could be speaking at once in the same room allowed pupils to listen in on other teachers than their own. No curtain or other divider separated the classes, which consisted of several benches full of students grouped by age and sex.

Each little change in church life brought an entertaining sense of novelty to the Franconia Conference young people: electric lights, evening services, changing the old seating arrangement (which had the women and girls seated in the middle between two tiers of raised benches where the men and boys sat), special speakers, annual conferencewide "mission meetings," an English hymnbook. In the Eastern District the East Swamp congregation, having completely discontinued German services, sent its German hymnals to Canada "for the use of the Russian Refugee Mennonites" in 1928.[9] Both the General Conference and Old Mennonites had just published new English hymnals. In the Franconia Conference two of the more "Dutch" congregations—Franconia and Salford—accepted the new *Church Hymnal* from Scottdale, but used a special edition containing an appendix of German hymns selected by their bishop, Abraham G. Clemmer.[10] This allowed their choristers to continue to lead them in a hymn by Christopher Dock, or such favorites as "Jesu, Jesu, Brunn des Lebens," "Komm, O komm du Geist des Lebens," or "Spar deine Busze Nicht." Their use would not die out completely at Franconia until about 1970.

"Special music," welcome in the Eastern District, was suppressed by the Franconia Conference leaders through conference resolutions. It was of course not forbidden as recreation in homes, where instruments might be played, and where young people gathered under leaders such as Abraham Clemmer of Line Lexington or George R. Swartley of Souderton. George's sons William and Warren were both musically inclined, Will having sung in the choir as a young man when his family attended the Indianfield Lutheran Church. On Sunday afternoons George required his family to sing around the parlor organ at home.[11] On occasion he led amateur men's choruses in homes. While the Franconia Conference did "encourage instruction in singing," care was to be exercised that "only faithful Brethren be chosen" as singing school teachers. Members were requested "not to affiliate themselves with choral societies, so that they infringe on the plain principles of our church. . . ."[12] The singing schools made a real contribution, as each succeeding generation learned to sing in a harmony that continued to amaze visitors from other denominations. In the Eastern District, West Swamp too had a notable tradition of congregational song, assisted for the past half century by an organ.

An enthusiasm for special singing, though it was not allowed in church, became more and more evident in parts of the Franconia Conference. Song leader Abram Rittenhouse of Plains, one of the many musical descendants of Deacon Abraham Clemmer (1834-1918) of Franconia, made an informal quartet with his three boys. As they husked corn in October 1921 they sang in four parts all day long. The father sang bass, Abe, Jr., baritone, Curtis second tenor, and Sam first tenor. Helping his cousins at their work was sixteen year-old John Edwin Lapp, recently baptized at Plains, who had bicycled out from Lansdale where the high school was closed for "institute-week." He "sang along" with the quartet, considering himself what was sometimes laughingly called, in Dutch, a mere "Mitsinger."[13]

By 1927 such eagerness to sing was toned down by the Franconia Conference. "All organized choruses, quartet, duet, or solo singing in churches or any other public gatherings shall no longer be continued," went the resolution. Singing was to be "congregational" rather than special; "talented members" (men only, of course) should be "encouraged to help lead the congregation."[14] When some men persisted in singing in quartets or groups at chapels and other places, they were "set back" from communion. Especially at Deep Run, where song-leader Sam Detweiler had sung solos in the congregation years earlier as a boy, was this prohibition hard to accept. Yet it was made to hold rather firmly until the mid-1940s. Millard Detweiler's male chorus might meet, but only to practice, not perform, in public. Weekly singing schools were led by such teachers as Warren Swartley,

Abraham Clemmer, Sam Detweiler, and Henry Bechtel, sometimes with
more than one in process, taught by the same teacher, at the same time.
Four-part a capella singing remained vigorous. When a large crowd was in
attendance, the singer's ears might ring with the volume of sound. It was
acceptable to sing at the top of one's voice. At the Franconia meetinghouse
some of the choristers deliberately shaped their mouths and cocked their
heads so as to project the sound clearly to the farthest reaches of the large
room.

A growing issue in the wider American church scene did not leave untouched the Eastern and Franconia Mennonites. Since before the beginning of the century there had been a developing polarization between
"modernists" and those who would eventually take the name "evangelicals." The term "Fundamentals" had also come into use before 1920.
Moody Bible Institute of Chicago was seen by evangelicals as a bastion of
sound teaching. When some midwestern Mennonites attended Union
Theological Seminary in New York or the Hartford Theological Seminary
or even the University of Chicago, Mennonites favoring Moody or the conservative Reformed Episcopal Seminary in Philadelphia took alarm. Of
course E. E. S. Johnson, pastor at Hereford, was a part of the Hartford
faculty. W. S. Gottschall, formerly of Schwenksville but now for some time
a preacher at the Ebenezer Church near Bluffton, Ohio, was an enthusiast
for Moody. Chairman of the General Conference Home Mission Board,
and a preacher in many pulpits in the General Conference, Gottschall
served as a speaker at the "Founders' Week" at Moody in February 1923.[15]
It was rumored that he would have liked to be president of Bluffton
College. Instead, he moved to a pastorate at Freeman, South Dakota.

At Bluffton a new institution named Witmarsum Theological
Seminary had recently been created by leaders of more liberal leanings.
Particularly prominent were John E. Hartzler and Paul E. Whitmer, both
former Old Mennonites (president and dean of Goshen College), and both
graduates of liberal theological schools. A number of Eastern District young
men came to this seminary (which existed for only eleven years), such as
Andrew Bechtel, Arthur Rosenberger, Austin Keiser, and Wilmer Shelly.
For one reason or another, these young men took pastorates in the midwest
when they graduated. Coming east, on the other hand, were men like
Daniel J. Unruh and G. T. Soldner, as well as the earlier A. J.
Neuenschwander. Unruh arrived in 1923 to preach at a new congregation
near Quarryville in Lancaster County, which had developed from an inde-
pendent revival among a Lancaster Conference congregation, Mechanic
Grove. Bishop leadership had been given by Jacob Snyder of the church at

John Edwin and Edith Nyce Lapp at the time of their wedding on September 15, 1926. (John E. Lapp)

Roaring Spring, over a hundred miles west, and the new congregation was accepted into the Eastern District.[16] The new pastor Unruh had studied at Moody Bible Institute, and became good friends with W. S. Gottschall.

A kind of difference in emphasis developed, over the next decade and a half, between Eastern District preachers who would recommend Witmarsum and Bluffton, and those who favored Moody. The latter were strongly "premillennial" in their teaching, using the "Scofield" Bible, filled with notes that provided premillennialist, dispensationalist interpretation of the text. In 1924 Howard G. Nyce, a student at the Reformed Episcopal Seminary, became pastor at East Swamp. Also a premillennialist, he would be followed as pastor by the eastward-returning W. S. Gottschall. From these years would date a new tendency for the East Swamp congregation to support Moody and later the Grace Bible Institute of Omaha, Nebraska (now Grace College of the Bible). Whereas the more traditional Arthur S. Rosenberger—for several years president at Bluffton—would lead West Swamp in a more specifically "Mennonite" emphasis, East Swamp would become a center of "evangelical" influence. Although showing these differing tendencies, and breaking up the old connection of belonging to a common "charge" or preaching circuit, the two congregations worked together peacefully in the conference relationship. A somewhat congregational polity in the Eastern District made such differences less of a threat to harmony than might have been the case in the Franconia Conference.

Pastor William S. and Nancy von Nieda Gottschall, as grandparents, around 1935. William, son of the well-known "Mose," is here in the closing years of his final pastorate at East Swamp. He had also ministered at his native "Gottschalls'," Bluffton, Ohio, and Freeman, South Dakota. The Gottschalls' missionary daughter and her Nebraska-born husband, Peter J. Boehr (back row), are shown here surrounded by their six children. The Boehr family was on furlough from mission work in China. Jennie died in March 1936, about the time her family was to have returned to China. (James J. Gerhart)

Before Arthur Rosenberger returned from Bluffton to West Swamp, he came home on a visit (1925) to ordain his own father, Seward, as elder of the congregation. Seward had been a public school principal in Philadelphia for many years, and a diligent lay worker and preacher in N. B. Grubb's First Church. Hoping to find the West Swamp pastorate a less stressful work than his school administration, the elder Rosenberger was disappointed to find his strength giving way after about four years of a much appreciated ministry.

Three other significant appointments in the Eastern District occurred in 1921 and 1923. At Schwenksville, idealistic young bachelor Freeman Hockman Swartz, originally of Pipersville in Bucks County, was ordained to take the place of "Bill" Grubb, who had moved to a church in Illinois. It was the beginning of a lifelong pastorate for Swartz, who would be visible and audible in conference work as well for decades. At Hereford, the devout, forty-five-year-old Elwood S. Shelly was appointed assistant to the much-traveled Pastor E. E. S. Johnson. Shelly, who for years had been practically blind, and his wife had made a modest living as "telephone operators" with Elwood memorizing the placement of the various sockets on his switchboard. He had carried pastoral responsibilities at Boyertown, Saucon, and West Swamp (later Bowmansville also). His two sons Paul and Andrew, still in short pants, would lead him to the pulpit and read the Scripture for him.[17] Both sons were destined to become leaders in the wider General Conference Church. Paul would be a professor at Bluffton, and Andrew executive secretary of the Board of Missions of the General Conference.

A new appointment at Souderton occurred when a "much loved" young minister, Reed Landis, resigned from his service of seven years to become pastor of the First Congregational Church in Germantown. He was also a "general representative" of the American Sunday School Union. The choice of a new pastor seemed to lie between young Arthur Rosenberger, now in Ohio, and another Bluffton graduate, Grover Thomas Soldner, thirty-one-year-old native of Indiana, and presently preaching at Summerfield, Illinois. Though the influential Detwiler family at Zion apparently preferred Rosenberger, Soldner was voted in, and when he came to Souderton, his Illinois pastorate was taken over by a native of Boyertown, Andrew S. Bechtel. The new pastor at Souderton never seemed to win the favor of Henry and Harry Detwiler, strong father-and-son supporters of Zion. When he wished to get into the church during the week Soldner had to ask Henry Detwiler, who lived next door, for the key. He confided later that during his whole term at Souderton (1923-31) he had had to ask for his salary check every time it was due, and that when he did so, Henry

Detwiler would often express doubt that there was enough money in the treasury to cover the salary. Yet Soldner was soon elected president of the Eastern District Conference, and Zion continued its strong growth pattern during his service, increasing by 100 members. The Soldners' little son, Paul, grew up to become a nationally renowned ceramic artist. Pastor Soldner, having been ordained by P. E. Whitmer of the Witmarsum Seminary, brought along to Zion a friendly relation with Bluffton College, which he had also attended. The seminary president, J. E. Hartzler, became a favorite speaker at Zion, and while there for a series of "Bible lectures" in 1924, he "broadcast" a lecture entitled "The New World" from "one of the large [radio] stations in Philadelphia."[18]

The Franconia Conference waited until 1931 to make a resolution regarding "the evils of the radio." The preachers were then admonished to condemn the cacaphony of "doctrines on the air," whether "worldly," "foolish," or "heretical."[19] Radios were becoming common in Franconia Township by 1926. Before long there was earnest discussion in some Sunday school classes at Towamencin, Souderton, and Blooming Glen, as "premillennialism," "eternal security," "assurance of salvation," and evangelism as taught by radio preachers entered the thinking of local Christians.

These themes, of course, were already being debated before the radio came. At the May 1921 Franconia Conference, the longest session in thirty years issued, as the fourth of six resolutions, a call for restraint in the current discussions on eschatology, and a faithfulness to traditional teaching:

> This conference feels the necessity of urging the leaders of the churches to teach the new birth, separation from the world, nonresistance and other church essentials relative to the welfare of the church, and not speculate on unfulfilled prophecy as the doctrine of the millennium.[20]

The three topics listed as "church essentials" were a combination much like what Preacher Abraham Godshalk of Doylestown had fostered, in the face of an "evangelical" challenge some seventy years earlier.

But this balance would not hold for everyone in the next three or four decades. In the Doylestown-Deep Run region the challenge was focused in the advent of a visiting evangelist, one Harold Harper, a pleasant young graduate of Moody Bible Institute. Former Methodist Mahlon Gross, now a Mennonite preacher at Doylestown, had Mr. Harper as a houseguest. The young man preached earnestly in local chapels and schoolhouses, drawing quite a few Mennonites who were impressed by his evangelical messages, the enjoyable choruses he taught, his object lessons, and his encouraging teaching on "assurance of salvation." The traditional Mennonite stress on humility, which had led people to say they "hoped" they were accepted by God through the work of Christ, was seen in the newer "evangelical" perspective to show a lack of faith. Now schoolchildren in the community discussed whether they were "saved." Several Mennonite preachers offered Mr. Harper their pulpits on a Sunday morning. Some members who had not been happy about the recent stronger Franconia Conference requirements regarding the "bonnet" began to prefer Mr. Harper's fervent preaching to that of their own ministers. Even Mahlon Gross at Doylestown was drawn, for a while, by the attraction of Mr. Harper's "eternal security" emphasis.[21]

These early 1920s were not a period of strong leadership among the Deep Run Old Mennonites. When Mr. Harper, who had earlier told his audiences to "leave your money at home," began collections to build a chapel of his own, his talk of being nondenominational was seen in a negative light by the more traditional people at Deep Run. Yet a number of Mennonites were making substantial contributions, and eventually about fifty joined the new "Grace Gospel Chapel" near Fountainville, including all but two of the children of song leader Sam Detweiler. The new group turned out to be identical in doctrine with the "Plymouth Brethren." Apparently before their new chapel was completed one of the new members, an elderly woman of the Deep Run Tyson family, died, and the funeral was held in the Deep Run Mennonite meetinghouse. Mr. Harper expressed his happiness that Mrs. Tyson had been saved. Minister Jacob Rush, speaking from the same pulpit a bit later, commented that she had been saved long before Mr. Harper had come to the community.[22]

It was just about this time that the lot for minister at Deep Run fell on little, high-voiced farmer Wilson Overholt. "Der kann net brediche!" scoffed Sam Detweiler (that man can't preach!). Later Sam, an influential school director and farmer, was asked to "make it right" with the new preacher. The latter worked faithfully at his new calling, thinking over his sermons while milking. He asked his old preacher-colleague John Leatherman, who was to live only a year or two longer, how to handle a difficult Bible text in a sermon. "Wann 'n Steh zu schwer iss," counseled the veteran preacher, "luss 'n leie" (if a stone is too heavy, let it lie). But one should "dig around" the stone, to see if some of the meaning could be worked loose.[23] Now and then Wilson, in his somewhat comical Dutch accent, would quote, in all seriousness, a stanza of Yankee poetry:

Ef you take a sword an' dror it,   Guv'ment ain't to answer for it,
    An' go stick a feller thru,   God'll send the bill to you.[24]

Though like many of his neighbors of that era, Wilson could not correctly pronounce "th," the people at the Norristown Mission liked to hear his earnest preaching. Once, when a Norristown member—a Jewish boy—who had gone astray hitchhiked out to visit Wilson at his farm, he found the little preacher at the morning milking. The sudden appearance of his lost friend so delighted Wilson that he impulsively threw aside the two buckets of milk he was carrying, to embrace the prodigal.[25]

Another unforgettable Franconia Conference preacher was ordained half a year later than Wilson, at Bally.[26] It was Elias Wasser Kulp, native of Towamencin, now farming a small place on the Bally side of Crow Hill. Thin as a rail, this raspy-voiced father of fifteen had been a scrappy sort of fellow before his conversion, and he carried a bit of his pugilistic style into his pulpit-manner. His wife, Elizabeth, a very devout woman, was a sister of Preacher J. C. Clemens of Plains. The two preacher brothers-in-law stood in friendly opposition on the eschatological question. Both, in recognition of their ability to keep the attention of an audience, were increasingly invited to hold series of "evangelistic meetings," in Lancaster and parts west, before such services were generally welcome in the Franconia Conference. Their styles of preaching contrasted sharply: Clemens had a golden, cheerful voice, and Kulp operated in a shouted, prophetlike demeanor. Kulp's wife, Elizabeth (Clemens) kept a detailed diary,[27] punctuated with prayers for her often-traveling husband, her church, her children, and sometimes, in loneliness on the hillside farm, for herself.

At Line Lexington there was an unusually forceful preacher, "Joe" Ruth. Many non-Mennonite neighbors took the opportunity to hear his magisterially orated sermons, delivered with his glasses pushed down on his nose, and with a forefinger wagging admonishingly. His colleague Aaron Freed had preached so loudly as well that for a while he lost his voice. In 1923 a younger man, farmer Arthur Ruth, was ordained to assist ministers Ruth and Freed. Before long Joe Ruth was also ordained bishop in the "Central" district, but he died about two years later. The lot for bishop then fell upon his nephew Arthur. Another farmer-preacher who had recently been selected as bishop was Abram O. Histand of Doylestown. In these decades the local papers tended to write detailed if somewhat distorted accounts of the lot-casting ceremony. When Edwin Souder of Rockhill was selected as preacher in July 1924, a local correspondent reported that after the lot had been cast amidst a congregation which filled the meetinghouse "to the doors," the young farmer "was at once anointed with great solemnity and kissed on the cheek by Bishop Abram Clemmer of Franconia, while the congregation sat in perfect silence." Souder was "literally," added the writer, "called from the plow to the ministry."[28]

One of the most shocking events of this era was death by shooting of a young home missionary. It was a former Vincent boy (baptized at Coventry), Arthur T. Moyer. He had been in the lot for minister when Henry Bechtel had been ordained at Vincent in 1914. He had also volunteered as a worker at the "Welsh Mountain Industrial Mission," an outreach of the Lancaster Conference among an Appalachian-like population on a forested range of hills projecting into the "Garden Spot" itself. Arthur had been teaching school there for some time, when on January 24, 1924, he was shot by a thief he had surprised stealing the mission's corn. He died after an excruciating ride to the Lancaster Hospital. Noah Mack, a Lancaster Conference bishop who had grown up at Bally (son of Bishop Andrew), preached Arthur's funeral sermon on the text, "As a man falleth before wicked men, so fellest thou. And all the people wept again over him" (2 Samuel 3:34). A little tract appeared in the Lancaster Conference, calling Arthur "A Missionary Martyr."[29]

In a few more years a lay missionary movement would break out among Franconia Conference young people. In 1924 a "chapel" had been built for the Norristown Mission, but most of the Sunday school children, reported worker Mary Mensch Lederach, seemed to leave after reaching their teens.[30] No services could be held on Sunday morning, as there was no ordained preacher at the Norristown Mission, and even the Sunday school had to wait until 1:30 in the afternoon, by which time one of the Franconia Conference preachers, such as J. C. Clemens, could be on hand. Some of the ministers traveled to help at the Philadelphia Mission, and at Doylestown Preacher Frank Swartz of Blooming Glen occasionally spoke on Sunday afternoons at "Everybody's Mission," a little venture organized in a second-story room by a retired Presbyterian.[31] Still other Franconia Conference ministers helped out at the Frazer Mennonite Mission in Chester County, a Lancaster Conference effort. The first benches for this work had come from the defunct Franconia Conference meetinghouse at Diamond Rock, in the hills south of Phoenixville.[32]

Had the plans of young nurse Miriam Detweiler of the Rockhill congregation been carried out, she would have been the first "foreign missionary" to go from the Franconia Conference. In 1926 the conference body approved her "call" to India, where she expected to serve under the "general" Mission Board at Elkhart, Indiana. These hopes were disappointed, however, when Miriam contracted typhoid fever, and was advised by her doctor against going. Later, having married Quintus Leatherman, she would serve with him for several decades in a mission church in London, England.[33]

In these same years, mission enthusiasm in the Eastern District was fueled by the return of Samuel ("S.T.") and Meta Moyer from India on their first furlough (1927). Zion Church was packed to the doors for the welcome home service.[34] On the home front, First Church of Philadelphia was led by Pastor Neuenschwander to cooperate with neighboring churches in a "Personal Visitation Evangelistic Campaign." Twenty-eight workers went out two by two to invite prospective members. The campaign netted fifty new members, "many" of whom came from other than Mennonite background.[35] The membership of First Church would thus remain in the upper 400's until the mid-1930s, when it would begin to dip sharply. A hint of the flavor of this highly organized congregation, six or seven decades after its founding, may be savored in some of the publicity materials by which Daniel M. Landis's Men's Bible Class sought new members. Visitors, on one card, were invited to "Experience the Great American Hand Shake."[36] The Second Church, where Silas Grubb was still vigorously active, was less seriously affected numerically. At Mechanic Grove and four missions in central Pennsylvania, outreach also continued, with fluctuating success.

By 1925 two additions to the Eastern District were taking shape west of the Susquehanna. The fruit-growing countryside north and west of Gettysburg in Adams County had seen a recent influx of Mennonites. Particularly prominent were Musselmans from the New Holland region, where Noah Mack, son of Andrew at Bally, was now a bishop. The Lancaster Conference congregation at Mummasburg near Gettysburg had a "liberal" wing favoring the allowance of life insurance, and unhappy with rigid dress requirements. Other issues included "congregational versus centralized authority, whether one could marry outside of the brotherhood, relate to other churches, and whether to endorse higher education."[37] Bishop Noah Mack, who felt he could "handle" the Musselmans he had known in Lancaster County, was called in to deal with the "liberals." By his own account, he "begged" them to "adjust themselves to the doctrine and discipline of the church...." When no agreement could be found, he said, "Let us not be spiteful, but let us meet with a smile and shake hands." As Mack later recalled it, "They smiled then and have done so since when we meet, but about half of the congregation left."[38] In June 1927, with fruit farmer A. W. Geigley as minister, the new congregation bought a building belonging to the "Christian Church" in the town of Fairfield, and added a new wing. "Scarred by the experience" of division, and without close ties to other Mennonite congregations, the Fairfield church traveled what one of its most stable members called a somewhat rocky and "loner's road" until 1941 (and after), when it would be taken into the Eastern District. Yet, although it sometimes "looked to other denominations for leadership," prophetic voices from within the congregation refused to let the Mennonite convictions die.[39] From the Musselman family would come the endowment of a new library for Bluffton College.

The other western addition to the conference came in 1928, when the independent Mennonite congregation of Richfield in Juniata County finally applied for admission.[40] Having enjoyed no conference affiliation for nearly half a century (but having a special relationship with the Lower Skippack Mennonite congregation), Richfield now added 140 new members to the rolls of the conference, just a year after the total had passed the 3,000 mark. Having been independent for so long, the Richfield Church would not always find its new Eastern and General Conference affiliations comfortable.

In this same year there were also new "home mission" stirrings farther east. As early as 1913, "about 35 members of the Deep Run Church" had been reported as living in the Lansdale-Chalfont area.[41] Eastern District preachers had also spoken at numerous meetings in the Harleysville Chapel, and Alvin C. Alderfer, the leading businessman of the expanding village, had long wished for an Eastern District congregation there. Alvin's mother had belonged to the large Salford congregation of the Old Mennonites, a mile from Harleysville, but he, having married a girl from Salford, had joined the Eden congregation at Schwenksville, where his serving as a "squire" was not forbidden. Since no Eastern District congregation seemed to take root at Harleysville, Alvin joined the efforts of people like Jacob R. Fretz, forty-two-year-old wholesale grocery salesman, and later banker, of Lansdale, to open up a "work" at last in the latter town. Jacob, son of the venerable Pastor A. M. Fretz of Deep Run, had two brothers also living in Lansdale. One of them, Allen R. Fretz, opened his home for a "cottage meeting" on February 2, 1928, attended by members of seventeen local Mennonite families. A series of such meetings followed, under the spiritual guidance of "Father" A. M. Fretz.[42]

The Eastern District took a strong interest in this development, but was also concerned about an opportunity in the general "Lancaster" area, where there was a continual if slow process of members leaving the Old Mennonite churches in search of more mission activity or cultural freedom. In addition to the small congregation at Mechanic Grove near Quarryville, there seemed for a while to be possibilities for a congregation in the Soudersburg area. Simon Landis of Elizabethtown occasionally attended conference sessions, and was given voting privileges. Conference Secretary A. J. Neuenschwander thought that it would be best to concentrate mission efforts on "Lancaster." But his motion, at the May 1929 conference, meeting at Altoona, "lost," and $1,000 of the annual budget was earmarked for a new work at Lansdale.[43]

In September 1929 "the Lansdale Mennonite Mission" was founded

Grace Mennonite Church, Mt. Vernon Street, Lansdale. The recently organized congregation purchased this building from the Evangelical Church on November 11, 1924. (Mennonite Library and Archives of Eastern Pennsylvania)

in the old building of the "Evangelical" denomination. Lay leader Daniel M. Landis of Philadelphia gave the first talk. A few months later the Lansdale Mennonites telegraphed the pastor of the Mechanic Grove congregation, Daniel J. Unruh, inviting him to be their leader. This young preacher of western "Russian" Mennonite background had recently studied at Eastern Baptist Seminary (earlier at Moody Bible Institute). He took hold of the Lansdale mission work with a will, as it became the Grace Mennonite Church with sixty-five charter members.[44] At first this was pretty much a reshuffling of memberships in other Eastern District churches. Deep Run, in particular, lost several dozen members in the exchange. But soon the evangelistic and constructive-spirited Pastor Unruh was bringing in new members from other backgrounds. Several of these people would enter full-time mission work in the next half-decade. In twenty years Grace would become one of the largest congregations in the conference.

Hereford, too, had a kind of outreach in these years of Pastor E. E. S. Johnson. In 1922 the congregation (Eastern Conference) had bought two buses to bring in people lacking their own transportation. One of the buses traveled through Boyertown, Bechtelsville, Eshbach, and Barto, while the other one picked up passengers from Pennsburg and East Greenville. Eventually as many as 100 persons, mostly children, took advantage of these free rides to church. Frank Snyder drove for at least fifteen years without pay. But most of the children, observed Pastor Johnson some years later, eventually "united with the churches of their own families, Boyertown, Hill Church, Niantic, and Huffs."⁴⁵

One little Sunday school girl who left a mark in the Eastern District was Antoinette Cupo of Germantown. The always-struggling congregation in the historic stone meetinghouse there had recently lost both pastor and deacon to death. On Easter Sunday, 1928, after a sermon by the venerable A. M. Fretz, Antoinette was called on to unveil a panel of stained glass just behind the pulpit, in the original back wall which was now the front of a Sunday school annex.⁴⁶ This window, which would somewhat incongruously catch the eye of every subsequent visitor to the old meetinghouse, memorialized the names of the recently deceased Pastor Anthony Shelly and Deacon Benjamin Bertolet, as well as previous Pastor J. W. Bayley, Sunday school Superintendent T. DeWitt Temple, and Deacon Henry Markley. The person in charge of the dedication of the window was the current superintendent, powerful-voiced Walter Temple, who commuted weekly from Wilkes Barre, and later from Allentown, to carry out his office. It would be Walter and his sister Eleanor who would successfully defend the ancient landmark against takeover by other groups, which might have meant the irretrievable loss of this symbolic reminder of the first permanent Mennonite congregation in America.

Thus, to a degree unmatched as yet in the Franconia Conference, the Eastern District congregations had "activity." Their conference sessions, held only half as often as those in the Franconia Conference, were three or four times as long, and filled with committee reports, parliamentary procedure, and sometimes debate. The Franconia Conference, still always meeting at the same place—Franconia—and on a Thursday forenoon, was often characterized by whispered conversations among the bishops seated at the front, while the other ordained men waited for the result. Whereas a half dozen of the roughly eighty delegates to an Eastern District session might be women, only men deliberated at the front of the Franconia meetinghouse—the largest hall in either conference. A single page of large type contained the published resolutions of a Franconia Conference session, in contrast to the thirty-five-page booklet containing the proceedings and reports of an annual Eastern District session.

There were also other forums for discussion in the Eastern District, such as the Sunday school or Christian Endeavor Conventions. At one of the latter, held at West Swamp in 1927, Jacob Fretz had proposed a young people's retreat for the conference, to be held that very summer. One was organized in the summer of 1928, at a YWCA-YMCA girls' camp at Green Lane. Sixty-eight young people registered, with four instructors including missionary Samuel T. Moyer.[47] In another decade this activity would be held on the conference's own campground. As in many other types of activity, it would be another eighteen years before the Franconia Conference would organize a similar program.

Of the nearly fifty congregations in both conferences, the one suffering perhaps the hardest blow in this decade may have been Upper Skippack (Franconia Conference). Once a fairly strong unit in conference life, it had not grown along with its sister congregation at Salford. It had struggled painfully over the acceptance of English, and never seemed fully to recover. In 1927 a number of the old Mennonite farms adjoining the meetinghouse grounds were taken by the new Eastern State Penitentiary. This resulted in some members moving out of the community, and weakened the congregation somewhat.

As we leave the 1920s, we may recall a sight common to those years— the Jewish peddler, heaving his "bindle" (a large, strap-bound pack of dry goods and notions) from his buggy to his shoulders, or opening it in a circle of fascinated children on the kitchen floor of many a Mennonite farmhouse. A symbiotic relationship held the culturally aloof Mennonites and these peddlers together. Some of the latter, such as Benny Ziv, were direct immigrants from Russia. Although they lived in Philadelphia, they would stay overnight with people such as Abram R. Moyers of Blooming Glen or Allen and Sallie Ruth of Line Lexington. Amelia (Mrs. Abe) Ruth, also of Line Lexington, actually clothed her girls with goods given her by peddlers who stayed at her house. One of them told Abe that when Abe came to the gate of heaven, it would be said, "Let him in. He was good to the Jews." Old Abe Levinson might wave his arms in indignation as he debated the Old Testament with farmer Allen Ruth, but there was no enmity. A Salford boy might gaze with dismay as peddler Isaac Fisher, staying overnight in the "back kitchen," wrapped himself in a prayer shawl that looked to the boy like an old rag. Young fellows might play mean tricks on the younger Abe Levinson, crossing the reins to his horse's mouth, or taunting him for eating sausage with pork in it when he stopped and asked for dinner. But the peddlers' persistence was endless, and they played on their customers' consciences. "She's hiding in there," fumed Abe Levinson about a young woman near Salford, "and then she has a white cap on!" One of the Goldberg brothers of Souderton, who went rapidly from pushing his clothes-bundle on a baby carriage to owning a large clothing store, wanted to marry a local Mennonite girl, but her father warned him off decisively.

As for Benny Ziv, he would eventually arrive at Abram Moyer's barn dead in his carriage, brought by a horse that knew the way. "Der Gaul iss gor net dumm," he had told a Lower Salford Mennonite (that horse is not at all stupid). Benny had stayed with the Moyers two nights a week for thirty years.[48]

By 1930 quite a few "non-Mennonite" names were on the rolls of Eastern District congregations, especially in Philadelphia, Allentown, or the mission congregations of central Pennsylvania. An Eleanor Temple at Germantown, a Nora Behrend of Philadelphia, or a Raymond Stubbs (originally of Zion) preaching at Bowmansville might be centrally involved in a meeting of delegates at an Eastern District conference session. By contrast, all Franconia Conference leaders were of local Mennonite "stock." Many of their non-Mennonite neighbors and potential converts felt this fact very keenly. After 1931 there would be an access of "new" names, resulting from a breakthrough into home missions. Yet it would be wrong to conclude that no "outsiders" had opted for membership in the Old Mennonite family of faith, in the centuries when there had been no "mission work" as such. From among the neighbors had come a significant number of hired-men, maids, and daughters- and sons-in-law whose family names by 1930 could also be called "Mennonite." Even though the "maiden-names" of the women were lost when they married (except in the "middle names" of their children), an impressive list of originally "non-Mennonite" names had accumulated in the Franconia Conference family. A partial list would include some from Baptist, Brethren, Catholic, Lutheran, Quaker, Reformed, and Schwenkfelder backgrounds:

> Alderfer, Althouse, Anders, Barndt, Beyer, Bishop, Cressman, Delp, Fly, Frankenfield, Frederick, Fulmer, Garges, Goshow, Guntz, Hallman, Hange, Heacock, Hedrick, Heebner, Jones, Keller, Kerr, Kooker, Kriebel, Krout, Krupp, Lewis, Long, Loux, Mack, Moore, Nase, Rice, Rush, Scheetz, Shisler, Smith, Stout, Swartley, Trauger, Wambold, Ziegler.

On the other hand, a possibly equal number of once-familiar names (*e.g.,* Buckwalter, Funk, Geil, Latshaw, Slifer, Showalter) were by now either entirely or nearly absent from the Mennonite family.

Chapter 15

"Conscience," "Discipline," and "The Original Concept of the Church"

(1930-1947)

It was in the 1930s, years of economic depression and unrest, when the dominance of the German *Muttersproch* had at last been broken, that the threshold to a new era of activity was finally crossed in the Franconia Conference. Of the five bishops, only two in the "Middle District"—elderly Jonas Mininger and Abraham Clemmer—were more German than English, and they would both die before the end of the decade, while the nation was still uninvolved in the spreading global conflict. In their closing years they had to deal constantly with a body of youth impatient for activity—church activity—at long last. Bishop Mininger, having been ordained a minister before 1900, hardly knew how to take it. "We want the young people in the church," he remarked at a Lancaster Conference session in 1933, "but we want them to stand by the church."[1] Why did they have to insist on singing in "quartettes" and even "sextettes," in chapels and places like that? It was Bishop Clemmer's lot to give a series of cautious consents to repeated requests for such things as evangelistic meetings, summer Bible schools, young people's meetings, and the opening of new "mission stations" by a spontaneously evolved corps of irrepressible young "workers" from his own bishop district.

More than twenty young people from the Franconia Conference attended the "Special Bible Term" at Eastern Mennonite School in Harrisonburg, Virginia, in 1930.[2] There, where sober plain clothes were the standard, social interaction itself often took the form of "cottage meetings," serving in "Rural" or "City Workers' Bands," handing out the evangelistic paper called *The Way*, attending "prayer circles," and singing in choruses. This demure activity, mingling social novelty with spiritual fervor, was

478

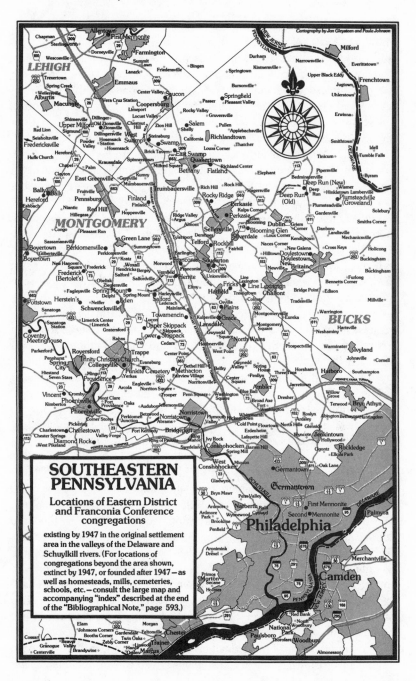

Cartography by Jan Gleysteen and Paula Johnson

SOUTHEASTERN PENNSYLVANIA

Locations of Eastern District
and Franconia Conference
congregations

existing by 1947 in the original settlement
area in the valleys of the Delaware and
Schuylkill rivers. (For locations of
congregations beyond the area shown,
extinct by 1947, or founded after 1947 — as
well as homesteads, mills, cemeteries,
schools, etc. — consult the large map and
accompanying "index" described at the end
of the "Bibliographical Note," page 593.)

fostered within a context of emphasis on spiritual "surrender." EMS President A. D. Wenger, mindful of concerns back home, urged his students to "be submissive to the Church. Never give her leaders trouble." Though the young people might be eager for activity, they should not "originate questionable innovations that are unfavorable to the ministry of [their] respective congregation[s], even though they are permitted elsewhere."[3] Students who returned from E.M.S. to the Franconia Conference, such as William G. Detweiler, Llewellyn Groff, David Nyce, Noah Mack, John Wenger, Fannie Good, or Laura, Ruth, and Susie Histand, brought with them the dual urge to do something and willingness to obey. The one thing that made the bishops most ready to permit new activities was an overt signal in the dress of the young people that the latter recognized the church's authority. Self-denial was routinely preached: "Others may—you cannot" was to be the dedicated Christian's motto.

William G. Detweiler,[4] baptized as a young man at Blooming Glen in 1917, had looked forward since boyhood to serving on a foreign mission field. Again and again his congregation had heard sermons from Mennonite missionaries on furlough from South America or India. Having taken his last year of high school at EMS, William went on to the unusual step of taking a bachelor's degree at Temple University, and teaching social studies in a North Philadelphia junior high school. He also studied at the Philadelphia School of the Bible, an emerging school of strong Fundamentalist stance, and volunteered for foreign work to the local Franconia Mennonite Board of Missions. The latter, usually meeting at the "Eastern Mennonite Home" in Souderton, asked William and his wife, Anna (Landes, of Skippack), to superintend their Norristown Mission, in replacement of Willis and Mary Lederach. While the Detweilers were living at the Mission (1928-31) Anna gave birth to identical twin boys, Bill and Bob. These future preachers proved quite an attraction to visitors at "the Mennonite Hotel," sometimes gaining, in their mother's opinion, more attention than was good for them. There remained the question of how William, Sr., could become a minister. The Franconia Conference at this time approved of only one method, the lot, and this had to be cast in a congregation—something the Norristown Mission, at this point, was not. But when William's home congregation, Blooming Glen, prepared to cast lots for a minister in 1930, his name was among the four candidates (one of whom, Titus Moyer, was said to have "gone through the lot" eight times without having it ever fall on him). This time the lot fell on Melvin Bishop, a short, impassioned preacher who would take up shoemaking as a means of income.

Around the time of this ordination Superintendent Detweiler had been visiting a Norristown couple who had moved to Pottstown, and holding cot-

Twins Bill and Bob Detweiler (b. November 29, 1929) at the Norristown Mission of the Franconia Conference, where their father William G. Detweiler was superintendent. With them is Naomi Hertzler. (Llewellyn Groff)

Another set of twin brothers who would be future preachers: Ray and Roy Yoder of Bally, born on February 7, 1938. Their mother, Elizabeth Kulp (Mrs. Henry) Yoder, is a daughter of one of the preachers of the (Old) Mennonite congregation at Bally, Elias W. Kulp. (James J. Gerhart)

tage meetings in their home. After a few months of such meetings, Preacher Jacob Moyer of the Moyer and Sons Feed Store in Souderton, the "field-worker" appointed by the Mission Board, preached to the gathering. And around Christmas (1930) the Mission Board appointed two young men from the Vincent congregation—Elmer and Arthur Kolb—to superintend a new Mennonite Sunday School in Pottstown. Thus an Old Mennonite congregation was born there fourteen years after the Eastern District had closed its own chapel in the same town. On the other hand, when the Franconia Mission Board sent a preacher to Allentown, where the Eastern District also had an established church, no tangible results followed (1930).

William Detweiler, seeing no opening in the near future for service as a minister or missionary under Franconia Conference auspices, now volunteered to the "General" Mission Board of the Old Mennonites at Elkhart, Indiana, and was assigned to a city mission at Canton, Ohio. Here he was ordained by 1933, and a few years later began to preach on the radio. This activity won him the disapproval of the bishops back home. A statement, "Members are not to broadcast," was added to the "rules."[5] Now the bishops rescinded their earlier approval of William's preaching in Franconia Conference pulpits. But a core of Mennonite supporters of William's radio work persisted in the Blooming Glen area. Some of the persons involved eventually opted for an independent congregation with a strong evangelistic emphasis (Calvary Church, near Souderton).

A mission outburst that rooted more consequentially into conference life occurred through the spontaneous emergence of several informal Bible study groups throughout the Franconia Conference. In a few years some of this thrust would be taken up into officially sanctioned "young people's meetings." Especially intense was the spiritual life of a "boys' meeting" in the Souderton-Franconia area in the late Twenties. A number of the zealous young men in this group came from the Souderton Sunday school classes of storekeeper Elvin Souder and clothing-factory worker Elias Nice. The "sparkplug" of this band (as one friend called him) was ebullient young dreamer Linford Hackman, who loved to read romantic tales of trapping and hunting in the Canadian North Woods. He had a Dutch accent as thick as cold apple butter, but a disarming and enthusiastic humor that ran like molasses in July. With his friend Llewellyn Groff, also an avid hunter and trapper, Linford imagined trapping and building churches in the Canadian hinterlands. Spreading out a map in a circle of his pious gang gathered in his home on the Cowpath Road, Linford excited his friends with a vision of a string of country churches in Canada taking their rise from the sober witness of the Franconia Conference itself. He even wanted to fly an airplane there. Jacob Moyer, the sometimes severe shepherd of the Souderton congregation, occasionally felt constrained to rein in what seemed to be Linford's irrepressible imagination.

The boys' group distributed *The Way* in Norristown, carefully mapping and dividing the town into "routes." Superintendent William Detweiler erected a large neon sign which glowed forth the message, "Jesus Saves," in front of the Norristown Mission, and the boys themselves now commissioned a huge billboard with an evangelistic Bible verse for the Bethlehem Pike near its intersection with "the 113." After several sorties by automobile into Canada had produced no opportunities for church building, Linford and Lewellyn looked at a field somewhat closer—the wooded range of hills that provided the "Ridge" on the northern horizon of the Branch and Skippack valleys. Among its boulder-strewn crevices, where substantial farming had never taken hold, where men from Souderton's Zion congregation had solicited interest a decade earlier, and where Walter Landis of the East Swamp congregation lived, the Franconia "boys" searched for lost souls. Steward Jacob M. Landis of the Eastern Mennonite Home told them he had been looking up at the Ridge for years, praying for a witness there.

Linford and Llewellyn inaugurated their efforts on March 22, 1931, with an impromptu prayer meeting at a sloping sprawl of boulders known locally as "the Devil's Potato Patch."[6] For the next year they and young fellow workers with a "vision" and "conviction" for witness moved about in the polyglot population of the poverty-stricken Finland and Rocky Ridge regions, helping find lost cattle here, sharpening an axe there, distributing "gospel tracts," and inquiring where a schoolhouse or other building might be rented for a Sunday school. They brought preachers Jacob Moyer and Menno Souder to speak in German at cottage meetings. Once the Mission Board refused their request to rent a dance hall for Sunday school. Finally the young volunteers managed to rent a log house among Italians, Polish, and blacks at Rocky Ridge, and Lewellyn Groff replastered an empty store near a defunct cigar factory beside a covered bridge at Finland. In March and May of 1931 the Rocky Ridge and Finland missions began regular services, with Franconian Conference young people, some still unmarried, hauling in multiple "loads" of community folks over sometimes almost impassable roads. Some of the people brought in seldom had such an opportunity to ride an automobile. "The mission board is backing us," wrote one young married woman to a pen pal at Johnstown.[7]

In the meetings there were an enthusiasm, a freedom of expression, and an intensity such as the workers had seldom if ever experienced in their home congregations. Some of the local people remained suspicious, and some hostile, but in the mission halls at both Finland and Rocky Ridge they

soon outnumbered the "workers." When the attendance was announced on
a Sunday morning, the number "from the community" was the important
figure. At Finland it soon climbed toward the eighties. In a year or two the
bishops of the Central district were asked to come and perform baptisms.
The very first community people to join at Rocky Ridge were Will ("Bill")
and Clara Anderson, an elderly black couple.[8] Their jovial spirits and joyful
testimony left an unforgettable impression on the young workers from
Franconia Township, and any other visitors. Clara, who would burst into a
peal of laughter and "back off" from the people to whom she was speaking,
could pray well in the meetings, generally using the words, "Father of
mercies and God of all comfort." She and Bill sang hymns together so impressively that they were eventually invited to sing at meetings across the
Franconia Conference area. It was a bit of the South brought into the staid
Pennsylvania Dutch circles. Clara, especially, was a personality, dishing up
her homemade ice cream, or serving her curious young visitors a meal of
raccoon. Bill, who could not read, took to standing at the door of the mission building, shaking people's hands as they entered; he said he wished to
be "a doorkeeper in the house of the Lord."

The Andersons accepted the plain coat, cape, and covering which were
the standard of the Franconia Conference they had joined, at least as the
rules had it. Nor were they the only black members at Rocky Ridge. Elderly
Willis Johnson and his wife lay ill and cold one Monday morning in their
impoverished home, when Linford Hackman, on a pair of snowshoes, and
another young worker, Abram K. Landis, came across the drifted hills to
help. Willis had become "very cautious" about white people, feeling that
he had been taken advantage of too often. But his heart warmed as the
young visitors went outside to bring in wood, built a fire, and cooked a
meal. "God sent you," the old man commented. Linford brought Dr. Paul
Nase from Souderton to treat the elderly couple, and in a day they felt better. Later, after his wife's death, Willis joined the Rocky Ridge congregation, along with other neighbors of over thirty different family names. One
local woman referred to the group as "The League of Nations." There were
ex-moonshiners. Later an intelligent black couple originally from Georgia,
James and Rowena Lark, joined.[9] James had been in the real estate business
and was not easily taken in. He would eventually become the first black
bishop in the Mennonite Church, founding churches in Chicago and
California.

Apparently the question of black members was new to the Franconia
Conference, and it was discussed at the October 6, 1932, session. But the
resultant resolution stated simply "that a colored applicant applying for
baptism at the Rocky Ridge Mission, be baptized and received into the

Clara and Will Anderson, the first members "from the community" at the Rocky Ridge Mission (1932), and the first black members of the Franconia Conference. (Llewellyn Groff)

Rowena (-1970) and James Lark (1888-1978), married in 1918, moved from the South to the Rocky Ridge area in 1927. Four years later, volunteer "workers" from the Franconia Conference started a mission there. Rowena soon attended and joined this congregation, and after several years won her husband to it as well. In 1944 they were called to Bible school work in a racially mixed community in Chicago, where in October 1946 James was ordained as the first black Mennonite minister, with the blessing of the Franconia Conference. (Mennonite Library and Archives of Eastern Pennsylvania)

Mennonite church."[10] A year and a half later, when fourteen new members were baptized at Finland after revival meetings by E. W. Kulp, one of them was also black—a middle-aged stone-cutter from Sumneytown. Alfred White too put on a plain coat and a little black bow tie. He sometimes surprised visitors from the "home" churches by conversing easily with them in Pennsylvania Dutch. A gentlemanly soul, Al lost few opportunities to narrate his escape, aided by a premonitory dream, from one of the famous powder-mill explosions of the Unami Creek area. He loved to share with young people the spirituals he had learned to sing in his southern boyhood.

Such was this urge for outreach among young activists in the Franconia Conference that at least nine new missions—mostly rural—were begun from 1930 to 1935. Six took permanent hold. Where the somewhat hesitant Mission Board itself took the initiative—at Allentown or Limerick—there was no success. Where it almost reluctantly followed a church planter like the urgent young Clayton Godshall, as at Spring Mount and Perkiomenville (1934), congregations developed. First an empty store, house, or factory might be rented, shortly to be filled with Sunday school children. Then young workers would be recruited among congregations in the Central bishop district. An attempt at Phoenixville produced no continuing church, but another at Lansdale—again closer to the Central district and drawing workers from the Plains congregation—did. By 1938 a tenth attempt, another rural mission, would successfully take place in the Haycock area, drawing personnel from the more eastern districts. This mission thrust, unparalleled in the previous history of either conference, would eventually more than double the number of congregations in the older fellowship. Whereas most of the numerical growth of the Eastern District was occurring through the expansion of the Zion and Grace congregations (and to some extent East and West Swamp), the Franconia Conference was establishing a string of new congregations on the periphery of their region. And in the process, the weak or nearly dead congregations at Methacton (Worcester), Boyertown, and Groveland (Plumstead) were also being revitalized.

Even though for decades few "community" people of leadership caliber would be incorporated into the new congregations, the new "posts" served as extremely valuable outlets for the expression of youthful faith and energy. Rather than opposing the strict cultural rules of the conference, the young workers often seemed more submissive than some of the home folks, whether "progressive" or traditional. Even after winning converts, the mission workers were willing (though sadly) to agree with the bishops in excluding from baptism those who proved unwilling to give up their life insurance or lodge membership. When the youthful friends Elmer Kolb and

Claude Shisler were both ordained in 1938, for Pottstown and Finland missions, without the casting of lots, it became dramatically clear not only that some of the grip of tradition had been broken, but that the Mission Board and the bishops trusted the active new generation. A year or two before this there had also been an ordination, at last, for the Norristown Mission, but here the lot had been used in spite of the fact that there were no candidates for the ministry at the Mission itself. Four names had been approved by the bishops from among nominations received from people all across the conference. The lot was then cast at the Franconia meetinghouse, and fell on a young worker at the short-lived Phoenixville Mission, Markley Clemmer.

Some people in congregations such as Franconia or Salford looked with critical eyes at their debt-carrying young members driving off in their automobiles to their mission work, not only on Sundays but on weekday evenings and Saturdays as well. "Sie sin' zu faul fa schaffe," might be the unsympathetic expression (They're too lazy to work). Yet these new Sunday school superintendents, choristers, and secretaries generally proved a stable part of conference life. It would even develop, eventually, that a significant number of them would represent the conservative side of conference thinking. Their mission congregations were the first to make evangelistic meetings, with speakers from "Lancaster" or even farther west, standard yearly procedure. A new periodical was sponsored by the Franconia Mission Board in 1937, significantly entitled *Mission News* (following the lead of the Lancaster Conference's *Missionary Messenger*).[11] This occurred just at the time when the Eastern District, long the host of the General Conference's *The Mennonite,* saw the editorship of the latter magazine transferred to Kansas when Silas Grubb's health began to fail rapidly. Another Franconia Conference development in 1937 was the new bookstore of J. Silas Graybill, a Lancaster Conference native who had married a Doylestown woman, and would be ordained a few years later as minister in the Doylestown congregation. Before long the store was given semiofficial recognition by the Franconia Conference as a source of literature, Sunday school gifts, and other supplies. Situated a block or two down from Allebach and Souder's on Main Street, Souderton, the store became a kind of Mennonite institution, evolving from "Graybill's" to "Herald" to the "Provident" Bookstore.

The urge to witness drove the Linford Hackmans and Llewellyn Groffs on to rural Minnesota, from where another Franconia Conference native, Irwin Schantz, would carry the witness north to the Indians of the Red Lake region of Ontario. Hackman eventually reached the Edmonton, Alberta, area, where he continued to kindle faith and missionary enthusiasm among northward emigrating Mennonites of other backgrounds. Also from Franconia, the Lester Hackmans became involved in mission

work in rural Louisiana, along with the John E. Wengers (Esther Wenger
was a daughter of Deacon Norman Moyer at Blooming Glen). The Nelson
Histands moved to a mission field at Culp, Arkansas. And although the
Franconia Conference had no foreign mission work of its own, at least three
of its young people went to Africa under the Lancaster Conference's mission board in the 1930s: Ruth Histand Moseman (Doylestown), John
Leatherman (Doylestown), and Noah Mack (Providence). Each had a
spouse from the Lancaster Conference.

If this outburst of mission spirit in the Franconia Conference in the
1930s has been given disproportionate space in the preceding pages, the
explanation might be that the writer of these lines, having been carried as a

The "Drs. Bauman" family, Eastern District missionaries to India, about 1935. L. to r.: Dr.
Harvey Rosenberger Bauman, Mary Harvella, Clara Ann, Albert Samuel, Kenneth, Dr. Ella
Garber Bauman (a native of Missouri), Elizabeth Ruth. (James J. Gerhart)

baby to the first meeting of the Finland Mission, and baptized in the old store building replastered by Llewellyn Groff, had a child's-eye view of the unfolding of the movement throughout the conference.

Mission-consciousness was also a significant feature of Eastern District life in the thirties. The Moyers and Baumans continued their work in India, and in 1936 the First Mennonite Church of Philadelphia, though now beginning its long and persistent decline, sent one of its members, Wilhelmina Kuyf, to China. Two years later Etta Davis of the Lansdale congregation went to the same country. Back from China on their second furlough came P. J. and Jennie May Gottschall Boehr (she was the daughter of Pastor W. S. Gottschall, now of East Swamp). As the date of their return to China neared, the ladies at East Swamp lovingly embroidered on a quilt the names of over eleven hundred friends, each of whom had contributed ten cents to the China work. The red-on-white quilt, filled with twenty-five circles of names, was presented to Jennie at the farewell service. But before her planned departure it was discovered that she had cancer, and the trip had to be cancelled. She died on March 4, 1936, murmuring, "Let the China missionaries know."[12] Two months later, a missionary meeting of the Eastern District, convening at West Swamp, sent a cablegram of "Conference Greetings" from Quakertown to China, congratulating the Mennonite Mission there on its twenty-fifth anniversary. The message was simply, "Philippians 1:2-6."[13]

The Upper Milford congregation shipped its old two-manual, foot-pedalled reed organ out to the Hopi Indian church at Oraibi, Oklahoma, in 1932.[14] Closer home, the new Lansdale church was growing so rapidly that the Home Mission and Church Extension Committee of the Conference could say, in 1933, that

> at no time or place in recent years has it been better repaid. When a church as a mission has an enrollment of two hundred in Sunday School and a membership of a hundred and thirty in three years' time, it speaks for itself.[15]

But the work at Mann's Choice or Napier, in central Pennsylvania, where the minister described a dirt road as "axle deep many times," was more of a "burden" to the committee. Finding only five faithful members left at Mann's Choice, the committee, meeting at Souderton in the spring of 1935, decided to close the mission, and concentrate on the more promising Napier.[16] Roaring Spring, once a thriving congregation, was also in a weak condition after the tragic death of longtime pastor Jacob Snyder.

In contrast to the situation in the Franconia Conference, the young people of the Eastern District Conference did not need to struggle, in the

1930s, for opportunity to practice the gifts of leadership. Both the Sunday School Union and the Christian Endeavor activities reached a peak of popularity in these years. The two conference-wide organizations held a joint rally in the wintertime. Prominent in "C. E." circles were such leaders as Walter Temple of Germantown, and May Markley, Morris Dehaven, and Norman Bergey of Eden. Young Bergey also served as an officer in the Perkiomen Valley and Montgomery County organization of the Christian Endeavour movement. This nationwide, interdenominational predecessor of Youth for Christ, so fervently fostered by N. B. Grubb in his heyday, provided a structure and procedure for Sunday evening programs of the youth of individual congregations. The young people would gather in the church two Sunday evenings a month, with their middle-aged parents often in attendance, to present talks on "topics" as suggested by a C. E. "quarterly." Although the "Old" Mennonites of Scottdale, Pennsylvania, and the Midwest also published helps for "Young People's Bible Meetings," their official use in the Franconia Conference was still rare at best. Such meetings trained young people to get up in front of a group, while providing a dimension of social interaction. The latter was particularly realized in periodic regional banquets and rallies which would be attended by many who were not themselves members of C. E. groups. Impressive and entertaining Christian speakers were engaged for these large gatherings, including a county judge, a New York City minister, and even, at Eden, the widely popular author of Christian fiction, Grace Livingston Hill.

The Sunday School Union (not to be confused with the larger American Sunday School Union), unlike the Christian Endeavour organization, had been native-born out of the Eastern District's own needs and vision. In the thirties, Allen R. Fretz of Lansdale was "Mr. Sunday School." Near the close of the annual convention of the Union held at East Swamp on September 25, 1937, a member of the East Swamp congregation rose and made a proposal that would have significant results for the Eastern District Conference.[17] The speaker was fifty-five-year-old bachelor J. Walter Landis, teacher of a Sunday school class of young fellows at East Swamp, a sometime tax collector and justice of the peace in Quakertown, and crippled since he had taken a nasty fall in a barn at the age of four. At a tax sale in 1929 he had purchased a run-down farm of over 100 acres straddling the Swamp Creek among the "sticks" and boulders near the hamlet of Finland. After his elderly mother, with whom he lived, had died, he moved to his recently purchased farm. Unable to walk without crutches, he never lost his enthusiasm for the church. For years he had been dreaming of establishing a "playground" for the use of Sunday schools of all denominations in the region.

J. Walter Landis (1882-1952), donor of the land for Camp Men-O-Lan, and his mother, Lucyanna Moyer (Mrs. Gideon) Landis (1857-1942), at their home in Quakertown. Walter was a justice of the peace, tax-collector, and Watkins products salesman. (James J. Gerhart)

A group from the East Swamp congregation at an Eastern District-sponsored Young People's Institute around 1936, at the University of Pennsylvania Boys' Camp along the Unami Creek between Finland and Sumneytown. (James J. Gerhart)

When nothing seemed to come of this dream, Walter had looked instead at the growing popularity of the summer "institute" and camp movement that had even spread among the "Old" Mennonites west of Lancaster County. The tenth annual Young People's Retreat of the Eastern District, held about three months earlier at a Green Lane campgrounds, had enrolled 153 participants. The question arose as to where the conference might have its own retreat grounds. In this context Walter Landis offered to donate whatever part of his farm the conference would wish to use. Here, he felt, the young people could come to have "mountaintop" spiritual experiences. Within two weeks, four ministers in "hiking clothes and high-top shoes" struggled through the "briery underbrush" up "to their armpits," to assess the possibilities of the completely undeveloped site. With some qualms, the conference began by accepting a plot of over twenty acres (later Landis donated the whole farm). Pastor Freeman Swartz of Eden, sometimes joshed by his fellow ministers as being "intoxicated with his own verbosity," was a sparkplug of support, and members of his congregation supplied much of the push for the initial stages. Among others involved were people like Alvin H. Alderfer and Norman Geissinger. The

Two Eastern District pastoral couples at what would be Camp Men-O-Lan, about 1937-1938. L. to r.: Eva Viola Renninger Nyce, Dorothy Kaufman Krehbiel, Olin Arthur Krehbiel (pastor of Grace Church, Lansdale), Howard Geissinger Nyce (pastor of the Allentown and Upper Milford Churches). (James J. Gerhart)

men of the Eden congregation put up the first building on the grounds.

No actual retreats were held on the grounds until the summer of 1941, when tents were used. A young retreater from Hereford, John Moser, suggested, in response to a contest for a name, that Walter Landis's name itself be involved. Freeman Swartz felt that the "first two syllables of Mennonite" could also be used. The name evolved, finally, from "Menno-land" to "Mennolan" to "Men-O-Lan," as rounded off by "a Philadelphia artist." Once publicity about the facilities began to appear, the Franconia Conference, whose mission at nearby Finland had now gotten a new church building and organized itself into a congregation, felt constrained to clear the air. One of its own members, black stonecutter Al White of the Finland congregation, had been employed by the new camp to blast out some of the rocks. "Due to the fact that we are receiving a number of inquiries about signs of Mennonite Retreat Grounds near Finland," ran a notice in the Franconia Conference *Mission News,* "we wish to inform the brotherhood that the grounds have no connection with our branch of Mennonites."[18] Yet within another decade the Franconia Conference would be renting the Men-O-Lan facilities for its own mission camps and youth meetings. This would be one of the earliest steps in a rapprochement between the two estranged conferences.

Later, the Eastern District attempted to establish a mission in a "Landis Memorial Chapel" in the renovated barn on the old farm, but no long-term success resulted. The neighboring Finland mission of the Franconia Conference did thrive, faithfully reproducing on a small scale the patterns of the older congregations from which its energetic young "workers" had come. Annual evangelistic meetings, with revivalists imported from other conferences, produced conversions in the community. An elderly widow, Mrs. Mary Ziegler, who joined the fellowship in its sixth year, soon thereafter donated to the congregation a fine parcel of land from her fruit farm less than a mile up the road from the rented store building that had served as meeting place since 1931. The plans for the new meetinghouse which was built on this lot in 1939 were drawn up by another recently received member "from the community," Gottlieb Traxel. A new minister had been ordained ten months earlier in the old store building—Claude Shisler, a linotype operator at the *Souderton Independent.* The bishops had broken ground for such a move half a year earlier than that by ordaining, in a similar manner, Elmer Kolb of the Vincent congregation to serve the emerging congregation at the Pottstown Mission.

Among the new faces in the Eastern District's pulpits was that of Ernest J. Bohn, graduate of Goshen College, and recently pastor of the General Conference church at Tiskilwa in his native state of Illinois. He re-

Mary Henry (Mrs. James) Ziegler (1866-1944), a member of the Finland Mennonite mission congregation, donated a tract of land from her fruit farm, on which the congregation built the first meetinghouse erected especially for a rural mission in the Franconia Conference (1939). As a woman, she was not allowed to speak at the dedication, though the "workers" would have appreciated this. (Claude M. Shisler)

placed G. T. Soldner at Zion in Souderton in 1931. An influential leader and officeholder in his new conference, Bohn would be its strongest ministerial advocate of Mennonite peace teaching as international war clouds grew dark. Arthur S. Rosenberger came back east to take the "Swamp Charge," consisting at this time of West Swamp, Bethany, and Flatland, but after four years was called to the presidency of Bluffton College, where he worked to regain for this institution the confidence of a somewhat suspicious eastern constituency. There were, of course, Bluffton enthusiasts in the Eastern District. A group of local students in 1931 and 1932 included J. Winfield and Millard Fretz of Grace Mennonite, Henry S. Detwiler of Zion, Homer Clemens of Eden, and Schwenkfelder Gerald Kriebel who often attended at Grace. At every session of the Eastern Conference the president of Bluffton spoke.

Back from a pastorate in South Dakota had come the elderly but still forceful William S. Gottschall. He served at East Swamp (and for a while at

Saucon) from 1930 to 1938, replacing Howard G. Nyce, a former railroad ticket agent at Lansdale who had studied at the theologically conservative Reformed Episcopal Seminary in Philadelphia. Nyce moved to the Allentown congregation, from which he served Upper Milford as well. A forceful pulpiteer, who resented "western" Mennonite criticism of lodge membership, he became president of the Allentown Christian Fundamentalist Fellowship in 1940.[19]

Of similar sympathies was W. S. Gottschall's replacement at East Swamp on the latter's retirement in 1938, genial young Harold Delbert Burkholder. A native of the Bluffton, Ohio, region, Burkholder preferred the emphases of the Moody Bible Institute and the Reformed Episcopal Seminary, both of which he attended. When Gottschall had reached retirement, the choice for his replacement lay between Erland Waltner, a young man from the South Dakota community which Gottschall had pastored, and Burkholder, from Gottschall's earlier pastorate in Ohio. Though Gottschall, himself a strong premillennialist, had suggested Waltner, the latter still had another half year to study in a course at the Biblical Seminary in New York City. The committee at East Swamp, not wishing to wait this long, invited Burkholder. When Waltner was free, a few months later, he was installed as the replacement for Silas Grubb, recently deceased pastor of Philadelphia's Second Mennonite Church.[20] These events confirmed the movement of the East Swamp congregation in a strongly "evangelical" direction. While pastor here, Harold Burkholder would become one of the founding fathers (and later president) of the Omaha, Nebraska, Bible Institute (later Grace College of the Bible). East Swamp grew under his leadership. A strong premillennialist, he would soon foster a "Prophetic Bible Conference" featuring such topics as "Will the Roman Empire be Resurrected?" and "Russia's Rapid Advance and Germany's Fate."[21]

In the Franconia Conference the bishops continuously resisted such teachings as "eternal security" and "premillenialism." Since "the turn of the century," they wrote, "outside influences were felt more than they had ever been before. Outside agencies began promulgating their doctrines," and because of lack of Bible study, "some of the members imbibed doctrines that are not in harmony with the 'Dort Articles of Faith.' " In 1938 the bishops sponsored the publication of a pamphlet on prophecy by Daniel Kauffman, well-known editor of the *Gospel Herald*, who claimed that "until about forty years ago" few "Mennonite leaders in America recorded themselves as being in favor of the literal-reign theory. The two main factors in bringing this about were the influence of the Moody Bible Schools and the circulation of . . . books. . . ."[22]

A letter to a Souderton-area woman from independent radio evangelist

George A. Palmer of Philadelphia, dated March 27, 1933, may illustrate the source of some of the Fundamentalist emphases:

> Dear Mrs. Derstine:
>   ... We are glad to know you are listening to our broadcast and that you enjoy it.
>   We also thank you for your gift of twenty-five cents toward our radio fund. . . .
>   Under separate cover we are sending you copies of the literature you request.[23]

In 1935, a Salford youth, Russell Weber, was elected president of a "Young People's Fundamentalist Fellowship" in Lansdale.[24] Particularly in the Towamencin congregation several families were enthusiasts for the Scofield Bible, and some attended the powerful preaching of Dr. Donald Barnhouse, Sr., at Tenth Presbyterian Church in Philadelphia. By 1939 there were weekly Bible study classes in several homes of such people from the Towamencin and Souderton congregations, sometimes attended by one of the Towamencin preachers, Warren Moyer. In 1942 the group would be using the Harleysville Chapel, and three years later would call a minister. In 1947 a lot would be purchased in Souderton for the "Grace Bible Church."[25] Another such movement, also drawing on Towamencin but much more centered among Blooming Glen members who supported William G. Detweiler's radio program, *The Calvary Hour,* would organize the "Calvary Mennonite Church" (between Souderton and Silverdale) in 1952. Although the original constitution called for the use of the prayer covering and anticipated joining "some Mennonite conference," the "evangelical" emphasis proved the stronger factor, and the name Mennonite was soon dropped.[26] Both "Grace Bible" and "Calvary" churches placed great emphasis on missions. The former was vigorously Fundamentalist, sending some of the young people to Bob Jones University; the latter claimed less doctrinal difference with the Mennonites than dissatisfaction with cultural restrictions. The years prior to the founding of Calvary had been an era in which the Blooming Glen congregation had experienced tension in its ministerial team, and some felt this was a contributing factor to the large outflux into the Calvary Church. Neither Grace nor Calvary kept an emphasis on the traditional Mennonite teaching against military service, but some young men from Calvary did choose alternate service.

If the main questions for those leaving were doctrinal and "evangelical," the drama as perceived by the Franconia Conference itself was a struggle against the loss of spiritual identity. No one spoke of "maintaining the right fellowship," or being faithful to "the old defenseless ground," but there was a continuity with what such older expressions stood for. "If there is any one thing which impresses a visitor at conference," wrote a young Rockhill member in 1936, "it is the grave concern there manifested lest the church become entangled with the world."[27] Bishops and ministers, with support from many (though not all) grass roots members, worked solemnly to keep a strongly bounded society. Their church customs had not significantly changed since the immigration of their ancestors two centuries earlier. Western conferences of the "Old Mennonite Church" saw a stability in this regard that they sometimes despaired of or considered inappropriate for themselves. "Franconia," wrote Dean Harold Bender of the now more conservative Goshen College, "has preserved in its customs and traditions more nearly the ancient Mennonite forms of worship, doctrine, and church government than any other American district. . . ." It might be regarded as "in several respects the mother conference of Mennonites in America."[28]

Bender, well embarked on a lifelong career of "recovering the Anabaptist vision," was an occasional visitor to the region, collecting old books for the historical library at Goshen or speaking, with Elmer Johnson, at a 250th anniversary meeting held by the "Historical Society of the Fran-

Harold Delbert Burkholder, native of the Bluffton, Ohio, area near the end of his pastorate (1938-1945) of the East Swamp Mennonite Church. (James J. Gerhart)

conia Conference District," on October 7, 1933. Similar observances at Germantown and Quakertown stirred up historical interest in the Eastern District, and in both conferences suggestions emerged that a history of eastern Pennsylvania Mennonite experience be written. When the Franconia Conference found among its membership a young college graduate capable of the work, and commissioned a book, the Eastern District, whose young pastor Freeman Swartz also hoped to write one, generously voted to make its own historical materials available for the Franconia-sponsored project.[29]

But there was little counterpart in the Eastern District to the sequence of identity-preserving resolutions issuing from the solemn twice-annual sessions of conference in the Franconia meetinghouse. Members were asked to withdraw from insurance and old-age pension plans, which were called by conference resolution in October 1936, "not in accord with the Biblical method of supporting the needy, I Timothy 5:4, which method has been observed by our church for centuries. . . ." The tradition of mutual aid was re-stressed as an essential element in the life of the Church.[30] Already the Board of Missions had added to its name "and Charities," as it sought to give more order to collections for the relief both of local farmers whose barns had burned and responses to pleas from beyond the conference area. Money was sent to recent "Russian" Mennonite immigrants in Canada and to other Mennonites who had experienced crop failure in the northwest. Money and even used farm equipment were shipped to Mennonite settlers in the "Green Hell" of the Chaco in Paraguay.[31]

Much of this money was handed informally to deacons, after announcements of the needs had been made from the pulpits. But the modern tendency toward institutionalization was also evident. In spite of scattered objections against the danger of impersonality in administrating mutual aid, a "Franconia Mennonite Aid Plan" (with deliberate avoidance of the term "insurance") was encouraged by conference action in 1935, during the heart of the Depression, and it began to function, with a state charter, on April 11, 1937. "326 policies" had been distributed by the fall conference that year, "enlisting $2,013,263.48 property value."[32] Members of conference congregations were "urged to withdraw from Non-Mennonite companies and place their risks in the Aid Plan." This would avoid "the unequal yoke" with "the world." Perhaps it was at this time that a local non-Mennonite insurance agent complained that Mennonites were running some kind of illegal insurance company. Although insurance of all kinds became more and more a fact of life, this "Aid Plan," with directors from all across the conference area, would also continue a vigorous, though almost noiseless function. Families who for reasons of scruples against anything so similar in form to an insurance company could not participate, were nevertheless often helped by collections in various congregations, when serious losses occurred.

Since, half a century later, the mood of the thirties would be difficult to imagine by many of its Mennonite characters' own grandchildren, a few glimpses into its life may be helpful: farmers J. Walter Bishop of Doylestown and Jacob Wile of Franconia receiving honors as leading potato growers in the state. Bishop being excluded from communion at Doylestown until he acknowledged, six years after he had attended the State Farm Show at Harrisburg, that he was "truly sorry" if he had offended his brothers and sisters thereby. Minister Alfred Detweiler silenced at Rockhill for having borrowed more heavily than he was able to repay. Bank President Clayton Gotwals of Souderton puffing on his cigar between sentences, while reading the conditions of the auction as the Union National Bank sold out Detweiler's farm equipment. Gotwals himself "standing" at repeated "counsel meetings" in the Franconia congregation (where he enjoyed meeting "the farmers"), thereby acknowledging that in his banking activities he had broken conference rulings. Souderton Old Mennonite Howard K. Alderfer, a thirty-seven-year-old clothing factory worker, declining jury service at a hearing in Norristown. Judge Knight of the Montgomery County Court, who felt Alderfer would "make a fine, conscientious juror," and that he should therefore "retain" him, asked him why, if his church did not completely forbid such service, he was unwilling. Alderfer said, though he had scruples against it, "I am in your hands, your honor, and I will do whatever you want me to. Still, I would very much like to be released." Judge Knight then let him go, calling him "perfectly honest" in his "reason," and saying that he did "not want to make any honest man do something that is repugnant to his religious views."[33]

More vignettes: the Franconia Conference resolving that its members should not participate in the forthcoming (1932) 200th anniversary celebration of Franconia Township. Pastor Ernest Bohn of Zion leading in prayer at the same affair. Young John C. Wenger of Rockhill, between studies at Eastern Mennonite School and Goshen College, conducting a group of young singers calling themselves the "Bucks Mont Male Chorus." Professor Russell Lantz of the Bluffton College Faculty directing an annual summer "Mennonite Musical Festival" of choirs from the Eastern District, in the Perkasie Park. Young people from the Franconia Conference attending the monthly Saturday evening song service at the Norristown Mission, and Horace Longacre and Elizabeth Goshow meeting there on a blind date. Paul Mininger, student at the University of Pennsylvania, being handed money to pay his tuition by quiet-spoken Steward Jacob M. Landis at the Eastern Mennonite Home in Souderton. Paul and his wife, Mary, living and having a common treasury with John and May Ruth of Lansdale. The five Franconia Conference bishops meeting at the home of Abraham G. Clemmer and deciding that their members may not belong to the new labor unions in the local clothing and hosiery plants, though they may contribute the equivalent of union dues to the union charity funds. The first Sunday morning services held at the Old Mennonite meetinghouse in Souderton in 1935, fifty-five years after its founding. Eighteen "market men" from the Blooming Glen congregation alone, plying their "routes" in panel trucks identified with their names, or standing in "stalls" in Philadelphia.

Still more: Reformed Mennonites or "Herrites" from Lancaster County attending the funeral of a daughter of one of their last members near the old Delp meetinghouse in Franconia Township, walking out of the house or upstairs when the funeral begins in the house, and later doing the same thing at the services in the Franconia meetinghouse, talking to each other in an apparent wish to avoid hearing what was being said by the minister.[34] Markley Clemmer, young mission worker at Phoenixville, saying good-bye to his friend from Doylestown, Minister John Leatherman, at the

Song leader Leidy Hunsicker and his wife, Della (Moyer), of the Blooming Glen congregation, in their butcher-shop in the village of Blooming Glen, 1938. (William L. Histand)

New York City Docks (1936). As Leatherman and his wife, Catherine (Garber), embark for mission work in Tanganyika under the Lancaster Board, Clemmer vows that he will either follow them or work evangelistically among people of African descent in America. Relatives at Doylestown, Line Lexington, and Salford passing around "the African letters" sent back from Tanganyika by the Leathermans and John and Ruth Histand Mosemann. The Franconia Conference voting in October of 1937 to prohibit television among the membership "either as an attachment for present radios or new radios with these attachments."[35]

A similar sequence of glimpses into Eastern District life might include the graduation of twenty-two-year-old Huldah Myers, a Sunday school teacher at West Swamp and future missionary to Colombia, from Ursinus College, and her beginning to teach school. Or the "tall gaunt figure" of Allen M. Fretz, "the Dean of ministers" in the conference at whose sessions he has been a familiar figure for half a century. A young Franconia Conference visitor calling Fretz an "aged yet youthful minister." At the age of eighty-one he was still carrying, noted Freeman Swartz, the next to "the heaviest preaching assignment in the conference" (Springfield, Perkasie and Deep Run).[36] "If he ever was excited he gave very little external evidence of it," remembered a younger relative. Yet his "soft spoken but crystal clear voice and sympathetic smile as he stood behind his lofty pulpit, girded by two pillarlike posts," at Deep Run, were making a lasting impression on the next generation.[37] A similar testimony was being left by his younger sister, Emmaline Detweiler, in the Zion congregation in Souderton. She had taught Sunday school in the primary department since her brother had performed her marriage to Henry D. Detwiler forty-one years earlier, when Zion was just beginning. She had also been vice-president of the Christian Endeavor Society when Henry was president, and helped him with the janitor work (their house was next to the church) for four decades. She had been the president all along of the Ladies Aid Society, and one of the organizers of a conference-wide "Orphanage Society." She would live to be Zion's oldest and most respected member.[38]

Nor should we overlook Henry S. Borneman, who grew up in the Boyertown congregation just now being merged with Hereford, and who is a well-known attorney in Philadelphia, as he publishes a colorful selection of his 300 pieces of Fraktur, begun in his childhood when his grandmother Esther Latshaw Stauffer had given him his first piece.[39] Then, too, we catch a glimpse of the elderly N. B. Grubb attending conference at Eden, and not finding anyone he recognizes on the sidewalks of his native Schwenksville, which still publishes the weekly *Item* he had founded more than fifty years earlier. And finally, Grubb and his son Silas, shortly before their deaths a few years later, receiving in Philadelphia a visit from an eager though slightly abashed young historian bent on writing up the history of the Franconia Conference, and including a shorter section on the Eastern District.[40]

In the brief encounter at the Grubb home in 1936 we may see a symbolic moment: the Franconia Conference is at last able to converse on an intellectual level with its Eastern counterpart. The old conference representative here is a young and enthusiastic face, whereas the Philadelphia men, once ebullient in their positions as pastors of a fourth of their conference membership, and long carrying the banner of Mennonite history, are now in an autumnal, somewhat reserved mood.

The young fellow, John Christian Wenger, was the son of a Lancaster Conference family that had moved into the Rockhill community thirteen years earlier, when he was thirteen. Father Martin Wenger had then served as custodian of the Rockhill meetinghouse and grounds, his family living in the sexton's house. Though there was some continuous tension among the Rockhill leadership, there was also a community tradition that blessed the budding church-consciousness of the young John C. Wenger, baptized in the Rockhill meetinghouse at the age of fourteen. The old minister Mahlon Souder, who died that year (his son Edwin being ordained in his place), left a distinct memory of godliness and neighborliness. His brother John worked affectionately as an amateur Mennonite historian, giving out little hand-drawn, colored Sunday school cards in the tradition of Christopher Dock.

A sense of the quality of spiritual community that informed the consciousness of the recently arrived Wenger family is preserved in the memoir of a non-Mennonite Sellersville neighbor, the well-known landscape artist Walter E. Baum. In a chapter entitled "Seen Through Young Eyes," he described the thoughts raised in his mind by the southwest view from his studio-window in Sellersville. There lay "the overlapping hills at Derstines"—site of the mill built by immigrant Michael Derstine two centuries earlier, and later of a local stop on the railroad. Since childhood, Baum (who had Mennonite ancestry on his father's side) had always seen these hills "as a boundary to rim the lands of the Mennonites," a "clear demarcation" between the community of the "plain folk" in the valleys beyond, and the citizenry of Sellersville, many of whom had Mennonite ancestry. Baum had gone to high school at Sellersville with Stella Derstine, now the wife of Blooming Glen minister Wilson Moyer, and knew such Mennonites boys as William Derstine and Preacher Mahlon Souder's sons.

An especially pleasant boyhood memory of Mennonite associations was that of going to Enos Detweiler's large woods near the Branch Creek at Cat Hill, after a "hickerniss sturm" in the fall. "Dozens of people" in a picnic mood would help themselves to the hickory nuts which "covered the ground" for acres. Baum writes that "it would be difficult to convey to the understanding of today's young people what they are missing in not being able to go to a woods like Detweiler's." Reflecting on the owners' old-fashioned permission for the neighbors to help themselves, the artist goes on in a very complimentary vein. "The Mennonite attitude was like that always, sharing their plenty with others!" As a boy, he states, he had "always stood in awe" of the plain-dressing people's ability to accept being "pointed at ... frequently with ridicule." As his "sense of values began to clarify," his "personal respect for the Mennonites increased." Though he could not understand how they and their faith could "fit into the scheme of this ultra-modern world," he found himself holding them "near the top in devotion. The Christian thread is more easily visible to me among these people than anywhere within the range of my experience."[41]

This overly generous opinion shows the possibility that an "outsider" to the Franconia Conference could be grasped by the power of its interior dream of a loving Christian family. In the year he was baptized into it, John C. Wenger entered the Sellersville High School, and in 1928 graduated as class president and valedictorian. A. D. Wenger, looking for students for the Eastern Mennonite School of which he was president, promised the eager student a reduced room and board in his own home if he would help with the housework while attending E.M.S. Four years later John C. Wenger had an AB from Goshen College (where to his home ministers' disapproval he had sung in a chorus), and was attending Westminster Seminary near Philadelphia. He was indignant when his name was withdrawn from "the lot" for a new minister to replace those silenced at Rockhill (the bishops later commented that the troubled situation required a more experienced person).[42] But a year later the twenty-four-year-old aspiring teacher and preacher was pleased to be asked by the Historical Society of the Franconia Conference to write a history of the conference. He could find time for this, it was felt, by taking off a semester from his studies at Westminster.

Chief promulgator of the project was John Derstine Souder, sixty-year-old farmer on the Souder homestead across from the Indian Creek Reformed Church on the Franconia Township side of Telford. A former postal worker and breeder of fancy poultry, Souder had been an enthusiast of local history since before his twenty-first year, when he had published a small history of Franconia Township. When his wife, Sallie, would die in 1937, he would turn increasingly to the solace of his "bee-hive"—a collection of notebooks on the history of the Bucks-Mont region, with special interest in the Mennonites. Most outstandingly, he would take up in earnest the now extinct art of Fraktur, and produce, by his own count, over 1,000 examples of it—some copied from pieces remaining in old family Bibles and some created from his own imagination—in the five remaining years of his life. Thus Henry S. Borneman, who published Fraktur, and John D. Souder, who practiced it, were pioneers in the recovery of this treasure-trove of forgotten beauty in the Pennsylvania Mennonite past.

On October 10, 1935, John Souder came to the Telford study of the seminarian forty-five years his junior, and the history project was inaugurated. It would take over a year of hard work. The retired farmer and the energetic student read a Psalm, knelt and prayed together, and then sang "My Jesus, I Love Thee." Day after day thereafter the old man came into the room, bringing "books, deeds and papers"—"bushels of stuff" that he had collected over a lifetime. He hauled his young friend "all over the country" to historical sites and homes where memories lived. Every afternoon he sat in Wenger's study for an hour, making the young re-searcher feel he was being told, "Produce, boy, produce!"[43] The result of this collaboration was an amazingly dependable and full collection of in-

John Derstine Souder (1865-1942), farmer on the Souder homestead on the Franconia Town-ship side of Telford, with one of his copies of local Mennonite *Fraktur*. He took a special interest in this art after the death of his wife, Sallie (Alderfer), in 1937. The chief promulgater of history in the Franconia Conference in his time, he claimed that he had produced 1,000 pieces of *Fraktur* after the age of seventy. (The Schwenkfelder Library)

formation, to which all later historians of the Mennonites would stand permanently indebted.

The industrious young author, though imbued with a reverence for the spiritual phenomenon he was describing, occasionally allowed himself an editorial comment. Noting that both the Blooming Glen and Deep Run churches had "a tendency to be less severe in their discipline"[44] than others in the conference, he went on to observe that "the Franconia Conference has always been troubled with the discipline question." His balanced youthful verdict was that "when discipline is very strict undue attention is apt to be given to externals, young people are driven from the church, and the danger of formalism faces the group."[45] With such sentiments members of the Eastern District would agree. Again, Wenger observed that "a reluctance to change" at Deep Run a few years earlier had possibly made some of its members "susceptible" to the preaching of an independent evangelist.[46] In his more cursory treatment of the Eastern District (his account was to serve thereafter as the main historical source for this conference as well), he maintained a rather even tone, though the Franconia Conference in these years was still feeling little if any sisterhood with its less conservative counterpart. The author did confess that he had been "disappointed" to learn of the Eastern District's refraining from dealing with the question of members taking military service in the Civil War.[47] He also remarked that in the reduction of "discipline ... to a minimum" in the Eastern District lay "one of the greatest points of difference between the two conferences."[48]

The finished book, entitled *History of the Mennonites of the Franconia Conference*, contained, among other valuable features, individual histories of each congregation in both conferences (though quite brief for the Eastern District), and two "ministerial lists," the idea for which Wenger had taken from a recent history of the Ontario Mennonites. The "lists" contained a surprising amount of historical detail from what might have been thought an inaccessible past. John Souder was proud of the book's 523-page bulk, and gave each bishop at conference a complimentary copy. These men professed astonishment at the size of the work just received from the press at Scottdale; they had expected something more of the size of the old *Kleine Geistliche Harfe*. The young author, having been paid a grand total of $410 for his pains, had already sailed for Switzerland, where he was to use his new book as a thesis in getting a ThD from the University of Zurich. This did not entirely meet with the approval of John Souder, who, though Wenger had written it all, felt that he was partly the author too. Shortly before embarking from New York on the S.S. *Europa*, Wenger had been married to a fellow Rockhill member, nurse Ruth Detweiler. Her

uncle Wilson Moyer had performed the ceremony (the Wengers had for a
time lived near Silverdale and attended at Blooming Glen, where Moyer
preached), and the attendants were Ruth's sister Miriam and brother-in-law
Quintus Leatherman.[49] Having "passed through the lot" when Markley
Clemmer was ordained for the Norristown Mission while the book was being written, Wenger saw that the role of minister in the Franconia Conference, a role he had strongly desired, was not immediately in the offing.
When he returned from Europe in 1938 he began a lifelong career of teaching at Goshen College and Seminary.

Meanwhile, war clouds lowered over Europe, and nations reeled in
economic depression. President Roosevelt still orated of neutrality, and
there were large peace demonstrations in New York City. The Eastern District had taken alarm at war trends as early as 1931, resolving to "re-affirm
our position on practical nonresistance and opposition to all forms of war
and violence, and the use of carnal weapons and urge our people to love
even their enemies as themselves...."[50] Miss Vivienne Musselman of
Philadelphia spoke "inspiringly" to the 1932 conference, meeting in
Philadelphia at the Second Church, of a new "Mennonite Peace Society."[51]
By 1933 the influence of the recently arrived pastor of Zion, Ernest Bohn,
was being felt on this topic. Conference resolutions, which he helped to
draw up, referred to "the fact that our denomination has historically stood
for the principle of love," and urged that, since "this principle is being
tested today as never before," it should be reaffirmed and that each congregation should have a special service to teach it.[52] Again in 1934 both

Franconia Conference young women in the mid-1920s. L. to r.: Stella Stout, Ruth Detweiler,
Grace Allebach, Gertrude Derstine, Bertha Alderfer, Verda Frankenfield. (Author's Collection)

"simplicity of living" and "Peace" were noted to be "fundamentals of Mennonite heritage," "whereas war cannot be reconciled to the teachings of
Jesus Christ our Lord...."[53] In 1935 the conference, taking note of "fe-
verish arming for conflict in ... many nations," again reminded the membership of "our non-resistance principle."[54]

The language grew stronger as war seemed more imminent. "Be it resolved," voted the 1936 Eastern District meeting at West Swamp, "that we
instruct our people in the historic Christian teaching of nonresistance, and
... urge our people to ... abide by it in any eventuality."[55] Again the
following year it was voted "to teach our young people the principles of
peace...."[56] Already A. J. ("Speedy") Neuenschwander, pastor of the
Swamp Charge, had represented the General Conference peace interests in
a personal interview with President Franklin Roosevelt (with Old Mennonite C. L. Graber).[57] The Mennonite Peace Society called a regional
meeting in October 1936. The Eastern District instructed its executive officers to keep the Mennonite convictions "before the Government authorities," and to let them know that "Mennonites cannot be expected to
take part in war."[58]

Such strong words were articulated by a "resolutions committee" composed of Huldah Myers, a schoolteacher from the West Swamp congregation, layman Samuel Snyder of the westernmost Roaring Spring congregation, and Olin Krehbiel, Kansas-born pastor who had just taken over
leadership of the expanding Grace Church in Lansdale. This committee
spoke for a highly concerned minority in the conference, but, as events
would prove, not a controlling conviction in the oncoming generation. The
Eastern District method of teaching the heritage, but allowing the individual to decide whether or not to abide by it, was about to undergo its
heaviest testing ever. What spiritually binding power would resolutions
expressing the ideal have over "our people"?

Pastor Bohn of Zion threw himself into the prophetic task, writing a
pamphlet, *Christian Peace According to the New Testament Peace Teachings Outside the Gospels,* and proposing, at the 1939 conference, a "Peace
Committee" for the Eastern District. The conference appointed to the committee its most outspoken layman on the subject, Robert Stauffer of the
West Swamp congregation, a conscientious objector in World War I. Also
chosen were two younger men, the new pastor at Second Mennonite, Erland Waltner, and Henry S. Detweiler, a protégé of Ernest Bohn at Zion.
Pastor Bohn was at "every meeting" of the new committee, and served the
peace "cause in numerous other ways."[59]

The war threat was of course only one of many topics for the Eastern
District in the 1930s. A ministers' aid plan was discussed at length, but not

enacted. The Bowmansville congregation experienced some friction, as Mennonites of "Russian" background who had moved to the community did not always merge easily with the locally born. In 1937 meetings began by the newer grouping in the "Steinmetz Meeting House" between Denver and Schoeneck. Within two years these worshipers, led by Elmer Hess, organized the "Emmanuel" congregation, which was accepted into the Eastern District in 1940.[60] A year later another "western" congregation, Fairfield, was likewise received.

Session after session of the conference involved discussion of procedural topics, revisions of bylaws, or parliamentary correctness. There was a "credentials committee" to certify delegates from the various congregations. The conference itself had begun, noted Freeman Swartz a decade later, "by being a deliberating and legislative body. Its very creation was caused by this struggle."[61] And there were ministers of the Eastern District, including Swartz himself, who appeared to relish the struggle of debate and parliamentary procedure. On this point there was a great contrast with the less democratic Franconia Conference, as the centennial of the great division approached. The Franconia Conference bishops continued to dominate the procedure as they had in 1847. They controlled access to information. Any topic which Bishop Abraham G. Clemmer of Franconia (died May 1, 1939) did not endorse could not come to the floor for discussion.[62] Members were told that they might ask questions at conference, but not "gainsay" a bishop. Six years after Abraham Clemmer's death it would still be stated that "no issue shall be brought before Conference if any Bishop opposes presenting the issue."[63] Decisions were often still being made by what could somewhat euphemistically be called a "rising vote" (the Eastern District also occasionally used this procedure, but on noncontroversial questions). The centralized power of the Franconia Conference bishops, which would fade sharply in the dynamics of the 1950s and 1960s, was now as strong as ever. It was strongly supported by a traditional consensus, weakest in the eastern section of the conference, but quite solid in the "Middle District" anchored around the largest congregation in the conference, Franconia.

Into this bishop tradition was introduced, in 1937, a young leader who would effectively carry its authority and promulgate its nonresistant theme through more than three decades of war and rumors of war. John Edwin Lapp, one of four children of Isaiah and Kate (Clemmer) Lapp, was born in the spreading town of Lansdale on September 11, 1905.[64] He grew up attending the Plains congregation, in the adjacent countryside. His father, from the Line Lexington congregation, having found his health too fragile to be a farmer, had worked in Philadelphia, then had a produce-wagon in

Lansdale, and died when John was eight. Kate Lapp had grown up on her father's farm—John D. Clemmer—in what by 1905 was rapidly becoming urban Lansdale. Her long-lived grandfather Abraham M. Clemmer had been deacon at Franconia, and stories of the 1847 division remained alive in family memory. Young John Edwin often stayed overnight with his Clemmer grandparents, in their large old farmhouse, still without electricity, in the middle of Lansdale. Here the fatherless boy both absorbed a sense of the traditional Franconia ethos and discussed with people born in 1836 and 1840 the tensions leading toward World War I.

Distributing newspapers morning and evening, John developed an interest in the world beyond Lansdale, but at the same time responded favorably to the spiritual community that assembled weekly in the old Plains meetinghouse (called "the Plain"). The gathering of friendly visitors after his father's funeral left a lasting impression on the eight-year-old boy. At the weekly meeting, Bishop Jonas Mininger's blunt German preaching was balanced with the kindly and even charming discourses of the history-loving, education-favoring J. C. Clemens, now living on a small farm on the Allentown Road.

John went to the Lansdale High School, at his mother's request (both of her brothers had studied beyond grade school, and neither stayed in the Mennonite fellowship). At the end of his second year in high school, J. C. Clemens gently prodded the tall young fellow, now under "deep conviction," to join a "class" of applicants for baptism at Plains, along with J. C.'s own son Paul and their Sunday school classmates Roosevelt Leatherman and Raymond Rosenberger. This occurred at an earlier age for John than was customary among his peers. John later wooed and married a farmer's daughter from Salford, Edith Nice, and at the age of twenty-five, after trying a variety of jobs, opened a grocery store in Lansdale (1930).

Having served as Sunday school superintendent at Plains, John found himself nominated for the "lot" when eighty-year-old Bishop Jonas Mininger finally called for ministerial help in 1933. The six candidates were all asked three questions from the "Minister's Manual," and whether they would "be willing to wear the frock coat"—the long, split-tailed descendant of their ancestors from the 18th century against which John Oberholtzer had rebelled ninety years earlier. By now it was not the "plain coat" which was the question for ministers, but the older version of the plain coat. More and more unordained men throughout the Franconia Conference were in these years taking up the "plain coat," in the renewed emphasis on nonconformity that had taken root after 1910. The second youngest candidate at the ordination service, John waited until only one book was left to choose. That volume contained the slip of paper with the verse from Proverbs, "The lot is cast into the lap, but the whole dispensing thereof is of the Lord."

Approaching his twenty-eighth birthday, the grocer-preacher found himself the youngest minister in the conference. The store business, in these years of depression, afforded no more than a bare living; five years later he would enter into partnership with another young man from the Plains congregation, Ralph Hedrick, who would eventually see the business grow into one of the region's leading grocery outlets. The bishops of the "Middle District" were pleased with the new young minister's dedication and ability to deal with labor union officials on the issue of exemption from union dues for Mennonites. When Jonas Mininger died in April 1937, John Lapp, not yet thirty-two, found himself once again the youngest in "the lot," this time "for a bishop." His older colleague at Plains, J. C. Clemens, was also a nominee. The meetinghouse at Franconia was filled by eight o'clock on the morning of June 1, 1937; about twenty ministers and bishops from the Lancaster Conference, sensing a historic occasion, were also in the audience. Once again, the lot fell on the youngest candidate, one of four with a high school education, and the only one for whom English was his only speaking language.

The new bishop was quick to note that Abraham Clemmer, now seventy, was the real influence on the "bishop board," and that this "board" performed what might be called an executive function. In fact, it would be called, for some time, the "Executive Committee" or "Board" of the conference. Conference Moderator Warren Bean of Skippack, and Bishop A. O. Histand of Doylestown, now well up in years, complained occasionally to Abraham Clemmer about the "pressure" they felt from the conservative demands of the large Franconia congregation on the rest of the conference. Occasionally someone would speak of the "rich Mennonites" of Franconia, hinting at an impression of arrogance.

Moving forthrightly into his function, John Lapp took as his role models the two older bishops from the congregations from which his grandparents had come—Franconia and Line Lexington. He admired Abraham Clemmer's discernment and articulateness in German (he himself could not preach in this language). Arthur Ruth, the somewhat younger bishop at Line Lexington (also in the Middle District), was, like Clemmer, a slightly built, short-of-stature farmer, and also very devout. In his pulpit-manner were traces of the stern oratory of his predecessor at Line Lexington, Bishop "Joe" Ruth. Arthur Ruth and John Lapp became the visible dual spiritual leaders of the central area of the Franconia Conference for the next two or three decades, unhesitant to discharge their solemn obligation to confront their audiences with serious exhortations in a manner scarcely imaginable by the generation of the less sober 1980s. Though neither used the old "singing" mode of preaching, their measured, scriptural cadences and traditional inflections evoked a sense of the eternity they contemplated, and the weighty call they heard inwardly to lead their people on the pilgrimage of a separate, obedient, mutually supportive, and nonresistant life. Lapp, in fact, took on his solemn responsibility so earnestly that some people, dissatisfied with the growing specificity of the printed rules of the Franconia Conference, were perturbed. His imposing physical height seemed to strengthen the authority he wielded.

In the summer of 1937 the aging but still vital J. C. Clemens attended the Old Mennonite General Conference in Oregon. He brought back a hand-written statement by church-statesman Harold Bender on concerns of peace and war. At the fall Franconia Conference, John Lapp's first as a bishop, the Bender statement was unanimously adopted as appropriate for the troubled times. After this action, Bishop Abraham G. Clemmer, though not the moderator, began a whispered consultation with three of the other four bishops (excluding young John Lapp). Then he rose and announced that in view of possible approaching emergencies there should be a "Peace Problems Committee" for the conference.[65] This was a significant step, since, unlike the Eastern District, the Franconia Conference had very few subdividings of its leadership functions. Receiving the body's approval, Bishop Clemmer then named J. C. Clemens, miller-preacher Jacob Moyer of Souderton, and the newly ordained bishop Lapp to the committee. This was about a year and a half before a similar committee was formed in the Eastern District at the urging of E. J. Bohn. Moyer and Clemens elected their younger colleague as chairman. Thus was inaugurated a lifelong leadership in the Franconia Conference on the central themes of peace and nonresistance. By 1941 Lapp would be elected to the Peace Problems Committee of the "Old Mennonite" church. As World War II drew on and magnified, he would become a close associate of Ernest Bohn of Zion, who held a similar position in the General Conference. At times they rode together on train trips to Washington, D.C. This rare fraternization of leaders from the estranged conferences resulted from the profound identification of the two leaders with the Mennonite teaching on peace. Lapp even suggested further development of this interconference fellowship, but another member of the Franconia Conference committee, whose relatives had belonged to Zion, declined approval. Bohn, who would find whole Sunday school classes from his large congregation joining the military in the approaching war, would resign and move to the midwest before the war was over.

The new committee's first action was to call for peace sermons in all the Franconia Conference congregations. One young man from Blooming Glen, Clarence Fretz, left for relief work in civil war-wracked Spain. As storm clouds darkened over Europe, a weekend teaching series was arranged in the Franconia Conference with Goshen professors Harold Bender and Guy Hershberger. While they spoke, over the Labor Day weekend of 1939, Hitler invaded Poland. On the following Armistice Day, November 11, the Eastern District too sponsored a "Peace Rally." Both conferences called for "relief" contributions, as news of war-ravaged victims became more common.

In the Eastern District, a quite forthright "Recommendation" on "Peace, War, Military Service, and Patriotism" was prepared by Robert Stauffer, Erland Waltner, and Henry Detwiler, and circulated to the ministers for study in the summer of 1940.[66] Calling the peace teaching "no new doctrine," but a reiteration of "an old age faith of the church which has been held precious by our forefathers from the time that the church was founded in Reformation times," the "Peace Committee" quoted ten New Testament passages teaching nonresistant love as the norm for Christians. Since "war is sin," the statement continued, we "can have no part in" it, either "personally" or by aiding those who do fight. Thus "we cannot accept service under the military arm of the government, whether it be combatant or non-combatant.... This applies to all wars...." Purchasing "war bonds" was also ruled out as acceptable for members. On the other hand, the committee expressed a willingness "at all times to aid in the relief of those who are in need, distress or suffering, regardless of the danger in which we may be placed in bringing such relief, or of the cost.... We are also willing to render such service as housing, road making, farming, forestry, hospitalization work during time of peace as well as during time of war." Finally, appreciation was expressed to the government for the privilege of not partaking in "the military machine," but being allowed to render other "service of national importance to our country...."

This vigorous statement was "adopted" by the Eastern District meeting at the Grace Mennonite Church in Lansdale on May 2, 1941. The phrase "Service of national importance" was a reference to a plan to open new "Civilian Public Service Camps," to be financed by churches supporting the conscientious objectors who would live and work in them. In the very month of the statement, the first of such camps opened, at Grottoes, Virginia, and by the end of the year a dozen Franconia Conference men had arrived.[67] The first stayed only a few months, but when the news of Pearl Harbor burst on the stunned nation on December 7, a much grimmer and long-term prospect arose for the boys who had already been drafted.

By this time the Franconia Conference had made its position clear. Every session for years already had closed with a rising vote to confirm the statement, "This Conference is still willing to continue in the simple and nonresistant faith of Christ." On May 1, 1941, the "young men in the draft age" were admonished "to be very careful of their conduct in public" and at hearings of the draft boards. "We should remember," read the conference resolutions, "that we cannot dictate to them and must never make any demands of them." No member was to work in "a Defense Industry making destructive war materials." Young men proving "not willing to file the Conscientious Objector papers" or refusing to "accept the Alternate Civilian Service" would "forfeit their membership" in the church.[68]

In comparison, the Eastern District, though having adopted a strong peace statement, did not attach any disciplinary conditions to its observance. On the day following its adoption, the delegates, expressing regret that a draft law had been put into effect, commended "those young men who have stood firmly in these times of testing . . . especially in taking their stand as conscientious objectors."[69] Later, advice was given on the purchase of "civilian" rather than "war bonds," for those who "wished to be consistent."

A special event of the year 1941 was the convening of the national "General Conference" in the facilities of the Souderton public High School, a half mile from the Zion Church, on August 17-22. Here "it was clearly specified" that the Eastern District would support the administration of the "Civilian Public Service" camps at the rate of $1.00 per member every six months.[70] This became a difficult goal to achieve; some congregations contributed "splendidly," while others seemed to prefer donating to relief. Eventually a total of $28,832.20 was reported as contributed by the Eastern District for the CPS program, and $41,060.74 for relief.[71] These figures apply to the years 1941-1947. Conference membership in 1945 was 3,698.

The larger Franconia Conference, with 4,551 less scattered members in 1945, donated $168,041.08 to the CPS program.[72] Whereas the Eastern District had about twenty-four conscientious objectors (6 percent of the total draftees),[73] the Franconia Conference had seventy-two.[74] Such comparisons must be made with care, however, since the factors in the two conferences were not the same. Fewer men in the Eastern District had the option of farm deferments, because of a greater urban membership. The percentage of men working on farms in the Franconia Conference actually rose during the war. Only 139 men were drafted from the conference membership, as the local draft boards, anxious to avoid long lists of conscientious objectors on their records, gave out over 700 farm deferments to Franconia Conference men.[75] The board at Lansdale was on particularly friendly terms with Bishop John E. Lapp, the head of the Board insisting on referring to the tall church leader as "Johnny."

It was a matter of sadness to Franconia Conference leaders that, of their 139 actual draftees, only half refrained from joining the military. Very likely most of the 700 farm-deferred men, thought the leaders, would have been conscientious objectors in obedience to conference standards, but the fact that half of those who *were* drafted had left the original teaching of the church—the first topic the Mennonites had explained to their neighbors after arriving in America—indicated that the renewed emphasis on discipline had not been a complete spiritual preparation for this crisis. Of the original congregations, Blooming Glen produced over a third of those opting for military service. Only five of its twenty-seven draftees chose conscientious objector service (though after the war six were "reinstated"). Deep Run also saw two thirds of its draftees become soldiers. By contrast, the conference's only "town" congregation, Souderton, sent all but four of its seventeen draftees to CPS.[76]

In the Eastern District 401 men were drafted[77] from a pool of members four fifths that of the Franconia Conference. Paul R. Shelly, son of the blind pastor Elwood Shelly, entered the Union Theological Seminary in the fall of 1942. He noted that his conference's "statements of policy" were "in accord with the biblical positions," but that "in practice the individual conscience decides." He tried to select a dissertation topic that would aid his conference "in their attempt to maintain their way of life better than they have in the past."[78] Shelly, who would soon be called to Bluffton as a Bible professor, would carry the logic of his concerns farther than was generally supported in the conference. In agreement with him was strong-willed Deacon Robert Stauffer of the West Swamp congregation. "Bob" had many contacts with Old Mennonites through his job of selling Ford automobiles for the Reliance Motor Company of Souderton. In the years after he had returned to Milford Square from Camp Meade as a World War I conscientious objector, Bob had even arranged to have bumpers painted black on cars he had sold to conservative Franconia Mennonite customers. Now, as he participated in the discussions with the men in Howard Shelly's "Live Wire Sunday School Class" at West Swamp, he was distressed to hear his younger classmates propose the installation of an American and a Christian flag in the West Swamp auditorium. A Christian flag was one thing, but Bob informed the class that a national flag, such as had already been brought to East Swamp and Bethany in Quakertown, could be put up at West Swamp only "over my dead body." The much-traveled pastor, A. J. Neuenschwander, tried to be diplomatic. He wasn't against it, he remarked, but what would be the good of it? West Swamp did not get the flag. Bob Stauffer and his friend Alvin Mumbauer then went to assist the struggling Saucon congregation (1944),[79] where young Ward Shelly, a former member of the nearby Mennonite Brethren in Christ congregation, was being introduced as pastor. Shelly also replaced A. M. Fretz at Springfield and Perkasie.

There was, of course, much more to life in these years than thinking about the war. On Crow Hill, where the Elias Kulps and Abe Gehmans lived behind Bally, a recently arrived New York author had taken up residence. For the next three decades Millen Brand would be watching, listening to, and writing poems about his Berks and Montgomery County neighbors of all religions, including members of both Old and New Mennonite congregations at Bally. Elmer Johnson, Schwenkfelder preacher for the new Mennonites, and Elias Kulp, his counterpart among the Old, as well as members of both their congregations, would make multiple appearances in Brand's book of poems entitled *Local Lives*, when it would finally appear in 1975. As Elias's wife, Elizabeth, would be recording her thoughts in her diary while her husband was off somewhere in a Mennonite community "holding meetings," Brand, in his study farther up on the Hill, might be evoking in poetically imagined soliloquies the spiritual and cultural idiom of the Berky or Longacre families.[80] Mennonite feelings about life and war would be given aesthetic expression in another of Brand's books, *The Fields of Peace*.

Speaking of books, there was a new volume in 1941 from the pen of Eastern District missionary to India, Samuel T. Moyer: *With Christ at the Edge of the Jungle*.[81] John D. Souder's pile of scrapbooks, bulging with photographs, drawings, and affectionate, opinionated research, were taken from his safe at the household auction after his death in September 1942 and placed by Elmer Johnson in the Schwenkfelder Library at Pennsburg. Thus in the same five-year period each of the two conferences had allowed its most significant historical collection to be removed to auspices other than their own (Silas Grubb's collection had gone to Bluffton).

At another household auction—at Fountainville, near Doylestown—forty of the more than 200 quilts from the sewing machine and needle of Hannah Overholt (Mrs. William) Gross, daughter-in-law of the Fountainville poet, were sold on April 24, 1942. Having begun to quilt as a nineteen-year-old bride in 1890, she had lost count of her production, but knew that she had given ninety quilt tops to the families of her six daughters and two sons. Some of the quilts had from 1,600 to 2,000 "patches" each. The Doylestown *Intelligencer*, featuring her plain-clothed picture on its front page, called her the "Queen of Bucks County Quilt Makers."[82]

A Lansdale woman, Kate (Mrs. Rhine) Bishop, of the Line Lexington congregation, was asked by the Franconia Conference to oversee a "Food for C.P.S." project. It consisted primarily of canning food from members' gardens. One congregation—Franconia—contributed over 2,000 cans.[83] In

the Eastern District, faithful church worker Anna Weiss and Deacon Robert
Stauffer, both from West Swamp, did the collecting.[84] A nurse in her forties,
Bessie Moyer of the Old Mennonite congregation in Souderton, stopped to
visit the CPS camp at Sideling Hill in central Pennsylvania, on her way
back from a weekend at the new Mennonite campground at Laurelville.
Learning that a nurse was needed at the camp, she immediately decided to
take the job, and spent twenty months there following September 1942.[85]
Among the "boys" who arrived at Sideling Hill in the following months was
Richard Detweiler, a newspaper reporter and member of the Blooming
Glen congregation, and a future moderator of the Franconia Conference.

In Franconia Township, nine one-room schoolhouses were at last
closed down and sold in 1941-1942, the children being sent to a new consolidated school along Route 113. This change gave impetus to a concern
for "parochial schools" in the "Middle District" of the Franconia Conference. It was now ninety years since the state-directed school system had
been accepted by Franconia Township, but in that time there had persisted
a very "local" sense, each set of farms around the nine schoolhouses retaining the feel of a neighborly cluster under the eye of parents and church.
Conference leaders responded somewhat cautiously to the calls for parochial schools, however, since there was very sharply divided opinion in the
"constituency" on this matter. Those who favored such schools could look
to the Lancaster Conference Mennonites, who had gotten a school of their
own several years earlier. Bishop John Lapp, and lay people such as Dr.
Paul Nase or realtor Robert Souder, both of Souderton, supported the parochial school idea, which did not achieve reality until the end of the war.

Some impression of the life of these years may be caught by a collage
of other glimpses. Farmer Earl Clemens visiting the Worcester (Methacton)
meetinghouse, where he was surprised to hear Bishop Warren Bean announce that he (Earl) was to be the new Sunday school superintendent.
Earl's cousin Paul Clemens's family also among those gathering to revive
the nearly extinct congregation, whose only surviving member was Harry
Davis. The aged Eastern Conference Pastor A. M. Fretz, in the last months
of his life, writing an exhortation to his Deep Run congregation, to "face
courageously" the task of maintaining the CPS camps and war relief,
reminding his flock that "by so doing, we are bearing witness to something
in which we verily believe."[86] Pastor Harold Burkholder of East Swamp
skipping his parents' fiftieth wedding anniversary to "hold meetings" at
Butterfield, Minnesota, where he was invited to a meeting in Omaha,
Nebraska, to plan for a new Bible institute of which he would later be
president.[87] Howard Nyce, pastor at Allentown, introducing to the Eastern
District session of May 1942 a Baptist preacher who was a member of an or-

ganization of which Nyce was president: the "Pre-Millennial Fellowship of
Allentown."[88] Bluffton graduate "Bill" Snyder, originally from the congregation at the Altoona Mission which was now about to be turned over to
the Salvation Army, going as a conscientious objector to Camp Luray in
Virginia. The young draftee then being called to the Mennonite Central
Committee headquarters at Akron, Pennsylvania, by Executive Secretary
Orie O. Miller of the Lancaster Conference. Neither Miller nor Snyder an-
ticipating, as the new worker arrived, that the latter would follow the
former in his office for a twenty-four-year span as executive secretary of
MCC's worldwide ministry.

More glimpses: *Life* magazine picturing young Harry Clemens, of the
Eden congregation, digging a foxhole in France.[89] The *Souderton Independent* printing Harry's letter home half a year later, reporting that,
"Thanks to the dear Lord," he had come through the "D-Day" invasion
"without a scratch."[90] An honor roll containing twenty-six names of men in
the armed services being put up in the Upper Milford Church. The news
coming to West Swamp that two of their young men had been killed in action. Young Maynard Shelly, of the West Swamp congregation, watching
Pastor Neuenschwander's sons joining the military as noncombatants, but
missionaries Harvey and Ella Bauman's son Ken choosing the conscientious
objector option. Maynard being quietly impressed by older church members at West Swamp that there was "another way" than the military. Bluffton alumnus Henry Detwiler of the Zion congregation, having made a decision not to enter the military, finding his black Ford car painted yellow
where it stood on the street at his home in Souderton. Henry meeting
Rockhill member Esther Detweiler, medical technologist at the Grand View
hospital, in a refugee camp in Egypt, were they were both working as
volunteers. The *Souderton Independent* printing another letter, from a
Harleysville soldier "Somewhere in Italy," stating that something ought to
be done about the "many so-called C.O.'s" who were skewing draft quotas
in the North Penn region.[91] A crowd of nearly 1,000 draft-age Franconia
men filling the Franconia meetinghouse on Sunday afternoon, April 16,
1944. The men singing, as "one great male chorus," the hymn, "Faith of
our Fathers," with a "degree of feeling and reverence" that at least one
young attendant had "seldom heard." Bishop John E. Lapp exhorting the
audience to live Christian lives consistent with their unpopular
conscientious objector stand, in order not to offend the community unnecessarily. The bishop reading from newspaper clippings, including a letter from a Line Lexington woman to the *Philadelphia Inquirer:*

We live in a community where conscientious objectors are very prev-

alent.... Let us draft every available conscientious objector immediately to fill the ranks of the infantry. Should they refuse to fight,
transport them to the front lines and let them kill or be killed.[92]

Mennonite marketmen wrestling with their consciences over how to stay
within the war-caused "ceiling prices" and still make a profit. A young Salford fellow questioning his Mennonite employer's practice of charging
more than ceiling price, and being told it was none of his business.

Still more: Bishop Lapp traveling to several dozen CPS camps, making
hundreds of pastoral interviews, and traveling over 25,000 miles, during the
war years, to both the camps and various committee meetings. Many other
pastors of both conferences also visiting the camps. The Franconia Conference declaring that names of men joining the military service were to be
announced in church.[93] Bishops Lapp and Ruth being called out to
Lancaster County to mediate in a church dispute in the Maple Grove congregation. CPS fellows from western General Conference churches at the
MCC headquarters at Akron attending "fellowship meetings" led by
Eastern District pastors in Lancaster—the beginnings of what would be the
"Bethel" congregation.[94]

Significant new leadership appeared in both conferences in the war
years. Lots for bishop were cast in the Franconia Conference three times in
the span of a year: "Andrew Mack's old district" was reactivated in part,
along with new mission congregations that had appeared since his death,
the choice falling unprecedentedly on one of the recently ordained mission
pastors—Stanley Beidler of Haycock. In the westernmost ("Schuylkill
Valley") district, farmer Amos Kolb of Vincent was chosen to aid the failing
Warren Bean, and at the opposite eastern end of the conference the lot fell
on butcher Joseph Gross, son of Deacon Abram, to replace A. O. Histand, of
the same (Doylestown) congregation. Perhaps the most striking ordination
of these months came in August 1944 when the lot for a second minister at
the Norristown Mission fell on a nineteen-year-old Goshen College student,
Paul Lederach. Within days this great-grandson of Minister Jacob Mensch,
as impressively tall as John Lapp, was invited to preach as a guest at his
father's home congregation, Salford, where he startled the fascinated
audience with a stern admonition for the men to get rid of their habit of
smoking. The eloquent new preacher would find himself ordained again by
lot a few years later, this time as a bishop, at the ripe old age of twenty-four.

In the Eastern District, the venerable A. M. Fretz finally passed on at
the age of almost ninety. His place at Deep Run was filled by a young
Ohioan, Russell Mast, and the congregation built a cabin at the new Camp
Men-O-Lan in their old pastor's memory. The "Swamp Charge," too,
remembered bygone leaders by naming the cabin its volunteers erected

Elvin Souder, Jr., of the Zion congregation (third from left) with a group of Paraguayan Mennonites and Mennonite Central Committee workers meeting for worship in Asunción, Paraguay. (Bottom) Photograph by Elvin Souder of Paraguayan Mennonite families, immigrants from Europe, with local transportation method. (Elvin Souder, Jr.)

"Ober-Shell," in honor of John H. Oberholtzer and Andrew B. Shelly. West Swamp built "Harv-Ella," for missionaries Harvey and Ella Bauman. First Mennonite of Philadelphia named its cabin "Wilhelmina," in obvious reference to their Wilhelmina Kuyf, who had returned to her mission work in China. At Zion in Souderton the vacancy left by departing pastor Bohn was temporarily filled by the resoundingly liberal pulpiteer and author J. E. Hartzler, now a professor with Elmer Johnson at Hartford Seminary. Russell Mast also helped at Zion. The new permanent pastor, installed in September 1944, was a fresh graduate of Hartford, the outspoken young South Dakota-native Ellis Graber. His bride, Delpha, a fellow-student at Hartford, soon introduced a popular annual performance of Handel's *Messiah*, and before long a new library would be organized and opened to the public as well as the congregation. Finding the well-attended services "so noisy you couldn't hear yourself preach," the young pastor shortly had a nursery organized for the many babies present. Graber and Harold Burkholder of East Swamp, each of whom served as president of the conference, represented the opposite ends of the theological spectrum within the body.

Back from seminary in New York came Paul Shelly. At a specially called meeting for Eastern District ministers at Grace Mennonite, he presented a paper on his aims for the Bible Department at Bluffton, where he had been called to fill a vacancy created by a controversial resignation. Shelly, it was clear, would have no problem being accepted as orthodox; he had imbibed from his blind preacher-father a deep sense of things Mennonite. His brother Andrew, installed as the new pastor of a congregation in Kitchener, Ontario, that had been without conference affiliation since its birth in 1924, was making plans to have it join the Eastern District.

In the CPS camps the draftees were somewhat dissatisfied, feeling that their work lacked true significance. The Franconia Conference sent each of its men a monthly allowance of $7.50. These funds and the canned goods prepared under the supervision of Nathan Keyser by volunteer women in the kitchen of the Eastern Mennonite Home were donated with a generosity that heartened the Peace Problems Committee. The Franconia Conference, stated their letter to the CPS men, had probably never in its history had a cause "that has enjoyed more loyal support from all of the congregations."[95]

A special case was that of Zion-member Elvin Souder, Jr., a son of one of the Old Mennonite partners in the "Allebach & Souder" clothing store. Elvin managed to find employment with a local farmer, which made farm deferment possible, but after a half-year concluded that he was not cut out for this kind of work. Under the auspices of MCC he left for service among the Mennonite refugees in Asunción, Paraguay, on whose behalf lawyer and MCC executive Maxwell Kratz of Second Mennonite in Philadelphia also expended many administrative efforts. Six months later, "Pop" Souder paid the way for Elvin's wife, Esther (a nurse originally from the Hereford congregation), and their small daughter, Jane, to join their husband and father in Asunción. Here both Elvin and Esther served for another year and a half.[96]

From the Franconia Conference, a Blooming Glen member, young dentist Earl Stover and his Kansas-born wife, Haidi (Enss), were among the first to go into foreign service. Earl, whose father had been one of the Franconia Conference conscientious objectors in World War I, had met Haidi, of General Conference background, as a fellow-student at Goshen College. In 1942, while taking accelerated dental training in Philadelphia, the newly married couple was recruited by MCC for a new work in rural Puerto Rico. When the La Plata Mennonite Hospital was finally opened in August 1944, they joined the staff, and Earl found himself the bearer of Puerto Rico's dental license #76. Although he had cleared his plans with the local draft board at Doylestown, and gotten the impression that this work was satisfying his draft obligation, Selective Service in Washington, D.C., only seemed to discover Earl's whereabouts in 1952, whereupon he was drafted for two more years. The young Stover family thus spent a full decade of dental and mission work on the island.[97] By the time they left, other Franconia Conference workers had joined them, including Esther Detweiler of Rockhill, Emma Landis of Salford, and William and Thelma (Derstine) Swartzendruber of Blooming Glen.

Soon after peace was declared in Europe, Thelma's brother, David Derstine, Jr., and his bride, Maxine (Troyer), left for relief work in Belgium, also recruited by MCC. The Derstines too had met at Goshen. When David had left home for his freshman year, his uncle Isaiah Derstine, a farmer at Franconia Square, had been displeased, and had offered David's father, "D. D." Derstine, a job for the young man on his farm, if that was what was needed to keep him from being drafted. Then when Isaiah had learned that Dave was thinking of marrying a girl from Indiana, his dismay had increased. His brother, he suggested, should try to break up the romance, lest the family feeling be lost through the introduction of a person who could not speak *"unser Sproch"*—our language (at this time some Sunday school classes were still being taught in "Dutch" at Franconia, and German hymns were sung regularly). Some months later, however, when Dave knocked at his uncle's farmhouse door at Franconia, the dubious farmer's reservations melted abruptly as, to his confused delight, Maxine Troyer began rattling away to him in his own idiomatic Dutch.[98]

More young people of both conferences left for relief work: Henry Detwiler (Zion) for Egypt (where he met Esther Detweiler from Rockhill) and Europe; Marvin Wasser (Deep Run West) for France; Paul Ruth (Line Lexington) for Europe; Jacob and Mildred Clemens (Plains) for Ethiopia. A new and wider consciousness was dawning. The Mennonite "family" in both its tightly bounded and more acculturated versions was about to enter a "watershed era" whose effect would be particularly strong on the Franconia Conference. The Franconia leaders were calling for a fresh wave of missions to absorb the spiritual energies of young people freshly stirred up. A group of young families was moving into the Rocky Ridge area with a hatchery, a stocking factory, and a dream of sharing the gospel as a whole ethos in the community of the young Mennonite mission there. Others were looking toward Vermont. And a few days before "V-E Day" the Franconia Conference approved the ordination of the first black minister in their whole denomination, James Lark.[99] This valuable member of the Rocky Ridge congregation, and his possibly even more devoted wife, Rowena, had been tapped by the larger church to lead a new "work" in a black community in Chicago. In Norristown, the first of the half dozen members of the Brown family who would join the Mennonite congregation was baptized. Two of his younger brothers would become Mennonite ministers, and one, Hubert, the first black moderator of a Mennonite conference (Southwest).

By the end of the summer of 1945, a special session of the Franconia Conference would grant permission, though withholding actual sponsorship, for a new parochial elementary school. In eight more years there would even be a conference-sponsored high school. In the new consolidated public schools Mennonite children had been exposed to strong war propaganda, and pressured to buy "War Savings Stamps" or assist in collection of rubber and metal scrap. Now the Franconia Mennonite Day School was organized by an association of Franconia Conference families, beginning with eighty students. By this time Old Mennonites in other conferences had already opened a dozen such schools. Yet it would have been unimaginable to Minister Abram Yoder and missionary-to-be Esther Freed, looking down across the Skippack valley from the steps of the old "Krupp's Schoolhouse" on the Cowpath, where they were the first teachers, that several decades later some 700 students would crowd the facilities of their expanded school. Even more surprising would it have been to be told that there would be a large gymnasium, since one reason many Franconia Conference parents did not want their children to attend the public high school was the physical education requirement, involving classes for which "gym shorts" were prescribed.

(Top) Henry and Neva Badetscher Detwiler of the Zion congregation in Souderton, in relief work with the Mennonite Central Committee in Europe just after the war (ca. 1946). (Bottom) MCC food distribution in Europe as photographed by Henry Detwiler. Many eastern Pennsylvania Mennonites helped to prepare such food. (Roger Detwiler)

One relief worker under the supervision of Henry Detwiler was Paul Ruth, son of Bishop Arthur and Florence Ruth of the Line Lexington congregation. Paul worked for a while on the island of Walcheren, Holland, which had been flooded as a result of wartime bombing. (Roger Detwiler)

As draftees drifted back home at the end of the war, the two conferences sought, in their differing manners, to reintegrate them into church life. The spring 1946 Franconia Conference sessions produced a statement bespeaking an unyielding stance:

> Ministers are admonished to contact those members who took military service when they return, to try to win them to the Faith. They shall be asked to relinquish all connections with the Veterans' Organization and if called again for service must promise to take the Nonresistant position. All insurance benefits are also to be canceled.[100]

In contrast, the young men who had taken the conscientious objector position were sent a letter containing a gift from the church for the purpose of "getting started" again in normal life. The letter, signed "Peace Problems Committee," commended these men:

> You have stood true to the nonresistant doctrine, and your name will remain with those who have borne a faithful testimony under test for the Christ who not only suffered but bled and died for you.[101]

In comparison, the Eastern Conference's methods of easing the reentry into church life may be sampled in the encouraging words of the Deep Run Congregation, where young Herbert Fretz was stepping just at this time into this grandfather's long-held pastoral position. The congregation now "resolved"

> that we express our praise and gratitude to Almighty God, who has so wonderfully preserved our young men from bodily harm and death during these past years of bloodshed, and that we heartily welcome back each and every one of them into the fellowship and work of our congregation.[102]

East Swamp also had a newly arrived young pastor, Abe Schultz, a native of Montana who had last served an Evangelical Mennonite Brethren congregation in Henderson, Nebraska. At a congregational dinner meeting held at Trainer's Restaurant in Quakertown, the new pastor asked the whole congregation to acknowledge their failures to follow Christ completely, rather than singling out the recently returned soldiers among them for special confession.[103]

Here, then, at the end of an era of global crisis and of the first century of its divided life, we shall leave off telling the story of this oldest Mennonite community in North America. We have watched it grow since Jan and Mercken Lensen took up their lot along a converted Indian trail in Germantown, and since nearly a thousand Palatines settled from Skippack outward, into an accumulation of over 8,000 baptized members. A century after it had split, this sundered household of faith was still worshiping in two uncommunicating communions, each persuaded that the other opposed, in its manner of maintaining the church, certain elements essential to the gospel of their Lord. Those for whom a distinct cultural identity was unacceptable were still crossing that painful divide in a one-way traffic, leaving behind little mutual affection or understanding. There were, certainly, individual exceptions to this general situation.

As for the older group, its plain clothes had grown ever more starkly distinct in the last four decades. Children were unaware that their parents, some of whom had discarded or hidden their youthful photographs, had once dressed as gaily as their non-Mennonite neighbors. At the same time, a considerable body of young people were grasping for spiritual expression and activity. Lay people as well as ministers often greeted "one another with an holy kiss" on the lips, as they met before and after meetings, under the long porch roofs or in the anterooms of large brick meetinghouses or miscellaneously rented mission halls. A solemn row of black-clad ministers,

(Top) Baptism at Blooming Glen in the new (1938) meetinghouse. Emma (Mrs. Abraham) Histand is greeting a newly received member with "a holy kiss" while her husband, Bishop "A. O." Histand is giving "the right hand of fellowship" to another new member. Three more young women who have just been baptized are still kneeling, awaiting the bishop's words, "In the name of Christ and his church, I give you my hand: Arise!" (Bottom) Communion at Blooming Glen. The members walk down the central aisle to be "served" with the cup by the bishop. As this is in process, Leidy Hunsicker leads a song on the theme of Christ's sacrifice. All the women, from 1911 until the late 1960s, wear coverings. (William L. Histand)

radiating a sacred authority, still looked out from the pulpit-benches on crowded weekend Bible conferences. "The ladies' side" of the meetinghouse presented a sea of coverings, with white or black "strings," depending on the degree of the wearers' conservatism. Whereas at Deep Run the men and boys still sat on the sloping "roost" on each side of the center section, neighboring Blooming Glen had built a less traditional, large meetinghouse, lacking the older long pulpit.

Well-polished automobiles sped back and forth to Paoli, where modest young men embarked on the "Pennsy" Railroad for CPS camps after brief furloughs. Marketmen drove their panel trucks home early on a Saturday afternoon for "Preparatory Services" (feetwashing) prior to the annual communion (Vincent had it twice yearly). Scripture-reciting bishops walked among the congregation with the communion cup, withholding it from a man wearing a mustache or a woman with short sleeves, as a deacon followed solicitously, filling the cup now and again from a demijohn of wine made from Concord grapes with Deacon Henry M. Ruth's mild recipe, or quietly bought in a Philadelphia State Store. Congregations knelt on uncarpeted hardwood floors for prayer twice in each meeting, the great, creaking transition providing valuable glimpses, to the younger generation, of those on the other side of the center aisle. At funerals, the whole audience filed slowly by the opened casket at the foot of the pulpit after the final song, the interminable line gradually evolving into a diagram of the departed one's *"Freindschaft,"* until at its end, with the ministers above them wiping their eyes, the ashen, tear-stained family itself stood around the body in a quivering silence, etching on the congregation's focused memory an indelible tableau of shared parting. Then Wilmer Nice of Harleysville (Zion congregation) or Paul Hunsicker of Souderton (Blooming Glen)—the "undertakers"—would "take charge."

The approaching great change in the Franconia Conference had hardly begun, though its tremors had awakened an aggressive vigilance in the bishops, who were reminded by occasional admonishing letters from their flock that they had been solemnly charged to "hold fast."

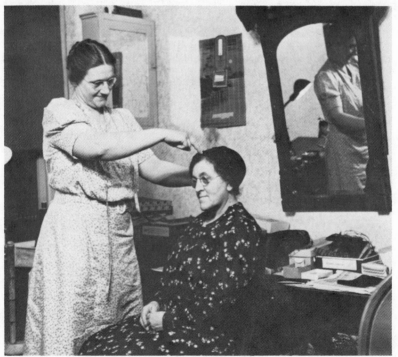

Ellen Moyer (Mrs. Elmer) Gross, of the village of Blooming Glen, fits a new bonnet on a customer, Elsie (Mrs. Walter) Smith, in 1938. (William L. Histand)

Wilmer Yoder of the Blooming Glen congregation on a "Cattle Ship" to Danzig in 1946, photographed by his fellow-volunteer Richard Rush of the Deep Run (Old) Mennonite congregation. (Richard Rush)

The atmosphere of Eastern District life was less severe, its people less culturally homogeneous. Conference sessions proceeded, as before, with dozens of resolutions realized through a careful parliamentary process. Fifteen committees reported annually, two or three including women as members (in the Franconia conference sessions the wives of the ordained men "kept silent," and sat off to the side and in the rear, if they came at all). The two churches in Philadelphia, long seen as expressions of the outward-looking spirit of the conference, now observing their membership dispersing as Philadelphia's population patterns shifted dramatically, called for the conference's prayers as they contemplated possible "changes" of program. A sprinkling of "western" Mennonites of "Russian" background, drawn by the eastern location of MCC headquarters, was appearing in conference churches, and a new congregation, emerging at Lancaster, would find a talented young Midwestern preacher of Anabaptist leanings, studying at Princeton (Donovan Smucker). Special music that would have awed the Franconia Mennonites (though they too were finally about to allow vocal groups) was common: a chorus, an octet, an organ, a violin solo, or a marimba duo. If there was almost no "discipline" in the sense of the once

A Franconia Township-Souderton (Old) Mennonite family in the plain clothes era. L. to r., front row: Joseph W. and Katie Derstine Hackman. Back row: Dorothy (Mrs. Paul Martin), Verna (Mrs. Ernest Moyer), Susan (Mrs. Edwin Moyer), J. Walter (m. Ruth Yoder), Wilmer (m. Alice Borneman), and Linford (m. Ada Clemens). (Susan H. Moyer)

mandatory "*Umfrage*" or counsel meeting as the Franconia Conference still practiced it, there was also, in Sunday school teachers, deacons, or spiritual young campers testifying during the evening devotions at Camp Men-O-Lan, a piety that would have startled those whose Franconia Conference orientation might have convinced them that such faith could not thrive without a rigid code of rules.

Startling, too, was the fact that though the Eastern District Conference had greater difficulty in holding its members to certain old Mennonite ideals, it produced leadership that could articulate those ideals more eloquently than most of the Franconia leaders themselves. One such person, now teaching at Bethel College in Kansas, looked back "at the end of a century," in 1947. Economist-sociologist J. Winfield Fretz had grown up under the preaching of A. M. Fretz at Deep Run, later attended Grace Mennonite Church in Lansdale, and after graduating from Bluffton College in 1934, had earned a PhD at the University of Chicago. In a somewhat pensive mood, he posed pointed questions about the "process of accommodation" he observed in the career of his parent conference. At its founding in 1847, its pioneers' "basic assumption," he noted, "was that the changes it advocated could be made without loss of basic religious values." As he considered "five religious principles . . . characteristically identified with the Mennonite faith" (simplicity, nonconformity, discipline, mutual aid, and nonresistance), Fretz felt "driven to say that on all these points there has been a loss of ground. . . . The Conference, as a religious group, has gradually adjusted itself to its environment. Adherence [to the five "principles"] has been weakened to the point of a faint flicker. . . . There is no indication that there is a testimony of greater or less vigor than is being given by any other evangelical Protestant group."[104]

Such a blunt assessment was read with solemn agreement by the few Franconia Conference readers who came across it in the magazine *Mennonite Life*. Yet their own fellowship would, in a decade or two, enter upon the same processes of acculturation here regretted.

Another observer at this same time, Professor Paul Shelly of Bluffton,

A harvest home service at the Deep Run (Old) Mennonite meetinghouse in 1938. Sam Detweiler is leading a song. Ministers and deacons seated in the pulpit include a number of visitors. L. to r.: Abram Yothers, Alfred Detweiler, Wilson Overholt, Melvin Bishop, John S. Hess of Lititz (the main speaker of the evening), unidentified, Daniel Gehman, unidentified, Henry Delp, Franklin Alderfer, and Harvey Meyers. (William L. Histand)

used a quotation from Pastor Silas Grubb to point up what he saw as an essential motif in the Eastern District outlook. "A man is answerable to his own conscience and not that of another," Grubb had written, and thus in World War I some Eastern District men had "preferred to be true to themselves rather than to traditions, sacred though they were...."[105] There was actually "a sense of pride," observed Shelly, in the fact that such individually based discernment could be tolerated, with the result that "members and leaders have been able to get along with each other even though there have been wide variations in belief and practice." While this helped to avoid controversy, the effect, Shelly thought, was that the conference thereby "sacrificed to some extent the original concept of the church as taught in the New Testament and by the Anabaptists"[106] who had brought this church into being.

As later events would prove, and as current trends were already suggesting, the Franconia Conference was in no position to consider itself

Photographed around 1946 by Paul Hertzler, who had grown up in the Norristown congregation, this group of Mennonite historians in the home of Harold S. Bender of Goshen, Indiana, includes a representative from the Franconia Conference and one from the Eastern District. L. to r.: Robert Friedmann, Ernst Correll, John C. Wenger (originally of the Rockhill congregation), Harold S. Bender, John S. Umble, Melvin Gingerich, Cornelius Krahn, and J. Winfield Fretz (originally of the Grace Mennonite congregation, Lansdale). (Mennonite Historical Library, Goshen, Indiana)

The first summer Bible school held in the Souderton Mennonite meetinghouse on Chestnut Street, 1944. (Marvin K. Landis)

above the same issues. It was poised at the brink of two decades of profound change that would drive it toward institutionalism and away from the folk-mind in which unarticulated beliefs could be taken for granted, or maintained by the decisions of bishops. A century after refusing to listen to the suggestion of a constitution, the Franconia Conference was drawing up one of its own.

Bishop John Lapp, by now the spokesman, though not yet the moderator of the Franconia Conference, was supplementing the informal financial "support" he received (and his wife, Edith, carefully recorded in a small notebook) with income from a small flock of turkeys tended by the growing family. He confessed that although he had been raised in nearby Lansdale, his heart was "more in the country than in the town," and he believed this was true for most Franconia Conference members. He would later recall with satisfaction that on the few acres surrounding the substantial brick house in the countryside along the Allentown Road, he, his busy wife, and the church community had "had our children to ourselves." Yet a powerful trend toward urbanization, bringing "a distinct effect upon the church life as well as the economic life," was unmistakable. Perhaps, in

An early evening service at the first Young People's Institute of Franconia Conference, on Labor Day weekend, 1946, at the Blooming Glen meetinghouse. Some of the talks were recorded on a wire-recorder by Clayton Godshall. (Mary Jane Lederach Hershey)

order to keep their way of life, some members of the conference would need to move to where there was still open, and cheaper, land. Bishop Lapp expressed the traditional approval of such a move, with the caution that it would be "much better for several families to locate in a given area than for one family to isolate itself entirely." Within fifteen years there would occur, indeed, a veritable exodus of young Franconia Conference farm families to western counties, mostly beyond the Blue Mountain that had, in colonial times, marked the limits of the German settlements. This would be the last distinct outward migration of Franconia Conference people continuing to seek a life on the land.

In such circumstances, what vision of its purpose and understanding of its character would guide the church? Closing our final chapter at the threshold of the era of television and the jet plane, we may ponder the words of a Mennonite bishop, this one a dozen generations later than Hinrich Kassel of the Palatinate, with whose definition of the church our first chapter concluded. For Bishop John Lapp in 1947, keeping "the right fellowship" was still central. Church members, he wrote, must "maintain a close unity with one another in the Lord Jesus Christ." Having been awakened to new outreach, we must not neglect the essence of our heritage.

> We must remember the Biblical principles of separation from the world, nonresistance to evil, mutual burden-bearing, and world evangelization and we must look for the appearing of our Lord. Then we shall be able to retain the proper relationship with our Lord, our church, the society about us, and those with whom we are employed. We will then perform our function as the light of the world and the salt of the earth, and have a distinct part in the program of our Lord Jesus Christ in being witnesses unto Him. [107]

Epilogue: Restoring the Right Fellowship

The cohesion and survival of the covenanted body of Mennonites is a striking phenomenon. Without sacrament or education or official status in European society, and even without buildings to meet in, they maintained their fellowship. In thickets along the Rhine, caves in Switzerland, a stone quarry in the Alsace, or a barn in the Palatinate, they met when they could, shared the Lord's supper, and held each other to faithfulness to a vision of a society beholden only to Christ. Their spiritual family survived vicious persecution, emigration, mixing of emigrant families in new locations, double and triple taxation, the chaos of war, and pietistic movements that, even as they renewed spiritual warmth, threatened to dissolve the covenanted family by reducing its concern for a "right fellowship."

Having straggled without plan into eastern Pennsylvania, this family "kept house," or maintained its fellowship, for 139 years after they first felt authorized to hold the Lord's supper in Germantown in 1708. Although the Revolutionary War opened a painful crack in their unity, producing a small body of "Funkites," for another seven decades the "Franconia Conference" experienced no major ruptures.

But then a polarization did occur. Historians will explain why, in terms of their favorite social, cultural, economic, or even ideological paradigms. For our purposes, might we paraphrase the Proverbs to say that where there is too narrow a vision, the peoplehood polarizes? And that each wing then retains only part of the original vision?

Did the Mennonites of the generations that built the towns along the North Penn, Perkiomen, and Reading Railroads give their descendants access to the story of maintaining the right fellowship? Was the "rich" Old Mennonite "man in overalls" who had worked all his life to develop his inherited farmland along the new railroad in Souderton into valuable real estate, and never, it seemed to a boy growing up in the New Mennonite Zion congregation, "spent a dime for pleasure," an inspiration to faithfulness, or a discouragement, to that boy? Was the Mennonite ethos that had been inherited by this man's generation likely to be favorably caught by the eager young people watching him? Is it not partly the responsibility of such humorless Pennsylvania Dutch materialists that many of their descendants have no rich and compelling vision of their "Zion"—their Anabaptist heritage?

But there is an equally challenging question to be asked of the young people, the ever-arriving new generation, who claim the banner of idealism. Is it not just as true that, once they do hear the story, once they are confronted with the spiritual claims of their Mennonite heritage, whether or not their parental generation has properly embodied its right fellowship, they still have a choice to make, an identity crisis to resolve?

For one confesses who one is in terms of the fellowship one considers to be the right one. The psalmist speaks of valuing spiritual identity above even the art by which it is often expressed. His harp—his aesthetic expression—must have a real place to be set; his mouth must have a particular song. If he forgets his Jerusalem—his identity—he may as well hang his harp on the willows, and let his tongue lie still, since the point of the song is gone. The secular audience, to be sure, finding the song aesthetically charming, may try to call it forth, but not because it cares for the singer's soul, or the covenanted family in which it was shaped.

Thus it was with a Mennonite woman of the Towamencin congregation in 1904. She had a son, talented on the violin, who was about to be faced with the life-changing call to be a simple Mennonite minister. The church, rightly or wrongly, required him to choose between its fellowship and the development of his aesthetic and commercial gifts. Though it cost them agony, he and his ambitious young wife obeyed the church in its narrow concept of the right fellowship, and he became a key voice in the transmission of a spiritual heritage. "This Sunday will never be forgotten," wrote his mother after hearing his first sermon, "when one of our children has to enter that holy pulpit and stand before God and men and teach from his holy word."

She also had a grandson, a budding pianist, who chose at the age of sixteen to be "baptized to" a local church that required no particular deviation from the surrounding generally Christian culture. "I would rather have see him Joyn a Concianious Meeting," confided the grandmother to her diary, "but may his garden angel keep him on the narrow way that leads only to Heaven." Thus, so often, was the issue addressed as a new generation came to the crossroads of identity: if obedience to the narrow way of

the gospel can no longer be kept in a disciplined fellowship, at least let there
be personal salvation! As it turned out, the musical grandson won the
plaudits of his community, and *his* son, in turn, recognition on a national
scale. But any question of maintaining across the generations a "right
fellowship" which bespoke Christ's society-reordering gospel had been
passed by.

And thus it was, too, for the highly respected pastor of the West
Swamp congregation, Arthur Rosenberger, who had served as president of
both his Eastern Conference and Bluffton College. A modest and devoted
servant of the church, he felt it difficult to answer questions raised by his
earnest brother-in-law, returned missionary S. T. Moyer. Because, he observed regretfully, in the Eastern District "we do not have solid Mennonite
communities" (he himself had grown up in Philadelphia), the young people
often "just gravitated along" with their "social environment" on matters
where the Mennonites had traditionally asked for hard choices. It would
certainly be preferable to have a pure church, "But we must deal with
people as they are and do the best we can to get the gospel of Jesus Christ
vital in their lives." If everyone who could not accept the Mennonite
emphases would be "ruled out" of the fellowship, "we would not have
much left." It was necessary, it seemed, to leave the strong Mennonite
teachings "up to the conscience of the new member as long as he professes
Jesus Christ as his personal Savior." It was Rosenberger's practice, he told
his brother-in-law, to tell new members who did not wish to accept adult
baptism or give up lodge membership or military service "that they must at
least be tolerant of our doctrines even if they cannot fully subscribe to all."

To this ambiguity had the logic of 1847 led, and a few decades later,
the Franconia Conference would be drawn toward it too. But in 1947, the
Franconia problem was at the opposite extreme. Its leaders knew all too
well just how the hair should be parted, the movies shunned, and brash
young people quieted into conformity to an increasingly ramifying code of
rules. Nor did they seem to reach out a hand of concern, even in sorrow, to
their estranged "General Conference" siblings living side by side with
them. They continued much in the spirit of their ancestors who, immediately after the 1847 division, had requested that the new group leave
them "in peace," and had treated the new conference with decades of what
was felt as "silent contempt."

By 1983, however, a change in attitude had occurred. There had always been individual exceptions to the general rule of alienation, and the
division had been briefly discussed without acrimony in young John C.
Wenger's Franconia *History* of 1937. Now the two conferences, which had
been consulting with each other peacefully and considerately for several

years, jointly sponsored a new writing of their divided history. It was no longer a matter of laying blame for the division, but of learning about ourselves, and about spiritual reality. And thus the question arises, what did our forebears mean when they could speak of maintaining right fellowship?

Their confessions of faith reveal that for centuries Mennonites claimed the gospel of Christ as a power that reconciled them, not only as individuals to their God, but also as social creatures to their fellow human beings. They had learned this not from philosophy but from the New Testament. They took from what they read there that although "all things . . . in earth or things in heaven" were *potentially* reconciled in Christ's sacrifice, within the household of faith this reconciliation should already become *actual*— take concrete form. Where Christ's cross was thus accepted as the key to life's meaning, a new order emerged. This was the Anabaptists' confession, the open secret of their witness, their evidence that God was at work in the world. This experience of radical reconciliation was not only for a church-within-a-church—a special group of unusually conscientious Christians—as Martin Luther had once proposed. The theology of salvation implied not only a psychology but a sociology as well. Since human life cannot be lived or have meaning in only the individual dimension, God's salvation must also extend to the other dimension—the social. In this dimension, too, the Anabaptists had "a real experience with the Lord." Here too they were empowered to "walk in newness of life."

This power to reorder human life, bringing the will of heaven into earthly relationships, was not, the Anabaptists believed, a mere ornament of the gospel, to be practiced if, when, and how the government felt it could be allowed. It was an essential part of the cosmic good news. Thus a distinct quality of mutuality, strengthened by the rigors of persecution, was taught into the very texture of Mennonite consciousness. To be defenseless like the Lamb of God, reconciled to each other in him, and mutually accountable to "bind and loose" according to his "rule" (Matthew 18) were the identifying marks of what Mennonites believed to be the "right fellowship"—the one that Christ had described and founded. It was certainly not right because it was Mennonite, but a group of people had found themselves called Mennonites as they tried to organize and maintain such a fellowship.

Transmitting this fellowship was the unmistakable mandate of their church. In the 20th century, the Franconia Conference was giving a persistent witness to this mandate by closing each of its sessions with the statement, "We are still willing to continue in the simple and nonresistant faith of Christ." This not only evoked a sense of continuity with the "old nonresistant ground" of the Anabaptist tradition, but was a continuing assertion that there was more to Christianity than claiming Christ as one's "personal Savior," and then experiencing "assurance of salvation" in one's heart. First be reconciled to your brother, Jesus had said, and then come to the altar to pray. Even John Oberholtzer, in the very opening paragraph of his controversial constitution, had acknowledged that it was necessary "to maintain christian order, conformable to Christ's teachings, in [the] community, that the name of God may ever be glorified. . . ."

Our story shows that neither clinging to tradition nor demanding new forms of the order had enabled the Mennonites of easternmost Pennsylvania to maintain one right fellowship. How could two groups of Mennonites unable to keep any fellowship between them teach the world which was the right one? Why had education, organization, and modernization been able to drive a wedge down the middle of the church?

The opportunity for damage had been provided by the emergence of two extreme mentalities, neither of which served the right fellowship well. The first one heard mainly voices from the past, on matters of ordering the church. It heard these voices with a clarity and power unimaginable to those tuned mainly to the present. What this backward-looking mentality knew was invaluable to the faith community, but its value was canceled by an accompanying dullness to the poignancy of genuine new needs, hurts, and dreams. This mentality felt the sanctions imbibed in childhood and adolescence as ultimate in form as well as content. It regarded its own stubbornness as faithfulness and courage. Sin was defined as change.

The second extreme mentality, characterized by a lack of sensitivity to the role of memory in the church, was tempted to ascribe positive value to things simply because they were not traditional. It had an inadequate sense of the seriousness of the risks it took with "the right fellowship," or of the irony of its tendency, while thinking it was leading the way out of tradition, to replace its own heritage with attitudes borrowed from other traditions, whether "evangelical" or "liberal." It was not sufficiently imaginative in its understanding of its own heritage. For this mentality, the experience of peoplehood, memory, continuity, and cross-generational covenant did not seem as compelling or sacred. They were often viewed as obstacles, rather than means of grace. To drop the "*Umfrage*" (Counsel Meeting) was thus felt as a kind of progress, rather than a loss of something essential to the right fellowship.

Yet we have seen, in the long story just told, that a strong sense of "our people" was not necessarily mere froth or idolatry. It was sometimes the very medium through which basic spiritual truth was conveyed. It was not tradition *per se* that Jesus, that great fulfiller of the law, condemned, but "empty traditions." The drama of our story is, after all, that two fellowships *were* maintained, though doubtless neither always behaved like the "right" one. A spiritual community, though in two pieces, did survive immigration, wars, the secular embrace of the macroculture, the wooing of the Methodist, Baptist, and Evangelical revivals, and the growing option of the independent American-type "Bible church" that did not have to give account of itself to a larger fellowship. Two *conferences,* or *councils,* one more loosely bounded and more rationally structured than the other, did continue to express the fellowship's desire to avoid mere congregationalism. That larger fellowship—the conference network—was considered part of what it meant to have a "right fellowship" in Christ.

Every year or half-year these two conferences gathered, separately, from across the triangle roughly sketched by the Delaware, Schuylkill, and Lehigh rivers (and from beyond, in the Eastern District), to acknowledge the importance of this wider relationship. A friendly dialogue between the two conferences, occurring by Eastern invitation, began at the centennial observance of "1847" in the Lower Skippack meetinghouse, when three groups—Eastern, Franconia, and "Johnson" Mennonites—reflected together. Twenty years later the conversation moved a large step forward, when they joined in the work of conserving their growing historical collections (1967).

In 1947 the two conferences were trying to express the meaning of the church in two opposite practices of communion: Franconia by requiring that it include acknowledgment of a lengthy code of rules, and be limited to people of "like precious faith"; Eastern by inviting Christians to approach the Lord's Table after consulting their private consciences. If the latter was not Anabaptist, neither did it reduce communion to the question of a mustache. But could either of these procedures reflect the right fellowship?

Both sides of the divided family, along with their failures, had important insights on this question. Each side would have to listen, if anything was to be learned, keeping in mind that the differences were real. A shallow ecumenism covering over these differences would show little respect, on either side, for the right fellowship of their common heritage.

But what more hopeful sign of reconciliation might there be than the two conferences listening together, at the 300th anniversary of their beginnings in America, to the story of their fellowship?

Notes

Chapter 1. "For the Sake of Their Faith" (1648-1681)

1. Yillisz Kasel, "Clagspruch in Krankbet," 22 pp. MS at MSHL, p. 22.

2. Harold S. Bender, ed., "Palatinate Mennonite Census Lists, 1664-1774," *MQR*, XIV (January 1940), 8-10.

3. "Palatinate," *ME*, IV, 110.

4. Gerhard Hein, "Zwei neue Quellenfunde zur Geschichte der Täufer in der Kurpfalz," *Der Mennonit*, XXV (January 1972), 12.

5. Gerhard Hein, "Die Herkunft der pfälzischen Mennoniten," *Pfalzer-Palatines*, ed. Karl Sherer (Kaiserslautern, 1981), 208.

6. Christian Neff, "Geschichtliches aus der Gemeinde Monsheim," *Mennonitische Blätter* LIX (February 1912), 11.

7. Wilhelm Niepoth, "The Ancestry of the Thirteen Krefeld Emigrants," tr. John Brockie Lukens, *Pennsylvania Genealogical Magazine*, XXI (1980), 201-202.

8. Walter Risler, "Täufer im bergischen Amt Löwenburg, Siebengebirge," II, *Mennonitische Geschichtsblätter*, XIII (1956), 40-41.

9. Classis of Amsterdam to Consistory in New Netherland, May 26, 1656, in Hugh Hastings, ed., *Ecclesiastical Records: State of New York*, I (Albany, 1911), 348-349.

10. See [Jeremias Mangold], "Ein Warhofftiger Bericht," reprinted in *Ausbund* (Germantown, 1785), 19-56, *passim.*

11. "Bern," *ME*, I, 291.

12. Quoted here from [Tieleman Tielen van Sittert], "An Appendix" [1664], *The Christian Confession of the Faith of the harmless Christians, in the Netherlands, known by the name of Mennonists* (Philadelphia, 1727), 34.

13. Heinz Schuchmann, *Schweizer Einwanderer im früheren kurpfälzischen Streubesitz des Kraichgaues (1650-1750)* (Kaiserslautern, n.d.), 5-8, 23.

14. Ernst H. Correll, *Das Schweizerische Taufermennonitentum* (Tübingen, 1925), 81.

15. Willy Winter, "Im Kraichgau nach dem Dreiszigjährigen Krieg," *Heidelberger Tagblatt*, January 22-23, 1974, 36. "Generallandesarchiv Karlsruhe 77/4336 Generalia," tr. Noah Good and Herman Guth, in Jane Evans Best, "A Bear Hunt in Europe," *Mennonite Family History*, II (January 1983), 10.

16. Correll, *Schweizerische Taufermennonitentum*, 81.

17. "Wolfsheim," *ME*, IV, 970-971.

18. *Ibid.*

19. William I. Hull, *William Penn and the Dutch Quaker Migration to Pennsylvania* (Swarthmore, Pa., 1935), 275-276.

20. Paul Michel, "Täufer Mennoniten und Quäker in Kriegsheim bei Worms," *Der Wormsgau*, VII (1965-66), 44 ("Sonderdruck aus 'Der Wormsgau' Siebenter Band").

21. Neff, "Geschichtliches aus der Gemeinde Monsheim" (see n.6), 11.

22. Michel, 22.

23. Neff, 11.

24. *Ibid.*

25. *Ibid.*, 12.

26. "Palatinate," *ME*, IV, 110.

27. Yillisz Kasel, "Clagspruch" (see n. 1), n.p. /11/.

28. *Ibid.*, /18/.

29. Thielman J. van Braght, *The Bloody Theatre or Martyrs Mirror of the Defenseless Christians*, tr. Joseph F. Sohm (Scottdale, Pa., 1950), 1125.

30. Bender, "Palatine Mennonite Census Lists" (see n. 2), 10-13.

31. Hein, "Herkunft der pfälzischen Mennoniten" (see n. 5), 211.

32. Bender, "Palatine Mennonite Census Lists," 13.

33. J. Ijntema, "Mennonites of the Netherlands," *MQR*, XI (January 1937), 27.

34. Van Braght, *Bloody Theatre*, 1125-1127.

35. Adolf Trieb, *Ibersheim am Rhein* (Worms, 1911), 70-71.

36. Neff, "Geschichtliches aus der Gemeinde Monsheim," *Mennonitische Blätter*, LIX

(April 1912), 26.

37. "Ibersheim," *ME*, III, 1. Trieb, 70.

38. Trieb, 56-57.

39. Edwin B. Bronner, *William Penn, 17th Century Founding Father: Selections from His Political Writings* (Wallingford, Pa., 1975) 10-12.

40. Sylvester K. Stevens, *Pennsylvania: Birthplace of a Nation* (New York, 1964), 29.

41. Hull, *William Penn and the Dutch Quaker Migration* (see n. 19), 280-284.

42. William Penn, *Journal of William Penn While Visiting Holland and Germany in 1677* (Philadelphia 1878), 79.

43. *Ibid.*, 167.

44. B. C. Roosen, *Geschichte der Mennoniten-Gemeinde zu Hamburg und Altona,* "Erste Hälfte" (Hamburg, 1886), 60n.

45. Hull, *William Penn*, 195-196.

46. *Ibid.*, 197-198.

47. *Ibid.*, 203. See also Friedrich Nieper, *Die Ersten deutschen Auswanderer von Krefeld nach Pennsylvanien* (Neukirchen Kreis Moers, 1940), 66.

48. Hull, *William Penn*, 204-209.

49. Stevens, Pennsylvania (see n. 40), 31.

50. H[inrich] K[assel], "Vom Christlichen glauben Taufe nachtmahl undt regel undt ordnung der menisten oder Tauffs gesinds gemeinde. Ein kurzes Endt wurff ge stelt durch J H Vor Einen Jungen, an kommenden Prediger, so viel als ein ABC wahr nach er sich durch die Hilfe desz Herrn Etwas Richten kann. ge stelt im Jahr *1681* Als ein Spiegel, darin man sich ein wänig be sehen kan umb dar nach zu Richten." 16 pp. MS in MSHL. On the page following the t.p. is the statement, "Dieses nachfolgende Geschrift ... geschrieben Im Jahr 1681 Im Majus nach dem ich ein wänig besser von meiner sehr schwähren Krankheit undt sehr harten fühber dasz ich vorhin die 30 wochen gehat undt da am lätsen noch 3 wochen alle dag mit grossen Ehelendt undt schwacheit gehat habe also hab ich disz ausz Drang meines ge müth auffs Papier ge setz und Hehr nach all auff dem bätt ge schrieben Von mir H K zu J H...." N.B.: a transcription of this document by Herman Oelsner, dated June 4, 1874, at the Juniata College Library, is filled with copying errors and/or changes.

51. *Ibid.*, n.p.

Chapter 2. "Only Ancient Forest" (1682-1700)

1. Berthold Fernon, ed. *The Records of New Amsterdam* (New York, 1897), I, 228; III, 65, 70, 221, 226, 236, 412; IV, 109; VII, 247.

2. *Ecclesiastical Records: State of New York*, I (Albany, 1901), 486-487; 505, 513, 555.

3. John Megapolensis and Samuel Drisius to the Classis of Amsterdam, August 5, 1657, in E. B. O'Callaghan, ed., *The Documentary History of the State of New York* (Albany, 1850), 106.

4. Harold S. Bender, "Was William Rittenhouse the First Mennonite Bishop in America?" *MQR*, VII (January 1933), 43.

5. E. B. O'Callaghan, ed., *Documents Relative to the Colonial History of the State of New York*, II (Albany, 1858), 176-177.

6. Quoted in Samuel Whitaker Pennypacker, *The Settlement of Germantown Pennsylvania and the Beginning of the German Immigration to North America* (Lancaster, PA, 1899), 258-259.

7. Leland Harder, "Pioneer of Christian Civilization in America," *Mennonite Life*, IV (January 1949), 48.

8. Pennypacker, *Settlement of Germantown*, 73-75, 106-108.

9. William I. Hull, *William Penn and the Dutch Quaker Migration to Pennsylvania* (Swarthmore, Pa., 1935), 243. For a further establishment of this date, see Ralph Beaver Strassburger, *The Strassburger Family and Allied Families of Pennsylvania* (Gwynedd Valley, Pa., 1922), 384.

10. Pennypacker, *Settlement of Germantown,* 193-194.

11. William Niepoth, "The Ancestry of the Thirteen Krefeld Emigrants," tr. John Brockie Lukens, *Pennsylvania Genealogical Magazine,* XXI (1980), 195. N.B.: The best summary of data relating to the so-called "thirteen families" of Krefeld immigrants to Germantown may be found in two articles appearing in a special printing of the Krefeld "Yearbook," *Die Heimat,* LII (1983): Guido Rotthof, "Die Auswanderung von Krefeld nach Pennsylvanien im Jahre 1683," pp. 2-11; and Charlotte Broecken, " 'Dutch Quaker' aus Krefeld, die (Mit) Gründer Germantowns 1683?" pp. 15-23.

12. Hull, *William Penn,* 244-245.

13. Pennypacker, *Settlement of Germantown,* 75, 108.

14. *Ibid.,* 81.

15. James Claypoole to Benjamin Furly, March 13, 1683, in Letterbook of James Claypoole, HSP.

16. Hull, *William Penn,* 181n.

17. Pennypacker, *Settlement of Germantown,* 108.

18. Claypoole to Furly, May 5, 1863 (see n. 15).

19. Claypoole to Furly, "1st month, 13th," 1682/3 (see n. 15).

20. Claypoole to Furly, May 18, 1683 (see n. 15).

21. Claypoole to Furly, June 5, 1683 (see n. 15).

22. Francis Daniel Pastorius, "Positive News from America," tr. Julius Friedrich Sachse, in *Letters Relating to the Settlement of Germantown* (Lübeck and Philadelphia, 1903), 9-12.

23. Bucks County Miscellaneous Streepers MSS, 195, HSP.

24. Niepoth, "Ancestry of the Thirteen Krefeld Emigrants" (see n. 11), 205.

25. *Ibid.,* 195.

26. Samuel W. Pennypacker, "Germantown Papers," a section in Pennypacker's Historical and Genealogical Notes, a bound, two-volume, generally unpaginated MS at the Pennypacker estate, Schwenksville, Pa.

27. Friedrich Nieper, *Die ersten deutschen Auswanderer von Krefeld nach Pennsylvanien* (Neukirchen Kreis Moers, 1940), 89. Pennypacker, *Settlement of Germantown,* 71.

28. Niepoth, "Ancestry of the Thirteen Krefeld Emigrants" (see n. 11), 198-205.

29. Hull, *William Penn,* 211-212.

30. Claypoole to Furly, June 15, 1683 (see n. 15).

31. Claypoole to Furly, June 19, 1683 (see n. 15).

32. Claypoole to Furly, July 3, 1683 (see n. 15).

33. Claypoole to Furly, July 7, 1683 (see n. 15).

34. [Herman op den Graeff], "A Letter from Germantown," February 12, 1684, in Sachse, *Letters Relating to . . . Germantown* (see n. 22), 34.

35. Hull, *William Penn,* 333-334.

36. Pastorius, "Positive News" (see n. 22), 34.

37. *Ibid.*

38. *Ibid.,* 12.

39. *Ibid.,* 14.

40. *Ibid.,* 23.

41. *Ibid.,* 14-15.

42. See "Map of Germantown, 1688," Pennypacker, *Settlement of Germantown,* 330-331.

43. Quoted in Pennypacker, *Settlement of Germantown,* 71-72.

44. Hull, *William Penn,* 334.

45. Pastorius, "Positive News" (see n. 22), 19.

46. Op den Graeff (see n. 34), 33-34.

47. Pastorius, "Positive News" (see n. 22), 29.

48. Hull, *William Penn,* 246.

49. Christian Neff, "Geschichtliches aus der Gemeinde Monsheim," *Mennonitische Geschictsblätter,* LIX (April 1912), 27.

50. H[arold] S. Bender, ed., "Palatinate Mennonite Census Lists, 1664-1774," *MQR,* XIV

(January 1940), 17.

51. *Ibid.*, 18.

52. Neff, "Geschichtliches aus der Gemeinde Monsheim" (see n. 49), 27.

53. Paul Michel, "Täufer, Mennoniten und Quäker in Kriegsheim bei Worms," *Der Wormsgau*, VII (1965-66), 47.

54. Walter Fellman-Monsheim, "Kreigsheimer Mennoniten und Quäker in ihrer Verschiedenheit," *Beiträge zur Geschichte der Mennoniten* (Weierhof, Germany, 1938), 23.

55. Strassburger, *Strassburger Family* (see n. 9), 384.

56. Hull, *William Penn*, 291.

57. Pennypacker, *Settlement of Germantown*, 170-172.

58. Wilhelm Classen to Silas B. Grubb, 1934, citing church records at Goch, SMG.

59. Ruttinghuysen purchased fifty acres in Germantown from Peter Keurlis on August 8, 1687. See "Germantown Papers," n.p. (n. 26).

60. Daniel K. Cassel, *Geschichte der Mennoniten* (Philadelphia, 1890), 76.

61. Harold S. Bender, "The Founding of the Mennonite Church in America at Germantown, 1683-1708," *MQR*, VII (October 1933), 230.

62. *Collections of the New York Genealogical and Biographical Society*, I (New York, 1890), 67.

63. Cassel, *Geschichte der Mennoniten*, 413.

64. Pennypacker, *Settlement of Germantown*, 64.

65. The entire document is printed in J. Herbert Fretz, "The Germantown Anti-Slavery Petition of 1688," *MQR*, XXXIII (January 1959), 50-51; also in Pennypacker, *Settlement of Germantown*, 197-199.

66. Hull, William Penn, 397-398.

67. *Ibid.*, 420-421.

68. Pennypacker, *Settlement of Germantown*, 106, 205.

69. Jon Butler, "Into Pennsylvania's Spiritual Abyss: The Rise and Fall of the Later Keithians, 1693-1703," *Pennsylvania Magazine of History and Biography*, CI (April 1977), 166.

70. Harder, "Pioneer of Christian Civilization" (see n. 7), 48. Pennypacker, *Settlement of Germantown*, 262. Pennypacker, "Germantown Papers" (see n. 26).

71. B[erend] C[arl] Roosen, *Geschichte der Mennoniten Gemeinde zu Hamburg und Altona*, "Erste Hälfte" (Hamburg, 1886), 76.

72. N. B. Grubb, ed. and tr., "Pro Copia Instrumentum Publicum," *MYBA*, 1910, 17-23. This was also published as a separate pamphlet by N. B. Grubb in 1909.

73. Niepoth, "Ancestry of the Thirteen Krefeld Mennonites" (see n. 11), 196.

74. Hull, *William Penn*, 250-251.

75. Pennypacker, *Settlement of Germantown*, 193.

76. Jan Streypers to Jan Lensen, May 5, 1698, Bucks County Miscellaneous MSS, Streypers MSS, HSP.

77. Andreas Ziegler, Isaac Kolb, and Christian Funk, "The 1773 Letter to the Holland Mennonites," in John C. Wenger, *History of the Mennonites of the Franconia Conference* (Telford, Pa., 1937), 397.

78. Samuel W. Pennypacker and others have confused deacon Jan Neuss with the Philadelphia silversmith Johannes De Nys.

Chapter 3. "They Are a Sober People . . . And Will Neither Swear nor Fight" (1700-1716)

1. Daniel Falckner, *Curieuse Nachricht from Pennsylvania*, tr. Julius Friedrich Sachse, Part XIV of *Pennsylvania: The German Influence in its Settlement and Development* (Lancaster, Pa., 1905), 44-45.

2. B[erend]. C[arl]. Roosen, *Geschichte der Mennoniten Gemeinde zu Hamburg und Altona* (Hamburg, 1886), 63.

3. Samuel Whitaker Pennypacker, "Germantown Papers," n.p., a section in Pennypacker's Historical and Genealogical Notes, a bound, two-volume, generally unpaginated MS

at the Pennypacker estate, Schwenksville, Pa.

4. Roosen, *Geschichte*, 59-60n.

5. W. T. Stauffer, ed. and tr., "Hans Stauffer Note-books," *PR*, X (July 1932), 97-98.

6. William Barton, *Memoirs of David Rittenhouse* (Philadelphia, 1813), 83-84.

7. Roosen, *Geschichte*, 63.

8. Harold S. Bender, "The Founding of the Mennonite Church in America at Germantown, 1683-1708," *MQR*, VII (October 1933) 236, 246. See also the extract of Pieter Verhelle, Jacob van Campen, Gerrit Roosen, and Jan de Lanoi to Claes Beerends, March 1702, reprinted in John C. Wenger, *History of the Mennonites of the Franconia Conference* (Telford, Pa., 1937), 405-406.

9. Pennypacker, "Germantown Papers" (see n. 3).

10. *Ibid.*

11. C. Henry Smith, *The Mennonite Immigration to Pennsylvania in the Eighteenth Century* (Norristown, Pa., 1929), 116.

12. Wilhelm Niepoth, "Jacob Gottschalk and his Ancestry," *MQR*, XXIII (July 1949), 47.

13. Wenger, *History of the . . . Franconia Conference*, 405-406.

14. Bender, "Founding of the Mennonite Church in America" (see n. 8), 227.

15. For proof of this date, see deeds recited in Ralph Beaver Strassburger, *The Strassburger Family and Allied Families of Pennsylvania* (Gwynedd Valley, Pa., 1922), 424, 455.

16. Samuel Whitaker Pennypacker, *The Settlement of Germantown, Pennsylvania and the Beginning of the German Immigration to North America* (Lancaster, Pa., 1899), 212.

17. "At a Council Held at Philadelphia, ye 15th 3 mo., 1706," *Minutes of the Provincial Council of Pennsylvania*, II (Harrisburg, Pa., 1838), 230.

18. "Stauffer Note-Books" (see n. 5), 101-107, *passim*.

19. See "Kolb" and "Rupp," *ME*. Daniel K. Cassel, *A Genealogical History of the Kolb, Kulp or Culp Family* (Philadelphia, 1895), 17-18. N.B.: Cassel must be used with caution, as his work contains frequent unidentified guesses. Tentative research suggests the following roster of members of the Thielman Kolb family of Wolfsheim, north of Alzey in the Palatinate (listed in December, 1685 as having five sons and two daughters): Peter, b. 1671 (a Mennonite bishop); Agnes (married Peter Galle); Anna, b. 1676 (married Balthasar Kolb); Henrich°, b. 1679; Martin°, b. 1680; Johannes°, b. 1683; Jacob°, b. 1685; Arnold°, b. 1687 (a person of this name and age emigrated from the Palatinate with the group including the family of Henrich Kolb in 1709); Dielman°, b. 1691; Maria (married Johannes Krehbiel). The names marked with an asterisk are those of persons emigrating from the Palatinate, 1707-1717.

20. Gerrit Roosen, Jan de Lanoi, *et al.* to Hermanus Schyn and the servants of the Doopsgesinde Congregation at Amsterdam, March 11, 1707, transcript at MHL. This is letter #2244 in J. G. de Hoop Scheffer, *Inventaris der Archiefstukken Berustende bij de Vereenigde Doopsgezinde Gemeente te Amsterdam*, "Tweede Stuk. Tweede Afdeeling" (Amsterdam, 1884), 449-450. The *Inventaris* contains a summary of each letter listed.

21. Jacob Gaetschalck, Harmen Karsdorp, *et al.* to "Hermanus Schyn and co-ministers," September 3, 1708, in Harold S. Bender, "Was William Rittenhouse the First Mennonite Bishop in America?" *MQR*, VII (January 1933), 44.

22. See letters #2245 (November 24, 1707) and #2246 (November 29, 1707) in Scheffer, *Inventaris*, "Tweede Stuk. Tweede Afdeeling," 450.

23. "The Rev. Dirck Keyser," *MYBA*, 1895, 20.

24. Bender, "Founding of the Mennonite Church" (see n. 8), 227.

25. *Ibid.*, 227-228.

26. Wenger, *History of the . . . Franconia Conference*, 398. The Bender translation from the German lacks this phrase.

27. Bender, "William Rittenhouse" (see n. 21), 45.

28. *Ibid.*, 46-47.

29. Among works that shed light on this episode, I have found the following useful: [Daniel DeFoe], *A Brief History of the Poor Palatine Refugees* (London, 1709); H. T. Dickinson, "The Poor Palatines and the Parties," *English Historical Review*, LXXXII (July

Notes for Pages 83-93   547

1967), 464-485; Frank Ried Diffenderfer, *The German Exodus to England in 1709*, Vol. VII, Part II, Publications of the Pennsylvania German Society (Lancaster, Pa., 1897); Daniel Häberle, *Auswanderung und Koloniegründungen der Pfälzer im 18. Jahrhundert* (Kaiserslautern, 1909); Walter Allen Knittle, *Early Eighteenth Century Palatine Emigration* (Philadelphia, 1937), 1-81; Oscar Kuhns, *The German and Swiss Settlements of Colonial Pennsylvania* (New York, 1901); J. G. de Hoop Scheffer, "Mennonite Emigration to Pennsylvania," tr. Samuel W. Pennypacker, *Pennsylvania Magazine of History and Biography*, II (1878), 117-138.

30. "Stauffer Note-books" (see n. 5), 107.

31. William I. Hull, *William Penn and the Dutch Quaker Migration to Pennsylvania* (Swarthmore, Pa., 1935), 388.

32. Strassburger, *Strassburger Family* (see n. 15), 460.

33. Jacob Landes, Samuel Meyer, *et al.* to "all the servants and bishops *(Eldesten)* of the Baptist (Tauffgesinden) Congregation in the Netherlands," March 3, 1709, in the Bibliotheek der Vereenigde Doopsgezinde Gemeente te Amsterdam, #1430 in Scheffer, *Inventaris* (see n. 20), "Eerste Stuk" (Amsterdam, 1883), 268.

34. N. van der Zijpp, "Rotterdam, das Tor zur Neuen Welt fur mennonitische Auswanderer im 18. Jahrhundert," *Mennonitischer Gemeinde-Kalender*, LXII (1962), 55-56; Knittle, 54, 68.

35. Ad[n] van Alkmar (Rotterdam) to the Lamb Congregation in Amsterdam, April 8, 1709, *Inventaris* (see n. 20) #2248; Jacob Jacobsz Verfolje to "the Teachers and Deacons . . . at Rotterdam," April 11, 1709, *Inventaris* #2249.

36. Knittle, *Palatine Emigration* (see n. 29), 74.

37. John Tribbeko and George Ruperti, "Lists of Germans Who Came to England in 1709," in *Immigrants to the Middle Colonies*, ed. Michael Tepper (Baltimore, 1979), 84-123.

38. *Ibid.*

39. Knittle, *Palatine Emigration*, 248-253.

40. *Ibid.*, 68-74; Diffenderfer, *The German Exodus* (see n. 29), 351-354; v. d. Zijpp, "Rotterdam" (see n. 34), 57.

41. Scheffer, "Mennonite Emigration" (see n. 29), 123.

42. Hull, *William Penn* (see n. 31), 387.

43. Scheffer, "Mennonite Emigration" (see n. 29), 123.

44. Pennypacker, *Settlement of Germantown* (see n. 16), 66.

45. Alan G. Keyser, ed. and Raymond E. Hollenbach, tr., *The Account Book of the Clemens Family of Lower Salford Township, Montgomery County, Pennsylvania 1749-1857* (Breinigsville, Pa., 1975), 129, n. 37.

46. Häberle, *Auswanderung* (see n. 29), 48-49.

47. "Stauffer Note-books" (see n. 5), 108.

48. Roger E. Sappington, "The Mennonites in the Carolinas, *MQR*, XLII (April 1968), 97-98; Knittle, *Palatine Emigration* (see n. 29), 100-102; Diffenderfer, *German Exodus* (see n. 29), 397.

49. Knittle, *Palatine Emigration* (see n. 29), 102-103.

50. *Ibid.*, 99.

51. Smith, *Mennonite Immigration* (see n. 11), 66-67, n. 2.

52. For two English translations of their letter (*Inventaris* #2253), see "On the Way to Pennsylvania," *MYBA*, 1911, 35, and Ira D. Landis, "For a Faith's Pure Shrine," *MRJ*, I (October 1960), 25.

53. Jones Detweiler, "Whitpain Township," in Theodore W. Bean, *History of Montgomery County, Pennsylvania* (Philadelphia, 1884), 1173.

54. Sappington, "Mennonites in the Carolinas" (see n. 48), 98.

55. A. J. Fretz, *A Brief History of Jacob Wismer* (Elkhart, Ind., 1893), 1-2.

56. "Heidelberger Widertäufer Schutzgeld," typed MS in the Heimatstelle Pfalz, Kaiserslautern, reproduced as an illustration in Clyde L. Groff and George F. Neuman, eds., *The Eby Report*, I (Philadelphia, 1975), 38.

Chapter 4. "In Their Own Way and Manner" (1717-1755)

1. Paul A. W. Wallace, *Indians in Pennsylvania* (Harrisburg, 1975), 138.

2. Abraham Harley Cassel, "Indian Reminiscences," transcribed and typed MS by Samuel W. Pennypacker in his Historical and Genealogical Notes MSS, a bound, two-volume, generally unpaginated MS at the Pennypacker estate, Schwenksville, Pa.

3. Jones Detweiler, "Whitpain Township," in Theodore W. Bean, *History of Montgomery County* (Philadelphia, 1884), 1174; Ralph Beaver Strassburger, *The Strassburger Family and Allied Families of Pennsylvania* (Gwynedd Valley, Pa., 1922), 363.

4. Pennypacker, Historical and Genealogical Notes MSS (see n. 2), n.p.

5. Strassburger, *Strassburger Family*, 428, 432.

6. J. G. de Hoop Scheffer, "Mennonite Emigration to Pennsylvania," tr. Samuel W. Pennypacker, *Pennsylvania Magazine of History and Biography*, II (1878), 126-129.

7. Evelyn A. Benson, "Martin Kendig 1710 Mennonite Pioneer Leader," *MRJ*, XVI (April 1976), 16.

8. Strassburger, *Strassburger Family* (see n. 3), 393.

9. Scheffer, "Mennonite Emigration (see n. 6), 130.

10. Benson, "Martin Kendig" (see n. 7), 16.

11. Strassburger, *Strassburger Family* (see n. 3), 415-416.

12. Both Dock and Ziegler and daughters named Catharina and Margaret, a possible reflection of mutual grandparents. A "Margaretha Duck" appears on the 1720 estate settlement papers of Germantown resident Conrad Jansen. See also Dock's will in Gerald C. Studer, *Christopher Dock: Colonial Schoolmaster* (Scottdale, Pa., 1967), 380-381. Ziegler's will is in Strassburger, *Strassburger Family* (see n. 3), 430-431.

13. Scheffer, "Mennonite Emigration" (see n. 6), 129-130n.

14. This and five subsequent "lists" in this chapter represent careful sampling from secondary sources, rather than definitive research, which would require a book in itself. The names in the "1717" wave seem to be almost all Palatine, with perhaps Grubb, Hunsberger, and Wenger suggesting a Swiss element (most of the Palatine names are also originally Swiss).

15. In this Palatine-Swiss grouping one notices that after 1717-18 the Salford area, next to Skippack, seems to be already filled up, and settlements farther out take place.

16. Strassburger, *Strassburger Family* (see n. 3), 419-420, 457.

17. William Brower, "Johannes Roth (Rhodes), or the Gleanings from the Life of a Pioneer Settler on the Schuylkill," *The Pennsylvania German*, X (January 1909), 119.

18. I am indebted for the details of this picture to the research of Alan G. Keyser.

19. Howard M. Jenkins, *Historical Collections Relating to Gwynedd* (Philadelphia, 1884), 88.

20. Strassburger, *Strassburger Family* (see n. 3), 415.

21. John C. Wenger, *History of the Mennonites of the Franconia Conference* (Telford, Pa., 1937), 15.

22. *Ibid.*, 317.

23. *Ibid.*, 317-318.

24. Cass K. Shelby, "The Ancestry and Family of Augustus S. Landis of Hollidaysburg, Pa.," *Report of the Thirty-First Reunion of the Landis Landes Families . . . August 19, 1950*, ed. Dorothy K. Landis (Bethlehem, Pa., 1950), 11-12.

25. A tradition remembered by John D. Clemmer (1836-1917) of Lansdale, Pa., told to his grandson John E. Lapp.

26. Brower, "Johannes Roth" (see n. 17), 121.

27. *Ibid.*

28. "Landes" and "Jus Retractus," *ME*.

29. Scheffer, "Mennonite Emigration" (see n. 6), 130; Brower, "Johannes Roth" (see n. 17), 121.

30. N. van der Zijpp, "Rotterdam, das Tor zur neuen Welt fur mennonitische Auswanderer im 18. Jahrhundert," *Mennonitische Gemeinde-Kalendar*, LXII (1962), 57.

31. Transcription by Elizabeth Horsch Bender of inscription in a Schwartz family Bible, 2pp., AMC.

32. Scheffer, "Mennonite Emigration" (see n. 6), 131.

33. *Ibid.*

34. See William Beery, *Beery Family History* (Elgin, Ill., 1957), 31-32.

35. Schwartz family Bible transcription (see n. 31).

36. Quoted in "Swearing the Immigrants," *PR*, I (December 1897), 52.

37. This list shows the edges of the Salford community being filled in, and a strengthening of the Saucon community.

38. Here the Goschenhoppen (later Hereford) and Swamp communities are achieving permanent strength.

39. Jacob A. Freed, *Partial History of the Freed Family and Connecting Families* (Souderton, Pa., 1923), 22-26. This is a quotation of the account by Samuel W. Pennypacker, "Bebber's Township and the Dutch Patroons."

40. A statement to this effect, which I have unfortunately not recorded, is among notes taken by Samuel W. Pennypacker from informal reminiscences of Abraham Harley Cassel.

41. Abraham Harley Cassel, comments on Christopher Dock, transcribed by Samuel W. Pennypacker in his Historical and Genealogical Notes MSS (see n. 2).

42. See his *A Simple and Thoroughly Prepared School Management* (written in 1750), in Studer, *Christopher Dock* (see n. 12), 271, 293, 296-308.

43. James Y. Heckler, *The History of Harleysville and Lower Salford Township* (Harleysville, Pa., 1886), 237-238.

44. Quoted from *The Pennsylvania Gazette*, October 5, 1732, in "Old Time News," *PR*, I (December 1894), 60.

45. "Twee naamlijsten van Doopsgezinde huisgezinnen uit de Palts, herwaarts gekomen om naar Pennsylvanie te reizen," #2281 in J. G. de Hoop Scheffer, *Inventaris der Archiefstukken Berustende bij de Vereenigde Doopsgezinde Gemeente te Amsterdam*, "Tweede Stuk. Tweede Afdeeling" (Amsterdam, 1884), 458. See a handwritten transcription in MHL.

46. Van d. Zijpp, "Rotterdam" (see n. 30), 61.

47. *Ibid.*, 62.

48. Scheffer, "Mennonite Emigration" (see n. 6), 132.

49. *Ibid.*

50. Wenger, *History of the . . . Franconia Conference* (see n. 21), 19.

51. Ralph Beaver Strassburger, *Pennsylvania German Pioneers*, ed. William John Hinke (Norristown, Pa., 1934) I, 62. See also C. Henry Smith, *The Mennonite Immigration to Pennsylvania in the Eighteenth Century* (Norristown, Pa., 1929), 37-40.

52. Of the following names, only Altdörfer (see n. 56, *infra*) has been carefully researched.

53. "Caspar Wistar's Letter of December 4, 1732," *PR*, II (1899), 120.

54. Charles H. Price, Jr., *A History of Christ Reformed Church at Indian Creek* (Telford, Pa., 1966), 6.

55. Smith, *Mennonite Immigration* (see n. 51), 197n.

56. Helen M. Stanley, *The Alderfers of America* (Allentown, Pa., 1972), 37-40.

57. J[ames] Y[ocum] H[eckler], "Notes about the Old Hecklers," handwritten MS, copy in MLAEP; A. J. Fretz, *A Genealogical Record of the Descendants of the Swartley Family* (Netcong, N.J., 1906), 1.

58. This is my count from the lists in E. Gordon Alderfer, *The Montgomery County Story* (Norristown, Pa., 1951), 266-273.

59. W. W. H. Davis, *History of Bucks County, Pennsylvania, from the Discovery of the Delaware to the Present Time* (Doylestown, Pa., 1876), 447.

60. Wenger, *History of the . . . Franconia Conference* (see n. 21), 154.

61. Scheffer, "Mennonite Emigration" (see n. 6), 132n; "Schwenkfelder Church," *ME*, IV, 488.

62. The writer has heard this story repeatedly from members of the "Old Mennonite" congregation at Bally, Pa., including minister Paul Longacre.

63. Henry S. Dotterer, "The Church at Market Square," *PR*, II (1899), 43.

64. "Saucon Mennonite Church," *ME*, IV, 434.

65. Wenger, *History of the . . . Franconia Conference* (see n. 21), 131.

66. James Y. Heckler, *History of Franconia Township* (Harleysville, Pa., 1960), 56.

67. Samuel W. Pennypacker, notation, "Note in a book belonging to A. H. Cassel," Historical and Genealogical Notes MSS (see n. 2).

68. Davis, *Bucks County* (see n. 59), 455.

69. Mrs Georges Carousso (transcriber), Philadelphia County Administration Book 'C,' *Pennsylvania Genealogical Magazine* XXII (1962), 263-264.

70. John F. Watson, "Notes of the Early History of Germantown," *Hazard's Register of Pennsylvania*, I (May 10, 1828), 289.

71. James Steel to Michael Ziegler, March 8, 1734/35, James Steel Letterbook, 1730-41, HSP.

72. Receipt for quitrent from John Newbery, June 10, 1735, signed "Witness my hand: Jacob Kolb," in possession of Alan G. Keyser.

73. Henry S. Landes (d. 1950), "Souder History," 42 pp. mimeographed genealogy (n.p., n.d.), 1, MLAEP.

74. Wenger, *History of the . . . Franconia Conference* (see n. 21), 18.

75. Priscilla L. Delp, *A Genealogical History of the Delp and Delp-Cassel Families* (Souderton, Pa., 1962), 17.

76. Ralph L. Johnson, "Family Bibles," *PR*, VII (July 1929), 90.

77. Roger E. Sappington, "The Mennonites in the Carolinas," *MQR*, XLII (April 1968), 106-107).

78. This fact was reported to me by John L. Overholt, Kilmarnock, Va., who has done considerable research on the Oberholtzer-Overholt families, some of whom were neighbors of the Wismers in Bucks County.

79. Davis, *Bucks County* (see n. 59), 556.

80. Wallace, *Indians in Pennsylvania* (see n. 1), 135, 139.

81. Adolf Trieb, *Ibersheim am Rhein* (Worms, 1911), 117-118.

82. Martin Kolb to C. Classen, May 18, 1738, Pennypacker Collection, MLAEP.

83. Christopher Saur, in *Der Hoch Deutsch Pennsylvanisch Geschicht-Schreiber*, October, 1739.

84. Martin G. Weaver, *Mennonites of Lancaster Conference* (Scottdale, Pa., 1931), 39.

85. Quoted in Peter Brock, *Pacifism in the United States from the Colonial Era to the First World War* (Princeton, 1968), 118.

86. "Jacob Godschalk, Martin Kolb, Michael Ziegler, Yellis Kassel, Dielman Kolb, and Heinrich Funk to "the ministers and deacons of the . . . Doopsgesinde congregations in Amsterdam and Harlem," October 19, 1745, *MYBA*, 1910, 25.

87. See Davis, *Bucks County* (see n. 59), 322-323.

88. "Zinzendorf, Count Nicholas Ludwig von," *ME*, IV, 1030.

89. Jacob Lichy, *Eine Warnende Wächter Stimme* (Germantown, Pa., 1749), 45-46.

90. "Notes," *PR*, I (1894), 57.

91. *Ausbund. Das ist Etliche schoene Christliche Lieder* (Germantown, Pa., 1742). Included in an appendix is "A True Account of the Brethren in Switzerland, in the District of Zurich, Regarding the Tribulation They Have Endured on Account of the Gospel" (my English translation).

92. Jacob Godschalck, *et al.* (see n. 86).

93. William T. Parsons, "The Bloody Election of 1742," *Pennsylvania History*, XXXVI (July 1969), 298.

94. Christopher Saur, *Geschicht-Schreiber*, June 16, 1743.

95. "Persons Naturalized in the Province of Pennsylvania," *Pennsylvania Archives, Second Series, II (Harrisburg, 1890)*, 302-309.

96. On Biery, see J. Hampton Hoch, *Hoch-High Family in America* (n.p., 1962), 19. On Ledterman, see I. John Leatherman and Emma Leatherman Candler, *All Leatherman Kin History* (Nappanee, Ind., 1940), 646. On Schleiffer see Charles Roberts, MS notes on "Henry Schleiffer, Immigrant," SL, under the listing, "Boppenmeier-Schleiffer."

97. Henry Z. Jones, Jr., and Annette K. Burgert, "A New Emigrant List: Bonfeld 1710-1738," *Der Reggeboge: Quarterly of the Pennsylvania German Society*, XIV (October 1980),17.

98. [Henrich Funck], *Ein Spiegel der Taufe mit Geist mit Wasser und Blut* ([Germantown, PA], 1744).

99. My translation from the German in the third edition (n.p., "Gedruckt im Jahr 1834"), 108.

100. [Tielman J. van Braght], tr. "Theophilus" [Alexander Mack], *Das Andenken Einiger Heiliger Martyrer* (Ephrata, Pa., 1745).

101. Jacob Godschalck, *et.al.* (see n. 86), 26.

102. Wenger, *History of the . . . Franconia Conference* (see n. 21), 272.

103. Henry Melchior Muhlenberg, letters published in *Hallische Nachrichten* (1749), extracted in Pennypacker, Historical and Genealogical Notes MSS (see n. 2).

104. *Ibid.*

105. "The verse from Deuteronomy 5:29," *Ibid.*

106. Jacob Godschalck, et al. (see n. 86), 26-27.

107. Wenger, *History of the . . . Franconia Conference* (see n. 21), 319.

108. Jesse F. Bechtel, "Rev. George Bechtel," *PR*, X (July 1932), 143-144.

109. "Kurze Nachrede einiger Mitglieder der Gemeine der Mennonisten, welche die Hochdeutsche Uebersetzung gegen die Hollaendische genau ueberlesen haben," *Der blutige Schauplatz, oder Märtyrer-Spiegel der Taufs-Gesinnten oder Wehrlosen Christen*, 3rd German edition (Lewistown, Pa., 1849), "zweiter Theil," 630.

110. Samuel W. Pennypacker, *Historical and Biographical Sketches* (Philadelphia, 1883), 172. "Lamech and Agrippa," *Chronicon Ephratense*, ed. J. Max Hark (Lancaster, Pa., 1889), 213-214.

111. Charles H. Glatfelter, *Pastors and People: German Lutheran and Reformed Churches in the Pennsylvania Field, 1717-1793*, I (Breinigsville, Pa., 1980), 21-22.

112. Studer, *Christopher Dock* (see n. 12), 267.

113. The passages quoted below are translated from Dock's original German by Elizabeth Horsch Bender of Goshen, Indiana. See Studer, 258.

114. Studer, *Christopher Dock* (see n. 12), 291.

115. *Ibid.*, 276.

116. *Ibid.*, 293.

117. *Ibid.*, 272.

118. *Ibid.*, 295.

119. *Ibid.*, 298.

120. *Ibid.*, 280.

121. For a fine reproduction see Frederick S. Weiser and Howell J. Heaney, *The Pennsylvania German Fraktur of the Free Library of Philadelphia* (Breinigsville, Pa., 1976) I, Fraktur #237.

122. See Joyce Clemmer Munro, "From the Records of the Old Goschenhoppen Lutheran Church," *Mennonite Historians of Eastern Pennsylvania Newsletter*, V (March 1978), 8.

123. Mary Jane Lederach Hershey, Harleysville, Pa., has as of this writing assembled a collection of photographic reproductions of well over 500 examples of Fraktur from Mennonite families of the Bucks-Montgomery-Lehigh-Berks-Chester area. This collection, the basis of an anticipated book, will greatly clarify the still-confused picture of eastern Pennsylvania Mennonite Fraktur.

124. Joy Derstine Harris, *Our Father's Lamp and Mother's Light: Ten Generations of the Dierstein Family in North America* (Harleysville, Pa., 1981), 231.

125. Wenger, *History of the . . . Franconia Conference* (see n. 21), 23. See Davis, *Bucks County* (n. 59), 570 for mention of "a widow named Barbara Rohr" who settled in Springfield Township.

126. Leah Margaret Rickert Goddard, "Early Rickert Family History," in Ruth F. Rickert, Rickert Family History, mimeographed (Rockville Centre, N.Y., 1982), 2-4.

127. Compare Wenger, *History of the . . . Franconia Conference* (see n. 21), 227 and Don

Yoder, "Fraktur in Mennonite Culture," *MQR*, XLVIII (July 1974), 316-317. The maker of the 1814 Fraktur cannot be the Rudolph Landes who arrived in 1749.

128. Rudolph Landes to "Cousin Rupp," April 13, 1787, in J. S. Hartzler and Daniel Kauffman, *Mennonite Church History* (Scottdale, Pa., 1905), 405.

129. Smith, *Mennonite Immigration* (see n. 51), 146.

130. See Ira D. Landis, "As Others See Us," *MRJ*, VI (April 1965), 16.

131. Jesse F. Bechtel, "Jacob Stauffer (Stover)," *PR*, X (July 1932), 142-143.

132. W. D. Huddle and Lulu May Huddle, *History of the Descendants of John Hottel* (Strasburg, Va., 1930), 7.

133. Henry S. Bower, *The Bower, Bechtel Stauffer Family* (Harleysville, Pa., 1895), 38.

134. *Pennsylvania Berichte* (Germantown, Pa.), August 1, 1749.

135. Heckler, "Notes About the Old Hecklers" (see n. 57).

136. A. J. Fretz, *A Brief History of Bishop Henry Funk and Other Funk Pioneers* (Elkhart, Ind., 1899), 628-629.

137. Osmund R. Fretz, "The Fretz Family From 1453 to the Migration," in Fretz Family Association, *Fretz Family History*, "Volume II" (Sellersville, Pa., 1975), [section 3], 99.

138. Muhlenberg, Letter to *Hallischen Nachrichten*, in Pennypacker, Historical and Genealogical Notes MSS (see n. 2).

Chapter 5. "Unlimited Freedom" and "The Flames of War" (1756-1786)

1. See Andreas Ziegler, Isaac Kolb, and Christian Funk to Wynand Peter Wynands, Wopke Molenaar, Sino van Abema, and John Cuperus, March 1, 1773, in John C. Wenger, *History of the Mennonites of the Franconia Conference* (Telford, Pa., 1937), 402-403.

2. Andreas Ziegler to Israel Pemberton, October 14, 1756, in Richard K. MacMaster, Samuel L. Horst, and Robert F. Ulle, *Conscience in Crisis* (Scottdale, Pa., 1979), 139-140.

3. *Ibid.*, p. 142.

4. *Pennsylvanische Berichte* (Germantown, Pa.), November 27, 1756.

5. Alan G. Keyser, ed., and Raymond E. Hollenbach, tr., *The Account Book of the Clemens Family* (Breinigsville, Pa., 1975), 9, 19.

6. Edward Matthews, "Lower Salford," *North Wales Record*, September 14, 1878.

7. *Pennsylvanische Berichte*, August 19, 1758 (Jacob Clemens); July 30, 1758 (Geissinger).

8. Ralph Beaver Strassburger, *The Strassburger Family and Allied Families of Pennsylvania* (Gwynedd Valley, Pa., 1922), 482-483.

9. Ralph Linwood Johnson, "The Van Vossen (Van Fossen) Family," *PR* (1934), 203-204.

10. James Y. Heckler, *The History of Harleysville and Lower Salford Township* (Harleysville, Pa., 1886), 293-298.

11. *Eine Restitution: Oder eine Erklaerung einiger Haupt-puncten des Gesetzes: Wie es durch Christum erfuellet ist. . . .* "Verlegt und zum Druck befoerdert durch die von Henrich Funcks hinterlassenen Kindern" (Philadelphia, 1763). Compare with this title the German translation of the heading of the "Zehnte Buch" of the *Enchiridion* of the Dutch Anabaptist writer Dirck Philips (1504-1568): "Von der Geistlichen Restitution: wie alles, was von Anfang geschehen, in Christo Jesu geistlich erfüllt und wiedergebracht ist."

12. *Ibid.*, 128.

13. *Ibid.*, 308.

14. Christian Funk, *A Mirror for all Mankind*, "translated from the German" (Norristown, Pa., 1814). My citation is from a reprint in *MHB*, XXXV (January 1974), 3.

15. Robert Levers to William Moore, October 31, 1781, in MacMaster, *et al.* (see n. 2), 339.

16. Gerald C. Studer, *Christopher Dock: Colonial Schoolmaster* (Scottdale, Pa., 1967), 379-380.

17. *Ibid.*, 359.

18. *Ibid.*, 265-266.

19. John Baer Stoudt, *The Life and Times of Col. John Siegfried* (Northampton, Pa., 1914), 18.

20. See copies of letters from a Jacob Gross in the "Weber Collection, Weyerhof," AMC.

21. Peggy Shomo Joyner, *Henry Roosen-Rosen* (Norfolk, Va., 1980), 51-53.

22. Albert Hagey King and Wm. Anderson Hagey, *The Hagey Families in America* (Bristol, TE, 1951), 455.

23. A. J. Fretz, *A Genealogical Record of the Descendants of the Swartley Family*, (Netcong, N.J., 1906), 1.

24. *Ibid.*, 1, 63.

25. [Julius F. Sachse, Daniel W. Nead, and Henry M. M. Richards], "Records of Indentures of (Individuals) Bound out as Apprentices, Servants, etc. . . . October 3, 1771, to October 5, 1777," *Pennsylvania German Society Proceedings*, XVI (1907), 146-147.

26. C. Henry Smith, *The Mennonite Immigration to Pennsylvania in the Eighteenth Century* (Norristown, Pa., 1929), 218, n. 170.

27. J. C. Williams, "St. James Church, Perkiomen, Evansburg," *Historical Sketches. A Collection of Papers Prepared for the Historical Society of Montgomery County, Pennsylvania*, V (Norristown, Pa., 1915), 361.

28. Johnson, "Van Vossen . . . Family" (see n. 9), 203-224.

29. Gysbert van der Smissen, "A Genealogy of the family of De Voss, arranged in order by Hendrick van den Berg and by his son Jan van den Berg . . . in the year 1791." Rearranged by Samuel W. Pennypacker, 1876. This significant MS is in the library of the Pennypacker estate near Schwenksville, Pa. In a prefatory note containing some erroneous history, Pennypacker records that he found the genealogy "in the summer of 1876 in the possession of the Rev. Henry A. Hunsicker of the Trappe who because of its being in the Dutch language had had little knowledge of its historical value. . . . It was the only copy in America. . . . I have translated it making a different arrangement of the material and numbering the descendants but preserving all the information contained in the original without any additions. Samuel W. Pennypacker, Nov. 18 1876." In entry #454 for Izaak Van Sintern, van der Smissen states that his information on the family of Izaak and Cornelia van Sintern comes from "an account given me by their oldest daughter Magdalena then widow of Martin Kolb under date of Oct. 28 1771 out of Skippack in Bebbers Township in the County of Phila in Penna, which I received June 2, 1772 in a communication from Hendrick Roosen dated Mar 2 1772 contained a genealogy of . . . four daughters to the number of 202 descendants."

30. Andreas Ziegler, *et al.* (see n. 1), 396-404.

31. A. J. Fretz, *A Brief History of John and Christian Fretz* (Elkhart, Ind., 1890), 99.

32. Christian Funk, *Mirror* (see n. 14), 4.

33. *Ibid.*

34. *Ibid.*

35. MacMaster, et al., *Conscience in Crisis* (see n. 2), 415-416.

36. Samuel Whitaker Pennypacker, *Annals of Phoenixville and its Vicinity* (Philadelphia, 1872), 103.

37. Quoted in E. Gordon Alderfer, *The Montgomery County Story* (Norristown, Pa., 1951), 124.

38. A. J. Fretz, *A Brief History of Bishop Henry Funck and Other Funk Pioneers* (Elkhart, Ind., 1899), 634.

39. Edward Matthews, *History of Towamencin Township* (Skippack, Pa., 1897), 11.

40. George Washington to William Howe, October 6, 1777, in Samuel Whitaker Pennypacker, "Pennypacker's Mills," *BHSMC*, XXII (Spring 1981), 320-321.

41. *Ibid.*, 32.

42. "From Brandywine Through the Perkiomen Valley to Valley Forge September and October 1777," *PR*, V (October 1927), 92-94.

43. Heckler, *History of Harleysville* (see n. 10), 383-384.

44. Pennypacker, *Annals* (see n. 36), 114.

45. N[athaniel] B[ertolet] Grubb, *A Genealogical History of the Gottschall Family* (n.p., 1924), 111-112.

46. MacMaster, et al., *Conscience in Crisis* (see n. 2), 474.

47. William H. Keichline, "Early History of Bedminster Township," *A Collection of Papers Read Before the Bucks County Historical Society,* V (1926), 268-269.

48. Abraham Gehman, letter to his in-laws, April 9, 1778, tr. Richard MacMaster in "Correspondence," *Mennonite Historians of Eastern Pennsylvania Newsletter,* VIII (May 1981), 6.

49. Christian Funk, *Mirror* (see n. 14), 5.

50. *Ibid.*

51. *Ibid.*, 4-5.

52. John L. Overholt, Kilmarnock, Va., telephone interview, March 13, 1982. Mr. Overholt, having long researched the Overholt-Oberholtzer pioneers in Pennsylvania, is preparing an article on "Oberholtzer Families of the Eighteenth Century."

53. *Ibid.*

54. MacMaster, *et al.*, Conscience in Crisis (see n. 2), 440.

55. *Ibid.*, 441.

56. Christian Funk, *Mirror* (see n. 14), 4.

57. *Ibid.*, p. 9. On Henry Funk, Jr.'s, attitude, see MacMaster, *et al., Conscience in Crisis* (see n. 2), 339.

58. Christian Funk, *Mirror* (see n. 14), 8.

59. MacMaster, et al., *Conscience in Crisis* (see n. 2), 335-338.

60. *Ibid.*, 513-516.

61. Calvin Ira Kephart, "John Kephart [1751-1822], Minister of the Doylestown Mennonite Congregation 1806-1822," *MQR,* II (April 1928), 119-120.

62. *Vorschrift* in the Mennonite Heritage Center, Souderton, Pa. From the Benjamin Altdörfer (1771-1840) family, Lower Salford Township.

63. *Pennsylvania German Fraktur and Color Drawings,* catalog of an exhibition at the Pennsylvania Farm Museum, May 19-June 30, 1969 (Landis Valley, Pa., 1969), plate 55.

64. *Vorschrift* by Martin Dättweiler, SL. The last line is as follows: "Marthin Däthweihler, Der hat Diesse Osterletz [Easter-present] geschriebn allhir in der Schul im Jahr 1769."

65. Pupil's writing booklet for Abraham Landes, in possession of Barbara Mininger, Elkhart, Ind.

66. [Christian Halteman?], "A 1782 Sermon," tr. Elizabeth Horsch Bender and ed. Leonard Gross, AMC, Hist. MSS 1-1-4, Box 51. For attribution, see John F. Funk, *The Mennonite Church and Her Accusers* (Elkhart, Ind., 1878), 58. Funk must be referring to Jacob, rather than Christian Funk. But Jacob would have been barely twenty-one in 1782. The other grandfather in question, Christian Halteman, would have been about thirty-eight.

67. N. B. Grubb, "Mennonite Reminiscences," typed MS, 6, SL.

Chapter 6. "We Will Keep House as We Understand It" (1787-1819)

1. Pauline Cassel, *History of Bedminster Bucks County, Pennsylvania* (n.p., 1976), loose map, "Bedminster 1783."

2. Frederick S. Weiser, "IAE SD: The Story of Johann Adam Eyer (1755-1837) Schoolmaster and Fraktur Artist with a Translation of his Roster Book, 1779, 1787," in *Ebbes fer Alle-Ebber, Ebbes fer Dich,* Publications of the Pennsylvania German Society (Breinigsville, Pa., 1980), 481-489.

3. Melissa Hough, "The History of Bangor," in *Slate Belt Bicentennial Heritage,* ed. Marjorie May, Maryann Repsher, et al., (n.p., 1976), 168-171. Ford W. Coolman and Rachel W. Kreider, *The Mennonite Cemeteries of Medina County with a Brief Historical Sketch of the Churches* (n.p., 1971), i-ii.

4. "Copy of the Last Will & Testament of Abraham Moyer, dec.," *PR,* IX (January 1931), 22-24.

5. W. W. H. Davis, *History of Bucks County, Pennsylvania* (Doylestown, Pa., 1876),

391-392; Joseph H. Wenger, *History of the Descendants of J. Conrad Geil* (Elgin, Ill., 1914), 15-16.

6. W. J. Showalter, "The Showalter Family," *Daily News Record* (Harrisonburg, Va.), August 7, 1933, typescript copy, HSP.

7. Reported by John L. Overholt, Kilmarnock, Va., and David G. Hall, Booneville, Mo., who have done extensive research on the Overholt family, in anticipation of publication of their findings.

8. A. J. Fretz, *A Genealogical Record of the Descendants of Martin Oberholtzer* (Milton, NJ, 1903), 132.

9. The information in the preceding two paragraphs is reported by John L. Overholt (see notes 7 and 11).

10. Davis, *History of Bucks County* (see n. 5), 411.

11. The three researchers whose recent work has made this account possible are Joel D. Alderfer, Harleysville, Pa.; Gary M. Kulp, Niagara Falls, Ont.; and John L. Overholt, Kilmarnock, Va. Joel Alderfer has found deeds and wills in the Bucks County Court House records establishing the identity of Dielman and Judith Kolb and their family. Gary Kulp cites such sources as "Return of the Loyalists & disbanded troops settled in the district of Canada West from Mill Creek" in the "Public Archives of Canada Series S-1"; "Lincoln Militia Return of 1818, Capt. William Crook's Company"; "Township Papers for Clinton Township"; and "Upper Canada Land Grant Petitions." John Overholt has carefully read the *Pennsylvania Archives* series and old periodicals for Overholt material, as well as innumerable warrants, deeds and wills in Philadelphia, Chester and Bucks Counties. Results of this research are anticipated in the periodical, *Pennsylvania Mennonite Heritage*.

12. Rudolph Landes to "Cousin Rupp," April 13, 1787, in J. S. Hartzler and Daniel Kauffman, *Mennonite Church History* (Scottdale, Pa., 1905), 404.

13. This material was located in "Return of the Loyalists . . . ." by Gary M. Kulp (see n. 11).

14. Gary M. Kulp, letter, July 24, 1983, citing an obituary of Susanna Kulp Griffin "in an old Methodist Newspaper, *The Christian Guardian*." Susanna is here said to have been born at "Peddlehouse" in Lancaster County, which I take to be a form of "Bettelhausen," an old nickname for the Strasburg area.

15. William F. Rannie, *Lincoln: The Story of an Ontario Town* (Lincoln, Ont., 1974), 164-168.

16. Christian Funk, *A Mirror for All Mankind* (Norristown, PA, 1814), reprinted in *MHB*, XXXV (January 1974), 8.

17. Funk, *Mirror* (see n. 15), 8.

18. A[ndreas] S[chwarz] Kolb to Isaac Kolb, October 3, 1792, Pennypacker Papers, MLAEP.

19. Davis, *Bucks County* (see n. 5), 563.

20. *Ibid.*, 555.

21. *Germantauner Zeitung*, February 6, 1787.

22. Abraham H. Cassel, "Franconia and Lower Salford Stories," *Historical Sketches. A Collection of Papers Prepared for the Historical Society of Montgomery County, Pennsylvania*, II (Norristown, Pa., 1900), 156-159.

23. Elisha S. Loomis, *Some Account of Jacob Oberholtzer* (Cleveland, Ohio, 1931), 83-84.

24. Edward Matthews, "The Clymer Family Was of Swiss Origin," newspaper clipping in Edward Matthews Scrap Book D-7, 45, Montgomery County Historical Society, Norristown, Pa.

25. James Y. Heckler, *History of Harleysville and Lower Salford Township* (Harleysville, Pa., 1886), 202.

26. Frederick S. Weiser and Howell J. Heaney, *The Pennsylvania German Fraktur of the Free Library of Philadelphia* (Breinigsville, Pa., 1976), I, #193.

27. *Ibid.*, II, #845.

28. [Gerrit Roosen], *Christliches Gemüthsgespräch* (Germantown, Pa., 1790).

29. Agnes Williamson Storer, *Elenore C. Custer, Her Family and Connections* (New Brunswick, N.J., n.d.), 141.

30. Kolb's Fraktur has as of this date not been studied as a body; Mary Jane Lederach Hershey has, however, collected and identified copies of more than a dozen pieces from his hand.

31. Donated in 1982 by Dr. George Gaugler to the Mennonite Heritage Center, Souderton, Pa.

32. This letter collection, under the heading, "Pennypacker Papers," is in the MLAEP.

33. My translation from a tape-recording of an elderly woman, Sallie Moyer Landis (b. 1867), in possession of Isaac Clarence Kulp, Jr., Vernfield, Harleysville, Pa. Another, earlier version appears in the MS "Hermonisches Melodeyen Buchlein über die Bekanteste Lieder im Marburger Gesangbuch" of "Jacob Ruth [son of Bishop David Ruth] Sing Schuler ihn der Niabritaner Schule," February 4, 1806, also in the possession of Isaac Clarence Kulp, Jr.: "Preceptor bin ich genand / Weil ich die jugend lere / Es gefelt mir wohl im ledigen stand / Und dass ist meine Ehre / Und wann die Schüler singen / So hör ich meine Freud / Gefall ich nicht den Menschen allen / Wann ich nur kann Gott gefallen / Das ist meine Lust / und das ist meine Freid." A song of this nature would fit schoolteacher Andreas S. Kolb (1749-1811), who was unmarried. The term "preceptor" may, however, be an originally non-Mennonite term. Cf. its use in reference to the career of a Reformed pastor, Lukas Hahn, born in Basel, Switzerland, in 1630, died at Neckargemünd in the Palatinate in 1690: "1649 Schulmeister in Graubünden, 1650 Diakon u. Präzeptor in Bretten, 1653 Präzeptor in Klingenmunster, Schulmeister in Hilsbach, 1653/54 Schulmeister in Weingarten, Germersheim, 1663 Pfarrer in Haag, 1681 Pfarrer in Bammantel. . . ." This résumé appears in Heinz Schuchmann, *Schweitzer Einwanderer im früheren kurpfälzischen Streubesitz des Kraichgaues (1650-1750),* "Folge 18" of Schriften zur Wanderungsgeschichte der Pfälzer (Kaiserslautern, n.d.), 6.

34. Tr.: "Then when I play the organ / Cheered with godly emotions, / And the congregation sings with me, / Oh how it rings in my heart!" See Abraham A. Meyer, *Christliche Lieder* (Milford Square, Pa., 1877), 95.

35. *E.g.,* a MS writing-practice booklet signed by Jacob Kratz, 1829-34, in my possession.

36. Weiser and Heany, *Pennsylvania German Fraktur* (see n. 26), II, #732. My attribution.

37. Ralph Beaver Strassburger, *Pennsylvania German Pioneers,* ed. William John Hinke (Norristown, Pa., 1934), III, 54. Johannes Smutz and Barbara Herstein are listed as immigrants, whereas the name Johannes Herstein appears under the heading, "Americans."

38. W[illiam] S. G[ottshall], "Bibles or Oxen," *MYBA,* 1906, 18.

39. This can be reviewed in letters by schoolteacher Andreas S. Kolb, writing to his parents in Germantown, 1792-94, in the Pennypacker Papers, MLAEP.

40. Alexander Mack to Daniel Lederman, ca. 1785, tr. Elizabeth Horsch Bender, copy at AMC.

41. A. J. Fretz, *A Genealogical Record of the Descendants of the Swartley Family* (Netcong, N.J., 1906), 63.

42. Storer, *Elenore C. Custer* (see n. 29), 46.

43. Davis, *History of Bucks County* (see n. 5), 391-392.

44. Sanford G. Shetler, *Two Centuries of Struggle and Growth* (Scottdale, Pa., 1963), 178-182.

45. Jacob Cassel Clemens, *Genealogical History of the Clemens Family* (Lansdale, Pa., 1948), 8. "Mt. Clemens City," *History of Macomb County, Michigan* (Chicago, 1882), 521. Christian's land was next to that of Tobias Newcomer. But *N.B.:* It seems possible that Michigan's Christian Clemens may be someone other than the son of Salford's John Clemens, who had his second mill near the site of present-day Doylestown, Pa.

46. A. J. Fretz, *A Brief History of Bishop Henry Funck and Other Funk Pioneers* (Elkhart, Ind., 1899), 580.

47. A. J. Fretz, *A Genealogical Record of the Descendants of Christian and Hans Meyer. . . .* (Harleysville, Pa., 1896), 328-329.

48. [Mrs. Simeon Kratz], "Valentine Kratz (1760-1824)," *MHB,* XII (January 1951), 2-3.

Davis, *History of Bucks County* (see n. 5), 411.

49. George S. Hunsberger, The Hunsbergers (Germantown, N.Y., 1969), 102-103.

50. Michael S. Bird, *Ontario Fraktur: A Pennsylvania-German Folk Tradition in Early Canada* (Toronto, 1977), 45. Illustration #19 should be credited to J. A. Eyer, and #20 to Andreas Kolb.

51. John H. Root and Ariel Dyer, *The Genealogy of the Root Family Who Came to Canada,* "Second Printing" (n.p., 1979), 14 (mimeographed).

52. For the location of Bien and Bechtel, see Frank H. Epp, *Mennonites in Canada, 1786-1920* (Toronto, 1974), 61, 82. On Clemens, see Ezra E. Eby, *A Biographical History of Early Settlers and their Descendants in Waterloo Township,* ed. & annotated Eldon D. Weber (Kitchener-Waterloo, 1971), 97, 102.

53. Fretz, *(Christian and Hans Meyer* (see n. 47), 329-331.

54. Jacob Gross, Abraham Wismer, Abraham Oberholtzer, Johannes Funk, Rudolph Landes, and Samuel Meyer, "Brief an eine Anzahl zur Mennonisten Gemeine gehörigen Familien," September 4, 1801, in *Briefe an die Mennonisten Gemeine* (Berlin, Ont., 1840, 10-11.

55. Fretz, *Christian and Hans Meyer* (see n. 47), 221-222.

56. Loomis, *Jacob Oberholtzer* (see n. 23), 74-75.

57. My account of this episode is based on a collection of five letters to printer Michael Billmeyer of Germantown, July 7 to December 5, 1803, by Deacon Jacob Kolb of Salford, Minister Jacob Oberholtzer of Franconia, and Deacon Martin Möllinger of Mellinger's. Noticed by Robert F. Ulle in 1978, the letters were then translated by Amos Hoover. Copies in MLAEP. See also Paul M. Yoder, "The Ausbund," in Paul M. Yoder, Elizabeth Bender, Harvey Graber, and Nelson P. Springer, *Four Hundred Years with the Ausbund* (Scottdale, Pa., 1964), 13-14; and Harold S. Bender's article, "Hymnology of the American Mennonites," in *ME*, II, 879-880.

58. Jacob Kolb to Michael Billmeyer, July 7, 1803, copy of translation by Amos Hoover in MLAEP.

59. "Gedruckt bey Michael Billmeyer, im Jahr 1803."

60. "Hymnology," *ME*, II, 880.

61. Hunsberger, *The Hunsbergers* (see n. 49), 650.

62. *Ibid.,* 603.

63. *Ibid.,* 657.

64. A. J. Fretz, *A Brief History of John and Christian Fretz* (Elkhart, Ind., 1890), 160.

65. The following account is drawn from Christian Funk, *A Mirror for all Mankind* (see n. 15), 9-11.

66. *Ibid.,* 11.

67. Fretz, *Brief History of Henry Funck* (see n. 46), 493.

68. Heckler, *History of Harleysville* (see n. 25), 28.

69. Fretz, *Martin Oberholtzer* (see n. 9), 109-110.

70. Hunsberger, *The Hunsbergers* (see n. 49), 567.

71. From a flyleaf in a Bible owned by Hiram and Mary Jane Hershey: "Diese bibel gehöret Mier Abraham Ziegler. Ich habe sie gekauft von der Elizabeth Ziegler."

72. Harold S. Bender, "Preaching Appointments for Bucks Co. Visitors in Lancaster Co. in 1813," *MHB*, V (September 1944), 1-2.

73. Gertrude Mohlin Ziegler, *The Ziegler Family and Related Families in Pennsylvania* (Zelienople, Pa., 1978), 36.

74. *Ibid.,* 171-172.

75. "Testimony from the Boyertown Case," *ODI*, 422.

76. Helen A. Stanley, *The Alderfers of America* (Allentown, Pa., 1972), 69.

77. Edward W. Hocker, *The Sower Printing House of Colonial Times,* Vol. LII, Proceedings and Addresses of the Pennsylvania German Society (Norristown, Pa., 1940), 118.

78. George F. P. Wanger, *A Genealogy of the Descendants of Rev. Jacob Price* (Harrisburg, Pa., 1926), 64-65.

79. Quoted from the *Norristown Herald,* August 27, 1817, in Theodore W. Bean, *History of Montgomery County* (Philadelphia, 1884), 502n.

80. John C. Wenger, *History of the Mennonites of the Franconia Conference* (Telford, Pa., 1937), 288.

81. MS records of West Swamp Congregation, MLAEP.

82. The Baptists' names were Griffith Jones and Joseph Matthias. See a MS record book for "Hunsberger's School," MLAEP. This school is also mentioned in Helen Kolb Gates, *et al., Bless the Lord, O My Soul* (Scottdale, Pa., 1964), 42.

83. I have been informed by previous owners of this farm, Mr. and Mrs. Irvin Kratz of near Morwood, Pa., that the designs remained in the barn until the 1950s, when the threshing area was remodeled.

84. Weiser and Heany, *Pennsylvania German Fraktur* (see n. 26), I, #239. Note: the attribution to an earlier Rudolph Landis (1732-1802) cannot be correct, since the Fraktur itself is dated February 11, 1814.

85. See hymn #21 in the "Zugabe einiger auserlesenen Lieder," *Die kleine Geistlichen Harfe der Kinder Zions* (Germantown, 1820).

86. *Ibid.,* hymn #17, stanza 3.

87. [John] O[berholtzer?]., "Der Christliche Gesang vor Alters und Jetzt," *CBB,* March 15, 1887. The author speaks of a time seventy years earlier in eastern Pennsylvania. At this time John Oberholtzer was about seventy-six years old.

88. Hymn #408 in the *Kleine Geistliche Harfe:* "Sag, was hilft alle welt. . . ."

89. Wenger, *History of the . . . Franconia Conference* (see n. 80), 415.

90. For the details of the following profile, see John F. Funk, *Biographical Sketch of Pre. John Geil* (Elkhart, Ind., 1897); and Philip Whitwell Wilson, *An Explorer of Horizons: William Edgar Geil* (New York, 1927) 282 ff.

91. Herman Gottschall to Jacob Gottschall, July 19, 1819, in possession of Isaac Clarence Kulp, Jr., Vernfield, Harleysville, Pa.

92. Wenger, *History of the . . . Franconia Conference* (see n. 80), 276.

93. Henry A. Hunsicker, *A Genealogical History of the Hunsicker Family* (Philadelphia, 1911), 22.

94. *Ibid.*

95. John Herr, *The True and Blessed Way Which Leadeth Beneath the Cross, to Heaven. . . .* (Harrisburg, Pa., 1816), 200.

96. Henry D. Hunsicker to Christian Herr, November 30, 1816, tr. and reprinted in Wenger, *History of the . . . Franconia Conference* (see n. 80), 416-417.

97. Heckler, *History of Harleysville* (see n. 25), 30.

98. John Hunsicker to Christian Herr, July 12, 1819, in Lancaster Mennonite Historical Library.

99. Herman Gottschall to Jacob Gottschall (see n. 91).

100. Anna Jane Waddington, *Eden Mennonite Church . . . 150th Anniversary* (Schwenksville, Pa., 1968), 5-6.

Chapter 7. "The Subject of Assurance" vs. "The Plain Duties of a Christian" (1820-1839)

1. David Beiler, *Eine Vermahnung oder Andenken* (n.p., n.d.—"geschrieben von Bischof David Beiler ungefähr im Jahr 1860"), 4.

2. Theodore W. Bean, *History of Montgomery County* (Philadelphia, 1884), 572-573.

3. A. J. Fretz, *A Brief History of John and Christian Fretz* (Elkhart, Ind., 1890), 187-188.

4. A. J. Fretz, *A Genealogical Record of the Descendants of Christian and Hans Meyer* (Harleysville, Pa., 1896), 160.

5. A. H. Cassel, Reminiscences recorded on June 13, 1889, by Samuel W. Pennypacker, transcribed in Pennypacker's Historical and Genealogical Notes MSS, a two-volume, bound set of legal-sized, generally unpaginated notes at the Pennypacker estate, Schwenksville, Pa.

6. *Ibid.*

7. Fretz, *John and Christian Fretz* (see n. 3).

8. *Ibid.*, 188.

9. Henry A. Hunsicker, "Local History Sketches," *Collegeville Independent*, September 6, 1906.

10. Jacob Stauffer, *Stauffer's Geschicht-Buchlein Von der sogenannten Mennonisten Gemeinde...*, *Zweite Auflage* (Scottdale, Pa., 1922), 137.

11. Fretz, *John and Christian Fretz* (see n. 3), 222.

12. *Ibid.*, 187.

13. John F. Funk, *Biographical Sketch of Pre. John Geil* (Elkhart, Ind., 1897), 23.

14. Bean, *Montgomery County* (see n. 2), 415.

15. Docket Book of Jacob Clymer, Esq., MLAEP.

16. *Ibid.*, 76, 86.

17. Pauline Cassel, *History of Bedminster* (n.p., 1976), 114. See also a paper headed, "Read by . . . Henry Eckel to John Leatherman . . . June 25th 1836," MLAEP.

18. Samuel Whitaker Pennypacker, *Autobiography of a Pennsylvanian* (Philadelphia, 1918), 18-19.

19. Isaac B. Tyson, "Genealogy . . . of the Tyson family" (1864). MS copy, 4, MLAEP. See also Edward Matthews, *History of Towamencin Township* (Skippack, Pa., 1897), 52. One of the last local people to speak Dutch was Peter Godshall Metz (1798-1886), farmer where the Skippack Creek crosses the Forty-Foot Road, in Towamencin Township.

20. Judith Ann Meier, "An Early History of East Norriton Township," *BHSMC*, XX (Spring 1977), 367.

21. Funk, *John Geil* (see n. 13), 23-24.

22. Isaac B. Tyson, "Genealogy" (see n. 19), 11, 13.

23. Der Menonisten: Oder Taufs Gesinden Gemeine Buch: Vor die Gemeinde in Bebberstaun Anno Dommini 1738, entry for April 25, 1825, MLAEP. Yet a local man, Henry G. Johnson, uses the term "Ältester" for deacon in his diary for October 2, 1832.

24. James Y. Heckler, *History of Harleysville and Historical Sketches of Lower Salford Township* (Harleysville, 1886), 29.

25. H. S. Hallman, *History of the Hallman Family in Canada* (Berlin, Ont., n.d.), 8-9.

26. Henry D. Hagey, *Some Local History of Franconia Township*, ed. Joyce Clemmer Munro (Souderton, Pa., 1979), 98, 231-232.

27. A. J. Fretz, *A Brief History of Bishop Henry Funck and Other Funk Pioneers* (Elkhart, Ind., 1899), 567, 571.

28. Elisha Loomis, *Some Account of Jacob Oberholtzer* (Cleveland, 1931), 87-88, 95-96.

29. Jacob Moyer to Christian Gross or Henrich Honsberger, October 9, 1826, tr. Elizabeth Horsch Bender, AMC. See also Lorraine Roth, *150 Years: Sesquicentennial of the Amish Mennonites of Ontario*, ed. Dorothy Sauder (n.p., 1972), 15.

30. Jacob Moyer to Christian Gross (see n. 29).

31. Jacob Moyer to Christian Gross, October 3, 1827, tr. Elizabeth Horsch Bender, AMC.

32. Jacob Krehbiel, "A Few Words About the Mennonites in America in 1841," tr. and ed. Harold S. Bender, 2nd part, *MQR*, VI (April 1932), 114-115.

33. The details on the Medina County story may be found in Ford L. Coolman and Rachel W. Kreider, *The Mennonite Cemeteries of Medina County* (n.p., 1971), ii-iii; 3-64, *passim*. A very suggestive survey of Franconia Conference emigrants and descendants in Ohio are in "Travel Notes of Samuel Godshalk, 1869," ed. J. C. Wenger, *MHB*, III (December 1942), 1-2. Exact figures on wagons passing through Easton in September-October, 1817, are in "Emigration," *Hazard's Register*, I (October 1828), 216.

34. Jennie Detweiler Weaver, "Reminiscences of 1839," 14 pp. MS written June 26, 1887. Copy received from Mrs. Weaver's great-great-grandson Gerald Weaver.

35. John Lapp [Batavia, Genessee County, NY] to "frends and relations," September 7, 1835, MLAEP.

36. Jacob Gottschall, travel diary in possession of Isaac Clarence Kulp, Jr., Vernfield, Harleysville, Pa.

37. A. J. Fretz, *A Genealogical Record of the Descendants of the Swartley Family* (Netcong, N.J., 1906), 22.

38. Martin Kindig to Jacob Gottschall, ca. 1823, consisting mostly of quotations from John Herr's writings, in possession of Isaac Clarence Kulp, Jr., Vernfield, Harleysville, Pa.

39. W. W. H. Davis, *History of Bucks County, Pennsylvania* (Doylestown, Pa., 1876), 860-861. See also an indenture between Philip Fretz, Samuel Smith, and Elias Cary Jun., and Thomas Carver, January 18, 1837, in Henry Wismer Papers, Fol. 1, Bucks County Historical Library, Doylestown, Pa.

40. Roger E. Sappington, *The Brethren in the New Nation* (Elgin, Ill., 1976), 165.

41. Isaac B. Tyson, "An entry from a journal," Isaac B. Tyson papers, n.p., MLAEP.

42. *Ibid.*

43. Isaac B. Tyson, "Genealogy of the Tyson Family" (see n. 19), 24-25.

44. Jacob and Maria Frey to Jacob Gross, September 5, 1839, MLAEP.

45. A. H. Cassel, Reminiscences (see n. 5).

46. A colorful picture of Abraham Detweiler Hunsicker may be constructed from details scattered through a series entitled "Local History Sketches" by Abraham's son Henry Alderfer Hunsicker, running in the *Collegeville Independent*, June 28-December 27, 1906.

47. Henry A. Hunsicker, *A Genealogical History of the Hunsicker Family* (Philadelphia, 1911), 67.

48. N. B. Grubb, "Rev. John H. Oberholtzer," *MYBA*, 1908, 35.

49. Oberholtzer family tradition related to me by a great-great-granddaughter of J. H. Oberholtzer, Mrs. Sara Louden of near Milford Square, Pa., July 13, 1981.

50. William H. Oberholtzer, "The Jacob Oberholtzer Family," printed family tree, "issue 2," July 7, 1981. This large sheet identifies Jacob Oberholtzer as having immigrated on the *Samuel* in 1732.

51. John H. Oberholtzer, Kurze Geschichte der Oberholtzer Familie, 8-pp. MS dated December 1891, MLAEP.

52. Also reproduced in Sandra Wilmot, "More Than Just Hearts and Flowers," *Americana*, X (September/October, 1982), 31.

53. Henry A. Hunsicker, "Church Division in 1847," *MYBA*, 1907, 20.

54. John Hockman, Jacob L. S. Gerhart, Christian Souder, *et al.*, handwritten certificate for schoolteacher William Hangey, dated 1852, in possession of Mrs. Lester Fitzgerald, Telford, Pa.

55. Ralph Wood, "*Der Bauernfreund:* A Newspaper of the Pennsylvania Germans," *BMCHS*, II (October 1940), 187.

56. William F. Dannehower, "The Sumneytown Academy," *PR*, III (November 1925), 72-73.

57. Fretz, *John and Christian Fretz* (see n. 3), 120, 256. Davis *Bucks County* (see n. 39), 820.

58. See Alexander Waldenrath, "Lost Goschenhoppen Region Newspaper Recovered," *BHSMC*, XX (Spring 1977), 389-391.

59. N. B. Grubb, "The First Mennonite Newspaper," *MYBA*, 1908, 6, 8.

60. Lyle L. Rosenberger, "Black Suffrage in Bucks County: The Election of 1837," *Bucks County Historical Society Journal*, I (Spring 1975), 29.

61. Samuel Whitaker Pennypacker, *Annals of Phoenixville and its Vicinity* (Philadelphia, 1872), 212.

62. Hiram Corson, "The Abolitionists of Montgomery County," *Historical Sketches. A Collection of Papers Prepared for the Historical Society of Montgomery County, Pennsylvania*, II (Norristown, Pa., 1900), 68.

63. Funk, *John Geil* (see n. 13), 41-42.

64. Bean, *History of Montgomery County* (see n. 2), 385.

65. A. J. Fretz, *A Genealogical Record of the Descendants of Henry Rosenberger* (Harleysville, Pa., 1906), 165.

66. Ralph Linwood Johnson, "Genealogical Studies of Some Providence Families," *PR*, XII (1934), 19-20.

67. "History of the Evangelical Association" (extracts from a book, 1894, edited by Bishop Ruben Yeakel), *PR*, VII (July 1929), 87.

68. Christian Gross to Jacob Gross and Jacob Frey, January 29, 1839, MLAEP.

69. A[braham]. Gottschall, *Wahre Gerechtigkeit Vertheidigt oder Ein Beweis, Wie man durch den Glauben wirklich soll gerecht werden* (Doylestown, Pa., 1837).

70. *Ibid.*, 12.

71. *Ibid.*, 14.

72. *Ibid.*, 3.

73. Funk, *John Geil* (see n. 13), 26.

74. Abraham Godshalk, Jr., *A Family Record* (Harrisburg, Pa., 1912), 108-110.

75. Abraham Gottschalk, *A Description of the new Creature* (Doylestown, PA, 1838). Abraham Gottschall, *Eine Beschreibung der neuen Creatur* (Doylestown, PA, 1838). The English version was printed by William M. Large, and the German by Joseph Jung.

76. Gottschalk, *Description*, quoted here from a reprint in Abraham Godschalk, Jr., *A Family Record* (see n. 74), 71.

77. *Ibid.*, 77.

78. *Ibid.*, 106.

79. *Ibid.*, 94.

80. *Ibid.*, 89-90.

81. *Ibid.*, 42.

82. J[oseph]. J[ung]. (printer), note at end of *Beschreibung* (see n. 75), 100.

83. Abraham Godshalk, Jr., *A Family Record* (see n. 74), 280-281.

84. Daniel K. Cassel, *History of the Mennonites* (Philadelphia, 1888), 247.

85. Garret Bean to Henry G. Johnson, January 28, 1838, in my possession.

86. Henrich Johnson, Notenbuch, A.D. 1826, MS currently on display at Mennonite Heritage Center, Souderton, PA.

87. Hunsicker, *Hunsicker Family* (see n. 47), 36-37.

88. "Testimony From the Boyertown Case," ODI, 422.

89. Edward W. Hocker, "Montgomery County History," *BMCHS*, XII (Fall 1959), 64-65.

90. John C. Wenger, *History of the Mennonites of the Franconia Conference* (Telford, Pa., 1937), 151-152.

91. Krehbiel, "A Few Words" (see n. 32), 111.

92. *Ibid.*, Part I, *MQR*, VI (January 1932), 49-50.

93. Jacob Krehbiel to John Lederach, July 7, 1839, in possession of Isaac Clarence Kulp, Jr., Vernfield, Harleysville, Pa.

94. "Palatinate," *ME*, IV, 111.

95. Christian Galle, "Die Familie Galle," *Mennonitische Geschichtsblätter*, XXXVI (1979), 61-62.

96. Amelia Mueller, "Jacob Ellenberger: Pastor, Teacher, Musician, Writer," Part I, *Mennonite Life*, XXXII (December 1977), 30.

97. Carl Justus van der Smissen to Benjamin Eby, May 19, 1840, printed by Heinrich Eby as *Zweyter Brief aus Danemark an die Mennonisten Gemeine in Canada* (Berlin, Ont., 1841), 23 pp.

98. Fretz, *John and Christian Fretz* (see n. 3), 240.

99. *Ibid.*, 254.

100. John Ziegler Gehman, Diary, tr. Raymond Hollenbach, December 1838, MLAEP.

101. [Andrew B. Shelly], "Pred. Christian Clemmer," *CBB*, April 1, 1883, 52.

102. Michael Landis to Jacob Gottschall, May 19, 1836, in possession of Isaac Clarence Kulp, Vernfield, Harleysville, Pa.

Chapter 8. "I Thought I Had a Perfect Right" (1840-1846)

1. [Edward W. Hocker], "Up and Down Montgomery County," *Norristown Times Herald*, August 16, 1965.

2. Advertisement carrying this date, by Samuel F. Shaeff of Center Square, Pa., as appearing in the *Norristown Herald and Free Press*, September 29, 1847.

3. John Ziegler Gehman, Diary, tr. Raymond Hollenbach, MLAEP, entries for July 14, 1833, and February 20, 1846.

4. Theodore W. Bean, *History of Montgomery County* (Philadelphia, 1884), 332.

5. James Y. Heckler, *The History of Harleysville and Historical Sketches of Lower Salford Township* (Harleysville, Pa., 1886), 60.

6. Charles|R.|Barker, "Neighborhood |News and Notices," *BMCHS*, XV (Fall 1962), 251.

7. *History of the Brethren Eastern Pennsylvania 1915-1965* (Lancaster, Pa., 1965), 296.

8. Ralph Beaver Strassburger, *The Strassburger Family and Allied Families of Pennsylvania* (Gwynedd Valley, Pa., 1922), 491.

9. George S. Hunsberger, *The Hunsbergers* (Germantown, N.Y., 1969), 657-660.

10. A. J. Fretz, *A Genealogical Record of the Descendants of Christian and Hans Meyer....* (Harleysville, Pa., 1896), 201-202.

11. S[amuel] M. Musselman, *Die Neue Choral Harmonie* (Harrisburg, Pa., 1844).

12. H[enry] A. Hunsicker, "Local History Sketches," *Collegeville Independent*, December 6, 1906.

13. Frederick S. Weiser and Howell J. Heaney, *The Pennsylvania German Fraktur of the Free Library of Pennsylvania* (Breinigsville, Pa., 1947), II, #840.

14. Heckler, *History of Harleysville* (see n. 5), 232.

15. "Appraisement of the Real & Personal Estate of Henry Rutt of new Britain Township...." January 20, 1757, Bucks County Court House, Doylestown, Pa. Located by Joel Alderfer.

16. Henry C. Mercer, "The Zithers of the Pennsylvania Germans," *Papers Read Before the Bucks County Historical Society*, V (1926), 487-490.

17. J. W. Richards, "Sermon," *Centenary Jubilee of the Ev. Lutheran Church of Augustus, Trappe, May 2, A.D. 1843* (Pottstown, Pa., 1843), 31.

18. Helen Kolb Gates, John Funk Kolb, J. Clemens Kolb, and Constance Sykes, *Bless the Lord O My Soul*, ed. J. C. Wenger (Scottdale, Pa., 1964), 26.

19. Edward W. Hocker, "Montgomery County History," *BMCHS*, XIII (Spring/Fall, 1960), 103.

20. Daniel Gross to Jacob Gross, Jacob Frey, and four others, November 1, 1842, MLAEP.

21. Henry A. Hunsicker, "Church Division in 1847," *MYBA*, 1907, 22.

22. John C. Boorse, "To the Montgomery County Historical Society" (dictated memoirs), sheet in box entitled "Politics" at Montgomery County Historical Society, Norristown, Pa.

23. Jacob Pennypacker, Diary, October 1, 1840. Bound MS, 2 vols., at Pennypacker estate, Schwenksville, Pa.

24. Hunsicker, "Church Division" (see n. 21), 22.

25. Samuel W. Pennypacker, *Autobiography of a Pennsylvanian* (Philadelphia, 1918), 48.

26. This list, on a sheet of paper with no heading except the date, May 16, 1840, is in the Jacob Hostetter Collection, AMC. Cawendrie & Winsen: Coventry and Vincent; Brawidens: Providence; Mardetsche: Methacton; Domensen: Towamencin; Auf der Blen: Plains; Deils daun: Doylestown; Dib Ronn: Deep Run; Schwammer Versammlunghaus: Swamp Meetinghouse; Frencone: Franconia; Bergese: Perkasie (Blooming Glen); Sakene: Saucon; Hosen Sack (Upper Milford).

27. My dating of this ordination, which differs from that given in John C. Wenger, *History of the Mennonites of the Franconia Conference* (Telford, Pa., 1937), 260, is based on the testimony of John H. Oberholtzer, in an eleven-page letter to minister Henry Nice, April 4, 1870, copy in SMGC.

28. Herbert Fretz, *The History of the Deep Run Mennonite Congregation Eastern Conference of Bucks County, Pennsylvania* (Bedminster, Pa., 1949), 12.

29. J. Riley Bergey, "David Bergey: A Sketch of his Life; His Career as a Minister," *MYBA*, 1918, 23-24.

30. A list of names for an ordination at Franconia, dated "1845," in the Henry Krupp

Papers, MLAEP. *Cf.* Garret Kolb, Diary (MLAEP), entry for November 17, 1845: "They made a preacher in Franconia today."

31. John H. Oberholtzer, *Der wahre Character von J. H. Oberholtzer* (Milford Square, Pa., 1860), 9.

32. John H. Oberholtzer, "Licht Uber die Mennoniten Trennungs-Geschichte und Ihrer Folgen in Ostpennsylvanien in 1847," a seventy-page MS in SMGC. On [p. 65] Oberholtzer refers to himself in a parenthesis in the third person: "Er war früher Grobschmid, auch Schlosser."

33. John H. Oberholtzer, "A Letter of John H. Oberholtzer to Unnamed Friends in Germany, 1849," February 7, 1849, tr. Elizabeth Horsch Bender, ODI, 403.

34. Oberholtzer to Nice (see n. 27), 3.

35. Oberholtzer, "Licht" (see n. 32), 17.

36. Oberholtzer to Nice (see n. 27), 3.

37. *Ibid.*, 2.

38. John H. Oberholtzer, "Testimony in the Boyerstown [sic] M. Church Lawsuit June 19. 1877," 16 pp. MS, paragraph #2, SMGC.

39. John C. Wenger, *History of the Mennonites of the Franconia Conference* (Telford, Pa., 1937), 155.

40. Oberholtzer to Nice (see n. 27), 2.

41. Oberholtzer, "Testimony" (see n. 38), paragraph #3.

42. "Testimony from the Boyertown Case," ODI, 425. Note: Oberholtzer's personally written version of his testimony differs somewhat from the official one reproduced in ODI.

43. *Ibid.*, 415.

44. *Ibid.*, 427.

45. J. Herbert Fretz, "A Pennsylvania Mennonite Church—West Swamp," *Mennonite Life*, II (October 1947), 35.

46. "Testimony" (see n. 42), 415.

47. Oberholtzer, "Licht" (see n. 32), 24.

48. *Katechismus, oder kurze und einfaltige Unterweisung aus der heiligen Schrift* (Doylestown, Pa., 1844).

49. [John H. Oberholtzer], "Vorrede," *Katechismus* (see n. 48), 4.

50. Mrs. Sara Louden, great-great-granddaughter of John H. Oberholtzer, near Milford Square, Pa., July 13, 1981.

51. Papers donated by Wynne Nyce, MLAEP.

52. Garret Kolb Diary, July 17, 1844, MLAEP.

53. Isaac Clarence Kulp, Jr., "Meetinghouses of Montgomery County," BMCHS, XXI (Fall 1977), 77.

54. Garret Kolb, Diary, August 30, 1844, MLAEP.

55. *Ibid.*, October 6, 1844.

56. Henry S. Bower, *A Genealogical Record of the Descendants of Daniel Stauffer and Hans Bauer and Other Pioneers* (Harleysville, Pa., 1897), 179.

57. Garret Kolb, Diary, November 14, 1844, MLAEP.

58. Oberholtzer, "A Letter . . . to Friends in Germany" (see n. 33), 423.

59. Record of Jacob Gottschall's funeral in Gottschall family papers, in possession of Isaac Clarence Kulp, Jr., Vernfield, Harleysville, Pa.

60. John F. Funk, *Biographical Sketch of Pre. John Geil* (Elkhart, Ind., 1897), 19.

61. Abraham Hunsicker to Christian Herr, January 29, 1848, ODI, 333, 335.

62. *Ibid.*, 335.

63. *Ibid.*

64. Garret Kolb, Diary, July 21, 1846, MLAEP.

65. Oberholtzer, "Testimony" (see n. 38), paragraph #13.

66. This picture emerges from details in two accounts by Edward W. Hocker in his "Up and Down Montgomery County" column in the *Norristown Times Herald*, March 23, 1925, and January 9, 1929.

67. "Johannes Bertolet," *PR*, II (November 15, 1889), 122. Anna Johnson Alderfer, "History of the Bertolet Family," 9 pp. MS read at the "Homecoming Anniversary" of the Frederick Mennonite Church (formerly Bertolets), April 24, 1977, copy in MLAEP. See also Daniel H. Bertolet, *The Bertolet Family* (Harrisburg, Pa., 1914).

68. James Riley Bergey, "Johannes Bertolet," *PR*, II (November 15, 1899), 122.

Chapter 9. "This Is Not Christian" (1847)

1. John H. Williams, "The History of Olney and Vicinity," *North Philadelphia News and Erlen News,* month and day unknown, 1933. Clipping in Joseph W. Hunsicker Collection, Montgomery County Historical Society, Norristown, Pa.

2. Abraham Hunsicker to Christian Herr, January 29, 1848, ODI, 335.

3. *Ibid.*

4. Abraham Grater to Henry Nice, April 26, 1848, ODI, 349.

5. David Allebach, "Hunsberger's Opinion Regarding Landes," ODI, 367.

6. Jonas Kratz, Henry Wismer, Maria Landes, Catharine Wismer, Catharine B. Wismer, and Susanna Conner, written appeal to the Franconia Conference, April 12, 1847, ODI, 371.

7. Allebach, "Hunsberger's Opinion" (see n. 5), 367.

8. Grater to Nice (see n. 4), 351.

9. Kratz, Wismer, *et al.* (see n. 6), 371.

10. John H. Oberholtzer, "Testimony in the Boyerstown [sic] M. Church Lawsuit June 19, 1877," 16 pp. MS, SMGC, 9-10.

11. Abraham Hunsicker, *A Statement of Facts and Summary of Views on Morals and Religion* (Philadelphia, 1851), 10.

12. Oberholtzer, "Testimony" (see n. 10), 9.

13. [John H. Oberholtzer], *Ordnung der Mennonitischen Gemeinschaft* (Allentown, Pa., 1847), 21 pp. For a recent English translation by Ernest G. Gehman, see ODI, 387-397.

14. "Constitution of the Mennonite Brotherhood" (see n. 13), ODI, 388.

15. Christian Herr, Jacob Hostetter, and four other Lancaster Conference bishops to Henry Nice, August 29, 1847, ODI, 363.

16. "Constitution," ODI, 391.

17. Herr, *et al.* to Henry Nice (see n. 15), ODI, 363.

18. "Constitution," ODI, 392.

19. *Ibid.*, 395.

20. *Ibid.*

21. *Ibid.*, 396.

22. "Testimony from the Boyertown Case," ODI, 423.

23. *Ibid.*, 424.

24. "Constitution," ODI, 396.

25. *Ibid.*, 394.

26. Herr, *et al.* to Henry Nice (see n. 15), ODI, 365.

27. "Testimony from the Boyertown Case," ODI, 423.

28. Oberholtzer, "Testimony" (see n. 10), 11.

29. *Ibid.*

30. "Constitution," ODI, 397n.

31. Grater to Nice (see n. 4), ODI, 351.

32. Oberholtzer, "Testimony" (see n. 10), 11. See also "Testimony from the Boyertown Case," ODI, 418.

33. Henry Nice to Abraham Grater, April-May, 1848, ODI, 361.

34. "Testimony from the Boyertown Case," ODI, 425.

35. *Ibid.*, 418: "nevertheless it will be read."

36. *Ibid.*, 425.

37. John H. Oberholtzer, "Licht Über die Mennoniten Trennungs-Geschichte und Ihrer Folgen in Ostpennsylvanien in 1847," 70 pp. MS in SMGC, 23.

38. "Constitution," ODI, 385, n. 3.

39. ODI, 361-362, n. 55 (see n. 15, *supra*).

40. This statement, missing in the version of the Herr-Nice letter tr. in ODI, 361-365, is in the version tr. by Ira D. Landis and H. S. Bender in "The Reply of the Lancaster Conference to the John H. Oberholtzer Constitution of 1847," *MQR*, XXIX (January 1955), 76.

41. Oberholtzer, "Testimony" (see n. 10), 6-7.

42. From the memories of John D. Clemmer, son of Deacon Abraham Clemmer, who was present, and Anna Landis, an eight-year-old girl who was also present, and told her grandson, Arthur Lapp.

43. James Gerhart, of the East Swamp congregation, reports hearing this version from older members there.

44. Oberholtzer, "Testimony" (see n. 10), 8.

45. Record Book of Swamp (Old Mennonite) Congregation, MLAEP.

46. Undated newspaper clipping, obituary of Samuel Musselman, calling him "for 40 years a faithful minister in the Mennonist Society." The dates in Wenger, *History of the . . . Franconia Conference*, 286, do not seem correct. See W. W. H. Davis, *History of Bucks County, Pennsylvania* (Doylestown, Pa., 1876), 454, where it is stated that Bishop Musselman died "in 1847 at the age of ninety."

47. Grater to Nice (see n. 4), ODI, 353.

48. Hunsicker, *A Statement* (see n. 11), 14.

49. O. O. Sower, "Einweihung der Schippacher Literarischen Halle," advertisement in the *Bauernfreund* (Sumneytown, Pa.), December 8, 1847.

50. Hunsicker, *A Statement* (see n. 11), 15.

51. "Constitution of the Washington Hall Debating Society," *PR*, VII (January 1929), 63.

52. A. J. Fretz, *A Genealogical Record of the Descendants of Jacob Beidler of Lower Milford Township . . . .* (Milton, N.J., 1903), 216.

53. *Bucks County Intelligencer* (Doylestown, PA), October 6, 1847, 2.

54. "Testimony from the Boyertown Case," ODI, 428.

55. *Ibid.*, 419.

56. *Ibid.*, 428.

57. *Ibid.*, 426, 428.

58. *Ibid.*, 426.

59. *Ibid.*, 419.

60. Oberholtzer, "Licht" (see n. 37), 42.

61. "First Session," October 28, 1847, MECMC.

62. "Testimony from the Boyertown Case," ODI, 419.

63. John Z. Gehman, Diary, November 20, 1847, MLAEP.

64. Herbert Fretz, *The History of the Deep Run Mennonite Congregation Eastern Conference of Bucks County, Pennsylvania* (Bedminster, Pa., 1949), 27. In a note dated October 5, 1982, author Fretz recalls that when he "interviewed old people on both sides" at Deep Run during a pastorate there in "1948, 1949," he found among them a tradition that the "old group" had begun to meet every Sunday in the midst of the 1847 controversy, though this had not been the practice earlier.

65. *Ibid.*, 12.

66. N. B. Grubb, "Mennonite Reminiscences," typed MS in SL, n.p.

67. Henry S. Bower, *A Genealogical Record of the Descendants of Daniel Stauffer and Hans Bauer and Other Pioneers* (Harleysville, Pa., 1897), 180.

68. Jacob B. Mensch to John S. Kurtz, February 15, 1887, ODI, 383.

69. Inventory of property of John D. Hunsicker, December 20, 1847, in Montgomery County Court House Annex, Norristown, Pa.

70. Story recounted by Linnaeus Kulp (1893-1983), Lower Salford Township, Summer, 1975.

71. Remembered by Alan G. Keyser, whose ancestral family has attended the "Lower Skippack" Mennonite congregation from before 1847 until the present.

72. Elmer E. S. Johnson, "Dr. Johnson's Remarks," *The Messenger*, I (April 1948), 4.

Chapter 10 "Our Reform" and "Our People" (1848-1860)

1. John H. Oberholtzer, "A Letter . . . to Unnamed Friends in Germany, 1849," February 7, 1849, tr. Elizabeth Horsch Bender, ODI, 403.
2. Abraham Hunsicker to Christian Herr, January 29, 1848, ODI, 341.
3. Henry Nice to Abraham Grater, "1848," ODI, 359.
4. John H. Oberholtzer, "Licht Über die Mennoniten Trennungs-Geschichte und Ihrer Folgen in Ostpennsylvanien in 1847," 70 pp. MS in SMGC, 53-54.
5. Oberholtzer, "Letter" (see n. 1), 405.
6. Nice to Grater (see n. 3), 361.
7. "Untitled Franconia Conference Minute of May 1848," ODI, 367-369.
8. Christian Herr to Abraham Hunsicker, April 17, 1848, ODI, 345-349.
9. Henry A. Hunsicker, "Local History Sketches," *Collegeville Independent*, August 1906.
10. F. G. Hobson, "Providence," *BMCHS*, X (April 1956), 132-133.
11. John Bechtel to an unnamed person, March 14, 1848, ODI, 343.
12. *Ibid.*
13. John C. Wenger, *History of the Mennonites of the Franconia Conference* (Telford, Pa., 1937), 252.
14. *Der Neutralist* (Skippack, Pa.), February 1850.
15. *Verhandlung des Hohen Rathes der Mennoniten Gemeinschaft*, a broadside containing minutes of the East Pennsylvania Mennonite Conference session of October 5, 1848, MSHL.
16. Henry A. Hunsicker, "Church Division in 1847," *MYBA*, 1907, 22.
17. Jacob Meyer to William Meyer, December 16 [1848], MLAEP.
18. Herbert Fretz, *History of the Deep Run Mennonite Congregation Eastern Conference of Bucks County, Pennsylvania* (Bedminster, Pa., 1949), 14.
19. *Ibid.*, 31.
20. Christian Gross to Jacob Gross, April 17, 1849, 153, tr. Elizabeth Horsch Bender, AMC.
21. Fretz, *Deep Run Mennonite Congregation* (see n. 18), 15-17, 23.
22. A. J. Fretz, *A Brief History of John and Christian Fretz* (Elkhart, Ind., 1890), 227-229.
23. For the Bowmansville "School Fight" story, see Charles D. Spotts, "The People of Bowmansville," *Community Historians Annual* (Lancaster, Pa.), IX (July 1970), 34-37; and A. G. Seyfert, "The Part a Lancaster County Pa. Mennonite Church Had in the Introduction of the Public School System," *The Mennonite*, April 3, 1930, 3-7, and April 10, 1930, 3-5.
24. Joseph F. Freed, "An Exhortation of Joseph F. Freed to his Little Son, Jacob," December 11, 1856, in Jacob A. Freed, *Partial History of the Freed Family and Connecting Families* (Souderton, Pa., 1923), 101-103.
25. "Fifth Session," May 2, 1850, MECMC.
26. Abraham Hunsicker, *A Statement of Facts and Summary of Views of Morals and Religion* (Philadelphia, 1851), 11.
27. Samuel K. Cassel to Samuel Moyer, November 29, 1850, MLAEP.
28. Abraham Grater, *An Explanation of Incidents That Took Place Among the So-called Mennonites* (Skippack, Pa., 1855), 7.
29. Hunsicker, *Statement* (see n. 26), 5.
30. "Im Namen der Mennoniten Gemeinschaft," undated broadside (after May 23, 1851), MSHL.
31. Hunsicker, *Statement* (see n. 26), 14.
32. *Ibid.*, 6.
33. See n. 30, *supra*.
34. Henrich Meyer to Samuel Meyer, January 22, 1851, MLAEP.

35. See the list of ordinations and baptisms from the Jacob B. Mensch papers, in John C. Wenger, *History of the Mennonites of the Franconia Conference* (Telford, Pa., 1937), 167-168.

36. [Edward W. Hocker], "Mennonites Not Always Successful in Avoiding Litigation, *Norristown Times Herald,* June 10, 1958.

37. Edward W. Hocker, "Montgomery County History," *BMCHS*. XII (Fall 1969), 117.

38. James Y. Heckler, "History of Skippack," MS in SL, taken from the *Montgomery Transcript* (Skippack, Pa., July-August, 1896), 54.

39. A run of the *Botschafter* is held by the Library of the Associated Mennonite Biblical Seminaries, Elkhart, Ind.

40. Ephraim Hunsberger, letter in *RB,* April 14, 1853.

41. John H. Oberholtzer, *Aufschluss der Verfolgerungen gegen Daniel Hoch, Prediger der Menonitten Gemeinschaft, in Ober Canada* (Milford Square, Pa., 1853).

42. John O. Clemens to Tobias and Magdalena Kolb, February 26, 1854, AMC.

43. John O. Clemens to Tobias and Magdalena Kolb, July 28, 1858, AMC.

44. Jacob Krehbiel to John H. Oberholtzer, April 4, 1859, in H. P. Krehbiel, *The History of the General Conference of the Mennonites of North America* ([Canton, OH], 1898), 35-37.

45. John H. Oberholtzer, "Unser Botschafter," *RB,* December 31, 1855. For a reproduction of the heading of Overholt and Donatt's *Star-Spangled Banner,* see Ellwood Roberts, *Old Richland Families* (Norristown, 1898), between pp. 36 and 37.

46. John H. Oberholtzer, "Leset dieses mit Ueberlegung," *RB,* December 31, 1855.

47. "Fifteenth Session," May 8, 1855, MECMC.

48. *Ibid.*

49. "Sixteenth Session," May 1, 1856, MECMC.

50. Anonymous handwritten note at bottom of a broadside, "Bischofliche Entscheidung" (1856), pasted on p. 170 of the Minute Book of the Evangelical Mennonite Church. Photocopy, MLAEP.

51. "Nineteenth Session," October 1, 1857, MECMC. J. H. Oberholtzer wrote to European Mennonites a year later (November 1858), asking how they dealt with the issues of prayer meetings and foot washing. See Samuel Floyd Pannebecker, *The History of the General Conference Mennonite Church* (Newton, Kan., 1975), 26.

52. William and Anna Schelly to Daniel and Markata Heigh, October 12, 1857, AMC.

53. J[asper]. A[braham]. Huffman, *History of the Mennonite Brethren in Christ Church* (New Carlisle, Ohio, 1920), 68.

54. Johannes Schantz to [Tobias Kolb], May 26, 1859, AMC.

55. "Twenty-fifth Session," and "Twenty-sixth Session," MECMC.

56. J. Battle, *History of Bucks County, Pennsylvania* (Philadelphia, 1887), 1067-1068.

57. J. H. Oberholtzer, *Der Wahre Charakter von J. H. Oberholtzer, Prediger und Bischof über mehrere Gemeinden in Ost-Pennsylvanien* (Milford Square, Pa., 1860), 13-14.

58. *Ibid.,* 19-20.

59. *Ibid.,* 23-24.

60. *Ibid.,* 78-79.

61. *Ibid.,* 114.

62. *Ibid.,* 105.

63. John Geil, "Farewell Address," in John F. Funk, *Biographical Sketch of Pre. John Geil* (Elkhart, Ind., 1897), 34-35.

64. *Ibid.,* 36.

65. A picture of Funk's boyhood is presented in Helen Kolb Gates, John Funk Kolb, J. Clemens Kolb, and Constance Sykes Kolb, *Bless the Lord O My Soul,* ed. J. C. Wenger (Scottdale, Pa., 1964), 20-37.

66. John F. Funk, Diary, May 5, 1855, AMC.

67. Gates, Kolb, *et al., Bless the Lord* (see n. 65), 23.

68. John F. Funk, Diary, September 2, 1855.

69. *Ibid.,* July 1, 1855.

70. *Ibid.,* September 23, 1855.

71. Gates, Kolb, *et al.*, *Bless the Lord* (see n. 65), 36-37.

72. For an understanding of these years in Funk's life I have found very helpful an unpublished paper by Joseph Liechty, "From Yankee to Nonresistant: John F. Funk's Chicago Years, 1857-1865," 44 pp., submitted December 19, 1979, at the Goshen Biblical Seminary, Elkhart, Ind.

73. Funk, Diary, March 30, 1858.

74. *Ibid.*, April 5, 1858.

75. *Ibid.*, January 23, 1859.

76. John F. Funk, "Account of John F. Funk's Trip to Illinois in 1857," 111, 113, John F. Funk Papers, AMC.

77. John F. Funk to Jacob Funk, March 20, 1860, AMC.

78. Funk, Diary, January 11, 1863? (pages marked November 28, 1862).

79. Henry D. Hagey, *Some Local History of Franconia Township*, ed. Joyce Clemmer Munro (Souderton, PA, 1979), 358.

80. *Der Bauernfreund* (Sumneytown, Pa.), February 27, 1856.

81. A. B. Shelly, "The Origin of the Mennonite Sunday-schools," *MYBA*, 1908, 26-28. See also Arthur S. Rosenberger, "100th Anniversary of West Swamp S.S.," *The Messenger*, X (July-August 1957), 10. Note also the following interesting description in a letter from Abraham K. Funk, twenty-two-year-old schoolteacher in Hilltown Township, to his older brother in Chicago, John Fretz Funk. The letter (in AMC) is dated March 11, 1862: "Some time ago I was on a visit up in Milford, and dined with Mr. [A. B.] Schelly (one of Milford's best School teachers) he informed me that he was teacher of a Bible Class that met every Sunday Afternoon at the Meeting House. The place where Rev. Jno. Oberholtzer preaches. I accepted an invitation to go with him as it was about 2 years since I had been there last, and was formerly acquainted with some of the people who assembled there. We soon arrived at the place, and entering the house found some 30 [80?] members present, among whom were almost all the young men and ladies of the neighborhood as well as men of upwards of 40 years old who took an active part in the discussions. With one or two exceptions all had German Testaments. The proceedings were highly interesting and instructive. It was pleasant to sit and listen—an edification for those interested—and a blessing to all."

82. Daniel Krehbiel, "Correspondenz aus Iowa," dated February 5, 1860, *CVB*, February 22, 1860, 63.

83. "Traktatenvertheilung in der Mennoniten Gemeinschaft," *CVB*, February 22, 1860, 63.

84. Krehbiel, *History of the General Conference* (see n. 44), 54.

85. John H. Oberholtzer to Henry Nice, April 4, 1870, SMGC. For another English tr. of this statement, see Krehbiel, *History of the General Conference* (n. 44), 56: "this denomination has never . . . constituted an ecclesiastical organization."

86. See John F. Funk to Salome Kratz, May 23, 1860, AMC: "Last evening Mr Preacher Overholt that is the Father of the Oberholtites and his co-laborer, Cousin Enos Loux were here. they were on their way to Iowa to attend some church convention. and I went with them to the Depot—and saw them safely shipped on the train toward their destination."

87. Krehbiel, *History of the General Conference* (see n. 44), 71.

Chapter 11. "Warfare: Its Evils, Our Duty" (1861-1865)

1. Donald A. Semisch, "The Bench and Bar of Montgomery County During the Civil War," *BHSMC*, XIII (Fall 1962), 170-171. Theodore W. Bean, *History of Montgomery County, Pennsylvania* (Philadelphia, 1884), 195-196.

2. Davis Hunsicker to Joseph Hunsicker, January 3, 1862, in "Letters of the Fifty-First," *BHSMC*, XIII (Fall 1962), 210.

3. Davis Hunsicker to Joseph Hunsicker, June 20, 1861, Montgomery County Historical Society Library, Norristown, Pa., "Letters A-4."

4. Davis Hunsicker to Joseph Hunsicker, January 3, 1862 (see n. 2).

5. Bean, *History of Montgomery County*, 207.

6. "Twenty-Seventh Session," October 3, 1861, MECMC.

7. See the list in Bean, *History of Montgomery County* (see n. 1), 211-221.

8. A. J. Fretz, *A Brief History of John and Christian Fretz* (Elkhart, Ind., 1890), 120-121. W. W. H. Davis, *The History of Bucks County* (Doylestown, Pa., 1876), 820 (Edwin Fretz).

9. A. J. Fretz, *John and Christian Fretz*, 154-155. Another member of the Deep Run "New Mennonites," Harvey Shaddinger, enlisted twice. See p. 241.

10. *Ibid.*, 334.

11. Abraham A. Godshalk, *A Family Record* (Harrisburg, Pa., 1924), 283-284.

12. Jacob Funk to John F. Funk, June 11, 1861, AMC.

13. J. F. Funk to A. K. Funk, July 8, 1861, AMC.

14. "Glenwood Hall," *PR*, I (February 1895), 84-85.

15. J. S[helly] Weinberger, "History of Freeland Seminary," *Ursinus College Bulletin*, XV (October 1898), 6.

16. Jacob B. Mensch to John S. Kurtz, February 15, 1887, ODI, 379.

17. A. K. Funk to J. F. Funk, December 8, 1861, AMC.

18. John O. Clemens to Jacob and Catarina Kolb, July 27, 1862, AMC.

19. H. P. Krehbiel, *The History of the General Conference of the Mennonites of North America* (Canton, Ohio, 1898), 82.

20. *Ibid.*, 113.

21. Cheryl A. Neison, "Arthur F. and Dorothy Hollis Barker...," *A History of Worcester Township* (Boyertown, Pa., 1978), 428.

22. Jacob S. Funk to John F. Funk, December 8, 1861, AMC.

23. Reported by Isaac Clarence Kulp, Jr., Vernfield, Harleysville, Pa.

24. A. J. Fretz, *A Genealogical Record of the Descendants of Henry Stauffer and other Stauffer Pioneers* (Harleysville, Pa., 1899), 113-114.

25. Joy Derstine Harris, *Our Father's Lamp and Mother's Light: Ten Generations of the Dierstein Family in North America* (Harleysville, Pa., 1981), 98.

26. Henry D. Hagey, *Some Local History of Franconia Township,* ed. Joyce Clemmer Munro (Souderton, Pa., 1979), 308.

27. Untitled handwritten account booklet, SL, VS15-5.

28. B. Whitman Dambly, "Where Washington Crossed the Skippack," *BHSMC*, II (April 1940), 112-116.

29. Reprinted in H. P. Krehbiel, *History of the General Conference* (see n. 19), 490-497.

30. John H. Oberholtzer to N. B. Grubb, August 30, 1890, copy in MLAEP.

31. William G. Gross and Samuel G. Gross to "Dear Cousins," September 14, 1862, in "One Hundred Years Ago," *MRJ*, VI (January 1965), 6.

32. "The Military Appeals," *Bucks County Intelligencer*, September 16, 1862, 2.

33. These seven cases are taken from a much longer list of affidavits selected by James O. Lehman from the uncataloged collection of documents in the Spruance Library, Doylestown, Pa.

34. *Bucks County Intelligencer*, August 19, 1962.

35. "Twenty-Ninth Session," October 2, 1862, MECMC. Signed, "H. O. Stauffer, Secretary."

36. *Die Geschichte der Trennung in 1847 und 1848 der Mennoniten in Ost-Pennsylvanien,* a broadside of 1863, tr. Elizabeth Horsch Bender as "History of the Division Among the Mennonites in 1847-1848," ODI, 410.

37. Jacob and Maria Landes to Tobias and Magdalena Kolb, May 7, 1863, AMC.

38. "History of the Division" (see n. 36), 410.

39. John F. Funk to Jacob Funk, October 17, 1862, AMC.

40. Jacob Beidler to Jacob Nold, October 26, 1862, AMC.

41. Obituary of Jacob Kulp, *Herald of Truth*, XII ("Extra for July, 1875"), 127.

42. "Alms Fund, Lexington Mennonite Congregation," March 27, 1863, English translation in MLAEP: "Received from members of the congregation for to defray expenses of Loeb

and others going to Harrisburg on account of drafted members. . . . " See also entry for April 6, 1864: "Paid Cash to Moritz Loeb $15.00."

43. Moritz Loeb to Tobias Kolb, January 12, 1864, AMC: "If you knew what I have done and borne for your and my friends while the drafts were on among us, perhaps you would gladly support Loeb's press."

44. John H. Oberholtzer, "Die Aushebung" ["The Draft"], *CVB*, October 29, 1862.

45. John Z. Gehman, Diary, October 21, 1862, MLAEP.

46. An obituary in an unidentified local newspaper calls him "for 40 years a faithful minister in the Menonist Society," and reports his burial on September 29, 1847.

47. Mary L. Bower (daughter of Joel Bower), MS note on flyleaf of Henry S. Bower, *A Genealogical Record of the Descendants of Daniel Stauffer*. . . . (Harleysville, Pa., 1897), MLAEP.

48. "Substitutes for Drafted Men," *Bucks County Intelligencer*, October 28, 1862, 3, col. 2.

49. Helen A. Stanley, *The Alderfers of America* (Allentown, Pa., 1972), 128-129.

50. John C. Wenger, *History of the Mennonites of the Franconia Conference* (Telford, Pa., 1937), 63-64.

51. This was related to me several years ago by Mrs. Mary Landis Wile, born 1892 in Lower Salford Township. Mrs. Wile's mother, Sallie Moyer Landis, was a niece of Frank Moyer.

52. A. K. Funk to J. F. Funk, January 29, 1863, AMC.

53. Abraham and Mary Leatherman to Samuel and Sarah Lapp, March 1863, William Gross Family Letters, MLAEP.

54. J. F. Funk, Diary, January 11, 1863 (pages marked "November 29-December 1, 1862"). AMC.

55. J. F. Funk, Diary, February 1-14, *passim*, AMC.

56. Peter Brock, *Pacifism in the United States from the Colonial Era to the First World War* (Princeton, N.J., 1968), 787.

57. John G. Stauffer to J. F. Funk, April 25, 1891, AMC.

58. See, for instance, "Exemptions Under the Draft," *Norristown Herald and Free Press*, October 13, 1863. "Exemptions Under the Draft," *Bucks County Intelligencer*, October 27, 1863.

59. The story of Abraham Bertolet's murder is covered in the *Norristown Herald and Free Press*, October 13, 1863; the *Bucks County Intelligencer*, June 30, 1863; and Robert I. Alotta, *Stop the Evil* (San Rafael, 1978).

60. Sarah (Mrs. Melvin) Gehman, a present-day member of Andreas Mack's Hereford congregation, reports this story as told by her husband's grandfather (February 20, 1982).

61. J. Paul Graybill, Ira D. Landis, and J. Paul Sauder, *Noah H. Mack: His Life and Times 1861-1948* (Scottdale, Pa., n.d.), 6-7.

62. "Aaron Moyer," *MYBA*, 1905, 34-35. "Rev. Andrew B. Shelly, *MYBA*, 1915, 17-19.

63. Henry B. Brown, Jr., "Talk Given at Trinity Church on Sunday, October 12, 1975," photocopy of 11 pp. typed MS, Ursinus College Library, Collegeville, Pa.

64. Abraham Grater, "Eine kurze Kirchen-Geschichte," 2 pp. leaflet dated December 22, 1864, SHL.

65. Edsel Burge, "Germantown Mennonites: A Search for Identity," *Friends of Germantown*, VIII (fall 1980), 4-5.

66. "Annual Conference of Christian and Reformed Mennonite Churches at Freeland— Full Report," *Norristown Republican*, April 18, 1864, 3.

67. "Thirty-First Session," October 1863," MECMC.

68. "Thirty-Second Session," October 6, 1864, MECMC.

69. Helen Kolb Gates, John Funk Kolb, J. Clemens Kolb, and Constance Kolb Sykes, *Bless the Lord O My Soul: A Biography of Bishop John Fretz Funk*, ed. J. C. Wenger (Scottdale, Pa., 1964), 53.

70. Related to me by a granddaughter of John Hagey's brother Joseph, Alma Hagey Mininger, October 2, 1977.

71. Henry D. Hagey, *Some Local History* (see n. 26), 307-308.

72. A. J. Fretz, *John and Christian Fretz* (see n. 8), 229-230.

73. Abraham A. Godshalk, *A Family Record* (see n. 11), 283-284.

74. See the lists in Theodore W. Bean, *History of Montgomery County* (see n. 1), 211-285, *passim.*

75. Family papers of Mrs. Sarah Schimmel Overholt, photocopies in possession of Marvin Rosenberger, Milford Square, Pa., present owner of what was once the John H. Oberholtzer residence.

76. These family traditions were reported to me by a great-granddaughter of David B. Overholt, Mrs. Sara Louden of near Milford Square, Pa., July 18, 1981.

77. "Petitions of citizens of the County of Bucks in the State of Pennsylvania, remonstrating against the appeal of the Commutation clause in the 'Act for Enrolling & Calling out the national forces'—Presented by Mr. Thayer of Penna Jany 11th 1864," in National Archives, Record Group 46, 38th Congress, HR 38A-H1.1, Amendment of Conscription Law. Two separate documents with identical petitions, one containing 121 signatures and the other 100. This significant material was recently located by James O. Lehman.

78. Richard E. Stauffer, *Stauffer, Stouffer, Stover and Related Families* (Old Zionsville, Pa., 1977), 188.

79. John G. Gehman to John F. Funk, December 11, 1890, AMC.

80. (Deacon) Jacob K. Overholt, The Church Record Book of the Deep Run Congregation Since 1858, "copied . . . by Jno. C. Wenger, Telford, Pa. 1935," 59, MLAEP.

81. Isaac Z. Hunsicker to "Dear friends" in Ontario, November 29, 1864, AMC.

82. "Patriotism of the Mennonites," *Bucks County Intelligencer,* April 4, 1865, reprinted in MHB, XL (April 1979), 6.

83. "Official Returns—Montgomery County, Election 1864," *Norristown Herald and Free Press,* November 15, 1864, 3. As the "most Mennonite" townships I have chosen Franconia, Lower Salford, and Towamencin. "Least Mennonite" though equally "German" are Frederick, Marlborough, and New Hanover.

84. Hereford tradition reported by Helen (Mrs. Solomon) Yoder, daughter of Joseph B. Bechtel, who grew up west of Boyertown at Greshville, Pa.

85. "Patriotism of the Mennonites" (see n. 82).

86. John F. Funk to the editor of the *Bucks County Intelligencer,* April 10, 1865, reprinted in "Patriotism and the Mennonites," *MHB,* XL (April 1979), 5-6.

87. John C. Wenger, *History of the . . . Franconia Conference* (see n. 50), 63-64.

88. John F. Funk, *Biographical Sketch of Pre. John Geil* (Elkhart, Ind., 1897), 39.

89. *Ibid.,* 44.

90. Related to me by Samuel C. Landis (1897-1979), a lifelong resident of the Harleysville area, member of the Salford congregation, and personally acquainted with Henry S. Bower.

91. Henry S. Bower, *A Genealogical Record of the Descendants of Daniel Stauffer and Hans Bauer and Other Pioneers* (Harleysville, Pa., 1897), 94.

92. "Thirty-Fourth Session," October 5, 1865, MECMC.

93. "Wichtig von Deutschland," *CVB,* January 1, 1866, 34.

Chapter 12. Faithfulness: Covenant or Mission? (1886-1890)

1. H. P. Krehbiel, *The History of the General Conference of the Mennonites of North America* (Canton, Ohio, 1898), 131.

2. "Mennonitische Friedensbote, Der," *ME,* III, 646. Krehbiel, *History,* 179-180.

3. Herbert Fretz, *The History of the Deep Run Mennonite Congregation* (Bedminster, Pa., 1949), 36.

4. Krehbiel, *History of the General Conference,* 160-163.

5. *Ibid.,* 163-164; 217.

6. Fretz, *Deep Run* (see n. 3), 36.

7. Abraham Wismer to Jacob B. Mensch, October 1867 (no day given), MLAEP.

8. Oral tradition reported to me by John E. Lapp, Souderton, Pa., September 29, 1981.

9. For Godshalk's very valuable record of his 1869 tour see "Travel Notes of Samuel Godshalk, 1869," ed. J. C. Wenger, *MHB*, III (December 1942), 1-2 and IV (June 1943), 3.

10. Harvey G. Allebach, "Reminiscences of Bishop Moses Gottschall," *MYBA*, 1923, 26-28. This charming piece was written about 1910.

11. See N. B. Grubb, *A Genealogical History of the Gottshall Family* (n. p., 1924), 90. W[illiam], S. G[ottshall]., "Samuel H. Longaker," *MYBA*, 1904, 30.

12. John C. Wenger, *History of the Mennonites of the Franconia Conference* (Telford, Pa., 1937), 380.

13. Seward M. Rosenberger, Joseph B. Bechtel, and Harrison Landis, *Fiftieth Anniversary of the First Mennonite Church of Philadelphia* (Philadelphia, 1915), 5-6.

14. Ibid. 7-8. See also Joseph Taylor, "In Memoriam Rev. Levi O. Schimmel," *MYBA*, 1904, 29. On January 19, 1873, the strife-torn Philadelphia congregation issued an invitation to J. H. Oberholtzer, who was about to move to the city, to be their pastor. The recently married Oberholtzer replied, cautiously, that he would be honored to serve there, but only after peace might be restored. See his undated letter, headed "Das Philadelphia Gemeinde, Friede und Heil, zum Grusz," in MLAEP.

15. "Thirty-Eighth Session," October 3, 1867, MECMC. Samuel Floyd Pannebecker, Open Doors: *The History of the General Conference Mennonite Church* (Newton, Kan., 1975), 61.

16. John H. Oberholtzer to Henry Nice, April 4, 1979, 11 pp. copy, SMGC.

17. "Forty-Seventh Session," May 7-9, 1872, MECMC.

18. Krehbiel, *History of the General Conference* (see n. 1), 432.

19. Ernst Correll, "President Grant and the Mennonite Immigration from Russia," *MQR*, IX (July 1935), 150.

20. "Pennsylvania Aid Committee," *ME*, IV, 141.

21. A tradition reported to me by James Gerhart, member of East Swamp Mennonite Church. See also "Pre. Jacob Beidler," *Herald of Truth*, XI (February 1874), 29.

22. "Russian Relief Fund," *Herald of Truth*, XI (April 1874), 78.

23. Ernst Correll, "The Congressional Debates on the Mennonite Immigration from Russia, 1873-74," *MQR*, XX (July 1946), 219.

24. "Das Mennonite Executive Aid Committee von Pennsylvanien an die Mennoniten Gemeinden in West-Preusen und Süd-Russland," April 16, 1874, broadside in Lancaster Mennonite Historical Library.

25. "Das Mennonite Executive Aid Committee von Pennsylvanien, an die Mennoniten Gemeinden in West-Preusen, Polen und Süd Russland," May 15, 1874, broadside in Lancaster Mennonite Historical Library.

26. William S. Hemsing, "Herman K. Godshall," *Souderton Independent*, July 22, 1937.

27. Samuel W. Pennypacker to [wife] "Dearest Virgie," August 11, 1874, Library of Pennypacker estate, Schwenksville, Pa.

28. John Shenk to Jacob Musser, December 4, 1844, "Aiding the Russian Mennonite Immigrants," *MRJ*, XV (April 1974), 22.

29. Hermon K. Gottschall, Gabriel Bear, John Shenk, and Jacob Shenk, letter headed, "Yankton, S.D. Oct. 28th 1874," MLAEP.

30. See Tobias Unruh, *Great Grandfather's Diary*, ed. Abe J. Unruh (Montezuma, KS, n.d.) [15-20]. "Two Russian Families," *Herald of Truth*, XII (January 1875), 8.

31. John Shenk to Jacob Musser, April 21, 1875, "Aiding the Russian Mennonite Immigrants," *MRJ*, XV (April 1974), 23.

32. John D. Souder, Scrapbook on "Germantown," SL.

33. *Herald of Truth*, XII (March 1875), 41.

34. "Unruh, Tobias A.," *ME*, IV, 786.

35. *New Holland* [Pa.] *Clarion*, July 31, 1875, 2.

36. "Died," *Herald of Truth*, XII (October 1875), 175.

37. "Died," *Herald of Truth*, XIII (August 1876), 143. Family traditions from John Swar-

tley (Susie's grandson), Telford, Pa.; Mrs. Beatrice E. Gross Stansel, Hutchinson, Kan.; and Alfred Dirks Myers, Sellersville, Pa. Mrs. Stansel also supplied photocopies of entries in the Isaac Gross family Bible. Two of these entries will be transcribed here. (1) "Den 24ten Januar 1875, als wir auf der reise nach America waren, ist uns eine Tochter zur welt Geboren, auf dem Groszen Welt Meer, vier Tage, Ehe Wir an Philadelphia anlandeten. wir gaben ihr den Namen Susanna Freudenport Illenois Dirks. Freudenport, und Illenois, Ist der name des Schiffes, auf welchem wir unsere überfahrt machten, nach America, Geschrieben von I G 1892." (2) "Johan Dirks, von Ruszland, ist Gestorben, den 9ten tag June 1876, seine Krankheit war, Auszehrung, er brachte sein Alter, auf 27 Jahr 10 Monat, und 17 Tag. Er liegt Begraben, auf Dem Mennonitten, Begräbnisz, in Franconien Taunschip, Montgomery County, pennsylvanien, So Jemand verlangen hat das Grab zu sehen, kann es gefunden werden."

38. This plaque, sent by Mennonites of the Freeman, South Dakota, area, is in the Mennonite Heritage Center, Souderton, Pa.

39. Records in the possession of the Salford Mennonite congregation, Harleysville, Pa.

40. Henry Krupp, Diary, June 15, 1903, and January 11, 1918, MLAEP.

41. "Correspondenzen," *CBB*, March 15, 1886.

42. Krehbiel, *History of the General Conference* (see n. 1), 212-213, 228-234.

43. J. Paul Graybill, Ira D. Landis, and J. Paul Sauder, *Noah H. Mack, His Life and Times* (Scottdale, Pa., n.d.), 6-7.

44. A tradition related to me by Mahlon D. Souder, son of historian John D. Souder of the Rockhill congregation.

45. John F. Funk, Diary, see entry following notation, "Sept 1st," 1875, AMC.

46. William S. Hemsing, "Herman Godshall" (see n. 26).

47. Deborah Bergey, "Liebes Lied," twelve quatrains dated "1873," MS in my possession. A granddaughter of Minister John Bergey of the Salford congregation, Deborah (1852-1907) married Henry B. Nice on November 17, 1877.

48. Samuel Godshalk, *Encouragement to Early Piety, for the Young* (Elkhart, Ind., 1880).

49. J. H. Battle, ed., *History of Bucks County, Pennsylvania* (Philadelphia, 1887), 1067-1068.

50. John C. Wenger, *History of the . . . Franconia Conference* (see n. 12), 115.

51. See n. 48.

52. John F. Funk, Diary, July 13, 1877, AMC.

53. William S. Hemsing, Diary, March 15, 1887. In possession of Henry Hemsing, Valley Forge, Pa.

54. Undated clipping from *Herald der Wahrheit*, containing a letter in which William Gross of Fountainville, over the date of March 1, 1890, states that he wrote the accompanying essay on the use of the German language eight years earlier.

55. Abraham A. Mayer, *Christliche Lieder. Gedichtet und zum Theil gesammelt von Abraham A. Meyer, an der Deep Run, in Bedminster Taunschip, Bucks County, Pa. (Gestorben am 16ten Mai, 1877, in seinem 83sten Lebensjahre)* (Quakertown, Pa., 1877).

56. "On the Death of Abraham A. Meyer," poem annotated "Written in German by H. M. Godshalk," tr. Samuel Godshalk, in Abraham Godshalk, *A Family Record* (Harrisburg, Pa., 1912), 133.

57. A. B. Shelly, "History of the Rise and Progress of the Sunday School Convention of the Eastern District," *MYBA*, 1903, 14.

58. John C. Wenger, *History of the . . . Franconia Conference* (see n. 12), 174, 195.

59. William S. Hemsing, Diary (see n. 53), April 23 and December 8, 1885.

60. John C. Wenger, *History of the . . . Franconia Conference* (see n. 12), 122-123.

61. [N. B. Grubb], "The Phoenixville Mennonite Church," *MYBA*, 1923, 22. John C. Wenger, *History of the . . . Franconia Conference* (see n. 12), 214-215.

62. William H. Speer, "How We Received Our Property from the Mennonites" (written "October 1st, 1898"), *Golden Souvenir Booklet*, Trinity Evangelical Lutheran Church (Bangor, Pa., 1928), 17-18. See also pp. 16 and 68.

63. Mrs. Henry Cassel, diary of a trip from Ontario to Pennsylvania, September 7 to

October 21, 1897, photocopy supplied by Lorna L. Bergey: "Took the train for bethlehem arrived in the morning at 5 O Clock changed cars for banker arrived at Abe Overholtzer at 8 O clock got breakfast and found them all well . . . next day Abe took us Out to see the Slate Works. . . ."

64. "Minutes of the Special Conference of the Evangelical Mennonites of Pa., and the United Mennonites of Canada, Michigan, Indiana and Ohio. Held in Upper Milford, Lehigh County, Pa." Unidentified clipping in "Scrap Book No. 3" of N. B. Grubb, 9-10, MLAEP.

65. A. J. Fretz, *A Brief History of Bishop Henry Funck and Other Funk Pioneers* (Elkhart, Ind., 1899), 150-153.

66. Herman Godshall to Jacob B. Mensch, July 22, 1879, Jacob B. Mensch Letters, MLAEP.

67. These traditions were reported to me by several persons, including Linnaeus Kulp, great-grandson of Bishop Jacob Kulp, and John E. Lapp, a follower of Jacob Kulp in the bishop's office at the Plains congregation.

68. John C. Wenger, *History of the . . . Franconia Conference* (see n. 12), 390.

69. Henry Godshall to Jacob B. Mensch, October 7, 1881, Jacob B. Mensch Letters, MLAEP.

70. *Ibid.*

71. William S. Hemsing, Diary (see n. 53), December 11, 1885: "Heard today that Charles Godshall was not in his right mind. He was but recently married. His mother was the same way long before she died." December 16, 1885: "He is not as crazy as people would make it appear, but he has for a long time been very queer. He is different now, looks like melancholy."

72. "Deaths," *Souderton Independent*, May 9, 1979, A4.

73. N. B. Grubb, "Mennonite Reminiscences," typed MS in SL, n.p.

74. Tradition reported by Mary Landis Fly, native of the Line Lexington-Doylestown community.

75. John D. Souder, "John H. Landis," *PR*, VII (October 1929), 115-116.

76. J. Paul Graybill, *et al., Noah H. Mack* (see n. 43), 7.

77. Samuel S. Haury, *Letters Concerning the Spread of the Gospel in the Heathen World*, tr. Marie Regier Janzen and Hilda Voth (Scottdale, Pa., 1981).

78. *Ibid.*, 53-54.

79. H. P. Krehbiel, *History of the General Conference* (see n. 1), 311.

80. "HKG" to S. F. Sprunger, editor of *CBB*, July 1, 1882, 98.

81. *Ibid.*

82. "Mennonite Evangelizing Committee," *ME*, III, 622.

83. On Andrew and John Godshall, see John D. Souder, Notebook on "Michael Derstine," 78, SL. On Jacob Loux at Lansdale, see "Local Notes," the Harleysville *News*, July 6, 1886, 3.

84. John F. Funk to Jacob B. Mensch, August 7, 1897, Jacob B. Mensch Letters, MLAEP.

85. John F. Funk, Diary, July 4-22, 1877, AMC.

86. *Ibid.*, July 19.

87. Deems Schimmel, Coopersburg, Pa., interview on May 17, 1982. See also an unidentified clipping from *The Mennonite* in N. B. Grubb's "Scrap Book No. 6," MLAEP.

88. "Seventy-Third Session," May 5, 1885, MECMC.

89. "Ein Mennonit von Pennsylvanien," "Berichte aus unser Gemeinden," *CBB*, August 15, 1882, 126-127.

90. See various unidentified newspaper clippings in N. B. Grubb's "Scrap Book No. 6," MLAEP.

91. Unidentified newspaper clipping, N. B. Grubb's "Scrap Book No. 3," MLAEP.

92. "Aus Unsern Gemeinden," *CBB*, June 15, 1884, 92.

93. "Seventy-First Session," May 6, 1884, MECMC.

94. David W. Bartow and Harold P. Bloch, *Upper Milford Mennonite Church, Zionsville, Pa.* (n. p., 1976), 11-12.

95. See "Eastern Mennonite Conference. Proceedings of the 76th Session," *TM*, II (July 1887), 132.

96. "Aus Unsern Gemeinden," *CBB*, November 1, 1883, 164.

97. W. S. Gottshall, "The Lot," *TM*, September 3, 1928, 3.

98. Jacob A. Freed, *Partial History of the Freed Family* (Souderton, Pa., 1923), 49.

99. This account is assembled from sources including: memories of Jacob M. Moyer (born 1879), Harleysville, Pa., recorded ca. 1960; "Selbstmord von Michael Alderfer," *Der Neutralist* (Skippack, Pa.), May 27, 1885; obituary in *CBB*, June 15, 1885, 6; "A Bank President's Suicide," unidentified newspaper clipping in N. B. Grubb's "Scrap Book No. 5," MLAEP; Helen M. Stanley, *The Alderfers of America* (Allentown, Pa., 1972), 129.

100. Recounted to me ca. 1945 by John Landis's granddaughter, Susan Alderfer Landis (1874-1962).

101. "Local Notes," *The Harleysville News*, November 1886, 3. "Mennonite Bishop Chosen," unidentified newspaper clipping in N. B. Grubb's "Scrap Book No. 5," MLAEP.

102. Herbert Fretz, *History of the Deep Run Mennonite Congregation Eastern Conference....* (Bedminster, Pa., 1949), 20.

103. Harvey G. Allebach, Reminiscences...." (see n. 10), 27.

104. J. Herbert Fretz, "A Pennsylvania Mennonite Church—West Swamp," *Mennonite Life*, II (October 1947), 36.

105. John G. Stauffer to John F. Funk, December 11, 1890, AMC.

106. H. P. Krehbiel, *History of the General Conference* (see n. 1), 427.

107. M. B. Schantz, "Ober-Milford," *CBB*, February, 1888, 6.

108. "Korr. d. 'B.-B' " [A. B. Shelly], "Correspondenzen," *CBB*, August 15, 1886, 6.

109. "The Church Awakening," *TM*, II (January 1887), 56.

110. Jacob B. Mensch, Record of Franconia Conference (privately kept unofficial minutes), May 1882, MLAEP.

111. See Mary Jane Hershey, "A Study of the Dress of the (Old) Mennonites of the Franconia Conference 1700-1953," *Pennsylvania Folk Life*, IX (Summer 1958), 45-47.

112. John C. Wenger, *History of the ... Franconia Conference* (see n. 12), 295.

113. Family tradition reported to me by a great-granddaughter of Enos Beidler, Dorothy Stover Schmidt, May 25, 1982. Another folk tradition from the Swamp area, reported by James Gerhart, is that Beidler was considered proud by some of his neighbors. They gossiped that he placed extra manure on the rows of corn closest to the road. It was thought that if the lot fell on him for the office of minister he would be somewhat humbled thereby. Local tradition also contains other examples of such use of the lot to influence certain men toward more loyalty to the church. Some felt this was the case with Rein Alderfer, ordained minister at Salford in 1915; several of his relatives had been drawn to the local mennonite Brethren in Christ congregation.

114. See records of David Fretz and of the Blooming Glen Trustees, MLAEP.

115. John G. Stauffer, "Eine Geschichte der Mennoniten," undated clipping in N. B. Grubb's "Scrap Book No. 7," MLAEP.

116. John C. Wenger, *History of the ... Franconia Conference* (see n. 12), 54, #21.

117. John G. Stauffer to John F. Funk, December 11, 1890, AMC.

118. Robert Friedmann, *Mennonite Piety Through the Centuries* (Goshen, Ind., 1949), 258-260.

119. This MS is in the SMGC.

120. John D. Souder, *History of Franconia Township* (Harleysville, Pa., 1886).

121. A. J. Fretz, "Preface," *A Brief History of John and Christian Fretz* (Elkhart, Ind., 1890), 6.

122. Though superseded by Herbert Fretz's *History* (see n. 102), A. J. Fretz's pamphlet remains interesting for its seven photographs of men from the Deep Run congregation.

123. "An Interesting Meeting," *Providence Independent* (Collegeville, Pa.), October 25, 1888.

124. Henry A. Hunsicker's twenty-five "Local Sketches" run from June 28 to December

27, 1906, in the *Collegeville Independent.*
125. "Religious," *Providence Independent,* February 14, 1889.
126. "History of the Mennonites," 4 pp. brochure advertising the forthcoming book by Daniel K. Cassel. The last page lists, under the heading "Endorsed By," Henry B. Moyer, John F. Funk, and Josiah Clemmer, as well as a "Committee of Conference (New School)": A. B. Skelly [sic], Allen M. Fretz, C. H. A. Van der Smissen.
127. Daniel K. Cassel, *Geschichte der Mennoniten* (Philadelphia, 1890).
128. Printed in St. Louis in 1895.
129. Carl Heinrich Anton van der Smissen, "Unsere Reise nach Ohio und Indiana," *CBB,* June 28, 1888, 6.
130. See a collection of newspaper clippings on the divorce of Abel and Sarah Gehman, N. B. Grubb's "Scrap Book No. 5," inside back cover, MLAEP.
131. John C. Wenger, *History of the . . . Franconia Conference* (see n. 12), 325.
132. William S. Hemsing, Diary (see n. 53), August 23, 30, 1885.
133. Lawrence A. Bartel, "How Zion Mennonite Church . . . came to be," *The Messenger,* XXX (March-April 1977), 6. Mrs. Ruth Bergstresser, Souderton, Pa., interview, April 27, 1983.
134. William S. Hemsing, Diary (see n. 53), October 8, 9, 1885.
135. H[erman] K G[ottschall], "Zur Beherzigung," *CBB,* January 21, 1889, 2.
136. "Ein Leser" to the Skippack *Neutralist,* "Mennoniten vor Gericht," undated clipping from the *Neutralist* (after January 2, 1889), in N. B. Grubb's "Scrap Book No. 5."
137. "Ein Protest, *CBB,* February 21, 1889, 2.
138. John G. Stauffer to John F. Funk, December 11, 1890, and April 25, 1891, AMC.
139. " 'The Mennonite Testimony for Peace,' by Rev. N. B. Grubb," unidentified clipping, reporting a speech made on December 12, 1889, in N. B. Grubb's "Scrap Book No. 5," MLAEP.
140. Daniel K. Cassel, *History of the Mennonites* (Philadelphia, 1888), 220.
141. Jacob B. Mensch to John S. Kurtz, February 15, 1887, ODI, 383.
142. Edward Hocker, "Up and Down Montgomery County," *Norristown Times Herald,* June 10, 1958, 10.
143. N. B. Grubb, "Mid-Summer Ramble," undated clipping from *TM* in N. B. Grubb's "Scrap Book #6," MLAEP.
144. Amos B. Kolb (1879-1973), interview, January 6, 1973.

Chapter 13. Two Paths into a New Century (1891-1920)
1. "Rev John Oberholtzer. Sketch of the Founder of the New Mennonites," *PR,* IX (January 1931), 40.
2. John H. Oberholtzer to N. B. Grubb, August 30, 1890, copy at MLAEP.
3. "Ninety-First Session," May 1, 1894, MECMC.
4. Copy of application in possession of Marvin Rosenberger, Milford Square, Pa.
5. "Saucon Church, Coopersburg, to Mark 211th Anniversary Sunday Afternoon," undated newspaper clipping supplied by Mrs. Edith M. Geissinger.
6. "Kurze Geschichte der Oberholtzer Familie" (December 1891), 8 pp. unfinished MS at MLAEP.
7. Copy in possession of Marvin Rosenberger, Milford Square, Pa.
8. "Ninety-Third Session," May 7, 1895, MECMC.
9. Records in possession of Marvin Rosenberger, Milford Square, Pa.
10. Cornelius Weygandt, *The Red Hills* (Philadelphia, 1929), 69-70. Other details from Harrison Landis (d. 1983), living on the former Jacob Detweiler farm, November 30, 1982.
11. "Zion Mennonite Church, Souderton," *MYBA,* 1910, 38-39.
12. See numerous newspaper clippings in N. B. Grubb's "Scrap Book No. 6," MLAEP.
13. Unidentified newspaper clipping (ca. 1893-1894) in N. B. Grubb's "Scrap Book No. 6," MLAEP.
14. James Gerhart remembers a man relating these facts in about 1930. Interview, April 24, 1982.

15. Jacob B. Mensch, Record of Franconia Conference (privately kept unofficial minutes), October 1899, MLAEP.

16. "The First Mennonite Church," large illustrated clipping from a Philadelphia newspaper dated November 23, 1894, in N. B. Grubb's "Scrap Book No. 6," MLAEP.

17. "Buried at Last," newspaper clipping in N. B. Grubb's "Scrap Book No. 6," inside back cover, MLAEP.

18. Joseph B. Bechtel, "A Brief Sketch of the Life Story of Rev. Nathaniel Bertolet Grubb," *MYBGCMC*, 1939, 26.

19. "Arrested by a Minister," *Philadelphia Ledger*, March 23, 1895.

20. Seward M. Rosenberger, Joseph B. Bechtel and Harrison Landis, *Fiftieth Anniversary of the First Mennonite Church of Philadelphia* (Philadelphia, 1915), 11.

21. J. B. Bechtel and N. B. Grubb, "The Mennonite Home for the Aged," *MYBA*, 1922, 43-45. See also miscellaneous newspaper clippings in N. B. Grubb's "Scrap Book No. 7," MLAEP.

22. L. J. Heatwole, *Mennonite Handbook of Information* (Scottdale, Pa., 1925), 128.

23. Papers of Deacon Henry C. Krupp, MLAEP.

24. Papers of Nora Gross Gehman, MLAEP.

25. Reported to me by the recently deceased Harvey Detweiler of the Deep Run (East) congregation.

26. Reported to me by Irvin Leatherman, formerly of Pipersville, Pa.

27. John F. Funk to Abraham Leatherman, February 18, 1892, MLAEP.

28. Paul M. Mininger, son of Hetty Kulp Mininger, interview, September 16, 1978.

29. *Ibid.*

30. Wesley Gross, "Mahlon G. Gross: Life and Labors," *Pennsylvania Mennonite Heritage*, IV (October 1981), 6.

31. For William G. Moyer see A. M. Fretz, *Directory: Mennonite Church, Deep Run Charge, January 1914* (Bedminster, Pa., 1914), 49. The family tradition of Bishop Rosenberger is remembered by his great-niece, Mary Landis Fly.

32. Jacob B. Mensch, conference record (see n. 15). May 3, 1894, MLAEP.

33. Jacob B. Mensch, Diary, November 20, 1897, MLAEP.

34. Wilmer Reinford, "The Jacob B. Mensch (1835-1912) Letters," *Mennonite Family History*, II (January 1983), 11-13.

35. Jacob B. Mensch, conference record (see n. 15), October, 1894.

36. Freeman Swartz, "Contemporaries in 1921," *The Messenger*, VII (Summer 1954), 14.

37. Harvey G. Allebach, *Echoes from Parnassus* (Berne, Ind., 1902).

38. Mary Lou Cummings, "Ann J. Allebach," *The Messenger*, XIX (November-December 1976), 4-6. "Biographical Sketches," MYBA, 1919, 18-20. See also *REDC*, May, 1913, 13; and May 3-5, 1914, 10.

39. J. W. Schantz, sermon excerpts reprinted in *The Messenger*, XIX (November-December 1976), 5.

40. "A Word of Introduction," MYBA, 1908, 18, 20. "Annie C. Funk," *MYBA*, 1913, 17-21. See also "Fiftieth Anniversary of the Christian Endeavour Society, Bally, Pennsylvania," *MYBA*, 1938, 19-20, and Christena Duerksen, "A Missionary on the *Titanic*," *Mennonite Life*, XII (January 1957), 44-46.

41. Helen Bechtel Yoder, Lancaster, Pa., and Jesse Bechtel, Media, Pa., interviews, November 13, 1982.

42. John F. Schmidt, "Mennonitisches Lexikon Distribution in America," *MQR*, XXXIV (July 1960), 211, 214.

43. Daniel G. Lapp, "To the converts at Doylestown," February 14, 1895, AMC.

44. Mark R. Wenger, "Ripe Harvest: A Research Study of Evangelist A. D. Wenger..." unpublished paper prepared for History Seminar at Eastern Mennonite College, March 8, 1979, 7-8.

45. John S. Coffman to Menno S. Steiner, November 19, 1896, quoted in Barbara F. Coffman, *His Name Was John* (Scottdale, Pa., 1964), 300-301.

46. Amos B. Kolb (1879-1973), interview, January 6, 1973.

47. Paul M. Mininger, interview, September 16, 1978.

48. Daniel Kauffman to Jacob B. Mensch, August 21, 1899, MLAEP.

49. A. Grace Wenger, "Amanda Musselman, 1869-1940," *Pennsylvania Mennonite Heritage*, V (October 1982), 7-16, *passim.*

50. Family records of Jacob D. Mininger, in possession of Mrs. Edward D. Mininger, Elkhart, Ind.

51. Mrs. Edward D. Mininger, interview, October, 1982.

52. A Doylestown tradition remembered by Deacon Oliver Nyce. See also Steiner's prospectus for a new edition of the Denner book, in the Muddy Creek Farm Library, Denver, Pa. Steiner advertised in the Harleysville *News,* October 17, 1900, and is mentioned in Jacob B. Mensch's diary for November 1900, and January 2, 4, and 12, 1901.

53. Amos B. Kolb (1879-1973), who told this story repeatedly, recounted it in an interview, January 6, 1973.

54. Local tradition remembered by Hanna Rittenhouse Clemens of the Plains congregation, granddaughter of a Franconia deacon.

55. A reminiscence of Linnaeus F. Kulp (1893-1982), who attended the ordination with his parents at the age of thirteen or fourteen.

56. "Three Franconia Boys Meet Sad Death by Drowning in Godshall's Dam near Morwood," undated clipping from the Harleysville *News* [May 1906].

57. "Rev. John W. Schantz," *MYBA,* 1917, 17-18. Paul E. Whitmer, "The Zion Mennonite Church, Souderton, Pa.," *Christian Exponent,* February 11, 1927, 43.

58. N. B. Grubb, "Thanksgiving Sermon," *TM,* December 13, 1906, 5.

59. John C. Wenger, *History of the Mennonites of the Franconia Conference* (Telford, Pa., 1937), 375. See also "Rev. H. and Mrs. van der Smissen," *MYBA,* 1905, 36-37.

60. "Statistics of Eastern District Conference, May, 1905," *MYBA,* 1906, 37.

61. For the Eastern District, see n. 60. For the Franconia Conference, see J. S. Hartzler and Daniel Kauffman, *Mennonite Church History* (Scottdale, Pa., 1905), 170-171.

62. Henry Wismer, will dated January 7, 1903, copy in MLAEP.

63. Jacob C. Clemens, Minutes of the Franconia Conference, May 7, 1908, MLAEP.

64. Amos B. Kolb, interview, January 6, 1973.

65. Reminiscence of Linnaeus F. Kulp (1893-1982), summer, 1975.

66. Elizabeth Cassel Clemens, Diary, July 18-27, 1903, photocopy at MLAEP.

67. William M. Moyer, notes for a talk given at the fortieth anniversary program at the Perkasie Mennonite Church, May 8, 1949, MLAEP.

68. Jacob C. Clemens, Minutes (see n. 63), October 5, 1911.

69. Sanford G. Shetler, *Preacher of the People* (Scottdale, Pa., 1982), 264.

70. Henry C. Krupp, Diary, August 27, 1911, MLAEP.

71. "Programme for the Bible Instruction Meeting to be Held in the Blooming Glen Mennonite Church Bucks County Pa. August 27th, to September 2nd, 1191" [sic], 4 pp. leaflet, MLAEP. Reproduced on p. 429 of this book.

72. Jacob C. Clemens, Minutes (see n. 63), October 5, 1911.

73. Amos B. Kolb, interview, January 6, 1973. At Vincent it was by and large "the Goods and the Kolbs" and Mrs. Jane Stauffer who were willing to wear "the bonnet," whereas the end of the affiliation of "the Funks and the Latshaws" seemed to be triggered by the new rigor of the conference requirement. An interesting case in the Vincent-Coventry congregation was that of Sue Funk Landis (b. 1861), daughter of George W. Landis, a "Feed and stock agent for the P. & R. Railway," living near Pottstown. Sue declined the new requirement, choosing to wear the slightly less modest "Kirche bonnet" (church bonnet) favored by conservative women from other denominations. She now stayed back from communion, though she continued to attend at Coventry until it was closed down a few years later. But she considered herself a Mennonite, and for the rest of her life sent persistent contributions to "Old Mennonite" mission causes, as these began to take shape. Whatever was left over from the monthly check from her parents' estate, after her living expenses had been met, was sent "out to Elkhart," or to

such causes as the Mennonite Mission in Kansas City or the later Franconia Conference missions. See Sue F. Landis to "Mennonite Gospel Mission, Kansas City," December 10, 1934, J. D. Mininger correspondence, AMC. Other information is from Fannie Good Greaser, a former employee of Sue Landis, interview, March 18, 1983. For Sue Landis's family see A. J. Fretz, *A Brief History of Bishop Henry Funck and Other Funk Pioneers* (Elkhart, Ind., 1899), 163-164.

74. Found in the Bible of Anna D. Roth. On the verso of the note is pencilled: "Baptized in the year of our Lord nineteen hundred and eighteen and received into fellowship in our Lord and Saviour Jesus Christ. In Franconia Mennonit [sic] Church."

75. Hanna Rittenhouse Clemens, interview, summer, 1975.

76. Amos B. Kolb, interview, January 6, 1973.

77. Jacob C. Clemens, Minutes (see n. 63), May 7, 1914.

78. Wesley Gross, "Mahlon G. Gross," (see n. 30), 9-10.

79. Nora Gross Gehman, "My Life," short sketch in a ledger, pp. 28, 34-35, Nora Gross Gehman papers, MLAEP.

80. Wesley Gross, "Mahlon G. Gross" (see n. 30), 8.

81. Barbara K. Freed to Joseph G. Ruth, "March 1916," copy by Cora Freed, MLAEP.

82. "The Mennonite Church of Allentown, Pa.," *MYBA*, 1917, 32. V[ictor] B. Boyer, "Why the Mennonite Church Appeals to Me," *TM*, August 9, 1928, 1-2.

83. "Our Missionaries," *50th Anniversary Zion Mennonite Church* (Souderton, Pa., 1943), n.p.

84. "Zion Mennonite Church, Souderton, Pa.," *MYBA*, 1919, 32.

85. "Our Churches in 1915," *MYBA*, 1916, 41.

86. Ernest Leitzel, "Introducing Richfield Mennonite Church, *The Messenger*, XXIX (March-April 1976), 10-11.

87. "Historical Sketch of the Mennonite Churches in Blair and Bedford Counties, Pa.," *MYBA*, 1921, 26-27.

88. "Eyewitness Accounts," *Mennonite Life*, XXX (September 1975), 19-20.

89. "A Plea for Toleration," *MYBA*, 1915, 34-35; "A Short and Sincere Declaration," *MYBA*, 1916, 17-18; "Declaration of Nonresistance," *MYBA*, 1918, 28-29; "A Declaration of Non-resistance and Loyalty to the Government," *MYBA*, 1919, 22-23.

90. William M. Moyer to John E. Hartzler, September 24, 1917, *MHB*, XVII (July 1956), 6.

91. Allen M. Fretz, *Directory: Mennonite Church, Deep Run Charge* (Bedminster, Pa., January 1917), n.p.

92. Henry C. Krupp, Diary, October 5, 1916, MLAEP. See also the entries for May 6, 1915 and January 11, 1918, referring to small amounts.

93. John C. Wenger, *History of the . . . Franconia Conference* (see n. 59), 56.

94. Willard Hunsberger, *The Franconia Mennonites and War* (Scottdale, Pa., 1951), 10.

95. "Drafted Mennonites Join Church," unidentified newspaper clipping in scrapbook of Mary Mensch Lederach, in possession of Mary Jane and Hiram Hershey.

96. "Ban Soldiers' Garb, Yet Will Enter Camps," Philadelphia *Public Ledger*, September 4, 1917.

97. "Would Join Army; Not to Bear Arms," Philadelphia *Public Ledger*, September 3, 1917.

98. Willard Hunsberger, *Franconia Mennonites and War* (see n. 94), 12-13.

99. Reported by Stewart M. Moyer, member of Zion Mennonite Church.

100. Herbert Fretz, *History of the Deep Run Congregation. . . .* (Bedminster, Pa., 1949), 25.

101. John E. Lapp, "The Mennonite Peace Testimony in the 20th Century," *Newsletter, Mennonite Historians of Eastern Pennsylvania*, VII (May 1980), 5.

102. As related by Warren Smith, Souderton, Pa., in 1975.

103. J. Herbert Fretz, "A Tribute to Osmund Rittenhouse Fretz," *Fretzletter* (newsletter of Fretz Family Association), (#48, July 1982), 1-2.

104. Recalled by James Gerhart, later president of the Men's Brotherhood.

105. Henry D. Hagey, *Some Local History of Franconia Township*, ed. Joyce Clemmer Munro (Souderton, Pa., 1979), 126.

106. "Biographical Sketches," *MYBA*, 1919, 20.

107. Willard Hunsberger, *Franconia Mennonites and War* (see n. 94), 13.

108. *Ibid.*, 12-13.

109. "Must Salute the Flag," undated, unidentified newspaper clipping in my possession. Norman G. Kolb, son of John W. Kolb, interview, September 9, 1981.

110. J. S. Hartzler, *Mennonites in the World War or Nonresistance Under Test* (Scottdale, Pa., 1922), 197-201.

111. Norman K. Berky, "Brotherhood of the Eastern District Conference," *YBGCMC*, 1945, 2.

112. John C. Wenger, *History of the . . . Franconia Conference* (see n. 59), 75.

113. *Ibid.*, 76.

114. Anthony S. Shelly, "The General Conference Session of 1920, at Perkasie, Pa.," *MYBA*, 1922, 27.

115. "Statement of Reasons for Opposition to Secret Orders," 4 pp. tract (n.p., n.d.). The last page lists A. M. Fretz as "Chairman," and M. H. Kratz and S. M. Rosenberger as "Members" of the five-man Committee.

116. John C. Wenger, *History of the . . . Franconia Conference* (see n. 59), 434.

117. Cornelius J. Dyck, ed., with Robert S. Kreider and John A. Lapp, *From the Files of MCC* (Scottdale, Pa., 1980), 20.

118. Orie O. Miller, "Our Relief Work in the Near East and Russia," in J. S. Hartzler, *Mennonites in the World War* (see n. 110), 210-213. "Kratz, Clayton," *ME*, III, 232-233.

119. Mary Dirks Janzen, "The Batum Story. God's Mercy and Man's Kindness" (55 pp. mimeographed booklet, 1974), 20, 45. Katherine Dirks Niebuhr, Wyndmoor, Pa., daughter of Henry and Agatha Dirks, interview, May 28, 1982.

120. John C. Wenger, *History of the . . . Franconia Conference*, 332-334.

121. Lena Stout (Mrs. Elmer) Moyer, interview, December 1, 1976.

122. Willis and Mary Mensch Lederach, interview, summer, 1976.

123. Mary Mensch Lederach, "The Limerick Interlude" (February 1978), 8. 24 pp. mimeographed MS, MLAEP.

124. RAFC, May 5, 1921.

125. RAFC, October 1, 1936.

126. "Our Missionaries" (see n. 83), n.p.

127. "Drs. Bauman Complete 37 Years of Missions," *The Messenger*, XVI (January-February, 1963), 5.

128. Linford Hackman, Carstairs, Alberta (formerly of Souderton), interview, May 24, 1977.

129. P[aul]. E. Whitmer, "The First Mennonite Church of Philadelphia, Pa.," *The Christian Exponent*, May 6, 1927, 139.

Chapter 14. New Faces, New Doctrines, New Congregations (1920-1930)

1. Jacob C. Clemens, Minutes of the Franconia Conference, May 5, 1921, MLAEP.

2. Norman K. Berky, "Brotherhood of the Eastern District Conference," *YBGCMC*, 1945, 3.

3. "Norris" [Edward W. Hocker], "Where the Plain People Have Large Churches," *Norristown Times Herald*, July 21, 1925.

4. "Norris" [Edward W. Hocker], "North Carolina to Commemorate Gen. Nash's Burial in Towamencin," *Norristown Times Herald*, June 9, 1927.

5. "Gilt Edged Securities Bring Excellent Prices," unidentified newspaper clipping, with pencilled note, "6/7/24," scrapbook of Mary Mensch Lederach, in possession of Mary Jane and Hiram Hershey.

6. Elvin Souder, Sr., taped interview by Dawn Ruth, summer, 1974.

7. Jacob C. Clemens, Minutes of the Franconia Conference, October 4, 1928, MLAEP.

8. "The Bench" [of the Souderton "Old" Mennonite congregation: Harvey C. Freed, Henry C. Krupp, Elmer B. Moyer, and Jacob M. Moyer], "Franconia Conference Resolution No. 5, of Oct. 4, 1928, As Explained to Souderton Church and Accepted by a Rising Vote." Mimeographed sheet in possession of James Gerhart.

9. "Jottings," *TM*, March 22, 1928, 8.

10. J. D. Brunk and S. F. Coffman, eds., *Church Hymnal Mennonite* (Scottdale, Pa., 1927). Special edition with "Deutscher Anhang. Compiled by A. G. Clemmer." 54 pp., 135 German hymns.

11. William |D. Swartley, "Singing—A Swartley Family Tradition," church bulletin of Franconia Mennonite Congregation, November 4, 1979, MLAEP.

12. John C. Wenger, *History of the Mennonites of the Franconia Conference* (Telford, Pa., 1937), 431.

13. John E. Lapp, interview, September 10, 1982.

14. Jacob C. Clemens, Minutes of the Franconia Conference, May 5, 1927, MLAEP.

15. "Chronicles of the Past Year," *MYBA*, 1924, 53.

16. "Mechanics Grove Church," *MYBA*, 1923, 35-36. See also "Calvary Mennonite Church (GCM)," *ME*, I, 495; "Mechanics Grove Mennonite Church (MC)," *ME*, III, 547.

17. Reminiscence of Howard Shelly, member of West Swamp Mennonite Church.

18. "Chronicles for the Past Year," *MYBA*, 1926, 42.

19. "Semi-Annual Session of the Franconia Conference Held October 1, 1931." Printed sheet of resolutions, MLAEP.

20. J. C. Clemens, Minutes of the Franconia Conference, May 5, 1927, MLAEP.

21. Wesley Gross, "Mahlon G. Gross: Life and Labors," *Pennsylvania Mennonite Heritage*, IV (October 1981), 7.

22. Remembered by Irvin Leatherman, formerly of Pipersville, Pa.

23. Remembered by Howard Leatherman, foster-son of Wilson Overholt. Preacher John Geil of Line Lexington (1778-1866) had spoken of "a man, plowing a field where there were stones, who told his friends that whenever he encountered a stone, too big to be moved, he plowed around it." See Philip Whitwell Wilson, *An Explorer of Changing Horizons: William Edgar Geil* (New York, 1927), 282.

24. James Russell Lowell, "The Biglow Papers, First Series," in Sculley Bradley, Richard Croom Beatty, E. Hudson Long, and George Perkins, eds., *The American Tradition in Literature*, 4th ed., Vol. I (New York, 1974), 831.

25. Frank Sturpe, Orrville, Ohio, interview, March 6, 1977.

26. John C. Wenger, *History of the . . . Franconia Conference* (see n. 12), 276.

27. Microfilm copy, MLAEP.

28. "Son Succeeds Father as Pastor of Church," unidentified newspaper clipping, scrapbook of Mary Mensch Lederach, in possession of Mary Jane and Hiram Hershey.

29. M. G. Weaver, *Arthur T. Moyer: A Missionary Martyr* (New Holland, Pa., 1925). 15 pp.

30. [Mary Mensch Lederach], "Mennonite Gospel Mission," 5 pp. MS written *ca.* 1928, in my possession.

31. Remembered by Oliver Nyce, retired deacon of the Doylestown Mennonite congregation.

32. John C. Wenger, *History of the . . . Franconia Conference* (see n. 12), 212.

33. Esther Detweiler, sister of Miriam, interview, December 1982.

34. "Chronicles for the Past Year," *MYBA*, 1928, 46.

35. P[aul]. E. Whitmer, "The First Mennonite Church of Philadelphia," *Christian Exponent*, May 6, 1927, 140.

36. Framed collection of photographs of Harrison Landis's men's Bible class, First Mennonite Church (Philadelphia), MLAEP.

37. Howard Y. Musselman, "Historical Sketch," *The Messenger*, VII (Winter 1953), 4-5.

38. J. Paul Graybill, Ira D. Landis, and J. Paul Sauder, *Noah H. Mack: His Life and Times* (Scottdale, Pa., n.d.), 71.

39. "Introducing Fairfield Mennonite Church," *The Messenger*, XXIX (September-October, 1976), 7.

40. B. S. Graybill, "Richfield, Penna. Mennonite Church, Juniata County," *MYBA*, 1929, 34. "Jottings," *TM*, May 10, 1928, 8.

41. *PEDC*, May, 1913, 12.

42. "Introducing Grace Mennonite Church," *The Messenger* [XXIX] (July-August 1976), 8.

43. *Report of the 131st Session of the Eastern District Conference . . . May 2nd-5th, 1929*, 13.

44. "Introducing Grace Mennonite Church" (see n. 42), 8.

45. Elmer E. S. Johnson, "Bus History," *YBGCMC*, 1938, 20-21.

46. Mrs. Wayne S. Getz, "Correspondence," *TM*, April 19, 1928, 7.

47. *131st Session* (see n. 43), 25.

48. Ziv, who came to the United States around 1900, died on October 20, 1942. Unidentified newspaper clipping from the Bucks-Montgomery County area.

Chapter 15. "Conscience," "Discipline," and "The Original Concept of the Church" (1930-1947)

1. "Bishops' Testimonies at Conference," *Missionary Messenger*, X (October 1933), 13.

2. Photograph of "Special Bible Term" at Eastern Mennonite College, Harrisonburg, Va., 1930, with handwritten identifications by one of the students, Fannie Good Greaser, MLAEP.

3. A. D. Wenger, "President's Message," *Eastern Mennonite School Journal*, "Commencement Number 1932," [5].

4. Anna Landes (Mrs. William G.) Detweiler, Orrville, Ohio, telephone interview, summer, 1976.

5. RAFC, October 7, 1937, "Seventh" resolution.

6. Jacob C. Kulp, "History of Finland Mennonite Church," 1. 71 pp. MS in possession of Jacob C. Kulp. This MS is perhaps the most detailed congregational history, including impressions of personalities, to have been written in the two conferences.

7. Susan A. Ruth to Edith Alwine, June 9, 1931, in my possession.

8. Abram K. Landis, Norman Mininger, and Ernest Moyer, talks given at 50th anniversary meeting at Rocky Ridge Mennonite Church, March 29, 1981. Tapes in MLAEP.

9. *Ibid.*

10. RAFC, October 6, 1932.

11. Vol. I, No. 1 of the *Mission News*, is dated March 1937. A letter on "Rocky Ridge" by Linford D. Hackman is dated March 12, 1937.

12. "In Memoriam: Mrs. P. J. Boehr," *MYBA*, 1937, 27.

13. "Missionary Program," *REDC*, April 30-May 3, 1936, 32.

14. Norman Geissinger, member of Upper Milford congregation, interview, June 20, 1982.

15. "Report of the Home Mission and Church Extension Committee," REDC, May 4-7, 20.

16. "Report of Home Mission and Church Extension Committee," REDC, May 2-5, 1935.

17. *Giving Thanks Unto God: Forty Years of Rich Blessings* 1941-1981. 40th anniversary booklet of Camp Men-O-Lan (n.p., 1981), 4.

18. "Field Notes," *Mission News*, V (May 1941), 6.

19. A. Warkentin and Melvin Gingerich, eds., *Who's Who Among the Mennonites* (North Newton, Kan., 1943), 184.

20. Reminiscence of James Gerhart, longtime member at East Swamp.

21. East Swamp Church Bulletin, Vol. I, August 18-25, 1940, MLAEP.

22. Daniel Kauffman, *My Vision of the Future* (n.p., 1938). "Published and Distributed by order of: The Board of Bishops Franconia Mennonite Conference," 8.

23. George A. Palmer to "Mrs. Derstine," March 27, 1933, in my possession.

24. "Harleysville," *Montgomery Transcript* (Skippack, Pa.), October 17, 1935, 1.

25. *Grace Bible Church of Souderton, Pa. 25th Anniversary* (Souderton, Pa., 1970), 7.

26. *Constitution and Doctrinal Statement of the Calvary Mennonite Church, Souderton, Pa.* (n.p., n.d.), 6: "We encourage the sisters to continue to wear the Devotional Covering." See also p. 9: "Relation to Conference. Our policy is to be determined when our membership with some Conference is established."

27. John C. Wenger, *History of the Mennonites of the Franconia Conference* (Telford, Pa., 1937), 52.

28. Harold S. Bender, "Introduction," John C. Wenger, *History* (see n. 27), vii.

29. REDC, April 30-May 3, 1936, 17.

30. RAFC, October 1, 1936.

31. RAFC, October 6, 1932. Agatha Stahl (Fernheim Colony, Paraguay) to Mrs. Philip Alderfer (Harleysville, Pa.), reprinted in "War Threatened Lives of Paraguay People," *Souderton Independent,* December 23, 1932. See also Resolution #7 in REDC, April 30-May 3, 1931, 35, and REDC, May 3-6, 1934, 38. For the Franconia Conference, see RAFC, October 5, 1933. Earl Anders, in those years a young farmer of Elroy, Pa., Franconia Congregation, remembers shipping a flat-bodied farm wagon to Paraguay. Interview, November 10, 1981.

32. RAFC, October 7, 1937.

33. "Bible Teacher Excused from Duty as Juror," *Norristown Times Herald,* clipping dated "February 1934," in scrapbook of Mary Mensch Lederach, in possession of Mary Jane and Hiram Hershey.

34. Remembered by Marvin Godshall, Franconia Township, who attended the funeral at the age of twenty-two. Interview, May 20, 1982.

35. RAFC, October 7, 1937.

36. Freeman Swartz, "Fifty Years in the Christian Ministry," *YBGCMC,* 1935, 23-24.

37. J. Winfield Fretz, "A Memorial," *YBGCMC,* 1944, 23.

38. "The Oldest Member," *50th Anniversary Zion Mennonite Church* February 7-14, 1943 (Souderton, Pa., 1943), n.p.

39. Henry S. Borneman, "Preface," *Pennsylvania German Illuminated Manuscripts,* "a corrected republication of the work originally published in 1937 by the Pennsylvania German Society as Volume 46 of its Proceedings and Papers" (New York, 1973), n.p.

40. Joyce Munro, "An Interview with John C. Wenger, *Newsletter, Mennonite Historians of Eastern Pennsylvania,* III (December 1976), 8.

41. Walter E. Baum, *Two Hundred Years* (Sellersville, Pa., 1938), 110.

42. Beulah S. Hostetler, "Leadership Patterns and Fundamentalism in Franconia Mennonite Conference, 1890-1950," *Pennsylvania Mennonite Heritage,* V (April 1982), 7.

43. Joyce Munro, "Interview with John C. Wenger" (see n. 40), 7.

44. John C. Wenger, *History of the . . . Franconia Conference* (see n. 27), 183.

45. *Ibid.*

46. *Ibid.,* 191.

47. *Ibid.,* 358.

48. *Ibid.,* 359.

49. "Sailing From N.Y.C. to Cherbourg, France on the S. S. Europe," *Souderton Independent,* April 8, 1937.

50. "Report of the Resolutions Committee," *REDC,* April 30-May 3, 1931, 35.

51. "Presentation of Aims of Mennonite Peace Society," *REDC,* April 28-May 1, 1932, 32. See also Irwin Bauman, "The Mennonite Peace Society," *YBGCMC,* 1932, 27.

52. "Report of Resolutions Committee," *REDC,* May 4 to 7, 1933, 34.

53. "Report of Resolutions Committee," *REDC,* May 3-6, 1934, 36.

54. "Report of Resolutions Committee," *REDC,* May 2-5, 1935, 36.

55. "Report of Resolutions Committee," *REDC,* April 30-May 3, 1936, 40.

56. "Report of Resolutions Committee," *REDC,* April 29-May 2, 1937, 42.

57. Willard Hunsberger, *The Franconia Mennonites and War* (Scottdale, Pa., 1951), 25.

58. "Report of Resolutions Committee," *REDC,* April 28-May 1, 1938, 41.

59. "Report of the Peace Committee," *REDC*, May 1-4, 1941, 31.

60. Mrs. Benjamin Unruh, "Emmanuel Church Dedicated," *The Messenger*, XV (May-June 1962), 7, 12.

61. Freeman H. Swartz, "The Origin and Development of Our Conference," part IV, *The Messenger*, I (April 1948), 3.

62. John E. Lapp, interview, July 30, 1976.

63. RAFC, May 3, 1945.

64. John E. Lapp (see n. 62).

65. *Ibid.*

66. "Report of the Peace Committee, *REDC*, May 1-4, 1941, 32-34.

67. Willard Hunsberger, *Franconia Mennonites and War* (see n. 57), 49-74.

68. RAFC, May 1, 1941.

69. "Report of the Resolutions Committee, REDC, May 1-4, 1941, 43.

70. Ernest J. Bohn, "General Conference Peace Committee Activities," *YBGCMC*, 1942, 4.

71. These are my computations from the annual accountings of the "Peace Committee in the *REDC*, 1941-1947.

72. Willard Hunsberger, *Franconia Mennonites and War* (see n. 57), 121.

73. J. Winfield Fretz, "Reflections at the End of a Century," *Mennonite Life*, II (July 1947), 34.

74. Willard Hunsberger, *Franconia Mennonites and War* (see n. 57), 44-45. Note on p. 44, however, that three of the seventy-two conscientious objectors transferred to military service.

75. *Ibid.*

76. *Ibid.*, 44.

77. J. Winfield Fretz, "Reflections" (see n. 73), 34.

78. Paul Rickert Shelly, "Foreword," *Religious Education and Mennonite Piety Among the Mennonites of Southeastern Pennsylvania 1870-1943* (Newton, Kan., 1950), v.

79. Recollections of Howard Shelly, member of West Swamp congregation.

80. Millen Brand, *Local Lives* (New York, 1975), 162-191, *passim.*

81. Samuel T. Moyer, *With Christ on the Edge of the Jungle* (Jubbulpore, 1941).

82. "Fountainville Woman Veteran at Quilting," *Doylestown Daily Intelligencer*, April 24, 1942, 1.

83. Willard Hunsberger, *Franconia Mennonites and War* (see n. 57), 102-103.

84. Ferne Alderfer, "Bessie Moyer Keeps Busy in Retirement Years," *New Horizons* (periodical for elderly members of Franconia Conference), IV (March 1981), 4-5.

85. A. M. Fretz, "C.P.S. Camps," *Home and Church, Directory of the Deep Run Mennonite Congregation*, January 1946.

86. Paul Kuhlman, *The Story of Grace* (Omaha, Neb., 1980), 121.

87. *REDC*, April 30-May 3, 1942, 5.

88. Reported in the *Souderton Independent*, June 24, 1943, 1, and July 15, 1943, 1. The issue of *Life* is here dated March 15, 1943, but this does not seem to be correct.

89. Harry A. Clemens, letter dated February 24, 1944, in *Souderton Independent*, March 23, 1944, 1.

90. Harold Ritter, letter dated February 24, 1944, in *Souderton Independent*, March 23, 1944, 1.

91. Quoted in Willard Hunsberger, *Franconia Mennonites and War* (see n. 57), 38-39.

92. *Ibid.*, 96.

93. RAFC, May 4, 1944.

94. Ray K. Hacker, *History of Bethel Mennonite Church* (Lancaster, Pa., 1972), 3.

95. Franconia Conference Peace Problems Committee, "Final Letter to C.P.S. Boys," in Willard Hunsberger, *Franconia Mennonites and War* (see n. 57), 135.

96. Esther Patterson (Mrs. Elvin) Souder, interview, January 24, 1983.

97. Earl and Haidi (Enss) Stover, interview, January 25, 1983.

98. David F. Derstine, interview, January 1983.

99. RAFC, May 3, 1945.

100. RAFC, May 2, 1946.

101. J. C. Clemens and Jacob M. Moyer, "Sample Letter Accompanying Monthly Allowance Checks to CPS Boys," August 8, 1945, in Willard Hunsberger, *Franconia Mennonites and War* (see n. 57), 134.

102. "Thanksgiving-Congregational Meeting-Minutes," *Home and Church. Directory of the Deep Run Mennonite Congregation,* January 1946.

103. Remembered by James Gerhart, member of East Swamp congregation.

104. J. Winfield Fretz, "Reflections" (see n. 73), 34.

105. Quoted in Paul R. Shelly, *Religious Education and Mennonite Piety* (see n. 78), 115. See also Paul R. Shelly, "The Mennonite Way of Life in the Eastern District Conference," *Mennonite Life,* II (October 1947), 39-40.

106. Paul R. Shelly, *Religious Education and Mennonite Piety* (see n. 78), 118.

107. John E. Lapp, "The Other Six Days," *The Mennonite Community,* I (July 1947), 29.

List of Donors

We gratefully acknowledge the contributions of the following persons and groups toward underwriting the cost of research, writing, and producing this history of the Franconia Mennonites:

FRANCONIA CONFERENCE

Ambler
Lauretta K. Walter Bochman
Floyd & Gladys Kulp
Warren Lambright

Bally
Anonymous
Gordon R. Beidler
Irene L. Gehman
Abraham K. & Drollene M. Gehman
Melvin S. & Sara Gehman
Daniel E. Longacre
Mr. & Mrs. James C. Longacre
Mr. & Mrs. J. Arland Longacre
Mr. & Mrs. Paul E. Longacre
Henry M. & Dorothy A. Martin
Mr. & Mrs. George S. Zeiset

Blooming Glen
Grace Allebach
Dr. & Mrs. James L. Conrad
Charles Hoeflich
Daniel L. & Alverna Yothers Hunsberger
Mr. & Mrs. John M. Hunsberger
Dr. & Mrs. Norman L. Loux
Mr. & Mrs. Joseph N. Moyer
Marie M. Moyer
Mr. & Mrs. Titus Moyer
Mr. & Mrs. Abram G. Rosenberger

Marcus L. & Evelyn B. Rosenberger
Mahlon A. & Miriam S. Souder
Paul & Grace Souder

Deep Run East
Friendship Class
Harold L. & Kathryn Moyer
Esther Yothers
Ruth Yothers

Doylestown
Paul & Grace Brenneman
J. Silas & Rebecca H. Graybill
Joseph L. Gross
Lester & Sara Heacock
Lawrence R. & Irma B. Nyce
Wynne J. & Grace Nyce
Richard & Ethel Rush

Finland
Claude & Naomi Shisler
In memory of Maurice H. Zeigler

First Mennonite Norristown
Mrs. Flora Willauer Bachkai
Ralph L. Freed
Rachel Clemmer Kauffman
Harold & Iona Weaver
Mrs. Mildred Oberholtzer Poley

586

Franconia
Anonymous
Mr. & Mrs. Levi C. Alderfer
Mr. & Mrs. Ernest W. Alderfer
Viola M. Alderfer
Mr. & Mrs. Donald Anders
Earl & Mary M. Anders
Mr. & Mrs. Curtis Bergey
Henry B. & Kathryn Z. Bergey
Mr. & Mrs. Horace L. Bergey
Willard & Anna S. Bergey
Henry & Donna Derstine
Paul A. & Stella B. Godshall
Mr. & Mrs. Mahlon M. Frederick
Elizabeth C. Hagey
Katie L. Hagey
Floyd M. & Naomi Hackman
Mr. & Mrs. Abram L. Kratz, Sr.
Mr. & Mrs. Jacob B. Kulp
Mr. & Mrs. Clayton H. Landis
Elizabeth A. & Verna A. Moyer
Nevin L. & Margaret B. Moyer
Susan Hackman Moyer
Mr. & Mrs. Willis Musselman
Harold K. & Dorothy K. Nice
Anna Stauffer
Mr. & Mrs. William D. Swartley
William Gotwals

Groveland
Vernon & Blanche Althouse
Paul L. & Thelma Harley

Line Lexington
Congregational Offering
Mr. & Mrs. J. Russell Bishop
Cora B. Freed
Jennie Sperling
William D. & Elizabeth B. Hallman

Methacton
Horace & Ruth Bergey
Glenn & JoAnn Brown
Ken & Polly Ann Brown
Mary K. Clemens
Grace E. Clemmer
Jay & Judith Clemmer
Anna Colflesh
Arlen & Shirley Delp
Dr. & Mrs. Melvin I. Glick II
Donald & Sarah Hunsberger
I. Wilbur Lapp
Mrs. J. Richard Stehman
Sarah Jeane Stutzman

Clayton & Margaret Swartzentruber
Paul R. & Betty Ann Wismer

Perkasie
George & Eva Hockman
S. Duane Kauffman
Robert S. & Rose A. Moyer
Abner & Virginia Schlabach

Perkiomenville
Isaac K. Alderfer

Plains
Anonymous
Ernest R. & Lois Clemens
Jacob R. & Mildred L. Clemens
Marcus A. & Helen S. Clemens
John W. & Joyce Clemmer Munro
Arthur K. & Lizzie Hackman
Ella K. Hackman
Walton & Karin Hackman
John & Edith Lapp
Russell Mumaw family
J. David & Betty Nyce
Henry & Charlotte Rosenberger
Arlin D. & Esther R. Shisler
Paul & Eva Swartley
David E. Yoder

Pottstown
Forrest W. & Ruth K. Essick
Elmer G. & Emily A. Kolb
Robert & Ruth Swartz

Providence
Congregational Gift

Rockhill
Mrs. Elizabeth H. Bishop
Thelma Felton
Cruz & Lois Wismer Hernández
Claude & Ruth Keller
Alma Keyser
Stanley & Velma K. Souder

Rocky Ridge
Anonymous
Mr. & Mrs. Elwood H. Halteman
Mr. & Mrs. Clarence Kooker
Mr. & Mrs. Ernest K. Moyer
Mr. & Mrs. Louis C. Steska

Salford
Anonymous

Adult I Sunday School Class
Mr. & Mrs. Harold A. Alderfer
Joel Derstein Alderfer
Sandy & Delores Alderfer
Sanford A. & Evelyn Alderfer
Verna Alderfer
Mr. & Mrs. Harlan A. Anders
Mr. & Mrs. Marvin A. Anders
Mr. & Mrs. Paul R. Clemens
Marvin M. & Beula Derstine
Donald & Diane Good
Paul & Isabel Glanzer
Fannie G. Greaser
Samuel Z. Greaser
Claude & Anna Groff
Wilmer M. & Perle B. Halteman
Lizzie M. Halteman
Hiram & Mary Jane Lederach Hershey
James Lederach Hershey
Mr. & Mrs. Sharon L. Hunsberger
Francis & Kathryn Kulp
Clyde & Anna Landis
Cyrus H. & Sallie M. Landes
Mr. & Mrs. Henry A. Landes
Mr. & Mrs. Larry D. Landes
Abram A. & Ruth R. Landes
Emma A. Landis
Esther N. Landis
Lizzie Etta Landis
Sallie M. Landis
Sara Kathryn Landis
Willis K. & Mary Mensch Lederach
Henry Weber Long
Mr. & Mrs. Vernon L. Martin
Richard A. Miller
Mr. & Mrs. Willis Miller
Claude & Shirley Moyer
J. Phillip & Betsy Moyer
Ella L. Ruth
John L. & Roma Jacobs Ruth
Leonard C. & Esther N. Ruth
Theona S. Sharrar
Willard & Marie Shisler

Souderton
Congregational Gift
R. Wayne Clemens
Oswin F. & Alverda Detweiler
Mr. & Mrs. Paul R. Detweiler
Mr. & Mrs. Harold Mininger
Mr. & Mrs. Nelson D. Moyer
Russell B. & Esther M. Musselman

Swamp
Grace V. Bertsch

Robert R. & Adeline W. Gehman
W. Norman & S. Viola Gehman
Henry & Carol Longacre
Horace W. & Elizabeth Longacre
Kenneth & Cora Longacre
Nelson N. Moyer
Mr. & Mrs. David S. Yoder

Upper Skippack
Congregational Gift
Robert & Ida Howell
Mae K. Reinford
Wilmer & Margaret Reinford
Earl & Linda Watson
Joshua C. Watson

Vincent
Mr. & Mrs. Mark Kolb
Mr. & Mrs. Paul W. Kolb
Mr. & Mrs. Paul W. Weaver

EASTERN DISTRICT

Bethel—Lancaster
Anonymous
Ray K. & Agnes R. Hacker
John & Ruth Nissley—Darwin, Trudy,
    Bernard & Rosemary
Melvin & Alta Shenk
Don & Virginia Ranck
William & Lucille Snyder
Delmar & Luella Stahly
Mr. & Mrs. Henry J. Toews
Arthur A. & Anna Mae Voth
Dr. S. E. & Helen B. Yoder
B. Earl Swarr

Deep Run—West
Paul N. & Barbara Detwiler
Kathryn Heacock
Russell W. & Grace M. Huber
Peter & Barbara Hunsberger
Chester & Ella Mill
Mr. & Mrs. James Derstine Kissel
Memory of Blanche Hunsberger Mood
Alvin & Ethel Moyer
David & Rosemarie Michels Moyer
Enos D. & Florence G. Moyer
Ray R. & Dolores C. Myers
Mr. & Mrs. Earl Ruster
Edward B. & Phyllis J. C. Tice
Bertha M. Wasser
Dennis R. & Dolores J. Wismer
Mr. & Mrs. Darwin Swartz
Harry & Margaret Ward

Eden
Mildred S. & Homer A. Clemens
Mr. & Mrs. Curtis F. Moyer

Fairfield
Congregational Gift

First Mennonite—Allentown
Edith & Armand Y. Geissinger
Leroy & Viola Weidner

Grace—Lansdale
Anonymous
Congregational Gift
Roy C. & Jean D. Clemmer
Mr. & Mrs. R. Lee Delp
Ferril & Anna Mae Derstine
Mr. & Mrs. Stanley R. Fretz
Wilbur & Marilyn Kriebel
Linwood A. & Gladys E. Kulp
Mr. & Mrs. David H. Hersh
Milton & Geraldine Harder
Willard S. & Katie H. Schwager

Hereford
Harvey J. & Kathleen Quenzer Bauman
N. James Gehman
Richard C. & Gladys E. Simmons

Indian Valley
Ernest M. & Helen B. Delp
Henry S. & Beulah Detwiler
John E. & Arlene Fretz
Julian S. & Louise Hagin
Wayne A. & Ruth Mumbauer
Harold R. & Karin T. Rittenhouse

Lower Skippack
Mr. & Mrs. Wilson K. Johnson
Mr. & Mrs. Howard K. Keyser
Harrison Irvin Yerger, Sr.

Pine Grove
Mr. & Mrs. Linford C. Good

Springfield
Marvin & Loretta Rosenberger

United Mennonite—Quakertown
Mr. & Mrs. Edwin Shelly
Fannie Clymer Stauffer
Dr, Stanley Moyer
Mr. & Mrs. Raymond W. Schultz

Upper Milford
Congregational Gift

West Swamp
Arthur & Marjorie Isaak
Daniel F. Meas
Mr. & Mrs. Arthur F. Mohr
Mr. & Mrs. James W. Mohr
Elmer & Mildred M. Mumbauer
Mr. & Mrs. N. Clarence Rosenberger
Richard A. Rosenberger
Mr. & Mrs. Wilmer F. Rush
Walter & Elizabeth Shelly
Mr. & Mrs. Henry D. Stauffer

East Swamp
James J. & Mildred H. Gerhart

Zion
Mr. & Mrs. Lewis L. Alderfer
Dr. George & Rhoda C. Gaugler
Mr. & Mrs. Gerald F. Hartzel
Harold L. Frederick, Jr.
John S. Keller
Mr. & Mrs. Ernest K. Landis
Esko & Alice Loewen
Stewart M. & Gladys L. Moyer
Paul L. & Elizabeth D. Musselman
Mr. & Mrs. Ralph E. Rosenberger
Patty & Elvin R. Souder

Dual Conference—*Germantown*
Congregational Gift

OTHER CONTRIBUTORS

John H. Burkholder
Mr. & Mrs. J. Winfield Fretz
Dayton E. Froelich
Carl H. Gottshall
Steven L. Hagey
Mr. & Mrs. Isaac L. High
Samuel L. Horst
Ken Hottle
Dr. & Mrs. Arthur J. Kennel
John M. & Naomi Kauffman Lederach
Paul M. & Mary S. Lederach
Philip B. & Ruth Lederach Rittgers
Charles N. Mininger
Ian H. Schiedel

Bibliographical Note

As this book continued to expand in size beyond the sponsoring committee's specifications, space for a bibliography became severely limited. The reader is therefore reminded of the hundreds of sources listed in the "Chapter Notes" of the preceding section.

The Mennonite Library and Archives of Eastern Pennsylvania (MLAEP), located as of this writing at the Christopher Dock Mennonite High School, Lansdale, Pa., contains a rapidly growing mass of manuscript and printed materials, not all tapped for the present work. This is the official repository of the two conferences studied in the present work. Included are shelves of local and family histories, many diaries, a remarkable collection of correspondence from numerous sources, and important personal collections such as those of Franconia Conference leaders Jacob Mensch, Jacob C. Clemens, John E. Lapp, and Elmer G. Kolb. Many congregational records and histories, printed and in manuscript, are available in various congregational boxes.

The most significant collection connected with the Eastern District Conference, assembled by Silas M. Grubb and his father N. B. Grubb, is in the Musselman Library at Bluffton College, Bluffton, Ohio. This includes unique manuscripts from the pen of John H. Oberholtzer, founder of the Eastern District, photographs, correspondence, and various records. However, a number of contemporaneous records are to be found in the MLAEP, supplementing but not duplicating the materials at Bluffton.

Other basic manuscript material is in the Menno Simons Historical Library at Eastern Mennonite College, Harrisonburg, Va.; the Mennonite Historical library and the Archives of the Mennonite Church, in separate buildings on the campus of Goshen College, Goshen, Ind.; the Historical Society of Pennsylvania in Philadelphia; the Schwenkfelder Library, Pennsburg, Pa. (includes the Samuel Pennypacker collection of European and Pennsylvanian Mennonitica and the John D. Souder scrapbooks); and in the holdings of the Samuel Pennypacker estate near

Schwenksville, Pa., recently under the supervision of Montgomery County authorities.

Much of the best writing on the 17th century backgrounds of Pennsylvania Mennonites is in the German or Dutch languages. An exception is the indispensable *Mennonite Encyclopedia*, whose four volumes nevertheless do not become as detailed on some local German or Swiss topics as does the *Mennonitisches Lexikon*, also in four volumes, issued by German Mennonite scholars. The Zurich background is presented by Ernst Corell, who draws on earlier scholarship in his valuable *Das schweizerische Täufermennonitentum* (Tübingen, 1925). Necessary for the Bernese picture, and the emigration story, is Ernst Müller's detail-rich *Geschichte der bernischen Täufer, nach den Urkunden dargestellt* (Frauenfeld, 1895), which utilizes Dutch sources and scholarship, and is, in turn, drawn upon for Delbert Gratz's *Bernese Anabaptists and Their American Descendants* (Scottdale, Pa., 1953).

Regarding the Mennonite migrations to Pennsylvania in 1683 and following, a spate of new material has appeared during the course of the editing of this book. Especially valuable on the Krefeld-Germantown migration is an article by G[uido]. Rotthoff, City-Archivist of Krefeld, Germany, "Die Auswanderung von Krefeld nach Pennsylvanien im Jahre 1683)," reprinted in *Mennonitische Geschichtsblätter*, XL (1983), 59-83. Another basic article is Helmut E. Huelsberger, "The First Thirteen Families: Another look at the Religious and Ethnic Background of the Emigrants from Crefeld (1683)," *Yearbook of German-American Studies*, XVIII (1983), 29-40. A recent *Festschrift* for long-time genealogy researcher Fritz Braun of the Heimatstelle-Pfalz in Germany is edited by Karl Sherer as *Pfälzer-Palatines* (Kaiserslautern, 1981); it contains fresh insight on emigrations from the Palatinate. Also helpful is a brief section on Mennonite names near the close of Annette Kunselman Burgert's *Eighteenth Century Immigration from German-Speaking Lands to North America. Vol. I The Northern Kraichgau*, Pennsylvania German Society, XXVI (Breinigsville, Pa., 1983). Much related material has been appearing intermittently in the two periodicals, *Pennsylvania Mennonite Heritage* and *Mennonite Family History*.

Unfortunately, although Dutch, German, and American scholars have drawn on it from time to time, the extremely valuable, even crucial Mennonite-related correspondence catalogued and summarized by J. G. de Hoop Scheffer in the Dutch *Inventaris der Archiefstukken Berustende bij de Vereenigde Doopzgezinde Gemeente te Amsterdam* (Amsterdam, 1884) has never in the ensuing century been systematically translated for the English reader. The fascinating story contained in this correspondence has yet to be fully told, but a readable account of some parts of it may be sampled in Nanne van der Zijpp's "The Dutch Aid the Swiss Mennonites," in Cornelius J. Dyck, ed., *The Heritage of Menno Simons: A Legacy of Faith* (Newton, Kans. 1962), pp. 136-158. A new interpretive account of the migration and settlement of Mennonites in the American Colonies is Richard K. MacMaster's *Land, Piety, and Peoplehood* (Scottdale, Pa., 1985), the first of four volumes in a projected series on "The Mennonite Experience in America." These works have superseded the pioneering C. Henry Smith's *Mennonite Immigration to North America* (Norristown, Pa., 1929).

The 523 pages of John C. Wenger's youthful *The Mennonites of the Franconia Conference* (Telford, Pa., 1937) will remain an indispensable resource on the history of both the Franconia and Eastern District Conferences. Much new material has of course surfaced and been printed since this publication, as in such periodicals as *Mennonite Quarterly Review* (especially the October 1972 "Oberholtzer Division" issue and the October 1983 issue which contains Germantown materials); the Franconia Conference *Mission News* and *Franconia Conference News;* the Eastern District *Messenger;* the *Newsletter* of the Mennonite Historians of Eastern Pennsylvania; the *Mennonite Historical Bulletin;* the *Mennonite Research Journal; Mennonite Life;* and others.

Two works that throw light on the 1847 division and the subsequent General Conference affiliation of the Eastern District are H. P. Krehbiel, *The History of the General Conference of the Mennonites of North America* ([Canton, Ohio], 1898), and Samuel Floyd Pennebecker, *Open Doors: A History of the General Conference Mennonite Church* (Newton, Kans., 1975).

The Conference minutes of the Eastern District may be read in an English translation by N. B. Grubb in a manuscript at the MLAEP, or in the published *Verhandlungen der Ost-Pennsylvanischen Conferenz der Mennoniten Gemeinschaft* (n.p., n.d.). Beginning with the May 1911 session, the Eastern District has published its *Proceedings* (variously titled) until the present. Private records of the Franconia Conference were kept for many years by Minister Jacob B. Mensch, and official minutes began to be kept in 1909. These, plus the minutes of many related organizations of both conferences, are preserved in the MLAEP.

Reproductions of a number of the hundreds of surviving examples of local Mennonite Fraktur art are included in the two-volume illustrated catalogue compiled by Frederick S. Weiser and Howell J. Heaney, *The Pennsylvania German Fraktur of the Free Library of Pennsylvania* (Breinigsville, Pa., 1976). Related items of Mennonite folk art are depicted in Joyce Clemmer Munro, *Willing Inhabitants: A Short Account of Life in Franconia Township, Montgomery County, Pennsylvania* (Souderton, Pa., 1981); and a forthcoming book of historic photographs and other visual materials from Lower Salford Township, by John A. Ruth, is to be published by the Harleysville National Bank in 1984.

Three other publications on related topics by the author of the present work are *The History of the Indian Valley and Its Bank* (Souderton, Pa., 1976); "The Story Behind the Franconia Conference's Outreach," *Franconia Conference News* (October 1976—November 1978); and *'Twas Seeding Time: A Mennonite View of the American Revolution* (Scottdale, Pa., 1976). On the latter topic, a broad background of source-material, meticulously documented, is presented by Richard K. MacMaster, with Samuel L. Horst and Robert F. Ulle in *Conscience in Crisis: Mennonites and Other Peace Churches in America, 1739-1789, Interpretation and Documents* (Scottdale, Pa., 1979).

Copies of five doctoral theses that treat topics related to the Franconia and Eastern District Conferences are deposited in the MLAEP. In the order of their appearance, they are: Paul Rickert Shelly, *Religious Education and Mennonite Piety Among the Mennonites of Southeastern Pennsylvania 1870-1943* (Union

Theological Seminary, published at Newton, Kans., 1950); Leland David Harder, "The Quest for Equilibrium in an Established Sect: A Study of Social Change in the General Conference Mennonite Church" (Northwestern University, 1962); Barbara Bowie Wiesel, "From Separatism to Evangelism: A Case Study of Social and Cultural Change Among the Franconia Conference Mennonites 1946-1970" (University of Pennsylvania, 1973); Beulah S. Hostetler, "Franconia Mennonite Conference and American Protestant Movements 1840-1940" (University of Pennsylvania, 1977); Robert Bates Graber, "The Sociocultural Differentiation of a Religious Sect: Schisms Among the Pennsylvania German Mennonites" (University of Wisconsin-Milwaukee, 1979).

In connection with the Tricentennial celebration of 1983, Joseph S. Miller, Marcus Miller, and Jan Gleysteen prepared a very helpful gazetteer of the main area described in this book. It consists of a published map entitled, *The Mennonites of Southeastern Pennsylvania,* and an accompanying 32-page booklet entitled, *An Index and Description of The Mennonites of Southeastern Pennsylvania 1683-1983* [Souderton, Pa.: Mennonite Historians of Eastern Pennsylvania, 1983].

Index

A Kempis, Thomas 221
Abolition 220
Academies 282, 410
Ackermanville 368
Acre, Caspar 107
Acre, Jacob 107
Acrostic 190, 365
Activity, Christian 418, 425, 478
Adams County 472
Aesthetic 190, 191, 214, 217, 227, 249
Affirmation 150
Africa 488
African Letters 501
Agricultural furloughs 446
Agriculture 218
Albright, Amos 171
Albright, Franklin 162, 171, 172
Albright, Jacob 172, 220
Alderfer, Abraham 188
Alderfer, Alvin C. 411, 436, 473
Alderfer, Alvin H. 492
Alderfer, Benjamin 211
Alderfer, Benjamin (son of Michael) 322
Alderfer, Bertha 506
Alderfer, Franklin 530
Alderfer, Henry (Upper Salford) 270
Alderfer, Henry A. 456
Alderfer, Henry O. 202
Alderfer, Howard K. 499
Alderfer, Isaac 240
Alderfer, Mahlon 446
Alderfer, Michael 204, 322, 328, 370, 380
Alderfer, Nancy 270, 359

Alderfer, Polly 270
Alderfer, Rein 575
Alderfer, Widow Mary 359
Allebach & Souder store 432, 461, 520
Allebach, Abraham 164
Allebach, Alpheus 432, 461
Allebach, Ann Jemima 411, 412, 413, 445
Allebach, Christian 98, 100, 361, 362, 363, 393, 435
Allebach, David 239, 258
Allebach, David K. 458
Allebach, Grace 506
Allebach, Harvey 411, 412, 423, 424, 439
Allebach, Henry 250
Allebach, Jacob 411
Allebach, John 361, 395
Allebach, Joseph 232
Allebach, Margaret Cassel (Mrs. Alpheus) 432
Allebach, Rockhill 434
Allegheny Trail 94
Allen, Jacob 459, 460
Allen, William 116, 125
Allentown 482
Allentown (Eastern District) congregation 436
Alms Book 113, 204
Alsace 28, 32, 132
Alsheim 89
Altdörfer 34
Altdörfer, Friedrich 110, 111
Ältester 204
Althouse, George 172
Altoona 433, 438, 439, 473, 517
Alzey 38, 73, 104
America (ship on which Pastorius arrived) 59, 60

American Legion 446
Ames, William 36, 37, 38
Amish 181, 205
Amsterdam 31, 47, 53, 54-56, 57, 72, 75-76, 81, 82, 82, 84, 90, 93, 112, 120, 124
An das Publikum (broadside issued by Eastern Conference) 296
Anabaptist Committee 32
Anabaptist teaching 531, 538
Anabaptists 27
Anderson, Clara (Mrs. Will) 484, 485
Anderson, Will 484, 485
Anne (Queen of England) 85, 87
Anteroom (of meetinghouse) 385
Antietam, Battle of 319
Anxious Year (1672) 42
Appalachian dulcimer, forerunner of 235
Appenzeller, H. G. 401
Apple, B. F. 368
Applebutter Road 400
Arapahoe Indians 375, 406
Arbitration 202, 296
Architecture 249, 397, 436
Arets, Lenart 57, 61, 66
Armentown 66
Arndt, Johannes, author of *True Christianity* 253, 400
Arnold, Gottfried 304
Aspisheim 26
Assembly, Menonite General (1971 ff.) 406
Assembly, Pennsylvania 118, 120, 153
Assurance of salvation 221, 222, 469

594

612   Maintaining the Right Fellowship

Schantz, Jacob 115
Schantz, Johannes 240, 302
Schantz, John 324
Schantz, Joseph 263, 284
Scheitholt (zither) 236
Schelly, Jacob 100
Schelly, William 284, 292,
 294, 301, 302
Schimmel, Georg 131
Schimmel, Joseph 404
Schimmel, Levi 314, 345
Schimmel, Owen 377
Schimmel, Sarah 300
Schlappe, Babe 42
Schleiffer, Heinrich 121
Schmutz, John 168
Schnebeli, Elizabeth 95
Schneider, David 349
Schomecker 30, 37
Schomecker, Arnold 30
Schomecker, Peter 31
School 113, 128, 139, 158,
 166-168, 189, 193, 211, 212,
 233, 516
*School-Management, A
 Simple and Thoroughly
 Prepared* (C. Dock) 128,
 129, 139
School, first Mennonite one in
 America 97
Schoolmaster 167
Schowalter family 131, 139,
 159
Schowalter, Anna 186
Schowalter, Christian 345
Schowalter, Henry 159
Schowalter, John 159, 186
Schowalter, Joseph 169
Schowalter, Ulrich 139, 159
Schrager 91
Schrager, Andrew 86, 89
Schrager, Katharina 86, 95
Schuler, Gabriel 165
Schultz, Abe 525
Schultz, Jonas 345, 372
Schumacher 37, 47
Schumacher family 80
Schumacher, Georg (Skip-
 pack) 106
Schumacher, George 38
Schumacher, Jacob 59, 64, 67
Schumacher, Jacob (immi-
 grant of 1731) 108
Schumacher, Peter 31, 38, 59,
 67, 68, 69, 73, 76
Schüpbach 100
Schutt, Elizabeth 170
Schutt, Jacob 170
Schuylkill 99, 101, 104, 116,
 142, 146
Schuylkill bishop district 142

Schuylkill River 55, 64, 65, 92,
 210, 218
Schwartz 106
Schwartz, Abraham 105, 106,
 111, 116, 135, 151, 153
Schwartz, Andreas 105, 106,
 166
Schwartz, Anna Kolb 106
Schwartz, baby Johannes 106
Schwartz, Elizabeth Hiestand
 106
Schweitzer, Mathes 105, 106
Schwenkfeld, Caspar 197,
 221, 457
Schwenkfelder Library 457,
 515
Schwenkfelders 111, 112, 118,
 135, 209, 221, 359, 372,
 410, 426, 457
Schwenkfeldian, The 457
Schwenksville 147, 194
Schwenksville congregation
 382
Schwerdle 111
Schwerdle, Johannes 140
Schwerdle, Philip 170
"Schwing dich auf zu deinem
 Gott" (hymn) 217
Schyn, Hermanus 81
Scofield Bible 422, 465, 496
Scottdale 170
Scripture Preacher 341
Second Mennonite Church
 (Philadelphia) 349, 402,
 423, 424, 437, 440, 495
Secret societies 292, 293, 294,
 295, 321, 449, 450
Sell, Abraham 202
Sellen, Hendrick 77, 142
Sellen, Jacob 136
Sellersville 320
Senn 34
Sensenig, Daniel 291
Sermon 156, 157
Settlement 372
Sevastopol 451
Shackamaxon 55
Shelly, "Widow" 269
Shelly, Abraham 203
Shelly, Andrew 520
Shelly, Andrew B. (A. B.) 304,
 313, 332, 343, 344, 352,
 353, 360, 375, 378, 382-384,
 388, 391, 395, 398, 413,
 437, 568
Shelly, Andrew R. 467
Shelly, Anthony S. 360, 364,
 414, 423, 436, 439, 449,
 458, 475
Shelly, Elwood 410, 467, 514
Shelly, Florence 410

Shelly, Maynard 517
Shelly, Paul 467, 514, 520, 530
Shelly, Ward 514
Shelly, William N. 269
Shelly, Wilmer 464
Shenandoah Valley 131, 159,
 336
Shenk, John 355, 357
Shenk, Michael 42
Shenkle, A. B. 297
Shetler, S. G. 416, 426, 427
Shisler, Claude 487, 493
Shoemaker, George (Canada)
 205
Shoemaker, Jacob 125, 204
Shoemaker, John 205
Shoemaker, Maria 205
Sideling Hill 516
Siebengebirge 27, 28, 30
Siegfied's Bridge 139
Siegfried, Col. John 139, 152
Siemens, Jan 61, 66
Signs, Gospel 483
Silk coat legend (Dirck
 Keyser) 82
Singer's Glen 159
Singing 177, 178, 179, 192,
 213, 462, 464, 517
Singing School 166, 217, 226,
 234, 432, 463, 464
Sinsheim 33, 36
Six Months in Bible Lands....
 (by A. D. Wenger) 418
Size of two conferences, rela-
 tive 278, 424, 425
Skippack 56, 57, 73, 82, 92,
 93, 96, 100, 108, 129
"Skippack Association for the
 Promotion of Useful
 Knowledge" 270
Skippack congregation 194,
 204, 249, 254, 278
Skippack Creek 79, 91, 111
Skippack meetinghouse 101,
 249, 250, 276
Skippack meetinghouse con-
 troversy 296
Skippack Pike 92
Skippack Road (later Skip-
 pack Pike) 94
Skippack, Lower 303, 369,
 395, 473
Skippack, the "head" of the
 Eastern Conference 294
Skippack, Upper 303, 321,
 476
Skulkers (draft-dodgers) 331
Slavery, "protest" against
 (1688) 70, 71
Slaves 308
Slides 458

John L. Ruth was born in 1930 and raised on a farm along the Northeast Branch of the Perkiomen Creek in Montgomery County, Pennsylvania. The nearby Salford Mennonite congregation, established by Palatine immigrants of 1717, had built its meetinghouse on land taken from the plantation of Henrich Ruth. But it was in the fellowship of a mission congregation established in 1931 by young "workers" from the Franconia Mennonite Conference—Finland—that John Ruth grew up and heard the witness of his parents' Christian and Mennonite heritage.

He attended the Lancaster Mennonite High School, some sixty miles west of Salford, graduating in 1948. Two years later, after a freshman year at Eastern Mennonite College, he was ordained a minister in the Franconia Conference, for a new Mennonite mission in Conshohocken, Pennsylvania. He graduated from nearby Eastern Baptist College (now Eastern College), and in 1968 completed doctoral studies in English and American literature at Harvard University.

From 1962 to 1976 he taught literature at Eastern College and the University of Hamburg, Germany (1968-69). An interest in filmmaking that grew out of a bicentennial commemoration of the death of Salford schoolmaster Christopher Dock (d. 1771) led to a collaboration with filmmaker Burton Buller of Henderson, Nebraska. Seven films resulted from that interest. Among them are *The Amish: A People of Preservation* (with John A. Hostetler); *Mennonites of Ontario;* *"606": The Persistence of Com-*

munity; *The Hutterites: To Care and Not to Care* (also with Hostetler); and most recently a film on Anabaptist backgrounds in the Alsacian city of Strasbourg.

Among other titles from his pen are a biography, *Conrad Grebel, Son of Zurich;* '*Twas Seeding Time: A Mennonite View of the American Revolution; The History of the Indian Valley and Its Bank;* four lectures entitled *Mennonite Identity and Literary Art;* and a history, currently in progress, of the Lancaster, Pennsylvania, Mennonite Conference. The latter community stems from the same European backgrounds as the Franconia and Eastern District conferences described in *Maintaining the Right Fellowship*.

Since 1972 John Ruth has served as an associate pastor on the leadership "team" of the Salford Mennonite congregation, and since 1976 has been supported in his historical and artistic efforts by a committee in the Franconia Conference. He is married to Roma Jeanette Jacobs from Hollsopple, Pennsylvania, and they have three children—Dawn Ruth Nelson, J. Allan, and Philip —and a granddaughter Sarah Ruth Nelson.